D. Magner

MAGNER'S
CLASSIC ENCYCLOPEDIA
OF THE
HORSE

A Complete Pictorial Encyclopedia of Practical
Reference for Horse Owners

Comprising

ALL SECRETS OF TAMING, CONTROLLING AND EDUCATING UNBROKEN
AND VICIOUS HORSES, WITH THE DETAILS OF BREAKING UP ALL HABITS
TO WHICH HORSES ARE SUBJECT; THEIR ABUSES, DISEASES AND
REMEDIES.

Also

FULL DESCRIPTIONS AND ILLUSTRATIONS

---

672 pages with over 900 illustrations

BY D. MAGNER

CASTLE BOOKS

This edition published in 2004 by

Castle Books ®

A division of BOOK SALES, INC.
114 Northfield Avenue
Edison, NJ 08837

Originally published in 1887
By D. Magner

ISBN 0-7858-1884-7

Printed in the United States of America

Leading Veterinary Surgeons Who Assisted In Preparing Special Articles in This Volume.

1. JAMES HAMILL, D.V.S. 2. T. BENT. COTTON, V.S. 3. PAUL PAQUIN, A.M.V.S.
4. A.J. CHANDLER, V.S. 5. JOHN A. McLAUGHLIN, V.S. 6. CHAS. A. MEYER, V.S.
7. D.G. SUTHERLAND, V.S. 8. DR. B.C. McBETH. 9. J.A. DELL, V.S.
10. S. BRENTON, V.S.

PREFACE.*

THERE are eleven million horses in the United States, and not one man in a million who knows how to educate them to the highest degree of usefulness. We say *educate ;* for the horse is an animal of high and spirited organization, endowed by his Creator with capabilities and faculties which sufficiently resemble man's to come under the same general law of education and government. Primarily, the word educate means to *lead out* or *lead up ;* and it is by the process of *leading out* and *leading up* a child's faculties that the child becomes a useful man, and it is by a like process that a colt becomes a useful horse. Now, teachers, like poets, are born, not made. Only a few are gifted to see into and through any form of highly organized life, discern its capacities, note the interior tendencies which produce habits, and discover the method of developing the innate forces until they reach their noblest expression, and then apply the true and sufficient guidance and government. The few who have this gift are teachers indeed, and, next to the mothers of the world, deserve the world's applause as foremost among its benefactors.

Next to child training and government comes horse training and government ; and which is the least understood, it were

---

* This preface was written by a gentleman well known in the world of letters, and especially famous, not only as a lover of fine horses, but as a high authority on all matters concerning them. Learning that I had in preparation a new work, he volunteered to write the preface, which is here given as a concise introduction to the author's own labors, with a high appreciation of the compliment paid him by the distinguished writer, in the personal allusion, the publication of which demands no apology when its high source is considered.

hard to say. Boys and colts, so much alike in friskiness and stubbornness, both are misunderstood and abused in equal ratio. The boys are shaken and whipped, and the colts are yanked, kicked, and pounded. That high-spirited or slow-witted boys become good men, and high-spirited or dull colts make serviceable horses, I conceive is due to the grace of God more than to man's agency,—that fine grace, I mean, spread abroad through and existing in all His creatures, which operates in regenerating continually, making the good better, and preventing those whose circumstances forbid their becoming good from becoming absolutely bad.

The author of this book is known to me as one of the gifted ones of the earth, because he is gifted to discern the nature of animals, and educate them for man's service. The possession of this gift suggested his mission, and well has he followed it, and by it been educated himself to a degree rarely, if ever, attained by man before. I doubt if there be on the globe his equal in knowledge as to the best method of training horses. Through this volume he seeks to give the public the benefit of his experience. I bespeak for it the careful perusal of the curious, and of those especially whose judgment and heart alike prompt them to seek for and promulgate knowledge, which, being popularized, would make the people more humane and horses more serviceable.

TABLE OF CONTENTS.

PART FIRST.

CONTENTS.

CONTENTS.

CONTENTS.

CHAPTER XXIV.

INTRODUCTION.

PRIOR to 1860, when I was first betrayed into giving some special exhibitions in the art of taming horses, there was but very little known on the subject, and what was known could not be regarded as more than the merest empiricism. Indeed, I had been under the impression myself at that time, that there was some great secret, giftedness, scent, or medicines by which vicious horses could be controlled and changed in character. This impression had misled me greatly ; and it was only by long-continued observation and practice that I was finally able, little by little, to grasp the subject in its true aspect, and learn the real principles of subduing and controlling vicious horses in a practically reliable manner.

The drift of my efforts and experiments which enabled me to do this, extended over many years, and during the first decade were necessarily but little more than a series of crude experiments, success being constantly alternated with more or less failure ; and, in fact, I was deeply interested in the study, and was far from exhausting it, when I left the road at the expiration of over nineteen years of the most exacting experience before the public, and extending to all the older-settled States of the country. But every failure, when made, had been only the means of suggesting new points, revealing to me new and more correct insight into the study, thereby carrying me forward, and enabling me finally to accomplish results in the

SUBJECTION OF SPECIALLY VICIOUS HORSES,

which were not only a source of constant interest and surprise to myself, but of astonishment to the best horsemen in the country and the world, because of reducing the principles of controlling and educating horses to the basis of an exact science, and not only revolutionizing all previous ideas of the control and management of horses, but saving fully eighteen-twentieths of the time usually required in their training, as well as making it entirely safe and simple to do. The power to change, as if by magic, the character of a horse that had perhaps defied all previous effort to be brought

2

under restraint, and proved in consequence to be practically worthless, frequently in the short period of less than an hour, could not but be accepted as a startling innovation to them, but, if possible, of more interest from the fact that these results were brought about by clear, well-defined principles of treatment, so plain, simple, and practical as to be easily understood and applied, and within the ability of any ordinary person to master and use.

These principles I was compelled to teach as a secret, for which I charged a fee of from five to ten dollars ; which instructions were necessarily limited to a few hours, and to a few representative citizens in each neighborhood that I visited ; and though I published a small work, which was included in the instructions, it was of necessity so written as not to impart these secrets, and would give no idea whatever of my methods and principles of treatment to persons who had not attended my lectures.

Though possessed, when young, of a remarkably strong constitution, the constant struggle and excitement forced upon me in so difficult a field for so many years, gradually undermined and impaired my health, until, in the early winter of 1878, I finally broke down so seriously as to be compelled to leave the road.

I now concluded to carry out at my leisure the purpose which had for some time been developing in my mind,—that of writing out the full details of my system, including such knowledge as I believed to be most valuable to horse owners, and that would bring it within the reach of people generally. I at first intended to make a work of only about three hundred pages, which would embody merely the simple outlines I gave to classes, with some additions to the treatment for sickness and lameness which I had already given in my old book. But after writing it up and preparing the illustrations I supposed necessary, I could see so much that should be added, that I was induced to re-write the whole matter, bringing it up to about six hundred pages, with about three hundred and fifty illustrations. When this was completed, I again found it necessary to make still more additions, until it grew upon my hands to the present size and number of illustrations of my regular book on this subject. With the enlargement of the work grew also upon me the desire to make the departments of **Shoeing, Sickness, and Lameness** equally satisfactory. With this object I made a special effort to secure the best veterinary skill I could command ; but in this I entirely failed, until fortunate in arresting the attention of DR. JAMES HAMILL, D. V. S., of New York City, formerly Professor of Pathological Shoeing in the Columbia Veterinary College, whom I found to have attended my lectures in that city in the winter of 1872, and who exhibited the kindest interest in my efforts, not only volunteering all the aid in his power to give, but securing for me the aid of two of his colleagues, DR. CHAS. A. MEYER, N. Y. City, and DR. JOHN A. MC LAUGHLIN, then of Jersey City, N. J., now of Providence, R. I., both of whom occupied high positions in the profession. DR. HAMILL gave me every aid in his power, not only in preparing the chapter on Shoeing, for which he was specially qualified, but in other departments, and in addition, placed the use of his fine library freely at my disposal.

The better to facilitate my work, I had these gentlemen dictate to me the outlines of treatment required, in the simplest language possible, with permission to make any changes I desired. It is but just, also, to them, to explain that the dictations by them were in all cases made without premeditation, the point in view being to give me the facts most clearly and in the fewest words. This was the more difficult for them from the fact that they were limited to my ability to take notes, as, on account of the peculiarly sensitive condition of my health, I could endure but very brief conversation, and but thirty or forty minutes' writing at one time.

I was also specially indebted to PROF. E. A. MC LELLAN, of Bridgeport, Conn., who was at the time Lecturer on Shoeing and Diseases of the Foot in Columbia Veterinary College, who gave me much valuable aid in that department. DR. B. C. MC BETH, of Battle Creek, Mich., also rendered me very important assistance.

After five large editions of the book had been published, and meeting with the greatest favor, it was strongly urged upon me by a leading book publisher, to add a STOCK DEPARTMENT that would in general character correspond with the rest of the work as it then stood. In support of his assertion, he stated that there was not a single really practical or reliable work published on the subject, and that if I would make such a book, I would not only be sure of a large sale, but confer a substantial benefit upon the farming community.

There had also been from the first repeated and urgent inquiries by my agents for such an additional feature, it being given as a reason that while farmers were greatly interested in horses, and needed the instructions given, they strongly desired also the additional departments suggested.

Influenced by these considerations, I was led to consider the matter seriously. But I found there was no single professional man in the country, so far as I knew, who could write up all the departments of such a work in the practical manner I required, as men even in the very first ranks of the profession are only proficient in certain departments, necessarily depending upon the aid of standard authorities. Then, there was no one man in the country whose time could be made available for the purpose, even at a high compensation.

In this emergency, and advised by veterinary friends, I determined upon the following plan, as that giving promise of the best and most satisfactory results : First, to obtain all the standard veterinary authorities in the English and European languages, especially those in German and French, embodying the highest and most reliable authorities on the subjects treated ; next, the employing of thoroughly trained scholars capable of translating and collecting the requisite facts from such authorities, and under my special directions write them out in the plainest language for the treatment of each disease ; and the matter so prepared, on each subject, to be submitted to one or more experts for each department, with instructions to make such changes and additions as in their judgment would be advisable to render the matter of the best practical reference. To do this work I employed three of the best scholars to be obtained in the country, one of whom was a regular graduate of one of our leading medical colleges. This work required of itself nearly a year's time.

In the meantime I consulted special friends in the veterinary profession to learn who were the best expert practitioners to make the revisions and corrections I required, and was so fortunate as to secure the aid of the gentlemen whose names are here given, and who co-operated with me in the most hearty manner.

LIST OF PROFESSIONAL EXPERTS.

JAS. HAMILL, D. V. S., 416 E. 14th St. New York City, formerly Lecturer on Shoeing and diseases of the Foot in Col. Vet. Col., Pres't Nat'l Vet'y Med. Ass'n, now Prof. of Oper. Surg'y and Horse Shoeing, N. Y. Col. of Vet. Sur. and Sch. of Com. Med.

CHAS. A. MEYER,* D. V. S., Editor Veterinary Gazette, New York.

JOHN A. McLAUGHLIN, D. V. S., Providence, R. I., ex-Veterinary Inspector N. J. State Board of Health.

D. G. SUTHERLAND, V. S., East Saginaw, Mich., ex-Pres't Mich. State Vet'y Ass'n.

PAUL PAQUIN, M. D., V. S., Columbia, Mo., Prof. Compar. Med., Direct. Exper. Labratory, State Vet'y Inspector, and Pres't Mo. Ass'n of Vet'y Science and Compar. Medicine.

T. BENT COTTON, M. D., V. S., Mt. Vernon, O., Pres't Ohio State Vet'y Ass'n, Vice-Pres't Nat'l Vet'y Med. Ass'n.

DR. B. C. McBETH, Battle Creek, Mich., Sec'y Mich. State Vet'y Ass'n, Hon. Mem. N. Y. St. Acad. of Science and Com. Path.

J. A. DELL, V. S., Ann Arbor, Mich., Pres't Mich. State Vet'y Ass'n.

A. J. CHANDLER, V. S., Detroit, Mich., Vice-Pres't Mich. State Vet'y Ass'n.

S. BRENTON, V. S., Jackson, Mich., Ex-Pres't Mich. State Vet'y Ass'n.

WM. JOPLING, V. S., Owosso, Mich., Treasurer Mich. State Vet'y Ass'n.

A. I. ROOT, Medina, O., author of "A B C of Bee Culture."

JOHN A. ADAMS, Horticulturist, Battle Creek, Mich.

---

* Deceased while this was being put in type.

The following explanations I deem also necessary in connection with the reference to these gentlemen :—

Dr. Cotton was highly recommended to me as a man ot much ability in the profession, by a prominent Eastern practitioner, and reference was made to his position among his *confrères* in the State, as assurance of his fitness for the work desired.

Dr. Paquin was known to me personally as a man of much more than ordinary attainments, and I made a special request that he would take charge of one or two of the more important departments. I am especially indebted to him also for translations from the French of analytical descriptions of the structure of the foot, he being known to me as an exceptionally fine French scholar.

I am also specially indebted to Dr. Meyer, not only for special papers, but for translations from the German on the structure of the foot, in which language he was a proficient scholar. In this respect, also, Dr. Hamill rendered me an exceptionally important service. Dr. Paquin, my best French scientific translator, was absent in Paris, engaged in special microscopic studies, and being unable to find a man competent to do the work, I explained the difficulty to Dr. Hamill, who stated that he would himself try to do it for me, and, to my surprise, I found him remarkably proficient, he being able to trace out readily every minute definition from the original, and adapt the explanations to the English, showing himself to be one of the most thorough scientific students of the structure of the foot in the veterinary profession.

Having personal acquaintance with Dr. Sutherland, who was at the time President of the Michigan State Veterinary Association, it occurred to me to send him sample chapters of the matter prepared, for his examination at the annual meeting of the Association at Jackson, and request him to refer me to those among the members of the Association competent and willing to take part in the work ; and through his aid, as well as that of the Secretary of the Association, Dr. Mc Beth, who also co-operated with me most cordially, I was able to secure the assistance of Drs. Dell, Chandler, Brenton, and Jopling, and Prof. Grange, of the Agricultural College.

The matter was now divided into sections and distributed to each of these experts, with freedom to make any changes or additions to the text they might deem necessary to make it most reliable and practical for reference. It was specially requested that the matter should be free from needless technicalities, and embody the most useful facts for the benefit of the class of readers for whom the work was intended. With the view of making this work as reliable as possible, special parts on the more malignant diseases were submitted to two or three in succession.

After the copy thus distributed had been all returned and put in type, it occurred to me that it would be a feature of special interest to my readers, to have the portraits of these professional friends engraved and placed in the work; and I was so fortunate (in some instances only after considerable persuasion) as to obtain permission to do so from those whose portraits are given; and I take great pleasure in presenting them as a good representation of the class of men engaged at present in the veterinary profession.

It is proper in this connection to state that should there appear any minor errors in the text, the responsibility for them must be entirely assumed by the author, as it was not possible, except at great inconvenience, after the matter had been put in type, to submit proofs to the gentlemen who had aided me in this work.

I may mention also that I made it a special object to have every detail of the work as fully and thoroughly illustrated as I could, as well as to include such features as would be most useful to the farmer. In carrying out this purpose I inserted in the stock department the large number of 800 figures, and in the horse department the still larger number of 950, among which are eighteen elegant plates. It is only necessary to state that there is no work heretofore published of this description that has more than a fourth of this number, and these usually of a very indifferent character, while this comprises the enormous aggregate, as will be seen, of 1,700, all having special reference to the text.

Particular attention is directed to the large number of illustrations of parasites common to the domestic animals; the great variety of figures illustrating the different diseases; the diversity of breeds of stock, particularly dairy cattle, sheep, hogs, and poultry. Certainly no work yet published can show any approach to the large number and varied character of the illustrations in these respects.

Interesting features will also be found in chapters on the Dog, on Bee-culture, the Growth of Fruit, including Insects Injurious to Fruit, and a Plea for the Birds, showing their value to the farmer.

The chapter on Bees, and that on the Protection of Fruit and Fruit Trees, will be found particularly interesting and valuable. That on Bee-culture was prepared with special care, under the supervision of A. I. ROOT, Esq., author of "The A B C of Bee Culture," and the highest authority on the subject, and includes the largest number of illustrations for the space occupied, that has yet been given on bees.

INTRODUCTION.

The chapter on Fruit was prepared by a leading horticulturist of large experience, MR. JOHN A. ADAMS, and will be found of great value and importance. The large number of fine and varied illustrations in this chapter, showing the insects that injure and destroy fruit, cannot but be of great interest, and with the text comprises knowledge of the greatest value to fruit-growers. I would call especial attention to this chapter, not only as a new feature, but for the practical character of its instructions and suggestions.

The Plea for the Birds should be read by every person of humane instincts. This paper is embodied mainly from an address by the famous and lamented REV. HENRY WARD BEECHER. This address was listened to by the author years before his death, and long before this work was prepared; but it struck him as so beautiful and valuable in every part, that he went at once to the stenographer and engaged him to furnish a copy for his special use. The addition of this chapter was in a good degree owing to suggestions of leading officers of the American Humane Society. This will be found one of the most interesting features of this work, because most useful and elevating in its influence, and being one of the finest pleas for the birds ever written, showing their value to the farmer, and the duty of protecting them. THE AUTHOR.

THE STANDARD
HORSE AND STOCK BOOK.

CHAPTER I.

PRELIMINARY REMARKS.

ONCE, while stopping with a farmer, as a matter of amusement I took a colt that had become unmanageable to him, and made him perfectly gentle. Upon learning what I had done, the farmer was so surprised at the result as to offer me fifty dollars for the secret. Without thinking, I proposed teaching him and ten of his neighbors how I did it, in addition to other points that might be of interest to them. In this I was entirely successful, and thus I was unintentionally drifted into the most trying and exacting field of effort that ever man engaged in, which continued nearly nineteen years. I was necessarily forced into contact with all sorts of people, who were continually trying to break me down, and in addition I had the most vicious and difficult horses

Fig. 1.— **Ideal Head of an Intelligent, Docile Character.**

forced upon me to experiment upon ; and that I succeeded at all seems to me even now so remarkable as to be beyond belief. But without realizing it, or knowing it at the time, the people who forced me to these trials were in reality my best friends, because proving the best instructors to me in the world ; and the experiments upon vicious horses were just what was necessary to give me the best opportuni-

Figs. 2–4.—**Extremes of Vicious Character.**

ties of observation and practice needed to master the subject. Now, in teaching classes I soon found it necessary to make such explanations of points and conditions as I could before making experiments ; and in like manner, before taking up the details of instruction, I think it necessary to refer to such points as will be most suggestive in the study of the subject. I may state that this is somewhat difficult here, because compelled to limit my explanations to less than one half of what I have been able to devote to it in my regular work on the horse, and also to omit many chapters of much interest to the general reader.

Many of the lower animals possess some qualities by nature that

Fig. 5.—**A Portrait of a Docile Family Horse.**

make them, in some respects, really superior to man. The dog, for example, can follow the track of his master through a crowd of strangers, though hours behind, and find him ; and he will also find his way home, though distant hundreds of miles—a fact that has been repeatedly proved. The ordinary sheep-dog will at command find and bring home stray sheep of the flock ; and the blood-hound can perform the still more remarkable feat of taking up the track of a criminal hours afterward, by the scent of a bit of his clothing, and pick him out from hundreds of others who had been his companions — a power that entitles even the commonest cur to our kindest consideration. The eagle and vulture, though miles in the

FIG. 6.—A very Intelligent, Docile Character.

air, can see the smallest objects of prey on the ground—a power far beyond that of man. Thus these superior qualities, exhibited so largely by the lower animals, seem to be a special provision of nature to guard them from danger and aggression, or to aid them in providing sustenance.

Now, this singular power of instinct appears to be a very strongly marked feature of the horse's nature. The wild horse of the prairie cannot be approached near enough on the windward side to imperil his safety; and even when cornered and unable to get away, his acts of biting, striking, or kicking are but his natural promptings to defend himself. It is also seen that no matter how wild a colt, when treated with such kindness as to win his confidence, he not only will not show fear of man, but become a pet. A good demonstration of this is shown in the remarkable docility of the Arab horses, which are always treated with the utmost kindness; and ladies who are specially kind to horses, it is known, can approach them anywhere, and make them such pets that they will follow, even into the house. Perhaps in no way is this peculiar instinct more strikingly shown than in the repugnance of exceptionally sensitive, intelligent horses to men who may be ignorantly or thoughtlessly cruel to them.

FIG. 7.—Intelligent, Courageous, but very Sensitive Nature.

Hence it is evident that the true ground of success in the subjection and education of the horse, or in breaking up and overcoming bad habits when formed, must be in proportion to the degree to which the efforts can be intelligently addressed to the line of these instincts, holding passive, combating, or overcoming them while addressing the understanding, without exciting his fears or resistance ; and it is absolutely imperative that in his education these conditions should not be disregarded.

FIG. 8.—One of the most Vicious Horses ever Subdued by the Author.

Another point : a horse may be moved to intense excitement and extreme resistance by even a momentary impression of fear, without any contact with or cause for feeling direct physical pain ; and again, in like manner, when properly treated, such fear may be overcome without resorting to treatment that would cause the least physical pain or injury.

Another important feature for consideration is the wonderful adaptation in the various domestic animals, not only to the several wants and requirements of man, but to the sections of the world in which we find them. Thus, for example, the Esquimau has not only a dog, but one peculiarly fitted by nature to his especial wants, acting not only as a fisherman and a hunter, but as a beast of burden, being in fact the only animal that could live and be of any use to him so far north. A little farther south, the Laplander has the reindeer, that lives on the moss peculiar to those regions, providing both sustenance and clothing for him, as well as being the very best means of traveling over those dreary, frozen plains. The Peruvians have the llama for carrying burdens over the Andes. The Arabs have the camel for their peculiar want, that of traveling over the arid, sandy

FIG. 9.—Nervous, Excitable Horse.

2

desert, and so constituted as to carry within himself a supply of water sufficient to last for many days.

Not only do we see here special families, demonstrating this

FIG. 10.—**A Vicious, Treacherous Nature.**

principle most strikingly, but such subdivisions of each as adapt them more perfectly for special uses. Now the horse, which is by far the most noble, valuable, and useful of all the domestic animals, in the management of which we are specially interested, shows this to a wonderful degree in size, disposition, and intelligence. For slow, drudging work, we have the coarse-grained, patient, heavy cart or plow horse, while for quick, long-continued exertion, we have the lithe thoroughbred, with the conformation of the greyhound, capable, if necessary, of running with the fleetness of the wind. From these extremes we have illimitable modifications, adapting them the more perfectly to the various requirements of man. Now, it is clear that the nervous, energetic racer or thoroughbred would be entirely out of place for the cart or plow, and the coarse-grained cart or plow horse for the quick, active exertion of speedy travel; and that to make each most useful he must be employed for such work only as nature best fits him for.

FIG. 11.—**Portrait of a Noted Vicious Horse.**

Dependent upon these physical conditions are others that have a still more important bearing upon the success of our efforts, because they are necessarily more obscure, and we are compelled to study them more carefully to win success, namely, the intelligence and disposition of horses.

To illustrate my meaning in part: It is clear that some horses

Fig. 12.—Sullen Treachery.

are very much more intelligent and quick to comprehend than others ; that some are by nature of the most perfect docility, while others have a large element of the naturally vicious, dangerous character. Here, then, we are compelled to study and learn, if possible, two things,—the conditions requisite for the best management of the sensitive, intelligent nature, as well as those that are dull, strong, and naturally vicious. In the first, we must study how to address and win the understanding directly, if possible, without a ruffle of excitement ; and in the management of the second, we must impress the intelligence in such a way as to win obedience most safely and easily.

This necessarily requires the careful study of the vital powers, dependent upon the following conditions : First, the intelligence, as dependent upon the volume of brain ; second, the physical strength, as dependent upon size and quality of bodily structure ; third, the peculiar phase and degree of the viciousness.

It is evident that when we have large brain, dense texture of body, good digestion, and large, deep chest, we have indicated, first, great natural strength ; second, great endurance, in consequence of ability to assimilate food ; third, capacity to oxygenate the blood rapidly, thus giving great endurance for long-sustained effort. Lacking these conditions to any extent, even though there

Fig. 13.—Sketch from Life of the most Vicious Mustang Pony the Writer ever Saw.

may be great energy and pluck, there will be less ability to resist well-sustained coercive measures.

Now, dependent upon the order of intelligence and bodily structure are certain peculiarities. For example, a full forehead, large, clear eyes, tending to brown in color, set well out on the head, eyelids thin, medium length from eyes to ears, ears pointed and of medium length, placed not very wide apart and high between them, and large nostrils,

F<small>IG</small>. 14.—**Sketch of a Vicious Stallion.**

will most always indicate the intelligent, steady, reliable, family horse ; while a forehead rather narrow, small, round eyes, set well back in the side of the head, eyelids heavy, long from eyes to ears, ears long and flabby, with a tendency to throw them back a little, nose rounding, and nostrils small, show the opposite, or a dull, sullen, treacherous nature. If the forehead be of a medium or good breadth, the eyes good size, clear, and setting well out, the lids thin, short from eyes to ears, ears a little longer than common, and

F<small>IG</small>. 15.—**Portrait of a Noted Vicious Horse in a Rage.**

nostrils large, there will be indicated intelligence, activity, but great sensibility ; usually termed the nervous, sensitive horse, that will not bear excitement.

From these extremes, again, we have illimitable modifications, dependent upon conditions referred to.

Figs. 1, 5, 6, and 7 give the best expressions of a naturally docile, intelligent character. Figs. 1, 5, and 6 are fine illustrations of the best types of the gentle family horse. Fig. 7 is the best type of a sensitive, but very intelligent horse, being a portrait of a noted Arabian horse. Fig. 9 is a good type of a very nervous, sensitive character. Figs. 8, 10, and 11

FIG. 16.—**Naturally Docile and Intelligent.**

are modifications of the dull, sullen, treacherous type. Fig. 10 is a portrait of a very marked case. Fig. 11 is also a portrait of a very noted vicious horse. Fig. 13 is that of a mustang pony, the most desperate, reckless creature the writer ever subjected to treatment. Fig. 17 is a portrait of a case that up to nine years old had proved utterly unmanageable, but whose character was made so gentle, after an hour's treatment, that it was afterward used as a family horse. Fig. 21 is a good illustration of the barnyard lunkhead. In addition there is seen to be a large number of illustrations showing combinations and contrasts of character which are deserving of careful study.

The size of bone, the texture of bodily structure, the length and color of hair, amount of hair in mane or tail, the action in moving, the size and expression of eye, the peculiarity of head, its length, breadth, etc., are subjects requiring the most constant and careful consideration in directing intelligent treatment.

Principles of Treatment.

In the subjection and education of horses, we have several natural difficulties to contend with. First: The horse is much stronger than man, and just so far as he in any

FIG. 17.—**" Wild Pete."   A Very Peculiar and Interesting Case.**

way learns that he can resist man's control, to that degree will he be encouraged and inclined to resist or combat him : hence, an indispensable condition of his successful education is that he must be given no opportunity to learn that he is not in every respect subordinate to man in physical power, until his character becomes fixed.

FIG. 18.—**Docile, Intelligent.**

Second: His methods of reasoning being dependent upon and limited to the observation and experience of his senses of seeing, hearing, smelling, and feeling, to prevent his becoming excited or frightened at objects and sounds with which he is necessarily brought in contact, he must be convinced in his own way, through these faculties, of their harmless and innocent character. Consequently, if he be treated according to these laws of his nature, he can be made to do willingly, without fear or resistance, anything for which he is by nature adapted.

Third: The horse, being unable to understand the meaning of articulated language, excepting so far as words are associated with actions, we must address his intelligence on this plane of his reasoning, because it is only by doing so that he can be expected to comprehend our wishes clearly.

Fourth: To the degree that the horse becomes excited, frightened, or confused, he must necessarily be both unable to understand what is required to be done, and correspondingly less inclined to submit to restraint in his management. Hence, whatever the treatment, it must be of a character not to confuse or excite him, nor to expose him to such excessive fear as would shock and derange his nervous system.

Taking these conditions in order, we see, for example, that if a horse learns to pull

FIG. 19.—**A Noted Vicious Horse.**

away, break his halter, resist the blacksmith in shoeing, or run away, etc., he will be encouraged to and try to do so afterward until the habit becomes fixed. On the contrary, when a colt is

3

first haltered, no matter how hard he may resist, if once taught to submit, he will not only readily follow without restraint, but will do so ever afterward ; or when the feet are taken up and handled until the operation is fully submitted to, or such restraint brought upon him as to compel submission, there will not only be obedience for the time, but all inclination to resist will be radically overcome.

FIG. 20.—**Strong-Willed, Intelligent Character.**

Now, the principle is the same in relation to other habits, or in overcoming viciousness. No matter how wild or unmanageable the horse may be, if he can be so treated that successful resistance becomes impossible, and he is shown that he will not be injured, there will not only be entire submission without the use of force, but if not excited or abused, he will remain permanently docile.

But it is imperative that there be at no point such an exposure of weakness as would encourage resistance ; for, though the method of treatment may be in itself right, if not carried to the point desired, the difficulties of the treatment will necessarily be increased to a degree liable to precipitate failure. For example, there may be strength to take up a colt's foot ; but if at any point of holding it it is pulled away, and control resisted, he will be inclined to resist afterward with as much energy as if there had not been sufficient power to take it up at all. Or, in teaching a horse to lead by the halter, if he resists successfully it will teach him to resist the efforts by pulling away. Now,

FIG. 21.—**Barnyard Lunkhead.**

the method of pulling on the halter may be all right, but the point of difficulty would be in not having power to carry it far enough. Not only this, but it is vital to·success to do it properly, or in such a way that there would be the least inclination to resistance. If, for example, in taking up the horse's foot, by standing forward of the hip, well up near the body, facing backward, one hand is rested against the hip, while at

Fig. 22.—Docile Expression.

Fig. 23.—Docile Expression.

the moment of taking up the foot with the other, there is firm pressure exerted against the hip, to throw the weight upon the opposite leg, the foot can be brought up easily, and then, when submitted to, the simple movement forward will bring it against the knees to be handled with safety as desired. In leading by the halter, if, instead of pulling straight ahead, which gives the horse great advantage to resist, the operator stands opposite the shoulder and pulls sufficiently hard to bring the horse off his feet a few times, he will soon follow unconditionally without the least restraint.

In a hundred different ways this principle is seen to be illustrated in consequence of the horse's not being sufficiently disciplined to make him entirely manageable in harness and fearless when under the tests of severe excitement. It is for this reason that horses that may have been driven for months, or even years, when managed with care, or not subjected to unusual causes of accident or excitement, are liable at some unguarded moment, when

Fig. 24.—Coarse, Low-bred Horse.

exposed to some exceptional strain, up to which they have not been tested, to become frightened and resist control, thereby resulting in constantly recurring cases of accident, as well as endangering the spoiling of the horse ; which would all have been prevented by the application and proper carrying out of necessary treatment in the first place.

Second : We see that when an object of fear or unusual sound is brought suddenly or unexpectedly to the horse's notice, or in contact with any part of his body, it is liable to excite the most intense fear and resistance ; whereas, if brought slowly and gently to his notice, letting him smell or feel of it until convinced of its harmlessness, it can be brought over and around him without causing the least fear or attracting his attention.   It makes no difference whether

Fig. 25.--Vicious.   Fig. 26.—Treacherous.

it is in driving to a carriage, letting the cross-piece come against the quarters, raising an umbrella behind him, the noise of a steam-engine, or anything else, the principle is the same.

Third : In relation to making him understand the meaning of special sounds or words of command.   If a man were simply to repeat the word "Whoa" to a horse, he might do it indefinitely without his being able to understand its meaning and object.   But if the horse were moved moderately, and immediately after the command he were pulled upon hard enough to make him stop, he would in a short time, when the word is repeated, learn to stop to avoid being hurt.   Or, in teaching him to back, if after the word is spoken the reins be pulled upon sufficiently to force him back, he will, after a few repetitions, learn, when the command is given, to go back freely, to evade the restraint and pain.

The better to illustrate this I will include here the details of teaching a few tricks.

To teach a horse to make a bow, first prick him lightly on the back with a pin, and repeat this until, in his efforts to avoid the annoyance, he drops his head, after which caress him, repeating the pricking until the head is again dropped, when again repeat the caress and give him something of which he is fond, and continue to alternate in this way with the pricking, caressing, and rewarding, until at the least motion of the hand toward the back he will drop his head.

To teach him to kick, simply prick him on the rump until there is an inclination to kick up, when, as before, caress him, and so repeat until the least motion of the hand toward the rump will induce him to kick up.

In teaching any kind or number of tricks, the principle is the same, the only difference being that instead of a pin, other means adapted to the requirements of the case must be used.

But one thing should be taught at a time, and that slowly and carefully repeated until thoroughly understood. The duller the horse, and the more complicated or difficult to the understanding the point to be taught, the less can be safely attempted, and the more time must necessarily be taken ; while the more intelligent the horse, and the simpler the thing required to be done, the more can be accomplished. And each point thus made should be made the foundation for the next, until the education is complete.

Again, to have prompt obedience, the same signal and word given in teaching the trick, or whatever is required to be done, must be repeated exactly, *even to the tone and pitch of the voice;* otherwise a horse is liable

Figs. 27–30.—Modifications of Good Character.

FIGS. 31–36.—**Extremes of Low-bred, Vicious Character.**

to become more or less confused and unable to understand or obey. The principle is the same in teaching a horse to do anything in or out of harness; the point being that such means or methods of treatment are to be used as will give the necessary control, and at the same time convey to the understanding in the most direct manner the idea of what is desired to be done.

Now, the principle is exactly the same in both preventing and overcoming viciousness or bad habits, no matter what their character or degree; the only difference being that instead of teaching a trick, or obedience in any respect, we must aim now to combat the habit already formed, simply repeating until there is entire docility and submission.

Again, in resorting to physical power, the nearer we are able to use it so as not to cause pain nor excite the belligerent nature of the horse, the better. If a man were strong enough to take a fighting bully by the shoulders and shake him so thoroughly as to show him that he had power to control the fellow as he pleased, and then treat him kindly and convince him that his intentions were good, it would have a better effect in impressing him with a sense of the man's mastery, and make him less inclined to resist, than if he had obtained control of him after a desperate struggle that would heat his blood and arouse his passions to the point of recklessness.

In like manner, if we could use power directly upon a horse, so as to restrain and control him as we wished, it would be far more effective than if the effort were of a character to cause him to become maddened and heated; or, if this be impossible, then the resorting to such indirect measures of coercion as will enable us to accomplish this most safely and easily.

Now, the treatment herein given does this

with far more ease, directness, and success than has ever yet been accomplished. It not only enables us to control with the greatest facility, frequently in a few minutes, not exceeding twenty or thirty, horses that had resisted all previous efforts to subdue or control them, and become practically worthless, but it gives the proper foundation for making the character safe and reliable afterward, its most remarkable feature being the startling results accomplished in so short a time, apparently changing the entire nature of the horse as if by magic.

This treatment is the outgrowth of the practice of over eighteen years of the most constant and exacting experimenting, and has been proved, by the results exhibited, to bring the control and education of horses as nearly as possible to the line of an exact science, conclusively showing that when horses become vicious or unmanageable, it is the result of ignorance or bad management, which the treatment herein given, if properly applied, would have entirely prevented.

I could include a great deal of other treatment, and much of it very good, but wishing only to give what is practical, I confine myself to such treatment only as I have found in my experience to be best.

Before taking up details, I would state that there is no difficulty in making a horse, even when of a very vicious character, gentle for a short time ; but the difficulty is to be able to hold and fix the character in such a way that he will remain gentle. This may be done in quite a variety of ways. Any method of lowering the vitality, such as bleeding, physicking, preventing sleep, depriving of food or water, subjecting to intense pain, or, in fact, any means whereby we can successfully lower the strength, will make a horse gentle. But the difficulty is that, however gentle he may be at the time, when the

Figs. 37–42. — Modifications of Well-bred Character.

effect passes off, or the horse regains his strength, there will be so great a tendency to gravitate back to the former condition that the treatment will nearly always result in disappointment.

While it is known that many persons have the power of controlling the will of others, or what is termed psychologizing them, and that some of the lower animals secure their prey in this manner, as exhibited by the snake in charming birds and small animals, various cases of which I refer to (particularly in discussing this subject) in my special work on the horse, the principle does not seem to work in the control of horses ; certainly it has not in my experience, and I have hundreds of times produced results before classes which seemed so remarkable to them that they would insist upon searching my gloves and clothes for some scent or odor which might account to them for the effect produced ; and even after this they could scarcely realize that it could be accomplished by the treatment illustrated before them. I have had members of classes repeatedly tell me in private that they knew I must have acquired my power by some secret not revealed to them, and be so confident of this that they would offer me large sums for it.

I necessarily acquired a certain expertness, the result of practice and accuracy of judgment in applying treatment, that often enabled results, in the control of certain types of resistance and character, that seemed very remarkable. This was frequently shown in the cases of horses afraid of a blanket, a buffalo-robe, or something of the kind ; in the control of a stallion so as to be led up to a mare and then called away ; the control of a wild and seemingly very dangerous colt that had been proved very unmanageable, so as to drive entirely gentle without breeching ; the making of a colt follow, or the making of a halter-puller when hitched stand quietly without attempt-

FIGS. 43–48. — **Modifications of Vicious Character.**

ing to pull. It was no unusual thing for me to do, when the case
happened to be good, within two or three minutes to be able to

FIGS. 49–51 —Three Types of Good Character.

throw a buffalo-robe as I pleased over the head or around the body
of a horse that had previously been quite seriously afraid of it,
without the horse caring much about it. In the control of a headstrong stallion, if a good subject, it rarely required more than four
or five minutes ; the hitching up and driving gentle of such a colt as
described, in six to eight or ten minutes ; the making of a halter-
puller stand submissive under the most severe excitement of being

FIGS. 52–54.—Coarse, Low Character.

whipped over the head, or the cause of the pulling thrown in his face,
without his pulling, in a couple of minutes.

Now, it is needless to add that if this treatment had been applied roughly or improperly, this control could only be obtained after
considerable severe treatment that would excite the horse greatly,
thus acquiring control only at the expense of considerable time

FIG. 55.—**Vicious Horse in a Rage.**

and trouble. This rule, in fact, runs through every phase of the treatment, in illustrating its success and applying it properly.

SUGGESTIONS IN RELATION TO PRINCIPLES OF MANAGEMENT.

If we tie down a horse's ear, or grasp it with the hand and twist it a little, it will be found that a horse that had been very nervous to shoe will often stand quite gentle to be shod. The jockey has learned that he can frequently make a bad kicking mare drive without kicking by tying the tail down to the cross-piece of the shafts or forward to the belly-band of the harness, so that it cannot be raised ; because disabling the tail creates such a sense of helplessness as to counteract the inclination to kick.

Sometimes checking the head high will accomplish the same result. Putting cobbles or shot in the ears will, on the same principle, sufficiently disconcert a balky horse to make him go right along. Blindfolding by covering the eyes only carries this to a greater extent, and will be found in most cases to make quite a stubborn horse work with excellent success.

FIG. 56.—**A Noted Vicious Horse.**

The secret of the first horse-tamer of whom I have any account —Dick Christian of England—consisted simply in tying up the fore leg, and then mounting and riding the horse until submissive. The next step in this direction was disabling both fore legs, and thus forcing the horse to lie down, which carried this principle to a greater degree of perfection. This was regarded a very rare secret, and was the basis of the methods practiced by Bull in England, Sullivan in Mallow, Ireland, Denton Offutt in Kentucky, and O. H. P. Fancher in Ohio, who were the first, most pretentious, and noted, before the advent of Rarey, who learned the secret of Denton Offutt,

F<small>IG.</small> 57.—An Incident in the Driving of a Noted Runaway Horse.

at the time a resident of Georgetown, Ky. This was the sole and only secret upon which were based Rarey's most extraordinary pretensions, and for teaching which he made $100,000 in England ; and probably much more than that was paid in this country for the same knowledge.

I may add, by way of explanation, that the control of Cruiser and other noted cases in England and France, upon which his reputation was based, although it was assumed to be, was not and could not have been accomplished by this treatment. Those interested in a full explanation of all the facts in regard to it, will find the details in the chapter on "Subjection" in my work, "Facts for Horse-Owners."

Various remedies have also been assumed to be used for taming horses under the pretense of a great secret, or the guise of fascination, on the principle of using certain scents for attracting and controlling certain wild animals or fishes. These means have about the same effect upon a horse as good apples, or anything else of which the horse is naturally fond. While it is true that horses may sometimes, for example, be strongly repelled by blood or the odor of poisonous snakes, and other dangerous animals, and that they are attracted and quieted by other scents, I have found nothing of the

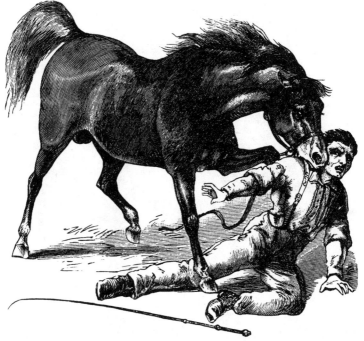

Fig. 58.—**The Famous Horse Jet, of Portland, Me., Subdued by the Author in Thirty Minutes.**

kind that would accomplish satisfactory results to me in their control, but little more than would be done by good apples, or the giving of anything else of which the horse is fond. Offutt and Fancher, before referred to, were the most pretentious in their use of such scents, the details of which I include in my other work.

Various alterations or modifications of this method of subduing horses were made at different times by different parties; but it was not until I was able to bring into use that here described as the First Method of Subjection, that the real power and effect of this principle of treatment was practically brought out; which has been the outgrowth of a great deal of practical experimenting requiring over fifteen years' time.

If in wrestling a man could be thrown directly upon his back as fast as he could get up, it is evident a much more effectual impression of his antagonist's mastery could be made than if he were permitted to carry on a doubtful struggle for half an hour, that would only occasionally bring him to his knees. The very doubtfulness of the contest would stimulate him to the utmost resistance until exhausted. But if he could be thrown at once, and as often as he could get up, his courage and confidence would be soon broken up, convincing him of the uselessness of continuing the struggle, and making the impression of mastery all that could be desired.

Fig. 59.—An Act of a Noted Vicious Stallion Subdued by the Author in Less than an Hour.

Now, the effect upon a horse will be the same. If the control can be made direct and positive, throwing him on his side as often as he can get up, the confidence which stimulates the resistance is quickly broken up.

The method here given as the First Method of Subjection, bears exactly this relation to that formerly used. It gives just the advantage and power that will enable any ordinary man to throw the strongest horse as quickly and as often as he can get up; in addition, he can hold him down or roll him back, as he pleases, thereby making it not only far more effective, but entirely obviating the objections to the old method.

I have called attention to these interesting facts: first, that the horse is governed in his actions by certain instincts or inherent powers, and that these must be studied closely as the foundation of his successful management ; next, tha. these constitutional differences are only provisions adapting him for special uses ; and that his character is clearly shown by the peculiarities of his bodily structure, actions, and more especially by the features of the head.   This will show, when looked at carefully, that resistance is only the expression of natural instinct, and that fear or vicious actions are not to be taken as indicating a degree of bad character or viciousness that should

Fig. 60.—The Thorough-bred.

be considered an obstacle in making the character good, simply requiring greater care and thought in meeting and combating the resistance, whatever it is, in the most simple, direct, and humane manner.   Though referred to before, it is so important that I call attention to it again here, that though the treatment may be applied just right, if not carried far enough, the failure may be as great as if improper treatment had been used ; and above all, that the better nature is to be won by patient, persistent kindness.   I have called attention, next, to the various methods of treatment taught me by the experience of many long years of observation, experiment, and study, and have tried faithfully to make the explanations as simple and plain as I could.

Now, it is indispensable that this chapter, at least certain parts of it, which are the key and groundwork of the detailed

Fig. 61.—A Good Model of Draught Horse.

instructions in subsequent chapters, should be read very carefully. You cannot understand these principles too well.

Fig. 62.—Shetland Pony.

There are also many points having close relation to this subject, and of great interest to the horseman, which want of space in a general work of this character compels me to omit: First, the inside history of Rarey's career, as a means of correcting the false impressions created by his pretensions and assumed success, because without it there was necessarily a certain mystery about the performance of this duty that could not well be made plain ; second, the details

Fig. 63.—Model of the French Norman Horse.

of the management and history of a large number of specially representative vicious horses, as suggestive aids to treatment in similar cases ; third, the outlines of my experience with reference to many cases and circumstances named, the better to authenticate the facts stated. There are also special chapters on other points having close and important connection with the instruction given on this subject. All these points are very fully given in my regular work on the horse, which can be referred to by those interested.

I would now call attention to what I deem the most important condition of success, which should be considered, above all others, as deserving of the most serious consideration, namely, the judgment and skill with which the treatment is applied.

It is generally supposed that the most important qualification for success in the control of vicious horses, is being a sort of strongish bully, gifted with power to master a horse physically, or whip him into submission. Now, no mistake could be greater. In many hundreds of instances, in fact, it was a matter of almost daily occurrence, horses were brought to me to experiment upon, which the most persistent efforts of the strongest and most pretentious or so-called best horse-breakers had failed upon,—horses that were sup-

Fig. 64.—The Horse Ready to be Thrown.   Old Method referred to.

posed to be so bad that nothing could be done with them. Such men were almost invariably members of my classes; and the results I was able to produce before them became of the greatest interest to them, because proving to them the necessity and value of bringing into exercise their highest intelligence and ingenuity in the performance of this duty; and that, in its true light, the study of the subject was one of the most interesting and instructive to which a thoughtful and intelligent mind could be directed.

Finally, above almost any other profession or business, the proper and successful management of horses requires peculiarly fine qualifications; and while in other directions one point of excellence may be sufficient to give a man marked success, this not only calls for a combination, but a very rare combination, of good qualities. First, a man must be fine and clear in his perceptions; that is, he

4   a

must be quick to see, delicate in feeling, with sufficient strength
of nerve to carry him through the severest trials without flinching
or showing weakness; added to these, sufficient persistence and
patience to follow up every point of difficulty, no matter how great
the obstacle, until successful. If I may so word it, he must
have the delicacy of touch and feeling of a woman, the eye of an
eagle, the courage of a lion, and the hang-on pluck of a bull-dog. If
he is lacking in any one of these qualities it is a matter of chance

Fig. 65.—**As the Horse is Liable to Rear and Plunge, in his Resistance to being Thrown.**

only, in critical cases, that there will not be accident or failure.

Now, if you have n't these qualifications, you can exercise at
least that very important one of going slow, studying your case
thoroughly, using the greatest care possible, and being patient in
your efforts. This alone will frequently enable you to do wonders.

Imagine yourself in the horse's place, unable to talk or understand what is wanted to be done or the object of restraint, incited
perhaps by great fear or the resentment of previous long-continued
abuse, to resist contact or restraint, and you will have the truest
instinct in pointing to the best course to be pursued. Not succeeding, even after great effort, should by no means imply failure; the
point is to look your difficulties over in their every phase, prepare

yourself more carefully, trust nothing to chance, and never think you cannot succeed ; and, with the exercise of reasonable patience and care, especially when aided by the instructions here given, the most ignorant and least fitted by nature for this work may accomplish wonders. Certainly, this will compensate largely for want of skill ; and, as time should not be considered, this can without difficulty be exercised by every one.

FIG. 66.—Usual Position before being Thrown.

In the next chapter we will take up the details of treatment, comprising three direct methods of subjection, followed by several indirect methods, which give such power and effectiveness in the control of vicious horses as practically to leave but little to be desired. These methods of treatment have been the outgrowth of a great deal of practical experimenting, and by them I was able to effect results in the subjection of vicious horses which it is conceded has never been equaled or approached in ancient or modern times ; and they give us the true foundation for the performance of this important duty with entire success.

CHAPTER II.

FIRST METHOD OF SUBJECTION.

AS before explained, disabling any part of the horse's body will produce in him a corresponding sense of helplessness ; and when we disable the whole body, or overmatch his powers wholly, we create in him a powerful sense of our mastery, and a corresponding sense of his own helplessness. The simplest and most effective means of doing this is by the method here given.

I give two rigs, one of leather and one of rope. The leather rig works well, is not difficult to fit, but is troublesome to make,

Fig. 67.—Mustang Ponies.

and expensive, costing from eight to fifteen dollars. The rope rig works equally well, and can be made of any old rope in a few minutes, at a mearly nominal cost. I include a description of each.

For the leather rig the surcingle should be made of two thicknesses of good harness leather, about three inches wide, and about eight or ten inches longer than the size of the body. The buckle should have two tongues, and be made of good wrought iron. When this rig is on and drawn tightly from the part over the backbone, a double strap, the length of the back, with a strong crupper, should be attached. Four or five inches on the off side should be fastened, at the front edge of this surcingle, a strong two-inch ring. On the

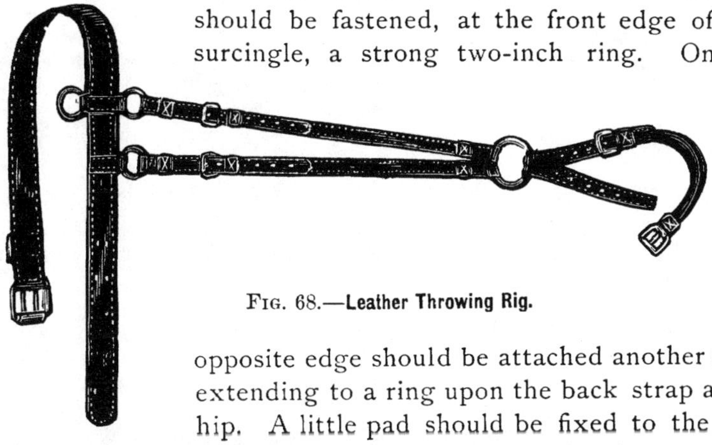

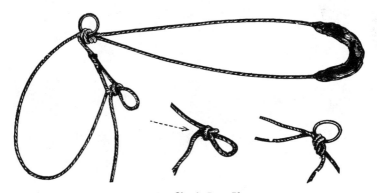

Fig. 68.—Leather Throwing Rig.

opposite edge should be attached another strap extending to a ring upon the back strap at the hip. A little pad should be fixed to the part coming across the back, to prevent bruising or chafing it.

For the rope rig, procure a three-fourths inch rope, eighteen or twenty feet in length. One that has been used enough to render it pliable is best. Make a simple loop about three inches long at one end, and double the rope about four feet from the loop. Pass over

Fig. 69.—Simple Rope Rig.

this double part a three-inch ring made of three-eighths rod. Measure the distance from the tail to where the saddle of the harness comes, to which bring the ring and make a simple knot of both ropes around it, regulating it to the length of the back as it is tightened. Next, put the double part under the tail, twist two or three times, and bring the part with the ring to its place about eight inches to the right of the back, with the loop toward the near side. While holding it in position, reach under the body, catch the oppo-

FIG. 70.—**Foot Tied Up.**

FIG. 71.—**Foot-strap.**

site end of the rope, bring it through the loop, and draw down to the size of the body. Now, while holding it in place by pressing down firmly upon it, make a simple knot in the rope, which forms a button and keeps it from slipping out. It is also necessary to protect the back and tail by winding the part of the rope coming under the

FIG. 72.—**The Rig as Arranged for Throwing.**

tail, and putting two or three thicknesses of cloth or blanket between it and the back.

Next, put on a strong strap halter with the nose part coming well down upon the nose, and draw it up rather close back of the jaw ; then take a piece of strong cord, made of the very best quality of hemp, (that used for the largest-sized war bridle, explained farther on, is best,) from five-sixteenths to three-eighths of an inch in diameter and about twenty feet in length, tie a hard knot in each end, and fasten one end around the rope or surcingle just above the ring. Pass the other end from above down over the strap of the halter back of the jaw, thence back and down through the ring referred to, until the slack is taken up. Now tie up the near fore foot. The best way to do this is to pass an ordinary hame-strap around the foot, thence to the belly-band, and buckle short.

Though this method, when properly carried out, enables throwing a horse on even very hard ground without bruising the knees or other parts, still it is very important, and adds greatly to the ease and safety of throwing, to have good soft ground. The best is

FIG. 73.—**Turning a Stubborn Horse around before Throwing.**

that which is free from stone, with thick, soft sod, as an orchard or meadow, a ploughed field, or a place liberally covered with straw or manure. Presuming that such a place has been selected, stand almost in front of the horse at the right, with a firm hold of the cord about seven or eight feet from the shoulder, pull gently, but firmly, as shown in Fig. 72. This will draw the head back to the side, and the body being thereby thrown out of balance, the horse is forced to fall over with a rolling motion on his side. If during the first trial he resists, let him have his own way a little while, and when in a good position, pull quickly, when he can easily be forced off his balance and made to fall over. In cases for which it is adapted, and if well done, the horse will be forced down so easily and naturally that nothing is left to be desired. Then he can be thrown as easily and just as fast as he can be made to get up. I have frequently been able to make nervy, strong horses jump up in this manner as often as ten times a minute. About twelve times is the limit of what such a horse will have the courage to get up before submitting, the treatment being always most effective when the horse resists it hard by trying to get up. If a strong-willed, headstrong fellow, disposed to resist hard, perhaps lunging forward, etc., as some horses are liable to do, take a firm hold of the cord and run around in a circle until

F<small>IG</small>. 74—**Usual Position of a Horse that Resists Strongly before being Thrown.**

he is made to follow, hopping steadily (as illustrated by Fig. 73), when stop, pull quickly, and he can be easily thrown over on his side.

As soon as the cord is given slack, the horse will usually jump up, when, by again pulling, he can be thrown, which can be repeated as often as he will get up. After being thrown, should he not try to rise, and it is desired to repeat the operation, stand behind him, keeping firm hold of the cord with the left hand (for position, see Fig. 78), and strike the belly with the hand or touch lightly with the whip, which will incite him to get up; on the instant of his trying to do so, pull quickly upon the cord, which will roll him back helplessly upon his side.

If the horse is specially sensitive upon the belly, quarters, or feet, first touch these parts with a pole while he is down until he will submit to it, then with the hand, until there is no inclination to resistance, which will be shown by the muscles becoming entirely

Fig. 75.—As the Horse will Usually Fall.

relaxed, and his becoming submissive ; after which he should be allowed to get up, when the handling or touching is to be again repeated carefully until submitted to unconditionally. But should the case resist very hard, and be somewhat difficult to throw, after

Fig. 76.—Type of Sullen Character upon which this Method will Fail.

getting him down once, simply roll him back as before explained, until he gives up, and the effect will be just as good, will be a great deal simpler, safer, and often save the horse from any strain that may result from rough or careless handling — an important point

Sometimes it is necessary to reverse the treatment, and throw the horse on the opposite side, before he will be entirely submissive ;

Fig. 77.—Position of the Horse when Down.

but after being thrown to the extent of making him lie down submissively, it will do no good to repeat the treatment.

Fig. 78.—Rolling the Horse Back when Struggling to Rise.

But in any case, if the impression produced by the throwing or rolling back is not sufficient to break up the horse's confidence and

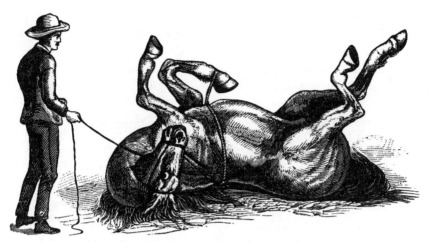

FIG. 79.—As the Horse will Sometimes Roll on his Back.

prevent a repetition of the habit, whatever it is, the treatment must be regarded as not sufficient for the case. For example, if the horse

FIG. 80.—As the Mustang or Wild Colt is Liable to Resist.

is a kicker, and persists in kicking after the full extent of the treatment, it must at once be supplemented by other treatment, until there is success; but if the habit is given up after being thrown several times, and he submits unconditionally, it would be good treatment, and all, in a general way, that is needed

On the other hand, if the horse drops, or lies down submissively, refusing to get up when touched or handled, it will do no good, and should not be tried further. It should not be used upon nervous, irritable, unbroken colts, and especially not on those showing a wild, sulky, or mustang nature. It should in no case be used on mustangs, as they are liable, as soon as the leg is tied up, to lunge,

Fig. 81.—As the Wild Mustang is Liable to Throw Himself.

or when pulled upon to throw themselves recklessly or sullenly down. For the subjection of such cases, it is not nearly so practical, safe, or effective as the other methods, particularly the Second Method, as will be found explained under those heads, for the reason that it is liable to excite them to the most violent resistance. In many cases, the moment a colt finds the leg tied up, it seems to frighten him, and he either resists desperately, or throws himself recklessly. But if a man is practiced in this, the moment the colt springs, pulling quickly against him will usually throw him over helplessly on the side; but if a man is not practiced, such an experiment had better not be attempted. In the course of my own experience, though frequently compelled to make experiments on horses entirely unsuitable to it, including colts, in the midst of a crowd, in very bad places, and under very unfavorable circumstances, and always feeling apprehensive of more or less danger, I never had an accident or seriously injured a horse in making such experiments.

I think it necessary to state again that mustangs should under no circumstances be subjected to this treatment. First, it will be found very difficult, in fact exposes to considerable danger, to attempt putting such a rig on a mustang,

FIG. 82.—**The Horse Subdued.**

as he cannot be approached or touched without kicking or striking violently, and when put on he is liable to resist, recklessly jumping around, and sometimes throwing himself over back—a cause of special danger.

The Second Method works well upon all these cases, and can be resorted to without difficulty.

SECOND METHOD OF SUBJECTION.

If one were to turn around rapidly a few times, he would become dizzy; were he suddenly to reverse the motion, the effect would be so intensified as to cause him to fall down helpless. The effect is the same upon a horse, and in the management of a certain class gives not only just the advantage needed, but almost unlimited power in their control.

I once had an exceptionally vicious horse brought me to experiment upon before a class. When hitched to a buggy, this horse had

FIG. 83.—**Method of Tying Halter to the Tail.**

been frightened to kick and run away, tearing the buggy to pieces. He was so˙ desperately afraid of a wagon that it was utterly impossible for even several men to put him in shafts, or even bring him near them. After working upon him for two hours, aided by members of the class, and resorting to every device of subjection known to me up to that time, my efforts were a complete failure, leaving me almost completely exhausted and chagrined at the result.

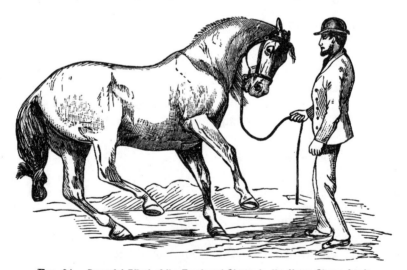

FIG. 84.—**Powerful Effect of the Treatment Shown by the Horse Staggering to the Point of Falling when Quickly Untied.**

Still, I felt bound to succeed ; but " How ? " was the question. At this juncture I happened to think that turning around quickly caused me extreme dizziness and helplessness. This I had learned years before.

I was aware that, in my extremely exhausted condition, it would be utterly impossible for me to turn so desperate, strong, and reckless a horse around sufficiently to do the least good; so it was clear that I was completely blocked in that way. At this juncture I remembered having once seen a dog in play catch his tail in his mouth and run around, when it occurred to me that possibly by tying the horse's head to his tail he would turn himself around. It was a forlorn hope, but, trying it, I found to my surprise and delight that he went around rapidly, and in a short time fell over, completely dazed and helpless. He chanced to be exactly of the right temperament

Fig. 85.—Position in which the Horse Falls, Confused and Helpless, when Turned too Quickly.

to be a good subject for this treatment; and, tying him a little short, he went round very quickly, and was consequently one of the best of subjects; but soon recovering from the dizziness he jumped up and went around again, with the same result. This he repeated three times in succession. (See Fig. 85.) I never witnessed a more desperate, insane struggle to resist restraint. As before explained, he was extremely nervous and afraid of being touched; so as he went round I brought the pole against his quarters until he was submissive to it.

I could not have been made more happy if I had been given a kingdom. It certainly was the best illustration I ever had of the value of ingenuity and skill. Here I had worked over two hours, until completely exhausted, with the aid of several men, and at that only making the horse so heated and thoroughly excited as to be desperate, and meeting with utter failure. It may be proper to say that before this I had used the old method of disabling the fore legs and making him lie down, carrying this to the utmost limit of what could be done with it, as well as following it up with other treatment. But now, without making scarcely an effort, there was the most complete and satisfactory success. Not only this, but besides having avoided all the cruelty and abuse to which I had necessarily subjected the horse, I had developed and brought to light one of the

Fɪɢ. 86.—Method of Holding the Strap while Going around with a Doubtful Case.

most important and valuable secrets yet discovered in the art of taming horses.

This method is wonderfully effective in the subjection of colts and vicious horses, especially those of a certain class of temperament, and in breaking single balkers. When combined with the other treatment, it makes easy and simple the control of horses that it would be both difficult and dangerous to subdue without. For example, a wild, dangerous colt, mustang, or vicious mule, which in many cases it would be exceedingly difficult and perilous to try to confine with straps or other rigging, with the aid of a simple halter can in this way be brought under control in a few minutes. Or, if in any case this is not sufficient to give the success desired, it will always give the required advantage to subject safely to the other methods of treatment. This we will call the Second Method of Subjection.

The conditions to be observed in its application are as follows:—

First, select a soddy place in a field or yard free from stones, stumps, or sharp fence corners. The place should not be too soft, such as a deeply-plowed field, barnyard manure, or deep straw. Heavy sod with considerable grass is the best.

Second, if there are sharp shoes on the feet, they should be removed before subjecting to this treatment; to neglect

Fig. 87.—As a Cold-blooded, Sullen Colt will Sometimes Stand Refusing to Turn when Tied.

this would endanger calking or cutting the feet badly.

Third, a strap halter should always be used. After catching

Fig. 88.—As the Sulky, Vicious Colt will Usually Kick when Touched.

the tail, take the strap of the halter between the teeth, so as to give freedom to use both hands, and tie the hair of the tail into a knot.

5   a

Divide the hair above the knot, pass the strap through, and tie into a half-hitch knot. The strap should be drawn just short enough to compel the horse to turn fast enough to divert his attention (something as in Fig. 83) and make him helpless, but not so short as to cause him to fall. The more nervous and excitable the subject, the longer the strap must be left at first, and the more sullen or cold-blooded the horse, the shorter it may be drawn. If at all doubtful as to the length, when the strap is run through the tail, be-

Fig. 89.—As the Sulky, Vicious Colt is Liable to Throw Himself if Tied too Short.

fore tying the strap double it in the hand, and go around with him a few times, as in Fig. 86, so that the necessary length can be exactly ascertained ; then quickly tie into a half-hitch knot, and let go. If tied the right length, the horse will keep moving in a circle as described ; but if too short, or forced up to the point of falling, the moment he staggers, pull quickly upon the end of the strap, which will pull it loose, and tie again the required length.

Sulky or cold-blooded colts, if tied very short at first, are liable to throw the head against the nose-piece of the halter, and if pushed are likely to rear up and fall over backward, as shown by Fig. 89. This can be easily prevented by holding the strap, as before, up near the tail with one hand, as before explained, and the part near the head with the other, and going around with him a few times, until he is slightly dizzy, then tie quickly and let go. Motion toward the head while passing, and so continue until he moves steadily.

FIG. 90.—A Vicious Colt as he will Usually Strike when the Pole is Brought near his Nose while Turning.

Now, take a pole or rake-handle eight or ten feet long and bring it gently against the legs or parts of the horse most sensitive, until there is complete submission to it. This he is likely at first to resist by kicking violently, but simply continue until all inclination to

FIG. 91.—A Vicious Horse as he will Usually Kick when Touched with Pole while Turning.

resist is overcome, so that after being untied he can be poled in any manner, or the feet can be taken up and handled without his show-ing the least resistance. Sometimes a young horse or colt will start all right, but when tested will not go sufficiently fast to enable his control. Under such circumstances, while moving, touch the nose lightly with a light buggy whip, and repeat until he is forced to the point desired to compel submission.

I soon learned by experience that by turning one way only, the impression upon the brain, after a certain point, diminished in pro-

Fɪɢ. 92.—The First Indication of Submission—Submitting to be Poled.

portion to the continuance of the turning, and that to maintain the effect it was necessary to turn the horse much faster. But even then after a certain time it would become inert. To remedy this I was induced to reverse the action, by tying in the opposite direction, which not only greatly increased the effect, but enabled me to re-peat the treatment to any extent desired with entire success. In bad cases, the horse should be turned one way up to the point of falling, then quickly reverse, at the same time poling, as before explained. It is necessary under such circumstances to watch care-fully, so as to be able, at the instant there is an indication of falling, to prevent it by quickly pulling the strap loose. The more frequent the reversing and the quicker the turning, the better the effect. In some cases it may be necessary to repeat it rapidly three, four, five, and even six times before it will be successful. To do this well requires care and quickness, and the horse should not be given freedom to run against anything. After the horse has submitted he should be thoroughly poled all over, the feet handled, etc., until there is entire indifference to it, then untied, and the same handling repeated. If the treatment has been properly carried out, there should be no difficulty at this point in handling the feet, poling, mounting, etc.

Fig. 93.—Taking up the Colt's Foot while Tied—One of the Tests in Determining his Submission.

This method of subjection is the simplest, the most humane and effective, all things considered, that has yet been discovered. It not only diverts the horse's brain from acting, but matches his strength so perfectly against itself, that without producing the least pain or injury he can

Fig. 94.—Method of Testing after being Untied.

be made almost entirely helpless. It will effect the entire subjection and docility of the average of the worst of wild, vicious, unbroken colts, no matter how dangerous, in about five to fifteen minutes, depending much upon how it is done, so that they can be ridden, have the feet handled, or allow anything to come against the quarters, etc. (See Fig. 94.) It gives, in connection with the war bridle, the true key for breaking single balkers. It is singularly well adapted for supplementing the other methods and effecting the control of extremely vicious horses that have partially or wholly resisted the other methods. It is the safest and best method of treatment for cases extremely averse to being ridden, bridled, or having the head handled ; also those which have the habit of striking. It is specially adapted for the subjection of mustangs. As an illus-

Fig. 95.—One of the Tests Frequently Given by the Writer in Proving the Effect of the Treatment upon a Notably Vicious Case, when Making Experiments before his Class.

tration of this, I have recently had reported to me a number of cases in Montana that had resisted all efforts to break them, which were easily controlled by persons who had obtained copies of my "Facts for Horse Owners," and that so quickly as to be the cause of the greatest surprise to them. One case in particular, estimated to be about sixteen years old, which had defied every effort to be ridden or handled, was controlled so perfectly within a couple of hours as to be ridden easily, and a short time afterward was driven in harness without difficulty. One was broken in Montana, by a lady, so well as to become such a pet to her that she could take it into the house with perfect freedom. It will not work well upon kicking, switching mares and colts of a slow, cold-blooded, sulky nature. There may also occasionally be found horses of a quick, nervous, and decidedly vicious character, that will at first seem to resist it or fall down too quickly. Upon such the Third Method should be used for a short time, to tone down their impetuousness, after which they will usually submit to this method without difficulty.

Though compelled almost daily to subject all kinds of horses to this treatment in small barns and other unsuitable places, and surrounded by a crowd of men, by being careful I never had a serious accident occur. Of course, in a field or open yard the danger would be immeasurably diminished. Still, I think it my duty to advise the greatest care to prevent accident, as it would be very easy to injure if not to kill a horse, if at all careless or reckless with a certain class. By going slowly at first and following up cautiously, there can seldom be an accident.

THIRD METHOD OF SUBJECTION.

It is well known that by hitting a horse at a certain point back of the ear, it is easy to knock him down ; also, if a horse were to throw himself over backward and strike this part on a hub or stone, he is very liable to be instantly killed. At the front part of the atlas bone, or the first of the cervical vertebræ, where it articulates into the occipital bone or back of the head, about an inch of the spinal cord is not covered with bone. If a knife or other sharp instrument were driven down at this point sufficient to penetrate it, it would cause instant death. Now, by bringing gentle but firm pressure upon this part, we have, if properly used, a very powerful and valuable method of subjection, and

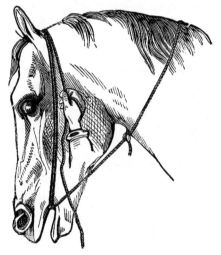

FIG. 96 —**Method of Applying the Cord to Put on Pressure.**

one which is singularly adapted, when necessary, to supplement the other methods of treatment. It is, however, like the other methods, especially adapted for a certain class of disposition and habit, not unfrequently making it easy to subdue horses upon which the other methods have failed, such as nervous-tempered, courageous, strong, wild horses that will not bear excitement or any form of treatment that would permit heating the blood. It is, however, a method of treatment that should be used with great care and judgment. It is easy, of course, to apply this form of pressure, but the point is to use it on cases for which it is suited, and adapted properly to enforce their submission. Not enough pressure, or applying it carelessly, would cause failure, while too much or too long-continued pressure would not only be needlessly cruel, but dangerous to life.

FIG. 97.—**Holding Cord when Through the Mouth.**

I found by experience that pulling sharply upon a horse with the second form of war bridle, which brings the main force of the pull upon this point, would often so unnerve and break up his confidence, that, though previously he could not be touched around the feet or body, he would now submit to such handling with entire docility; and that putting the center of a cord under the bridle so as to rest upon this point, and bringing both ends through the rings of the bit, and carrying back for reins, would usually make a pulling horse drive submissively, in a short time, to a slack rein. I was not, however, led to make any special effort to study out the key to this principle of subjection, until, in a chance way, I heard of a man who, in breaking colts, brought a cord moderately tight two or three times around the head. This, with the remembrance of the effects before referred to, led me to experiment carefully with a cord in this way. But, finding it gave but little more advantage than the common war bridle, I abandoned its use.

At this time I carried canvas, visiting only large centers, which gave me all the opportunity I wished for using the First and Second Methods, and I rarely found a horse that would not submit to these methods of treatment. One day, however, a vicious, kicking mare was brought in that resisted the utmost resources of my regular treatment; for, once warming up in harness, she would kick, in spite of all that could be done, in the most desperate manner. The extremity in which I was placed led me instinctively to try what could be done with this treatment by carrying it to the utmost limit, and, without stopping to reason upon the matter, I kept on not only winding the cord, but drawing it pretty tight, until I used nearly one hundred feet of hard, well-stretched war bridle cord. I now let her stand about eight or ten minutes, when, upon trial, she seemed to be entirely submissive, after which I put her in harness, and she drove entirely gentle. Not being sure what the ultimate result would be, either as to her remaining gentle or not causing injury to her, I told the owner that if she proved to be injured in any way to report to me, and I would satisfy him for any damage. Two weeks later, he informed me that she had remained entirely gentle, and was all right.

I was now led, as opportunity permitted, to experiment carefully, so as to learn the conditions of carrying out this treatment with most success, and its exact effect upon different classes of cases. I found that for ordinary cases the average of three war bridle cords, of about eighteen feet, each drawn so as to give a moderate pressure, that is, a pulling tension of about four or five pounds, (in some cases a little more would be necessary,) and the time of pressure from five to eight or ten minutes, according to the case ; and that in some exceptionally bad cases one or two extra cords would be required, and the time of its continuance somewhat longer ; in very extreme cases from fifteen to twenty minutes.

Fig. 98. — **Cord when On.**

I did not give this method of treatment to classes, but held it as a reserve until after my experiments in New York in 1872.

Method of Applying it—Special ·Points of Importance.

The simplest and best way of applying this method of treatment is as follows : Take a small, firmly wound, smooth hemp cord, about five-sixteenths of an inch in diameter, that has been well stretched, and about eighteen feet long, such as we use for the small size of war bridle.* Tie a hard knot at one end and a loose tie or knot about eighteen or twenty inches from this end, bring around the neck, and slip the end knot through the loose tie as for the first form of war bridle ; stand a little in front, and at the left of the head ; bring the cord through the mouth, and pass it over the

---

*Finding it difficult to get a cord of the proper size, strength, and smoothness, I have it manufactured especially for this purpose, and supply it to subscribers at closest rates.

head where the halter rests, pulling down gently; thence through the mouth again, and hold firmly with the left hand, while the right

is again passed over the head and pulled down as before. (See Figs. 96 and 97.) And so repeat to the end of the cord, winding for the first three or four turns rather loosely, then gradually, with each repetition, pull a little tighter. Always use care to bring it over the tongue, so as not to tangle or bruise it.

Now take another cord and tie to the first one, so that when pulled down the knot will come on either side of the head, but not at the top or in the mouth. Draw this cord

FIG. 99.—Touching the Horse's Quarters with Pole while the Cord is On.

as tightly as thought necessary for the case, and continue to wind until three cords are used, according to the degree of resistance to be controlled. Fasten carefully by bringing the end under the other coils, and tie it so that it will not slip or get loose.

The principle involved is that the greater the strength of will and power of resistance on the part of the horse, the more cord must be used, the tighter it must be drawn, and the longer it must be left on. The average time it should be kept on is from six to ten minutes

In no case of even extreme resistance should it be left on longer than from twenty to twenty-five minutes. Unless in a small place, where there is not sufficient room to run around, attach a strap or cord to two or three of those around the head and hold by it, or tie to a hitching post.

FIG. 100.—Manner in which Some Horses Kick when Touched with Pole.

The success of the treatment will now depend upon what is done after it is applied, as it will practically do no good to put on pressure and do nothing more; that is, the efforts must now be directed industriously to combat and overcome the resistance, whatever it is, until there is submission. For example, if a kicker in harness, while the pressure is on take a small pole or rake-stale and bring against the legs and quarters, as shown in Figs. 99 to 102. If the case is very vicious, this will usually be resisted very hard, the horse kicking violently. This is not to be accepted as a cause for discouragement or fear of failure, as in reality all the best subjects for this treatment resist hard at first. Simply continue the poling gently until there is entire submission to it. Sometimes a horse may submit in five minutes ; if he does, simply uncoil the rope to the last three or four winds, and hold so while the pole is again applied to the quarters.

Fig. 101.—**Manner in which a Vicious Horse will Kick when Touched with Pole.**

If there is no resistance, unwind and turn the last cord into the first form of war bridle, and while holding it test again carefully.

This is about the course required with the average of good tempered, sensitive horses that have learned to kick. If, however, the case is one of plucky, determined character, that resists violently after a reasonable effort, without there being any indication of submitting, the best course will be to draw the cord a little tighter. In some extreme cases one or two extra cords may be added. A horse of decided courage and determination will usually not only resist very hard at first, as stated, but the eyes will fairly snap with fury. If, however, the cord is put on properly, and the poling applied gently and persistently, it is rare that it will not be submitted to in from five to eight minutes.

Fig. 102.—**Submitting to the Pole after being Subdued.**

When there is submission, the most prominent signs will be submitting to the pole, the ears dropping a little, the eyes softened in expression, with a slight indication of panting. There is also, in some cases, profuse sweating, which is always a favorable indication. One of the nice points of success is to force to the point of submission quickly, and as soon as made, as quickly removing pressure, but continue the poling as before explained, until after entire freedom.   The result

will usually be very remarkable, a horse that had perhaps been one of the most determined and violent of fighters becoming as docile and gentle in appearance as if he had been always so.

While being subjected to this treatment, the central point of observation should be the

Fig. 103.—**Manner in which Some Extremely Vicious Horses will Resist when Subjected to Pressure.**

eye.   So long as there is fire in it, and the ears are thrown back, no matter whether the horse kicks or not, it is an evidence that he is fighting hard, and the pressure must be kept on.   On the contrary, when there is a general ceasing of resistance, the eye is softened in its expression as if going to sleep, breathing accelerated, panting a little, and especially if there is rapid sweating, it is sure evidence of unconditional submission.   No matter if these indications are shown in even two or three minutes, the result will be just as effective as if it had been left on ten. In fact, as soon as these indications are shown, the cord must be taken

Fig. 104.—**As Some Desperately Vicious Horses will Throw Themselves when Subjected to Pressure.**

off at once. To keep on pressure any longer would not only be entirely unnecessary, but abusive.

The treatment should now be carried out for driving, as directed for kicking and other habits, under those heads.

If bad to shoe, while the pressure is on attach a rope or strap to the foot, and pull back and forward as in Fig. 108 until the toe rests upon the ground, and there is submission. The cord should then be immediately taken off the head, as before explained, and turned into the war bridle, when the leg is to be repeatedly tested.

Fig. 105.—**The Horse as he Stands when Subdued.**

As stated before, all good subjects for this treatment will resist hard at first, and make a determined fight, but when they do give up, will be found entirely manageable ; while those that do not resist when touched while the pressure is on, are, as a rule, not good subjects for it.

This method of subjection reveals the horse's character exactly, whatever it is. If one of great courage and spirit, he will usually, while under pressure, fight at first with great fury, but finally submit unconditionally ; but if of a sulky, treacherous nature, while the pressure is on he will often stand sullenly, doing nothing. In such cases the Second Method must be depended upon, in connection with the others.

The success with which some kickers can be subdued and broken of the habit by this method, will often be most remarkable. It is especially adapted to the subjection of courageous, determined, sensitive horses, that will not bear excitement or heating of the blood. It also works well upon biting, striking, vicious stallions,

especially when used in connection with the other methods. It works extremely well upon mules, seldom requiring more than ten minutes to subdue even those of the worst character.

Cases upon which it will not work well, and for which it should not be used, are young, unbroken colts, sullen or cold-blooded horses of any character, and, once in awhile, a class of high-strung, sensitive horses of great courage and endurance, that become excited, strike, and resist hard. Such cases are, however, somewhat rare. It is not adapted for balkers; if it

FIG. 106.—**Mouth as Usually Kept Open when Cord is on.**

must be used upon such, let it be after subjecting to the First or Second Methods, or both, and then but for a few minutes. The reason this method should not be used upon colts, is that they will in the first place usually resist any attempt to put on the cord, or bite and chew upon it to a degree that will bruise or cut the cheeks, which is very troublesome to treat.* (See Fig. 107.) Besides, colts can be controlled so much easier and better by the Second Method, that there is no necessity for using this upon them.

There will occasionally be found an old horse that will bite upon the cord like colts. In all such cases the treatment must at once be abandoned, and dependence placed upon other methods. Those that cut or bruise the cheeks are usually of a surly, obstinate nature, the sullen disposition being prominent, which

FIG. 107.—**Appearance of Mouth when Biting upon the Cord.**

will usually be denoted by the small, clear eye, set well back on the side of the head, eyebrows rather heavy, fullness below the eye, long between the eyes and ears, ears rather long and heavy, and small nostrils. In a very extensive practice of many years, I found no practical means of preventing horses' biting in this way,

---

*For special treatment for such possible bruising of cheeks, see Bruises of Cheek.

so that when we had such cases we found it to be the best course to abandon it at once.

This method of subjection is so arbitrary, and in ignorant hands can be so easily made the basis of injury and abuse, that for a long time I have been very reluctant to give it to my classes, or publish it, fearing they would misuse its advantage ; but with anything like ordinary care, it is not at all difficult to determine the cases for which it is suitable, and to avoid needless abuse by it. It is always advisable, before applying this treatment as well as in the application of other methods of treatment, to look the horse carefully over in a general way. Then, if not sure of the character test a little to be able to determine it with accuracy.

Fig. 108:—**Pulling the Foot Back—Bad to Shoe.**

If a nervous, excitable, coltish-acting fellow, that has perhaps been seriously frightened in consequence of carelessness or accident, the Second Method may first be used. Should this fail, or not produce satisfactory results, then this method may be tried. To make its application plainer, first bring the cord through the mouth once and pull down rather tight. Should this be submitted to, it is safe to proceed. But if the horse strikes violently, or resists, showing a disposition to bite upon the cord, especially after two or three coils have been used, it had better be abandoned and other treatment used. Or, if it is desired to subject the horse to the First Method first, and the cord cannot be put on with safety, subject to the Second Method for a few moments, then resort to the first, after which the impression can be fixed by this.

FIG. 109.—Pulling Head of a Vicious Horse around to Avoid his Fore Feet should he Strike, and Observing that the Cord Comes Right in the Mouth.

The First Method cannot be repeated with much assurance of success. If the horse will not get up after being thrown, you will have accomplished all that you can by this treatment. Also the Third Method will, as a rule, prove a success or failure after the first trial. It cannot be repeated with success, and should not be tried. Whatever is attempted by this method must be done at the first trial. But if the horse will bear it, this trial can be carried to a considerable extreme of pressure, and be continued for some time, though it should not exceed twenty-five minutes, except in very extreme cases. One horse, of a certain temperament and character, may be able to stand pressure for fifteen minutes as well as another especially sensitive horse, perhaps, would the same only two or three or four minutes. So that each case must regulate just the extent and amount of pressure needed. These points I have learned by experimenting for a good many years on a great variety of horses. I would repeat, that the point is to make all the impression possible with

FIG. 110.—Looking at the Opposite Side to See that the Cord Comes Right, and Determining the Amount of Pressure Necessary.

it when used, and then, if there is failure, resort to other methods.

THE WAR BRIDLE.

FIRST FORM.

I will take up, next, a means of management so simple, yet so practical and valuable in its effects, that it is in some respects indispensable, because it gives us in certain ways a degree of control not attainable by any other means. Certainly, for so simple a means, when skillfully used, it has a wonderful effect. It would not seem possible, until witnessed, that an ordinary unbroken colt or stubborn horse, entirely unbroken to lead, could be taught in a few minutes to follow around anywhere, without the least restraint, even watching a man, turning and following him in any manner, like a trained dog. If a horse is restless and will not submit to have the harness put on, resists being bridled, cleaned, or curried, restless in shoeing, or being a little nervous when ordinary objects of fear are brought around him, etc., this gives almost immediate control, in addition to being the foundation for other important management.

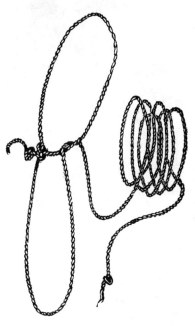

FIG. 111.—**First Form of War Bridle.**

Then, it can be modified in a variety of ways to increase its power, so as to show such a degree of restraint upon certain classes of viciousness as to appear most startling. But while it may frequently enable the accomplishment of what may seem very remarkable results, it cannot in reality be accepted as more than subordinate or supplementary to the other methods. It will be all that is needed in controlling and making gentle all ordinary colts. It is the best of all means for teaching a colt or horse to lead or follow by the halter. In fact, eight tenths of all ordinary cases, with a little care and patience, could be controlled easily by this simple method of treatment alone. It was by this means that I was led to advertise with confidence to be able to control any unmanageable, headstrong stallion so successfully that within ten minutes I could lead him out to a horse or mare and stand off eight or ten feet and call him to me

FIG. 112.—**First Form of War Bridle.**

by word of command only ; and yet simple as this method may seem, it took me fully fifteen years to catch the full points of its value.

DETAILS OF ITS APPLICATION.

First, concerning the quality of cord, and its length. It is very important to have the best possible quality of fiber, and size about right. The point is to have the cord as small as possible, yet sufficiently strong to give assurance of its not breaking under the most severe strain to which it can be subjected. I have found the best to be that made from the very best quality of long-fiber Missouri hemp, wound very hard, yet in such a way as to be as flexible as possible. I used the same cord for the War Bridle that I did for the Third Method of Subjection, and found it necessary to have it made specially for this purpose, as I could not find any in the market suffi-

FIG. 113.—**Smallest Size of Cord Used—Five six-teenths of an Inch in Diameter.**

FIG. 114.—**Largest Size of Cord Used—Three eighths of an Inch in Diameter.**

ciently fine and strong to be suitable. The size should be from five sixteenths to three eighths of an inch plump in diameter, and in length from fifteen to twenty-two feet. The average length used by me was from eighteen to twenty feet. We cut them this length, or divided a roll into four parts, and then we used them as required for either purpose.

For the simplest form of War Bridle, take such a piece of cord, tie each end in a hard knot, and make another knot or loop about twenty inches from one end ; bring this end around the horse's neck, and pass it through the loose knot or loop, regulating the size of the loop to that of the neck. Next, catch the end hanging down, and pass between the cord and neck, forming a loop with the free end on the near side. Pass the loop this forms through the mouth, or over the lower jaw, as shown in Fig. 112. This we will term the First Form of War Bridle.

This, it will be noticed, gives considerable pulley power sideways and back upon the mouth. The method of using it is as follows :—

Stand opposite the shoulder, about four or five feet away from the head, and give a sharp, quick pull or jerk, when instantly give slack, using more or less force, according to the amount of resistance to be overcome. This will be found to give great power, being sufficient, unless the horse is very heavy and slow, to pull him around easily, when by repeating a few times he will come around freely without being pulled upon. Now, go to the opposite side and repeat the pulling until he will come around in the same manner. The force of the pull must necessarily be regulated to the resistance of the horse, a quick, nervous

FIG. 115.—**Double-Draw Hitch.**

horse requiring but two or three light pulls to bring him off his feet and make him follow around freely ; whereas a dull, stubborn, or slow horse may be required to be pulled upon with a good deal of force, and the pulling repeated quite a number of times to produce the same effect.

After doing this, by stepping sideways and ahead, the horse will follow promptly, in circles, right or left ; then gradually enlarge your circle, until you go straight ahead, and he will follow freely. But should he be a little slow, or not follow promptly as desired, simply repeat the pulling a few times as before, when he will follow freely in any manner, though the cord be thrown over the back, and will afterward do so equally well with the control of a common halter.

It will be noticed that this form only gives power sideways. If you were to go in front of the head and pull forward, it would only throw the head up and back, in fact making the horse resist following, and expose your weakness to him.   When we want power to bring the horse straight ahead, should it be necessary, simply change to the Second Form, as shown in Fig. 117, when by pulling a few times he will be made to come ahead as freely as before sideways.

The next step, naturally, is to handle the horse around the shoulders, hips, and legs.   If this is done carefully and gently, as directed under that head in Colt-Training, there will not often be much resistance.   But should there be, and this means not be sufficient to overcome it, for this or other minor troubles recourse may be had to the regular treatment laid down for such resistance.

Fig. 116.—Second Form of
War Bridle.

SECOND FORM OF WAR BRIDLE.

Take off the cord as now on, and make a single loose knot or loop about a foot from the end.   Put the end knot through the loose knot or loop, and draw sufficiently tight to prevent its slipping out. The loop thus formed should be only just large enough to go over the lower jaw, because the larger the loop the less power will be obtained.   Next pass the cord from the off side over the head where the halter rests, and down through this loop back of the jaw, until the slack is taken up as shown in Figs. 116 and 117.

Now, step a little sideways and ahead, and pull gently, holding the cord taut, and you will find that you have reversed the previous order of working by its giving you power to bring the horse straight ahead. Now, give a sharp pull

Fig. 117.—Second Form of War Bridle as it
Should be Adjusted.

as before, when you will find that you will be able to pull the horse right to you ; but if you do not the first time, you can at farthest after a few repetitions. A quick, nervous horse may jump right to you on the first pull, and will follow in the most prompt manner afterward, while one of a slow and sullen nature may resist quite hard for a while, but will always yield in time.

As a means of breaking horses that lag when handled or pulled upon by the halter, or refuse to lead to any point, as, for example, through a door (a common habit), this form of the War Bridle will be found to be by far the best means of management, and becomes the foundation of success in the breaking of double balkers, as shown under that head, making it a very easy matter now to control such cases.

I would call particular attention to the fact that the cord must be put just at the point on the head, back of the ears, where the halter or bridle rests. If by chance it should be placed

FIG. 118.—**Cord too far Back on the Neck, with Loop on the Lower Jaw too Large. Will not Work.**

three or four or more inches back, as shown in Fig. 118, the secret of its power will be lost.

Putting this part over the head about half way back on the neck, drawing down tightly with the hand, or tying moderately tight, as shown in Fig. 119, will be found all that will be required in the control of all ordinary cases bad to bridle, handle top of head, harness, etc. If tied down, it should not be kept so at longest more than a minute or two.

THE DOUBLE-DRAW HITCH FORM.

This gives nearly three times the power of the ordinary forms of the War Bridle. It can be changed or modified in two or three ways, as may be necessary, and is a very practical and valuable means of control. I may mention here, that this has been the principal secret (for in difficult cases I could not succeed without it) of performing the apparently impossible feat of being able within ten minutes to control so easily any headstrong or lunging stallion, when great power is required, as before referred to.

Fig. 119.—**Method of Tying Down to Make Horse Submit to be Harnessed, have his Head Handled, etc.**

First, put on a cord as for First Form of War Bridle; but instead of bringing the cord down through the loop, bring it from below up; then pass it over the head and back through the mouth, thence through the loop this forms on the near side. (See Fig. 115.) If desired, this can be modified so as to give still greater power by bringing the cord across under the upper lip, instead of through the mouth, or by making another loop over the head in the same manner, and by bringing it under the upper lip.

By experimenting a little with this, it will be found to increase the power wonderfully. A horse so stubborn and sullen that he can hardly be moved or seem to be influenced by the First Form, can be lifted almost bodily out of his tracks by this, giving all the power necessary for making such a horse follow in a few moments. Where a horse is restless, or somewhat unmanageable, such as resisting the feet being taken up, having a blanket thrown over him, the head handled, etc., he can sometimes be made to submit readily by bringing the cord, after the First Form is adjusted, forward under the

Fig. 120.—**Manner of Tying.**

upper lip and right around over the head, and through the mouth, and holding moderately tight. But it should not be held so more than a minute. Should it be resisted very much, it will be better to resort to regular coercive treatment.

There is quite a secret in using the War Bridle. It is, first, in getting the right position and distance from a horse ; second, the method of pulling, which is the point here to be explained. Wind the cord once around the right hand, not very tight, while it is passed through the left a little in advance of the right. And now for the secret : it is giving a sharp, quick jerk with both hands, like the cracking of a whip ; not a long, heavy, dead pull, mind, but a quick little jerk, as it were, and instantly slack. You will, of course, place one leg a little forward of the other to give pur- chase ; the rest must be done by the force of the arms only. I have frequently been able to illustrate this by jerking heavy horses around freely by pulling upon the cord lightly but quickly with my naked hands, with- out the least injury

FIG. 121.—**Modification of Second Form.**

to them ; while strong, heavy men, though pulling quite hard in a slow, indifferent way, could scarcely move them, and at that bruise their hands quite seriously.

I may say that in hundreds and hundreds of cases, men who had joined my classes and to whom had been shown and explained every point of its application, and had its effect illustrated to them, would often catch the points only so crudely or imperfectly that they would follow me fifteen or twenty miles to attend another class and have them again explained to them. This is one of my reasons for being so explicit in giving such full details of this principle of man- agement, and which must necessarily be frequently referred to in connection with other methods of treatment.

I am just in receipt of a letter from a gentleman in California, who, in relating his success in breaking mustangs, after stating that he had broken mustangs easily that had been given up by others, said he had made a wager that he could make a sixteen-year-old mustang that had not been touched for three years, follow him in thirty minutes, and that he did it so well in seven that it would follow him anywhere and thereby astonished those who knew the mustang. And this he did with the War Bridle.

The simplicity of this form of control makes it very difficult to realize its real value ; neither is it too much to say that it requires considerable practical skill to bring out its full power.

If limited to the various forms of the War and Patent Bridles, there should be no real difficulty in being able to control certainly more than half of the average colts and vicious horses in the country.

"W," OR BREAKING BIT — TRAINING THE MOUTH.

Whatever we do with the horse, however successful our treatment, we must ultimately come to the control of the mouth ; and if not successful in this, no matter how good our treatment otherwise,

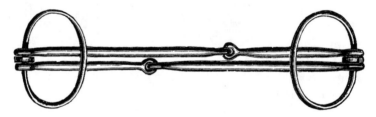

FIG. 122.— " W," or Breaking Bit. Half Size.

it must necessarily be regarded as seriously defective. This matter of getting good control of the mouth, simple as it may seem, bothered me more to catch the points of doing successfully, than any other treatment here referred to. And it is naturally one of the most difficult points for horse men to contend with successfully. This is usually sought to be done by bitting, that is, putting on a bitting-rig, checking the head up, and letting the colt fight it until he gives up, and in the management of runaways, depending wholly upon such bits as will give direct power. The difficulty is that while the horse may be controlled in this way, the disposition to continue the habit is not overcome, which is the real point important to accomplish. Then, in many extreme cases, the resistance may be so great that it is not possible by any means heretofore in use to hold the horse.

It must be borne in mind that this method (bitting) brings dead pressure only upon the mouth, and necessarily cannot teach the idea (which is the real point to be attained) of submitting the head up and back to the easy and flexible restraint of the bit, and give assurance of having the horse entirely submissive to easy restraint of the bit under any possible impulse of excitement.

The common methods of treatment are defective in various ways, and are the direct causes of the many accidents and cases of trouble experienced in the use of driving horses. The colt is simply subjected a short time to a bitting-rig ; there is, perhaps, success in driving him double, or putting him before the plow with another horse, until gentle. It is a matter purely experimental, also, of being hitched up single. If the colt is exceptionally intelligent and good-tempered, by using extreme care there is perhaps success in hitching him to a buggy. Now, if he moves off and finally drives ordinarily well, he is presumed to be a gentle, broken horse. Indeed, there would seem to be no other reasonable course of management. This is the fatal error, and the prime cause of our trouble. To explain this, we will presume now to make an experiment or two. The horse appears to be entirely gentle and manageable, and so he is, as far as he has been trained. But let the rein be caught suddenly under the tail, let one of the traces get loose, the breeching-strap break, or some other derangement, in itself trifling, occur, and the colt is startled, frightened, kicks by impulse, or springs ahead, to free himself from the supposed danger. There is no assured control by the bit ; he has never been made to feel it ; the consequence is, he rushes against it, runs away, and the horse is spoiled. And this is about the history of nearly all runaway kickers, with their incidental troubles. These were the horses I was almost constantly required to experiment upon before my classes. And it always became a matter of the greatest surprise to the best horsemen witnessing my experiments, to see with what success I could drive such in a short time, under the greatest excitement, entirely gentle, submitting freely to what before would have made them kick and run away. The secret of course was that I went to work first to remove the cause in the most direct manner, thereby making the foundation for greatly lessening the resistance to the bit. For example, if kicking was the cause of the indirect resistance, the first point I aimed at was to overcome that, then to go directly to the control of the mouth until successful.

Now, these points were what a long course of, I may say, very ignorant and often blind experimenting forced me to learn. I was soon compelled from necessity, as stated, first to make the horse in a general way perfectly gentle, and then come directly to the point of resistance, whatever it was. Then, another point I learned was that making one part of the body gentle is no assurance that the other will be so. For example, making the forward part gentle, would not make the hind part so ; that I could make one foot submissive to be shod, and yet leave the other foot as difficult to handle and control as ever ; that making a horse fearless of a handkerchief when brought around his head or in front of him, no matter how indifferent to it he became, if thrown from behind, under his belly, upon his hips, or behind him, would be as likely to frighten him as if he had not seen it before.

In a hundred ways these little points could be shown, and are fully explained in details of treatment under special heads. But because these conditions are not understood, or those requisite for overcoming them are not known or understood, these troubles necessarily follow. Now, in no respect is this more strongly shown than in the management of the mouth. By experimenting a little upon a variety of horses with the War Bridle in teaching to lead, it will be found that a horse will sometimes at first resist with such persistence that the united strength of several men would not be sufficient to make him lead ; yet, by repeating, as explained, the short little pulls in such way as he is the least able to resist, the horse will in all cases soon learn to follow in any manner, even running after the trainer, without being pulled upon or perhaps without the use of the halter at all ; and he will do this ever afterward.

Now, the principle is exactly the same in obtaining such control of the mouth as will enable securing unconditional submission to the slightest restraint of the bit, — a point that took me at least twelve years of the closest observation and practice to catch the idea of intelligently, and even up to the time of leaving the road I was constantly learning new points of advantage in this respect. The results I would sometimes be able to bring about in doing this were really striking, in many cases truly wonderful. Though a digression, I will refer to a few illustrative cases in point.

A runaway horse, eight years old, the last time hitched up, jumped over a toll-gate, ran away, had not been driven for over a year afterward, and was regarded utterly unmanageable. After thirty minutes' treatment he was driven down a steep hill to a buggy, without breeching, the wagon running against his heels, guided by a six-year-old boy who sat near me on the seat ; and the horse remained gentle afterwards.

A strong, large-boned Western horse, in New York City, nine years old, was sold for $275, on condition that he could be driven to a cart. He was hitched up to a heavy dump-cart, with both wheels blocked, two men held him by the head, and two in the cart held the reins. He resisted all restraint, and ran away, and was purchased for fifty dollars. This horse, though utterly unmanageable, was controlled so perfectly within an hour, that the slightest restraint of the reins was sufficient to guide and control him under any excitement, in driving to a single buggy ; and this without breeching, the cross-piece coming against the quarters.

A five-year-old colt, in Toledo, Ohio, a runaway, and so desperate that the only way he could be held in harness with success was to hitch him between two heavy horses, tied back to them by the head,—this horse, in less than an hour's time, was made entirely manageable, was driven next day through the principal streets perfectly gentle without breeching, and remained so.

In Cleveland, Ohio, a trotting-horse that had defied with such determination every effort to be controlled in single harness as to be regarded as practically worthless, submitted perfectly within an hour, and as a special feat, in the meantime having the treatment repeated, in addition to being trained, was driven next day on the square without reins or breeching, by the control of the whip only.

These cases, with others equally striking that could be referred to did space permit, were thus made manageable to the control of the bit by training the mouth with the "W," or Breaking Bit. The full details of these cases, with thirty-six others, are given in my special work on the horse, under the heading, "Illustrative Cases," the better to illustrate there the treatment to be pursued in the management of such cases. These results, so far as training the mouth, I could accomplish with a greater or less degree of success, and with different kinds of bits ; but found the "W," or Breaking Bit, here given, the simplest and best.

It is not a bit for driving, though it may in some cases be used as such. The secret of its success is not so much in the bit as in the manner of using it, which in principle is practically the same as that given for the War Bridle. As explained in the use of the cord, there may be at first the most determined resistance to it ; but by repetition of the treatment the horse will in a short time not only cease resisting, but will follow anywhere. The impression made in this way is never forgotten, the horse afterward leading by the merest restraint of the halter.

In the same manner, when there is at first an effort with this bit to control or force the submission of a headstrong horse, there may be the most desperate resistance to it ; but by repetition of the treatment, sometimes requiring considerable perseverance, there will in a short time be such complete submission to it that the horse can be held or controlled afterward, even under the greatest excitement, by the lightest restraint of an ordinary bit. This principle of training is also illustrated in "Halter-Pulling," and in fact in every step of subjective treatment.

The length of the bit should be regulated to the size of the mouth, so that when pulled upon, the bars will come at right angles with the jaw on each side. The average length is eight and three fourths inches from center to center of ring-holes when put together. This makes the length of the short bars three and three eighths and the long bars five and three eighth inches from center to center of holes. It may be made much shorter, but it would proportionately lessen the lever power of the bars upon the jaw, which is the key of its success. The bars should be made of round cast-steel rod, filed and polished perfectly smooth, about five sixteenths of an inch in diameter. Between the bars, at the ends, there should be a small, thin washer. The rings should be made of iron wire, about two and a half to three inches in diameter. The bars especially should be filed and polished perfectly smooth, so as to leave no rough corners or surfaces anywhere. A round, stiff piece of leather may be stitched inside the rings ; while this may be dispensed with, it is desirable to have it on.

A great variety of bits are made on this principle, but their construction is so faulty that they do not work well. They are mainly defective in being too short and rough. This bit will not bruise or cut the mouth. Some of the points which took me a good many years to learn, were, that there was no practical advantage in making the bars twisted and rough for the purpose of hurting more ; that the lever power was the point of its success, and that it would work just as well when the bars were smooth as when twisted and roughened, making the serious objection of cutting and tearing the mouth.

The point of its use is, when put in the mouth the reins are to be brought back through the shaft lugs so as to bring a straight, even pull upon the mouth backward, and prevent the horse from turning around. A specially important point is that the hand parts of the reins are large and soft, so as to give good hold upon them. Now, stand behind, just beyond the reach of the heels, with a rein twisted once around each hand, and after moving the horse moderately, call "Whoa!" sharply, instantly following with a sharp, quick, raking pull. The variation of the pull in the arms should not be more than two or three inches, blended with the direct pulling, which should be with the energy of the strongest blow from the shoulder, the principle simply reversed. In this way, after the command of "Back" or "Whoa" is given, whichever it is, repeat at short intervals. In all ordinary cases the submission will be quick and easy; but in plucky, bad cases, the resistance may be very determined. In fact, in exceptional cases it may be so great that it will seem impossible to make the horse yield; but this should not by any means be accepted as a reason for discouragement.

If the horse warms up much, and becomes sullenly indifferent to the pressure of the bit upon the mouth, by repeating the lesson it is rare that he will not be found to submit in a few minutes. At any rate the lesson must be so thorough that there will be unconditional submission. In all my experience I never found more than half a dozen cases that did not submit to two or three lessons. Success will depend upon how it is done, the main point being to make the horse submit, if possible, before he warms up, persevering and repeating till there is success. But should the horse become so warmed up as to make it necessary to repeat the lesson, he must be allowed to stand long enough to become entirely cool. The better way would be to let him stand over night, or even longer. In most cases, when the lesson is repeated, he will be found to respond immediately, because the mouth has now become very sensitive; but if not, the only thing to do is to go on as before, carefully, until successful.

Another very important point is, if the case is known to be a very serious one, and resists with decided courage (this has special reference to large-boned, rather coarse, but very plucky, determined horses), to move the horse at first very slowly, until the point is gained of making him stop and come back at a slight pull. In my own practice I moved the horse on a very slow walk, and repeated making him stop until he would do so without being pulled upon, then stop and come back, until he would respond to the pull of the bit with the elasticity of a spring. Then I moved him a little faster, and repeated until he could be moved to a sharp trot, and would stop instantly at command without being pulled upon, no matter what the excitement. This I would repeat over and over until I could put the horse on a run and do it; and if his character had been such as to make him at all seriously doubtful, this lesson was repeated after he had got cool. This is what I called testing what had been done. In most cases the horse will be found entirely manageable ; but he may, when pushed up sharply, resist quite hard again. If so, the point must be fought out at once, and most thoroughly.

The next step is to put before a wagon. In my own experience, I made it a point always, in such cases, to force the horse back suddenly against the cross-piece ; in fact, I impressed him with such power as to entirely discourage him from the least offer of resistance. I then moved the horse a little, pulling the wagon behind him. He being submissive to this, I now attached the harness, got into the wagon and started him again, very moderately, and as before repeated the starting and stopping until I could push him out on a run, and make him stop at command. The lesson in all cases was made without the breeching strap being buckled.

Frequent reference will be made to this bit in different parts of the work, more especially in Colt Training, Running Away, and Runaway Kickers. It will also in many cases be found good treatment for breaking up the habit of pulling on one rein. It is the best means, also, of teaching a horse to stand or back.

More extended details in the application of this bit will be found in the chapters on "Colt Training," and "Running Away."

FOUR-RING, OR UPPER JAW BIT.

As training the mouth by the Breaking Bit is not always desirable on account of the work of doing it, and the lack of skill and practice in using it, I include other forms of bits which will enable the control of horses more directly and sometimes with great success : 1. The Four-ring Bit ; 2. The Half-Moon Bit ; 3. The Spoon

FIG. 123.—Improved Four-ring Bit.

Bit ; and 4. The Patent Bridle. Other bits might also be used with success. We describe first the Four-ring Bit.

In controlling a horse by the head, we find that one of the most sensitive parts of the mouth is the roof of the upper jaw. If we take a common snaffle bit and slide two rings over the mouth-pieces, and connect them by a strap passing loosely over the nose, when the reins which are attached to the outside rings are pulled upon, the center of the bit will be forced upward against the roof of the mouth, producing such acute pain that but few horses can pull against it with much force.

This bit has been in very general use for a number of years, but I do not know when or by whom it was invented. Frank Leslie, of *Leslie's Weekly*, who witnessed some of my experiments in New York City, told me that while in Europe he saw an illustration of such a bit in an old Grecian work. While the bit works fairly well when not pulled upon very hard, its power would be almost wholly lost by the rings sliding to the ends of the bars if the resistance against it were at all severe. To prevent this I devised an obstruction to the rings at a certain point, beyond which they cannot slide. (See Figs.

Fig. 124.—Improved Four-ring Bit.   Patent Applied for.

123, 124.) By this improvement the bit will rest easily and naturally in the mouth, yet be held firmly in place in spite of any degree of pulling upon it.

This bit will usually work well upon hard pullers and side-reiners, especially those that, as they warm up, have more inclination to lug or pull. I have known many horses that would pull so hard upon a common bit as to draw the wagon by the reins, yet would, by the use of this bit, when properly adjusted, submit to an easy rein. It is also one of the simplest and safest means to make a horse stand to be shod. For this purpose, when the bit is in the mouth, take a common War Bridle cord, tie one end into the near ring, and pass through the opposite ring till taut, and tie. Then bring the cord around the horse's neck as for Second Form of War Bridle, with the cord well back upon the neck, and pass down back of the jaw. This will be found of special value to horse-shoers, because, with rare exceptions, it compels most horses bad to shoe to stand gentle while being shod.

The main point of success in this bit is, first, in having it made right, as shown — the bars a little longer than the ordinary bit, and either constructed so that there is an obstruction at the ring at the inner end of the bar, as shown in Fig. 124, or the bar slotted, as shown in Fig. 123. In either case, the bars must be filed smooth, so as to make the play of the ring free and easy.

But the most important point is its proper adjustment to the head. It should be made to hang a little low in the mouth ; next the strap across the nose should be made of nice soft leather, from an inch and a quarter to an inch and a half wide, the ends buckling nicely into the rings. This strap must come right straight across the nose, and be buckled short enough so that when the bit is pulled upon, the full pressure of the center of the bit, or the ends of the bars, where they come together, will be brought firmly and

strongly against the roof of the mouth, yet not fitted so tightly that it will press uncomfortably against the upper jaw when the bit is not pulled upon. If the strap across the nose is in the least too long, the point of advantage will be practically lost, and there must be disappointment. This is a point that must be looked to carefully.

FIG. 125.—**Four-ring Bit as Arranged for Use.**

The ordinary simple forms of this bit, as generally sold by harness-makers, are not made properly, and in addition they are never properly fitted, and consequently will rarely give the satisfaction expected.

When in Cleveland, Ohio, a gentleman reported to me having a very fine, fast-gaited driving horse in every respect all right, except that he would pull so hard that he became practically unmanageable. I adjusted this form of bit carefully, when he would drive in any manner, fast or slow, to a slack rein, scarcely showing any resistance.

A very fine driving mare owned by a physician in Battle Creek, Mich., was perfectly gentle and fearless, but she would pull the wagon with the reins,— if in the least excited could not, in fact, be held down at all. I adjusted a bit as described, when she drove entirely gentle, in fact he told me that his wife could drive her afterward.

A great many interesting cases could be referred to, showing the value of this bit when properly made and adjusted. It will not work well on horses that throw the nose up very high, as by the horse doing this, it will be found that its advantage will at once be lost. Neither is it adapted for rapid speeding.

THE HALF-MOON BIT.

The point of this bit is in having the lower or inner side drawn to a thin edge. The edge can be made straight, or a little concave. The edge should be about as thin as an old twenty-five cent piece, and filed very smooth, but not sharp enough to cut. The point is

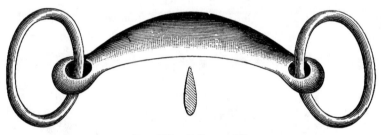

FIG. 126.—**Half-moon Bit.**

that the small surface brought against the jaw, when pulled upon at all hard, will necessarily cause so much pain that it will not be resisted. It will in many cases work very nicely, while in some cases it will not work well at all; it will usually work well on spirited, energetic, headstrong horses. There should be round pieces of leather adjusted inside the rings.

This bit will enable driving many headstrong horses easily. The simplest and best form of check for this is arranged about as follows: Put on a small steel bit partly bent, and pass a closely-fitting strap from each ring across the nose. To keep it in place, another small strap should extend from the center of it to the head-piece. The gag-runners should be attached to the bridle, well up on the head-piece, on a line with the ears. The check-rein should be attached to this bit, and drawn short enough to throw the head well up.

The next point is to so conform the driving-bit that it cannot be resisted. This is accomplished by making the part of the mouth-piece coming against the jaw so thin that more than an ordinary pull

7   a

upon it will hurt so severely that there will be no inclination to pull against it ; next, it should be made circular in form, so that it will give sufficient lateral restraint to prevent pulling or lunging sideways. The length should be from four and seven eighths to five inches from center to center of holes, the bend about one inch forward from a line drawn across the center of the holes, with the edge filed down to about the thickness of the back of an ordinary knife-blade, and rounded to prevent cutting. This will make the surface bearing against the mouth so narrow that the most plucky horse can scarcely pull against it. This bit will be found very effective for the management of spirited, pulling, and lunging horses.

THE SPOON BIT.

The Spoon Bit simply causes sensibility in the mouth in another way, namely, by the pressure of the spurs or flanges against the outside of the jaw to the degree the bit is pulled upon.

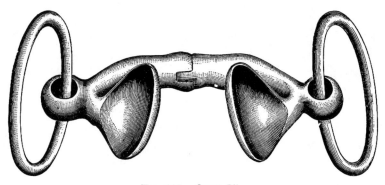

FIG. 127.—Spoon Bit.

It will be found in many cases to work very nicely, though it is not a bit that gives much power. It is more like the Four-ring Bit in compelling an easy submission of the mouth to the guidance and restraint of the reins. The illustration will sufficiently explain its construction.

In using any of these palliative bits upon horses known to be liable to run away, it is in all cases advisable to put on one or two foot-straps, to be carried back into the wagon, and the horse carefully tested, when, if he should resist the bit and lunge ahead, he can be at once disabled by pulling one foot from under him. Should this be resisted, follow immediately by pulling the other foot from under him. This is, of course, simply a precautionary measure.

THE PATENT BRIDLE.

When the horse is found to be extremely reckless in resisting the bit, and especially when the case cannot be subjected to the regular treatment to be trained out of the habit, it is very important to be able to bring sufficient power upon the mouth to restrain and hold the horse safely. If, in addition to this, the force of the restraint can be made to impress the horse in such a way that he will be disinclined to repeat it, a very important point will be accomplished. This we can now do very successfully by what we here denominate the Patent Bridle, which is especially adapted for the control of extremely headstrong or lunging horses

During my early experience, I found an excellent method of driving hard-pulling, runaway horses was to bring a

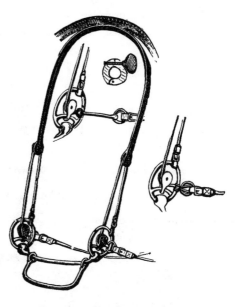

FIG. 128.—Outline of Patent Bridle.

small cord across over the head under the head-piece of the bridle, then pass the ends through the rings of the bit, and then attach the reins. Then, when the horse pulled, the purchase would be brought directly across the top of the head, and it was found to work in

FIG. 129.

many cases very finely. I made various modifications of this, but when I made the point of training the mouth out of resistance by the Breaking Bit, there being no special necessity for this kind of treatment, I abandoned it. But knowing the inability of many to do this with the requisite success, in addition to often requiring considerable work to do it well, to meet this emergency I devised the Patent Bridle, which carries this principle to the highest degree of perfection.

It sometimes requires considerable practice as well as much

hard work to train a horse successfully by the Breaking Bit ; also to make a bad puller, or horse having a hard mouth, sufficiently sensitive to submit to the control of an ordinary bit.

This is an ordinary bit with a pulley in each ring. A small, oval strap passes under the head-piece of the bridle, at each end of which is a pulley corresponding to those attached to the bit. Tie or buckle the ends of the reins into the rings of the bit, pass them up

Fɪɢ. 130.—Patent Bridle for Headstrong, Lunging, Runaway Horses.   Patented Oct. 20, 1880.

through the pulleys on the ends of the round straps, thence back through the pulleys in the bit rings. On the ends of these round pulley reins is stitched a small, strong string. Another round, extra bit of strong, flexible material (used only for severe cases) is attached to the main bit. (See Figs. 128, 129.) This bridle gives great pulley power, up and backward, against the most sensitive part of the mouth, under the upper lip, making it almost impossible to resist an ordinary pull upon the reins. In addition, the fulcrum of whatever power is used being brought, by the rounded strap before referred to, directly upon the spinal cord (as explained in Third Method), makes it a direct and powerful means of subjection ; so that if there is courage to pull for any length of time, the horse finds himself so overmatched that he will soon cease the resistance, and drive with an easy or slack rein, when the extra bit, if used, can be removed.

In using this bit upon a dangerous or doubtful horse, I would advise first heading up a long hill, and then pulling upon him steadily, as may be necessary until he gives up. A rubber connecting the ends of the bit to the rings on the pulley-reins makes the action of the bit upon the mouth the same as any ordinary bit. If at any time there should be much resistance, the rubbers stretch sufficiently to give play to the reins upon the pulleys, which will compel submission,— a very important point in the management of plucky, treacherous horses.

In breaking a horse to lead, simply reverse the reins through the pulleys so as to pull ahead. By catching both reins and pulling sideways and ahead, it will give such purchase that the horse can be lifted right or left, or ahead with as much or more power than by the War Bridle.

For halter-pulling, pass the reins or cord attached to the rings through the ring or hole in the manger, and form the end into a noose around the body of the horse back of the shoulders. The instant he begins to pull, the punishment becomes so severe upon his head that he will soon be afraid to pull. This is the only practicable means for breaking bridle-pullers. It is equally effective for breaking double-balkers. For such, the cord is tied to the end of the pole (as explained under the head of " Balking "), when, if the balker does not go, the gentle horse jerks him out of his tracks, making it a very easy and effective method of managing a double-balker.

THE FOOT-STRAP.

On the same principle, a second foot-strap can be used, when there will be power to control either one or both feet as may be desired. It must be used before the horse gets under much headway, for, if allowed to get under much motion, and then have both fore feet pulled from under him suddenly, it would throw or tumble him over upon his head.

Another objection is that in throwing the horse forcibly upon the knees, unless the ground is very soft, or the knees well protected by pads, there is serious danger of having the knees bruised or cut. A horse can be very easily ruined in this way ; for, should the synovial membrane of the knee-joint be cut through or ruptured, which can be easily done, it would surely result in spoiling the horse.

Both legs can without difficulty be pulled from under the horse at the same time with a single strap, and it would work very well so far as bringing the horse upon his knees in a soft spot, and disconcerting him when moved moderately in harness only, and would enable the control of quite a bad colt, but cannot be safely hazarded when hitched to a wagon, and especially if the ground be at all hard, and the horse is per-mitted to go at all fast, for the rea-

FIG. 131.—**Foot-strap.**

son, before explained, of the danger of tumbling the horse over on his head, and bruising and cutting the knees. If this is attempted, it should be done by the use of two straps.

During my early experience, in fact the second colt I used the foot-strap upon, the owner was elated with the idea that he was allowed to hitch up his colt, and though entirely manageable, to show a friend his power he let him out on a sharp trot a little down hill, when he pulled the opposite strap suddenly from under ; the consequence was that the poor colt was thrown directly upon his face, his knees badly cut, and the skin torn from his forehead and nose, in fact injuring him most seriously.

Driving a colt around in harness, where there is plenty of straw or very thick sod, throwing him upon his knees repeatedly, which can be easily done with a single strap, by passing it through rings attached to a strap on each fore foot and back to the belly-band, will of course enable throwing the horse squarely, without any difficulty ; but it subjects the horse to such a severe jar as to need-lessly strain and worry him. The use of both straps does this far more safely and effectively, because it enables pulling one foot or the other as may be desired—a great advantage. Should this be used, and the horse resists with energy, the more direct methods of subjection should be used.

A single strap can always be used to advantage, and sometimes a double one as a means of security, which can be put on quite easily. An ordinary piece of good, strong clothes-line, bed-cord, or webbing can be used to advantage, which can be attached to the feet as simple reserve power, should the horse attempt to lunge ahead, but when found submissive to the control of the mouth, are of course to be removed.

THE BREAKING RIG.

When a colt or horse is dangerous or reckless in his resistance, it is very convenient to control him by means that will require but little if any practical skill, and for this purpose I have invented the Breaking Rig, which will be found a valuable acquisition to the other methods here given.

To break a kicking, runaway horse or colt, all that is necessary is to carefully harness him in the rig so that he will not break loose, and let him go as he pleases. The more he struggles to free himself, or tries to kick and run, the quicker he will be broken, while the

FIG. 132.—**Simple Form of Breaking Rig.** **Patented July 6, 1880.**

trainer can sit quietly behind, touching and poling the horse where sensitive until he becomes submissive and gentle. The rig should be constructed as follows: First, set an upright post firmly in the ground. Next, have two shaft-arms, about twenty feet in length, so fitted that one end of each will turn upon the post. At the outer end of both of these shaft-arms should be fitted a spindle, and a wheel from a lumber or farm wagon. Separate the ends of the arms at a distance of eleven or twelve feet, or so that the horse can travel between them without touching either. Next place two bars across from one shaft-arm to the other, the inner one about three feet eight inches from the hub of the wheel, the outer one about two feet from the inside one at the horse's shoulders, and three feet at the quarters, so that an average-sized horse can travel easily between them. Have holes or mortises made through the shaft-arms, and the ends of the bars fitted to them.   The inner one should be fast-

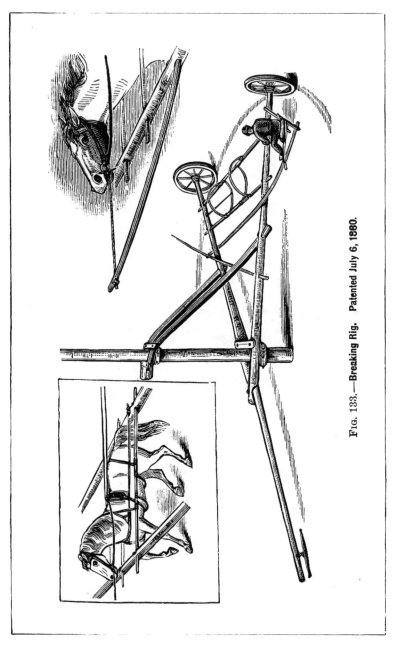

Fig. 133.—Breaking Rig.   Patented July 6, 1880.

ened permanently, but the outer one so fitted that it can be taken
out and reversed, to allow driving the other way.   It is best to have

the holes or mortises duplicated, so that the bars can be adjusted to fit the size of the horse.

If the wheels are not high enough to support the frame arms, put an extra piece of scantling on the upper side, and make the mortises or holes high enough to bring the bars where the shafts would come in driving. The simplest way of fastening the horse in the rig is, after he is harnessed in place, to pass a strap under the body from one bar to the other, another over the body and shoulders, and a third over the hips.

No matter how vicious or headstrong a runaway horse may be, the faster and more determinedly he runs in this rig, the sooner he will from necessity become gentle. He has not the liberty to rear up, throw himself, or kick. If he undertakes to run he will be carried round in a circle so rapidly as to become completely dizzy, and would fall helpless if not confined and supported. If sensitive about having the head, neck, or hind parts touched, he can now be handled until he is entirely submissive to it. If he is afraid of an umbrella or robe, these objects can be brought around him until he is submissive. If he is afraid of a carriage-top, open and shut an umbrella before his face, over, and behind him, until he is fearless of it. If afraid of having the rein caught under the tail, and inclined to run under such circumstances, he can now, with entire ease and safety, be made to submit to it.

With such a rig made, which is very simple and easy to construct, the green colt, kicking runaway horse, or those of other dangerous habits in harness, such as fear of top, umbrella, or robe, etc., can be easily broken by any one. The point is to adjust the rig to the horse, so that he will not be hampered or feel any serious restraint, except when he struggles to resist ; and then let him go or drive him as explained, until, under the most trying tests, he is proved to be submissive and docile.

Not only this, but it will also be found very effective for breaking single balkers,— a very important advantage. By modifying the rig a little as shown in Fig. 133, the pole may be allowed to extend to the opposite side of the circle, to which a gentle horse can be attached. Now, with the War Bridle cord on, of course after being previously subjected to it as explained under the head of balking, it is adjusted to the pole in front. If the horse will not go when commanded, the gentle horse at the opposite end of the pole can be started up, when his whole power, if necessary, can be brought upon the cord, which will soon bring the horse forward off his feet, when, after a few repetitions, he will stop and start freely at command.

Chapter III.

COLT TRAINING.

THE successful teacher aims first to gain the confidence of his scholars, so that he can address their understanding clearly. But were he to transform himself into a dangerous monster, whipping them while talking in an unknown language, indicating by his actions that he would kill or injure them, they would become so frightened and excited that their first impulse would be resistance or a desperate struggle to get away.

Now this is the impression made upon a wild, unbroken colt when hurt, frightened, or excited, in the effort to train and control him, and which in a proportionate degree must increase the difficulty of his successful management.

Fig. 134.—**Simple Way of Haltering a Dangerous Colt.**

It is important, on this account, that every step in the management of these cases be of a character to prevent and overcome fear, when the instruction and training can be carried forward to the degree of the colt's ability to understand, and there is perfect obedience.

In the first place, it is important to discriminate as to character, whether naturally gentle, very wild, or vicious. On this account, for convenience, I will divide them into three classes: First, colts that are naturally gentle, but nervous. Second, colts that are somewhat wild and unaccustomed to being handled. Third, those that are not only wild, but vicious and dangerous. The—

FIRST CLASS

Usually require but very simple treatment. The first important point is to teach the colt to lead. The War Bridle is by far the best and simplest means of doing this; but as this may not be available, I will explain how it can be done in most cases very easily

FIG. 135.—Testing a Doubtful Colt before Subjecting to Treatment.

with a common halter. Put on quietly a simple rope halter that fits nicely upon the head, the nose-piece extended well down; tie the noose back of the jaw into a knot, to prevent its slipping or drawing tightly upon the jaw.

Now stand opposite the shoulder, take a firm hold of the hitching-part, and give a sharp, quick jerk, which will pull him around toward you. This pulling to be repeated at short intervals until he will come around freely without being pulled upon, when go to the opposite side and repeat the same. Now gradually increase your circle to a line straight ahead, until he will follow in any manner. If the colt is a little heavy, perhaps sullen, tie up the near fore leg, when he can be pulled around easily. Once yielding, give the leg freedom, when he will follow freely. After leading well, catch the halter up near the head, and go around with him on a sharp walk at the same time, and bring a pole (one end of which being well back of the arm) against the quarters. The pulling around will sufficiently disconcert the colt to allow this without much resistance, when repeat, and he will soon learn to submit, after which repeat on the opposite side. It would, however, be much better to put on the War Bridle if available, and after pulling right and left two or three times, bring a pole against the quarters, legs, and flanks, as before explained. If there is submission to this, it will be all that is necessary to do, and will be just as effective as if the colt was subjected to the severest treatment.

FIG. 136.—About the Length the Halter Should be Tied.

Now handle the feet gently. There is quite a sleight in doing this. The point is, when on the near side to rest the left hand against the shoulder, and as the other is run down to the foot to press the body from you, throwing the weight upon the opposite foot, when the near one will be relaxed, and can be taken up easily. While holding the halter with the left hand extended back to the hip, and holding it short enough to pull the head partly around, pass the right hand down over the leg and along gently, until the fetlock is reached. Now, as there is an effort to lift the foot, press from you with the left hand, and the foot can be easily brought up. At first do not lift it very high, gradually repeating until it can be taken up on a level with the knees. This submitted to, remove pressure with the left hand, and move forward under the leg, the left arm and elbow coming over the leg above the gambrel, so as to hold it firmly between both knees and hammer it lightly, then put down and take up again. In this way repeat a few times, gradually hammering harder until there is no fear or resistance. This to be repeated on the opposite side.

Now mount the colt quietly. The best course is to stand opposite the shoulder with the left hand grasping the halter and mane, the right resting upon the back. While standing right up to the horse, make a little spring upward, and on the instant of doing so throw the right arm forward so as to bring the part a little forward of the elbow, across the back and hold the body so poised a little

Fig. 137.—Pulling the Foot Back with Cord.

while. If the submission is at all doubtful, it is better to repeat this two or three times, at each time bringing the body up a little higher, or until the breast will come across the horse's back. This submitted to, gently bring the right leg up over the back, and gradually assume a sitting position. Be careful at this stage to caress and talk to the colt. At each progressive step it will help your efforts greatly to give him some little present of an apple, or something else of which he is fond ; then go on more boldly, and in a short time you can get off or on as you please.

It is desirable at this stage to accustom a colt to sliding back over the hips, and touching the heels against the flanks. There is quite a sleight in doing this. It is this : While across the back with the leg partly over, catch the halter or bridle rein short enough to pull the head around a little toward the left shoulder. Now gradually slide back, touching both heels gently against the sides, until you can slide back over the hips. Should he at any point resist or jump, you can instantly slip over to the near side, and the head in the meantime being pulled around toward you, throws the hind part from you. Simply repeat until he can be mounted and will submit to all this in any manner. In teaching to drive in harness, the first thing to do is to accustom the colt to have the hind parts and flanks touched without resistance. The simplest way of doing this is as

FIG. 138.—Pulling the Foot Forward.

follows: Take an ordinary pole, something like a rake-stale, and see that there are no rough corners or points on it. While standing opposite the shoulder, with the right hand holding the pole, its end resting back under the arm, bring the other end quietly to the mane and scratch along carefully, gradually extending back over the body and legs, then go behind and rub down between the legs, belly, etc., until submitted to.

TRAINING THE MOUTH.

The next step is to train the mouth. There are two ways of doing this—by putting on the Bitting Rig and accustoming to the bit for some time, and driving directly with the bit. In my practice I trained the mouth directly with the bit. If the bitting method is adopted, the course to be pursued is to put on a bridle with an ordinary smooth snaffle bit and leave it on until accustomed to it, then put on any ordinary rig and check at first so as to bring but little restraint upon the head, leaving it on thirty or forty minutes. Next day check a little shorter, and let him run in a yard, or be led by the side of another horse. At each repetition check a little shorter, until the head is brought as high as he will bear, and submit to it. If this

Fig. 139.—The Colt as he Stands after Treatment.

course be adopted, be careful not to draw too tight at first, nor leave on too long. Many a colt is ruined or killed by this kind of imprudence. The error in bitting usually is that the colt is caught and entirely held by force and, while perhaps greatly frightened and excited, the rig is put on and the head checked up high and fastened there mercilessly. The result is that if a colt of much temper and courage, he is liable to get mad, rear up, and throw himself over back, which frequently results in his being killed. In any event he is worried and excited to a degree that causes serious harm. Another thing: if left on too long, he becomes tired, and to relieve himself he rests the head upon the bit, and thus learns the habit of lug-

ging and pulling upon the bit in driving, a very unpleasant as well
as mean habit.   He is also, from this cause, liable to learn the habits
of refusing to rein but one way, or pulling on one rein, throwing the
head down when pulled upon, refusing to stand, or to back.   These
were habits that I had to contend with almost constantly in colts
partly broken that were brought me to experiment upon.

A very good and simple Bitting Rig can be made as follows:
With an ordinary bridle with snaffle bit and gag-runners, fit a simple surcingle with loops at different points on both sides with
crouper attachments, as shown by Fig. 150.   Next take a piece of
cord about the size used for War Bridle, and place the center over
the water hook, or to be held by a strap connecting it with the saddle part.   Now pass the ends forward through the gag-runners down

Fig. 140.—**Wrong Way of Teaching Colt to Lead by Halter.**

through the rings of the bit on each side, thence back through the
loops on each side of the surcingle, and tie into the hip-ring of the
back-band, sufficiently short to give the restraint required.   The
higher the cord is held on each side, the greater the tendency to pull
the head up and back, while the lower it is, the greater the tendency
to pull the nose in ; so the hight on each side should be regulated
to suit the case.   While by this means there is restraint upon the
head up and back, the sliding of the cord through the rings and gag-
runners gives sufficient freedom for the head to be brought down to
relieve fatigue.

Other breaking rigs, and some very good ones, are in use ; the
only objection to them is their expense and complication, there being
in some cases arrangements of cross-bars put upon the saddle-part to
give more fulcrum in pulling the head up and back.   It is evident
that the end to be attained is to teach the mouth to be submitted freely
up and back to the flexible restraint of the bit in driving.   Now, bit-

ting only holds the head to a fixed position of restraint, and does not give the idea of doing this practically, which, as stated, is the point to be attained. This I learned to do easily with the Breaking Bit as follows: Put on an open bridle with smooth snaffle-bit a little longer than common if attainable, with harness which should be so fitted as to rest easily upon the body. I was in all cases in the habit of giving the head entire freedom, and I made it an important point that the horse could see me, consequently used no blinders. The reins should be brought back through the shaft or lug-bearers.

FIG. 141.—**When Pulled upon Very Hard, is Liable to Rear and Throw himself over Backward.**

Get directly behind and drive the colt around slowly. When he pulls ahead, give a little raking jerk, then slack instantly, and so repeat. Do the same for throwing the head down and lugging, which will bring the head up and back, simply repeating until the mouth is submitted freely to moderate resistance and held in position. Sometimes the colt will fight this quite hard. If he is at all sullen, and resists hard, the Breaking Bit must be substituted. It will require a good deal of work to make your point, and at best can only be accomplished imperfectly with anything like an ordinary driving bit. In such a case you are to substitute the Breaking Bit, which enables you to make your points very easily and quickly. Even

8   a

with this there will be sometimes quite a hard fight for a time. Simply persevere, being careful not to lacerate or bruise the mouth. When the colt resisted too hard, I found it better to stop until he became cool, and then repeat, when the point could be made very easily.

It will be noticed, in making a horse lead with the War Bridle, that he may at first resist very hard indeed. It would seem to an

Fig. 142.—Right Way of Pulling to Teach the Colt to Lead.

inexperienced person that he could not be made to lead at all, but by perseverance it will be found that the horse will give up unconditionally. The principle is the same in training the mouth in this way with the bit. A horse may resist for a time with great determination. Simply keep cool, go slowly, repeating as stated, and he will soon learn to submit unconditionally. In any event, there must be perseverance until the point is made and the mouth submitted to the slightest restraint if necessary. The lesson should be repeated in driving to wagon.

The details now will be the same as for the management of the next class, which can be referred to.

SECOND CLASS.

Among this class there will sometimes be found a colt that may develop quite a bad character, and it is necessary to proceed cautiously. First learn, if you can, what you have to deal with. If a colt is at all mild, and not easily approached, it is best to turn him quietly into a moderate-sized room or carriage house. There should be no stalls which he can run into, or corners to run against and hurt himself. It would perhaps alarm him too much to try to catch him and put on a halter, and besides, there would be danger of his getting hurt. This difficulty can be easily overcome as follows: Get a pole about ten feet long, and drive two nails into it,

FIG. 143.—Simple Method of Making a Sullen Colt Follow Instantly.

about eight inches apart, the first about one inch from the end. Take a common rope halter and form a slipping-noose with the part which slips through it back about two feet, hanging the part which goes over the head on the nails of the stick, so as to be easily adjusted upon the head. (See Fig. 134.) If the colt is not very much excited or frightened as the halter is extended toward him, he will reach out his nose to smell and examine it. While he is trying to gratify his curiosity in this way, bring the slipping part under his jaw, while the head part is passed over and back of the ears, when by turning the stick half round, the halter will drop upon the head. Now, by pulling upon it, the slack will be taken out, and the halter will be upon him securely.

Should you try to teach him to lead now, he may resist so hard as to become very much excited and worried. Even with the War

Bridle on it is not always policy to try it at this stage. The best course to pursue is to subject to the Second Method of Subjection. Reach out as carefully as you can until you can get hold of the tail. It must usually be done very quietly. Tie it into a knot, and run the halter through, drawing short enough to bring the body into a half circle. Catch the cord and hair with the right hand, and with the left catch the hitching part well up toward the head, and go around with him a few times as shown in Fig. 86; then tie into a half-hitch knot, and let him go around. Be careful not to tie so short that he will go around too quickly, as this would make him so dizzy that he would fall down. As you let go, motion the hand toward the head as he passes, or catch up a pole which is ready and motion toward the head, and touch lightly around the

FIG. 144.—The Colt as he will Usually Follow after Treatment.

hind parts. This to be done only when he is going slow, which will force him to go rapidly; and in this way continue until he becomes so dizzy that he will submit himself to be poled around the legs and body in any manner. In most cases this is a very simple operation, and entirely safe; but there are frequently cases that require considerable care and judgment. For example, should a colt be of a sullen, reckless character, if he is tied too short at first and then let him go his own way, he may lunge and throw himself. This can always be avoided by holding the strap part of the halter when passed through the tail with the hand, and then going around a few times until he is a little dizzy, and in the meantime pull just the length required and make fast by tying into a half-hitch knot, when give freedom. Should he go too fast, or there is danger of his falling or throwing himself, catch the end of the strap and pull loose. This is a very nice point, and one that must not be neglected, whereas, if tied too short at first, causing him to go too fast, it is important that the strap be instantly pulled loose and tied longer. In either case, the point is to regulate the going around just enough to make him dizzy and no more. There is nothing made by letting the colt fall, and especial care must be taken to prevent his throwing himself.

Now proceed with the poling. Touch every part of the body that is in the least sensitive while going around, until submitted to ;

Fig. 145.—Teaching a Colt to Follow with the Whip.

then untie and do the same. I mean by this that when he will submit to being touched on any part with the pole, go to the opposite side and repeat until there is no fear or resistance shown. Every part of the body must be touched. Usually the feet can be taken up now and handled.

Next get on the back. These points should be made thoroughly. As a general thing, this will require but a few minutes' effort, and the change will seem wonderful. All his fears and sensibilities apparently having left him, he acts the part of an entirely gentle colt. But some colts, and those too that may appear quite gentle, may resist very hard when touched or tested in this way, striking and kicking with great fury. This is not to be accepted as a cause for discouragement. Simply force up sharply to the point of helplessness, and, if resisting this very hard, reverse quickly and tie the other way, and thus repeat until there is entire submission. It is very rare that even a colt of this character, when this treatment is applied properly, cannot be made perfectly gentle within from eight to twelve minutes.

　　If the case is a bad one, after making this point, proceed as follows : Put on the War Bridle and make him follow thoroughly. There will usually be but little trouble in making the colt follow with this in a few minutes. Now take up the feet, as before explained. If this should be resisted, punish a little with the cord by pulling

Fɪɢ. 146.—Colt as he will Follow after being Trained with Whip.

right and left once or twice and repeat. As a general thing there will be but little trouble experienced. Sometimes it may be found quite difficult to take up the hind feet without getting hurt. In such a case simply tie a flexible piece of rope or webbing to the hind foot, and while held at the head by an assistant, pull the foot back. This may at first be resisted quite hard, but simply keep repeating until it is submitted to unconditionally. Now gradually catch the foot with the hand, and so repeat until it can be handled without difficulty. (See Figs. 138 and 139.) The opposite foot must be treated in the same manner. If this is resisted very hard, turn to instruction on " Bad to Shoe," where full details are given.

　　The next step is to drive in harness. I found I could accomplish my end quicker and better by putting on a nice, smooth

Breaking Bit, with wide leather inside the rings to prevent its being drawn through the mouth, then pass the reins back through the shaft of the harness, and stand behind, holding the reins far enough away to avoid being kicked or hurt. Now touch gently with the whip, and gradually let the colt go any way he will, straight ahead. When he will do this nicely, teach him to stop by calling "Whoa!" sharply, and immediately giving a short, sharp, raking jerk, just enough to stop him, but immediately slack. Usually the horse will resist this by trying to go ahead. Simply repeat until he will get the idea and stop promptly at command. It is important that this

FIG. 147.—Bringing the Pole Against the Quarters.

is repeated until thoroughly learned. Now gradually make him go sideways by pulling the line to the right or left. In any event, this must be persevered in until the colt will stop and start, turn sideways, or in circles, as required. Do not commit the error of trying to back him or make him back too freely. While it is advisable to teach him this now, it must be done very cautiously. Simply call "Back," and pull him back just enough to bring him off the feet a little, if you can, backward. This to be repeated until he will move back by pulling gently upon the reins and saying "Back." Let this be the object of two or three short lessons, so as to get him to come back at command, but not to go back too freely for this reason: If a colt is made to come back too easily, should he become frightened at anything in advance of him, and especially if pulled back suddenly, he is liable to go back too far, and thus learn the habit of running back, turning around, upsetting the wagon, and getting away, one of the worst habits a horse can acquire.

This point of coming back accomplished, now stand a little sideways and bring the pole across against the quarters, then between the legs and under the body until it is submitted to unconditionally. Next bring back against the pole or rail anything about as high as the cross-piece of shafts when in harness, as shown in Fig. 147.

This submitted to unconditionally, with sufficient control of the

Fig. 148.—Bringing Pole against Quarters when First Driven in Harness.

mouth to hold a colt under any degree of excitement, the next step is to drive in shafts. If he becomes excited or stubborn at any point, particularly if he resists the bit hard, the better way will be to put him away until cool, when by repeating the lesson he will soon work in. At this point there is great danger of spoiling the mouth, because when the blood becomes much heated the sensibility of the mouth becomes so blunted that he will bear to have it cut to pieces without seeming to feel it; but when over the excitement it will be so sensitive and sore that he will be liable not only to yield too freely, but, as before stated, acquire the habit of running back; hence the necessity of being careful in this respect. The course I found easiest and best was to get two poles, something like hop poles. about twelve feet long, lay them down in the form of shafts; about six feet from the forward ends lay on a piece of pole and make fast with pieces of rope or strap, so as to make the poles at this point about three feet apart ; now hitch the colt into these poles without breeching, and drive along as shown in Fig. 153, repeating the lesson until he can be turned right or left, back against the cross-piece, or submit to any excitement, and can be held and managed easily.

This point accomplished, you can next hitch to a wagon. If available, get a two-wheeled cart, which would be much better. Before hitching to wagon or cart, be sure that all fear of any rattle or noise from behind is thoroughly overcome. Next, when the shafts are brought up behind and the colt put in, run the cross-piece against the quarters two or three times and push them right

FIG. 149.—**Method of Backing the Colt against Rail or Pole.**

and left against the body, then shake and rattle the wagon, then move him along a little, pulling the wagon behind. Now attach the tugs and breeching-straps, and if you wish to give the utmost security, attach a piece of cord or strap to the near fore foot, and hold as a third line. Now, should the colt try to lunge ahead, simply take his foot, when he will become disabled. Usually there will be no resistance. It is simply a measure of precaution. Found safe, take off and drive moderately.

Another point: The colt should always be hitched where the road is wide and level, or in a field, giving a chance to drive around and turn easily. At first let him go any way he will, giving him a moderately slack rein. If the previous work has been well done, the colt will be as gentle and indifferent to excitement as an old horse. But if not subdued and made thoroughly gentle and fearless, as before explained, there is danger, in exceptionally bad cases, of his getting frightened and kicking, and thus a great point is lost. It is, in fact, almost fatal to success to let a colt by carelessness or accident resist at any point, as it makes him cunning and doubtful,—a condition that sometimes requires very careful, thorough work to overcome.

There should be no effort to make a drive until the colt is accustomed to turning, stopping, and starting, but not to backing; let that come after the going ahead and stopping is thoroughly es-

Fig. 150.—**Simple Form of Bitting-rig.**

tablished, when repeat the lesson on backing a little. At first, the driving should be confined to a walk, then gradually let out to a moderate trot, being careful not to drive to the point of exhaustion. If the colt steps well, and it is desired to cultivate a fast trotting gait, there is more necessity for going slowly. First, let him out on a smooth, moderately descending road, holding up often, and speaking to him kindly. Gradually he can be let out faster and a little farther, but not to the point of breaking, nor so far at any time as to cause fatigue. If it is intended to hitch to top carriage, drive around first with an umbrella held over the head, bringing it over the back. Next, lead him around so that he can look into the top and smell of it, then lead him into the shafts and hitch.

The custom of using blinders on horses, especially as usually put on, in a haphazard way of pressing against and covering up the eyes, is an abomination which should be dispensed with in driving. They are admissible only when the horse is lazy or cunning, watching the whip, etc. Any horse of intelligence and courage will always drive more reliably when able to see around and behind him.

FIG. 151.—**Strained, Unnatural Position of the Head when Checked High.**

If it is desired to drive the colt double, it is equally necessary that he should be subjected to sufficient treatment, such as training the mouth a little, making him gentle to being handled before being hitched up. It is important that this driving should be carefully repeated, and at each time of hitching up that the shafts should be run against the quarters as before described, so as to make the horse thoroughly accustomed to being touched around the quarters and legs. If allowed to stand a few days or longer, before hitching in, he should be tested carefully.

FIG. 152.—**The Head as Nature Designed it Should be Carried.**

It is important that all these precautions be taken in the management of sensitive young horses. If it is well done, there will be no danger of the colt becoming frightened, kicking, and running away from any little accident such as the breeching strap breaking, the cross-piece touching the quarters, catching the rein under the tail, etc., as there is close connection in these cases with excessive fear. See chapter on Fear.

THIRD CLASS.

In this class are to be found sometimes colts of the most difficult character to manage. Some of the worst cases I ever handled in my life were colts partly or wholly unbroken. Among this class we found our greatest average of subjects to be experimented upon before classes. They were usually colts that had been either greatly frightened or excited to kicking and running away, or were naturally so vicious and dangerous as to be very difficult to go near or handle at all with safety. If kickers, they would kick in the most reckless and desperate manner, making it impossible for even two or three men to hitch them in shafts and be able to hold them without their kicking or running away.

In the management of these cases it is necessary to prepare thoroughly. A very important point is to have a roomy place, with soft or sodded ground, or ground covered with something that would make it soft and prevent slipping. The first thing to do is to get the halter on safely and with the least excitement. Next get the horse under sufficient control to be able to subject him to requisite treatment. The Second Method is by far the simplest and safest in accomplishing this. After turning around quickly almost to the point of falling, untie quickly, and tie the other way, following up until submissive to being handled. If the colt be of a mustang character, this will be found by all odds the best treatment. In some cases this may not be sufficient to accomplish your point. If a colt three or four or more years old, and if of a disposition to be safely used, subject to the First Method, throwing rapidly and just as long as the horse will get up. Then perhaps it would be advisable to subject again sharply to the Second Method. This is the course we frequently pursued with great success, but then we had the advantage of knowing the treatment best suited and applying it most successfully.

Next put on the War Bridle, double-draw hitch form, and make all the impression with that you can. If this be done properly, the colt must be very bad indeed that will not yield to it in a short time. In very serious cases we resorted at once to the Third Method, making all the impression we could with it, and again going back to the Second Method. In some critical cases we had to depend almost wholly upon the Third Method. But usually the Second or First will be found sufficient, and certainly, in connection with the double-draw hitch form, there should be no real difficulty experienced in making your point.

It is of course indispensable that the conditions and principles in applying these methods of subjection should have been read and studied carefully. Another important point to bear in mind : When the case is known to be a very serious one, prepare yourself thoroughly. First, as stated, you must have a suitable place to work in ; second, you must have everything necessary to work with. Nothing should be left to chance. Your War Bridle cord must be of such size and quality that it will not break or give way at a critical time. It is a cause of the most serious embarrassment, if not of failure, to use anything that would break or give way in making your experiments. You must look to the point of even being dressed properly. I mean by this that you should be stripped as if working for your life, because at certain points it is necessary to be very quick and

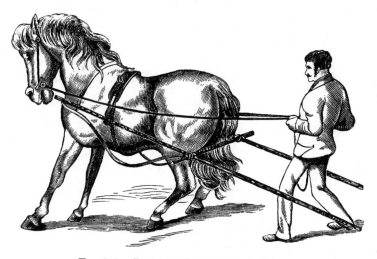

Fig. 153.—Testing the Colt by Driving in Poles.

ready for any emergency. In my practice I made it a great point to have a supply of apples or something else of which horses are fond, and the moment I made the subject submit unconditionally I appealed at once to his better nature by the kindest treatment, but in the meantime kept on handling him industriously, and thus continued until the horse was cool and over the excitement, when, after resting awhile, I repeated the handling in the same manner, and then, if necessary, I in part repeated the treatment. In this way I kept on until I felt sure of success. I may repeat that it is simply a matter of exercising care and being thorough. No risks that can be avoided are to be taken. As stated under that head, the Third Method cannot be repeated with success, neither can the First. Whatever is done with these methods must be done at once. The after-treatment to be given the same as described, simply using, if anything, more care. The point with these cases is to make every step thorough, and from every point gained make the next, until the colt can be hitched up and driven with safety. In our experiments before classes we were usually able to hitch up these cases in from fifteen to twenty-five minutes. For one who is not practiced, and I presume my reader not to be, the point is first to make the colt thoroughly gentle, and second, making the point sufficient to driving to poles and cart after thorough control of the mouth.

In the management of mustangs, which properly comes under this head, the point is to get to the horse and make the first movement with him with safety. This will sometimes be found very difficult, but certainly there is no treatment that works so well upon the mustang nature as the Second Method, and it must be depended upon mainly for such cases.

Fig. 154.—Sullen, Obstinate Colt, as Sometimes Brought for Treatment.

TEACHING A SULLEN COLT TO LEAD.

Sometimes the colt is so sullen that it will be found very difficult to at first make him lead by the head. The younger the colt the more sullen will be this resistance. Sometimes the temperament is such that the colt will fight very hard. Where you find such, the best way is to resort to strategy, which will usually enable making your point easily. Take two War Bridles (one not being sufficiently long), unite the ends, and make a noose, which bring around the body, the noose under, and bring the cords forward between the fore legs. It should be placed about half way between the shoulders and hips. Stand in front, a little to the left, and while holding the halter with the left hand give a little sharp jerk upon the cords, which will contract the noose around the body, and so hurt and frighten the colt that he will jump ahead. Simply repeat a few times, when he will follow around freely.

Sometimes doubling the cord and bringing the two under the tail, then twisting them two or three times over the back, knotting them together in front of the breast, and pulling in the same manner, will work better. The objection is that some colts will kick when the pressure of the cord is felt under the tail. It will in any event be found a very nice means to make a sullen, unbroken colt lead quickly. It took me a good many years to learn this simple trick. Once a colt was brought in that sulked so badly that he could not be made to lead. On the impulse of the moment, I took the War

Fig. 155.—Colts as Usually Made to Follow on a Run by a few Minutes' Treatment before the Class.

Bridle, brought it under the tail, and gave a quick, sharp pull forward. The consequence was, he jumped nearly ten feet ahead, and, in fact, I had all I could do to hold him. This worked very well until I found a colt that it caused to kick, which I remedied by bringing the noose around the. body as described. Once a man in Pennsylvania offered to join my class if we could make a colt he had lead. He stated that the colt was five years old, and could not be led ; he would be satisfied if we could make the colt lead across the barn. I directed one of my men to go to the man's place, to put a halter on the colt, and put on the cord under the tail, as described, and bring him along. The first the people knew he had him running after him into the inclosure. We then of course trained him by the head with the War Bridle to make him follow, which we did in a few minutes.

TRAINING TO LEAD WITH WHIP.

Another method of teaching a sullen colt to lead, and one that works very nicely if done properly, is by training with the whip. After putting on a halter, bring a short whip over the withers, so that the lash will strike the side of the head below the eye (see Fig. 145), and commence tapping lightly until the head is turned around a little from it, when stop and caress. This to be repeated until the colt will step around toward you to avoid the annoyance of the whip. Then step ahead a little and touch with the lash over the

FIG. 156.—Proper Method of Hitching the Colt at First.

hips, which will cause him to come ahead, and so continue until he will follow anywhere. This is a little feat of training, but the result that can be accomplished with it in a few minutes will often be wonderful. During my first tour in Maine, in 1863, I advertised to make any wild colt follow me into the open street within ten minutes with the whip only, not having anything on him. I did it in this way: At first I used a belly-band and surcingle, to prevent the horse getting away—that is, when he tried to move I pulled the foot from under him; but he can be held just as well with a halter, and it is much simpler.

HITCHING THE COLT.

This is very simple and easy to do by the method here given, but by the old method of treatment is liable to be a very serious matter. After teaching a colt to lead well and making him gentle, provide yourself with a cord sufficiently strong (largest size War Bridle is the best); this should be doubled, and make a noose around the body ; bring forward between the legs, pass through the rings in the manger and tie into the halter, hitching about as long as you usually would a horse to a post. Be careful to hitch in such a position that he cannot run around. In a large stall will be the best place. The moment you are ready, let the first impression be a sharp one by exciting him to go back with a lunge, but the cord around the body will hurt him so that he will usually jump and spring ahead. Simply repeat until he can be made to go back. It is important that this point be well made, so as to break up all inclination to pull afterward. I would hitch in this manner for a day or two. Very full instruction will be found under the head of " Halter-Pulling " on this point, which can be referred to.

9   a

Chapter IV.

EXCESSIVE FEAR—ITS EFFECTS.

IT is quite wonderful to what a degree the nervous system can be shaken or deranged by sudden fright or intense fear. So susceptible is the mind to this influence that not infrequently very trifling causes in themselves make such an impression upon children

Fig. 157.—The Colt Excited by Fear.

and sensitive persons as to produce convulsions and insanity that may in some cases end in death. Even large audiences are sometimes so panic-stricken by the cry of fire, or some other cause of danger, as to seem insensible to reason. Under such circumstances, many men and women become so demented that they are most likely to do just what they should not. For example, they will try to save things of no value, and leave valuable property to be destroyed, throw mirrors and other fragile articles from upper story windows, without realizing they must be broken ; be unable to dress, or will get on garments the wrong way, etc.

(130)

Now the horse is liable to be excited and deranged in the same manner. It is well understood how difficult it is to get horses out of a burning building ; and if by blindfolding, etc., they are taken out, when given freedom their confusion and excitement is so intense that they are apt to rush back into the fire. On the sudden approach of a train, or blowing of the whistle, a horse in crossing the track is liable to become so paralyzed that it cannot be forced across

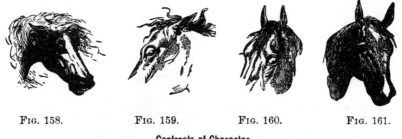

| FIG. 158. | FIG. 159. | FIG. 160. | FIG. 161. |

Contrasts of Character.

in time to prevent a collision. It is not uncommon to have a horse frightened to death in this way.

To illustrate, I will include an account of a few such cases that comprise the record of a few days only : —

"In Rochester, N. Y., the other day, a horse was so frightened at an engine letting off steam, that it trembled, and in a moment fell dead from fright."

"At White Plains, N. Y., a horse was so frightened by a locomotive whistle that he dropped dead."

"Two very remarkable cases of horses being frightened to death occurred in Fairmount Park, Phil., within the past few days. Last Thursday the horse of P. Wallace, of Seventeenth and Catherine streets, became unmanageable, through fright at a train of cars on Mifflin Lane. The occupants of the carriage alighted, and Mr. Wallace undertook to drive the horse off to quiet it, when it dropped dead."

"During Monday the horse of Mr. Zeiss, Ridge Avenue and Jefferson Street, ran away from fright at a passing steamboat. Guard Ledlie caught the animal, when Mr. Zeiss said he could then manage the horse, and started off. The horse went off all right for about 60 yards, when he again ran away and went 15 or 20 feet, when he dropped dead."

Colts or unbroken horses are especially susceptible to fear. Almost every step in their management, as shown in Colt Training, lies in overcoming resistance excited by fear. It is the principal cause of kicking and running away, as well as many other annoying or dangerous habits, which make the horse partially or wholly worthless for use.

A colt that once had the habit of feeding around and poaching in neighboring yards, was so gentle and indifferent to fear that he could scarcely be driven away. In order to frighten him off, an old tin pail was tied to his tail and a dog set on him. At first he cared nothing about it, but when he started to run, the pail rattled and thumped against his heels so severely that he became frightened, and kicked. The faster he ran, the more the pail rattled and thumped against his legs, and he ran until he was exhausted. As the result, his nervous system was so shaken and injured that afterward the stirring of the grass, or drawing of a stick on the ground behind him, would so excite him that he would scringe, switch, and kick.

The effect is the same upon a colt or horse which by some accident or imprudence has been excited to kick and run away while

Fig. 162.—Excited by Fear.

hitched to a wagon. The striking of the wagon against the legs in kicking, makes him think it is the wagon hitting and hurting him, and he tries in the most desperate manner to get away or free himself from it ; so the fear, kicking, and running are increased until freed from the wagon, disabled, or caught. Thus the wagon becomes the same in respect to frightening and exciting the horse and spoiling him, that the tin pail was in frightening the colt. The same effect, of exciting and frightening the horse as by sudden or unexpected contact with objects or sounds, are produced in various ways. Now, as these difficulties are entirely preventable by proper treatment, the importance of understanding and applying it can be appreciated.

A horse's way of reasoning is limited to his experience in seeing, hearing, and feeling. When convinced in this way that an ob-

4

ject or sound will not hurt him, no matter how objectionable or repugnant it may have previously seemed in appearance, it will be regarded with indifference. It is remarkable also what a degree of insensibility to fear, or how much confidence can be inspired when subjected to proper treatment. For instance : Let a pole be brought suddenly or unexpectedly against the quarters of a wild colt, and he will instantly jump, snort, and kick, showing the greatest fear of it. If this be repeated for a few times, the fear, kicking, and effort to get away will be greatly increased. If, on the contrary, the pole were slowly and gently brought to the nose, so that he can smell of it, then passed over the mane and back, gently rubbing the parts, and gradually extending it over the hips and across the quarters lightly, increasing the force of the contact as he will bear, at the same time attracting his attention and quieting his fear by stroking the head, talking to him, or giving apples, etc., a few repetitions, requiring in all perhaps not more than ten or fifteen minutes, will make the colt entirely fearless and indifferent to being touched.

I was once present when a team of four horses was harnessed for the first time to a band wagon. With the first note, the horses were excited to such intense fear that it was only by the greatest effort they were kept from running away, though the band stopped playing instantly. I directed the men to get out and go back about fifteen rods. In the meantime, I took the most excitable horse by the bridle, stroked his nose, talked to him quietly, and directed the others to be treated in like manner. They were greatly excited ; the one I held fairly shook with fear. After a few minutes, I directed the band to commence very lightly upon one or two instruments at first, the others afterward to gradually start in. This slight commencement was repeated several times before the horses would bear it without showing great excitement. I then directed them to play louder, and increase the tone gradually until up to the full force of all the instruments and drums. This point made, while playing they came forward very slowly, got in and commenced again in the lightest possible manner, gradually increasing the sound until they played again with full force. I now directed the band to keep quiet while the team was driven a short distance, then, as before, commence lightly and slowly, gradually playing louder until the horses appeared indifferent to the sound. The result was that in less than twenty minutes the band paraded the streets, playing as they pleased, the horses entirely gentle, in fact, appearing to enjoy the music. Here we see such marked excitement and fear shown from hearing a sudden, unexpected sound, as to precipitate the most violent resistance, and the contrary of soon quieting down and becoming indifferent to it, by convincing the reason that it would not cause injury. As the resistance of colts is almost wholly excited by fear, I had necessarily to give a very full explanation of their management in reference to preventing and overcoming excessive fear, which should be referred to ; but their management is so intimately connected with this chapter that I will, at the expense of some repetition, give further details.

Suppose we wish to accustom a colt to the sight of a piece of

Fig. 163.—**Nervous, Excitable Nature.**

paper or a white handkerchief. It is first brought to his nose so that he is able to feel of it, and see it plainly, then rubbed against the head and neck until it ceases to attract attention. If now the operator were to step behind or opposite the flanks, and throw it suddenly behind or under the belly, it would be very likely to excite as much fear and resistance as if he had not before seen or felt it. The difference of position makes it appear a new object of danger to be avoided. Familiarized with it at the head, it should be thrown down carelessly in front, then a little farther back, occasionally rubbing it against the head and nose, and so repeating until it can be thrown anywhere around or under the body ; this must also be done on both sides of the body alike.

A spirited horse that may have been driven for years to a wagon, gentle, would be just as likely to kick and run away should the breeching break and let the cross-piece or whiffletree come against the quarters, as if he had previously known nothing about them. And so in relation to other objects or causes of resistance. This is particularly noticeable in breaking colts, as shown by the fact that making one side or leg gentle will not make other parts so ; both sides must be treated alike. It is on account of these conditions not being understood (the details of which are given in Colt Training, Kicking, etc.). that so many accidents occur from the use of horses supposed to be gentle and safe. They are gentle so far as they have been broken or accustomed to certain objects or sounds ;

but when subjected to changes, the impulse of kicking, running away, etc., is as liable to occur as if they were entirely unbroken. Hence we say that the great majority of such accidents are the di-

FIG. 164.   FIG. 165.   FIG. 166.

Contrasts of Character.

rect result of ignorance and bad treatment.   For details, see preceding chapter on Colt Training.

FEAR OF RATTLE OF WAGON.

If the horse is afraid of the rattle of a wagon, restrain or overcome his resistance as may be necessary by one or more methods of subjection.   Next, accustom the horse to being touched on the quarters, etc., with a pole.   Put on the harness with Patent Bridle or Breaking Bit, to insure holding him easily, bring him in front of the shafts, and have some one rattle the wagon until the horse is regardless of it.   Now carefully put him between the shafts, and let

FIG. 167.   FIG. 168.   FIG. 169.

Contrasts of Character.

the wheels and body of the wagon be shaken again ; then drop the shafts upon the ground and repeat.   Should the horse at any time try to run ahead, pull him back sharply until he will stand quietly without resistance.   Now hitch him up and drive moderately at first, making a noise by a stick running across the spokes, etc.   Gradually let him out to a trot and run, compelling him to stop occasionally at the command to "Whoa." In the meantime, as there is submission, treat kindly. This will not usually be found a difficult habit to overcome. In making experiments before classes on this kind of cases, which were very common, it rarely required more than fifteen or twenty minutes to hitch ¡up and drive such safely, even without breeching.

JUMPING OUT OF THE SHAFTS.

To make a colt entirely safe and reliable in shafts, he should be thoroughly accustomed to objects striking against his quarters or legs. It is not sufficient that he is accustomed to being touched around the tail, or even flanks; for though brought to submit to

Fig. 170.   Fig. 171.   Fig. 172.

Contrasts of Character.

this, there will be no assurance of his being gentle should the shafts strike lower down on his quarters or legs. In my practice I always made it a point, even after the colt was proved gentle, standing between the shafts, to pull them against the legs both ways, letting them drop down sharply on the ground, until he is entirely indifferent to their noise or contact. When a horse is not properly trained to this, if the breeching is not unbuckled when he is unhitched, there is danger of his becoming frightened from the breeching pulling the shafts sideways against the legs, and bringing its pressure upon another part. Under such circumstances a horse, if at all sensitive, is apt to become very much frightened, kick, and jump around until loose, and is ever afterward, the moment unhitched, ready to jump out of the shafts. The habit, as a rule, is easy to overcome. Simply accustom the quarters to be touched, and treat practically as before explained.

TOP CARRIAGE.

A little care in preventing excessive fear will save a great deal of trouble. In no respect is this more strongly illustrated than in the fear of a top carriage. Because a horse drives gentle to an open carriage, it is taken for granted he must know enough to drive to one with a top, and hence the trouble. The horse should first be driven around moderately, the driver carrying over his head an open umbrella, which appears to the horse like the top of a carriage. It should be shaken around and over the horse's body gently until it does not attract his attention in the least. Now lead the horse to the carriage, and let him feel and smell of the top, and while doing so, raise and lower it. Then lead him around the carriage, shaking and rattling the top at intervals. Next lead him into the shafts so as to bring the head over the dash. If sensitive, caress

FIG. 173.—Simple Treatment—Bringing the Pole over the Back and Quarters until no Fear of it is Shown.

and talk to him, and reward as before. Turn the horse around in the shafts, lowering and raising the top until it can be brought up and thrown back without attracting his notice. While the top is up, put the shafts through the lugs so as to bring the horse into position, attach the harness, and start him on a walk or moderate trot, repeating the raising and lowering of the top until it is disregarded, when he can be driven right along.

If an extreme case, it will be necessary to first compel submission by subjective treatment, and getting thorough control of the mouth with the Breaking Bit or Patent Bridle. There must be no half-way work. Make every step sure, and go slowly until the horse can be put in shafts as before explained, and driven without showing fear. This work must in all cases be done out of doors. It may also be necessary to repeat the lesson once or twice, so far as leading around, feeling and smelling of the carriage, are concerned. It is only a matter of a little work and care in this way to make almost any horse entirely gentle and fearless.

OBJECTS EXCITING FEAR WHILE RIDING OR DRIVING.

In overcoming the horse's fear of objects while riding or driving, very much depends upon the treatment. If but partially broken, and sensitive, it will help very much to put him through a course of subjection. Sometimes, horses so exceedingly sensitive that they can hardly be driven with any degree of safety, after being treated are entirely fearless in driving. This is seen in the effect

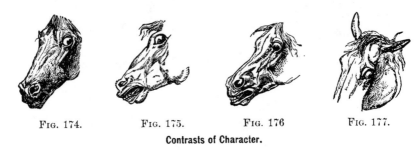

FIG. 174.   FIG. 175.   FIG. 176   FIG. 177.

Contrasts of Character.

produced by the treatment upon the wild colt. The subjection of "Wild Pete," referred to at the conclusion of this chapter, is a good illustration of the remarkable effect of this treatment.

If the horse drives gentle, but is afraid of some special object, such as a white stone, stump, sheep, etc., take all the precaution possible against his seeing such things suddenly and unexpectedly. As soon as his alarm is excited, if at all violent, the best way is to stop him, speak encouragingly, and hold him quiet until his alarm subsides, then let him go on, quieting him until the object is reached or passed by.

Many horses that may appear perfectly gentle, and perhaps used for family driving with entire safety, are consequently supposed safe under any circumstances. No mistake can be greater. A horse may be all right, but suppose a threshing-machine or a threshing-machine engine were suddenly met: these are entirely new, and may suddenly frighten the horse. Do not undertake to drive against such objects; you had better turn around and drive the other way, or lead quietly as you can, ordering the engine to be stopped if necessary. These precautions should be taken with any peculiar object when met; if not, your horse is liable to become so reckless as to resist control and be spoiled. You cannot afford to take the risk, and no man who has any regard for his family should undertake it.

Many horses comparatively safe are liable to be frightened by suddenly meeting a drove of sheep, load of hay, white cow, sprinkling wagon, etc. For safety, it is better for a few times to get out and take the horse by the head and hold or lead him in part. Particular care should be taken not to expose him to the sudden meeting of a brass band and drums or anything of the kind. If he is a crazy-headed fellow that seems all right until he sees something and then loses his senses, lunging into the fence, or turning around quickly, there is so much danger of being upset that unless there is certainty of making him thoroughly safe, he should be condemned for such use. If he will keep well up to the bit, there should be no trouble in preventing his going sideways by either the Breaking Bit or Patent Bridle.

The Bit gives power in but two ways,—sideways and ahead; so if the horse will not go against it and runs back when suddenly frightened, or turns around quickly, there is practically but very little power to prevent it, except what can be done with the whip and speaking sharply. Hence the great danger and imprudence of using such horses for single carriage driving.

A ROBE.

The sight of a buffalo robe will sometimes excite great fear in a horse. In ordinary cases the fear of it can be easily overcome as follows : While holding the horse by a halter or War Bridle, which would be better, stand on the off side of the head, and bring the robe up to the right side, so that he can see and smell of it. If this is borne, with a quick jerk-like movement swing it over the head, covering it completely, and go around with him, keeping on either side of the head until he will stop and stand quietly. The first movement determines the success or failure of the experiment. The point is to get it over the head so quickly that the horse cannot see the movement, when the terror of it will almost immediately subside. Then draw it backward and forward, finally pulling it off and throwing it on, and so repeat until it can be thrown over the body or around the horse in any manner.

If there is failure by this method, which is something of a

sleight, take the following course : First, get good control with the War Bridle. Next, while holding the horse firmly with one hand, with the other bring the robe gently to his nose, letting him smell and feel of it, when, gradually, as he will bear, bring it up over the head, neck, and body ; then stand off a little way, and throw it upon him, and repeat until it can be thrown upon him at a distance of eight or ten feet without exciting fear. Both sides must be treated alike.

No matter what is done, the treatment must always commence at the nose and head, and gradually work back, as before explained.

Fig. 178.—**Letting Colt Feel and Smell of Umbrella.**

To overcome all fear of the robe, it may be necessary to repeat the lesson several times. If the robe cannot be brought near the horse with safety by the control of the War Bridle, the resistance must be overcome by First or Second Methods of Subjection. The Breaking Rig, if available, would be still simpler and better. Occasionally there may be found cases in which the intensest fear may be shown, for which the treatment should be made exceptionally careful and thorough.

When treated by Second Method, the horse may strike and kick so recklessly as the robe is brought near, it may be necessary to hang it upon the end of a pole to bring it near the head with safety. It will aid greatly to give the horse apples, etc., after submitting.

UMBRELLA OR PARASOL.

For an ordinary case of a horse being afraid of an umbrella or parasol, bring one, while closed, gently to the nose, passing it back over the head and neck ; then open it a little and repeat until it can be fully spread and brought over and around the body generally. Now go off some distance and again approach slowly, and

FIG. 179.—Bringing Umbrella over the Head.

hold it over the head. If at any point there is much fear evinced, close it and let the horse see and smell of it, when again repeat the experiment ; so continue until the horse can be approached in any manner while swinging the umbrella over the head, without attracting notice. No matter how well the horse behaves, the umbrella should not at any time be forced upon him so quickly or unexpectedly as to excite him. To do so would endanger undoing the good impression previously made. The lesson should be repeated as for other objects.

SOUND OF A GUN.

If the horse is afraid of the sound of a gun, first snap caps some distance from him, gradually going nearer and repeating until it can be done over the body, neck, and head, occasionally patting and rubbing the head and neck with the hand ; then repeat, putting in small charges of powder and coming nearer, and so continue until a full charge can be fired over or near the horse, as desired.

HOGS AND DOGS.

Sometimes a dog or hog by running under a colt will excite intense fear.   If very bad, get good control by subjecting to First and Second Methods, and drive around in harness in a small yard where there are hogs, until they will not attract attention.   Next, hitch to a wagon, and repeat the driving slowly.   These cases usually require several repetitions of treatment.

RAILROAD CARS.

When a horse has been frightened by a locomotive or train of

cars, it is sometimes a very difficult matter to overcome the fear, mainly on account of the inability to control the movement of the cars.   The simplest and best course for all average cases will be about as follows :—

Drive the horse around in harness, so far away from the engine as not to excite much fear, and gradually drive back and forth in long circles, and closer, stopping occasionally to give a piece of apple, or something, talking and rubbing the head and neck awhile.   Sometimes it may be advisable to use the War Bridle ; but, as a general thing, it would be better to teach him confidence by

FIG. 180.—The Press Horse of Gowanda, a Noted Runaway Kicker, after being Subdued.

driving around near the train.   This should be repeated until he can be driven around, and quite close, without offering resistance. Now drive around to a wagon or sulky ; if to a wagon, get one that will allow turning short circles without upsetting.   To work surely, it is necessary to work slowly.   Of course it will be necessary to have absolute control over the mouth.   In this way a horse can be driven with comparative safety near or about moving or stationary trains. Anything like complicated rigging for the control of such horses will be found comparatively worthless.   If the horse cannot be driven with safety after the treatment given, the risk is too great ; he had better be discarded for driving near the cars.

It may be asked, how I have been able to make horses so fearless of the cars that they can be led up to an engine or driven near, with indifference. The course I have usually pursued is as follows: First get the horse under good control by a course of subjection, usually by the First or Second Methods, or both; then make arrangements with the engineer to let off steam plentifully, and rush the horse, with the harness on, into it until completely covered, when he will soon cease to care anything about the noise, etc. If this cannot be done, drive him around, gradually going nearer the engine until indifferent to it.

Much depends, in the first place, upon getting the horse under good control; second, in the management while in the neighborhood of the engine. A good way, sometimes, is to blindfold the horse and drive near the train until quiet, then let him see out of one eye, gradually moving him around, and let him see out of both eyes. Very much can be done in this way. The horse should be hitched to a wagon and driven at every available opportunity about or near the cars.

Fig. 181.—**Wild Pete.**

There is one point to which I would call particular attention: The horse may appear perfectly gentle after being treated, but when the position is changed, as when taken from a building into the street, or from the street into a building, or if allowed to stand for some time, he will upon trial seem to be as much afraid as ever, but upon repetition of treatment it will require only a very few minutes to make him as fearless as before.

INSANITY.

It is not uncommon to find horses intensely afraid of some particular object, as blood, or the sound of the cars, etc., while perfectly indifferent to other objects or sounds. The causes we cannot always trace, though we can see the effects. In all ordinary cases, there is but little difficulty in overcoming such fear by proper treatment, but it is possible to find cases so extreme as to render it

difficult, if not impossible, to make them reasonably safe.   I am satisfied that many of the extreme cases of this character which I have
treated, have been the effect of prenatal causes.   But the nervous
system can be so impressed by direct causes of fear and injury, as
stated, as to destroy life or produce insanity.

One of the worst horses I ever handled was a small bay, in Ver-
mont, that was perfectly gentle, except being afraid of the shafts
touching one quarter.   This was caused by the shaft having run
into his quarter.   Ordinary cases of this kind yield to treatment in
a few moments.   Some nervous systems are susceptible to very intense impressions when once excited, and there will be correspond-

FIG. 182.—**Wild Pete in the Act of Running Away.**

ing difficulty in overcoming them.   Therefore success must be
determined as much by the intensity of the habit as by the treatment.   The success of the treatment will depend upon the directness with which the brain can be influenced ; but success in getting
up a reaction and changing the character as desired, must be
equally the result of the amount of resistance, viciousness, or derangement of the nervous system.   These are points which should
be studied, since frequently even a minor habit, or apparently trifling
form of resistance, may cause a great deal of trouble to be overcome,
because of the intensely susceptible as well as positive character of
the case.

I will include here reference to a very interesting case of this
kind of nervous susceptibility, from a number in my special work,
to show the decided effect of proper treatment.

This was a nine-year-old bay pony, owned by Mr. Smawley, a
livery keeper in Petroleum Centre, Pa.   This pony was so wild and

reckless that he was in that region of country known by the name of Wild Pete. Every effort to break him had failed. It usually required two men to hold him while being groomed. He could be ridden, but it was utterly impossible to do anything with him in harness. Once when a harness was put on him, he became so frightened and reckless that he jumped and got away, and when found, all the harness excepting the collar had been torn or shaken off. His fear was so great that he was frightfully wicked in his resistance.

When I visited the place in 1869, I was confronted with this horse. All said, "Let us see you drive Wild Pete," regarding it as a good joke that they had a horse that could "beat the horse-tamer."

Fig. 183.—Pole Rig.

Upon examination, I found him a small, closely-knit fellow, possessing great action and power of endurance. His forehead was broad, and the head in all respects well formed. To test him, I put on the War Bridle, tied up his near fore foot, and while holding him, with the lash of a straight buggy whip barely touched his quarters. This frightened him so intensely that he sprang over six feet into the air, kicked violently, pulled away from me and although on three legs, repeated this jumping and kicking for over half a mile.

I stated to the people that I could not break such a horse in a barn, but would form a class, and on the following day I would drive him before them without breeching, entirely gentle and fearless, and that the money for the instructions might be deposited in

10   a

the bank, to be delivered to me on fulfillment of this condition. As this was one of the most interesting and marked cases I had found in all my experience, and as it represents a large class of nervous, unmanageable colts, I will include the full details of the treatment used :—

I first arranged with the owner to have him taken to the Titusville trotting park, eight miles distant, and there I subjected him carefully to Second Method, which was exactly adapted to his temperament. I touched his quarters very lightly at first, which he resisted by kicking, snorting, and jumping in the most desperate manner. But I persisted in the effort, repeatedly reversing both ways

Fig. 184.—**Wild Pete, as he Appeared Next Day after being Subdued.**

until he was compelled to submit to it, but not sufficiently to hold gentle. This so toned him down that I was then able to subject him without difficulty to First Method, which, as he resisted with great courage, was consequently very effective in his case, but not by any means sufficient to make him submit to be harnessed or put in shafts. I subjected him again to Second Method, and now succeeded in making him entirely gentle to submit to having a pole brought against his flanks, etc.

The next step was to drive him, which I knew I could not safely do. To accomplish this, I improvised the pole rig for shafts, referred to in chapter on Colt Training. As soon as he found himself between the poles and was allowed to move, he seemed for a few moments to exert all the energy of despair in trying to get away. But expecting this, I was prepared to meet it and hold him, though his resistance at this stage was very determined.

This simple rig, though a chance outgrowth of incidental necessity, proved not only just the thing for the emergency, but a valuable acquisition for the management of colts and horses generally of this character. Turning right or left, the poles come against the legs ; in backing, the ends stick into the ground, bringing the cross-piece firmly against the quarters. There is no danger of their breaking, and by their use the quarters can be accustomed to being touched or run against by the shafts in driving. Submitting to this he was practically broken, and at once harnessed before a wagon with breeching straps loose, and driven back to the American House, much of the way with the cross-piece striking the quarters, proving him perfectly gentle. That evening I drove him to Petroleum Centre, and the next day, as promised, exhibited him in harness, proving him a model of docility.

An incident peculiar to this case is here worthy of mention : Upon visiting this place about three years afterward, Mr. Smawley informed me that the horse had been used as a family carriage horse and was one of the safest in that part of the country, but that it was impossible to shoe him with the halter on, while with the bridle on he was perfectly gentle to have his feet handled. While treating him, had I taken up his feet after the harness was removed, and accustomed them to being handled and pounded upon for a few moments, he would have been just as gentle while being shod with the halter on as with the bridle. As it was, he could associate submission only in the manner the treatment was used, and this carried it no farther than driving with the control of the bit, hence the docility to allow the feet to be handled while it was on.

CHAPTER V.

KICKING.

K ICKING is the most common as well as most dangerous habit we have to deal with. It not only destroys the value of the horse most seriously, but makes his use, when it is possible to use him, so unreliable and unsafe as to be a constant menace of danger and loss. The greatest average of test subjects brought me to experiment upon before classes were in nearly all cases kickers rang-

Fig. 185.—The Effect of Bad Treatment.

ing over the unbroken colt that kicked when touched, the colt that would kick and run away, the one that could not be harnessed or hitched with safety, determined runaway kickers, and especially horses that kicked when approached, or from mere habit. We often had horses brought us that had been experimented upon so much as to make them so thoroughly vicious and dangerous in their resistance as to be practically worthless. A great many interesting cases illustrating this could be referred to did space permit ; but to show the value of the treatment here given when properly applied, I will refer only to a few cases, as an aid to the reader in making experiments.

First. A five-year-old stallion, owned in Northern Indiana, that had resisted all treatment. This horse was naturally very gentle, but had been frightened in driving, and could not be put in the shafts. He was driven entirely gentle in twelve minutes before the class.

Second. An eight-year-old trotting-horse in Cleveland, O. This case would kick and run away in spite of all that could be done. The utmost effort made to break him had failed. The disbelief in my efforts was so great, that, for a test case, I was compelled to buy him at a large price, and was entirely successful in bringing him under the most perfect control in about forty minutes ; and to the surprise of everybody he was driven next day on the square perfectly docile, without bridle reins, or breeching.

Fig. 186.—Treatment that only Confirms the Habit.

Third. In Mansfield, O., a thoroughbred trotting-mare, seven years old, had kicked from the time she was three years old, and, in defiance of the utmost effort, became entirely unmanageable. This was a severe test case, no one believing that she could be broken. She was controlled with entire success and driven in the street within an hour, and proved afterward one of the gentlest and finest driving mares in the country.

Fourth. A seven-year-old horse in Putney, Vt. This was a pony horse of remarkable courage and pluck, would run away regardless of all that could be done, and was one of the most desperate kickers I ever saw. Upon a test, he pulled six men by the bit, three men to a rein, across the floor, and this with the Breaking Bit in his mouth. He was brought under perfect control in about three quarters of an hour, and proved afterward as gentle and manageable as any family horse could be.

Fifth. The Hetrick horse, of New York, a large Western sorrel horse, was sold for $275 on condition that he could be driven. He had been hitched to a cart both wheels of which were blocked, and

FIGS. 187–192.—**Contrasts of Character.**

though held by three men, he ran away, tore the cart to pieces, and proved utterly unmanageable. This horse was bought for $50, and brought to me to experiment upon as a test case. He was brought under such complete control in less than an hour after I was able to get my hands upon him (which was a difficult matter to do with safety), that he could be driven anywhere without breeching by the control of an ordinary bit only.

Sixth. A four-year-old colt in Ravenna, O., of so exceptionally wild and dangerous character that he could only be brought in between two long ropes. It certainly seemed impossible to hitch this colt in harness, because if touched on any part of the body it would be impossible to hold him, and yet, without any serious difficulty, he was driven entirely gentle in thirty minutes without breeching.

Seventh. A four-year-old colt of trotting blood, in Lancaster, N. H. This was one of the most nervous, impulsive kickers in that country. This horse was sent over forty miles to one of the best horse-breakers in that country to break, who, after working with him two weeks, gave him up as hopeless, but was driven entirely gentle without the least excitement or danger within forty minutes.

Eighth. A runaway kicker in Brookville, Pa. This horse had not been in harness for two years, and was regarded as entirely unmanageable. After thirty minutes he was driven down hill without breeching by a little boy.

Ninth. A seven-year-old horse in Norwalk, O., had not been in harness for over a year, and was regarded as hopelessly unmanageable. Two horse-breakers who visited that country, worked upon this horse for two weeks, resulting in seriously injuring the horse, and leaving him worse than he was before. This case was entirely controlled in less than fifty minutes' treatment, and was driven next day eight or ten rods distant in the street without breeching, by word of command only.

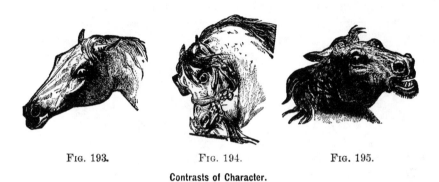

Fig. 193.   Fig. 194.   Fig. 195.

Contrasts of Character.

These apparently remarkable results were accomplished by one or more of the methods of subjection, with the Breaking Bit described in the second chapter. These, with a great many other interesting cases, are referred to in detail in my regular book on the horse. We had cases of this character brought to us almost daily to be experimented upon, and it was very exceptional cases that we could not hitch up and drive within fifteen to twenty or thirty minutes. Occasionally we would find cases that we could not control

Fig. 196.   Fig. 197.   Fig. 198.

Contrasts of Character.

in one or even two lessons, but it was seldom we experienced any real difficulty in doing so by careful repetition of the treatment, the main point being to apply the treatment carefully and properly.

I think it advisable to call attention, first, to the common causes of kicking. In Colt-Training and Fear special attention is called to the fact that making one part of the body gentle gives no assurance of making other parts so ; or accustoming a colt to an object such as a piece of white paper, blanket, or other ordinary causes of exciting fear, making him gentle to having it brought near or placed upon one part of the body, is no guarantee of his being fearless of it when brought to other parts ; that making one

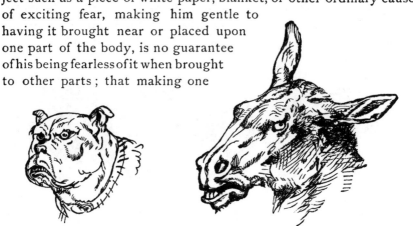

Fig. 199.   **Ideals of Sullen, Treacherous Natures.**   Fig. 200.

part gentle in handling will not make another so. Thus, for example, we bring a handkerchief to the nose, and it is soon submitted to. Now, if it be suddenly thrown under the belly, or over the back, and especially if thrown from behind, it will be found to excite as much fear as if the horse had not before seen or felt it. So in accustoming the body to being handled. Making the fore legs gentle to be handled is no assurance of the hind legs being so. In making

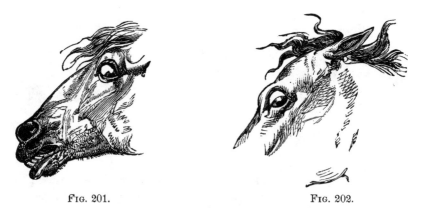

Fig. 201.   Fig. 202.

Ideal Expressions of Determined, Fighting Kickers.

experiments, I frequently illustrated this very clearly by making one of the hind legs or quarters gentle to being handled or taken up, yet showing that the opposite leg would be resisted as much as if the other parts had not been touched. This is particularly the case in relation to the hind quarters. Now, when a colt or horse is broken as ordinarily done, and goes off all right when put in harness, it is taken for granted that he is as gentle and safe as can be expected. He has not been subjected to any treatment that would assure his docility when touched from behind ; consequently, if, by carelessness or accident, the rein is caught under the tail, or the breeching strap breaks, or there is some other cause of derangement that lets the cross-piece or whiffletree come suddenly against the quarters, these parts being practically unbroken or not accustomed to such contact, the horse is liable to be so frightened and excited as to kick, and once started

FIG. 203.   FIG. 204.

Points Showing the Expression of Confirmed Kickers.

in the habit, there is increased inclination to do so until confirmed in it. Now, all this can be prevented without the least difficulty by fifteen or twenty minutes' proper treatment, as explained in the chapters referred to (Colt-Training and Fear), requiring only, excepting in very serious cases, the very simplest treatment, and even when the case is very dangerous or vicious, the treatment is not at all difficult, so that in point of fact nearly every case of this character, no matter how vicious the colt in the light of our present knowledge and experience, may justly be accepted as invariably the result of ignorance and bad treatment. In the first chapter I have explained that the principle of teaching the horse to do anything is exactly the same as in overcoming a habit, the only difference being that it is reversed, so that the key to success is in being able to combat the habit directly and thus overcoming all inclination to resist. If it is a matter simply of overcoming fear, as in the case of a green colt, the first thing to do is to accustom all parts of the body to be touched and handled until there is no fear or resistance. It will be noticed that a nervous colt may at first resist very violently, but in a short time, if properly done, all this fear will seem to cease, and there will be perfect submission to being handled as desired.

If it is a matter of teaching a colt to kick, the point first is to get him started in the act, gradually repeating and encouraging for doing so, when by its repetition the horse will be taught to kick as

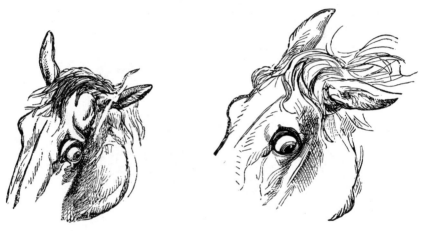

Fig. 205.   **A Good Expression of the Sullen Kicker.**   Fig. 206.

a trick or habit. Now, when the habit is formed, and we wish to break it up, the point is, if the colt has been excited by fear, to overcome that cause of fear, which is not at all difficult. Next, when learned as a habit, no matter how vicious or persistent it is, the point is to combat it most directly until it can be overcome, when the better nature is to be brought into co-operation, and thus even the most reckless case can be easily broken of the habit. Now, in the cases referred to in the commencement of this chapter, this is just what I did by the advantages of the treatment here described. In the case of a simple colt, or one that has been spoiled in breaking, no matter how wild or reckless, if unable to overcome the resistance by simple good management, I simply subjected to either or all the methods of restraint or control described, until the habit was given up, when all that was necessary to do was to treat the case gently, at the same time accustoming the horse to being handled until all inclination to repeat the resistance was entirely overcome.

DETAILS.

For convenience we will divide kickers into three classes : *First,* colts that have been spoiled in their breaking ; *second*, vicious, kicking, runaway horses ; *third*, those that are simply kickers, otherwise gentle, but thoroughly confirmed in the habit. Among these might be included a great many modifications, but as the treatment is very much the same, and in a great measure depends upon the use of the

Fig. 207.—Showing the Impulsive, Dangerous Character of Bad Kickers when first Brought for Treatment.

means of control described, it would only confuse to try to give minute details.

FIRST CLASS.

These will usually be found very simple and easy to manage. I would advise first to study your case carefully, if not quite sure of the character of the resistance and disposition. I mean by this, whether the horse will show very much resistance at first or after being roused, which will usually be found the worst cases. The colt that is simply nervous and kicks a little can be controlled very easily by the use of the War Bridle, double-draw hitch form, by putting it on and making the horse feel your power a little, then accustom the hind parts to being touched with a pole, as explained in Colt Training. If this is resisted, simply punish with the cord until the poling will be submitted to unconditionally.

I will presume that there is not a Breaking Bit available, and only the ordinary resources of the stable at hand. In such a case, put on next a well-fitting harness with an ordinary bit. The longer the snaffle bit, the more power and effectiveness. Treat precisely as advised for the colt, by poling behind and backing up against the rail, so as to come against the quarters where the cross-piece of shafts will strike. This thoroughly submitted to, drive around, at the same time poling industriously until there is no fear of it. Then hitch to poles as directed in that chapter, and make the point thor-

Fig. 208.—As some very Bad Kickers will Act when Touched.

ough of accustoming the quarters to being touched or being pressed against without resistance.

If there is much fear of the wagon, and the case is at all doubtful, put on the foot-strap, and first put in shafts without breeching, as explained for colts, and make the point thorough of submitting to the rattling of the wheels, shoving the cross-piece against the quarters, etc., then hitch in cautiously, holding the foot-strap as a reserve power. Continue driving until there is assurance of the case proving safe.

Second Class.

Among these will frequently be found some very serious cases. They are usually young horses that have been frightened, kick violently, and run away. Now, let me tell you that there are certain temperaments that may make you serious trouble and require care-fulness to manage successfully. They are usually horses of good dispositions, very intelligent, but sensitive, and if thoroughly fright-ened, the effect may be very serious indeed. In any event, if there is much fear, it must be thoroughly mastered. The course usually pursued is to hitch up the horse as carefully as possible, and then try to drive him. This generally only leads to increasing the trouble, by giving the horse an opportunity to resist again, and thus

Fig. 209.—As the **Desperate Kicker sometimes Resists when Subjected to First Method**.

be only more confirmed in the habit, the very point we should try to avoid.

Take the horse first into a quiet corner of a well-sodded field, back yard, or carriage-house with floor well covered with some soft material. See that there are no idlers lounging around to criticise and annoy you ; prepare yourself with every necessary requisite for your experiments, even having provided your supply of apples, sugar, salt, or something else of which the horse is fond. Make up your mind that you will not lose your temper, and that you will work slowly and carefully. Try first the Second Method. If car-ried out properly, the case should be quite a bad one that cannot be controlled by it so far as making gentle out of harness. There is quite a sleight in using this treatment, and if not just understood, you should read very carefully explanations of it under that head. Send the horse around at first rather slowly, until sure that he will bear it, then gradually push up to the point of falling, and if known to be very bad, reverse quickly. Lose no time in doing this; it must be done as quickly as possible, so as to give the horse no time to concentrate his efforts in resistance. At any rate, keep on till the poling is submitted to unconditionally. If, however, you find the case resists very hard, try now the Third Method. This in sensi-

Fig. 210.—As Extremely Bad Kickers Resist when Touched while Pressure is On.

tive, nervous kickers, is certainly very effective. Do not put it on very tight at first, and see what the effect will be. The key of its use is, after being put on, to pole the hind parts until there is no re-sistance. If the poling is resisted for some time, put on tighter, and repeat. Usually a few minutes' pressure will be sufficient. If you have a good place and a rig, and you are at all handy, it would also have a good effect to use the First Method. This will work wonderfully well in some cases, but, singular as it may seem, it may not work at all with satisfaction in others, (if not quite clear, read explanation on page 56,) and it might be supplemented in such cases by either or both of the other Methods. But as this is a matter of experiment, I cannot really describe here the cases it will or will not work upon. At any rate, either or both these Methods of treatment found most convenient and easy to use may be tried until in a general way the horse is made gentle, then carry out your control with the Breaking Bit. A very full explanation of the use of this bit, as applying to these cases, will be found under that head, and should be read carefully. As there stated, there is a great sleight in its use. First get thorough control of the horse in harness, so that he will stop immediately, and come back against the poles or anything else. This point must be made at all hazards, and must be made without much working of the mouth, if possible, for fear of making it too tender. After he will stop and start, start him

Fig. 211.—Test often Given by the Author in Proving the Horse's Docility after being Subdued.

out on a run, and make him stop immediately at command without pulling.

This point made, then hitch cautiously to poles, or cart, or whatever is most convenient at hand, and carry out your control as described in Colt-Training. The whole point is to be careful and thorough. If your horse kicks with you once successfully in shafts, you have practically lost all you have gained. This must not be permitted on any condition ; so that the point of real success is to make your groundwork so thorough that when you come to driving in shafts, you are able to make it with certainty. If you are at all doubtful, resort to any measure by which you can prevent the horse's resisting. The foot-strap will in ordinary cases be your simplest measure of doing this. Should the horse develop a sullen **or** sulky disposition if subjected to Second Method, it may be necessary to touch him sharply upon the nose with the whip to force him to go along sufficiently quick to produce the effect desired. You may try the First Method, and if you fail, then you must depend upon the Third.

You may meet with the difficulty of his biting upon the cord. This is so rare, however, that it is hardly worth mentioning ; but if you should find such difficulty, this treatment must be abandoned at once. With good management there will be but little trouble.

If a colt is very wild and much afraid of a wagon, the case is liable to be a very serious one. If a very nervous horse, you must

Fig. 212.—As the Horse usually Drives in Harness after being Subdued.

be particularly careful so as not to injure him. Take your time, and make every step slowly and thoroughly, trusting nothing to chance. These cases will sometimes resist with great fury, striking and kicking most violently. The First and Second Methods will usually be your best treatment upon these. If you have a good assistant, you can work sometimes with excellent advantage by putting on two foot-straps, when your assistant can pull one or two feet from under the horse, thus bringing him repeatedly upon his knees. The objection to this is that it worries the horse greatly, and unless the ground is soft and free from stones, there is danger of bruising and cutting the knees ; besides, the effect is not nearly so good as can be obtained by the treatment described. If the patent Breaking Rig, explained in Chapter II., were available, it would save considerable work in this way. The horse is then held helpless in shafts, as it were, when he can be driven as desired. When the Third Method is used, while the pressure is on bring the poles against the quarters industriously. Usually at first the horse will kick hard, but it is rare that there will not be submission in a few minutes.

These points made, gradually remove the pressure, and while doing so keep rubbing and bringing the poles against the quarters and flanks, until there is unconditional submission, then continue as explained, driving in harness and wagon. The greatest average of the worst horses I ever found have been iron-gray, sorrel, and black, though I have occasionally found bays extremely bad. It should

Fig. 213.—A Test to which the Horse should be Subjected before being Subdued.

seldom require more than thirty or forty minutes to bring a very bad horse under control by these combined efforts of treatment.

THIRD CLASS.

I have in my mind now about the worst class of kickers we have to deal with. They are either cases that have been made thoroughly vicious by excessive fear or running away, or those that are so naturally vicious, and kick and strike so recklessly as to seem to be beyond the reach of any kind of treatment. There is a class of men who think it is bravery to be reckless with dangerous horses. In point of fact, I have found such men to be usually the greatest cowards. In experimenting before classes, I would frequently have men who would be disposed at first to censure me for appearing to

11 a

be overly cautious. I will illustrate by referring to a special case in Michigan. A farmer brought in a five-year-old colt to be experi-

FIG. 214.—One of the Tests Usually Given by the Author before the Class, Proving the Horse's entire Submission in Harness.

mented upon. He stated that he had been driven in harness, but had got the better of him. I at once saw the colt to be a very dangerous one, and was acting so cautiously with him that the man openly censured me for presuming to be so timid, and he was about walking up to the horse to show me how easily he could handle him. I simply said, " Wait a moment ; you do not know your danger ; I will show you what kind of a horse you have here, and then if you think best you can handle him as much as you please." I took a small pole and reached it out toward the horse's nose, when immediately he reared and struck at it with the viciousness of a wild mustang. I next touched the hind parts, when he jumped into the air and kicked with such fury as to clear the floor at once. I then said to the owner, " Let me see you go up and handle him now." Said he, " I would not go near him

FIG. 215.—**Norman Horse. Naturally Gentle.**

for a thousand dollars ; I had no idea he was so bad." I taught him and the class a bit of a lesson that I think they never will forget. I then went on carefully until I could get to the horse safely, when I soon had him under perfect control, and he became as gentle to be managed and driven as any ordinary colt, not requiring in all more than thirty minutes.

FIG. 216.—**The Best Type of Intelligent, Courageous Nature.**

These cases are liable to resist with great recklessness. It is a specially important condition of success that everything needed for treatment should be carefully at hand, and of the best quality. It is almost fatal to success, and especially so in the management of a critical case, to have anything break when a horse is making a determined struggle of resistance. There should be great care taken not to get injured. The selection of ground, or the place where the work is to be done, is

Fig. 217.—Surly, Dangerous Character.

a very important consideration. In fact, every emergency must be carefully provided for. I have in my mind now a representative case. A five-year-old colt had been harnessed several times, but each time kicked himself loose and got away. He was brought in at Gallupville, N. Y., and is referred to on page 414 in my regular work. This was a strong, large-boned, courageous colt, extremely afraid of being touched, and could not be hitched to a wagon. As we were compelled to make experiments in a wagon-house with a plank floor, and with a large number of people around, it required the best of management to control him with safety. We tried first the Second Method, but could not under the circumstances carry it far enough to be at all effective. The First Method would have worked well upon this case, but could not be safely used on a hardwood floor. I concluded, however, that the Third Method would be sufficiently effective, and subjected him to the highest pressure we could prudently use with four cords. Upon touching the hind parts, he kicked with such fury that he threw the shoes from both hind feet with so great a force that they dented the wall deeply on the opposite side. This resistance was continued for fully twelve minutes. It was a struggle of the most severe character, but after about fifteen minutes he submitted to being poled. We next subjected him sharply to the Second Method, reversing a few times, and now making the impression sufficiently strong to submit unconditionally. The rest of the treatment was the same as previously described. When harnessed, he resisted control of the mouth very hard, but finally came back to its restraint, and was driven before the class with entire success. As this was a well-known case, I requested that he be taken to the adjoining town the next day afterward, where, after a little repetition of treatment, he was hitched up and driven in the street perfectly gentle, when he acted just as docile and manageable as any family horse.

A six-year-old horse of about the same character, near Lake

Champlain, N. Y., had been badly frightened, and was utterly unmanageable. We had a large, roomy place, giving us opportunity
to use the Second Method with safety, and dependedupon it mainly,
requiring but very little treatment with the Third Method. This
was a splendid subject, fighting every point very hard, but finally
submitting unconditionally. The First Method could have been
used with decided advantage, had we had a good place.

I will refer to one more among this class. The Hetrick horse,
referred to on page 149, was perhaps as fine an illustration of a
thoroughly vicious horse as I ever handled, and as good an example
of successful treatmentas I have ever given. The difficulty was to
get this horse, but after being able to do so, he submitted readily to

FIG. 218.—Expression of most
Obstinate Cases.

FIG. 219.—Most Difficult Type of
Character to Break.

the Second and First Methods, his resistance being characteristic
of the mustang, striking, kicking, and snorting with great violence.
The Third Method could not safely be used upon him.

The best illustrative case showing extreme resistance excited
from fear, all things considered, was that referred to on page 144.
This horse, though nine years old, was a perfect maniac in his actions. He even could not be harnessed, and his management was
one of the clearest in showing the good effect of proper treatment
of any I ever handled in all my experience. This case could not
have been broken in any ordinary building with a hard floor. In
fact, to be successful it was necessary to have every condition favorable. To handle this case safely, I was obliged to go eight miles,
as I could not get a suitable place to handle him short of this ; but
the result was perfectly successful.

FIG. 220.—**Extreme of Bad Character.**

Now, the point in the management of those cases, as will be noticed, was in applying treatment properly, being careful, and making the treatment sufficiently thorough until successful. I was in all cases in the habit of making the after-treatment such as to win the confidence of the horse, so that when I did succeed I had the subject perfectly cool and quiet, yet entirely gentle. As before stated, the horse must often be carefully tested, and if necessary the treatment in

part repeated until there is certainty of his being safe.

I think it advisable, in conclusion, to refer to a specially serious case where I came very near failing on account of being unable to use treatment suited to the temperament, mainly to show the importance in critical cases of using such treatment as the case will best bear. A man I

FIG. 221.—**Ideal of Bad Character.**

had started in the business, who had traveled with considerable success for several years, visited New York, where his success attracted considerable attention. A very fine-blooded horse, of specially vicious character, was brought in for treatment, with orders to this man to break him or kill him, horse was not worth anything unless he could be broken. Everything was

FIG. 222.—**Sullen Nature.**

FIG. 223.—The Malone Horse.

done to this case for a week to subdue him or so break him down that he could not resist, but the horse being one of great vitality and courage, the man was unable to subdue him, and gave him up, stating that he could not be broken. Circumstances required that I should give special experiments in New York, and this case was selected as the best subject to experiment upon first. I had pledged myself to forfeit one thousand dollars if I could not subdue in forty minutes any horse that could be produced, and in the limits of a box-stall, without throwing, exciting,

FIG. 224.—An Incident of the Malone Horse. Result of an Effort by a Horse-breaker to Drive Him.

or whipping him, and this was supposed to be the best test case that could be found.

I knew this man would use the First Method, and supposed also

that he would use the Second, as it was a part of the treatment I
had instructed him in ; but not being a man of much ingenuity, he
could not catch the points of its success, and did not practice it.   I

Fig. 225.—The Malone Horse as Driven Next Day after Treatment, on the Square,
without Bridle, Reins, or Breeching.

knew the class of horses that must resist this treatment, and that
the points were decidedly in my favor to be able to control him by
the Third Method, which I had kept up to that time a secret.   To

Fig. 226.—The Hettrick Horse after
being Subdued.

my surprise, when the case was
produced, I found it was not at all
suitable for the Third Method ; but
as I had promised to control the
case by treatment they had never
seen, and supposing also that they
had seen the Second Method, I was
forced to do the best I could with
the Third.   The case, as I suspected, resisted it very violently,
the features of serious objection
being his showing the true mustang nature, striking desperately,
and biting upon the cords.   I however succeeded in making the case
gentle, and making what appeared

to be a great success; but both cheeks were so bruised that I knew when he became cool, they would be sore and appear

Fig. 227.—The Hettrick Horse as he Resisted when Approached while Tied to the Pole.

seriously injured. I kept the horse in my possession, until the inflammation subsided, when I subjected him to the Second Method, not requiring in all more than fifteen minutes, and made him perfectly gentle.   Could I have used this Method in the first place, I could have controlled him without the least injury or excitement in about thirty minutes.   I refer to this case to show how nice a point it is to use the treatment adapted to the case, and the temperament must determine this.

SWITCHING KICKERS.

When a horse is greatly excited and irritated by fear or abuse, his nervous system is liable to become so sensitive that he will squeal and switch.   This is more common to mares, which are more impressible than horses ; consequently, when badly spoiled, they are more difficult to break.   In this form it becomes involuntary resist-

FIG. 228.—The Hettrick Horse as Driven in the Street next Day.

ance, or a species of insanity, and in extreme cases very difficult to overcome.   The point is, if possible, to make a sufficiently strong, counteracting impression to overcome this.   Very much will depend upon how much the nervous system has been shaken, and the peculiarity of disposition.   Some of the worst kickers I have ever handled were colts which had been greatly frightened and abused in breaking.   The course I pursue with such is about as follows :—

If the case is one that will bear impressing sufficiently to overcome the kicking, I subject to regular treatment as advised for ordinary cases, directing my attention particularly to accustoming the quarters to being touched.   Failing in this, I use direct means of restraint, such as the kicking-straps or overdraw checks.   The kicking will now punish so severely that there will soon be fear to repeat it.   The straps should be used in driving for some little time after the inclination to kick is overcome.

KICKING-STRAPS.

These straps should be cut at least two inches wide; they should be made of two thicknesses of good harness leather, sewed together and fitted so they will come nicely around the leg between the fetlock and gambrel. There should be a strong wrought-iron D stitched on the front sides. The insides should be lined with soft, thin leather, or buckskin, to prevent chafing the leg. If no Patent Bridle is available, use a strong, well-fitting halter, with the strap passing back between the legs over the belly-band; or it may be attached to the belly-band by a piece of rubber. Next, take a strong hempen cord, not less than five eighths of an inch in diameter, firmly wound, or a good piece of leather made round like a rein, run it through a pulley or ring attached to the halter-strap a little back of the belly-band, and extend to the rings of the foot-straps. The point

FIG. 229.—Stevens Horse after being Subdued.

is to have the rig so regulated that the position of the horse will be perfectly natural in traveling; but should he run or kick, both legs coming back at once brings the whole force directly upon the nose. The straps should be kept on until the pain caused by the kicking makes the horse so much afraid to kick that he will not repeat it.

Sometimes the straps are connected with the bit so that the horse will kick directly against the mouth. But this is objectionable because when the kicking is severe against the mouth it will be cut and bruised, besides it is liable to break the jaw. Even when kicking against the nose, by the restraint of the halter, there is possible danger of injuring the spinal cord at the juncture of the head with the spinal column. I never had an accident occur from such a cause, though I used the treatment a great deal in my early

FIG. 230.—The Ravenna Colt.

experimenting. I have heard of one case in Maine of a horse breaking his jaw by kicking against the bit, and one in Ohio, killed by the
severity of the shock upon the neck.

It will be found then when the horse kicks against the mouth or
nose, he will soon learn to throw the head down to give greater
length between it and the legs, as this destroys the force of the blow.
With the use of the Patent Bridle the force of the kicking throws the
head up, and at the same time punishes with such severity that
there will not be much inclination to repeat it, and the habit will
soon be overcome.

Fig. 231.—Kicking-strap as Arranged for Use.

Twenty years ago, a very bad mare defied my utmost efforts to
stop her kicking, and as a matter of experiment I passed a rope from
the bit to the hind leg below the fetlock, and thence back to the opposite side of the bit, and held it in my hand while I excited her to
kick. After a few repetitions she gave up unconditionally. By this
means I succeeded in breaking her of the habit, but the rope chafed
and tore the skin so badly upon the legs that I had much trouble in
curing them. To guard against this in other cases, I put on straps
to which I attached rings, and passing the rope through them as before, I irritated her to kick, repeating until there was submission.
But as this could not be carried out in driving, the kicking-straps,
with the connection made to the bit, were devised ; after which the
pulley arrangement was added. These straps are best adapted to

kickers with the nervous system so weakened that the habit is in a great measure involuntary.

OVERDRAW CHECK.

The overdraw check can be modified in various ways, according to the case. Sometimes a simple overdraw check is all that is necessary. If more power is desired, in addition to the check, the restraint can be carried to the hips, thence to the shafts. (See Fig. 235.) So that in the act of kicking, as the quarters are elevated, the restraint will be instantly brought upon the head, throwing it so high as to disable. This principle of control was learned by the writer under the following circumstances: In 1861, when in Henderson, Jefferson Co., N. Y., a half-witted fellow offered to instruct me how to drive any kicking, runaway horse. He said, "Bring the center of a slender rope of sufficient length to the top of the horse's head, and pass the ends down through the rings on each side of the bit, and thence back into the wagon as reins." I afterward used

FIG. 232.—Tail-strap.

this means of control, and found it would work well in some cases, though not in all. I gave the idea to a man named Hartman, in Lancaster, Pa., who modified it into what was afterward known as the "Hartman reins," which he patented. A great improvement in this for kickers, is to pass the reins over the hips to the shafts as explained.

Checking the head high will sometimes hold in restraint a strong-willed, treacherous horse, that is liable to lunge sideways, or pull heavily. It will usually work well when a horse is a little irritable, and simply needs a little restraint to keep him inside the point of resistance, the same as the tail-strap acts in preventing the horse from kicking by keeping the tail confined and helpless. The simplest and best way of checking the head high is to pass the check rein through gag-runners, which should be attached to the head part of the bridle well up near the ears, and buckle into an extra bit, which is to be held up against the roof of the mouth by

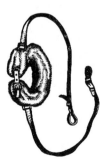

FIG. 233.—Tail-strap Detached.

means of a strap passing over the nose. This form of checking the head up and back will be found very effective.

A common method in use years ago for kickers was to put a triangular piece of iron, in form like a V, between the collar and bit, the central point resting on the collar ; and with both ends attached to the rings of the bit, it held the head up in position as desired. A strong-headed, doubtful horse will frequently drive with entire safety when the head is helplessly held up in this manner ; but the check before referred to is the simplest and best means.

Sometimes the horse will kick only when the rein is caught

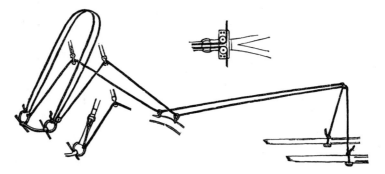

Fɪɢ. 234.—**Simple Method of Forcing the Head up, and Preventing Kicking by the Elevation of the Hips.**

under the tail. If he is simply irritable, and hugs the rein, the eas- iest way to prevent it is to wind an ordinary crupper with cloth, or cover nicely with chamios skin, or soft leather, until one half to two inches in diameter, as may be necessary. (See Fig. 240.) This be- ing larger than the rein below makes it impossible for the horse to hug the rein with sufficient strength to hold it.

When the tail becomes very sensitive from the continued chafing of the parts, its action becomes involuntary. In such cases it must be confined to make the horse safe. This can be easily done by buckling a small strap around it under the hair about two thirds down the dock, from which, on each side, extends a small strap to the hip-straps, and fasten short enough to prevent the tail from switching around and catching the reins.

Hɪᴘ-Sᴛʀᴀᴘ.

If the horse is irritable around the hips, but drives all right so long as restrained, or unable to bring the hind parts up, simply strapping him down will sometimes be all that is necessary to do in order to use him with safety. The best way to do this is as follows : Attach a loop to the harness between the hip and tail ; through this pass a strong two-inch strap with ends attached firmly to the shafts on each side. There be should pieces of leather or iron screwed to the under sides of the shafts to keep the ends in place.

Two points must be kept in mind in order to be successful : 1. The shafts must be so stiff that they will not bend much ; 2. The strap over the hip should be so strong that it will not break, and just tight enough to be drawn straight when in place, but not so long as to give any freedom to raise the hips.

Fɪɢ. 235.—The Horse as Disabled when there is an Effort to Kick.

Four-Ring Bit.

The four-ring bit by its power will sometimes throw the nose up, and occasionally make a doubtful, headstrong horse drive all right ; but it is the best adapted for the management of headstrong luggers. Sometimes a strong-headed puller that cannot be held by an ordinary bit will drive gentle with this. The effectiveness of this bit is in the pressure of its center against the roof of the mouth. As made heretofore, when pulled upon very hard, these rings would slide in so far as to prevent the desired purchase against the palate. To prevent this, I devised the slot, or obstruction.

Sometimes the Patent Bridle will work quite well in the management of kickers.

For the Breaking Rig, see illustration with description in first chapter.

It may be asked, "Is there any medicine by which you can make a horse gentle?" See "Medicine" in "Subjection."

KICKERS IN STALL.

In the first place, for the management of kickers in the stall, a great deal depends upon the size of the stall and the adroitness of the man in approaching the horse. A very narrow stall makes it somewhat difficult, if not dangerous, to approach even many gentle horses. Such stalls are not only an abomination for the increased danger and inconvenience they cause in going around a horse, but

FIG. 236.—**Simple Method of Controlling the Head.**

for not affording sufficient freedom for the horse to lie down and step around. It is no reason for stalls being so constructed because somebody who should know better makes them so. If the stall is large, there will be better opportunity to keep out of reach, and, unless the horse is very vicious, there will be no difficulty in going around him with comparative safety.

Then, much depends upon the character of the man. A courageous, determined horse soon learns to become aggressive toward a naturally timid man who seems afraid to approach him. If a horse is very vicious in his stall, he is like any other dangerous brute upon which nothing short of a thorough course of subjective treatment will produce any impression. But if irritable or cunning, a sharp lesson with the War Bridle until he will follow promptly will usually be sufficient ; after which it may be left on for a day or two.

The treatment for all ordinary cases should be about as follows : First, put on the War Bridle, second form, which may, if the case is stubborn, be turned into the Double-Draw Hitch Form, and make him feel its power sufficiently to follow promptly. Lead him into the stall, and while holding the cord, step in and out repeatedly, making him, during the time, keep his hind parts turned in the opposite direction. This treatment may be accompanied by giving apples, etc.

If the case is important, and it is desired to be very thorough, after putting on the halter, put on the War Bridle, second form, with the part going through the mouth running through the rings on either side of the halter to keep it in place, and the part over the head well back upon the neck. Now pass the cord back to the end

of the stall and tie to a ring or post, leaving it sufficiently long to give the horse room to step around as usual when tied by the halter. When it is desired to go in, if he does not step around at command, untie the cord and give a sharp pull upon it, which will bring the head around,

Fig. 237.—Fig. 236 in Use.

throwing the hind parts to the opposite side, when he can be approached with safety. This may be repeated when first put on for a few times, to teach the idea of stepping around when commanded. After a few repetitions he will soon learn, when approached and commanded, to step around.

Fig. 238.—A Noted Vicious Kicker.

There is a great sleight in approaching vicious horses when in stalls, the disregard of which may sometimes cause a naturally gentle horse to kick if approached or touched unexpectedly. First, no matter how gentle a horse is, there should be no effort to go near or approach before attracting his attention by speaking to him. If at all doubtful, the course should be about as follows: When behind, a little to the near side, look directly at the horse's head and say sharply, "Get around!" repeating until the eye is caught. A great deal depends upon the expression of confidence and authority shown. An intelligent, courageous horse will discern instantly any lack of confidence or power, and become correspondingly aggressive.

At first the horse may look back and try to measure your strength and be disposed to question your advance. It will be a matter of will power now. Look at him with all the firmness you can, and repeat the "Get around!" with the most thorough vim of expression. If a man of any nerve, but few horses will disobey. If he steps around, no matter if the ears are put back and the eyes partly closed, showing an inclination to kick, there will seldom be

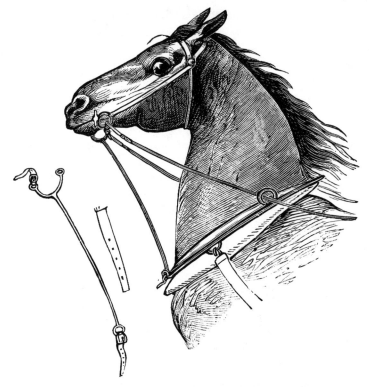

Fig. 239.—A Simple Method of Keeping the Head Elevated to Prevent
Kicking while Driving.

much danger. The eye kept firmly upon that of the horse, will discover any movement almost before it is made ; so reach the end of the stall fronting the horse, with head slightly turned to hold the eye, and make a quick, gliding leap or long step toward the shoulder. After getting well forward of the hips there will be little danger ; watching the opportunity in this way, and moving quickly, will permit getting beyond reach of danger before the horse can kick.

This is really the only secret of getting around or into the stall of a doubtful horse without getting hurt. (See chapter on "Stallions.") By observing closely, the intentions of the horse will always be revealed by the expression of the eye and his actions. Danger is shown by the ears being thrown back, eyes partly closed, lips drawn back, and mouth perhaps partly open. If the horse will not move when commanded, but holds his position firmly, especially if one having a dark, lurking eye set well into the head, thick eyelids, and heavy ears, the character is treacherous, and needless risks should not be hazarded. What such a horse does he will do quickly without warning. But if he seems to yield, no matter how bad he is, and there is quickness in getting into the stall, as explained, there will be but little danger.

I have frequently been able to go into the stalls of horses that were very dangerous, and have never been kicked or hurt while doing so. Many times the horse would kick the stall, but by a sharp, ringing command sufficient to disconcert, and by jumping quickly, I could always get to the shoulder or head without being touched. In many cases I have been compelled to take the chances from necessity; but by observing these precautions, and calculating my chances carefully, I would be able to get by, though at the instant of doing so the horse would kick the stall behind me.

Fig. 240.—Crupper as Wound to Prevent Catching the Rein.

When desiring to get out, pull the head around after, bringing the hind parts well around to the opposite side. The instant the halter is let go, step or spring beyond reach.

WHILE HARNESSING.

The habit of kicking while harnessing is always the result of carelessness or bad treatment. Were the horse treated kindly and the harness put on gently until accustomed to it, there would be no trouble. Not being accustomed to the breeching or the crupper under the tail, a sensitive horse is liable to kick when feeling pressure upon those parts. I have frequently found horses gentle after the harness was on, yet they would kick violently when the attempt was made to put it on; while others would kick only after it was on. All that is necessary to do in such cases, is to put on the War Bridle, and after giving a few sharp pulls with it, hold firmly in the left hand, and while keeping it taut upon the month, with the right spread the harness gently over the back and hips. The pressure of the cord upon the mouth will hold the attention of the horse sufficiently to allow putting the crupper under the tail and buckling.

To break up the habit, it may be necessary to repeat this treatment two or three times, punishing sharply for any resistance, and encouraging by kind treatment for allowing it to be put on and off as desired. After gaining the attention by the War Bridle, it may be drawn down and tied as in cut 119, page 86, but not kept so more than thirty seconds to a minute ; after which the harness can be put on or off as desired. It is very important in these cases to associate kindness with the treatment by giving apples, etc.

Fig. 241.—As a Bad Case of this Character will Usually Resist before Treatment.

Resistance to having the collar put on, or the neck touched in consequence of having been made sore, is sometimes a formidable difficulty, as the horse may show great viciousness, striking or kicking violently. If the treatment named is not sufficient, then more force must be used ; but with care, the War Bridle will be found sufficient. In such cases, attention must be given to having the collar large enough to permit putting easily over the head. Or if an open collar, it should be unbuckled and put on quietly over the neck. In addition, particular attention should be given to curing the parts, if sore. A great point also in the management of such cases is in winning the confidence of the horse to bear having the sensitive parts touched by scratching the mane and other parts, and imperceptibly approaching the sensitive parts until it is borne ; then follow by caressing, giving apples, etc.

There may be cases also where resistance to the harness upon the hips, or crupper under the tail, will be very violent. In such cases a regular course of subjection may be necessary. One of the worst cases the writer ever handled was of this character, compelling to resort to the First, Second, and Third methods, which were in part repeated to break him of the habit.

KICKING AND BITING WHILE GROOMING.

The habit of kicking and biting while grooming, is in all cases the result of bad treatment. A sharp curry-comb or card is raked recklessly over the legs and belly, regardless of cutting into the skin. The horse may snap, kick, and almost lie down upon the ground in the effort to avoid or relieve the pain ; but no more attention is given to this than to kick and pound as a means of compelling to stand quietly. Sharp curry-combs, or any instrument that will hurt, should not be used upon such horses. Should the horse be over-sensitive, the result of former bad treatment, restrain a little with the War Bridle until he will submit to

FIG. 242.—As the Horse will Stand Quietly to be Harnessed after Treatment.

being cleaned as directed. In such cases, it is always advisable to commence at an insensible part, and work gradually to the part at which the grooming is resisted.

BAD TO BRIDLE.

Most horses will submit readily to be bridled, by giving a short lesson with the War Bridle, and tying down as explained, when the bridle can be put on or off as desired. Care should be taken to have the bridle large and easy fitting. As there is submission, give more freedom until there is no resistance. Should the horse show viciousness, and resist this treatment, then subject to Second

Method, and while tied, handle the head and put on the brible
When untied, restrain with the cord, being careful in such cases to
work gently, rewarding liberally for obedience.   Able once to take
off or put on the bridle without force, repeat for some time, holding
the attention by giving apples, etc.   Such a horse should be bridled
with care for some time, to outgrow the sensibility.

CHAPTER VI.

RUNNING AWAY.

THOUGH the treatment for this habit is, to a great extent, given under the heads of "Kicking" and "Fear," yet in bad cases it is liable to be so troublesome to manage that I deem it necessary to consider it more definitely here. The main point is to make the mouth manageable to the restraint of the bit. But if there is much viciousness or resistance, it is necessary to tone it down or overcome it by a general course of subjection, when the control of the mouth can be made more easy and certain. For example : A nervous, excitable colt, so unmanageable as to be both difficult and dangerous to put in shafts by any control that could be brought upon the mouth, after a proper course of subjective treatment which would overcome his fear and excitement, would be found to offer but little resistance to the control of even a common bit. The effect is the same in the management of headstrong, runaway horses, moved by some special cause of excitement, such as the rattling of a wagon or other object.

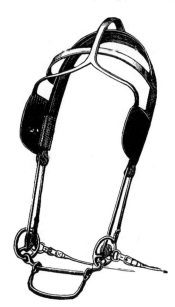

Fig. 243.—The Patent Bridle.

There are three principles of controlling the mouth : 1. By training, as done with the Breaking Bit ; 2. By a form of bit that will prevent the horse from pulling against it, on account of the pain it may cause ; 3. By obtaining such power upon the mouth and head as will control the horse directly.

Of course these conditions run more or less into each other in the different forms of bits given, the point in all cases being to use such a form of bit or method of treatment as will safely and easily effect the control desired. The Breaking Bit is undoubtedly the best for making a hard mouth submissive and flexible. The Half-moon

Bit will in many cases also work well. Its thin, bearing surface, when pressed hard against, hurts so keenly that but few horses will have the nerve to resist it. The Spoon Bit also, in many cases, works excellently by the pressure it brings upon the jaws laterally, thereby making it a good form of bit for cases that will not rein easily, or that will pull on one side. Next comes the Four-ring Bit, which, with its improvement, is a very simple but powerful means of controlling doubtful, headstrong, lugging horses. It is particularly well adapted for the easy driving of side-reiners. The fourth and last is the Patent Bridle, which has been designed by me especially for the direct control of headstrong, runaway horses.

The power of the Patent Bridle is so great that when properly adjusted it is very difficult for a horse to make any prolonged resistance to it. It acts in three important ways : First, in its most severe form it will produce such intense pain in connection with its great power upon the mouth, that it is very difficult for the most courageous horse to resist its restraint ; second, in proportion to the resistance, if any, it brings such a pressure upon the spinal cord that it becomes difficult to bear up against it for any length of time ; third, its impression is so great upon the nervous system that should it be resisted hard for some time, there will rarely be any inclination to pull against it afterward.

It is proper to add that these combinations and forms of bits may be varied in different ways to an almost unlimited degree. Properly used, great results can be accomplished with the Breaking Bit alone, as before explained. It requires more work, but is the only bit I have found that works satisfactorily in making the mouth sensitive to the control of an ordinary snaffle bit. As will be noticed in the chapter on " Kicking," it was by the use of this bit that I was able to perform my best results in the control of runaway kickers. If the mouth is stiff and hard, and it is desired to make it flexible, put on the harness with this bit in the bridle, run the reins through the shaft-bearers, and get directly behind. Now slowly move the horse on a moderate walk, and suddenly call, " Whoa ! " following instantly with a quick, raking jerk upon the reins. Repeat at short intervals, until at the moment the command is given the horse will stop instantly to avoid the hurt of being pulled upon. Then gradually increase the gait to a fast trot or run, making him stop as before.

At this point it is necessary to be very thorough. There should be no half-way work. The submission must be of the most pronounced character. After this is done in harness, so that when the horse is put on a keen trot or run, he will stop instantly without being pulled upon. Then, when hitched to a wagon, repeat slowly

FIG. 244.—A Lunger as he Usually Starts.

until he can be let out on a rapid trot or keen run, and will stop instantly at the least intimation of the command to do so, and this to be done without the breeching-straps being buckled. He must show the most thorough submissiveness when everything is apparently wrong.

In most cases the horse will submit in from ten to fifteen minutes; but if badly set in the habit, and plucky, the resistance may be so strong that this cannot be done in one lesson. The difficulty is, if the horse warms up very much, the sensibility of the mouth becomes so blunted or destroyed that he will bear the severest pulling upon without flinching. Then the best plan will be to put him away until cool, when by a few minutes' repetition of the treatment the mouth will usually be found so sensitive that he will submit unconditionally. In this way it can be determined how much to do without danger of harm. This point accomplished, hitch to a wagon, and repeat the same treatment. The course pursued by the writer, as before explained, is to let the horse go a few steps, call "Whoa!" and give a sharp, raking jerk to force him back a little. Repeat so far as necessary to establish the point of stopping and coming back, then, as before, let out a little faster until proved safe when on a fast trot or run. This point is to be made very thoroughly. If it is thought advisable, the bit can be left on for a few days in driving, but usually this will be unnecessary; for if the horse is properly trained, he can be controlled by an ordinary snaffle bit.

The Half-Moon Bit.

The Half-moon Bit, an illustration of which is given, will sometimes work very nicely upon headstrong pullers. It seems to work best when the head is well checked up, as shown in Fig. 246. The bit is very simple, merely a circular mouth-piece, with the inner part filed down to about the thickness of the back of an ordinary knife-blade, and rounded to prevent cutting. This makes the bearing surface against the mouth so narrow that even the most plucky horse will not have the nerve to pull very hard against it, while its circular form prevents pulling sideways. It should, however, be tried cautiously upon a dangerous horse.

Spoon Bit.

The Spoon Bit is so constructed as to bring the edges of two flanges, when pulled upon, upon each side of the lower jaw. Fine illustrations of this are given in Figs. 247 and 248. In some cases of badly trained mouths, or of moderately headstrong horses, it will be found to work very nicely. One point of advantage is its mildness, it being only a simple snaffle bit until resisted. It works especially well in the management of horses that rein hard.   It is not a

FIG. 245.—Showing the Power of the Patent Bridle.

bit that is adapted for headstrong, dangerous lungers, as it does not give sufficient power for such cases.

A valuable form of bit, and one which works exceedingly well for the control of some headstrong, pulling horses, is a

simple bar made flat or concave on one side, and rounded on the other, from five eighths to three fourths of an inch wide, with a piece of rounded leather inside the ring on each end, as shown in Figs. 249 and 250. The flat or concave side is used when the horse pulls, or is inclined to resist the bit. When the mouth is sensitive and manageable, s i m p l y turning the rounded

Fig. 246.—The Half-moon Bit Adjusted.

side against the jaw makes it extremely easy on the mouth. The length must be regulated to the size of the mouth, or about the average length of driving-bits.

Four-Ring Bit.

The Four-ring Bit, Figs. 123, 124, full explanation of which is given in Chapter II., page 94, which can be referred to, is peculiar in respect to the sensibility it causes upon the mouth. While it is not a bit that gives much direct power, the effect is such that but few horses, outside of lunging, runaway horses, can successfully pull against it. Hence a horse that with an ordinary bit may pull so hard as to make it extremely difficult to restrain or control him, more especially one that as he warms up will pull harder, will sometimes scarcely pull at all upon this bit, driving so easily as to hardly straighten the reins.

It is not, however, to be risked too much in the driving of a really dangerous horse ; for, as before stated, its success depends more upon the sensibility it causes upon the roof of the mouth than upon any real power it otherwise gives. Consequently, should the horse lunge recklessly against the bit, the pain it inflicts not being sufficient to hold him in check, he is liable to get away. When used upon a doubtful horse, he should be carefully tested with it, first by driving around a little in harness, then as described in the use of the Half-moon Bit. The foot-strap may be used to enable testing the horse sufficiently hard to know with certainty to what degree he will submit to the restraint. This bit also works very nicely on side-reiners, or those that pull on one rein.

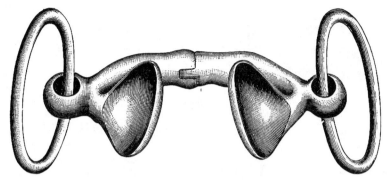

FIG. 247.—First Form of Spoon Bit. Easy on the Mouth.

PATENT BRIDLE.

The Patent Bridle, described on page 184, is undoubtedly the most powerful means yet introduced of controlling a headstrong, runaway horse. It does not require any practice or work other than fitting the head-piece and bridle to the head, and setting the horse back a few times. It gives two important points of advan-

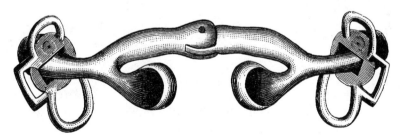

FIG. 248.—Second Form of Spoon Bit. Gives More Power.

tage: First, it is as any common bit in the mouth until resistance is excited, when by an ordinary pull such power is brought upon the mouth that the strongest horse cannot well resist it; second, it brings direct pressure upon the spinal cord so as to affect the whole nervous system most forcibly, and break up the inclination to pull; so that when a horse submits to it once, he will usually drive with an ordinary bit and slack rein. This is one of the most important secrets in making a horse safe in harness. Now when everything is all right, it is reasonably presumed that a horse must be safe. It is a point of testing up to the point of what the horse will usually bear, repeatedly. There must be no nonsensical timidity or mock sentiment shown in doing this. The greatest humanity is to make the horse as safe as possible to those using him.

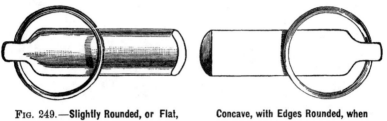

FIG. 249.—Slightly Rounded, or Flat, when not Desired to be Severe.

Concave, with Edges Rounded, when More Severity is Required.

LUGGING, OR PULLING UPON ONE REIN.

The quickest and simplest way to break up this habit is to put on the Breaking Bit, also the First Form of the War Bridle. But instead of bringing the cord through the mouth, bring it through the rings of the bit. Pull sharply on one side opposite that on which he lugs, until he will bring the head around freely without being pulled upon. Now tie up the cord, take down the reins, and drive around. If he pulls in the least, repeat the lesson, until he learns to yield

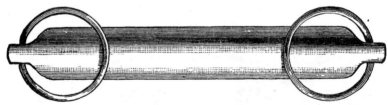

FIG. 250.—Rounded Side of the Bar.

promptly to the restraint of the reins, when he ought to drive to an ordinary bit; or the Breaking Bit can be kept on for a day or two. This treatment will make that side of the mouth as tender and submissive to restraint as the opposite, and he will pull evenly.

The Spoon Bit and Four-ring Bit, just referred to, work especially well for this habit.

WILL NOT BACK.

This is the result of bad training of the mouth. Ordinarily it is a very simple habit to manage, but I have found a few cases exceedingly stubborn and difficult to break. First, in the management of colts. If a colt is very young, or of a cold-blooded, sullen nature, he will usually sulk and resist the bit when pulled upon to back. With the Breaking Bit, however, it is a very simple matter to do in most any case of this kind. During my early experience, I usually made this point by putting on the War Bridle, first form, and standing at the shoulder, then giving a sharp, quick jerk sideways and back, and thus repeating until forced to go back a little, then stood in front and pulled back moderately until the point was made. Another method, practiced upon such cases by me with success, was, to put on a foot-strap and surcingle; instead of putting the strap over the belly-band, bring it forward, then, after the foot is pulled up, press back gently upon the head, at the same time letting the foot go down; it will be put down about ten inches back of the other, making a short step backward. This is to be repeated until the colt will go back freely. Another excellent method was taking an ordinary jack-knife, or the end of a stick brought to a dull point, and press gently back inside the shoulder blade, at the same time pressing back upon the head gently. The colt will usually go back to free himself from the pain, when caress and repeat.

I have used all these methods with success. When I caught the point of training the mouth with the Breaking Bit, I practically abandoned the palliative methods, and depended entirely upon them, by training the mouth as described under that head in Colt Training. Extremely bad runaways would sometimes resist the bit in the most desperate manner. It was not unusual for horses of this character to pull from two to three men on a walk, even against the Breaking Bit, with the recklessness of insanity. Such horses were usually submitted to the restraint of the bit freely until excited, the very point that had to be overcome. Now we managed all these cases by simple, sharp little jerks, as explained under the head of "Running Away," and repeating. If the horse became warmed up and sullen, which would destroy the sensibility of the mouth, we would stop, and repeat after he became cool, when, of course the sensibility of the mouth would be greatly increased, then repeat until there would be perfect submission. The principle is the same in teaching an extremely bad colt to back. There is quite a sleight in using this bit in these bad cases. It is, when directly behind, with the reins loose enough to come on each side of the quarters, to give such a quick, energetic pull that the horse is brought back before he can concentrate his will to resist. It should be a little series of surprises in this way. Let him stand quietly, and suddenly give a sharp little raking pull, at the same time repeating the word "Back." I have often been able in this way to take horses that seem to be very bad, and lift them bodily from the ground backward in a few minutes. This will usually work well with warm-blooded horses. If the case is of a cold-blooded nature, eye small, eyelid thick, long from eye to ear, the eye well into the head, if a large boned, strong horse, you have one that will fight like a bulldog. If possible, the point is to get him off his feet the first time. Should he become a little warm, stop and repeat ; at any rate, keep on until successful. There should be no exception—we never had one. We had cases that would resist very hard, and required two or three lessons, but we never found a case that we could not break. Be careful not to cut or bruise the tongue.

This is the point I forgot to mention before. When the horse will sullenly resist the bit, you can easily bruise or cut the mouth without his feeling it. The treatment for bruises, should you have trouble in this way, is dousing heavily with cold water ; bathing with callendula is probably the most effective treatment. This remedy has the best effect in removing swelling, etc., that the writer has ever used. It seems to have the best healing effect.

During 1869, when I was in Painesville, Ohio, a man brought in a runaway horse of the worst character. He stated that he would wager fifty dollars that if excited he could not be held by the reins, and wished the trial made. The Breaking Bit I then used had short bars, with square, twisted corners. With this in his mouth the horse resisted six men, or three to a rein. Upon examination of the mouth, I found the tongue to be very badly cut. Using callendula, which was given me a short time before by a practitioner in Cleveland, Ohio, cured the tongue in three days. We had no trouble in breaking the horse with the usual treatment of the Breaking Bit.

CHAPTER VII.

BALKING.

IF a naturally gentle horse be hitched to a tree or other immovable object and commanded to pull, he would at first pull all he could; the second time he would not pull with quite so much confidence as at first; while the third or fourth time he would pull but little, or perhaps not at all. To whip and urge him now to pull

Fig. 251.—**As the Horse will Sometimes Stand, Regardless of the Most Severe Whipping.**

would only start him in the habit of balking. Or, if a horse is overloaded or so exhausted that he cannot pull the load, and in this condition is whipped and urged to go, he will balk. Or, if he starts too quickly, and is pulled back violently and whipped till confused and excited, the habit of balking is begun. Hence we see that this habit is purely acquired, the same as kicking and other habits, for which there can hardly be a reasonable excuse.

Balking horses are of two kinds: Double-balkers and single-balkers. Balkers in single harness may be divided into two classes: First, horses that refuse to go at all; second, those that will not pull unless given their own way. The mule and ox, and horses having similarly patient, cold-blooded natures, have little inclination to this habit; while nervous, warm-blooded, fine-grained horses are easily taught the habit.

In teaching a colt to drive, let him go slowly at first and as he pleases. There should be sufficient room so as not to require short turns, as pulling short around before learning to rein is liable to confuse and irritate him to balk. If there appears any inclination to stop, or if he refuses to go, the driver should sit quietly in the wagon, fix the harness, or do anything to take up time until the horse gets over his fret. If he does not feel sure of his going, let him get out and move the colt a little to the right or left, speaking to him kindly, and it is rare that he will not move off without knowing that he has balked. If he has an irritable disposition, and appears unwilling to stand, particular care should be taken to teach him thoroughly the lesson of stopping and starting, as described under the head of Colt Training. If the habit is only partially learned, and especially if the colt is of a warm-blooded nature, it is by all means advisable to win him out of the habit by kind treatment, if possible. I will illustrate by referring to a peculiar case in my early experience :—

I often traded horses, and not unfrequently got very bad ones. Among them was a small pony mare, nine years old,—a confirmed balker. This I did not know until after I had traded for her. I harnessed her carefully in the shafts, but she stood stubbornly. Upon touching her with a whip, she threw herself down. I saw at once that she was one of the very worst of balkers, and that in the effort to break her she had been subjected to a great deal of whipping and abuse. I unhitched her, got her up, tied up the harness and reins, and went into an orchard close by and filled my pockets with apples. I then led her to a back road not much used, and standing near her head with a switch in my hand, touched her lightly over the hips, saying, "Get up!" This caused her to start. After going a few steps, I called "Whoa!" at the same time pulling upon the reins, when she stopped, for which I gave her a piece of apple, and stroked her nose and head. This I repeated until she would start and stop at command.

This point gained, I next untied the reins, and while standing at the shoulder and holding the reins slack in my hands, I repeated the command for starting, touching her for a few times lightly over the hips. At each repetition I stood a little farther back, until able to get directly behind her, and make her go or stop at command. I then took her to the top of the hill and hitched her up. This was the critical point of the experiment, and I did not propose to take any chances of failure. I commenced again at her head, rewarding as before, until I was able to get on the step, and finally into the wagon, at each repetition being careful to reward her, even getting out of the wagon to do so. It was soon quite amusing to see how eagerly she would reach round her head in anticipation of her reward. Now I required her to go a little farther at each time of starting, until able to drive fifteen or twenty rods ; then I took her out of harness, and put her in the stable. The next day I hitched her up again, and commenced cautiously as before, spending only a few minutes, but requiring her to go farther and faster until on a sharp trot or run. I repeated this lesson again next day until she could

be driven as desired. The point of success was that I made the lessons short, and was careful not to do more at a time than she would bear. I could even make her stop in a mud-hole and stand as long as I wished her to, and then at command she would pull out willingly. Those who knew the mare were quite surprised to see me drive her, and regarded it as a great feat. In reality it was no feat at all, but merely the result of a little patient management, which it is not difficult for any one to practice. This mode of treatment is especially

FIG. 252.—Slow, Patient Nature,—not Disposed to Balk.

adapted to nervous horses that will not bear pushing.

   There is nothing that so tries a man's temper and patience as a sullen balker. One may resolve to be patient, but after reasonable efforts with kind treatment, and failing, he determines to see what a whip will do. Some men in anger will strike a horse over the ears, twist and pull his tongue severely, and yet not be able to make the animal flinch. A balking horse of spirit, thoroughly maddened by such treatment, may resist the most severe punishment. Horses have been known, when excited in this way, to sullenly stand even the burning of straw under them. The skin on the legs and body is so thick, and has so little sensibility, that when the blood is thoroughly warmed up, the severest whipping or pounding can be scarcely felt, and it becomes only a means of intensifying the habit. The usual method of whipping, kicking the belly, hitting back of the head with a club, etc., while often liable to kill or seriously injure the horse. can really have no beneficial effect.

STARTING THE BALKER.

Sometimes very simple treatment will start a balky horse, as kicking the leg lightly below the knee until he lifts his foot ; passing a string over one of his ears, and tying it down ; letting the horse inhale a little ammonia or red pepper. These are very common tricks, and will sometimes disconcert a horse sufficiently to cause him to start. The following has been considered a great secret in the treatment of balkers, and will in some cases work with considerable success.

MEDICINE.

Take the oslets or warts growing inside a horse's leg, dry, and grate them fine, and keep in a tightly-corked bottle, as they lose their strength quickly and evaporate on being exposed to the air. About three-quarters of an hour before the horse is to be driven, blow a thimbleful from a quill into his nostrils. This has a soothing effect, and will cause the horse to go off all right.

An old man who had been a successful horse-breaker, told me that he had used it forty years, and never failed to make a horse go as he desired with it ; that he seldom repeated it more than two or three times. When a horse takes a dislike to other horses and kicks at them, the oslets from a vigorous horse, or from the one objected to, used as above, will in most cases overcome such aversion.

Sometimes stepping before a horse and moving him to the right or left a little, and stroking his nose, or pulling his ears gently, etc., will cause him to start. Grasping both nostrils with the hand to prevent his breathing until he struggles for freedom, and turning him a little sideways at the instant of letting go, will frequently start quite a bad horse. Tying the tail to the cross-piece will frequently start him, as a horse will always pull by the tail. Blindfolding is one of the simplest and best methods of starting a stubborn balker. After being blindfolded, he should be allowed to stand a few minutes, then move him right and left a few times, say encouragingly, "Get up," and the horse will usually pull steadily against the collar and move off all right. Tying up the fore leg, and compelling him to stand on three legs till tired, will usually be a very effectual means of starting a balker, and frequently after a few repetitions it will break up the habit. This method works best on nervous, impulsive horses.

A MAINE MAN'S METHOD.

"When a horse balks, take him out of the shafts, tie the bridle rein into the tail short enough to bring his body into a half circle, and make him go around four or five times. This will make him dizzy ; then put him in shafts and he will go off all right. If one lesson will not break him, repeating it will be sure to do so."

This is merely palliative ; it will frequently enable starting a balking horse, but is not by any means adequate for breaking up the habit. It will be seen farther on that it is part of my regular treatment for this habit. I invented it and taught it in that State nearly twenty-five years ago ; and the idea of managing balky horses in this way was given by me as a simple method of starting a horse, but not of breaking up the habit.

A mare in the habit of balking, although occasionally driving well for weeks at a time, one day got into one of her balking tantrums. Her owner, becoming angry, determined to kill her. Taking a gun from the hands of a sportsman who happened to be standing near, he fired the charge of shot into the body. It did not kill her, and on recovering, she was put to work as usual. It was found afterward that whenever she balked, simply pointing a stick at her was sufficient to make her start at once.

A horse employed in drawing limestone to a kiln from a quarry close by, was in the habit of balking. One day he refused to pull, and, in defiance of the strength of several men who caught and held the wheels to prevent the accident, backed over the precipice, falling about thirty feet. The cart was broken to pieces, but the horse escaped with slight injury. He was put to work as usual, but was never known to balk afterward.

A farmer who was once a member of my class made the following statement in relation to his managing a balker : He had a mare that would sometimes work well for a week, and then, perhaps, at a critical time would stand stubbornly, resisting all effort to move her. One day while drawing in oats she balked. After working with her a long while, he resolved that she should go or starve. He drove a stake down in the ground, and tied her to it ; then putting a sheaf of oats a few rods distant, he went off. This was at ten o'clock in the morning. About five o'clock he returned and tried to start her, but she would not go. He tied her again to the post, and let her stand until morning. Then he unhitched her, took the reins and tried to start her, but she would not pull. During the afternoon he tried her again, when she went. Upon reaching the sheaf of oats, he let her eat it. He now drove her home, unharnessed and fed her, then put her to work. She worked all right for a few days, and then balked again. This time he let her stand forty-eight hours, then fed her, when upon trial she went all right, and he kept her at work. She never balked afterward.

Another man of much tact with horses informed me that he always succeeded with balkers by the following treatment: When a horse balked, he unhitched and put him in the stall, and stationed a man behind him with a whip. Every minute or two the man tapped the horse on the quarters with a whip, just enough to annoy him. This was kept up for twenty-four hours, the regular feed and water being given. If he refused to go upon being tried, he was put back, and the same treatment kept up to prevent his going to sleep, until he would go as desired. It was rarely, after one or two lessons of this treatment, that a horse would not work in all right. Innumerable instances of breaking very bad horses in this way have been brought to my notice by horsemen who have been members of my classes.

It does no good, practically, to subject a horse to treatment in a barn, or where not accustomed to balk. It should be carried out as nearly as possible where in the habit of resisting. Any means that will disconcert a horse when he balks is a step in the right direction. But if we have in addition power to move him as we wish, we have the key of compelling the entire submission of balkers that have defied the greatest efforts to break or drive them. This we can obtain by the Second Method, and other treatment here given.

Regular Treatment.

The course I usually pursue, and which I would advise in the management of bad cases, is about as follows: Put into the wagon, ready for use, a good strap halter, a War Bridle, a light bow whip that will not break, and some good apples. Hitch up the horse as if to make a journey, and let him go as he pleases until a level, isolated piece of road is reached. Now if he does not balk, provoke him to do so. Get out quietly, unhitch him, tie up the reins and tugs, put on the halter over the bridle, and subject him to Second Method both ways until well off his balance. If hitched up now he will be likely to go off all right, but will be apt to balk at some future time. As the object should be to effectually break up the habit, it is necessary to make the lesson very thorough.

This treatment makes a powerful impression upon him in two ways: First, to convince him that there is power to make him move any way desired, which is the point to be established, as he does not know the difference between going sideways and straight ahead. Second, it disconcerts him in the most powerful manner, and thus prevents or overcomes the inclination to resistance. But it is also necessary to create sufficient reserve power to force him to move should he again refuse to go. To do this, put on the War Bridle, first, or double-draw hitch form, and lift him right and left. When he follows promptly, change to second form. Now pull upon him sideways and ahead. As he yields, gradually pull more on a line with the body until he will come ahead promptly.

Next, tie up the cord loosely in the terret, take down the reins, run them through the shaft-lugs, and get directly behind. Say "Get up!" pulling one rein a little, and, if necessary, touch the quarters sharply with the whip. After going a short distance, call, "Whoa!" If he does not stop, force him to do so by a slight pull of the reins. Repeat this until he will stop and start at command, then reward by giving some apple. Repeat the driving, stopping, and starting until he works in all right and is over the excitement of the treatment, then hitch to a wagon, when will come the real test. Stand near, and in a low, gentle tone say, "Get up!" and repeat the starting, stopping, and rewarding as before, until he will go as desired. If a very bad case, it will be necessary to make the impression as thorough and complete as possible, and it would be best to put him away until the next day, when he should be tried, and, so far as found necessary, the treatment repeated until under good control.

Although the horse may go a few times as commanded, yet, after hitching to a wagon, he may balk again. If so, take down the cord, stand in front of him—a little to the right or left—and give a sharp jerk, repeating until he will go at command. Should this be resisted, which is not at all improbable, repeat the previous course of treatment, which, in some cases, may be supplemented by the other methods of treatment. It is advisable to test the horse hard before putting to regular work. A great point after the coercive treatment, is to win his confidence by giving him apples, etc.

RESTLESS BALKERS, OR SUCH AS WILL NOT STAND WHEN GETTING IN OR OUT OF A WAGON.

If, when a young horse is hitched to a wagon, he is allowed to start as he pleases a few times, he is liable to acquire the habit of becoming impatient, so that as soon as hitched up, if not allowed to go his own way, he may get mad and balk. Or if whipped to start quickly, and then pulled back upon, or if made to stand too long while getting into or out of a wagon, he may acquire the habit of

balking. A short lesson in teaching to start and stop, as directed in
" Colt-Training," would prevent this. As it is a very common as
well as annoying form of balking, I will include the details of a simple treatment, which can be easily practiced by any one :—

First, teach the horse to stand (see " Will Not Stand," page
201) with the harness on, as explained to stand with the Breaking
Bit ; then tie up the reins, give a good sharp lesson with the War
Bridle, and put him in shafts. If he balks, overcome it with the War
Bridle. If of a quick, nervous disposition, this treatment should be
sufficient ; but if of a decidedly resolute, plucky character, regular
coercive treatment by Second Method, etc., may be necessary. But
as there is usually little inclination among owners to resort to coercive treatment, for the benefit of such I include the details of simple, winning treatment :—

Before putting the horse into the shafts, adjust the harness.
Get directly behind, with an ordinary carriage whip touch the hips
lightly, and say sharply, " Get up ! " After going a short distance,
call, " Whoa ! " and pull lightly upon the reins to make him stop.
When there is prompt obedience, give a little apple, etc. Continue
driving and stopping until a good foundation is made for the next
step. Next, turn the carriage to face a barn or high fence, and quietly hitch the horse in ; then go to his head, caress, talk to him, and
give him some apple. Be in no hurry, but hold his attention in this
way several minutes. When you want him to move, walk ahead a
little and say, " Get up ! " or " Come ! " After going a few steps, stop
and repeat the rewarding.

There will be less inclination to rush ahead when a barn or high
fence is in front, and you are standing directly before him. In addition to this, his attention is attracted by the apples. In this way repeat until the obstruction is reached, when it will be easy to turn or
back short around. Gradually get back opposite his head and shoulders, with each repetition going farther back till the wheel is reached,
when mount the step and get into the wagon. Repeat this until the
horse is obedient to wait for the driver to get in, stopping and start-
ng as desired. Now drive farther, and take some one in with you
as if to take a journey. First, drive where the horse is least likely
to resist, but finally in front of the house, or other place, where there
has been most trouble. The hitching and unhitching should be repeated, and his attention held as before with apples, etc., in the
meantime talking, walking around, and rattling the wagon. A little
care should be used, especially after idle spells, to hold the attention
by giving apples, etc., or have some one stand at his head and talk

to him, but not to take up the reins until ready to start. If in a barn, keep the door shut until ready to start.

WILL NOT STAND.

Usually it is not difficult to teach a horse to stand unless there is inclination to balk. If a young horse that is simply a little impulsive, treat the same as directed for teaching colts to stand. Usually, with an ordinary mild bit, there will be an inclination to pull against it and fight its restraint. If this is the case, the Breaking Bit can be used as follows :—

First, with the harness on, train to stop as explained in Colt Training. When first hitched to a wagon, let it be away from the place where accustomed to be hitched. I prefer to turn the horse's head toward a high fence or barn, because there is less inclination to go ahead when such an obstruction is in view. Then get in and out repeatedly, occasionally giving him an apple, etc., for some time. Now move him around, standing him a little farther off at each repetition, and gradually more sideways, until he will stand with his body parallel to the barn or away from it. Next, repeat the lesson where in the habit of being hitched, until he will stand as desired.

When hitched in, have the reins in the hand or within easy reach. The moment he starts, give a sharp pull that will make him stand, go to the head and stroke it for a while, then go back to the wheel. For the least resistance, set him back sharply with the reins. When desired to start, take him by the head, and, after going a few steps, call "Whoa!" If he does not stop promptly, pull sharply upon the reins until he will do so. Reward for standing ; punish for moving. Having once learned to stand and wait, get on the step and make a noise ; this submitted to, get in quietly and sit down. Repeat the stopping, starting, and waiting, until the impression is fixed upon the mind. After he will do this properly away from the house, he should be taken where in the habit of resisting, and the lesson repeated, if necessary.

Horses of this character are sometimes very sensitive, and require nice management, because they are so easily taught to balk. The point is to impress thoroughly the idea of stopping, and make it so habitual that when the horse is most impulsive during cold and chilly weather, it will not be forgotten. A very good plan, should the case be a little doubtful, and seem in danger of working into the habit again, would be to have some one stand in front of him, or near the head, and stroke the nose a little, but not touch the reins. This will disconcert the horse sufficiently to make him stand while getting in, when by stepping out of his way he will move off quietly.

If the Breaking Bit is not available, the following course of treatment, though requiring more time and care, will be found to work very well: Put on the foot-strap, call "Whoa!" at the same time pull upon the foot-strap, which will pull the foot up and throw the horse upon three legs. After a few repetitions, he will stop rather than be pulled upon and tripped. Now put him before a wagon, carrying the foot-strap back as a third rein. If he starts, simply pull the foot from under a few times, or until he will stand as desired. In some cases, the foot-strap may be put on both fore feet, as a very determined horse may lunge forward upon three feet. If when one foot is taken up there is inclination to lunge forward, simply pull the other foot from under, which brings him forward upon his knees. This treatment should be given on soft, sodded ground, or sandy road free from stones, to avoid bruising the knees.

Put the Breaking Bit into the bridle and commence cracking a whip, yelling, or anything else to attract his attention. If he moves, punish by jerking him back sharply, and say, "Whoa!" Then repeat, cracking the whip, etc., until he will stand quietly under the excitement. When he will stand while in wagon, get out and caress him, walk around carelessly, crack the whip, etc. The instant he starts, call "Whoa!" and jerk him back again. When he will stand, go to his head, caress, give an apple, etc.; so repeat the lesson until he will stand quietly. At first, the cause of excitement should be moderate, gradually increasing each time. The reins should extend back into the wagon over the seat, so they can be caught quickly when necessary. In this way the horse is made afraid to start for fear of being punished. If it is desired to make the effect still more thorough, boys can be made to run around, make a noise, etc.

A simple way to make a horse stand without being hitched, is to buckle or tie a strap or cord around the near fore foot below the fetlock, and tie the other end around the shaft back of the cross-piece, bringing it short enough so that, while not interfering with the limb while standing, it prevents its being brought forward in the effort to stop or go ahead. A horse will stand quietly by spanceling the fore legs together; that is, tying two small cords around the fore legs about six or seven inches apart. As soon as the horse finds he cannot step, he will stand quietly.

DOUBLE BALKING.

When a horse throws himself back in the breeching sullenly, with his head over the other horse's neck, as if to say, "Make me go if you can !" it will try a man's patience very much, and unless he

FIG. 258.—Arrangement for Breaking a Balker in Double Harness.

knows how to overcome the difficulty, he will be likely to retaliate
by kicking and pounding, which is likely to do more harm than

good. Many horses are led into this habit by badly fitting collars, that either choke or make the shoulders so sore that it becomes painful to push steadily or firmly.

When hitched to a load, care should be used to prevent pulling so hard and long at a time as to get out of breath. Neither should a stop be made in a soft place, or where a steady, heavy pull to start will be required. The team should be kept fresh, and encouraged by stopping often and giving the horses a chance to recover breath. In pulling up hill or very steep places, a good rest should be given before starting. If one or both horses become confused, and balk, let them stand until they recover fully. Then stand in front, take both by the head, and move them to the right or left. It is sometimes advisable to turn them both ways. When you get them to move together, say gently and encouragingly, "Come, boys!" or any word to which they are accustomed. Much depends upon the tact of the driver in bringing them up against the collar with assurance, and in helping them to break the force of the dead pull in starting, by moving partly sideways. If the wheels are sunk in the mud, and the power and willingness of the horses to pull out is doubtful, a part of the load should be thrown off; better do this than run the risk of spoiling the team.

Horses compelled to pull hard should not be checked up. Let the head have full freedom. Sometimes a horse is so stubborn that he will not go, even when not required to pull any load. Always be governed by circumstances, such as the horse's disposition and the difficulty to be encountered. If of a sensitive, nervous disposition, try either of the following tricks, which in many cases will work very nicely : First, tie a strap or cord to the end of the tail, bring it forward between the legs and attach it to the hame ring of the gentle horse, or to the end of the pole. Tie it so short that unless the horse will come forward promptly to his place he will be pulled upon sharply. Or double a piece of cord (that used for War Bridle is best), pass the tail through the center, and twist the ends of the cord three or four times and tie to the hame ring of the gentle horse or to the end of the pole. Or, again, a noose may be formed of a small chain or rope around the body back of the shoulders, and tied to the end of the wagon tongue. Now when the gentle horse is made to start, the pull becomes so severe that it startles and disconcerts the balky horse from his purpose, and compels him to go ahead.

After adjusting either of these rigs, start the gentle horse quickly so as to make a sharp pull upon the balker, which will surprise and force him to jump ahead. After a few repetitions, he will jump ahead to avoid being hurt. If the cord under the tail causes the horse to kick, it should not be used.

BEST TREATMENT.

First, put on (under the ordinary bridle) the Second Form of War Bridle, bring it under the head-piece, and, as in the case of balkers in single harness, pull sideways and ahead, slowly repeating until the horse comes freely without restraint. This lesson should be made very thorough.

To prevent chafing or cutting the hands, gloves should be worn, or the cord may be wound around a piece of broom handle or other stick with which to pull upon. This done, get a stiff pole or

FIG. 254.—Patent Bridle Used for Breaking Double Balkers.

sappling about three or four inches in diameter, and about ten feet in length, or so long that it will extend about thirty inches beyond the horse's nose. Bore a hole about two inches from each end, and fasten the large end of the pole to the inside end of the gentle horse's singletree. When the horses are hitched up, pass the War Bridle through the hole at the other end of the pole, and draw it short enough so that when the horse is up in his place there will be little, if any, restraint upon him, and make fast. Next, pass a cord under the pole from one hame ring to the other, making both ends fast, and leaving it just long enough so that when both horses are in their natural positions, there will be no slack. Then pass another cord around the pole and tie both ends into the gentle horse's hame ring, regulating the length so it will hold the pole over the wagon-tongue in position. Or have a ring made about one half to three fourths of an inch larger than the pole. Attach a cord or strap to connect this ring with the hame rings on each side. This holds the pole in position over the wagon-tongue, and is a better way than the first, but more troublesome to make.

If there are stay chains on the doubletree, they should be removed, so as to give it free play. Get into the wagon (there should be no load) and start the gentle horse quickly. The balker of course refuses to go. The instant the gentle horse starts ahead, if the adjustment is properly arranged, his whole power is brought directly upon the balky horse's head, compelling him to start. Finding he must go, it will usually be but a very few minutes' work to make him so afraid of being pulled upon and hurt, that he will be the first to start at the command. This accomplished, put on a little loading, gradually increasing it until he learns to use his strength reliably. To fix the impression thoroughly, it may be necessary to keep the pole on a few days.

The Patent Bridle will be found to work very nicely in the management of these cases. The reins are simply reversed, so as to pull ahead instead of back, and tied to the end of the pole.

This method of treatment makes the breaking of double balkers a very simple and easy thing to do. It gives power to force the horse into obedience without danger or cruelty. I will refer to a few cases, showing the ease with which horses of this character can be broken by the treatment given.

CASE No. 1.—At Great Barrington, Mass., an Irishman proposed to join my class and pay a double tuition fee, if I would promise to break his horse of balking. I told him if he would join the class I would teach him the principle, and if he could not make his horse work perfectly gentle when he went home that evening, he could so report next day at West Stockbridge, where I was engaged to lecture, and I would return his money. He was extremely suspicious and incredulous as to my terms, but finally joined the class. The following day he was at the next town, so well pleased that he stated publicly to his friends that in ten minutes he was able to make the balky horse work as well as the gentle one, and that he could fully indorse all my statements.

CASE No. 2.—At Brunswick, Maine, a man introduced himself to me, and stated that he teamed for a living; that his whole property was his horses; that one of his horses balked, making his team worthless; that his only object in going into the class was to break this horse of the habit.

I assured him that I would put him in the way of breaking his horse without difficulty; and that if he could not make him work and pull as desired when he went home in the afternoon, on the following morning he could come to me and get his money back. Next day he stated that in less than ten minutes he was able to make this horse work just as well as the other.

CASE NO. 3.—When in Northern New York, in 1876, a man introduced himself to me as an old scholar, who had attended the lectures a few years before, and desired to come into my class again. He said that he had not had occasion to make any use of the instructions until about a year before, when, in plowing, one of his horses balked. He was for some time puzzled to know what to do, when it occurred to him to try this method of treatment. He had forgotten the details, but remembered the general plan. He took a three-fourths-inch rope, and put it on the Second Form of War Bridle, as described for balking. He next took a rail from the fence, and tied one end to the gentle horse's singletree ; to the other end he attached the rope. He then started the gentle horse, and jerked the balky horse out of his tracks two or three times. Using his own language, " That 'ere horse did n't wait to be pulled upon the second time, but pulled as if for life, and never offered to balk afterward, though I put the plow down to the beam."

It was by mere good luck that this man succeeded, considering the crude, imperfect manner in which the treatment was applied. It is hardly safe to risk attempting to make a bad horse go directly in this way. He should be made to yield first to the War Bridle until very sensitive to its restraint, then the pole should be adjusted very carefully. If too short, or so limber that it will bend much, the experiment will be liable to fail.

OVERLOADING.

There is a general inclination among teamsters to overload. This is very common in large cities. While engaged in making illustrations for this work in New York City, I daily passed through Fulton and other streets, and frequently took a side street to avoid witnessing the abuse to which horses were subjected in consequence of being overloaded. It was no unusual thing to see a team whipped severely while pulling to their utmost power, and finally compelled to stop for want of strength to go farther. A team never should be compelled to draw more than it is able to pull easily over the worst parts of the road. This should be the rule. The strain and pulling in this way will sometimes injure a horse more in a few minutes than working reasonably hard all day.

When a horse is unaccustomed to work before a wagon or plow,

is unsteady and easily irritated, especially in plowing, it is advisable
to let him go around a few times before putting the plow into the
ground. A little patience at the beginning, in this way, will frequently enable working a horse in gentle that would otherwise be
easily spoiled.

CHAPTER VIII.

BAD TO SHOE.

THE average of these cases are very simple and easy to manage, but there will occasionally be found among them horses of the most difficult character to control. Ordinary cases of this character were of almost daily occurrence, and usually required but a few minutes' time to make them stand gently to have the feet handled as desired. But we were liable at any time to have a horse of this character that would test our power to the utmost, and such cases frequently made us a great deal of trouble. In the chapter on "Colt-Training" I have given instructions on

FIG. 255.—As a Vicious Horse will Sometimes Act while being Shod.

handling the feet, page 108, which may be referred to in connection with this.

By the use of a little patience and tact, it is rare that even very sensitive colts cannot be made to submit the feet to be handled and pounded upon as desired ; and once done, unless there is some special cause for disturbance, it can always be done. It is true there is occasionally a young horse that is naturally so wild and vicious as to resist all ordinary good management in the effort to take up and handle the feet ; but with our present methods of treatment, even these cases submit readily to control in a short time.

If a colt of ordinary good character, give a short lesson with the First Form of War Bridle, when the feet can be taken up without difficulty. The efficiency of this simple method of control, in making

14   a   (209)

colts submit to be ridden, led, or handled, is very remarkable ; and in no respect is it greater than in allowing the feet to be taken up and handled. Pull right and left sharply a few times with the War Bridle, or sufficiently to make the colt come around without being pulled upon ; then step back, holding the cord rather tight, pass the right hand lightly down the hip and leg to the fetlock, and lift the foot gently ; at the same time, with the left hand, press hard against the hip, so as to throw the weight of the body upon the opposite leg, which will enable taking up the foot more easily. If sensitive, lift it but a few inches at first, and then let it rest again upon the ground ; then again slide the hand lightly down the limb, and lift a little higher than before, repeating until in a position to rest upon the knees with the gambrel under the arm. With the right

FIG. 256.—As the Horse will Stand after Treatment.

hand hammer the foot lightly, put it down and take it up a few times, then stop and caress.

This point made, bring the foot gently forward, in position as if to clinch down the nails. Should the colt at any time jerk or pull the foot away, let go and give a few sharp pulls with the cord, and go on as before until the foot can be taken up and hammered upon as desired. The opposite foot must be treated in the same way. To take up the fore foot, rest the left hand upon the shoulder, pass the right lightly down the limb to the fetlock, and at the instant of lifting the foot, as before explained, with the other hand press upon the shoulder to throw the weight upon the opposite leg, which will relax the near one, and make it easy to be taken up. Take up and let down a few times, tapping it lightly, and repeat until it can be pounded upon quite hard ; then bring forward upon the knees, and proceed the same as before. The foot should not be held at any time so long, or grasped so awkwardly, as to produce fatigue, or frighten so that it would excite inclination to pull away. By being careful at first but little difficulty will be experienced in making any ordinary colt submit the feet to be taken up and hammered upon as desired. Should the colt be so wild or vicious as to resist the War Bridle, subject to Second Method until so dizzy and helpless that he stops turning.

While the head is still tied around, as before, rest one hand upon the hip, pass the other quickly from the gambrel down to the fetlock, and lift the foot forward. If submitted to, but little more need

F<small>IG</small>. 257.—**Pulling the Foot Back while Controlled with the War Bridle.**

be done ; but if resisted, send around again until helpless, when the effort should be repeated. If submitted to, untie the halter and repeat the handling. Sometimes, after the head is given freedom and the dizziness passes off, the colt may, unexpectedly, kick violently. To avoid being struck, stand well forward, and far enough out from the hip to be out of range of the foot, and, as before, while balancing the body by resting the left hand upon the hip, with the right cautiously, but firmly, lift the foot forward. Should the colt kick now, the hand will simply be carried back with the foot without doing harm. When the foot is freely submitted, step forward so as to come well under the hip, bringing the foot upon the knees. If in this position he kicks, the foot will simply be thrown out and back from the knees, so that there will be no danger of accident. If the case is still unmanageable or doubtful, put on the double-draw hitch form of War Bridle. While an assistant is holding the cord (see Fig. 257), buckle a rein, or tie a cord around the foot below the fetlock. Get directly behind, out of reach, and pull the foot back. This will usually be responded to by a sharp kick, or the foot pulled forward with energy. If so, let the War Bridle be jerked upon once or twice as punishment. Repeat the pulling at short intervals until the foot will finally be given back freely,

FIG. 258.—The Colt as He will Stand after Treatment.

and rested upon the toe. Now step forward to a point a little back of the shoulder, with one hand take a short hold of the strap, at the same time resting the other upon the horse's back, and pull the foot forward repeatedly. Usually this will be submitted to; if so, catch the foot and bring it forward and back, to test its flexibility or submission to control. If, however, it is resisted, or the control is still doubtful, pass the strap over the neck, back between the fore legs, and up under the part over the back. Pull short enough to bring the leg well forward under the body, and tie into a half-hitch knot. This will bring the weight and pulling of the leg directly across the back and neck in a way that disables greatly.

Next touch or lightly slap the leg until it is submitted to freely, when more freedom should be given by giving loose a little. When freely given to the hand, untie, carry the leg back and forward to test it, when take in both hands and pound upon it, as before explained. After the foot is submitted unconditionally, keep on handling for some time, giving apples, etc. The opposite foot must, practically, be treated in the same manner, and according to the degree of resistance.

The blacksmith's shop is no place in which to handle colts. The fire and hammering add to the general excitement, and greatly increase the difficulty of making the horse submit the feet. In addition, it is not the blacksmith's duty to expose himself to be injured or hurt, or to lose

FIG. 259.—**Simplest Method of Making a Nervous Horse Stand to be Shod.**

time in trying to shoe a wild, unbroken colt. Such colts should always be handled at home until proved gentle, which, by following out the instructions given, will not be found a difficult task. I have often found horses that, in consequence of fear or abuse in a blacksmith's shop, could not be shod there. I will refer here to but one of many cases in point.

FIG. 260.—**Blindfolding a Nervous Horse to be Shod.**

During my early experience, while at a town in Southern Pennsylvania, a horse was brought forward for treatment that could not be shod, his particular cause of resistance being fear of the blacksmith's leather apron. When first taken to the shop for the purpose of being shod, the hammering and flying sparks greatly excited him, and as the smith came forward to take up his foot, the appearance of his leather apron became an object of intense fear. In a short time the colt became so violent that he would not allow any one with an apron to go near him.

The owner and smith concluded they had a sure thing in this case with which to beat me, and came twelve miles for the purpose, leading the horse. They said they would both join the class provided I would make the horse sufficiently gentle to allow a man with a leather apron on to go near enough to handle him. At the same time they told their friends secretly that I could do nothing with the horse, and that they came there for the express purpose of showing me up as a humbug. All felt so sure that the horse would beat me that a large number joined the class to see the fun, expecting of course they would get their money back. I subjected the

horse quickly to the Second Method and War Bridle, not requiring in all more than six or eight minutes, when he could be handled without the least difficulty, being perfectly regardless of the apron. I ordered the horse taken to the shop, and accustomed to the sparks and ham-

FIG. 261.—As the Cord may be Adjusted for Control of Simple Cases.

mering; to be treated kindly, giving apples, etc.; also to be shod a few times outside the shop, to make sure of his docility.

To show the simplicity of what may appear difficult, it is worthy of mention that at the same place, a party of three men — a father and two sons — were employed over three hours in trying to lead a six-year-old colt, pulling, pushing, and backing him by main force, to the place of exhibition, a distance of not over one fourth of a mile. The conditions were that I must make him follow me freely across the barn floor. A few sharp pulls with the War Bridle were sufficient to make the horse run after me, not requiring in all more than two minutes, proving so conclusively the ignorance and bad management of the parties that they were laughed at and ridiculed by the entire class. (See Fig. 155.)

Confirmed in the Habit.

As the main object in the management of most cases is to make them submit to be shod with the least trouble, I will first give the simplest treatment for doing so. Indeed, this simple treatment, with a little care, will often be sufficient for the control of even very bad cases.

Fig. 262.—Simple Method of Using the Cord for the Control of Horses Bad to Shoe, Harness, etc.

If the horse is very sensitive and excitable, but naturally gentle if given his own way, a great deal, of course, depends upon the good management of the shoer, but as much on the aid of the owner. Try the following course : When the smith is in position, and ready, his left hand resting on the horse's hip, let the owner, or some good, quiet man, catch the horse's ear with one hand, squeezing or twisting it a little ; with the other stroke the nose, or grasp the muzzle, and hold firmly but gently, at the same time talking to the horse kindly.

If there is resistance to this, try blindfolding. Tie a blanket, or something convenient, over the eyes, at the same time rubbing the nose, etc. With care on the part of the shoer, cases that have proved very difficult to shoe will submit at once to be shod as desired. If these expedients fail, put on the cord, the First, or Double-Draw Hitch Form, and make the horse feel its power by giving a few sharp pulls right and left. Then step back to the hips, pull the head around a little, keeping the cord taut, and take up the foot, punishing instantly for any resistance. Or, stand to the head, and keep the cord drawn rather

Fig. 263.—Method of Putting on the Cord when the Horse Proves Very Stubborn.

tight to hold the attention of the horse while an assistant takes up the foot. If the horse is very stubborn, bring the second turn of the cord over the upper jaw, under the lip. This part being very sensitive, a slight pressure hurts so severely as to disconcert the horse

sufficiently to make him submit. Or the cord, Second Form, can be put on, with the loop brought over the upper jaw, and pulled sufficiently taut to force submission. In either case, gradually let up as the horse submits. In no case should the cord be held tight more than half a minute at a time.

The four-ring bit properly used will sometimes work extremely well in making a horse submit to be shod. The bit is put into the mouth with an ordinary head-piece, and the strap closely ad-

Fig. 264.—Showing the Manner of Letting up on the Cord as the Horse Submits.

justed across the nose. Now tie the end of the cord to the near ring, pass it around and tie to the opposite one back of the jaw; then pass over the neck, well back and down behind the jaw, as for second form of War Bridle. Now, by pulling down upon the cord, the joint of the bit will be forced up against the roof of the mouth, which hurts so severely that the horse is at once disconcerted, or disabled sufficiently to permit the foot to be taken up. The amount of pressure or force of the pulling must be regulated according to the resistance. If there is submission in a short time, the lightest pressure will be sufficient to make the horse stand quietly to be shod. There is this to be said about this method of

Fig. 265.—Four-ring Bit. Method of Pulling down on the Cord.

treatment, as well as that of the War Bridle: If it works at all, it seems to work so well as to leave nothing to be desired. But if it fails, the failure will be equally marked. It is, however, but just to add that though in many cases failing, the power of the War Bridle or four-ring bit, when properly used, is sometimes wonderful, the horse at once submitting unconditionally.

Tying the head to the tail so as to keep the head bent around pretty well, will sometimes make a horse submit to be shod, but not often. This means, with that of putting the cord under the upper lip, which I copy below, has been of late so extensively published as an infallible means of making the most vicious horses stand to be shod, ridden, etc., that I think it necessary to give some explanation of them here :—

"MASTERING VICIOUS HORSES.

"Recently an exhibition was given at the corner of Ninth and Howard streets of a new and very simple method of taming vicious horses, which is claimed to be superior to any in use. The first trial was with a kicking and bucking mare, which, her owner says, has allowed no rider on her back for five years. She became tame and gentle in as many minutes, and allowed herself to be ridden about without a sign of her former wildness. The means by which this result was accomplished consisted of a piece of light rope, which was passed around the front jaw of the mare, just above the upper teeth, crossed in her mouth, and then secured back of her neck. It is claimed that no horse will kick or jump when thus secured, and that a bucking horse, after receiving this treatment a few times, will abandon his vicious ways forever. A very simple method was also shown by which a kicking horse can be shod. It consisted in connecting the animal's head and tail by means of a rope fastened to the tail and then to the bit, and drawn tightly enough to incline the horse's head to one side. It is claimed that it is absolutely impossible for a horse to kick on the side of the rope. At the same exhibition a horse which for many years had to be bound on the ground to be shod, suffered the blacksmith to operate on him without attempting to kick while secured in the manner described."

This is from the same piece as the Maine man's method of breaking a balking horse, referred to in "Balking." As I brought both these methods of treatment into use, and have had almost unlimited experience with them, I think I am able to determine their value with more ac-

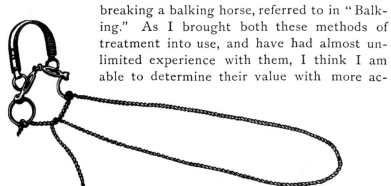

FIG. 266.—The Cord as Used with the Four-ring Bit.

curacy than it is possible for inexperienced persons to do. While they will secure the control of many, even quite bad cases, as explained, they cannot by any means be depended upon for the control of really difficult cases. They were used by me almost daily under circumstances like the following :—

After subjecting a horse to the Second Method, while still tied, the effort would frequently be made to take up the foot ; but it was rarely, unless thoroughly subdued, that the foot would be submitted. The same is true of the cord, or War Bridle. It was often a matter of considerable importance to be able to control some cases quickly, and I would, as an experiment, try the most simple and di-

Fig. 267.—Pulling the Foot back to Test the Horse's Submission.

rect methods of management. I have experimented in this way thousands of times before and after regular subjective treatment with the War Bridle, and cannot regard it as more than palliative, since it would, in a great many cases, prove entirely inefficient. Even with the Double-Draw Hitch, its most powerful and effective form, which until recently we kept a secret, and used only as a reserve, we could not depend upon it. Twenty-five years ago the War Bridle was my principal resource for controlling colts and bucking horses to ride. But it is entirely inferior to the Second Method for the control of bad cases. Simply tying the head to the tail, and sending the horse around until dizzy, then mounting from the outside, so as not to get entangled by the strap, the horse will be found so helpless that he cannot buck ; should he attempt it, he would simply be carried around the more rapidly until submissive.

The matter of breaking bucking colts and horses was a common, and, sometimes, a very formidable difficulty to meet. One of the worst cases I ever came across was a ten-year-old mule in Central Mississippi. It was proved absolutely impossible, even by the restraint of any kind of rigging, to mount or keep upon this brute's back. In fact, the case was so bad, and the people felt so sure that I could not ride her, that they made up a large class for me, knowing they would get their money back if I failed to do so. I simply subjected her to the Second Method sharply, and in less than fifteen minutes rode her as I pleased. This would have been impossible by the palliative means referred to. She was a good representative of the mustang nature. This is the only method of treatment by which

Fig. 268.—As the Foot will be Rested upon the Ground after Submitting.

a strong, determined bucker can be safely and easily mastered.

It was frequently the case that we would have for our main subject a horse that was particularly bad in shoeing. As a test of success, it would be often required that the horse be shod in a blacksmith's shop. Now after being subjected to regular treatment, there would usually be but little trouble in taking up and hammering upon the feet as much as desired at the place of treatment; while we would sometimes have all we could do, even by the most severe use of the War Bridle, to handle such in the shop.

Treatment for Very Vicious Cases.

Very much depends upon the disposition of the horse and the treatment pursued. In most cases the following will be found easy and effectual: Subject to the Third Method, using more or less pressure, according to the case. While the cord is on, attach a strap or rein to the hind foot, and pull back as previously explained. At first there will usually be great resistance, the horse kicking with great spitefulness, or pulling the foot forward energetically. But however much he may resist at first, it must not be accepted as a cause for discouragement. Simply keep pulling the foot back at short intervals until there is no resistance. When given freedom, it will be rested upon the toe, then pull forward and back as before explained. In some cases it may be necessary to tie forward by bringing the strap over the neck, back between the legs, and making fast to hold the foot firmly until all resistance is overcome. Treat the opposite foot in the same manner.

This was the treatment pursued by us with the most success in the management of the worst cases. A good deal of course will depend upon the use of tact and good management, as before explained. A coarse-grained, passionate man can very soon undo a great deal of good work. In the management of these critical cases a great point is made by having a good, quiet man to stand at the head and stroke the nose, and it is needless to state that the smith should be a man of considerable patience ; but when the case is serious it should never be shod in the shop. All this should be done where free from the excitement and annoyance of such a place. This is a point I would particularly impress upon the reader — to attend to accomplishing your end well at home, then take such precaution as you can without exciting or annoying the horse much when it becomes necessary to shoe him at the shop.

To give an idea of the power of this treatment when properly applied, I will refer to its effects upon a few special cases.

At Bellows Falls, Vt., a paper-maker owned a fine horse, which, though otherwise very gentle, was extremely hard to shoe. A traveling horseman of much experience and a great deal of pretension, visited the place and made a small class. The owner, wishing to have his horse broken, brought him in to be experimented upon. According to the gentleman's statement to me, this man worked with the horse about half a day, injuring him very severely,— in the owner's language, " almost killed him." The result of it all was that the horse beat the man completely, and was more reckless and determined in his opposition than before. I requested the gentleman to let me see the horse. Finding him to be naturally of a good disposition, and that his resistance proceeded mainly from excitement, I told the owner we would have no difficulty at all with the horse, and succeeded in making him perfectly gentle in about fifteen minutes.

The day following, at the next point we found an eight-year-old mare, considered impossible to shoe. The temperament being suitable, we subjected her to Second Method and War Bridle, which made her entirely submissive in about ten minutes. The next day, at Putney, Vt., the kicking, runaway horse was presented. Reference is made to these consecutive cases to show the frequency with which exceptionally vicious horses were brought for experiment and the success in their treatment.

In the management of many cases, either or both the First and Second Methods may be used with advantage in connection with the Third Method, but it should always be done at home, where there is time and privacy to apply and carry out the treatment properly.

LEANING OVER.

There are occasionally horses that will allow the foot to be taken up, but will lie down or lean over upon the blacksmith while it is held. Usually a few pulls with the War Bridle, repeating them for each occurrence of lying over, until he learns to stand without leaning, will be sufficient. If this is resisted, subject to Second Method. While the head is tied around, take up the foot and test until he will stand squarely. If there is any inclination to lean over after the head is given freedom, disconcerting a little with the cord should be sufficient. Sometimes it is advisable to stand at the head ready to punish, while an assistant takes up and holds the foot as if to shoe. Though a horse may for some time be sullen and persistent in leaning over, it is not usually a difficult habit to overcome. Once compelled to stand, it is seldom necessary to repeat the lesson.

It should have been stated in the proper place that there must be no effort to push against the quarters; but the moment there is an effort to lean over, the foot should be instantly dropped, and the punishment with the War Bridle made somewhat severe, and this repeated until there is submission.

Chapter IX.

HALTER-PULLING.

HALTER-PULLING is one of the simple habits that not only cause great annoyance, but seriously injure the value of a horse, by making him unsafe to be left hitched in the street. A horse subject to this habit may stand all right when not excited, but will be ready to break his neck in the attempt to pull loose should a bit of paper, or anything else, be suddenly thrown down in front of him. There was no habit that troubled me more to learn how to manage than this one. It was easy enough, with a little

FIG. 269.—As the Colt will Naturally Resist when Pulled upon Straight Ahead.

care, to keep a horse from pulling for a short time, but the difficulty was, in bad cases, to break up the habit.

When there is an effort at first to lead a colt by the halter, the moment the pressure is felt upon the head there will be an inclination to resist or pull back. If the halter is a rough, hard, rope one, with the slipping-noose back of the jaw, when pulled upon the pain inflicted will increase this tendency to resist and pull away (Fig. 269). In the same manner, when a colt is tied and his freedom restrained, there is a natural inclination to resist and pull back; and if after a violent struggle the halter is broken, the habit of pulling will be learned. Usually, the younger the colt the more stubborn will be the inclination to pull, and often he will struggle so desperately as to throw himself down. Not only this, but there is danger

(222)

of straining and injuring the neck by the violence of the jerking and pulling. I have known of colts pulling so hard as to make the neck stiff, deforming and spoiling them ; and in a few cases even killing themselves by dislocating the neck. Yet there was practically no better remedy in use than to hitch by a halter so strong that he could not break it. The point was to be able to so hitch the colt as to induce the least inclination to pull, and that when he did pull he could not break away, strain, or otherwise injure himself.

The first successful experiment I made in the management of this habit was to pass the hitching part of the halter through the ring in the manger, thence back over the belly-band, and tie to the hind foot, leaving it so long that the horse could step around as usual. When the horse pulled, the strain came directly upon the hind leg, which prevented his pulling se-

Fig. 270.—As the Colt is Liable to Break Loose when Hitched in the Usual Manner.

verely. After submitting to this, I next tied the hitching part around the fore leg above the knee, so that should he pull, the leg would be pulled forward to the manger. But I soon discovered two objections to this method : First, there was danger, by this violent pulling upon the leg, of causing serious lameness ; and second, when afterward hitched directly by the head, there was a liability of his repeating the pulling.

To avoid this, I took a cord of sufficient length, brought the center under the tail like a crupper, bringing both ends forward over the back, twisting a few times, and then knotted them together in front of the breast. I then passed the ends through the rings of the halter, and tied to the post or manger. When the horse pulled, the strain came directly upon the tail, which, in the case of a colt, would cause him to jump ahead, surprised and frightened. I soon learned, however, that a stubborn horse accustomed to the habit, would quickly learn to pull against it, or pull as bad as ever when it was taken off. I also found that it was apt to make the tail so sore that there was not only liability to cause the horse to kick when pulled upon, but afterward, should the rein be caught under the tail, or he be otherwise irritated.

I then devised the plan of making a noose of the cord, and placing it well back around the body, bringing both cords forward between the legs, and through the hole in the manger, thence back to the halter, and fasten. Thus two important improvements were made ; namely, the serious objection of making the tail sore was removed ; and, instead of tying directly to the post or manger, passing it through the ring or hole in the manger, and tying to the halter back of the jaw, the restraint was brought directly upon the head as if ordinarily hitched, but with the advantage of greatly disabling and punishing, while the horse could not strain or injure himself in the least, no matter how hard he pulled.

If the subject were a colt, the moment there was an effort to pull, the sudden tightening of the cord around the body frightened and hurt him so much that it compelled an instantaneous jumping ahead, and after repeating two or three times, all inclination to pull was entirely overcome. It was necessary to hitch him in this way only a few times, when he could be tied by the halter directly, without knowing it was possible to pull. If while hitched in this manner he was frightened by a robe, or a piece of paper coming suddenly in front of him, he was soon convinced of his inability to pull loose. and consequently the inclination to do so was broken up.

For especially bad, sullen pullers, however, I found this was not of itself sufficient to break up the habit. It was easy, of course, to prevent the horse from pulling while the rig was on, but when taken off, and the horse tied as usual by the halter, there was liability of his again repeating the pulling. To overcome this difficulty, I was led to the expedient, when there was an effort to pull, of inflicting such intense pain as to disconcert the horse from his purpose, even while under the greatest excitement, and on this point I was successful. To give something of an idea how I was led to do this, I will refer to a chance incident :—

Two colts that pulled very hard upon the halter — one of them desperately — were brought me to experiment upon. The one that pulled the worst provoked me so much by his intense pulling, that to frighten him out of it I whipped him very hard upon the tip of his nose, where there is the most sensibility. Though he made a supreme struggle, I soon succeeded in this way in making him so afraid to pull that, no matter how excited afterward, he could not be made to go back. The other horse submitted in a few minutes, requiring but a slight punishment. Meeting the owner afterward, he informed me that the horse that pulled the hardest at first never did it afterward, while he had considerable trouble in breaking the other one of the habit.

This led me to experiment upon this principle all I could. When I found a bad case, I treated it, if possible, in private, and was invariably so successful that I soon became convinced that I could in this way force the most stubborn pullers into submission in

Fig. 271.—As a Horse of Sullen Temper is Liable to Throw himself down when Pulling.

a few minutes. In making these experiments, I found that in many cases the lesson must be repeated, in order to fully break up the the habit, and that it was fatal to success to let the horse feel that he could resist at any point. Nothing with which the horse is tied should give way. Even the breaking of the whip, or the inability to force to the point of complete submission, would be equivalent to defeat. In all cases the experiment should be made at the place where in the habit of resisting, or as near it as possible.

The Patent Bridle will be found to give still more power, and is indispensable in the breaking of bridle-pullers. In using this, reverse the reins through the pulley, so that instead of passing back, they will run forward. (See Fig. 273.) Now, the moment the horse pulls, the punishment upon the head becomes so severe that he will be afraid to repeat it.

Having learned these points, I advertised, among other apparently difficult feats, to make any halter-puller in two minutes so that he could not be made to pull upon his own halter when hitched. Many amusing incidents could be given, showing an effort to break me down in this respect. I will give here two illustrative cases, one of them among the worst halter-pullers the writer ever saw :—

On the morning of my engagement at a large town in Northern New York, happening to step into a livery-stable, I found several men standing around, laughing and yelling at a mare hitched in the stall. She had a rope under her tail, against which she pulled with great desperation, sitting back upon the ground and bracing herself with her fore legs. There was no lunging, but a steady, reckless

Fig. 272.—The Halter-puller Trying to Pull Loose.

pull, which settled the cord its thickness into the flesh of her tail. In explanation, they said they were stirring up and practicing the mare to have a good subject for me ; that they knew she was the premium halter-puller of that country, and they proposed to fix her so that she would beat me.

She was ten years old, of medium size, brownish-black in color, of the most courageous, plucky character imaginable, and one of the worst possible halter-pullers in the country. She would undoubtedly have defeated me had I not, in this way, become aware of her extremely bad character, and prepared for the emergency. It was a preconcerted plan to spring the mare upon me, and defeat me, and thus make an excuse to get their money back. Though I had never seen so bad a halter-puller before, I determined to put a bold front on the matter, and pass for all I was worth.

In forming a class, I told the people they were to distinctly understand if I could not control the mare in two minutes so that she could not be made to pull when hitched by her own halter, I would give every man his money back ; with this understanding I made a large class.

It now became important for them to defeat me, and for me, if possible, to succeed. Fearing my whip would break, I secured an extra one, of the best quality I could find, stripped off my coat and vest, attended carefully to every detail of hitching, and doubled the usual strength of the cord, to guard against the possibility of breaking. The moment the mare was tied, she went back with all the fury of a maniac. But she had no more than done so when I sent the lash of the whip across the tip of her nose, repeating as rapidly and with as much force as I could. The struggle was a desperate one, and the excitement and anxiety to see which would beat was intense. At the fourteenth or fifteenth blow, the whip broke ; dropping it and catching the other, without losing a blow, I followed up the str uggle Had this whip broken, failure would have been inevitable ; but fortu- nately it held out, and at about the thirtieth blow she jumped ahead. But true to the instincts of her desperate pluck, she immediately went back again. The punishment, however, was too hot for her, and after the third stroke she bounded into the air, completely con- quered ; for, in defiance of the utmost effort, she could not be made to pull back. I was consequently voted " All right." So great was the exertion on my part, that after she submitted I was out of breath and completely exhausted.

I told the owner afterward that if he wished to break the mare successfully, he must not permit any fooling with her ; he must lead her quietly to the stable, back her into the stall, tie her head to the post, and let her stand until cool and over the excitement, when the impression would be so intensified that she would not repeat the habit ; and as a matter of precaution to test her as thoroughly as he could, then hitch her as I had done. I met the owner a week afterward, when he told me there were not men enough in the town t o make her pull hard enough now to break a tow string.

At Marion, N. Y., where I made a large class many years be- fore, I found a twenty-four-year-old mare that had not been hitched for ten years ; also a daughter and grand-daughter of the mare,— all confirmed halter-pullers. To catch me, nothing was said about the character of the subjects until the time of making the exper- iments. The youngest mare was led in first, and proved a decidedly good subject, yielding unconditionally in about a minute. They next led in the mother, a twelve-year-old mare, saying, " We have another case we wish tried." But, upon trial, she yielded, if any- thing, more readily than the first. They laughed, and said, " Now let us have the old mare ; if he can stop her from pulling we will give it up." This revealed the plot, and she was the reserved case upon which they depended to defeat me. Upon trial, however, the old mare proved no more difficult than the others,— in fact, not making near so good a contest as the first. Almost daily there were horses of this character brought me, many of them extremely bad ; but in no case was there failure. (Details of hitching a colt, and accustoming to stand hitched, are fully given in "Colt-Training," and can be referred to under that head.)

In breaking up this habit, no possible chances of failure should be taken. First, the cord must be so light and pliable as not to be noticeably felt around the body, yet so strong that it cannot be

Fig. 273.—**As a Horse will Rear and Jump Ahead after Pulling.**

broken by the most desperate lunging. If heavy and clumsy, it would teach to discriminate between being off or on. Second, the manger, post, or ring through which the cord plays, should be so strong or solid that there will be no danger of giving way. If it is a hitching-ring, and small or rough, it should be wound with leather or something to prevent its cutting the cord. Third, the horse should be first tied where in the habit of pulling hardest, or where most accustomed to pull. The degree of freedom should be about the same as when ordinarily hitched by the halter, and the point of tying or playing through the ring should be about on a level with the breast. As before explained, in ordinary cases all that will be necessary will be to hitch in this way, and frighten him back a little at first by whatever excites him, until he refuses to go back, when all inclination to pull will be overcome. While in serious cases, especially if of a plucky, determined character, punishing sharply with a whip will be necessary.

It is important also that the whip be of the right length and best quality, as in many cases the want of this precaution would be sufficient to cause defeat. It should be from five to six feet long, rather stiff, with a bow top made of buckskin, and a good hard lash. It must be of such good material that there will be no danger of its breaking, and so easily handled that the end of the nose can be struck with quickness and precision. If long and unwieldy, it cannot be handled with the effectiveness necessary, as there is danger of hitting around the eyes and head, which must not be done.

Another point: The horse must not at first be hitched where he cannot, if necessary, be punished with the whip; when he goes back, punish instantly. When he jumps forward, make a noise, crack the whip, or anything else, but do not strike him. It is advisable to let him stand quietly where treated until cool. He may, when left alone, try to pull again once or twice, but this will only fix the impression the stronger until he will give

Fig. 274.—A Test to which the Halter-puller was usually Submitted by the Class after Treatment.

up the contest. Next, he should be tested at other points, though not very severely. If he pulls, the punishment should be quick and sharp until submissive. It does no good to break a horse only sufficiently to make him stand quietly when not excited or frightened. To be effective, he must be made to stand quietly, regardless of any of the usual causes of excitement. Unless this can be done, the horse should not be risked hitched in the street, or at any place where exposed to causes of fear. Hitching to a limb of a tree, which will give when pulled upon, will prevent the habit during the time hitched, but when tied to an unyielding post or manger, he is again liable to pull.

Running Back in the Stall when Unhitched.

For ordinary cases of running back in the stall when unhitched, tie a little longer than for halter-pulling ; then untie the halter, and

the horse will run back to the point of being disabled and hurt. This will cause him to jump ahead. Repeat, at each time tying a little longer, until the nose will come on a line with the back end of a stall, when he should be hit sharply across the nose until he jumps ahead. This will in a short time make him afraid to run back. As a precaution, it is advisable, the next time he is unhitched, to have a cord on, so that should he try to

FIG. 275.—First Method of Making a Horse Stand in Harness without Hitching.

run back he could be caught by the cord attachment and punished as before.

Whenever I had a particularly bad case of this kind, I hitched the horse as before explained, but with the cord or rope so long that when he went back it let the nose come just outside the stall. I would then stand outside, while some one unhitched him, or made him go back. The moment he went the length of the cord, he was

stopped with a jerk, when I stood ready to punish him by hitting him across the tip of the nose once or twice, causing him to jump ahead. A few repetitions of this would make him so afraid he could not be made to go back. I have at different times created considerable amusement in the management of these cases,

FIG. 276.—Second Method of Making a Horse Stand without being Hitched.

FIG. 277.—How to Hitch a Horse to a Tree or Smooth Post so that the Strap or Cord will not Untie or Slip Down.

by making it impossible for the owner, after the experiment, to back the horse out of the stall. Treated in this way, the management of these cases is easy and simple.

STANDING WITHOUT BEING HITCHED.

It is sometimes quite important to have a horse stand without being hitched, as there may be no hitching-post at hand. This can be done in two ways: First, by buckling one end of a strap around the foot below the fetlock, and the other end to the cross-piece of the shafts, just short enough to hold the foot in a perpendicular po-

FIG. 278.—Taking up the Colt's Foot while Tied—One of the Tests in Determining his Submission.

sition. When the horse tries to step, being unable to carry the foot forward, he is rendered helpless. It is always advisable to try a horse before leaving him in this way, as it is barely possible he may lunge forward upon three legs if badly frightened ; but only wild, impulsive fellows are liable to do this. Another way is to simply tie the fore legs together, as seen in the cut. This method is specially valuable in making saddle-horses stand without being hitched.

It is also important to be able to hitch a horse to a tree or smooth post in such a manner as to prevent the cord from slipping down. I give an illustration of a method for doing this, which is so plain that it does not need any further description.

CHAPTER X.

STALLIONS.

THERE is no class of horses that require more careful management than stallions. They have more intelligence than other horses, and are quicker to take advantage when carelessness or weakness is shown. They are also more courageous in their resistance. In addition, the character of their resistance — biting and striking — is far more difficult to combat. Mistakes can be made in breaking mares and geldings without doing much more harm than to increase the labor of their subjection ; but in subduing a stallion, a mistake, or even slight carelessness, is in many cases fatal to success. The whip should never be used upon a horse of this character ; for there is great danger, if at all spirited or courageous, of his becoming in consequence aggressive and vicious.

FIG. 279.—Portrait from Life of Old Hambletonian, Sire of the Hambletonian Trotters.

A young horse that is very gentle, allowing himself to be handled and caressed around the head, etc., can, by bad treatment, easily be made so vicious that his whole character is changed. A great many cases of this kind have come under my observation. At one time, a gentleman who had previously attended' one of my lectures, told me that he and his brother owned a fine stallion in company. The horse was naturally quite gentle, but one day his brother, becoming impatient with him, hit him sharply with the whip ; the result was the horse ever afterward held such an antipathy against him that he could not safely go near or handle him in any way, while toward himself the horse was perfectly gentle.

The " Gifford-Morgan Horse," sold to Fred Arnd, of Bath, N. Y., and mentioned in the last part of this chapter, is a striking case in point. Had I not been in Bath at the time, and able to treat him properly, he would have been entirely unmanageable and worthless.

FIG. 280.—As Vicious, Headstrong Stallions Usually Resisted before Treatment.

During my early experience, when in Utica, N. Y., as a test I was required to experiment upon a horse owned by Mr. Roberts, a prominent citizen. This horse had been perfectly gentle and used by the family for driving. Mr. Roberts, employed a groom **to** take care of the horse, who, to show him up and play smart, was in the habit of whipping him. The owner discovering this, the man was discharged. Mr. Roberts afterward, while trying to

handle the horse, was suddenly pitched at by him and seriously injured, and would have been killed had not two men who were near by clubbed him off with a rail. Six months after the accident he had not recovered sufficiently to leave his room, the horse in the meantime running loose in a large stall, and so vicious that no one could go near him. This case was a good subject, and submitted to treatment readily in about twenty minutes, being driven and handled with as much success as before. This case is referred to as No. 13 in "Subjection," in my book on

Fig. 281.—**The Roberts Horse.**

the horse.

I could refer to a great many interesting cases where the character had been spoiled by rough, bad treatment, and I found no horses more susceptible to treatment than they, being almost the best subjects to experiment upon before classes. I have in my mind a particularly good one, treated in Herman, N. Y. This was a finely bred seven-year-old horse, taken from Canada, where it was reported he had killed a man ; at any rate, he had not been taken out of his stall for seven months, and was supposed to be entirely unbroken to harness. The only clew I could get to his disposition was that he was well-bred, and I was confident that he would be a good subject when once able to get him before the class. So confident was I of this, that I promised not only to make him entirely gentle, but to drive him in harness without breeching in forty minutes, and failing to do so would return the money. This case not only submitted readily to treatment within that time, but was tested several weeks after and proved entirely gentle. He was led behind a buggy to a point twelve miles distant, and hitched up by me and driven in the street without breeching. Of course, it was insisted that the horse should be treated with great kindness, and he certainly behaved as gentle as any family horse.

I refer to these cases to show to owners the necessity of employing good, careful men to take charge of their horses. A coarse-grained, passionate man should not be employed at any price. Habits of intemperance should in all cases be sufficient to disqualify a man for such work.

There is no class of horses that submit more readily to treatment when taken in time, but they are the hardest to reform when the treatment is not right, or when, by the inefficiency of the owner or groom, they are afterward allowed successful resistance. On this

Fig. 282.—**Vicious Stallion in a Rage.**

account I have thought it advisable to refer specially to the management of these cases here.

Treatment for Headstrong Stallions.

If a colt is simply unbroken and impulsive — perhaps nipping a little — he can be easily made gentle by subjecting him lightly to the Second Method and following it with the War Bridle. Sometimes a horse of this character is perfectly manageable until led near other horses, when he will try to pull away. I will refer to two or three such cases: While at Pennington, N. J., a horse that pulled away so badly he could not be taken into the streets at all if other horses were in sight, was reported for treatment. He was subjected lightly to the Second Method, and then brought under thorough control by the War Bridle, when he was led home as manageable as any horse.

Well-bred, nervous-tempered horses of this character will always prove easy subjects to manage ; while those of a sullen, cold-blooded, or draft order may be found quite difficult, and require

Fig. 283.—As the Headstrong, Vicious Stallion, after Treatment, could be Called Away from a Mare or Horse. Tests of Control Given by the Writer before the Class upon Horses of this Character.

very careful treatment. It is seen that for these simple cases a short lesson with the most severe form of the War Bridle should be all that is necessary. Stand opposite the shoulder, four or five feet away, and give a sharp pull, repeating slowly until he will come around promptly. This lesson must be made sufficiently thorough to overcome all inclination to resist, no matter how tried or excited. Five or ten minutes' treatment, when properly done, should be sufficient to break up the habit.

Treatment for Very Vicious Stallions.

Vicious stallions require very careful management. In determining the treatment, a great deal depends upon the temperament of the horse, and how greatly his resentment has been excited. A horse that seems the worst is not always the hardest to break ; in fact, if he has never been fooled with much, he may be, in many instances, the very easiest to manage ; and when once subdued by the methods of subjection given here, it will not be difficult to hold the character good by careful after-treatment.

Fig. 284.—**Method of Placing the Hand, and Bringing it Quickly to the Head, in Approaching a Vicious Stallion.**

If a stallion of moderately good disposition be partially broken or subdued, and that for a number of times, it may be very difficult to afterward make him reliably gentle. Or when once thoroughly subdued, if he is whipped or managed in such a way as to again excite him to resist, it would require the most thorough course of treatment to produce the same degree of docility as before ; for by such successful resistance the horse is taught a degree of cunning and treachery that it is next to impossible to break up. On this account it is of

FIG. 285.—**The Stallion "Jet."**

the greatest importance that the treatment of these cases, when once undertaken, should be very careful and thorough.

For a really dangerous horse whose head cannot be reached with safety, the best course is to subject him first to the Second Method, which will give sufficient foundation to use the other methods with more success. Subject him next to the First Method, throwing rapidly as long as he will get up, or until he will not try to resist. It is rarely this will not make the horse, in a general way, submissive; but as it is necessary to make the impression as intense as possible upon these doubtful cases, this treatment should be followed with

FIG. 286.—**" Jet" as Led into Portland before being Subdued.**

the Third Method, and in some cases it may be advisable to repeat again with the Second, after which the War Bridle should be used.

It is almost needless to state that there should be the most careful attention, while going around the horse, to keep such a restraint upon him as will prevent his biting. A very little carelessness, such as taking the eye off from his, turning the back to him, or relaxing restraint upon the head, would encourage aggression, and practically undo all that had been done. It is easy enough to subject the horse to the various methods of treatment given, but it is not so easy to exercise that prudent after-watchfulness which is an indispensable requisite in fixing and holding the impression made.

Fig. 287.—"Jet" as Led Home after Treatment.

In going into the stall, the trainer should give the horse an apple or two, or something he likes, to win his better nature. It is also important that the horse be worked or driven enough to keep him a little sore or tired.

Above any other class of horses, stallions seem the best able to determine the strength of character of a man from his actions ; and in approaching them in the stall it is almost fatal to success to show any timidity or weakness in voice or manner ; whatever the feeling of doubt, nothing but the most perfect confidence and firmness must be shown. Fencers always look each other in the eye to see an indication of the intended movement, and to be ready to ward off the attack. In the same manner are the intentions and movements of the horse in a great measure revealed.   In approaching a

Fig. 288.—The Fred Arnd Horse as Led out of the Stable to be Subdued.

vicious horse in the stall, a fixed, determined expression of the eye
and manner will sometimes so disconcert him that he will stand un-
3

decided what to do until approached and made helpless.   The usual course to pursue is about as follows : When within reach of the horse, look him firmly in the eye, and say, " Get around ! " or any other word of command, in a way to make him feel your power.   If his eye quails, approach ; if not, stand still.   It may be a duel of a few minutes to determine which will give up.   Should he yield, approach softly, midway between his head and quarters, so as to keep him, as it were, undecided and unbalanced.   If standing too near his quarters, he is liable to kick ; if too near his head, to strike or bite. The point is to keep him undecided until the shoulder is reached ;

Fig. 289.—The Fred Arnd Horse as Seen by the Writer Four Years
after being Subdued.

then pass the hand quickly up the neck to the ear, thence down, grasping the nose-piece of the halter.   He is at such a disadvantage now that unless very violent he cannot do harm.   Should he, however, attempt to strike or bite, grab the mane at the shoulder with the other hand, and so keep the head turned straight from you.   But should he prove too much, the only alternative is to get out of the way.   Presuming, however, that he is under good control, the point now is to disable him.   Have a cord ready, throw the doubled part over the neck and pass over the lower jaw ; bring the other part down through the loop tight, and tie into a single hitch.   Now put on another cord, and if necessary tie up one leg to prevent kicking, get him out of the stall and subject him to treatment, modifying it according to the case.

Should the horse show a cool, daring expression of eye, with ears thrown back, and standing sullenly, and seemingly indifferent, no chances should be taken. Such a horse will wait until within reach, when he will kick, strike, or bite so quickly that no firmness or quickness of action would save a man. In such a case resort to any means most convenient and safe that will give sufficient control to enable subjecting him to the regular treatment. If no halter or bridle is on, the following course may be adopted : Put on a halter as described in "Colt-Training," tie up the head, put on a bridle, or one or two War Bridles, get him out on a sodded place, and subject him to treatment. Of course, if the stall or room is large enough, he can be subjected to treatment there.

The point of making the horse sufficiently gentle to be handled and used while free from rigging or restraint of any kind, must be thoroughly established as a foundation upon which this after-treatment must be based. Unless this can be done, the horse cannot practically be made safe. In my experience with these cases I make the lesson, if I can, a quick, overpowering rush of force, which breaks up all resistance, and makes him submit before he warms up, being careful not to strain, bruise, or overheat the horse.

Sometimes stallions, especially of this character, are liable to develop very peculiar whims in the way of affection or hatred. I will give here a very marked case, formerly owned by me. A ten-year-old Gifford-Morgan stallion, owned in Bath, Steuben Co., N. Y., was of a fine, intelligent, docile disposition naturally, but when excited he showed an undercurrent of great will and courage. He was raised in Gowanda, N. Y. I bought him for the purpose of training him to drive without reins, and succeeded in making him drive very nicely, holding him gentle. For a stallion, he was singularly free from all inclination to bite, and other habits of viciousness. Later, I sold this horse, with another, for breeding purposes, to Fred Arnd, a hotel-keeper, in Bath, N. Y. Mr. Arnd (who was somewhat intemperate in his habits) one day perceiving the horse acted as though about to bite, whipped him severely. Happening in the stable at the time, I found Arnd in the horse's stall, and greatly excited from the exertion of whipping and kicking. I told him emphatically that he must not whip and abuse the horse in that way. If he did, he would surely in a short time make him so vicious he could do nothing with him. I advised him at once to give the horse some apples, and handle and caress him until over the excitement. But he disregarded the advice, and about a week afterward I again heard a row in this stall. Proceeding to the place, I found Arnd with hat off and face red with passion, in the act of whipping and kicking the horse. I again told him in the most positive terms that he could not whip and abuse the horse in that manner without spoiling him, and that he must on no condition repeat it. As before, I urged him to treat the horse kindly, give apples, etc. ; but, as before, my advice was disregarded, and as the result, in less than a week afterward he came to me and said, " That horse is so vicious no one can go near him. I am afraid he is completely spoiled. If you can and will break him for me, I will do anything you require."

I found the horse perfectly furious, with eyes like balls of fire, and ready to jump at any one who might approach. He did not seem to have the least recollection of me, and it was with the greatest difficulty I was able to get him out of the stall, and across the street into my tent. I subjected him first to Second Method, following with First, which he resisted furiously. I threw him fully a dozen times before he gave up the contest, when he quieted down, and seemed to fully recognize me. I talked to him and caressed him now for some time, walking around with him, when he would follow me around perfectly gentle. I now directed

FIG. 290.—Vicious Stallion in the Act of Biting.

him to be placed in the care of a quiet, careful man, and instructed him to make it his business to visit the horse frequently in his stall, give an apple or two each time, caress and talk to him, and on no account to allow Arnd to go near or in his sight until I advised it. The treatment was continued two weeks, the horse acting just as gentle as before. Now while standing at his head I directed Arnd to come inside the door of his stall. The horse knew him instantly and became greatly excited, but I managed, however, to keep him quiet while Arnd was near him.

I soon afterward left the place, but at the expiration of about four years I again visited that part of the State professionally. At Merchantsville, in the same county, I was surprised to find this horse. I was informed that at the moment Arnd would come near, the horse would become furiously excited, and seem ready to jump at him, but was perfectly gentle toward others. Convinced that he could not manage him, he sold him to his present owner, a resident of Merchantsville, who used him for breeding purposes and for a family driver.

Fig. 291.—**Godolphin Arabian. From Stubb's Picture. By J. C. Beard.**

The man told me his wife could hitch up the horse and drive him as well as any old family horse, and he could take him out in the street by the halter and play with him with all the freedom he could with any pet horse. "But," added he, "were he to see a bald-headed man it would make him so furious he would kill him if he could get at him." Mr. Arnd was bald-headed, and the horse retained his peculiar repugnance to such an appearance. I took him into the streets by the halter, and found he was just as obedient to the whip as when I owned him, over four years before.

Young horses of this character, no matter how apparently vicious or unmanageable, were the best subjects to handle before

Fig. 292.—**Godolphin Arabian, the Noted Sire of the English Thoroughbred. From Stubb's Painting.**

classes, and I always preferred them when I could get them, as they were so quick to respond to treatment. Indeed, many of the most noted cases referred to in my regular work were stallions. There is a point, however, to which I desire to call special attention in relation to treatment of these horses.   If the horse is well-bred, or of a warm-blooded character, not fooled with very much, no matter how vicious he may appear, his treatment should be simple and easy, but the vital condition of success will be in making the after-treatment good.   There must be no fooling or carelessness.   It will be particularly dangerous to whip or scold very much.   The point is to watch the case carefully, repress without punishment if possible, and win the good nature.   It requires a cool, well-balanced man, in a word, to manage these cases with success ; but if the horse is cold-blooded, of a sullen type, and especially if of the draft order, and has become thoroughly vicious, while there may be no difficulty in making such a case submissive for a time, he will be almost sure to break over, and in most cases will be liable to become as bad as before.   I have reference to cases now that have been fooled with, and have become thoroughly fixed in vicious habits.

An Act of the Mustang Pony Refered to with Illustration on Page 30,
And in " Facts for Horse Owners," Page 443, where Full
Particulars are Given.

CHAPTER XI.

CHECKING AND BLINDERS.

CRUELTY OF CHECKING.

IN sitting, walking, or standing, every person knows how tiresome it is to maintain one position very long, and that a frequent change of position is equivalent to resting. It would be compara-

FIG. 293.—**Horse in Nature.**

tively easy to move the hand up or down, which could be done almost indefinitely without much inconvenience; but to hold it in one position perpendicularly or horizontally, would soon become extremely tiresome and difficult; in fact, so much so that it would be impossible to hold it out horizontally longer than a few minutes. A French subordinate officer, as a punishment, marched his soldiers all day without allowing them the regulation freedom of changing the position of their arms, which so injured them that it was regarded sufficient cause for inflicting upon him the penalty of death.

Now, checking horses and forcing them to hold their heads unnaturally high and keeping them thus arbitrarily in a fixed position, as I notice to be generally practiced, frequently all day, while perhaps being rapidly driven or worked hard, must

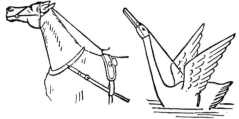

FIG. 294.—**The Horse with Over-check.**

be almost equally trying and painful for them to bear, and in connection with the use of blinders is so much of a fault that it cannot but be regarded as the greatest ingratitude and crime to so faithful and useful a servant.

(246)

This custom of using arbitrary checks upon horses for giving fictitious style to them in driving, at the expense of a great deal of comfort, freedom, and vital force, is of the same foolish character with various senseless customs of both civilized and savage nations, such as the cramping of the feet of Chinese women, or the wearing

FIG. 295.—Let the Drivers Try It.

FIG. 296.—A Gentle Family Horse; Showing the Discomfort and Pain of High Checking.

of the finger-nails to such a length as to interfere with the freedom of the hands, flattening the heads of Indian children, and the tattooing of the body by African and other tribes. The custom of checking, in the hands of ignorant people especially, has become so very common as to demand the most serious effort to prevent it.

CROPPING AND DOCKING.

In accordance with these ridiculous notions, introduced, perhaps, by some titled fool, it was the custom in England, about forty years ago, to crop horses' ears and manes, illustrations of which are given from an old English work, showing the method of doing it. Thirty years ago, in this country, this was carried to such an extreme by many, that it became the point of ambition of the professional dealer to have a horse with the shortest and most elevated tail, with a short tuft of hair hanging to it. To show that this is true, I give an illustration of such, copied from the English work before named.

FIG. 297.—The Family Horse Trying to Relieve himself from the Restraint of the Check.

FIG. 298.—One Position of Head of the Horse Referred to in Text.

HIGH CHECKING.

Soon after the inauguration of trotting, it was found that horses of certain temperament and form could be made to trot more reliably and faster by holding the head checked high, and soon considerable ingenuity was displayed in the development of the best methods of doing this. This was resorted to with the same object with which toe weights and other means are now used, to hold and force more reliably in the trotting gait.

Down to about fifteen years ago, the check in general use consisted of a simple strap, the ends of which were attached to the rings of the bit, passed through the lugs on each side attached to the throatlatch, and back to the saddle-hook. The shorter the strap, and the higher these lugs were placed, the higher the head was necessarily drawn up and back. A good illustration of the extreme of such checking is shown in Fig. 151.

Various improvements were made on this method, based mainly, now, in addition to the points explained, in raising the lugs, or in attaching them well up

FIG. 299.—The Horse Trying to Relieve himself from the Torture of the Overdraw Check.

near the head-piece of the bridle ; next in passing the strap through the rings of the bit, and attaching to the cheek-pieces of the bridle, making the purchase straighter up on the head, and giving considerable pulley purchase up and back upon the bit. Various modifications have been made of this form, in connection with powerful curb bits, with the object of elevating the heads of fancy carriage teams in the principal cities of this country and England.

FIG. 300.—Throwing the Head up to Obtain Relief from the Check.

Finally, a change was made,—that of passing the strap, one end of which was divided and connected with the rings of the bit, back over the head, and attaching it to the saddle-hook, which was called the Kimball-Jackson check. The next change was that of placing an extra small steel bit in the mouth, with a strap attached across the nose to hold it in place, which was connected to an extra strap passed up to the top of the head-piece, on which a patent was taken. It was introduced, I believe, by a man named Carroll. This was improved upon by an extra strap, bringing the check-lugs rather high on the bridle, and connecting the rein directly with this extra bit.

Fig. 301.—One of the Positions the Horse Assumes in trying to Obtain Relief from the Pain of the Check Referred to in the Text.

The next step was to attach branches of a straight strap directly to the nose-piece or rings of this extra bit, and pass it back over the head to the water-hook,

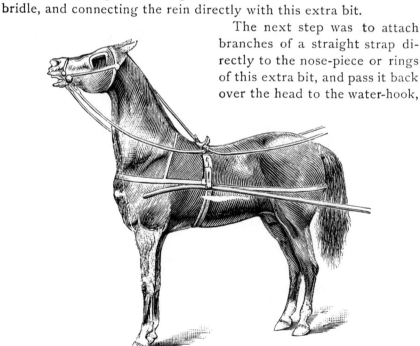

Fig. 302.—As Driving Horses are Frequently Checked up, Referred to in Text.

as now used, not only simplifying it, but giving the most arbitrary power of keeping the head elevated. No matter what the form or temper of the horse, this form of check holds the head up so arbitrarily that the horse is helpless to resist it, giving the appearance of style, especially in those that carry the head rather low, and hence their popularity with dealers.   These improvements were brought into use, as has been stated before, by the professional trainer, for the sole purpose of making horses trot steadier and faster ; but on account of the appearance of style which they forced

FIG. 303.—**The Head as Usually Drawn up with the Overdraw Check.**

the horse to indicate, and the pride most people exhibit in trying to give their horses the semblance of superior form and style which it conveys, as well as to intimate, as far as they can, the efforts of the professional trainer of trotters, they have, during the past decade, come into very general use.

It may be worthy of mention that this check is peculiar to this country, not being, as far as I know, used in any other country, only the old form, with its modifications, being used in Europe. In England it is known as the " bearing-rein."

In originally using this check, or bearing-rein, upon driving horses, the object has been to use only so much restraint as would prevent the horse from throwing the head down below the breast, and to curtail the head to its natural position, or slightly below it, which is not seriously objectionable.

The want of a proper training of the mouth (which is fully explained on page 88, and also under "Colt-Training") frequently leads plucky, spirited horses to so lunge or pull recklessly against the bit as to make them unmanageable and dangerous. This it is

FIG. 304.—**The Extreme Torture of the Bedouin or Gag Bearing-rein.**

sought to overcome by different forms of severe bits. When giving instructions and making experiments, I had almost daily lunging, kicking, and runaway horses of the worst character brought forward to be experimented upon,—horses that when used at all, could only be driven by the most severe form of bit ; and I was invariably able to drive such without a check, giving the head entire freedom, and I may say, without breeching as well, the most interesting feature of which was the simplicity of treatment with which it could be done.

In a certain class of lunging, headstrong horses, I call attention under that head to checking the head high to repress resistance ; but it is given as palliative treatment, in the absence of a better. I call attention to it also to prevent a horse from kicking, because it is difficult for a horse to kick when checked high. But it is given

as a simple means of control, as other treatment is given for objectionable habits, and does not apply at all to the use of the check
upon gentle horses in their driving.

Even those most humane in intentions and feelings are liable
almost daily to subject the most gentle horses to this very serious
cause of discomfort and pain. To illustrate somewhat the extent of
this, I will refer to two cases coming to my notice in one evening,
just previous to writing this paper. A banker, who had a promis-

Fɪɢ. 305.—Comfort.

ing three-year-old trotting colt, which he purchased for his own
driving, having him hitched up one day, invited me to ride. The
colt's head was checked so extremely high as to make it unpleasant
for me to witness the pain and discomfort of the horse in trying to
relieve himself from the restraint. Fig. 302 is a good illustration.
I took particular pains to explain to the gentleman that this was
not only entirely unnecessary, but a cause of real cruelty, and that
I was confident he would not intentionally subject his colt to such
needless pain and discomfort, when brought to his notice. He,
like thousands of others, had scarcely an idea what the check was
for. He "liked to see the head kept high, as it made the colt
appear better;" "it was the method of hitching up trotting horses,
and his colt ought to trot," etc. But notwithstanding my utmost
efforts, I could not persuade him to leave off the check.

The same evening I saw a gentle family horse driven by two girls. The horse, one of the kindest of animals, was checked as high as he could be made to carry his head ; and while driving on a walk it was really painful to notice the strained manner in which the poor creature stepped, taking up his feet and putting them down almost like a blind horse, because the nose being pulled up so high, the blinders prevented his seeing the ground before him, at the same time working the mouth and throwing the head right and left in the

Fɪɢ. 306.—Showing the Discomfort and Torture of High Checking.

effort to free himself from the severe restraint. For a good illustration of these positions, see Figs. 296 to 301.

This is only a fair illustration of how many favorite driving and family horses, including even some work horses, are unintentionally checked up, and compelled to remain so for hours at a time, no matter how worked.

But while the check is less objectionable for light driving, it is not only abuse but real cruelty to use restraint upon the head of the draft horse in this way, as it to a great extent disables the horse from drawing heavy loads. This need not be demonstrated ; any man of observation can see it, and it is finely illustrated in Fig. 308.

A high English authority, Prof. McBride, says :—

"I most heartily concur in what has been said about the bad effects of the foolish custom of using the check-rein. It is a very common cause of roaring in the horse, which statement is indorsed by all veterinarians, seven hundred in England alone."

Figs. 302 and 303 were drawn and engraved expressly for me, showing the great discomfort of horses checked high, though the

Fig. 307.—The Ordinary Side Check, Giving an Easy Rein.

artist did not fully catch my ideas in his orders, and consequently did not express the position as fully and clearly as desired ; in any event, they are not overdrawn.

For the privilege of copying Figs. 293, 294, 295, 306, and 307, which tell the story very plainly, I am indebted to Hon. T. E. Hill, of Chicago, Ill., the author and publisher of "Hill's Manual" and other works. They are taken from "Hill's Album," a very fine family work.

Figs. 323, 324 are from photographs of what are termed "burrs" that have been used by drivers in New York City upon the bits of their horses, and are here given for the purpose of showing their effect upon the horses. The side view (Fig. 319) shows the ends of the tacks as they extend through the leather. These burrs were placed on the bit on each side of the mouth, so that the least pull of the reins would force the ends of the tacks against the cheeks, thereby producing great excitement and pain. The one copied from was taken from hundreds of others like it in Mr. Bergh's office. Fig. 317 is given to show their effect upon the horses. It is copied by permission from a plate owned by the Humane Society.

Fig. 308.—**The Check-rein on Work Horses.**

Horses are unintentionally subjected to excessively cruel abuses by ignorant, thoughtless persons, a fair illustration of which is shown in Figs. 321, 322. What as story it tells! What a degree of abuse of a fine horse is here shown! See his head tied up helplessly while pushed, perhaps abused, to gratify the pride of a couple of thoughtless simpletons! And yet this is only what can be seen almost daily by any observant person in every village and town in the country.

BLINDERS.

The horse should be able to see plainly. By far the finest and most expressive feature of the horse's head is his eyes. They are also the most useful ; he depends upon them most largely, and he should have the greatest freedom in their use. The better to prove this, and to show their location and position in the head, I give illustrations copied from life (Figs. 312, 313), showing how singularly well adapted they are to enable a horse to see not only on each side, but behind and before, as may be required, and the necessity for giving them the utmost freedom for doing this. Nature, who does everything right, most wisely requires this, and it is but the hight of ignorance and folly in any one to assume to change or interfere with her plans.

FIG. 309.—Showing the Position of the Eyes in the Head.

During my early public experience, when I gave exhibitions in driving horses without reins, it was noticeable that every motion of the whip, though held directly over the horse's back, was promptly obeyed,—that the horse, in fact, could be controlled quicker and better by the simple motions of the whip than ne could by bit and reins, giving the very best demonstration of this singular power.

Instead of making the horse unsafe, he is really made safer and more tractable by his being able to see everything around him plainly, that is, when he is so trained, this being the important condition in making him safe. Now, not only are blinders a serious obstruction to the horse's seeing clearly, but they are often a cause of much injury by striking

FIG. 310.—Showing the Position of the Eyes.

against the eyes, or by being pressed upon them. In pointing out this cause of harm lately, I found a piece of wire connected with the ornament of the blind, which became raised and pressed into the eye almost a quarter of an inch, so as to cause serious injury. The blinders had been pressed close up to the side of the head, and against the eye to such a degree as to attract my notice. This is a common occurrence, as the clinch of the wire holding the ornament either extends beyond the surface of the leather, or becomes raised more or less, and hence is a very common cause of injury to the eye. I have frequently found the outer edge of the eye abraded and raw from this cause.

A horse is naturally suspicious and afraid of anything he does not plainly see, or does not comprehend the nature of, and hence he must either be prevented from seeing objects at all, or be permitted to see them plainly. Any one can understand that if compelled to look through a small slit or narrow space,

Fig. 311.—Fashion. The Blinders as now Formed. The Eyes Completely Covered.

it not only in the first place increases the difficulty of seeing, especially while moving, making it very trying on the eyes, but it makes it clearly impossible to see things as plainly as if the eyes had entire freedom. This is just the effect blinders have upon the horse's eyes.

Now, of late years, in the large cities especially, the fashion has become quite common of making the blinders not only very large, but in the form of a bowl, that is, hollow in the center, and the edges brought forward in saucer shape, carrying it to such an extreme that they really cover up the eyes and prevent the

Fig. 312.—The Eyes so Covered that the Horse Cannot See.

horse from seeing at all, or but very little out of the front corner of the eye ; and harness-makers throughout the country are foolishly adopting this plan of forming blinders.

REPRESENTATIVE CASES.

I made a special effort to obtain the aid of an artist to make photographs of representative cases, so as to have an absolutely correct illustration of a good average of them, but found it so difficult to secure one to do this that I was compelled to be satisfied with drawings, which, while not just what I wanted, give a very good idea of the form and position of blinders upon the heads of fashionably equipped coach horses, including

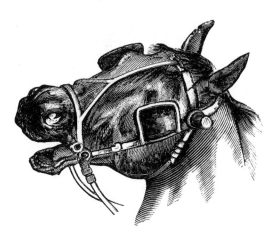

FIG. 313.—**The Fashion in the Country.**

the opposite of rough specimens to be often seen in the country, which will be noticed with interest.

In experimenting upon such horses as were brought to me before classes for illustrating the effects of treatment, I always gave the fullest freedom of sight, no matter what the object, and could always soon make the horse entirely indifferent to the object or cause of fear. This is, in fact, one of the most important essentials of success.

THE HORSE SHOULD SEE.

A horse can be driven to a top carriage with close blinders, when he cannot without ; this is because he was never permitted to

FIG. 314.—**The Old Farm Horse with Blinds.**

see the top while in this position, and if permitted to see it suddenly or unexpectedly, it would be liable to frighten or excite him very seriously, and would be dangerous to have him do so. This is frequently illustrated very forcibly by taking off or changing the bridle on a horse while hitched to a carriage. The horse being thus permitted suddenly to see the top behind him, which is now an entirely new object to him, will often show such violent fear as to resist all restraint and run away. One of two things must

be done ; viz., either cover up the eyes so that he cannot see the top, or give him entire free- dom in seeing it, when the cause of the trouble will be easily overcome.

It is true that blinders may be used in certain cases to over- come natural defects, the same as other appliances are used to overcome certain difficulties ; but they are only necessary, when at all, on account of im- proper or defective education.

First, a lazy horse will drive steadier and better when he

Fig. 315.—The Corners of the Blinders Dang-ling against the Eyes.

cannot see the motions of the whip, because such will learn to watch the whip when raised for punishment and jump to avoid it,

and then slack up again until the effort is repeated. But if blinders are used upon such horses, they should be so formed that they will not interfere side- ways or forward, or in any way injure or touch the eye. They should merely prevent him from looking back.

Second, a horse which has an ugly looking head, or a serious defect in an eye, or has suffered the loss of an eye, will be improved by the use of skillfully applied blinders, which will serve to con- ceal the defects ; and this, as before explained, was the cause of their intro- duction.

Third, if the horse is but imperfectly trained, and not accustomed when hitched to a top carriage to see it, the careful covering of the eyes with blinders will enable driving of the horse with com-

Fig. 316.—Blinders Striking against the Eyes.

parative safety so long as the blinders are kept so, and will pre- vent the occurrence of a large portion of the accidents that are of

FIG. 317.—**Horses Excited by the Torture of the Burrs Shown Below.**

daily repetition throughout the country, resulting in such frightful loss of life and property.

I would repeat that there would be no more necessity nor sense in using blinders upon horses driven in harness, if properly trained, than there is in using them upon horses under a saddle ; and who would think of disfiguring and encumbering a horse's head, no matter how poor, with blinders when used for the saddle ?

Look at these matters in a reasonable, practical manner.

Imagine yourself in the horse's place, and try to feel how you would

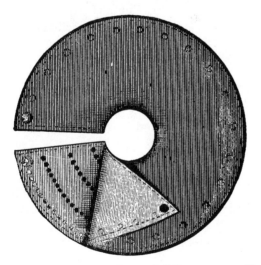

FIG. 318.—**Burrs. Half Size.**

FIG. 319.—**Side View, Showing Length of Tacks. Half Size.**

like to be hampered and disabled as horses are forced to be while subject to the arbitrary control and often to the most unreasonable abuse of a vain or ignorant driver, while compelled to work hard. Treat the horse in the same spirit of generosity you would be yourself treated under like circumstances. Then there are other points. There is often shameful neglect of horses when hitched. They are left unsheltered and uncovered in the cold and rain, while their riders or drivers are in some drinking saloon, toasting their shins in comfort, drinking from the cup that exhilarates only to deprave or destroy the best impulses of their natures. With a

Fig. 320.—All Day in the Storm.

brain on fire with excitement, or benumbed with torpor, the poor horse is driven home again, heated and exhausted, to be followed perhaps by a chill that often seriously injures or destroys the poor animal by causing inflammation in the feet (founder) or inflammation of the lungs (pneumonia), etc. They are unnecessarily lashed and savagely jerked upon the bit,

Fig. 321.—In the Hands of Fast Young Men.

without reason and without mercy. They are clubbed, and kicked, and cursed, and, in fact, treated with every conceivable indignity practiced by barbarous tribes upon captive prisoners. There is no spectacle more calculated to excite the pity and sympathy of the benevolent and philanthropic, than the faithful old family horse, worn down with serv-

Fig. 322.—Ruined by Fast Driving.

FIG. 323.—The Effect of being Improperly Broken.

ice, overloaded and whipped into hard drudgery in his last days, when he should be released from work and permitted to end his life in peace. Surely there is no domestic creature toward which civilized man displays so much in humanity as toward this constant and faithful companion of his labors and pleasures ; and it would seem that no man with the least claim to being considered a gentleman would need to be appealed to to treat his horses with humanity, if not with kindness ; yet it is unfortunately the case that such appeals, made by disinterested men and women of humane impulses and by our humane societies, are often unheeded or regarded as the merest sentiment.

FIG. 324.—Beaten by a Cruel Master.

FIG. 325.—The Last Days of the old Family Horse.

It should not be difficult for one to see that a reasonable sense of responsibility should prompt to the most considerate care of every animal on the farm. Not only does kind treatment make them more easily managed, but imperceptibly the feeling is felt in the home, making the relations of life more beautiful and happy.

CHAPTER XII.

THE MULE.

WE frequently had mules brought in to experiment upon, and often found them exceptionally good subjects. A mule when vicious is supposed to be not only very dull but extremely bad, and if the treatment is not made right, becomes really very difficult to manage ; but when managed according to the experience of our later years, we always found this animal among the very best

Fig. 326.—A Favorite Mule.

of subjects. No matter how bad the character of the mule, or how vicious the resistance, he always works in, in a short time, entirely gentle. The treatment we used with most success at first was the Second Method, and it was rare that we found one that did not submit to this readily. However, it was not in all cases the clear success we could desire, and we then depended upon the simpler methods of treatment, making sometimes a good deal of work ; but when we struck the Third Method in connection with the Second, we found mules to yield to treatment very readily. I have in mind two cases which will fairly illustrate others.

When I was in Cleveland, O., after having very decided success for a week or two, the subjection of the Malone horse in the first place attracting very wide attention, parties from the West Side brought over one evening an extremely vicious mule, they feeling sure that it would break me down. I was asked if my treatment would work upon mules. I answered, "Yes." A man spoke out, "Bring in that mule." I found a very fine, large fellow that had been used to a cart, would kick violently, and would not have the feet handled. I subjected him rapidly for a few minutes to the Second Method, using the War Bridle a little in addition, when he submitted unconditionally within six or eight minutes. The success of the experiment was a cause of great merriment, and was regarded as a great feat. In point of fact, the greatness of the feat was entirely owing to the great susceptibility of the mule to control.

FIG. 327.—Mule Team as Driven in the South.

At a small town in Central New York certain parties made a great effort to break me down, and depended mainly upon a very vicious mule to do so. This mule had been hitched to a fence outside, and outrageously abused by being punched with a sharp stick, making him perfectly reckless. In this condition he was brought in for treatment. He was subjected rapidly to the Second Method for a few minutes, followed by the Third Method, and became perfectly gentle within ten minutes, and was driven without breeching.

The mule, I think, is, if anything, more susceptible to treatment than the horse, and he is usually more abused and less cared for than the horse. The popular opinion in relation to him is not at all favorable ; but I have found that mules could learn anything about as easily as any intelligent horse. When I was in Fostoria, O., a man there had a small mule that appeared to be half starved, and, as a matter of pity more than anything else, I was led to buy him. We trained this mule to throw boys, and to do anything that the ponies could do. He would squeal, laugh, and do many amusing tricks, and could throw any living man. I sold him when in New York for five hundred dollars to circus men.

I would advise in all cases very kind treatment to mules. Subject rapidly for a few minutes to the Second Method ; it will rarely be necessary to use more, and if the case is not made vicious there should be no exception. If a mule is treated gently, given little presents, and flattered, and especially if spoken to kindly when approached in the stall, there should be no more trouble in approaching him than a horse. It is a matter of a little care and good management. I include here an illustration of mules as driven in the South, and it is but just to state that I have never been more interested than to see common negroes drive a team of from four to six mules before a spring wagon with a single line. Indeed, I am candid in admitting that it was a greater feat of nice training than any we were able to give in driving horses without reins ; and I often felt like taking off my hat to those negroes in admiration of their remarkable success as teamsters. A negro rides the near pole mule, then a long rein is extended forward to the lead one, and either pulling or jerking indicates to this leader which way to go ; and, so far as I could see, they could be driven as accurately around a corner or any point as could be done with the best of management with reins.

The treatment of sickness and injuries for mules is practically the same as that for horses. For bruises or saddle gall, I think it advisable to state here that, being so simple, there is nothing superior to cold water. Remove pressure from the part, and bathe thoroughly in cold water. This method, simple as it is, stands over all others for allaying acute inflammation. Simply pour on pure cold water, and repeat as may be necessary. In some cases, as described in the medical department, hot and cold water alternated may be better. It will depend upon the amount of constitutional disturbance caused by the intensity of the pain.

CHAPTER XIII.

MISCELLANEOUS HABITS.

CRIBBING.

THIS is a habit for which there has been no practical remedy. Many claim that it is caused by indigestion, and that by neutralizing the gas generated in the stomach in consequence, a horse will cease to crib. Mr. O. H. P. Fancher, who thirty years ago traveled extensively as a professional horse-tamer, and who is specially referred to in the first chapter as claiming to tame horses by the use of certain scents or medicines, was the most pretentious advocate of this theory; but I have never known, on any reliable authority, of any case being cured by use of medicine. It has also been claimed that cribbing is caused by the teeth pressing too closely against one another, a reliable remedy for which is sawing between them. I have known of a great many cases treated in this way, but without any success, except that in some cases the habit is prevented for a time by the soreness produced by the filing. Driving wedges between the teeth has also been resorted to, the effect of which would be so much pain as to prevent the horse from cribbing for some time.

FIG. 328.—**A Horse in the Act of Cribbing.**

A horse will not crib on anything that is lower than the knees, consequently a practical way to prevent the habit is to tear away the manger, and feed the horse from the floor or from a basket.

To break up the habit the only practical remedy is punishment, as hereafter explained.

Saturate the manger, neck-yoke, and straps, if inclined to bite them, with kerosene oil. Rubbing the parts bitten upon with strong fly-blister, may next be tried; or get cayenne or red pepper pods, boil down to a strong decoction, and wash the parts the horse may be inclined to bite upon thoroughly with the solution. To be repeated at least once a week, for a month or more. The object is to make the lips and mouth so sore as to prevent the inclination to bite. This method will often work very satisfactorily ; but, like the treatment first advised, must be done thoroughly to be effective. Covering the parts with sheep-skin will seldom do any good.

W. D. Gross, of Kutztown, Pa., advertises a device for the cure of cribbing, for which he claims much. It is simply a thin plate of metal placed over the upper front teeth and fastened by small bolts. This will, of course, make the gums sore, if pressed upon to any extent, and will undoubtedly work well, and is worthy of trial ; the objection is the difficulty of fastening the plate to the teeth. Cribbing can be stopped

Fig. 329.—The Halter Adjusted for Cribbing.

by buckling a wide, flexible strap, moderately tight, around the neck. It should be from three to three and one half inches wide. A narrow strap will not work well.

Fig. 330.—Throat-strap with Tacks.

When in Bath, N. Y., many years ago, I noticed that a horse when cribbing at a post in the street contracted the larynx and muscles of the neck forcibly during the act. Instantly it occurred to me to make the experiment of putting such an adjustment upon the throat-latch as to cause sharp pain when there was an effort to repeat the act. I went to a harness-shop, procured some six-ounce tacks, drove them through a strip of leather about half an inch apart, and filed the points sharp and of equal length. I laid this bit of strap on the inside of the throat-latch, so as to bring the points of the tacks under the larynx, and kept it in place by winding each end and the center with a piece of waxed-end. I now buckled the throat-latch long enough so that it would not touch the neck when eating or swallowing, yet so close as to bring the points of the tacks sharply against the throat at the least attempt to crib, and stood by to notice the effect. The first time the horse tried to crib he was hurt so keenly that he jumped almost from the ground. In a short time he tried it again, with the same result; the third time he only gave a little nip, and then stood quietly for some time. I now had him changed to another location, with a man close by to note the results. He reported that the horse did not crib any more during the afternoon. I have broken several horses of the habit by this means, and think if the adjustment is made right, and continued long enough, it will be found to be very effectual. Success will depend upon the care with which this is kept adjusted. If there is large muscular development of the neck, the strap must be buckled shorter than when the neck is well cut out, as it is termed. Make the reproof severe at first; then keep the tacks so adjusted as to touch sharply when the habit is repeated.

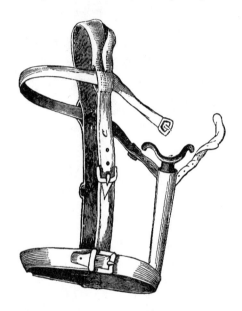

FIG. 331.—**Halter as Used by the French.**

If the throat-latch is not on a line with the top of the head, the tacks cut the jaw a little below the juncture of the head with the neck. If this is kept on a few days or weeks, and then taken off and again adjusted carelessly, there is likely to be a failure. If the horse finds he can crib once with this on without hurting himself seriously, he will be encouraged to repeat the effort, and will soon punish himself severely to do so. But if punished at first, and this is kept where it will hurt keenly at the least attempt to crib, and is left on a few weeks, it ought to be successful. It will not do to buckle a strap around the neck. The adjustment must be made to the strap of the halter, and the halter must fit nicely to the head. It must be made like a bridle, with brow-piece, so that it will not shift or move on the head. A boy broke five horses of this habit a few years ago ; but he became careless and failed on the sixth. There is, once in a while, an old horse of determined character that will crib in defiance of this or any other means. Such cases are, however, rare. A young, nervous-tempered horse will yield readily to the treatment, and but few horses will attempt to crib while wearing a muzzle.

Since writing the above I find in a French work an illustration which I copy, giving the same idea but much more complex than the method before given. It is included, however, as a point of value, and can be studied in connection with the explanation given.

If a strap be buckled rather tightly around the neck, a horse will not crib while it is on. This is, however, but a simple preventive. There is also the objection that gradually the horse may learn to resist, to overcome which the strap has to be buckled tighter, which of course obstructs the circulation, and causes inflammation, thus producing serious and permanent injury. If a strap is used for this purpose, it should be fully three inches wide, and buckled just tight enough to prevent the inclination to crib. A wide strap works a great deal better than a narrow one, and is less liable to do harm.

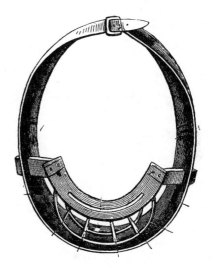

FIG. 332.—Throat-strap as Used by the French.

WIND-SUCKING.

Sometimes a horse sucks wind without the habit of cribbing. I include a cut of a form of bit to prevent this, for which much is claimed. A practical horseman of experience gave me the point. He claimed that it would work perfectly in preventing the inclination to crib and suck wind.

Procure a piece of gas-pipe about seven inches long. Drill a hole across each end, through which put in rings, as seen in cut ; next, drill four or five holes, as shown in cut. The theory is that the gas in the stomach cannot escape through the mouth on account of its being closed, and that instinctively the horse will bite on something to open the mouth and throw off the gas. With this bit in the mouth, the air passes through the small holes in the center, and out through the ends. (See Fig. 333.)

The gentleman referred to positively assured me that in several cases known to him it worked with perfect success.

PUTTING THE TONGUE OUT OF THE MOUTH.

If the tongue is put over the bit, have a piece of thin sheet-iron about two and one half inches wide and five inches long, with the ends rounding, and the edges filed smooth. Drill two small

holes (Fig. 336) near each edge, at the center, and fasten to the bit. Shorten the cheek-pieces of the bridle, so that the bit is drawn well up in the mouth. This piece of iron renders it impossible for the horse to get the tongue over the

FIG. 333.—**Bit Made of Gas-pipe, for preventing Cribbing and Wind-sucking.**

bit. The simplest and best way of preventing this is to have the smith make a mouth-piece, as represented in Fig. 335, which is seen to be bent up, and comes so high in the mouth that the horse cannot get the tongue over ; this works well, and is not inconvenient to drive with. It should be bent up at least two and three fourths to three inches, come well out to the cheek-pieces,

and be filed smooth to prevent cutting or chafing the mouth. (See Fig. 335.) The tongue is sometimes, but not often, put out under the bit. For such cases the following treatment will work well :—

Get three medium-sized bullets, and hammer them out to about an inch and a half in length. Drill a small hole through the end of each. Tie one to the center of the bit by a little piece of wire through the joint. Attach the others to the bit about an inch from the center (one on each side), so as to play loosely.

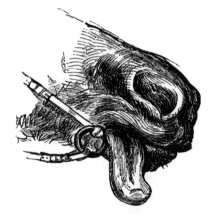

FIG. 334.—**Manner of Putting the Tongue out.**

When this bit is in the mouth, these extra arrangements will so disconcert the horse that in his struggles to get them out of the way, he will forget to put his tongue out. (See Fig. 337.)

The next best way is to buckle a strap around the nose so that the mouth cannot be opened. This, of course, prevents the tongue being put out, and in a short time the habit will be broken up. There are bits now made for this habit, which may be obtained of dealers.

Pawing in Stall.

A horse will not paw much unless he can hear the noise ; so a good method of preventing this habit is to muffle the foot by tying a piece of blanket around it. Next, by attaching a piece of chain or clog to the foot, as follows : Get a piece of chain about ten inches in length, run a short strap through one of the end links, and buckle it around the foot above the fetlock ; or a piece of light chain can be fastened to a small block, and attached to the foot in the same manner. When the horse attempts to paw, the clog or chain rattling against the foot so discon-certs or hurts him that he will repeat the movement but a few times.

Fig. 335.

Kicking in Stall.

Kicking with one foot against the side of the stall is a habit which many horses are liable to learn, and, like pawing, it is some-times very annoying ; therefore it is important to be able to prevent or overcome it. In the first place, it is rare that a horse will learn to kick against the side of the stall if it be large and roomy. Large stalls are, in all cases, very important for the health and comfort of the horse, as well as for convenience in going around him. The simplest and best way of preventing this habit is to pad the side of the stall, which will prevent the sound of the striking, when the in-clination to kick will soon be overcome. Or, attach a clog or piece of chain to the foot, as explained for pawing.

Another method is to tie some thorny bushes together, and sus-pend them over the place kicked, so as to swing freely when struck· When the horse kicks, the rebound will bring the bushes against the legs, so frightening and hurting him that the attempt to kick will be repeated but a few times. A clog may also be hung over the place struck or kicked, which, when struck, would react in the same way, and thus prevent a repetition of the habit. Making the stall wide, and padding the sides as explained, are the most simple and practical methods for preventing this habit.

GETTING CAST IN THE STALL.

This is mainly caused by being confined in a stall that is too small. When the horse rolls and turns upon his back, he is so cramped and restrained by the narrow walls that he is unable to roll himself back to regain his feet. Sometimes the division of the stall is so short that in the effort to roll, his body comes across, and in contact with, the ends, and, the head being held fast by the halter, it is impossible for him to get up; so a large, roomy stall would of itself be almost a complete remedy.

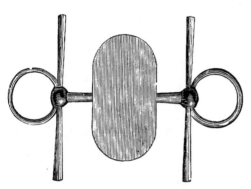

FIG. 336.

The simplest way to prevent it is to tie one end of a piece of rope or cord to the beam or flooring directly overhead, and the opposite end to the head-piece of the halter back of the ears, leaving it just long enough to allow the horse to reach his nose to the ground. As he lies down and tries to roll, being unable to bring the top of his head to the ground, he is disabled from rolling. A small ring should be stitched to the top of the halter, to which the strap or cord can be easily and securely fastened when necessary.

Some horses are liable, by pawing, to get the fore foot,

FIG. 337.

and in some cases even the hind foot by scratching the head with the leg, over the halter-strap, thereby becoming tangled and helpless in the stall. The halter should be hitched higher than common, though long enough to permit the horse to lie down easily.

Jumping over Fences.

Every dairyman knows that a cow or ox will not attempt to jump a fence, pull it down, or run, while a board is over the forehead, attached to the horns in front of the eyes; this simple means will usually work well upon cattle, but will not do upon a horse, because it gives too much freedom to see over the nose.

If a horse or mule, put on a halter that fits well to the head—a five-ring halter is best. Next, find a piece of fine leather (an old boot-leg will do), about as long as the head, and from four to five inches wider than the head is at the eyes. Attach a string at each corner. Attach the upper corners by the strings to the halter, where the brow-piece is attached to the cheek-piece. Tie the cords attached to the lower corners back of the jaw, being careful to leave freedom enough for the jaws to act when eating. Let the ends now pass over the throat-latch, and make fast. The horse is simply disabled from looking ahead or over the nose, which will disconcert him sufficiently to prevent jumping or throwing the fence down. If an ox or cow, attach the upper corners to the horns, and pass the strings around the neck instead of over the throat-latch.

Tender-Bitted.

Use a large, smooth mouth-piece, with leather cheek-pieces, so as to let the bit rest about an inch lower than usual in the mouth. Next, try winding the bit with a piece of chamois-skin which has been saturated with tannin or alum, to harden the mouth.

Kicking Cows.

Many years ago a man who attended my class in Herkimer Co., N. Y., reported to me that he had a very bad kicking heifer, and as a matter of experiment, he put the War Bridle on her and gave her a sharp lesson with it, as directed for breaking a colt to lead and drive. After a few minutes' treatment, he found that she stood perfectly gentle to be milked, and he had no more trouble with her. Some time afterward, while in the dairy counties, I gave this point to my classes, and I have since had a good many especially bad kicking cows brought forward to be experimented upon, the treatment in all cases proving successful in a few minutes.

One of the most amusing incidents that occurred in making these experiments was at a little town near Jamestown, N. Y. At the time I carried canvas, and after getting through the regular experiments, a notoriously bad kicking cow was brought in for treat-

18   a

ment. As usual, a few pulls of the War Bridle made her stand to
be milked as gentle as could be desired. While the class were amusing themselves over the ease with which the cow was controlled,

and somewhat at the expense of the
owner, with the cord still on, she
suddenly, and without warning,
rushed through the wall of the canvas, almost tearing down the whole
tent, and ran through the main
street of the town toward home.
Every dog in the street took after
her, making a most ludicrous scene,
no one appearing more amused
than the owner. He came into the
class on condition that I would
make the cow gentle to be milked
at home. He never came back to
report on the success of the ex-

FIG. 338.—Arrangement of the Cord for
Leading a Cow.

periment. The course of treatment is about as follows :—

Put on the War Bridle, second form, pull right and left a few
times ; then stand off at a safe distance, and pull a little upon the
teats. If there is resistance, punish ; so repeat, until there is no resistance. Sometimes the teats are sore, and the pain caused by
milking is very severe. Take Goulard's extract 2 oz., sulphate zinc
2 oz., lard 2 oz., and rub upon the parts a few times. This is a favorite remedy among dairymen for sore teats, cake in the bag, etc.
This prescription I know to have been sold for fifteen dollars, and it
is prized by dairymen in Northern New York, where the medicine
is sold especially for their use.

To Lead a Cow Easily.

Tie a rope around the head under the horns, bringing the knot
over the ear. Now bring the rope forward and under the ear, again
forward over and under the cord. By pulling now, the cord will
tighten around the ear, hurting so severely that the cow will lead
freely.

CHAPTER XIV.

TEACHING TRICKS.

IN this chapter I give the portraits of my old group of trained horses and ponies, whose performances were regarded with such great interest by all who witnessed them, that for a number of years I was compelled to give an extra exhibition daily for the benefit of ladies and children, for which a regular admission fee was charged; and it was universally conceded that these exhibitions were more interesting than those of any circus. The performances of Blind Billy were regarded as especially remarkable, from the fact of his being totally blind. He was, without question, the most remarkable performing horse that has ever been exhibited in this or any other country. I give a very fine portrait of this remarkable horse, sketched by a leading artist.

The details of teaching a few tricks, which I give in this chapter, will be of special interest to farmer boys, who may desire to train their colts in this way. A horse seems more intelligent and tractable when trained to perform a few simple tricks, such as telling the age, kissing, bowing his head, kicking up, turning right and left, or following with the whip, etc., all of which any intelligent boy can easily train a colt to do.

In training a colt or horse to perform these tricks, there should be no hurry or effort to teach more than one thing at a time. Make the lessons short, and repeat until thoroughly learned, when another can be taken up; but do not continue the lesson long enough to excite or confuse the horse.

To Follow by the Whip.

One of the simplest and most interesting tricks to teach a horse is to follow at the motion of the whip, without bridle or halter. It is even quite useful, as it teaches a horse to follow at command from one part of the barn to another, or to come out of his stall without attempting to get away. Full details of teaching this trick are given in the chapter on " Colt-Training."

To Nod His Head, or Say " Yes."

To teach a horse to bow, or nod his head, prick him lightly on

the back with a pin, and continue until in his effort to avoid the annoyance he drops his head ; then instantly stop the pricking and

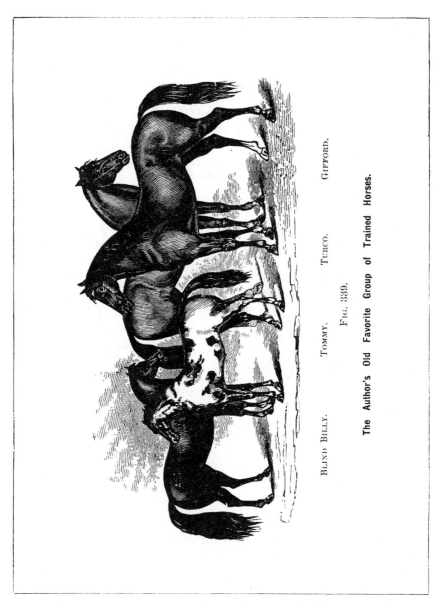

BLIND BILLY.   TOMMY.   TURCO.   GIFFORD.

FIG. 339.

The Author's Old Favorite Group of Trained Horses.

caress him. Repeat the pricking until the head is again dropped,
when caress and give him something of which he is fond. Continue
to alternate in this way with the pricking and caressing, until at the

instant a motion is made toward the back, or even to take a pin from the coat, he will drop his head.

To Shake His Head, or Say "No."

To teach a horse to say "No," prick him lightly on the top of the shoulder with a pin until he shakes his head, when stop and reward him. Repeat the pricking until at the least motion toward the withers the horse will shake his head.

Fig. 340.—**Blind Billy.**

To Tell His Age.

To teach a horse to tell his age, prick him lightly on the back part of the leg until, to avoid the annoyance, the foot is lifted, or there is an effort to paw ; for this, stop and caress him. Repeat until the least motion toward the leg will cause him to paw the ground.

In teaching this trick, the body is naturally bent a little while in the act of pricking the leg, and by repeating, the position will soon indicate to the horse that he must paw. This position is to be maintained until he paws four, five, or six times, or as many times as he is years old, when the position is changed, and the pawing ceases.

To Kick Up.

To teach a horse to kick up, simply prick him on the rump with a pin until there is an inclination to kick up, when, as before, stop and caress him. Repeat until the least motion toward the rump will

FIG. 341.—**Blind Billy Running after and Catching his Trainer when Playing Blind Man's Buff.**

induce him to kick up; then touch with the whip, and repeat until at the mere motion of it he will kick up.

These tricks may be made quite interesting by talking to the horse somewhat as follows: "Tommy, I want you to tell how old you are; will you do it?" and signal for the horse to shake his head,

FIG. 342.—**Blind Billy Kicking up.**

as if refusing. Then exclaim, as if surprised, "Oh, you can't tell your age, I suppose, without being paid for it! Will you do it if I give you a lump of sugar?" and signal for him to nod his head. You can now signal for him to tell his age, and when he has done so, it gives him an air of sagacity which is very amusing and interesting. Again, you may ask: "What will you do to one who does not treat you well?" Then signal for him to kick. His prompt obedience, of course, indicates to the spectators that he understands what is said to him, when in reality he is only obeying the signals which have been taught him. The nice point lies in giving the signals in such a manner that they will not be noticed or understood by the spectators.

Teaching to Kiss.

Kissing is a very simple trick to teach a horse, and it adds greatly to the interest of those already explained. Stand facing the horse, with the right side turned partly toward his left shoulder, and let him take a piece of apple from your hand, which is held toward his mouth. Bring it nearer each time, and finally let him take a piece in the same manner from between the lips. When he does not reach forward promptly to take the piece of apple from the lips, prick him with a pin at the point of the shoulder. Repeat until he gets the idea of avoiding punishment by bringing his mouth to that of the trainer when desired. Now put the apple farther into the mouth, which

Fig. 343.—Blind Billy Walking on his Knees.

will compel him to open his lips to get it. Commence lessening the size of the apple, finally giving it to him as a reward after he has performed the trick of bringing his mouth to that of the trainer. This will teach him that by doing this he will escape punishment and receive reward.

To Lie Down.

Fig. 344.—Blind Billy in his Great Act of Walking Erect.

A horse is taught to lie down or to sit up principally by means of the whip or bridle, as follows: Tap the horse smartly across the shins until he will drop upon his knees. This method, however, requires a good deal of care and judgment, or it will occasion needless pain and punishment before the horse is made to submit. I will give the following method, which, though slower, is better calculated for amateurs :—

Tie the bridle-reins into a knot back of the neck, throw your strap over the back, under the body, and tie to the near foot below the fetlock. Now pass the right hand well over the back, and take a short hold of the strap. Cause the horse to step toward you, and pull the foot up. Then pass the left hand around the reins, pull back and down upon them in such a manner as to turn the head a little to the off side, at the same time pulling down steadily but firmly on the strap over the back with the right hand. As the horse goes down, gradually pull the near rein, so as to bring the head to the left, at the same time pressing down and from you firmly with the right, until the horse will lie down. Now pass the end of the strap through the ring of the bit, draw through gently, step over the neck, and as

Fig. 345.—Tommy.   Sketch from Life.

the horse attempts to get up, pull him back, until he lies quiet. Rub and caress him, and after lying a few minutes, say, "Get up, sir!" Repeat in this way a few times, until the horse will lie down readily. Then while holding him on or near the knee with the strap, hit him on the shin of the other with a small whip, until he will bring it under and lie down. After a while he can be made to come on his knees and lie

Fig. 346.—Tommy in his Vicious Act of Defending the Ring.

down by simply pulling the head down a little and hitting the leg with the whip, at the same time saying, "Lie down, sir!" repeating until the horse will lie down to the motion of the whip.

To Sit Up.

When the horse will lie down promptly, put on him a common collar, and while down take two pieces of rope, each about ten feet in length, tie the ends around the hind feet, carry them forward between the fore legs, and bring them once around the collar. Now step on his tail, take the bridle-reins in the right hand, while holding the ends of the rope firmly in the left. Give a little jerk on the reins and say, " Get up, sir!" When the horse throws out the forward feet and springs to raise himself on the hind feet, he finds himself unable to complete the effort, on account of the hind feet being tied forward under him, and so brings himself in a sitting position.

Fig. 347.—**Tommy as the Model Riding Pony.**

Instantly step forward, holding the ropes firmly, rub and caress the head and neck a little for a few seconds, then as you see the effort to keep up becoming tiresome, let loose and say, " Get up, sir!" By repeating in this way a few times, the horse will soon learn to sit up when commanded, without being tied.

Fig. 348.—**Tommy in his Great Act of Throwing.**

To Throw Boys.

To teach a horse to throw boys, first make him kick up as before explained. Then have plenty of straw on the ground, put a boy on his back, and while holding the halter make the horse kick up sharply by pricking, or touching him with the whip. The instant he kicks up, have the boy throw himself forward over the shoulders, for which give the horse a caress and a piece of apple. Repeat until he will, at the motion of the whip, make an effort to get the boy off. When he has done this, put on a larger and stronger boy, so that he must make a greater effort to get him off. Watch the point carefully, and see that the boy comes off when the horse makes an effort to throw him, otherwise he will soon become discouraged. By persevering in the treatment, he will soon learn to throw the most expert rider. But it will be noticed that he will make a greater effort sometimes than at others. When he does not seem to work well, put on a poorer rider, and work up again gradu-

ally. When the horse makes a particularly good point, give him apples, and caress him, for encouragement. It is important now to teach the horse to throw his rider only when commanded, or at a signal. To do this, when the boy is on, lead the horse a short distance around the ring, and then signal for him to throw. Repeat in this manner, also letting him go around alone with the boy on his back, until he will go on a sharp trot or run, and throw when commanded.

Fig. 349.—Tommy as the Gentle Pony.

I trained a pony to throw so expertly that he would at times turn a man or boy over in a double somersault, and bring him down squarely upon his feet. The best throwing pony ever exhibited in this country was admitted to be "Tommy." (See Fig. 348.) He has been exhibited in all the principal places in the North ; and although the best riders, from the bare-back circus-rider to the mustang-trainer on the plains, have tried, no man has ever been able to sit squarely upon his back one minute after the horse was signaled to throw him. His performances in this way have been regarded as wonderful. He will even carry two boys on his back for a while, and then at the motion of the finger throw them both. This sometimes afforded a good deal of amusement. First, if a boy was indicated to him as being good, he would allow him to ride as long as he wished, and then to safely slide off behind down to the ground. Then another boy would come who perhaps used tobacco, or had some other vice, when the pony would throw him immediately. Again, if there was a sharp political campaign, a Democrat and a Republican boy would mount him at the same time, and the one who could ride him the longer time could declare his party the victor.

To give something of an idea of the wonderful performances of these ponies, especially the expertness with which Tommy could throw a rider, I give some extracts from the press :—

Last night a large number of our leading citizens, by special invitation, were present at Prof. Magner's exhibition on Champlain Street.

The first exercise was performed with Blind Billy, a pony stone blind. He sat down as commanded, and walked upright on his hind legs several times around the ring. A handkerchief was thrown down in the ring, and the pony ordered by his master to find it. After walking around a few minutes, the pony came to a stand and seized the article in its mouth. Several other interesting tricks were performed by this blind pony, but the most laughable scene took place when the spotted wild horse, Tommy, was introduced. He presented every appearance of a wild steed, and ran restively about with distended nostrils and fiery eye, his mane bristling like the quills of a fretful porcupine, but at the approach of his master he became as tame as a lamb. Every one was invited to try their equestrian skill on Tommy, and all who tried were thrown to the ground, tenderly, but in the twinkling of an eye. Mr. Magner offered $100 to any one who would ride Tommy one minute. Several tried, but none were rewarded with success. One ambitious gentleman threw off hat, coat, and vest, and said he "would be d——d if he did n't ride him." Tommy was too

FIG. 350.—**Tommy in his Vicious Act—Chasing a Boy out of the Ring.**

much for him. He was thrown several times, and finally concluded that he had better let Tommy have his own way.—*Cleveland Leader.*

FUN ON THE PARADE.

The parade yesterday morning presented such a lively scene as has not been witnessed for some time. The occasion was the exercise of some trained horses by Mr. Magner. Straw was plentifully strewn on the ground, and expectation was high while the arrangements were going on. A cordon of boys and men were arranged. a rope placed in their hands, and a ring formed around the straw, into which soon pranced the first animal. This one cut up all sorts of circus capers, the most notable and most heartily applauded feat being the dexterous unseating of a small colored boy, who had the hardihood to allow himself to be placed astride the animal. Next came a totally blind animal, which performed miraculous antics at bidding.

The last feature was the crowning one. A spotted horse was led into the arena amid the plaudits of the vast assemblage present on the ground, and the Reform Club, which appeared *en masse* at the windows. After various gesticulations by the horse, a challenge was sent to the multitude for some one to mount. A large darkey essayed the task ; but no sooner had he pronounced himself " Ready," than Spotty raised his hindermost legs, lowered his he..d, and l. d. went careering through the air. " Golly, boss ! dat hoss can't do dat again ;" and so up he went again, to be treated the same way, only more so. A fairer complexioned auditor then attempted it, but he was treated in like manner. In fact, it is quite impossible for any one to remain seated when that horse takes a notion to unseat him. The prompt unseating of these two worthies so amused the multitude that Mr. M. thought they had had fun enough for one day, and so announced the show over.

His class in this city was a large one, numbering over forty members, comprising our leading citizens, all of whom acknowledge the superiority of his system over those of other trainers who have visited this locality.

Fig. 351.—**Turco and Gifford, as Driven without Reins.**

His power over untamed horses is said to be marvelous.—*New London (Conn.) Evening Gazette.*

A Wonderful Performing Blind Horse.

Among Prof. Magner's fine troupe of horses is one that is blind. This beautiful pony — for he is beautiful — is a wonder. He seems to understand every word said to him, and will perform the most difficult feats with an ease and rapidity that is surprising. He will go to any part of the ring, find and bring a handkerchief, take it from his leg, or any part of his body, go lame, go right or left, back, go ahead, sit down like a dog on either side, squeal like a pig, roll over, walk and kick on his knees, put his ears back and forward, kiss, with many other tricks, showing the greatest intelligence and most skillful training.

He was not touched with a whip during the whole performance. The professor simply stood at the center-pole, and talked to him as he would to a boy. He is, without doubt, the finest and most remarkable performing horse in the world.— *Cleveland Leader.*

An Exciting Incident.

Mr. Magner's tent is crowded daily to witness the performances of his wonderful ponies, and attend his lectures. One of these beautiful ponies, among other amusing performances, will throw any one from his back. Yesterday, when Tommy was introduced, a crack circus-rider came forward to ride him for the reward of one hundred dollars. He stated that he came to Buffalo to get the money, as he could ride Tommy, or any other horse, as long as he pleased. At this turn in affairs a general stir was manifested, which culminated in the most intense excitement. It was proved that no ordinary man could ride the cunning little fellow, as shown by his performances for weeks. But here was a trained athlete, that could turn a somersault on a horse bare-back without being thrown ; would it be possible to throw him ? There were serious apprehensions that he could not. Mr. Magner stood silent a moment, with the reserve characteristic of him, contemplating the intruder, as if to say, "You may, perhaps, do it, but not if I can prevent it ;" while the other stood with folded arms, showing the most perfect confidence in himself.

It was a scene worthy the brush of a painter. The immense throng present were hushed into silence, waiting for the contest. A signal brought Tommy upon a run. The whip was passed around his nose quietly, when the athlete was invited to come forward, who, disdaining help, lightly bounded upon the pony's back ; but before he had time to say Jack Robinson, Tommy commenced a series of gyrations that would astonish an Indian, and sent his man fully six feet into the air. It was beautifully and grandly accomplished ; but would he, could he, do it again ?

The trial was made, and, as before, the pony went into the air with the quickness of lightning, and, after a little more prolonged effort, sent his man heavily to the ground. But the contest was not yet over. All the desperation that pride and confidence could excite seemed to be now called into the actions of the man for a final test. He mounted more carefully, and, with a grasp of iron, awaited the onset. It soon came ; for Tommy, seeming to be now conscious of the task upon him, twisted and turned and jumped as if a demon, his eyes flashing fire, until, with a tremendous bound, he sent the man high in the air from his back, this time fully vanquished. It was a grand performance. Many, with feelings of intense admiration, crowded forward to caress the noble little fellow, while Mr. Magner seemed as proud of his pet as if he had won a kingdom. It was the finest and most exciting exhibition we ever witnessed.—*Buffalo (N. Y.) Courier.*

DRIVING WITHOUT REINS.

Thirty years ago driving a stallion without reins was regarded as one of the most interesting feats of training ever exhibited. That a spirited horse, or a span of them,—stallions,—could be driven, guided, and controlled by only a whip, seemed so remarkable that people came in crowds many miles to see it done. Yet it is one of the simplest feats of training, and one of the finest illustrations of the ease with which even horses of naturally bad temper can be made manageable when properly treated. I but refer to it here, as the limited space at my disposal will not admit of giving the details of this feat of training. Those specially interested to learn it will find full particulars in my work, "Facts for Horse-Owners."

CHAPTER XV.

EQUESTRIANISM.

THAT there is no exercise to be compared with horseback-riding is conceded by all well-read physicians, as well as by all ladies and gentlemen who have given it a test. One has only to look at a person returning from a ride on the saddle to see at once

Fig. 352.—**Horseback-riding.**

the beneficial result. The tinge on the cheek, and ruddy glow on the whole face and neck, is a positive assurance of the fact. It will prove a sure cure for dyspepsia in its worst form, if one will but persevere in the delightful recreation. But some one will say, "Oh, I cannot ride horseback ; it is too violent an exercise." And why? Simply because the attempt is made without any knowledge of the art, if it may be so called. The fundamental principle of the art of learning to ride is to learn one thing at a time, and learn to do that well, before attempting to do anything else. The first thing to learn is how to sit upon a horse. One should become perfectly at home in a saddle upon a constantly moving horse, so that whether it walks, trots, canters, shies, or jumps, he will either not lose, or will immediately regain, his position. The proper seat is a firm one in the saddle, with the legs below the knee free, and the body above the waist supple and pliable. Whatever movement the horse makes, whether to the right or left, or tipping backward or forward, the hips must conform to it, while the legs from the knees downward

are free to obey the rider's will, and the upper part of the body retains its balance by accommodating itself instinctively to every
movement. If the upper part of the body be kept rigid, its effect
will be to remove the hips from their place in the saddle. If, on the
other hand, it be flexible, it will yield and sway with every movement, and will be left free to obey the motions of the saddle.

In Tommy's act of throwing the boys, described in another
chapter, whenever a boy or young man would sit in the saddle
rigidly, with a firm grasp of the mane, no matter how strong or sup-

Fig. 353.—**An Insecure Position.**

ple he might be, the pony would throw him with great ease, and
with the force of a bullet, from his back; but when a young man
came in who would sit and balance himself on the pony's back as if
with the greatest carelessness, harmonizing the motions of his body
freely with those of the pony in the attempt to throw him, it would
frequently require the greatest effort to dislodge the rider.

The position assumed in the saddle should be with the weight
of the body supported directly under the hips, the spine curved inward, and the head and chest thrown backward. We give two illustrations from Leach, showing the insecure and the secure positions in
riding. The rider in the first illustration exhibits the greatest caution and timidity, with his body bent forward, and his whole at-

titude one of rigidity. The second illustrates the freedom with which the body may be managed when the seat is secure. When a landsman first goes to sea, he finds it extremely difficult to adapt himself to the motions of the vessel, stumbling and falling like a child learning to walk ; but with practice he soon gets what is termed his "sea legs." The principle is the same in learning to adjust one's self to the motions of the horse in riding.

The learner should make no attempt to guide or manage his horse, nor even trouble himself how to mount and dismount. Let

Fig. 354.—A Secure Seat.

him get into the saddle, turn his toes inward, press his knees against the saddle, but not his calves, bringing the flat of the thighs in the largest contact with it. Curve the spine inward, and throw the shoulders back. Let the arms hang listlessly by the side. Holding mainly by the knees, shift the seat from side to side and from front to rear, with as little swaying as possible of the upper part of the body. Continue this practice, no matter how long it takes, until the seat is firm, and the learner can move in any direction while keeping the spine curved inward. When the rider has accustomed himself to the slow motion of a walk, let the speed be increased, until finally the horse is galloped with a long bridle-rein, under all his motions, and the rider feels comfortable and easy, and has learned to depend only on his thighs and the flexibility of the body to maintain his position.

Having perfectly accustomed himself to the seat, the pupil may now put his feet into the stirrups, and learn their use. They should be used as a matter of comfort and convenience, as it is fatiguing to ride with the legs dangling at the horse's side. In walking, a gentle

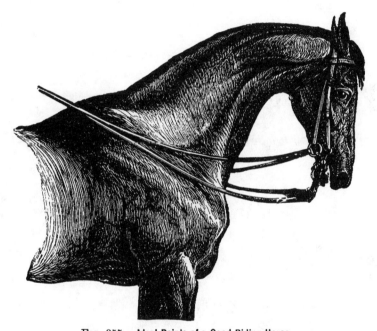

FIG. 355.—Ideal Points of a Good Riding Horse.

support of the stirrups keeps the body from swaying from side to side as the horse moves. In trotting,—when stirrups are almost indispensable,—they permit the horseman to either " rise to the trot," or to distribute the shock in " riding hard" between the feet, the seat, and the thighs, so that it is no longer a shock, but becomes a quick, easy movement. The stirrup-leathers should be so adjusted that the iron will just touch the bottom of the feet, giving them support without raising their position, while the inner part of the thighs, as far down as the knees, are pressing firmly and immovably against the saddle, and the legs below the knees hanging vertically.

In ordinary riding it is best to have the ball of the foot touch

19   a

the stirrups, as the play of the ankle-joint gives more elasticity to the support. But in galloping or leaping it is best to "drive the feet home," and carry the stirrups in the hollow of the foot. We consider the wooden stirrup in common use in this country to be the safest and best.

The main office of the stirrups is to rest the legs, while at the same time they assist in maintaining a proper position. But in case of any sudden start, the knees and thighs should be at once performing their duty of grasping the saddle. They cannot do this if the

Fig. 356.—A Good Model of Riding Horse.

weight is thrown too much upon the feet. It is also important to learn how to stand in the stirrups while the horse is in motion, turning so as to look to the rear, to throw the weight first on one foot and then on the other, and to assume every possible position rapidly and easily; for all this adds to security, freedom, and grace in the seat.

The following is the correct manner of mounting by the aid of the stirrups: First take the reins in your left hand just over the horse's withers. Stand with your right side to the horse, not too near, and put the left foot in the stirrup. Grasp the horse's mane with the rein hand, the pommel of the saddle with the other, give a spring with the right foot, and vault into the saddle, throwing the

FIG. 357.—Position in Mounting.

leg back and over the horse. Now rest the balls of the feet in the stirrup, and close the knees against the horse to keep a firm seat while trotting fast.

It is impossible to ride really well on an average horse without a curb bit; but it is impossible to ride well on any horse unless the curb bit is properly made and adjusted. And no one can either ride with pleasure or become really a good horseman on a horse that is in constant pain from an ill-fitting bit.

The beginner should use the reins of the snaffle only, grasping a rein in each hand at a length that will give him command of the horse. The proper manner of holding the reins, is, however, in the left hand, the curb reins divided by the little finger, the snaffle reins divided by the middle finger, the ends of both sets carried up

FIG. 358.—Army Bit.

through the hand and secured by the thumb, which should be uppermost, and pointed to the ears of the horse. By bending the wrist to the right, so that the knuckles come uppermost, the horse is turned to the right. By bending the wrist to the left, so that the finger-nails come uppermost, the horse will be turned to the left. There

FIG. 359.—Ordinary Bit.

should never be tension on the two bits at the same time. The horse should be ridden upon the curb; the snaffle should be used to fix the hight of the head, and occasionally to take the place of the curb to freshen the mouth.

Particular attention should be given to having the saddle adapted to the size of the person who is to use it. If it is too large for the rider, it will not only give him discomfort, but will increase the difficulty of acquiring a seat.

FIG. 360.—Holding the Reins.

Invalids, or those not accustomed to horseback-riding, should select a horse that is gentle and fearless, easily managed, sure-footed, and elastic in action. A riding-horse should not be used in harness, as this soon destroys the elasticity and smoothness of action necessary for easy riding. If the horse is at all vicious and unmanageable, he should be subjected to such treatment (as explained under that head) as will insure his entire docility and easy management. This is particularly necessary before attempting to ride him in the street.

Much of the foregoing instruction will apply to ladies learning to ride horseback. The lady should so sit upon the horse that her weight will fall perpendicularly to the back of the horse, her face directly to the front, her shoulders drawn back, and her elbows held to her sides. She will permit her body, from her hips upward, to bend with the motions of the horse, in order that she may preserve her balance. The right knee will hold the upright horn close in the bend of the knee. The left foot will be thrust into the stirrup to the ball of the foot, and the heel will, as a rule, be carried down. But when the heel is elevated, the upper part of the left knee should find support in the side horn, and for that end the stirrup-leather should be given such a length as will permit this. A lady should never be mounted on a weak or stumbling horse.

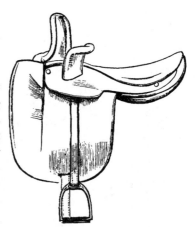

FIG. 361.—Ordinary Side-saddle.

The reins are to be held in the left hand, as already described, and in a line with the elbow. The whip should be carried in the right hand, with the point toward the ground. It takes the place of the right leg of the man, and the horse should be trained to answer to its application in exactly the same way as to the pressure of the man's leg. The horse should never be struck with the whip upon the head, neck, or shoulders, as such whipping will render him nervous, and may cause him to swerve.

It does not come within the limits of an abbreviated article of

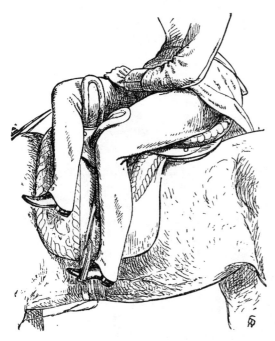

this character to give the details for the training of a horse to the different gaits and tricks of which he is capable under the saddle, as there are a great variety of works imparting this knowledge in full, which are easily accessible by those who desire it. With these suggestions, and sufficient practice, any one may enjoy this, the best of all modes of exercise.

If people would generally adopt horse-back-riding, they would starve out half our doctors, and would

Fig. 362.—Position in the Saddle.

live in the enjoyment of much better health than they now do. I will give here one of the many cases of restoration to health from this exercise that have come under my notice: A lady (whose name I will omit) came into my riding-park in a hack from her home about a mile distant. I arranged a stand so that she could step upon it, and sit down in the saddle without any effort. I led the horse around at a walking pace for about twenty minutes, when she dismounted, quite exhausted, and was taken home. The next day she came again in the carriage, and took another short lesson, and so continued to do three or four times a week for about four months. During this time she gained in strength to such an extent that at the expiration of the time she rode by car to Boston, a distance of twenty-five miles, did some shopping, thence to Cambridge to dine with her mother, and then returned home and rode ten miles on horseback. At the end of her ride she said to me:

"I feel no more fatigued than I did this morning when I started for Boston."

This is only one of the many cases that have come under my observation of regaining health from this exercise. Let every one have good practical training if possible, but get the exercise at all events, if you cannot have the training.

In corroboration of what Mr. Robinson says on the beneficial effects of horseback-riding, I copy the following paragraphs from a

Fig. 363.—**A Good Position.**

valuable little work on "Horseback-Riding from a Medical Standpoint," by Dr. Durant, of New York :—

Horseback-riding, as we have seen, is one of the most energetic modifiers of the circulation ; it distributes the blood equally to every part of the capillary net-work, giving to each part its due proportion, by maintaining a due tension in every part by equalizing the temperature ; it prevents equally anæmia and hyperæmia, and sanguineous stagnation, by the impulsion which it gives to the circulatory phenomena, and aids nutrition by the acceleration of the respiratory and digestive phenomena. It is by its effect upon the reactions of the blood to the nervous system that horseback-riding produces such a happy influence.

The effect of horseback-riding upon the functions of the system is especially remarkable upon that of digestion. It stimulates the appetite, excites and perfects digestion, favors absorption — in fact, to use a trivial expression, "It makes the bits go down." These are not the only results of the new energy imparted to the functions which we have studied, all of which concur in the accomplishment of this special one; it exercises a special influence upon the muscular fiber of the coats of the stomach and the intestines. These viscera may be considered as fairly suspended in the abdominal cavity, where they are barely held and limited in their movements by the folds of the peritoneum. Each shock from the horse shakes them and makes them roll, as it were, upon each other, and causes the changes in the relations of the convolutions of the intestines. These shocks and knocks and rubbings act as a mechanical excitant upon the muscular fiber, which in consequence contracts with more energy, preserving, however, the peculiar character of the fiber-cells ; that is, of contracting slowly and successively, the action of the fiber being increased and the peristaltic contractions acquiring more power, there results from it a more intimate mixture of the juices and aliments in the stomach, a more perfect chymification of the food, and a more prompt and complete absorption of matters already digested ; and, lastly, all those which have as yet escaped the process are brought into the portions of the intestines where their metamorphosis is effected.

FIG. 364.—An Ideal of the Family Horse.

Chapter XVI.

BREEDING.

ONE of the primary points of success in any enterprise is to start right, and in no respect is this more true than in the breeding of horses. The law of like producing like is inexorable ; consequently, to raise good horses, good horses must be bred from. Many farmers who are keenly alive to other interests, are

Fig. 365.—Arabian Mare and Colt.

singularly thoughtless and imprudent in this. If a mare is broken down, and unfit for labor, no matter how coarse or badly formed she is, or what the evidence of constitutional unsoundness, she is usually reserved to breed from.

On the same principle, no matter how coarse the stallion, if he is fat and sleek, and if his use can be obtained cheap, he is selected for the same purpose. The most ignorant farmer is particular to select the largest and soundest potatoes, the best quality of oats, wheat, etc., for seed, because he has learned that this is true economy ; yet there is the utmost disregard of this law of prudence in the breeding of horses and farm-stock in general. This sort of economy is like paying a quarter for a chicken and giving a dollar to get it carried home.

It costs just as much to raise a poor, coarse-blooded colt, as a fine-blooded one. The cost of feeding and care is really the same, the only difference being in the use of the horse. The first will possibly sell, when five years old and trained to harness, for from a hundred to a hundred and fifty dollars. The other is worth from two hundred to a thousand, and possibly more. The first will scarcely sell for the cost of feeding and care. The second insures a large profit, and this for a little additional first cost. The fact is, breeding from poor, unsound horses is so much a detriment, that it would be a damage to any one to be compelled to breed from such stock, if given for the purpose.

In Russia, Prussia, and Austria, the breeding of horses is controlled by the government, each one having large breeding establishments, where those wishing, can procure sound stallions, devoid of all hereditary diseases. Each stallion is furnished with a certificate from the government. No other stallions are allowed to serve mares, under a penalty. The result is that you will scarcely find an unsound horse, except from accidents, etc. Hereditary diseases, such as ophthalmia, roaring, rupture, spavin, ringbone, curby hock, spongy feet, etc., are scarcely known. It would be a source of undoubted economy and benefit to the breeders, if the legislature of each State would enact such laws, by appointing competent inspectors to grant licenses to those free from blemish or hereditary diseases or unsoundness.

A few years' breeding, under such restrictions, would materially increase the value of horses in each State, and thus be a real blessing to owners and the country.

In selecting a stallion, first look carefully at his head. The nostrils should be large and well defined ; eyes full, bright, and clear, and good breadth between them ; the ears lively, rather short and tapering, and the head high between the ears. Next, see that the throat shows no enlargement of the glands, indicating a tendency toward a whistler or roarer. The shoulder should be oblique, strong, and high, the fore leg not tied in under the knee, for such are liable to spring.

The feet should be of good size, and of sufficient depth to give strength to the quarters. Spongy and flat feet should be rejected. The loin should be strong, the back well coupled, quarters broad from point to point of hips, and running nearly straight out to the root of the tail. The stifle should stand low and well out ; hocks strong and broad ; no puffs or windgalls, as these indicate weakness.

As a colt from such a horse may at an early age show indications of blood spavin and thoroughpin, look at the inside of the hock for an enlargement at the point of what is called a jack spavin or curb. Next, see that there is no enlargement at the edge of the hoof, known as ringbone. Weak eyes, blindness, poll-evil, fistula of withers, or in fact any unsoundness, should be sufficient cause for rejecting a stallion. I need not enlarge upon the fact that the mare should be selected with the same care.

The reader will be aided in the study of disposition, bodily form, and the general characteristics of good and bad animals, by reference to the illustrations already given, and especially those in the following chapter. These will enable the mind to grasp these points better than it would be possible to do by the most extended verbal descriptions.

The following from a leading writer on selection is so much to the point that I cannot do better than to copy it :—

To be successful in breeding, special attention should be given to the particular variety of horse required. If heavy draught horses, or even trotting roadsters, or ponies, are required, both the sire and the dam should be selected with special reference to these points. Desired effects can in a great measure be produced by proper crossings. If the mare is light-boned, or defective in this or in any other respect, select a horse that possesses the contrast of greater strength. But to insure certainty of what is wanted, the mare and horse should be as near the type of what is desired as possible, though not related. Disposition should be an important consideration, as its inheritance will be as certain as that of physical qualities.

CARE OF THE MARE.

The mare is said to be with foal eleven months, or three hundred days ; but it is not uncommon for mares to have fully developed foals in much less time, and in many instances mares have been known to go four or five weeks beyond this time. Time should be so arranged in putting mares, that the colts will come at a time when there is some grass, as the mare will do better not to be confined to dry feed.

The virgin mare, or one that has not had a colt for one season, must be put when she is found in season. The mare that has had a colt will be found in season, and should be put on the eighth or ninth day after foaling ; some prefer the eighth, others the eleventh. Good judges claim that it is dangerous to go beyond the tenth, as the mare is apt to come off her heat soon after, and if allowed to go to a later period, the sucking of the colt is likely to reduce the mare too much to allow conception to take place, and thus a year's service of the breeder is lost.

After putting a mare, the days for trial are the ninth after service, the seventh after this, the fifth after this again. Some commence again, commencing with the ninth day, and follow up as before, making forty-two days. Twenty-one days being the period elapsing between a mare's going out of heat, and coming in again, making her periodical term thirty days. Twenty-one days is claimed to be sufficient to prove a mare.

Reference is made elsewhere in this work to the importance of protecting the breeding mare from excitement, abuse, etc. Especial care should be exercised in this matter, as fright, exposure to bad weather, improper feeding, or any influence that would seriously disturb the normal condition of the nervous system, will have its certain effect upon the colt, often to the great loss of the owner.

The mare and colt should be well fed, and protected from storms. The theory of working a mare hard, and half starving the colt, is the poorest kind of economy, since the mare needs generous feed and rest, to renew her strength and make her milk, by which of course the colt is nourished and made to grow. When size and strength will indicate that it is time to wean, which is usually in five or six months, put the colt in a quiet pasture, away from the mare, where it should be closely looked after. A little oats (better if bruised) should be given daily.

The conclusion of careful breeders is, that it is much better for a colt to run in pasture than to be confined in a stable. If the colt is intended for farm use, castration may be performed when six months old ; if, however, the withers are light, it should be postponed until the head and neck fill up to the degree required, and this may require from one to two years, or even more. If the head is large and heavy, early castration is advisable. Colts should be generously fed, and protected from the inclemency of the weather in winter. They should be treated gently ; may be broken early to harness, if treated gently and with care. This, however, is hazard-ous, as there is danger of over-driving young colts if they are driven at all. Many seem to take pride in trials to which they subject two or three-year-old colts. It is not what they can do, but what they ought to be required to do.

Fig. 366.—An Arabian Horse.

CHAPTER XVII.

STABLING.

THE stable should be built on a dry, airy location, facing the south when possible. It should be warm, well ventilated and lighted, and so constructed as to prevent the exposure of the horse to sudden changes of temperature. The stall should be suffi-

FIG. 367.—As a Horse Usually Stands while Resting in a Field.

ciently large to allow the horse to turn around or lie down, with conveniences for feeding. The width should not be less than six feet, but when practicable it would be better to allow each horse ten or twelve feet, to admit of a reasonable degree of exercise. This is not merely a great convenience to the horse, but it has considerable influence in preventing swelled legs, getting cast, etc. It is also important in that it permits a safer approach to a doubtful or vicious horse. It is the common custom to make the floor inclining backward, but this practice is unnatural, as shown by the fact that the horse, when left to choose his own position in a field, will almost invariably stand with his fore feet the lowest. (See illustration.)

The floor should be level; and to permit this, and at the same

(301)

time keep it dry, it should be constructed as follows : Incline the
floor backward about two inches, making it water-tight, with an
opening or drain at the back end for the water to pass off. Arrange
upon this an extra floor of slats about an inch to an inch and a
quarter thick, and five eighths to three fourths of an inch apart·
The back ends should be two inches thicker than the front, to compensate for the slope of the floor underneath, and thus give a level
surface for the animal to stand upon, while the water can pass between the slats and drain off. This upper floor should be made in
two parts, so as to open from the center upward, and stand upon
edge while the lower floor is washed or cleansed as desired. This is
the method of construction in one of the most perfect stables in the

country, to an examina-
tion of which the author
is indebted for the idea.

The door should be
large, with an extra one
of slats, which can be used
during warm weather ex-
clusively for light and
ventilation. It would also
be well to have screens or
mosquito - netting over
the door and windows, to
protect the horse from
flies,—a great annoyance
to sensitive animals.

FIG. 368.—The Accepted Method in General Use.

One of the most serious objections to stables as they are usually
constructed throughout the country, is the lack of proper ventilation.
Usually they are nothing but close boxes, and entirely too small for
the number of horses kept in them. The doors and windows are
closed, and the bedding, saturated with ammonia, is tucked away
under the manger. If there is an upper flooring, it is made the receptacle for hay, so that it not only obstructs any possible ventilation through the stable, but by becoming impregnated with the
poisoned air below, it is rendered unfit for food. Any one going
into such a stable, especially during warm weather, will have the
eyes immediately affected by the escape of ammonia, which, with
the contamination of the air, caused by being breathed over and over,
makes it even sickening to breathe any length of time.

It is evident that to supply the wear and tear of bodily structure, the food must not only be good, but of sufficient quantity to

supply nourishment to the body. Now, a horse can live days, and even weeks, without food, while he cannot live five minutes without air.

It is needless to enter into details as to the quantity of air a horse breathes in any given time, as every intelligent reader has a good idea of this ; but the fact that a horse will quickly die when deprived of air is not so forcibly impressed upon the mind. Now, it is evident that if the blood is not oxygenated by means of pure air passing to the lungs, the system will soon be poisoned ; thus it is seen how necessary it is that there should be plenty of air in the stable, and as pure and free from contamination as possible. If it becomes impure in consequence of there being too many horses in the stable, and also loaded with ammonia from the bedding, it can-

not properly purify the blood or carry away through the proper chan-nels the broken-down, worn-out particles of mat-ter, and thus permit a proper nutrition of the body. Instead of this, all the various conditions of disease are engendered. This is particularly notice-able as the source of oph-thalmia, grease, glandular swellings, etc. Now, if pure air were obtained only at a great expense, it might

Fig. 369.—Objectionable Method of Tying.

be a reasonable excuse for not furnishing it in necessary abundance ; but the fact that it is obtainable in all cases with a very little trouble and care, renders this neglect little less than a crime, for which there should be no excuse or apology.

An abundance of ventilation in stables may be supplied in vari-ous ways, but the simplest and best is substantially as follows : A chimney or opening through the ceiling may be made in the form of a dome or cupola. The top should be roofed over, and have lateral openings by means of weather-boards. The most convenient or comfortable stable the writer has ever seen had such a ventilator, which was so regulated that it could be partly or wholly closed, as desired. This was accomplished by means of two cords attached to opposite edges of a revolving door, and adjusted in the lower part of this opening or chimney. Another special convenience was a contrivance for obtaining and measuring grain to be fed, which was so ingenious that I give a description of it: The grain was conducted from the loft to the feeding-floor by a spout in which were two slides. Pulling out one of these slides a few inches permitted the escape of two quarts, and the other one of four quarts, of grain, which was deposited in a drawer beneath. In the bottom of the drawer was a screw, with a handle projecting from the side of the spout. Moving this handle right and left a few times shook the bottom like a sieve, and thus removed all the dust and dirt, leaving the grain clean, fresh, and ready for use.

I have found two features about the stables as usually constructed through the country, which are so faulty that I would urge

FIG. 370.—Rack too High.

the necessity of having them corrected. First, in the construction of mangers and racks. The manger, an open trough, is usually so high that a horse of medium hight can barely reach over and put his nose to the bottom. Extending over this manger is a rack so high that the horse can scarcely reach the hay from it. There is usually more hay packed into this than the horse can eat at one time, so it is suffered to remain there until it becomes stale and sour from the horse's breathing upon it, and the exhalations from the bedding, which is usually packed during the day under the manger. When the horse reaches for the hay, the dust and dirt which have accumulated are thrown over his head and eyes. In the first place, the horse does not like to eat such trash; second, it is difficult for him to reach it; third, he is liable to be annoyed, if not injured, by the hay and dirt filtering into his eyes and mane.

The nearer the horse is made to feed in the stall as he does in the field, the better. But if compelled to eat grain from the ground, there would be waste. To avoid this, a receptacle must be provided in a corner about on a level with the shoulder, from which to eat grain; but the hay should be measured and put in a corner on the ground, where it can be easily reached. If there is not too much given, the horse will eat it clean.

The importance of this is now so well understood that all first-class horses are fed in this way. For the ordinary work horse, or for country stables, a simple low rack or manger, one side made into a box or receptacle for the grain, and the other part for hay, is all that is necessary. If two horses are kept together, the stall should be about twelve feet wide, with grain-boxes at the right and left, and the manger for hay in the center. Horses accustomed to working together will always agree when kept in the same stall, especially when they have separate mangers, and are prevented by their halters from interfering with each other's grain. The

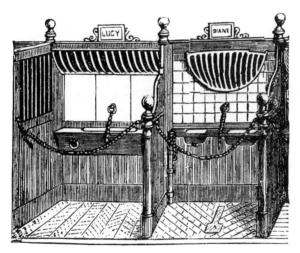

Fig. 371.—The Accepted Form of Single Stalls.

mangers and racks should be on a level, and about three feet and four inches from the ground. The manger should not be less than sixteen or eighteen inches deep; eighteen inches from front to back, and twenty or twenty-two inches in length. For one horse, the rack should be about four feet in length. The advantage of such a manger and rack is, that all the hay that is put into it will be eaten clean. There will be less danger than by the common high rack of putting more hay before the horse than he will eat at the time, and thus his mussing and spoiling it will be prevented. It will entirely obviate the objection of dust and seeds falling upon his head and into his eyes, or of pulling the hay out and wasting it under his feet.

Some horses are inclined to throw their hay out with their

20   a

noses. This can be effectually prevented by nailing two or three
bars across the upper part of the crib from the back to the front.
The hitching ring should be on the off or farther side, to prevent the
strap from being caught by the foot.   If the horse is a greedy eater,
and disposed to throw the grain out of the box, it can be prevented
by putting a few round cobbles in the bottom, thus compelling him
to take his grain slowly.   The division between the stalls should always be high enough to prevent the horses from interfering with
each other.   If windows are near, they should be so high as to prevent any current of air from striking directly.

CHAPTER XVIII.

FEEDING AND WATERING.*

HAY, corn-fodder, oats, and corn constitute the principal food of horses in this country; hay and oats in the Northern States, fodder and corn in the South. The food should be of the quality and quantity to impart strength, vitality, and elasticity; and this requires some discrimination and care, as the food should be harmonized both to the condition of the horse and the severity of the labor to which he is subjected. As a rule, the stomach should not be distended with food when prolonged, energetic effort is required. This is to be especially guarded against in the feeding of hay. Greedy eaters can and often will eat so much hay as to unfit themselves for active labor, and it usually results in heaves or broken wind. Heaves are always found in the teamsters' or carters' stables where there is no care in feeding. This disease is never found among racing horses, from the fact that the utmost care is used in selecting the food and feeding in small quantities, or in adapting it more perfectly to the wants of the system.

It has been demonstrated beyond doubt that the reason horses improve so much in wind by eating prairie hay is, that it is so coarse that they cannot eat it fast enough to overload the stomach. The quantity of hay should be carefully regulated, and never as much given as the horse will eat if at all voracious. The majority of owners pack a large rack full, either allowing liberty to eat too much, or making it unpalatable and unhealthful by being breathed upon. From eight to ten pounds is about the average quantity for an ordinary roadster, to be allowed in twenty-four hours, more or less, according to the size, the kind of work, and the quantity of grain given. Dusty or moldy hay should never be fed, as it is liable to produce various forms of disease.

The food should be clean, and perfect in quality. Hay is most perfect when it is about a year old. Horses would perhaps prefer it earlier, but it is neither so wholesome nor so nutritious, and may

---

* The main points of this paper were dictated by Dr. Summerville, of Buffalo, N. Y., to the writer while studying with him.

cause purging. When it is a year old, it should retain much of its green color and agreeable smell.* Blades of corn pulled and cured in the summer are unquestionably much better than hay. I should certainly prefer this kind of fodder to any kind of hay, for fine horses. It is strange that it is not prized more highly in the North.

Oats make more muscle than corn; corn makes fat and warmth. Hence, the colder the weather, the more corn may be given, and the harder the work, the more oats. Oats should be a year old, heavy, dry, and sweet. New oats will weigh from ten to fifteen per cent more than old ones; but the difference is principally water. New oats are said to be more difficult to digest, and when eaten in considerable quantity are apt to cause flatulency or colic, and derangement of the stomach or bowels. The same may be said of corn. If not sound and dry, it may be regarded even much more dangerous than oats, and should not be fed. Doing so will be at the hazard of the consequences above mentioned.

The quantity of oats given daily may vary from eight to sixteen quarts. If the horse is large, and the work is severe, a little more may be given. Corn should be fed in the ear, and like oats must be regulated in quantity to the size and labor of the animal; from five to twelve good-sized ears are a feed. I give a larger proportion of feed at night, and less in the morning and at noon. There is ample time for digestion during the night. There is not during the day, if the labor is severe. Experience proves that some mildly cooling laxative food should be occasionally given. A bran mash, made by pouring boiling water on eight or ten quarts of wheat bran, covered over until cool and fed at night, from one to three times a week, is the finest and best.

Carrots are a good laxative and alterative before frost, but are too cold and constipating during cold weather. They may be fed in October, November, and December, but in the Northern States not later.

I feed Irish potatoes, from one to three quarts, with the usual quantity of grain, from two to three or four times a week, and would recommend their use. Feeding a small quantity of roots and giving bran mashes keep the bowels open and the system in a healthy condition. Without them constipation is probable, and this is one of the primary causes of diarrhea, colic, or inflammation of the bow-

---

* In packing or stacking hay, salt should be slightly sprinkled through it so as to destroy insects. It also aids in preserving it bright, and makes it more palatable and healthful for the horse.

els. If it is desired to make a horse fat in a short time, feed corn-meal and shorts, with cut straw, to which add a pint of cheap molasses. Nothing like this for recruiting and filling up a horse that is out of sorts or poor.

If the horse is exhausted, or when sufficient time cannot be allowed for him to eat and partially digest a full meal, he may be greatly refreshed by a draught of warm gruel, or, in summer, of cold water containing a small quantity of meal.

COOKING THE FOOD.

My attention was some time ago called to the advantage of cooking feed for horses. Those who have given the most careful study to the principles and best methods of alimentation, state, first, that well-crushed grain is not only more readily masticated, but more easily digested ; second, that cooking the feed enables the animal to assimilate a far larger percentage of the nutrition than from the same amount of grain fed in its raw state. The amount of grain is claimed to be from 20 to 30 per cent. According to report, the Germans have long used cooked feed for their army horses, and found it to excel all other kinds of feed in giving greater strength to the horse, and increasing his power of endurance. It is also claimed by the most successful stock-breeders in England and on the Continent, that horses and cattle thrive better, and are far healthier, when fed on cooked feed than when fed on any kind of raw feed.

I copy from a circular published by the Chicago Steam Cooking Feed Company, some of the advantages of cooked feed for horses :—

1. Many horses are so voracious and eat so rapidly, that they do not properly masticate their feed, and, in other cases, the grain is too hard to be properly masticated.

2. It is estimated that more than one half of the diseases which afflict horses, are induced by the use of uncooked feed, and its bad effects upon the digestive apparatus.

3. The hard, flinty covering of raw grain can neither be properly ground by the teeth, nor is it soluble in the stomach, and most of it passes from the stomach undigested.

4. All energy expended in attempts to assimilate certain parts of raw feed, is just so much waste and positive loss.

Among the advantages of using properly cooked feed for domestic animals are the following :—

1. Cooked and ground feed is much more palatable for the animal, and is very easily masticated.

2. The hard, dry covering of grain, when it has been steamed and ground, be-

comes as nutritious as any part of the grain, and adds just so much to its food properties.

3. The entire grain is digested and no portion of it wasted ; nor is there any loss in the efforts of the stomach to do the work of the cook and the grist-mill.

4. The loss in feeding raw grain is changed to gain in the cooked feed, a smaller quantity of the cooked grain giving a larger proportion of animal strength.

5. The primary cause of much illness and derangement of digestion in animals is removed by the use of properly cooked feed.

It seems to the writer that cooked feed is especially important to horses having weak digestion, and for old, enfeebled horses.

When a horse is " off his feed," by overeating or want of proper exercise, the better way is to reduce his usual quantity of grain one half for three or four days or a week, when he will eat again as well as ever.

I here give Mr. Bonner's system of feeding :—

In the morning, at five o'clock in summer and six o'clock in winter, each horse is given two quarts of oats. At nine o'clock two quarts more are given, and the same quantity is given again at one o'clock. Before feeding, each horse is given all the water he will take, unless he is to be driven, in which case the allowance is cut short a little. At five o'clock in the afternoon the allowance of hay is given, usually about ten pounds to each horse ; and none is given at any other time during the twenty-four hours. At nine in the evening each horse is given a warm supper, prepared as follows : For ten horses twenty quarts of oats are put into a large kettle and boiled, after which is added about the same quantity of wheat bran by measurement, with the proportion of a teaspoonful of salt to each horse. The whole is thoroughly mixed, and, when sufficiently cool, each is given his share. If not driven, each horse is walked from half an hour to an hour daily, and the greatest care is taken not to expose them needlessly for a moment without blankets.

The following is the routine pursued with Dexter :—

At six every morning, Dexter has all the water he wants, and two quarts of oats. After eating, he is " walked " for half an hour or more, then cleaned off, and at nine has two quarts more of oats. If no drive is on the card for afternoon, he is given a half to three quarters of an hour of gentle exercise. At one o'clock he has his oats again, as before, limited to two quarts.

From three to four he is driven from twelve to fifteen miles ; after which he is cleaned off and rubbed thoroughly dry.

He has a bare swallow of water, on returning from the drive, but is allowed free access to his only feed of hay, of which he consumes from five to six pounds.

If the drive has been a particularly sharp one, he is treated, as soon as he gets in, to a quart of oatmeal gruel ; and when thoroughly cool, has half a pail of water and three quarts of oats, with two quarts of bran moistened with hot water.

Before any specially hard day's work or trial of his speed, his allowance of water is still more reduced.

It is a very bad practice, and one that should never on any condition be permitted, for grooms or teamsters to give any kind of medicine, either for tonic or diuretic purposes. Many a fine horse is completely ruined by ignorant grooms and owners, who think they can help nature by giving niter and other strong medicines, that are never admissible except in certain emergencies, and then should be given only very cautiously.

I am satisfied that many veterinary practitioners give not only too much but too strong medicine, which, though of apparent advantage for the present, must ultimately result in serious harm to the health of the horse. Clean, good feed properly prepared, and given in quantities according to the needs of the animal, is safer and better than to be giving medicine for every little change of condition.

If the horse is out of sorts, overfed in proportion to his work, becomes dainty, or the depurative processes are obstructed by the feeding of too much or of too highly concentrated feed, let up on the grain, and feed more bran mashes or green food.

Old horses that are not feeding well, or are running down without apparent cause, should have the teeth carefully examined (see article on the " The Teeth "), as sometimes the horse cannot grind his feed. The simplest way of making an examination, is to catch the tongue, and, with the hand closed, let its under part rest upon the lower jaw, with the end of the thumb forced upward against the roof of the mouth. (See illustration of giving ball.) This will compel the horse to keep his mouth open, so as to enable looking into it or passing the hand far enough back to examine the teeth. If they are found to be the cause of the trouble, they should be filed down, as directed under that head.

WATERING.

If a large quantity of cold water is taken into the stomach while the system is agitated, by the circulation being so increased as to open the pores of the skin freely, it is liable to chill the stomach and close the pores of the skin, and thus excite some one of the common alimentary derangements, as colic or inflammation of the bowels, etc. Hard water, especially cold well water, is more liable to cause mischief in this way than soft water. Hard water will affect some horses so much as to almost immediately cause the hair to look rough or staring, and derange the appetite. Horses that are raised and worked in a country where the water is strongly impregnated with lime, are troubled with intestinal calculi ; *i. e.,* stone in the bladder. Hence soft water should be given, if convenient ; but if well-water be given, especially during warm weather, it should either have the chill taken off or be given very sparingly.

The best time to water a horse is about half an hour before feeding. While driving, the rule should be, little and often. None, or only a swallow or two, should be given at the close of a drive, until cool. If very warm, the horse should be walked moderately where there is not a current of air to strike him, from ten to thirty minutes. If any danger is then apprehended, the chill should be taken off the water if very cold, and given sparingly, or only a few swallows at a time. The common custom is to give about a half bucketful. The safer course would be to give less and repeat.

The rule for ordinary use should be, to give a small quantity often during'the day, and let the animal pursue his journey or labor immediately after. If allowed to stand, the system is liable to be chilled, and the absorbents closed, which is the common cause of laminitis or founder, although this disease may not develop itself until twelve or twenty-four hours afterward. Any cause which will chill the horse — either cold winds or cold water -- will be almost sure to produce this disease.

Chapter XIX.

HOW TO TELL THE AGE.

IT is sometimes very important to be able to determine the age of a horse ; and as this is indicated most surely by the teeth, I have had made, under my special supervision, a large proportion of the illustrations here given, which will be found the fullest and most

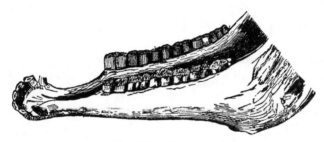

Fig. 372.—The Teeth.

complete published in this country. I encountered very serious difficulties in obtaining these illustrations, as I found it next to impossible to give the artist an idea of the changes occurring in the teeth and form of the jaw with age, but they are as accurate as I could se-

Fig. 373.—One Week Old.

cure. I have tried also to make the description so simple as to enable any ordinary person to determine the age of horses with considerable accuracy, or so nearly as to prevent being seriously imposed upon. In doing this, I have not hesitated to appropriate the language o others when adapted to my purpose.

Fig. 374.—Six Weeks.

At first the jaw is small, and to accommodate the position, temporary, or what is termed milk teeth, are grown ; these are succeeded by permanent teeth, as the jaws become larger and stronger. As the front teeth, or nippers, only are usually studied to note the changes which determine the

(313)

age of a horse up to eight years, I will try to give such an explanation of them as will serve to aid the general reader in catching the

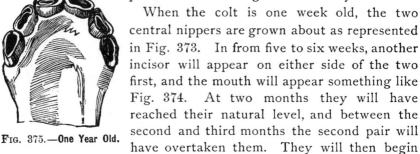

points of these changes most clearly.

When the colt is one week old, the two
central nippers are grown about as represented
in Fig. 373. In from five to six weeks, another
incisor will appear on either side of the two
first, and the mouth will appear something like
Fig. 374. At two months they will have
reached their natural level, and between the
second and third months the second pair will
have overtaken them. They will then begin

FIG. 375.—One Year Old.

to wear away a little, and the outer edge, which was at first
somewhat raised and sharp, is brought to a level with the inner one ;

and so the mouth continues until some
time between the sixth and ninth months,
when another nipper begins to appear on
each side of the two first, making six
above and below, and completing the
colt's mouth ; after which the only observable difference, until between the second and third years, is in the wear of
these teeth.

The teeth are covered with a polished,
hard substance, called enamel. It spreads
over that portion of the teeth which ap-

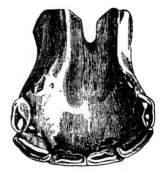

FIG. 376.—Twenty Months.

pears above the gum ; and not only so, but as they are to be so
much employed in nipping the grass, and gathering up the animal's

FIG. 377.—Two Years.

food (and in such employment even this
hard substance must be gradually worn
away), a portion of it, as it passes over
the upper surface of the teeth, is bent inward and sunk into the body of the teeth,
and forms a little pit in them. The inside
and bottom of this pit being blackened by
the food, constitutes the *mark* of the teeth,
by the gradual disappearance of which, in
consequence of the wearing down of the
edges, we are enabled for several years to

determine the age of the horse.

The colt's nipping-teeth are rounded in front, somewhat hollow
toward the mouth, and present at first a cutting surface, with the

outer edge rising in a slanting direction above the inner edge. This, however, soon begins to wear down, until both surfaces are level, and the *mark*, which was originally long and narrow, becomes

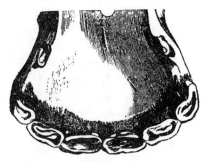

shorter, and wider, and fainter. At six months the four nippers are beginning to wear to a level. Fig. 375 will convey a good idea of the appearance of the teeth at twelve months. The four middle teeth are almost level, and the corner ones becoming so. The mark in the two middle teeth is wide and faint; in the two next teeth it is darker, and longer, and narrower; and in the corner teeth it is dark-

FIG. 378.—**From Two and One Half to Three Years.**

est, and longest, and narrowest. At the age of one year and a half, the mark in the central nippers will be much shorter and fainter; that in the other two pairs will have undergone considerable change, and all the nippers will be flat. At two years this will be more plainly marked. Fig. 377 is intended to show the appearance of the mouth at this stage.

Fig. 378 is intended to show the appearance of the mouth at two and a half to three years old. The next is intended to show it at three and a half years old. The two central permanent teeth are growing down, and are larger than the others, with two grooves in the outer convex surface, and the mark is long, narrow, deep, and black. Not having yet attained their full growth, they are lower than the others. The mark in the two next nippers is nearly worn out, and is wearing away in the corner nippers.

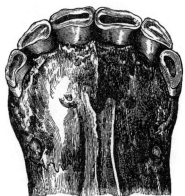

FIG. 379.—**About Three and One Half Years.**

Between three and a half and four years the central nippers have attained to nearly their full growth, and the second pair will have so far displaced the temporary teeth as to appear through the gums, while the corner ones will be diminished in breadth, worn down, and the mark become small and faint.

At four years the central nippers will be fully developed; the sharp edge somewhat worn off, and the mark shorter, wider, and fainter. The next pair will be up, but they will be small, with the mark deep, and extending quite across them.

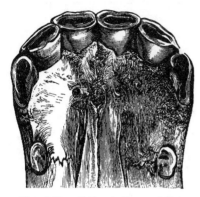

FIG. 380.—**At Four to Four and One Half Years.**

FIG. 381.—**At Four Years.**

At four years and a half, or between that and five, the corner nippers are shed, and the permanent ones begin to appear, something like Fig. 380 The central nippers are considerably worn, and the next pair are commencing to show the marks of usage. The tush has now protruded, and is fully a half inch in hight; externally it has a rounded prominence, with a groove or hollow in the inside.

At five years the horse's mouth is almost perfect. The **corner** nippers are quite up, with a long, deep, **irregular** mark on the inside, and the other nippers **are** showing the effects of increased wear. The tush is much grown, the grooves on the inside have almost or quite disappeared, and

FIG. 382.—**About Four Years.**

the outer surface is regularly convex. It is still as concave within, and the edge nearly as sharp as it was six months before.

At six years the mark on the central nippers is worn out. In the next pair the mark is shorter, broader, and fainter; and in the corner teeth the edges of the enamel are more regular, and the surface is evidently worn. The tush has attained its full growth, being nearly or quite an inch in length; convex outward, concave within; tending to a point, and the extremity somewhat curved. The horse may now be said to have a perfect mouth, as all the teeth are produced and fully grown.

At seven years, the mark, in the way in which we have described it, is worn out in the central nippers, and fast wearing away in the corner teeth; the tush also is beginning to be altered. It is rounded at the point, rounded at the edges, still round without, and beginning to get round inside.

At eight years the tush is rounder in every way; the mark is gone from all the bottom nippers, and it may almost be said to be out of the mouth. There is nothing remaining in the bottom nippers that can afterward clearly show the age of the horse. The upper nippers will give some indications, but nothing certain.

After the age of eight years, there are no points that will enable determining age with any degree of accuracy. A horse that is fed on corn will show an older mouth than one that is fed on oats and sloppy feed.

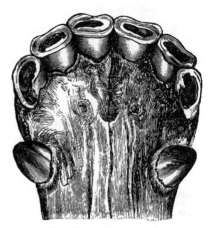

Fig. 383.—At Five Years.

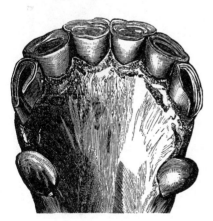

Fig. 384.—At Six Years.

The usual time for determining a horse's age is in May; but a colt may come any time between then and fall, so that the wearing away of the teeth or disappearing of the marks or cups may in some cases indicate the horse to be older or younger than he really is. These conditions must be taken into consideration.

At six years the teeth are rather short, flat, or wide, and the gums run across them horizontally, something like Fig. 384. After the eighth year the gums begin to recede from the center, and the teeth become longer in appearance. By looking at Fig. 390, showing twelve years, we can see that the gum is receded and run to a sharp point at the center of the teeth. At twenty years, the teeth are considerably narrower and longer, and the gums are drawn back sharper.

By observing the face of the teeth, there will gradually be seen a change to the triangular form, which can best be seen and de-

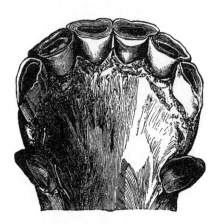

FIG. 385.—**About Seven Years.**

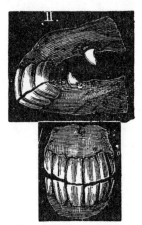

FIG. 386.—**At Eight Years.**

scribed by Figs. 395, 396. From the age of four-teen, we see this is more noticeable, the middle nippers gradually increasing and extending out to the corner ones, as indicated by Fig. 397. From fifteen to eighteen this triangular form be-comes laterally contracted, so that at about twenty and afterward the teeth become biangular. As before explained, there are great peculiarities in the form of the teeth with advanced age. The most common is shown by Fig. 397. I include a somewhat rare form shown by ex-treme age. (See Fig. 398.) Many curious

FIG. 387.—**At Eight Years.**

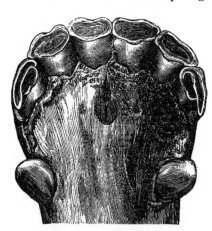

FIG. 388.—**About Eight Years.**

tricks and methods of telling the horse's age after eight years old have been shown the writer at various times, such as wrinkles about the eyes, root of the tail, etc., none of which give the idea so correctly as the genera appearance of the teeth and ab-sorption of the jaws. In young horses the edge of the lower jaw is round and full ; as the horse becomes older, this edge becomes sharper and thinner.

The most unique trick shown the writer of telling the age was the following :—

FIG. 389.—**About Six Years Old.**

If a gold ring be attached to a hair pulled from the tail or mane of a horse, and suspended directly above his head between his ears, it will oscillate, like a pendulum, just the number of times the horse is years old, then stop and repeat. I have repeatedly made the experiment, and it certainly seemed to repeat the age of the horse ; but I could not feel satisfied that the motion of the ring was not in a great measure controlled by the involuntary movement of the hand. The man who gave the idea made the experiment in the presence of the writer, with apparent success.

FIG. 390.—**About Twelve Years Old.**

Jockeys frequently resort to cutting down the teeth of aged horses, so as to simulate as much as possible the appearance of the mouth at eight or nine years of age. This was formerly done by sawing or filing, but more recently there has been invented, by Dr. Lancer, a leading veterinary surgeon of New Jersey, a very ingenious instrument for chipping off the teeth, so that the front nippers can be cut down very quickly and easily by any amateur. But the breadth of the teeth and other changes of form, as explained, will expose the deception ; also the deep hollow and gray hair about the eyes, with the under lip con-

FIG. 391.—**About Twenty Years Old.**

siderably pendant. This treatment is called " Bishoping," from the name of the man who introduced it in England, and is practiced very largely by jockeys in the larger cities of this country, especially in New York.

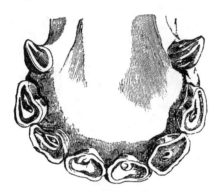

FIG. 392.—About Eleven Years of Age.

FIG. 393.—Mouth of the Mare at Thirteen Years.

I wish to call attention to the fact that horses, especially those advanced in years, are liable to have the teeth in wearing overlap one another, become very rough, and wound the inside of the cheeks ; or the grinders become irregular in length when they do not come opposite each other in shutting, or the teeth become carious and break away when not correspondingly worn with the others, shoot up to a degree to penetrate the jaw, causing soreness and inflammation, and seriously interfering with eating.

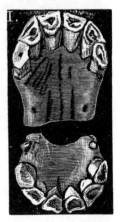

FIG. 394.—Mouth of the Mare at Thirteen Years.

The writer saw a very interesting case of this kind at the Columbia Veterinary College, in which the unobstructed tooth had seriously penetrated into the upper jaw. In the endeavor to relieve the pressure of the parts, the animal evidently masticated the food wholly upon the opposite side of the mouth ; in consequence of this the teeth on this side were so worn down that both upper and lower jaws were twisted around more than an inch out of line.

Sometimes caries, or ulceration of a tooth, produces such serious disturbance that there may be an enlargement of the parts, growth of fungus, or necrosis of the parts. This, too, is much more common than is suspected. Prof. Cressy, of Hartford, called my attention to a case in which a back tooth in the lower jaw became ulcerated, causing much enlargement of the jaw. He first removed the tooth, then divided the skin at the lower edge of the jaw, and with a drill made a hole through the bone. Through this hole he put a seton to keep the parts open until a healthy healing process should be produced. A strong preparation of carbolic acid was put upon the seton, and dressed once a day, which finally effected a perfect cure.

When the horse, without any apparent cause, is running down, munching, or eating his food but slowly, especially if there is any lateral action of the jaw, examine the mouth carefully to see whether

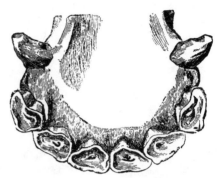

FIG. 395.—At Fourteen Years Old.

there is any noticeable cause of trouble in the teeth. If rough and irregular, they should be rasped down. The method of doing this is now so well understood as to scarcely need explanation.

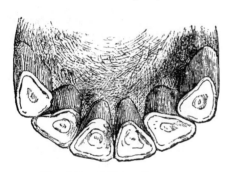

FIG. 396.—At Sixteen Years Old.

The rasping down of all irregularities should be carefully done, and if there is a decayed tooth it should be removed by a veterinary surgeon who is conversant with the simplest and best method of doing it. There are regular horse-dentistry implements in general use for this purpose, which can be easily obtained. If the tooth has grown down below the level of the others, it should be rasped or sawed off to the proper dimensions, and carefully watched afterward so as to remove any undue growth harmful to the opposite parts.

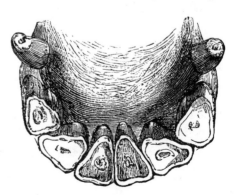

FIG. 397.—From Seventeen to Eighteen Years.

If there is any enlargement of either jaw, more especially of the upper one, with perhaps a running sore offensive to the smell; and if in addition there is offensive matter running from the nostril on that side, the trouble may be suspected as arising from a carious tooth, and the jaw on that side must be carefully examined.

FIG. 398.—Extreme Age.

FIG. 399.—Ideal Colt's Mouth.

It may be asked, How is it, if the trouble arises from a carious tooth, that the matter comes from the nostrils?

Answer: By the imprisoned matter forming a sinus into the nasal cavity.

The treatment for all such cases is, first, in the removing of the

FIG. 400.—Irregular Growth of Teeth.

offending cause, namely, the tooth itself, and also, as far as possible, the dead or diseased parts, and favoring a healthy condition of growth by cleansing out the parts with a strong solution of carbolic acid or chloride of lime, or any good disinfectant. Next, protect the parts from the lodgment of particles of food, by filling with a pledget of tow saturated with the tincture of myrrh, or any good healing astringent, and dress once a day. If there is diseased bone or fungus growth, it should be treated the same as for other difficulties of the same kind.*

---

* Since writing the above, my attention has been called to an article in the *Journal of Comparative Medicine and Surgery*, of April, 1883, by Dr. Robert Jennings, of Detroit, Mich., in which he refers to a large number of cases of this description.

FIG. 401.—A Model Form.

FIG. 402.—The Famous Eclipse Thoroughbred Racing Stallion.

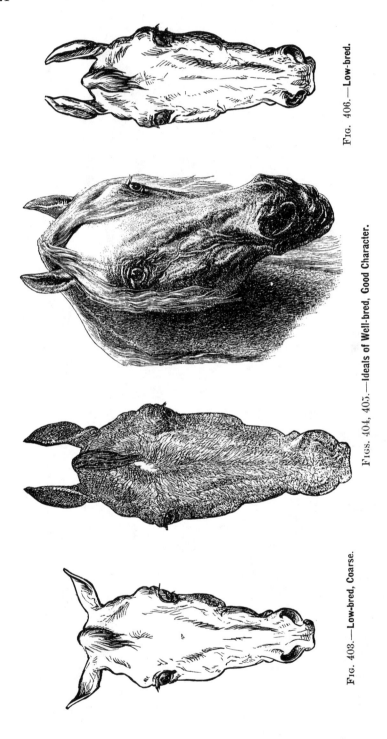

FIG. 406.—Low-bred.

FIGS. 404, 405.—Ideals of Well-bred, Good Character.

FIG. 403.—Low-bred, Coarse.

Fig. 407.

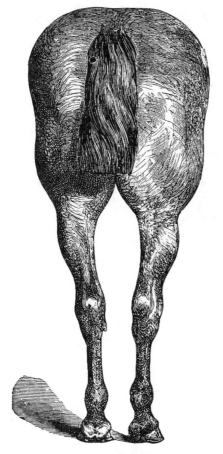

Fig. 408.   Fig. 409.

Fig. 410.

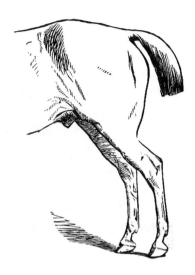

FIG. 411.

FIG. 412.

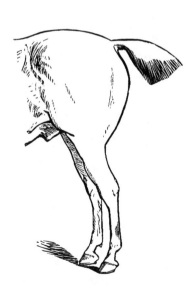

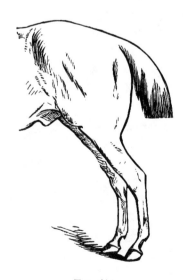

FIG. 413.

FIG. 414.

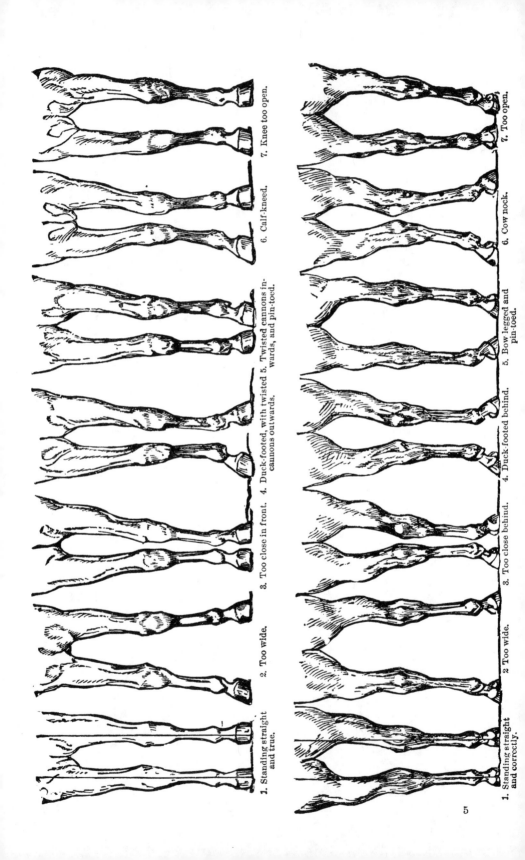

1. Standing straight and true.   2. Too wide.   3. Too close in front.   4. Duck-footed, with twisted cannons outwards.   5. Twisted cannons inwards, and pin-toed.   6. Calf-kneed.   7. Knee too open.

1. Standing straight and correctly.   2. Too wide.   3. Too close behind.   4. Duck-footed behind.   5. Bow legged and pin-toed.   6. Cow nock.   7. Too open.

CHAPTER XX.

SHOEING.

PRELIMINARY EXPLANATIONS.

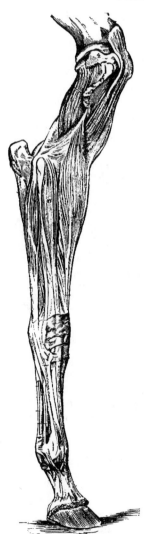

FIG. 429.—**The Foot and Limb with Hoof Skin Removed.**

DURING my early experience I was induced, by the advice of friends, to give what instruction I could on shoeing. With this object, I had prepared models of the hoof, and the best forms of shoes, and was frequently led to give short lectures on the subject. It was not, however, until I visited New York City, in 1872, and had several conversations with Mr. Robert Bonner on shoeing, that I was able to obtain anything like a correct idea of the principles of doing this. I found that what was published in books accessible on the subject, was but the merest rubbish, calculated in many respects to seriously mislead and do harm. Mr. Bonner had just purchased the mare Princess, the famous old competitor of Flora Temple. Her feet were badly contracted, and the tendons of the legs greatly thickened, causing her to move almost as sore and stiff as a foundered horse. He assured me that before I left the city the feet would look entirely natural, and that she would travel with as much freedom and ease as a colt. From my knowledge of the subject, it seemed utterly impossible to cure such a case ; and yet, to my astonishment, in less than three months afterward she was perfectly well. I was startled, first, to find that I knew nothing of the subject ; second, that there was so little known about it practically ; and third, that a gentleman for his own amusement proved to me that he had a far deeper and more correct knowledge of it than doubtless any man of his time.*

At any rate, I was now led to study the subject in an entirely different light, and though far from being able to give the instruction on this subject I would like to do, for want of the requisite knowledge, I have done the best I could to make the instructions so simple and practical that they will at least serve to correct some of the wretchedly bad treatment practiced by shoers. I have tried also to include such illustrations of the

Fig. 430.—Lateral View of Horse's Foot after Removal of the Hoof.

structure of the foot as would show its various parts most clearly, with other features of most interest to shoers.

The bones of the foot are so nicely adjusted and balanced by the ligaments and tendons of the limb, that there is no unequal strain brought upon any joint, but each assists in supporting the others. But if the heels are raised too high, or the toe left too long, there will be correspondingly increased strain brought upon the ligaments and tendons supporting the back or front part. In like manner, raising or lowering the

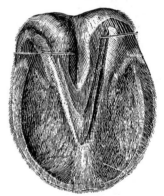

Fig. 431.—Inferior View of Foot with Hoof Removed.

* Indeed, this is conceded now by even the leading members of the veterinary profession, as will be seen by the following statement by Dr. Going, formerly veterinary editor of the *Spirit of the Times,* which I copy from his Veterinary Dictionary. He says :—

"It is said that no man has ever yet reached perfection in any branch of art, science, literature, industry, etc.; but while I am unprepared to join issue with the assertion, I can safely say that the nearest approach which has ever been made in this connection (horse-shoeing and the study of the horse's foot) has been made by Robert Bonner, Esq., of New York, who, had not the *Ledger* already made him famous, would undoubtedly have obtained widespread renown through his almost superhuman knowledge in this department. I have had the pleasure of conversing with him on this subject, and am pleased to have an opportunity of stating the impression the conversation made upon me."

inner or outer quarter would produce a lateral strain upon the joints and ligaments, which must ultimately cause the foot to grow out of line, and induce serious injury. Consequently, the point to be attended to in removing excessive growth of the wall in preparing it for the shoe, is to preserve or restore the natural angle and direction of the hoof. This is one of

Fig. 432.—**Coffin Bone Showing Internal Lateral Cartilage, Internal and Posterior View.**

A, coffin bone; B, internal aspect of the lateral cartilage.

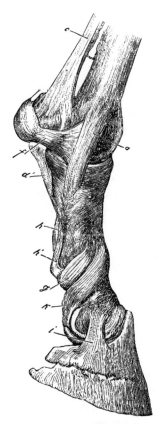

Fig. 433.—**Lateral View of the Pastern Bones and Ligaments.**

the important points, in doing which successfully the genius of true skill and success must be shown. A large number of illustrations are given showing good forms and positions of the feet and legs, with faulty forms. Also the various lines of movement of the feet when in motion. These are to be studied in paring the feet to change or modify the action as may be desired.

First, in preparing the foot for the shoe, the aim should be to cut away so much of the wall as would be a surplus of growth, or so much only as would bring it back to its natural form and adjustment. As a rule, the wall should be lowered to the level of the unpared sole. The sole and frog should on no account be pared or touched by the knife, nor should the heels be "opened." The horny sole and frog, unlike the wall, do not grow indefinitely ; but when they have attained a certain thickness, they throw off the superfluous or old horn in flakes or scales. This natural thickness of the sole and frog-horn is an essential condition for the

a, Lateral ligament of the fetlock; i, Anterior lateral ligament of the coffin joint; c, Suspensory ligament; f, Lateral sesamoidal ligament.

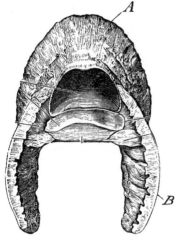

Fig. 434.

A, ospedis or coffin bone; B, transverse section of lateral cartilage.

maintenance of the foot in health and its protection from injury. In any event, about all that is necessary to do is to remove those loosened and detached flakes, which, were it not for the shoe, would have exfoliated themselves. Cutting away more than this becomes a serious cause of injury. The angles between the bars and crust should be moderately pared out, as accumulations here, with continued pressure of the shoe, are apt to induce corns. The frog does not require paring more than the removal of ragged parts, and even these better not be touched.

Second, the shoe should be in form, so that when on, the adjustment of the foot, or its power to obtain hold or grasp upon the ground, will be what it was before being shod, and yet sustain the wear for the time it is intended to be on.

Third, it should be nailed on firmly, yet so as to break or weaken the wall of the hoof as little as possible, and not interfere with the freedom of the quarters or enlargement of the foot as it grows.

In its natural condition the outer rim or wall of the foot comes in contact with the ground first; second, the frog and outer edge of the sole; third, the center of the foot

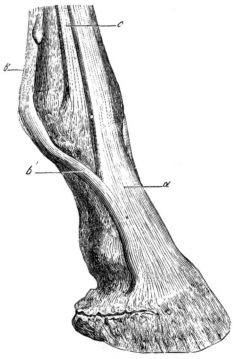

Fig. 435.—Anterior and External View of Right Front Foot.

a, Exterior pedis ligament; b, Suspensory ligament.

and spaces between the bars and frog. To show this more clearly, three sectional drawings are made from half-size casts, showing the concavity of the foot at different points between the heel and turn of the hoof, and the necessarily great disturbance of this relation by the form of shoe usually put on. Fig. A shows the foot at the point of the heels as it rests upon the ordinary thick shoe, with calks raising the frog and sole so unnaturally high from the ground that there can be no contact of those parts with it necessary for obtaining moisture and preserving a condition of health. In addition it will be noticed that in the way shoes are usually fitted, the bearing surface is very much concaved, tending to crowd the quarters together. Fig. B shows the same, with form and fitting of shoes as they

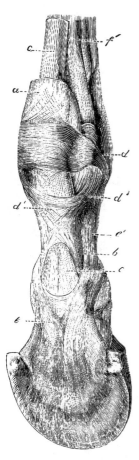

Fig. 436.—**Right Front Foot, Posterior and Slightly Lateral View.**

a, c, Perforans tendon; f, Suspensory ligament.

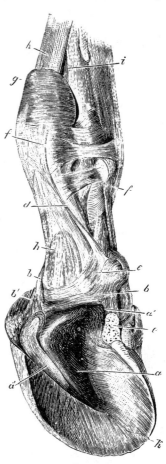

Fig. 437.—**Inferior, Lateral, and Posterior View of the Right Front Foot, Showing Ligaments of Tendons.**

a, Sensitive frog; h, Perforans tendon; f, Suspensory ligament.

should be ; Figs. C and D show the same at relative distances between there and the turn of the foot ; D, at the widest part, representing a heavy shoe. (See page 347, Figs. 472–475.)

If a colt's foot grows too long or out of line, it should be leveled down so as to make the adjustment natural, the outer edge rounded a little, and the colt driven barefoot.

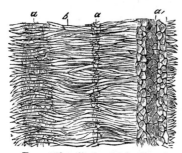

FIG. 438.—**Horizontal Section of the Horny Frog.**

a, Horn tubes: b, Cells between tubes.

It is noticeable that excessive wear is always at the toe, and that the heels rarely suffer, even on bad roads, and this being true, tips or thin steel plates only should be used, and that thick and high heeled shoes are not only certainly unnecessary but seriously injurious—that, in fact, in all cases the best shoeing for the feet, for all roads and seasons, when in a good condition of health, must be such as will permit them to be as nearly barefoot as possible, or, at least, that the posterior part is so, yet sustaining the attrition of wear to which they may be subjected, prevent slipping, and best preserve the natural adjustment of the feet.

TIPS OR THIN SHOES.

If tips or thin steel plates are to be used, simply trim off the wall in front down to a level with the sole, and adjust to, and nail on, with four small nails, a small thin strip of steel or iron a little broader than the thickness of the wall. Steel would be best, because it admits of being made lighter, and wears longer. The heels and frog should not be interfered with unless one heel is much higher than the other, when it should be lowered sufficiently to restore the proper adjustment. The objection to tips is that, as the toe is growing, the heels are wearing, which in time would be likely to increase the strain upon the flexor tendon and its appendages. This disproportion of wear would be more rapid and noticeable should the roads be wet and gravelly, as moisture and grit soften the horn and cause it to break and wear away more rapidly, but not so much as may be supposed on paved streets and mud roads. The writer saw

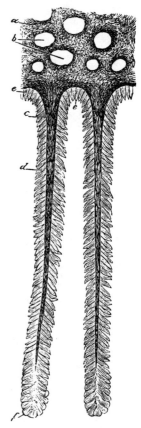

FIG. 439.—**Horizontal Section of Horny Wall Enlarged.**

a, Wall with horny tubes; b, Horn tubes; c, Horn laminæ.

several horses in New York City that had been shod with tips with decided benefit to the health of the feet, and without any apparent disproportion or wearing down of the frog and quarters, though the iron was worn down fully a quarter of an inch. The parts became, as it were, hardened and polished, thereby resisting the wear almost as much as the iron.

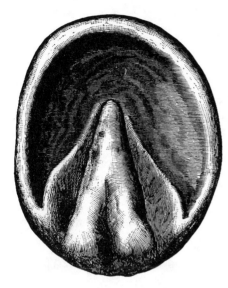

Fig. 440.—**Colt's Foot Three Years Old.**

As there has been much discussion among writers in relation to the use of tips, or thin-heeled shoes, I requested Dr. Hamill and Dr. McLellan, the two best veterinary authorities on this subject in this country, to give me a statement of the cases for which, in their judgment, tips would or would not be adapted. I give herewith the reply of each, and invite the attention of the reader to the points made, and the reasons given therefor. Prof. Hamill says :—

* * While I am a firm advocate of frog and sole pressure, and have driven my own horses for years over the pavements of New York City with nothing on the feet but what is known as the English tip or toe-piece shoe, which gives the foot the entire freedom of all its natural movements, yet I must say it would be absurd to attempt to shoe every horse in this way. There are any number of cases where this system would be *injurious* to the foot, and even to the limb. But as the foot, or rather that part of it inclosed within the hoof, is the object oftenest under consideration, I shall explain briefly how it may suffer from extreme frog-pressure. (One point which we should always keep in view is a due proportion, or equal distribution of the weight in all parts of the hoof, and by no other system can the foot be healthy.)

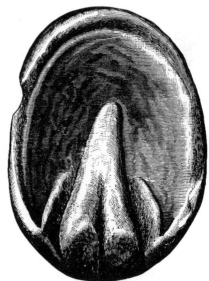

Fig. 441.—**Colt's Foot Four Years Old.**
From a Cast.

Any foot that is thin in its general structure, but more so in its vertical position, or from top to bottom, and with the frog full at its pyramidal eminence or body, is not a proper foot for frog-pressure.   In such feet the plantar cushion, or what is

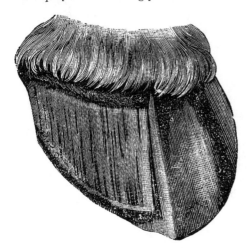

known as the fibrous or fatty frog, is very thin, is easily made weaker by absorption through extreme pressure or irritation on the horny frog, and therefore offers very little protection to the great flexor tendon where it passes under the navicular bone.

But I may be asked, How could this in any way cause injury, if the navicular joint be perfect, as the tendon requires only a slight cushion underneath?   My answer is, that there is a *double* impingement of the tendon, owing to the navicular bone descending on the tendon every time weight is thrown on the limb, the proof of which is the pain caused

Fɪɢ. 442.—**Half Hoof Removed.**

by this action on the internal structures of the hoof.   I ask, Where is the shoeing-smith who has not seen the agony of a horse while standing on one bare foot on the level floor while the other foot is being shod, and the relief which followed when the shod foot was placed on the floor?   I may be told that such feet

have been previously weakened by bad shoeing and bad care, and that a horse which never had been shod would not suffer in this way.   Those who make such assertions are entirely ignorant of the anatomy and physiology of the foot.

My answer is, that when a horse first comes to the world he has *no* frog development, and for the first year of his life, while walking on a level, can have *no* frog-pressure.   It is only animals that are raised on low or marshy land that have a great development of frog.   Horses belonging to mountainous countries have very little frog, and generally narrow or apparently contracted feet, which is no evidence of disease.   Witness the ass and the mule for example ; and I may add that although wide heels are generally desirable, they are no evidence in themselves of perfect health.   I am well aware that most thin heels, and generally thin feet, have a large

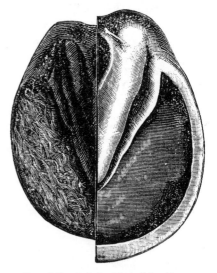

Fɪɢ. 443.—**Inferior View of the Above.**

frog, but the depth of such a frog is more apparent than real, as it will be found on close investigation that the flexor tendon and navicular structure are lower or nearer the ground-surface in such a foot.   Therefore we must discriminate in all cases, as one mistake may cause irreparable injury. To be definite, we can safely give extra frog and heel pressure in all cases where the hoof is deep at the quarters, where there is a tendency toward contraction and atrophy of the frog, where the obliquity of the pastern is not too great, *and where the feet and limbs are perfectly sound and well proportioned.* (This latter will narrow the circle more than most people are aware of.) No thoughtful man would dare to throw extra weight on the sole and frog of a foot that had long suffered with navicular disease, however excellent this would be as a preventive. Neither

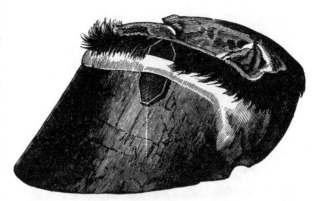

Fig. 444.—**Showing the Coronary Band.**

should we throw extra weight on the posterior parts of a foot or limb where there is any soreness of flexor muscles or tendons, or any ligament involved, as it would entail greater tension on the parts, while the opposite is what is required, viz., flexion or relaxation.

I say distinctly, we should only carry frog-pressure to the extent of bringing into activity all the elastic structures of the foot, which increases the circulation of those parts so liable to atrophy, *and only through the circulation* can we keep up or restore the health, vigor, and growth of frog, sole, heels, and quarters of the horse's foot.

Fig. 445.—**Showing Inside of Hoof.**

Prof. McLellan says :—

In reference to the use of tips, I give you only an outline. They are useful in the case of corns, in quarter-cracks, in thrush, in interfering, and in fitting the horse to run at grass. They are not applicable to feet that have thin, flat soles, with low heels. They are not applicable to heavy work horses with flat feet and prominent frogs (such frogs are liable to suffer bruises when so exposed, the resulting inflammation extending frequently to deeper and more vital structures). They are not applicable to feet having navicular disease. They are not applicable when, in applying them, it is necessary to disturb the normal relation of the bones of the limb.

22   a

They will be found particularly useful in strong feet that have corns in both heels, and in the case of bad interferers.

TRIMMING.

Before preparing the foot for the shoe, the smith should go in front and look at it, so as to determine better its adjustment. Sometimes the foot may be run over by having one side too high or the toe worn off excessively. If it is desired to be particular, he

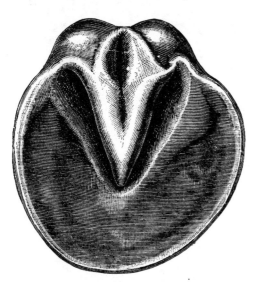

FIG. 446.—The Foot Natural.

should see how the feet are carried in a sharp trot; whether too high or too low; or whether he travels too close, endangering interfering or cutting — using the words of a high authority, "to see whether there are any traces of bruising or cutting on the inner sides of hoofs, fetlocks, or knees." He should also see how the old shoe has been worn. The foot can then be taken up, when a look from the heel forward will enable an observing shoer to determine how much and what part is to be cut away to level it to the proper proportion, and the faults, if any, that can be modified or corrected. If the horse travels high, the shoes must be light; if low and subject to stumbling, they may be increased in weight a little, and the toe somewhat rounded; if liable to strike, then set close under the wall with edges filed smooth.

The point is to cut away or remove the surplus growth in the easiest and best manner, which depends more upon the deftness and ingenuity of the man than upon the use of any special means. The wall should be reduced to nearly or quite on a level with the outer margin of the sole. The bearing surface of the entire wall should be made level, so that an even bearing surface of the shoe will rest upon it fully. The rasp should now be passed around the toe, to cut away the sharp edges and bring it to the size required. Practically, this should be little more than rounding off the sharp edges of horn to prevent splitting.

The principle is the same of leveling and preparing the feet of horses that have previously been shod. In such cases, to take off

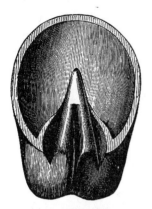

the shoe the best method is, after the clinchers are cut off, to raise both heels slightly with the pincers, then pry forward and across the foot a little, when the nails can be pulled out one by one. It is seriously objectionable, as generally done, to pull off the shoe by force, as the severe wrenching endangers tearing the hoof and straining and injuring the foot. This would be especially objectionable if the hoof be thin and the horse sensitive. Next, any stubs or nails should be removed.

Fig. 447.—Foot Excessively Pared.

While it is simply intended to pare down the wall to its natural form, if it is thin and weak, growing but little, especially at the heels, where there is great difficulty to grow sufficient wall for the support of the foot, no more should be removed than is barely necessary to level it. As before stated, there should be no interference with sole or frog, excepting to chip or cut away the portion of the old horn which could not be exfoliated. Frequently the heels are too high, or the toe too long ; in either case, whatever the excessive accumulation or growth of horn, it should be cut away until the foot is brought back to its natural form and adjustment. Sometimes there is excessive accumulation to the amount of half an inch or more at the heels, or even of the whole wall of strong, upright feet, yet to the ordinary observing shoeing-smith it may not appear excessive, because cutting away so much would make the foot

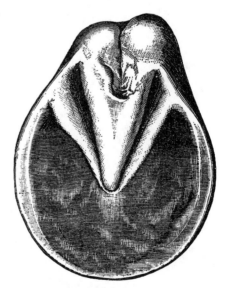

Fig. 448.—Foot after Four Years' Shoeing.

appear to him to be unnaturally small. Several specimens of abnormal growth of feet are given. Fig. 495, page 355, taken from life, is a good representative case, and was seen by the writer at

Fulton Ferry, New York City. It is that of a pony mare driven before a huckster's wagon. The right foot was so contracted by this excessive accumulation of horn, that its mobility was entirely destroyed. It will be noticed that the toe of the shoe is carried forward something like a sled crook, to enable a rolling motion upon the ground. It was pitiable to witness the pain and misery this poor animal exhibited. She walked with a crippled, sensitive motion, and while standing would put out one foot, then the other, but mostly the right one. The case could have been easily relieved of pain

FIG. 449.

FIG. 450.—**Too Short and Upright.**

FIG. 451.—**Too Oblique.**

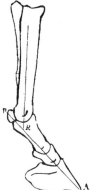

FIG. 452,—**Natural Obliquity of Ankle.**

and soreness, by simply cutting down the feet and thoroughly soaking and opening the quarters, as explained in treatment for "Contraction." The dotted lines represent the point to which the horn should be cut away, showing an excess of accumulation of over three inches.

FIG. 453.—**Heels too High.**

FIG. 454.—**Too High on One Side.**

THE SHOE.

The shoe should, in form and size, little more than cover the wall, excepting at the heels where it should be so much wider and longer as to compensate for the growth of the foot, and be heavy enough to sustain the attrition, or wear, for the time it is expected to be on. But should this require an excessive thickness, then the bar may be made wider, to permit more wearing surface. It should fit closely all the way around to the bearing surface prepared for its reception, so that it may give to the crust all the support it can receive, and carry out in its ground surface, as nearly as possible, the form of the wall before it was cut away. It is a rule, recognized by the best

authorities, that the sole should not rest upon the shoe, except around the toe where the outer edge is left full and natural. But if the wall is cut down close, and the sole rather thin (which, as explained before, in no case should be done except for pathological reasons), it is advisable, if it comes too near the iron, to lower the part coming under it. As a rule, the bearing surface should be level, and the ground surface concave, or the inner edge of the ground surface so beveled off that it will not harbor stones and dirt, and be so stiff that it will not bend.

As before stated, if the horse is expected to be driven only occasionally, and upon common dirt roads, the wear will be but little,

FIG. 455.—**Too Short.**

and the shoes should be correspondingly light; but if much travel is required, on stony or macadamized roads, the weight should be sufficient to sustain such wear. The addition of a small bit of steel, hammered well into the toe, and tempered, would add greatly to its durability. It would be much better to make them wholly of steel, as they would be very much lighter, equally stiff, and less liable to bend.

In a condition of health, from a light family driver to the heavy draught horse, the principle of shoeing is the same; the size, thickness, and

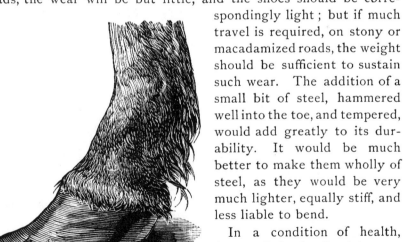

FIG. 456.—**Foot too Long.**

weight only differing so as to adapt to each case, with the difference that when exceptional power is necessary, as for draught horses, or to prevent slipping, calkins must be used. As a rule, nothing more is wanting, unless necessary for extra wear, than just iron enough to protect the outer crust of the foot, and prevent its breaking. More iron than this becomes extra weight, and causes fatigue in carrying, like thick, heavy-soled shoes or clogs.

It is a question among English authorities whether a shoe should be "rounded at the toe" (a practice known as the French system) to aid mobility.

A moderate rounding at the toe would seem desirable in all cases where there is want of mobility. It is especially desirable when the horse is a little stiff or sore, as it enables him to travel much easier. This is proved when the mobility of the foot is destroyed, and there is necessity for using a rounded shoe to conform with the action. Illustrations of a large variety of shoes of different forms are given, which can be studied.

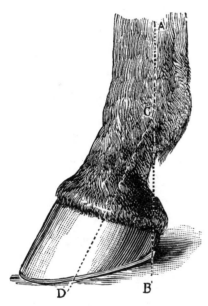

Fɪɢ. 457.—Shoe Properly Adjusted.

Prof. Williams, of Edinborough Veterinary College, advises that the calkins and toe-pieces should be done away with for all kinds of horses except those used for

Fɪɢ. 458.—Thin Shoe for Light Work.

Fɪɢ. 459.—Faulty, Bad Form of Shoe.

heavy draught in towns where the streets are paved and steep. It is urged that all horses required to go beyond a walking pace are injured by shoes with turned-up heels and toes. Farm horses and those employed on macadamized roads are better without than with toe-pieces, although the pace at which they are required to go is never faster than a walk. In fact, all horses, when possible, should be shod with a flat shoe.

NAILING.

The object of nailing should be to hold the shoe firmly to the foot without injuring the wall, and leave the foot as independent of the restraint of the shoe at the quarters as possible. The nails should be driven where there will be most secure nail-hold; more or less as well as heavier nails being necessary, in proportion to the thickness of the wall, weight of the shoe, and severity of the work. The wall is thickest and strongest at the toe or front, and becomes thinner and more flexible toward the quarters and heels, especially

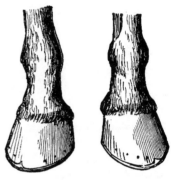

Fig. 460.—Toes too Wide.

at the inner heels, where it is sometimes extremely thin and flexible.

There has been much speculation during the past few years in relation to the cause of this quarter's giving out before the other, as nature evidently intended it to stand strain and wear equally with other parts. The cause, undoubtedly, is the interference in its mo-

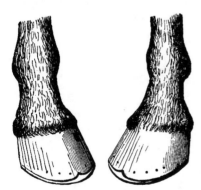

Fig. 461.—Extreme Toeing In.

bility by bad-fitting shoes and nailing so far back as to interfere with the flexibility of the quarter. This being true, it is evident that the principal nailing should be at the toe and front, because there is more horn there to nail to, and less liability to do harm by separating and breaking the fibers of the wall. They should not extend any farther back into the quarters than is barely necessary to give a safe hold of the shoe to the foot. The fewer and smaller the nails driven, the better, providing they are sufficient to hold the shoe. But much will depend, in doing this, on the accuracy of the fitting, thickness of the wall, and weight of the shoe.

If the nails are driven well back on the outer quarter, and only round in the toe of the inner side, for the purpose of affording more freedom to the quarters, it will be found that as the foot grows, the shoe will be carried to the outside quarter and toe to such an extent that the inner heel of the shoe will be drawn inside of the wall at the

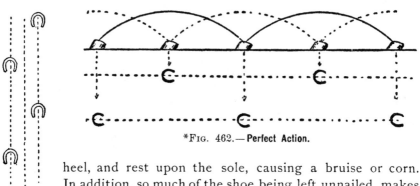

*Fig. 462.—Perfect Action.

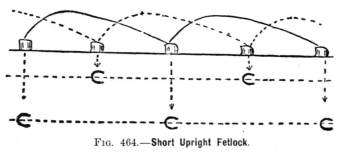

*Fig. 463.

Perfect Action.

heel, and rest upon the sole, causing a bruise or corn. In addition, so much of the shoe being left unnailed, makes it liable to get loose and work under the quarter, which would cause a rapid wearing or breaking down of structure. All things considered, the best way is to nail back to the turn of the wall securely. Or the nailing may be extended a little farther back on the outside, and shortened a little on the inner side, in any case giving both quarters all the freedom compatible with security, in retaining a firm hold of the shoe. As the foot grows, the shoe will be brought forward so evenly under it as not to do harm.

For ordinary light shoes, six to seven nails, evenly distributed around the front part, should be sufficient, sometimes extending the outer nail a little beyond or nearer the quarter than the inner one.

Fig. 464.—Short Upright Fetlock.

But if the shoes are heavy, and the work hard, as for draught horses, heavier nails, and from seven to eight in number, will in most cases be required. A small, thin clip turned up at the toe, and one at the outer quarter, will help greatly in holding the shoe firmly in position; but they should be turned up thin, and set well out on the edge of the shoe.

---

* In connection with figures 462, 463, see page 328.

But very little of the wall should be cut away, so as not to weaken or injure it ; but sufficient to enable bringing the shoe to its position. The shoes should not be hammered down tight to the wall, but simply sufficient to rest easily against it. Next, if the foot is broken, or much weakened by old nail-holes, punch the holes where there is soundest horn to nail to, as shown by Fig. 596. A thin shoe will not admit of any fullering, because it weakens the shoe, without giving any special advantage in nailing. The stamp form of punching the holes should be used ; that is, the hole made larger at the surface and smaller at the bot-

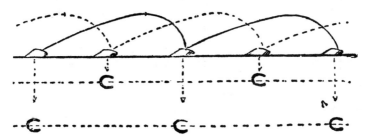

* Fig. 465.

Too Close. * Fig. 466.—Action with Low Heels and Oblique Fetlock.

tom, so that the nail-heads will fit into it exactly.

The method of driving the nails is next worthy of consideration. There are two methods ; one, starting the nail rather near the outer surface and driving high, called the English method, which is practiced very generally in this country ; the other, starting the nail deep and bringing out low, known as the French method, which leading authorities concede to be the best. If the nail is driven very near the surface, it is liable to chip or break the horn out, which injures and weakens the wall very much ; whereas driving deep and bringing out low, insures a good hold, and the wall will be almost grown out by the next shoeing. Consequently they should be punched deep over those points where the wall is thickest, and less so toward the quarters where it is thinnest, or proportionately farther from the outer margin of the shoe.

The common method of fullering all shoes alike, and bringing the nails at the same distance from the edge, can be no more adapted for all kinds of feet than can the size of the shoe itself. This straight-jacket way of punching

*Fig. 467.

Action that Strikes.

* In connection with figures 465, 466, 467, and 470, see page 327.

all alike, brings the nail-holes at the same location at each repetition of shoeing, so that if the shoe becomes loose, or is pulled off, this part of the wall is liable to be torn off, or so split and broken

Fig. 468.   Fig. 469.

Thin-heeled Shoe Advised by Prof. Williams of Edinborough Veterinary College.

as to leave only a soft, imperfect horn. In resetting such a shoe, it becomes necessary to put it farther back under the foot in order to gain secure nail-hold. Not only this, but the portion of the projecting wall being cut down to the shoe, leaves it deformed and injured to an extent that

several months' growth cannot repair. But if the holes be punched over parts that would give as secure hold, the shoe can be nailed on sufficiently firm to hold it without doing harm, and thereby preserve the symmetry of the foot In such a case it may be necessary to nail rather close to the heels ; but even this had

*Fig. 470.

**Faulty Action.
Too Wide.**

better be done for a short time than risk injury and

Fig. 471.—**Foot Prepared for Shoe.**

malformation by the method named.

If by carelessness or otherwise a nail should be driven into the quick, which will usually be known by the horse's flinching, it should be pulled out at once ; or should a horse show soreness after being taken out of the shop, the foot should be examined carefully by tapping over the part, and the nail at the point of soreness pulled out. (For more details, see treatment for Pricking and Rucking.)

CLINCHING DOWN THE NAILS.

When the nail is twisted off, the end should be filed down to the proper length, and, with the corner of the rasp or little punch, cut out the pith or raised part under the clinch, and turn down lightly but firmly. The common custom is to make a deep notch with the corner of the rasp, which extends across the face of the hoof from one nail to the other.

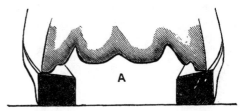

FIG. 472.—Foot at Point of Heel on Thick Shoes.

This is so injurious that it should not be permitted even to the smallest degree. No rasping of the outer surface of the wall should be allowed, excepting to touch or smooth any roughness of the clinches, and to round of the edge of the

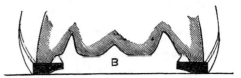

FIG. 473.—Shoe Fitted as it Should Be.

FIG. 474.—Adjustment between Heel and Turn of Foot.

wall dawn near the shoe. It has been explained under the proper head, that the inner surface of the wall soft and spongy, and that as it approaches the outer surface, it becomes hard and

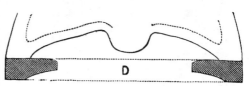

FIG. 475.—Adjustment at Turn of Foot.

bony, and the fibers closer and denser, and that over the surface is a sort of skin or thin covering of enamel, that prevents too rapid evaporation of moisture ; and it is necessary to retain intact this strong fibrous horn, as well as its outer covering, so as to hold the nails firmly, as well as to prevent the excessive evaporation of moisture which would follow.

Should the shoe be too short, which is liable to happen, to remedy the difficulty it is the common custom to set it back under the wall, and rasp the thick, strong wall, extending out over the shoe, down to it. Or, should the shoe be too straight or narrow for the foot across the points of nailing, to drive the nails so deeply as

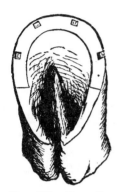

not only to endanger pricking, but greatly to weaken the wall.

The excessive rasping not only destroys the strongest part of the wall, that best able to retain the nail-holes and support concussion, but causes a serious internal disease not usually understood, which shows its effect in an absorption of the

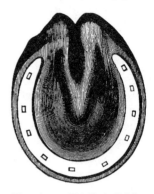

Fig. 476.—**Tips. From the French.**

Fig. 477.—**Thin Strip Set in Hoof. From Lafosse.**

bone beneath. Fig. 523 is a good illustration of this. The specimen from which it is drawn was obtained from Dr. Hamill. The small sketch is full size, and shows the exact appearance of its surface, and small points of horn which are over a quarter of an inch long, extending out like pegs.

Shoeing the Hind Feet.

There is usually so little

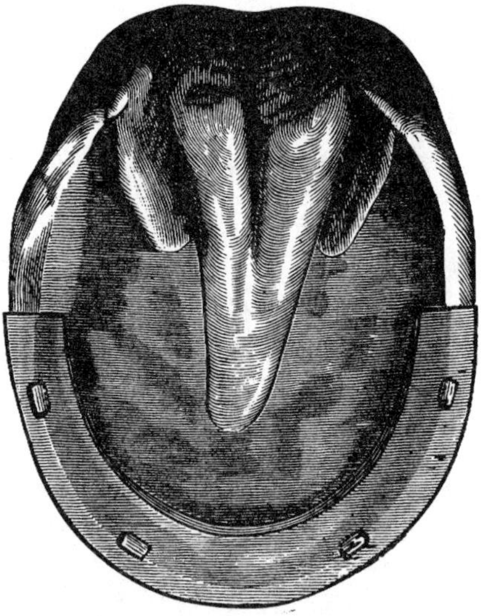

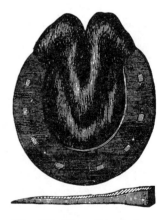

Fig. 478.—**Tips Applied to the Colt's Foot.**

Fig. 479.—**Thin Shoe. From Lafosse.**

trouble with the hind feet, that it is scarcely necessary to give any directions as to their management. The horn is thickest at the quarters, and the principal nailing should be done there. Some-

times there is a curling under or
contracting of the heels, which
may be the cause of more or less
inflammation, extending to the
sheaths of tendons and other parts
of the leg; in such a case, if
thought advisable, either or both
quarters can be treated as explained under that head in "Contraction."

PRICKING AND RUCKING.

I think it advisable, in this connection, to say a few words about
pricking, which is more common
than many suppose. It is not unusual, indeed it is a very common

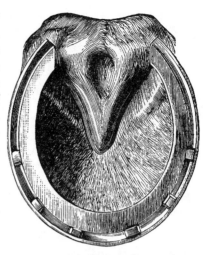

FIG 480 —Shoe Adjusted. From the German.

occurrence, to drive the nail too near the quick or into it, and thus
by a little carelessness cause great harm. First, if the nail be driven
so as to go to the quick, in which case the horse may show it by
flinching, it should in all cases be pulled out at once, and the hole

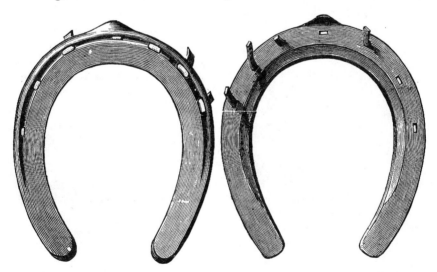

FIG. 481.—Model Shoes.   FIG 482.—Showing Location of Nails.

be left vacant. If this is done, no harm will follow. Sometimes
the smith, especially if he expects to be scolded, will drive the
nail down, which in a few hours or next day will show itself by

making the horse lame ; or the nail may be driven so deeply as to go near the soft parts of the inner edge, and when the point strikes

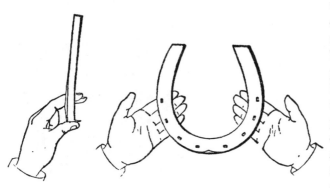

the hard horn of the outer surface, it may bend inward or press upon and break through to the sensitive parts. This is called rucking, as shown in Fig. 508 The nail should be pulled out at once.

FIG. 483. —**Examining the Shoe.**

Another cause of harm is what is termed fitting and drawing the nails too closely. If the nails are driven rather deep, and clinched down firmly, they are liable to bend inward and press upon the sensitive parts. This is called pinching. If present when the horse is shod, and it is noticed that the nails are driven rather deep for the thickness of the wall, insist upon their being driven farther out.

An ignorant or thoughtless man may claim there is no danger, though he is driving the nails much too deep. Should the horse show soreness or lameness within three or four days after being shod, especially if he puts

FIG 484.—**Location of Nails.**

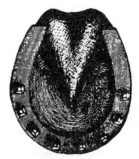

FIG. 485.—**French Method of Nailing**

the foot forward to ease it, give the matter attention at once. First rest the hand lightly upon the hoof to discover whether there is any unusual heat, and if so, at what point ; next take a light hammer or small stone, and tap lightly round over the nails, until the horse

flinches, when the of-
fending nail or nails
can be discovered and
pulled out. If this is
done soon after being
shod or during the
same day, all that may
be necessary to do is to
leave the nail out.

I have had excellent
success by pouring a
little callendula into
the hole. In one case,
where there was con-
siderable soreness a
few hours after being
shod, though the horse
was quite lame on ac
count of the nail being
driven too deep, after
pulling out then ail, a

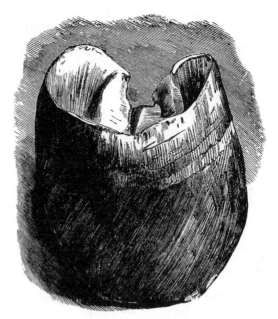

FIG. 486.—The Hoof of a Fore Foot Showing the Bad Effects of Excessive Rasping.

little callendula was poured in, and the shoe again put on, and the
horse in a few hours was free from lameness. But if he shows lameness in a day or so after being shod, cut away the wall from around

FIG. 487.—Shoe Properly Adjusted and Nailed.

the hole, so as to
let out any mat-
ter which may
have formed.
Next poultice the
foot until the in-
flammation sub-
sides, then cover
the hole with a
little digestive
ointment (which
is made by melt-
ing together equal
parts of tar and
hog's lard, and
stirring till cool), over which put a little tow and put on the shoe.

CONTRACTION. ITS CURE.

For hundreds of years there has been great effort made to pre-

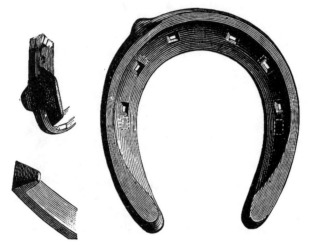

Fig. 488.—**Good Model of Concave Shoe.**

vent and cure contraction. I give a variety of figures showing some forms of shoes and methods of expanding the quarters.

Contraction may be divided into three classes: 1. A general compression, or drawing in of the wall upon the vascular structure; 2. When but one or both quarters are drawn in; 3. When the heels are curled in, or pushed forward under the foot. The prevention and cure of contraction must depend upon removing excess of horn, frog-pressure, freedom of the quarters, or, if necessary, opening them mechanically as desired, and upon moisture. Any of these conditions lacking, there must in serious cases be partial or entire failure, no matter what the means or methods used. If the feet could

Fig. 489.—**Ordinary Calks.**

have conditions that would afford natural moisture, and the shoes be made so thin that the frog and sole could have reasonable contact with the ground, the quarters so free that they could expand with the growth of the feet, there could be but little if any contraction.

FROG-PRESSURE.

We see that in all cases where there is reasonable

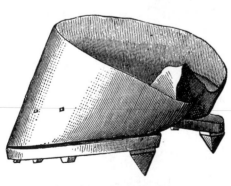

Fig. 490.—**Adjustable Calk.**

frog-pressure, the frog becomes larger, firm-
er, and more elastic ; while raising the frog
from contact causes it to become small and
hard, the quarters to draw in, and the whole
foot to diminish more or less in size. But if
not accustomed to pressure, it should be
given gradually, in connection with keeping
the feet thoroughly softened, so as not to
excite inflammation or soreness. It would
not do for a man accustomed to wearing
boots for years to suddenly go barefoot on
rough, hard ground. The skin on the feet
is so thin that they would be made sore,
and would be liable to serious inflammation. In like manner it would not be prudent to bring the heels and frog of a horse's

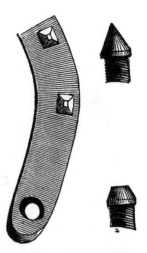

FIG. 491.—Adjustable Calks.

foot that has long been protected by shoes, suddenly to the ground.
If there is but little contraction, with fairly good condition of the
feet, all that will be necessary to do is to level down the feet, and

FIG. 492.—Model of Shoe for Express Horses.
From Dr. Hamill's Collection.

FIG. 493.—The Goodenough Shoe.

remove any surplus of old horn from the sole, put on thin-heeled
shoes, and keep the feet soft by moisture.

The next simplest and best method would be to use the convex
shoe. See Figs. 552 –554. After leveling and trimming out the
foot properly, as before explained, cut away or weaken the arch be-

23   a

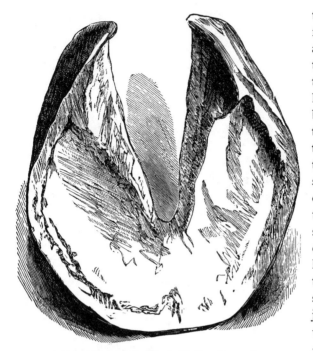

FIG. 494.—**A Dried Hoof with Frog Removed.**

tween the bars and frog sufficiently to allow of some elasticity of the quarters, then fit the heels nicely to the bearing surface of the shoe. In doing this, care should be taken to leave them sufficiently deep to e n a b l e matching the bevel of the shoe nicely without cutting away or lowering the wall too much. No horn should be left projecting inside, as it would form a wall against the inner edge of the shoe, and prevent the heels from spreading. Of course, no nails should be driven back in the quarters. As before explained, the frog should gradually be given contact with the ground. As the quarters are opened, the shoe can be taken off, made larger, and reset, until the foot is reasonably expanded, when a level bearing-surface may again be used.

But for anything like a bad condition of contraction, more direct and positive treatment will be necessary. For example, if the foot is badly contracted, the frog small, and sole forced upward acutely, the whole internal structure, in fact, locked and tied, as it were, by the severe compression of the wall, three conditions are necessary: First, complete elasticity of quarters and sole; second, power to open quarter so as to relieve pressure, and allow the sole to settle back to its natural position; third, gradual frog-pressure so as to restore a

FIG. 495.—**The Frog.**

healthy condition of circulation and strength of parts. The first important step in the treatment is to thoroughly soften the feet. The simplest way of doing this in the stables is by tying two or three thicknesses of blanket around the feet and keeping them wet about twenty-four hours; or better, fill two small bags with bran, put a foot into each, and tie a string loosely around the top of the bag and leg above the fetlock. Put each foot into a bucket of water, and afterward pour on water to keep wet; or the horse can be made to stand in mud till the feet are soft.

FIG. 496.—**Mobility entirely Destroyed in Right Foot.**

There is usually a large accumulation of horn, especially at the heel, all of which must be removed, and the wall leveled down to its proper dimensions. Next, with the drawing-knife pare out the sole; not enough to make it bend to pressure, but more than beyond the removal of the old horn. Then with a small knife, which should be made expressly for the purpose,—let the blade be made straight, with a cutting edge on both sides, and the end turned about a quarter of an inch, tempered and ground down to a keen edge, so as not to cut a channel much more than one eighth to three sixteenths of an inch wide, — weaken the wall between the bars and frog, by scraping or cutting out the bottom of the channel back to the point of the

FIG. 497.—**Showing Great Excess of Horn.**

heel so much that when pressure is brought upon the heels outward, there will be no impediment to their opening freely at their upper edge. To do this, commence well forward near the point of the frog, and cut back, following the line of the arch carefully. Particu-

lar care should be taken not to cut so much at any part as to cause
bleeding. On this
account the op-
erator should feel
his way cautious-
ly, cutting deeper
as he goes back.
The bar should
be cut away to
within three quar-
ters of an inch
from the point of
the heel. No more
should be cut
away from the
rest of the bar, or
part coming un-
der the clip, than

FIG. 498.—**Shoe too Wide and Long. Bearing-surface
too Concave.**

may be necessary to give a straight shoulder for it to rest against.
Both sides must be treated alike. If the part has been cut through
in the least, it should be protected after the shoe is on by melting
a little resin and tallow
into it, and covering
with tow.

FIG. 499.—**Concave Bearing-surface of Shoe 498 at Heel.**

There have been
many ignorant and
pretentious quacks,
who have presumed to
weaken the heel by

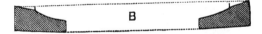

FIG. 500.—**Concave Bearing-surface of Shoe 498 between Heel and Turn of Foot.**

sawing in between the
bars and frog. Only a
very small point can be
reached in this way,

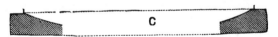

FIG. 501.—**Concave Bearing-surface of Same at Turn of Foot.**

without cutting to the quick. The saw cannot be used here at all
with advantage. The point is to weaken the horn at the bottom
of the cleft so that it will spread freely, and this can be done properly only with the cutting-knife. The proper flexibility of the
heels can be judged by a slight pressure with the hand.

This done, our next object is to remove the compression of the
wall. To do this, fit to it a rather thin, flat shoe, made of good iron.
At the heels it should be made a little wider and longer than the

foot, and the nail-holes punched, as in Fig. 565. Lay on the shoe as intended to be nailed, and with a pencil make a mark over the inside of the bar at the point of the heel on both sides. This done, accurately punch or drill two holes through the iron, about three sixteenths of an inch in diameter. If it can be done, it would be better to have the holes beveled on the inside of the bar, extending up and back at the point of the heel. Next, take two little pieces

Fig. 502.—View of Hoof with Marked Depression across the Front, and a Corresponding Bulging downwards of the Sole.

of good iron or steel, about three fourths to seven eighths of an inch long, by about three sixteenths thick, and about five eighths of an inch wide. Cut down the end until it will fit the hole in the

Fig. 503.—Model Thin-heeled Shoe.   Fig. 504.—Light Hind Shoe.

shoe, and rivet it, as shown in Fig. 557. These are now to be warmed and bent, and, if necessary, filed so as to lie flat against both heels, and just long enough to come a little short of touching the soft horn above it. Next weaken the shoe a little on both sides, which may be extended over a much larger space than shown in Fig. 558; or if the shoe is not very heavy, it may be spread

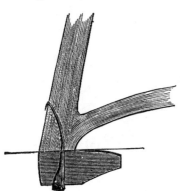

FIG. 505.—**Sole and Wall Cut away too much.**

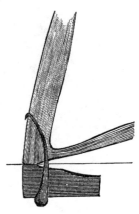

FIG. 506.—**Wall not Cut away Quite Enough.**

without weakening. Regulate so as to come a little forward of the point where the hoof begins to draw in. If the shoe is thin, the inner edge should be turn up and formed into a clip, which, with a little care, can be filed and fitted. But if the shoe is at all thick, it would be somewhat difficult to do this; for if the clip is turned up so that the shoe is too large or too small, a very tedious, annoying bungle would be the result. In addition, it would be difficult to make the clips sufficiently long to enable bringing pressure as high up against the wall as it will admit, which is a very important point toward opening the upper part of the hoof.

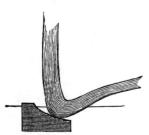

FIG. 507.—**Heel as it Usually Rests on the Shoe.**

The method before given, which necessity compelled me to devise and adopt, makes this simple and easy to do; and except the shoe is so thin as not to admit of punching or drilling, it will be found by far the simplest and best method of forming the clips. When properly adjusted, nail on carefully. The nails around the toe may be larger than those driven in the quarters; and while driven so as to give a good hold, and rather high, if the feet are at all sore and tender, great care should be taken that the hammering is not too heavy, nor the nails driven deep. The clinches should simply be turned down lightly. If the hoof extends out over the shoe at any point, it should be no reason for more rasping than merely to round off the edges of the horn. Let

it alone. It is frequently the case that one quarter is more contracted than the other ; in fact, it is not unusual to have one side
of the heel very much drawn in, while the other may be very little, if any, contracted ; so that two conditions must be met ; namely,

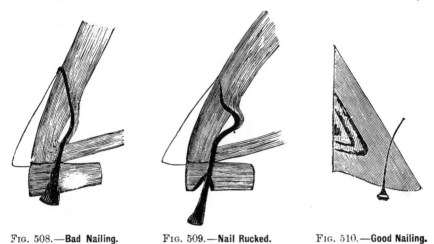

FIG. 508.—**Bad Nailing.**   FIG. 509.—**Nail Rucked.**   FIG. 510.—**Good Nailing.**

first, to open either heel as little or as much as may be desired,
independent of the other. This the spreaders (which have been
devised and patented by the writer) will enable doing in the most
perfect manner. Simple as these spreaders are, the writer has
found it very difficult to have them made properly. On this account he has found it necessary to have them made according to an

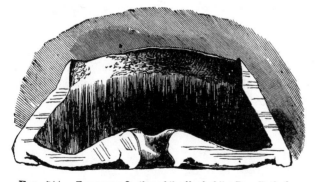

FIG. 511.—**Transverse Section of the Hoof of the Fore Foot of a
Work Horse in which the Sole had Become Convex.**

exact pattern,
and they will be
furnished at a
moderate price
to those desiring
them.

However nec-
essary it may
be to have this
part of the work
well done, it is, in
reality, but a
preparatory step
for what follows.

First, if tongs or a screw be used to spread the shoe, the pressure
being made equal on both sides, the side which is weakest must do

all the bending—opening that quarter too much without affecting the other at all. Another cause of difficulty is not having the tongs convenient with which to spread the shoe, and it is put off too long ; and when finally attempted, done so roughly, or opened so much as to cause violent inflammation and lameness. With the spreaders, this difficulty is entirely overcome.

FIG. 512.   FIG. 513.   FIG. 514.

Shoe Should Conform to Foot. The Shoe Being too Small and Badly Abjusted, the Foot is Compressed and Necessarily Injured.

OPENING THE HEELS.

The method of doing this should be about as follows : First, measure between the heels of the shoe carefully, by cutting a bit of straw or stick the exact length between them, and then estimate how much each heel will bear opening without causing soreness. Unless the foot is very soft and elastic, it is hardly prudent the first time to open them more than a quarter or three eighths of an inch. It is well to first open the quarter most contracted, which, until brought out to balance with the other, should be opened the most. Then measure again and spread the opposite side. If opened too much, or enough to cause soreness, a few light taps of the hammer against the outside will set it back. The feet should be kept soft by stopping with flaxseed-meal, and tying two or three thicknesses of blanket around, and wetting occasionally. In the course of an hour or two examine the condition of the feet carefully. If the horse puts out one foot, or indicates the least soreness, the quarters have been opened too much,

FIGS. 515, 516.—Very Common Result of Wearing Small, Bad Fitting Shoes.

and they must be at once knocked back sufficiently to relieve the undue pressure, and be kept wet. It is rarely, however, that the spreading of a quarter, or even three eighths, of an inch, will at first cause any soreness. On the contrary, it always gives relief. Still I think it necessary to use care. The horse can be driven or worked moderately, if desired. In two or three days the spreading can be repeated, but now not so much as before, and again in three or four days following, and so on at longer intervals.

If the foot has been properly prepared, two points will be accomplished by this spreading, namely, the severe compression upon

| Fig. 517.—**Natural Position.** Good Shoeing. | Fig. 518.—**Effect of Contraction** and Soreness. | Fig. 519.—**Extreme Case** of Contraction and Soreness. |

the vascular structure and coronary ring will be immediately relieved, and the sole, which in all cases of this character has been forced up, as shown, to an acute angle, will straighten and let down. To aid this, the sole must, by paring, be made so flexible that, as the foot is opened, it will settle down and come back to its natural condition. The soreness resulting from the compression of the parts will be removed, and a better condition of circulation and nutrition result. By this course the mobility will not only be restored, the horse travel with more freedom and confidence, but as the hoof grows down it will become thicker and of a better fiber.

As before explained, to bring about a healthy condition of circulation and nutrition, the frog must necessarily be given contact with the ground to the degree it will bear, which should be provided for by the thinness of the shoe. In some simple cases, nailing **the** shoe to the heel, as shown in Fig. 558, may be sufficient to hold the quarters firmly enough to enable spreading them as desired. The objection is that the wall is so thin at the point of the heels, that it may be difficult to get a good nail-hold without pricking or breaking out; besides, the nailing cannot be repeated. The nails should be small and driven very carefully, getting as much hold as the horn will admit of. The supposed objection to this plan of opening the quarters is, that it prevents their natural elasticity by their undue confinement. But this is not a valid objection; because in the di-

Figs. 520, 521.—How a Horse Stands when Sore-footed or Lame.

rection it is desired to give them freedom outward, it only facilitates it, while at the same time it gives a certainty and positiveness of relief that cannot well be secured in any other way.

In fact, herein lies most of the success in the management of all conditions of contraction. In my experience I never have found a smith who could catch the points of properly preparing the foot and fitting the shoes for such cases. In every instance I have been compelled to stand over the shoer and dictate every movement or do part of the work myself. First, the want of judgment in preparing the foot; second, in adapting the weight of the shoe to the foot, and fitting the clips so as to enable opening the quarters easily and surely as desired.

MR. ROBERGE'S METHOD.

Since writing the foregoing my attention has been called to a very simple and practical method of opening the quarters for the cure of contraction, which is used with marked success, and illustrated in Fig. 566, devised by Mr. David Roberge, a practical horseshoer of great ingenuity and skill, located at No. 106 West Thirtieth Street, New York City. Various methods of opening the heels on this plan are given, which are from French and other authorities, to show the great effort that has been made by mechanical means to overcome this difficulty. But Mr. Roberge, by giving more length to the spring, and simplifying its construction, makes it all that can be desired. The

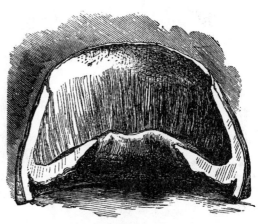

FIG. 522.—Anterior Section of a Hind Hoof Made Vertically across the Center, Showing the Thickness of Wall.

spring is made of steel, the exact proportion and adjustment of which is shown in Fig. 567. The wall is first weakened by sawing down slightly between the heel and frog, when the spring is placed

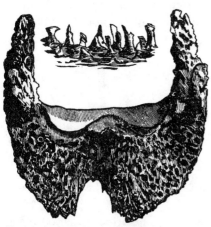

FIG. 523.—The Effect of Internal Inflammation, Caused by Excessive Rasping and Other Causes of Injury.

in position with so much force given to it as may be thought necessary to press the heels outward as desired. The shoe is then nailed on over it, as ordinarily done. The pressure is gradual and constant, and must prove just the thing where both quarters will admit of equal pressure. But should one quarter be much more contracted or unyielding than the other, it does not seem to the writer that it would work so well, because the full pressure would then be thrown on the weaker quarter. But this, it is claimed, can be obviated by nailing the shoe well back on the quarter of the opposite side, which would prevent that side from being acted upon

This spring, with particulars, can be obtained by addressing the patentee, Mr. Roberge.

ROLLING MOTION SHOE.

I also give illustrations of a form of shoe devised and largely used by him with great success, which he has patented. The object

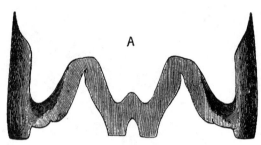

to be attained is, where there is want of mobility, or much soreness and inflammation, to so form and adjust the shoe that the foot will partly roll upon the ground, thereby relieving the strain and irritation. To use Mr. Roberge's words,

FIG. 524.—Transverse Section of a Model Hoof at the Quarters.

" This shoe, by allowing the foot to roll upon the ground, gives the foot the advantage of an extra joint, and to that degree relieves the strain or want of mobility, which causes lameness or soreness." Consequently, it not only enables the horse to travel easier, but aids in making a cure. This principle of treatment he has studied very closely, and it is remarkably successful.

This principle of treatment has long been in use. I give an illustration from Lafosse, showing a side view of the hoof fitted for the

FIG. 525.—Showing the Usual Arch of the Sole. FIG. 526.—Showing Effect of a Little Contraction. FIG. 527.—Sole Bent Upwards. Effect of Contraction.

shoe ; also a specimen of the French shoe. The principle is to turn up the shoe at the heel and toe about the thickness of the iron. Mr. Roberge's shoe differs essentially from this, in that he gives a curvature sideways as well as with the length of the foot. What he terms his " best shoe," and which is the most unusual, is Fig. 568, which is a thin plate hammered into a rounded or bowl shape, the

exact proportions of which are preserved in the drawings given.
Fig. 570 is a side view, which will give a good idea of the relative
proportion of the curve. By this form of shoe the foot has perfect

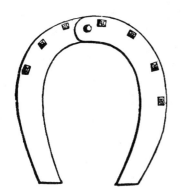

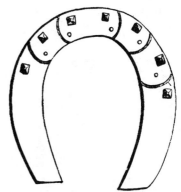

FIG. 528.—**Hinge Shoe. From the French.**   FIG. 529.—**Form of Shoe Devised in England
for Preventing Contraction.**

freedom of motion either way. If the foot is feverish or dry, wet
sponge or oakum is pushed in between the shoe and bottom of the
foot. Fig. 572 is a view of the same made a little heavier, the same
form of circle being preserved, with the difference of the central
part being removed with cross-section of the same. The shoe from
which this drawing was made was claimed to be the same that was
worn by Dexter when he made his fastest time to road wagon.
Figs. 575, 576, show the method of putting on calkins. In conversation with the writer, Mr. Bonner stated that David Roberge was one
of the very foremost living students of the principles of shoeing. He
is an unassuming, practical man, but is wonderfully successful.

QUARTER-CRACK.

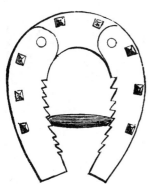

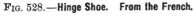

FIG. 530.—**Form of Shoe Used
by the French for the Cure
of Contraction.**

This is the one difficulty next to contraction which seems to have baffled the
skill of the best veterinary authorities
and horsemen to prevent or cure ; because
in extreme cases they had no practical
treatment beyond that of a bar shoe, cutting away the horn so that the part back
of the split would have no bearing upon
it, or supporting the weak parts by
drawing the edges together with nails,
or fastening on a plate with screws, all
of which are merely palliative, and not
to be depended upon. It would, of course,

be easy to grow the foot down by keeping the horse in a stall or small yard where the ground is soft, but when put to work it would be liable to split down again as before. Consequently it has been one of the most vexatious and annoying of difficulties, because to do this it was necessary to keep the horse idle from three to six months; and then, when put to work, if by chance he were driven sharply over hard or frozen roads, the quarter was liable to burst, which would again make the loss of use necessary. Or it became necessary to resort to the palliative measures referred to, and thus in time the value of an otherwise good horse would be destroyed.

FIG. 531.

FIG. 532.—Shoe Made in Sections and Riveted together to Prevent Contraction.

We see, in the first place, that the whole trouble arises from the hoof becoming contracted or too small for the internal parts. This will be most noticeable at the inner quarter by the wall becoming straight or drawn in sharply a little below the hair, the part at which the split invariably occurs. This is proved by the fact that the

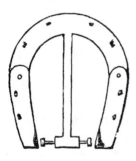 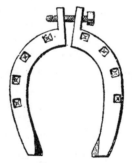 

FIGS. 533, 534, 535.—Different Forms of Shoes for Cure of Contraction.

quarter is most liable to burst or split when the hoof is dry and hard, or when concussion is increased by driving on hard roads. This tendency to split is also increased by the inferior quality of horn grown; because the contraction of the parts, or pressing of the wall in against the soft parts, so obstructs the circulation that there

is not sufficient blood
to grow sound, tough,
healthy horn. On
this account the only
reliable and practical
cure is opening the
quarters sufficiently
to remove pressure
until the new horn is
grown, which can be
done to any degree
desired, as follows:
First, cut down be-
tween the bar and the
frog of the inner
quarter, as explained
for contraction, until
it will yield readily
to pressure. Next cut

FIG. 536.—Ordinary English Shoe.

away the edges of the wall to the end of the split; then make a
crease with the firing-iron at the edge of the hair. If the spilt extends well up into the coronary band, this can be omitted, and instead, the iron touched lengthways with the split. If, however, the
quarter is properly
opened, such inter-
ference with the firing-
iron will be unneces-
sary, as the horn
would usually grow
down sound without
it. Now, fit a shoe as
explained for contrac-
tion, putting a clip
only upon the inner
side (as shown in Fig.
585). The opposite
side is to be nailed
well back to counter-
balance it. When the
shoes are nailed on,
with the spreaders
open the quarter all

FIG. 537.—Bearing-surface of Ordinary English Shoe.

it will bear without producing soreness, or about a quarter of an inch. This done, fill the crack with a little melted resin or tallow, over which put a little tow to prevent gravel or dirt from working into the quick. It is next advisable to stimulate the growth of tough, healthy horn. This can be done with hoof liniment, which should be put on, as explained, two or three times a week. The hoof should not be permitted to become dry or hard, which can be easily prevented by stopping with flaxseed-meal and tying two or three thicknesses of blanket around the foot, and keeping wet while standing in the stable. The horse, if necessary, can be put to work as usual. In the course of a few days, spread a little more, or as

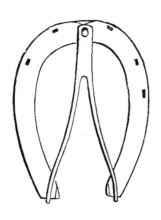

Fig. 538.　　　　　　　　　　　　　Fig. 539.

Forms of Spring Used for Spreading the Quarters.

much as may be necessary to make the hoof sufficiently wide to remove all pressure from the weak part. When grown down, the cause will be removed.

If an ordinary case, with but little drawing in of the quarters, simply lower the inside quarter a little so as to remove pressure from the upper edge of the wall, and put on a level shoe. Next, with a firing-iron burn a slight crease across the upper edge of the wall, keeping the foot soft, and stimulating the growth by applications of hoof liniment. This will enable growing the wall down without its splitting back. But if the quarter is drawn in perceptibly, then in addition to the creasing, the quarter must be given entire freedom, by cutting down between the bar and frog. The details of a very interesting case, and explanations of how I learned this method of treatment, and its success, will be found in connection with this part of treatment in my special work on the horse.

SAND CRACK, OR FISSURE AT THE TOE.

This is usually the result of a diseased condition or ulceration of the upper anterior part of the coffin-bone, caused by injury to the part. In a large number of dissections made by Mr. Gamgee, to whom I am indebted for treatment here given, he found cases of the

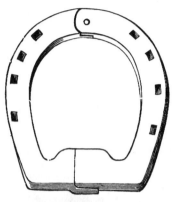

pyramidal process to be common, and a depression down in front to be also frequent. The front of such feet is weak and deficient both in hoof and bone. The bottom of the foot must have nothing removed from it except to level it down at the quarters. The front of the hoof should be left rather long and deep, the shoe to come well back under the quarters, and clips to be taken up, one on each side of the toe. When the shoe is applied, the clips are

FIG. 540.—**Hinge Bar Shoe for Cure of Contraction.**

neither to be let into the wall nor roughly hammered up to it, but to be drawn just tight enough to support and hold the part firm. For treatment of the fissure, take tar and resin one ounce and tallow a quarter of an ounce, and melt together.

Apply this while warm to the fissure of the hoof and coronet, then place a layer of tow over this dressing, and bind the wall of the foot with a broad tape, to support its position and keep the part firm. A cure in bad cases is not to be expected.

CORNS.

Corns are usually to be found at the inner heel, or at the angle between the bar and the crust, and are caused by the shoe pressing upon the part. This will be most likely to occur should the wall break down, or be cut away so much

FIG. 541.—**Spring Inside Shoe Riveted to Toe Part for Expanding Quarters.**

as to let the shoe rest upon the sole, or should the shoe be nailed well back on the outside and toe, as then, if left on too long, it will be drawn outward and forward so much that the inner heel will be

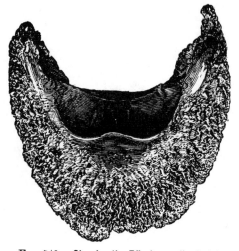

FIG. 542.—**Showing the Effect upon the Pedal Bone of Sole Bulging Down.**

the quarter is very much contracted, the space between the bar and quarter being greatly lessened, it causes such bruising or pressure upon the soft parts as to excite inflammation, or cause a corn. The usual remedy is to cut away the parts so that the shoe will not rest upon it, and put on a little caustic, or touch it with a hot iron, which destroys sensibility, and changes the condition of secretion. Butter of antimony or salts of niter are favorite remedies; then melt in a little tar, resin, and tallow, and cover with a little tow to prevent gravel or dirt working into the tender part. The usual way in severe cases, is to put on a bar shoe, so as to enable removing all pressure from the sore part. This mode of treatment, however, as usually done, is only palliative, not curative. The horse will travel better, but if the shoe is left on a little too long, or presses upon the part in the least, or should gravel or

drawn under the quarter, and rest upon this part, bruising it. When the sensitive sole is thus bruised, the effused blood mixes with the horny matter and makes a red spot, and if the irritation is continued so as to produce very much inflammation, ulceration may take place, which would, in some cases, be sufficient to affect the inner wing of the coffin-bone, and cause matter to break out at the coronet. Sometimes when

FIG. 543.—**Representation of the Last Six Bones of the Foot, Showing Great Change of Structure.**

dirt accumulate between the part and the shoe, inflammation and lameness will follow. The only remedy for this is to remove the pressure. But in time by this treatment the difficulty is only aggravated and made worse. Hence the usual assertion that "corns cannot be cured."

Gifford, one of my old performing horses, had a very bad bruise (corn) on one of his inner heels, which, if not carefully attended to, caused serious lameness. After being troubled with it about seven years, it had grown to such proportions as to involve the entire angle at the heel, so that the horn was broken quite through, and the sensitive structure partly

FIG. 544.—Showing Bearing-surface of Shoe Shown in Fig. 544.

ulcerated. At the close of the season's business, there was considerable inflammation and soreness in the entire foot. All palliative measures having failed, it finally occurred to me to try the experiment of removing all pressure from the part, and turning the horse out to grass. But there was another serious difficulty, to which, in part, some of the soreness might be attributed. By the contraction or curling under of the outer heel, it had become so weak that it could scarcely be made to support his weight in traveling, so I decided to treat this at the same time. The division between the bar and frog of this side was well thinned out to make the quarter flexible. Next a thin shoe of untempered steel, a little more than an eighth of an inch thick, was made to fit accurately to the wall (as shown by Fig. 588), the end being turned up for a clip, and fitted nicely to its place. The part of the opposite heel of the shoe coming over the

FIG. 545.—Form of Concave Shoe Used by the French for Expanding the Quarters.

corn, was entirely cut away, leaving simply sufficient to cover the wall, which at this point was very thin. The shoe was now fastened on sufficiently to hold it firmly in place, but with very small nails.

There was no rasping or attempt to beautify the foot in any way. Figs. 586 and 589 give a very good idea of the appearance of the foot before and after the shoe was put on. The quarter was now carefully opened about three eighths of

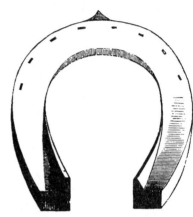

FIG. 546.   FIG. 547.

Devices for Cure of Contraction Used by the French.

an inch, without causing any irritation. Nothing was put over the bruise or corn, nor was it meddled with in any way. The horse was now turned out to grass daily. At first he moved very tenderly, though not lame. In a week the heel was again opened a little more, and again at intervals until opened out as desired. In a few weeks the tenderness, fever, and inflammation subsided ; and at the expiration of three months the corn was entirely cured, there being a healthy growth of sole over the part, leaving only a slight appearance

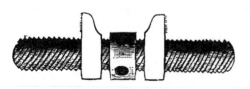

FIG. 548.—**Screw for Spreading Shoe.**   FIG. 549.—**The Shoe as Adjusted.**

of redness, on account of not being entirely grown out. The contracted quarter was also out to its natural position, the change for the better in all respects being very gratifying. An ordinary flat shoe was now put on, when he traveled as well as ever. The majority of such cases can be easily cured while the horse is kept at his usual work, by putting on an open shoe if the foot will bear it, if not, a light bar shoe, with the part coming under the corn entirely cut away, leaving only sufficient to cover the wall. It will not matter whether the bar is cut away or not, as there will be nothing over it to harbor gravel or dirt. It would be advisable to fit the shoe carefully, or even drive two or three nails, to know exactly the position of the shoe upon the wall. Then mark the part to be cut out, when the nails can be pulled out, the

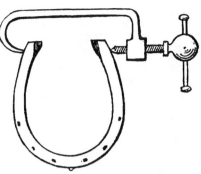

FIG. 550.—The Shoe Made Wider than Foot, with Clips at the Heels for Opening the Quarters. A French Device.

part cut or filed away properly, and the shoe again nailed in place.

The success in the treatment of the case referred to, led me to believe I had made an important discovery, as I had not found it laid down by any authorities on shoeing. Since then, upon investigation, I have found that the principle was well understood by many old authorities, though the method of treatment, as will be seen, was slightly different.

On page 96 of Freeman's work on "Shoeing," published in 1796, he says :—

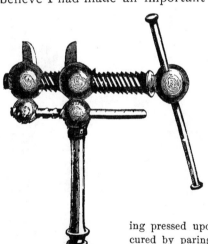

FIG. 551.—Form of Screw Used by the French for Spreading the Shoe.

I have frequently bought horses whose feet, on examination, proved to have corns, occasioned by ill-made shoes having pressed upon them. These were, in general, easily cured by paring the feet properly where the grievance lay, and turning the horse out without shoes for two or three months.

In the supplement to Coleman's work, published in 1802, the writer found, for the cure of corns, the shoe cut away over the corn, as shown by Fig. 587.

Bracy Clark's work, published in 1809, gives an illustration of a shoe with that part which would come over the corn entirely cut away.

The half-moon shoe, or tip, by Lafosse, referred to hereafter, is claimed to cure corns. Cæsar Fiaschi, of the sixteenth century, gives a figure of a three-quarter shoe, almost the same form as that of Bracy Clark's, for this trouble. White's work, published in 1820, says :—

> The only thing to be done is to take off the shoe, and turn the horse out to grass. In slight cases, however, this may not be absolutely necessary, and is often inconvenient, but it is by far the best plan, and I may add, *perhaps the only effectual one,* when a radical cure is desired.

WEAK HEELS.

If from any cause there has been much fever in the feet for some time, in consequence of being driven on hard roads, or being partially foundered, there will be diminished supply of horn, so that the wall will not only grow slower, but thinner. (See reference to inflammation and Figs. 555, 556.)

FIG. 552.—**French Convex Shoe.**

Sometimes the heels are cut down so closely that should the shoe work loose, and wear or break down the quarters, it would be

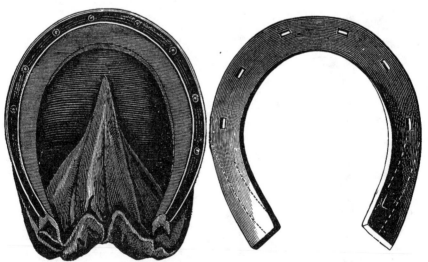

FIG. 553.—**Bracy Clark's Convex Shoe.**
From his Book Published in 1819.

FIG. 554.—**Ordinary Convex Shoe.**

easy to produce a weak, low condition of the heels. This may cause a great deal of trouble, on account of the slowness with which the horn grows to supply the increased wear. This morbid condition of inflammation also produces another very marked effect, namely, that of separating the wall from the sole, or what is termed becoming shelly. Sometimes, if the shoes are badly fitted and made too wide at the heels (as explained under the head of "Contraction"), they will soon cause a weak, bad condition of the heels, the quarter gradually giving way or breaking down; and if the foot is at all flat, the sole and frog become liable to settle, or are made convex.

One of the most marked cases of this kind the writer ever saw was that of a cart-horse, brought to his notice in Central Pennsylvania. The feet were broad and flat, with the heels drawn in to a point so that there was scarcely any bearing of them upon the shoe. The result

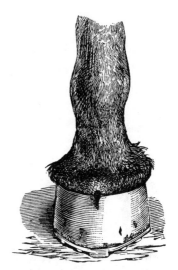

Fig. 555.—The Foot of a Pony that had been Calked, Referred to in Text, after the Inflammation had Subsided, Growing Nearly a Quarter of an Inch Larger.

of this was that the horn wore or broke away until the line of bearing was over an inch above that of the frog. To remedy the difficulty the calks were raised correspondingly high to keep the frog from the ground. (See Fig. 594.) This horse traveled with great difficulty, even on a walk.

The course most likely to give success in the management of these cases, is to use a wide shoe that will give a large bearing-surface to the weak parts, and sustain them. Of course, nothing more should be cut away from the heels than is sufficient to only level them a little. Special care should be taken to prevent them from breaking and wearing down by the shoe, which may be done by placing a piece of leather between the bearing-surface and shoe. As the horn will usually be

Fig. 556.—The Foot Drawn in and Deformed from Long-continued Inflammation Caused by a Nail being Driven into the Foot, the Hoof Growing About Half an Inch Larger after the Inflammation Subsided.

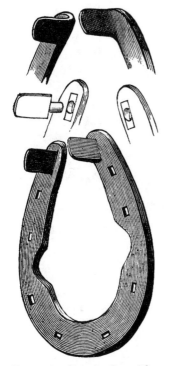

Fig. 557.—Shoe for Cure of Contraction. Devised by the Writer.

very brittle and weak, it is advisable to use great care in fitting the shoe, with thin clips on each side. At any rate, the shoe must be fastened on so firmly that it will not get loose. In some cases it may be necessary to bring the bar down so as to enable a more accurate line of adjustment to the shoe and frog.

When in Massachusetts, in 1876, a leading horseman called my attention to a fast-trotting stallion that had weak feet, and which caused him a great deal of trouble. He wished to know how to shoe them so as to improve their condition. I found the feet in good shape, but the sole and wall were very thin and weak, the effect, undoubtedly, of the horse being slightly foundered or overheated. I advised putting on a shoe that would support the sole and frog, the space between the shoe and frog to be packed with oakum. He objected that this would not do, as the horse would not bear any pressure at all upon the sole. Some time afterward my attention was called to a very high indorsement from this gentleman of a certain form of patent shoe that had been used on this horse. It stated that it enabled the horse to travel as well as ever, and that its utility was all that could be desired. I was interested to know just what kind of a shoe had been used, and when again in that vicinity, I found one at considerable trouble, of which I give an accurate drawing. (See Fig. 598.) While it may be evident that in many such cases the shoe could be made to support the entire sole, if hammered out of iron,

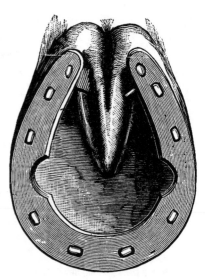

Fig. 558.—The Shoe Adjusted.

the increased weight would make it seriously objectionable. The fitting of a thin piece of steel plate, as shown in Fig. 598, would enable this to be done with but little addition to its weight. The manner of putting it on was simply by bringing the whole surface of the wall and frog to an even bearing, to which the shoe was carefully adjusted.

Fig. 559.—**Spreaders in Position to Open the Heels.**

Next, the space between the shoe and bottom of the foot was filled with oakum, to which was added a little tar and resin, so as to form an even but firm support all the way round.* The drawing of the oakum, as it appears in Fig. 601, is an exact illustration of that which was used upon the shoe named, though only the back part of it is shown. Parties who had used the shoe upon feet which had become sore and tender from driving upon hard, stony roads in the city and neighborhood, stated that it enabled the horses to travel much better. If the foot is sore and sensitive, supporting it with a bed of oakum in this way will serve to break concussion, and consequently make the horse go better for a time. But for contraction, quarter-crack, coffin-joint lameness, etc., for which it was advertised as a cure, it cannot benefit beyond the effect of slightly breaking concussion, as explained. It would be just the thing for weak heels and for any condition

*A preparation of tar, beeswax, hard soap, and resin, melted and formed into a salve, to be used with oakum as a packing, was given the writer by a horseman of much experience, claiming that it softened the feet and stimulated the secretion of horn.

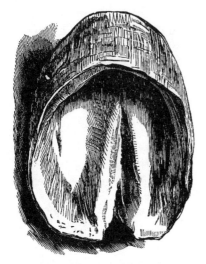

FIG. 560.—**Back View of a Hoof Greatly Contracted, the Effect of Long-continued Inflammation.**

where the sole and frog need support. As it is, however, seriously objectionable to cover the whole bottom of the foot when it can be avoided, I include cuts of an improvement by which the whole bearing-surface of the frog and heels, the important parts, can be supported without the sole being excluded from moisture or air, which is important for the secretion of healthy horn. In such a case, if desired, the plate instead of being let to the inner edge, can be extended across the quarter so that the upper surface will come even with the shoe, and be riveted on.

INTERFERING.

The main point in the management of interfering is to have the shoe close under the wall at the point of striking, and the offending part shortened or straightened a little, and to have no nails driven there, the clinches of which would soon rise and cause cutting. The edge of the shoe should be beveled under a little, and filed smooth. There is usually a good deal of carelessness in letting the shoe extend outside the crust at the point of the heel. It should set well under the wall all the way round, and the wall be filed smoothly to it. In addition, in some cases, the horse will travel better to lower the inside heel a little ; in others, to raise it. It is in all cases advisable, however, if the horse

FIG. 561.—**Showing two Openings Caused by Corns.**

can be made to travel without striking, to keep the adjustment natural by paring the foot level and making the shoe of an equal thickness all the way round, with perhaps the inner part straightened a little.

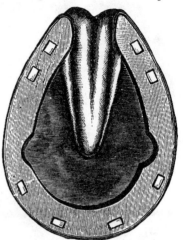

Sometimes colts driven to a sulky, when a little leg-weary, may strike badly ; in such a case the ankle must be protected. In all cases where the ankle is cut, the swelling and soreness increase the difficulty, and should be guarded against by covering. If the irritation is kept up, and this is not done, it may result in permanent enlargement of the part, which would afterward increase the liability to be hit. This can be prevented only by coverings, or by being protected by the ordinary simple means, until the inflammation

FIG. 562.—**Shoe as Nailed on to be Spread.**

subsides and the injury heals. Prof. McLellan says on this subject :—

Treatment for interfering, to be rational, must take into account the causations. Thus, if the toes turn out — a very common cause of interfering — they should be inclined in all that is possible. This can be accomplished by bending the outside web of the shoe from its inner to its outer border, making the edge through which the nails are driven, quite thin. Or if calks are used, the toe-calk can be welded nearer the inside than the outside toe, and the toe-calk beveled at the expense of its outer extremity. If the knee is banged, but light shoes are indicated. Lightness in the shoe is always desirable in the hind feet, and if the season of the year permits, tips will be found very effective in prevention of interfering. The nails should be left out of the hoof at the point where it strikes, because the clinches are liable to become raised or loosened, and do injury.

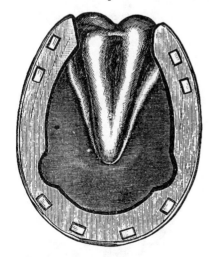

FIG. 563.—**As the Heels Appear after Being Spread.**

CLICKING, OR OVERREACHING.*

This is a term applied to the striking of the hind shoes against the forward ones during progression. It may be due either

* Contributed by Prof. McLellan.

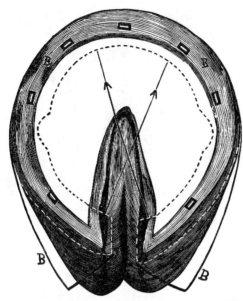

FIG. 564.—**Badly Contracted Foot. The Lines B B Show the Degree to which the Foot may in Time be Spread.**

to a faulty conformation, to weakness, or to disease. In seeking to remedy the defect, we must endeavor to discover its cause. If it is due to defective form, we may so adjust the hoofs and apply the shoes that the feet shall be placed upon the ground in such relation to the body as to modify in some measure the fault of form. In some cases the toes of the forward feet must be reduced all that is possible, and the toes of the hind feet lengthened. In others, weights or heavy shoes upon the forward feet answer a good purpose. In some, weights upon the outside of the hind feet overcome the difficulty.

If the hind feet are placed upon the ground well forward when the animal is at rest, heel-calks of extra length will be found useful.

Weakness, as a cause of clicking, is shown in colts and in horses that have diseased hind feet. In the first, the animal is not able, or has not learned, to dwell upon the hind feet to give to the body that forward impulse that comes from the *long push;* in the second, pain prevents the extension. In the case of the colt, shoeing must be supplemented by good driving,—the animal should be kept up to the bit, and the head well checked up, and should not be fatigued by overdriving. In the case where the clicking depends upon a diseased condition of the foot or leg, the removal of the cause is the indication. As general rules for the prevention of clicking, the toe of the forward hoof should be reduced all that it will bear ; the shoe should be short, both at the toe and heel ; the heels of the shoe should be beveled at the expense of its ground surface ; when the toe should be beveled, giving the shoe, when applied, the appearance of one partly worn. In many cases concaving the ground surface of the shoe is useful. If the toes are long and the heels extremely low, thick-heeled shoes or heel-calks are indicated.

The hind shoes should be light, and long at the heels, giving the heels of the shoe as wide a bearing as possible. In case the toe

FIG. 565.—**Simple Form of Shoe for Spreading the Quarters.**

of the hind foot is much worn, and as a consequence the hoof spread at its plantar surface, clips should be drawn up from each side of the shoe, so as to grasp the wall at its widest part. No attempt should be made to fit the shoe to the squared and shortened toe ; but give it the natural form, and let it project at the toe to that extent that would indicate the length of the hoof were it unworn. Heel-calks upon the hind shoes are applicable to nearly all cases.

In all cases of overreaching or clicking, adjusting the hoof and shoe so that the inside quarter and toe of the hoof are higher than the outside, will assist in overcoming the difficulty.

STUMBLING.

Stumbling is usually associated with some diseased condition of the foot. In the prevention of this disagreeable

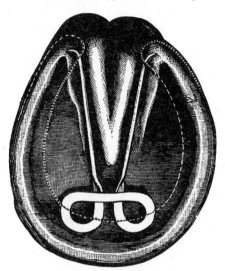

Fig. 566.—An Outline of Mr. Roberge's Spring, with its Position on the Foot.

Fig. 567.—Thickness of Spring. Full Size.

Fig. 568.—Width of Bar. Full Size.

and dangerous habit, particular attention must be given to cutting the hoof. Reduce the hoof all it will bear without injury ; see that the hoof is of equal depth on each side of the toe. This you can ascertain best by standing in front of the horse and comparing the two sides. In fitting the shoe, bend up the toe, giving it the rounded appearance of one well worn. If calks must be used, weld toe-calk back to inner margin of web, making it low. In the stable use wet swabs to the feet.

SHOEING FOUNDERED HORSES.

If the mobility of the foot is destroyed, as the result of chronic founder, or other cause of morbid inflammation, mobility must be aided by rounding the entire shoe or toe. If the foot is entirely stiff, the shoe must be so formed that it will roll upon the ground, which can be easily done by leaving the inner edge of each side wide, and turning down in a half circle, as shown in Fig. 609.

If the sole is broken down, or the wall separated at the toe, the result of acute inflammation or founder, weight will be thrown more upon the heels. For such cases the shoe must be so fitted as to extend well back under the heels ; and if the sole is thin at the toe — bulging down — it may be supported by letting a thin flange of iron extend well back under it ; or fitting a steel plate across the part so as to give an even support all the way round, and the adjustment made easy by packing with oakum, though in most cases the sole will not bear pressure, and is simply to be protected by a wide shoe. The shoeing of such feet must be in a great measure experimental ; consequently the ingenuity of the owner or smith must be exercised to conform with best advantage to the condition of the case. First, do nothing that will irritate or make the foot

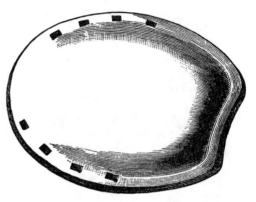

Fig. 569.—Roberge's Best Form of Shoe to Aid the Mobility of the Foot in Lameness.

sore. It simply must be supported to the best advantage, and the mobility aided by rounding the toe, or setting the calks well back under it.

SPECIAL CAUSES OF INJURY.*

Fig. 570.—Side View of the Above, Showing the Curve.

I add references to a few authorities, showing the bad effect of paring the sole and frog excessively, rasping the outer surface of the hoof, and the use of thick, badly-fitting shoes. I will call attention first to the most prominent authority, Prof. Coleman, from whose teachings all the modern works in this country have been principally guided in their instruction. In January, 1792, a Veterinary College was started in London. A short time afterward Edward Coleman was appointed Chief Professor. I cannot do better here than to copy from Prof. Gamgee's work on "Shoeing," pub-

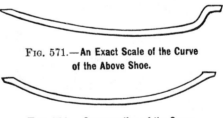

Fig. 571.—An Exact Scale of the Curve of the Above Shoe.

Fig. 572.—Cross-section of the Same.

---

* The illustrations in this article overrun the text, and this will explain why they are not placed opposite the matter referring to them.

lished in London in 1874, in relation to Coleman's teaching. He says : —

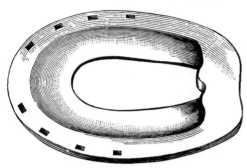

FIG. 573.—**Ordinary Form of Rolling Motion Shoe.**

"In England, since Prof. Coleman ruthlessly destroyed the empirical knowledge of the old masters, and substituted for it a system of fantastic and often cruel notions, we have been a prey to endless speculative theories. The result is that with the best horses in the world, we have a far larger proportion of lame ones than are to be found in any other country. * * *

"It was a kind of teaching on the foot and on shoeing that did the incalculable and, I fear, almost irreparable damage which has brought suffering on horses and shortened their existence, which has spoiled farriers, by leading them astray on false pretexts, and has entailed discredit on the English Veterinary School. * * *

FIG. 574.—**Cross-section of the Same.**

"One change, among others introduced by Mr. Coleman, has entailed, I believe, a more lasting damage on the art farriery than any of his many other crotchets, which have unfortunately become thoroughly parts of English horse-shoeing. He introduced the drawing-knife, and made it supercede the buttress for preparing the feet for shoeing. The buttress is the instrument still in use for paring down the wall surface to receive the shoe everywhere except in

FIG. 575.—**Side View, Showing Degree of Curve.**

England and parts of the New World, to which English hands and language have carried our modes of shoeing, such as it has become only within the present century.

"Old men can remember the buttress's being in general use throughout Great Britain ; but the way it was banished from English practice is known to few ; and its supercedence, and these remarks on the effects of the change, may astonish many. The drawing-knife, or searcher, as it was called, a small, hooked.

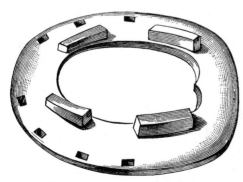

FIG. 576.—**Ground Surface of Above, Showing Method of Putting on Calkins.**

crooked little instrument, was formerly kept for the purpose of exploring wounds and extracting foreign bodies from the foot, and was to that extent in vogue on the Continent as well as in England. But theorizing, and a fancy for a change, led the professor to order the general use of the little hooked knife instead of such a broad, level tool as the buttress. He had unfortunately conceived such notions as that the sole of the foot did not bear the weight of the animal, that it was necessary to pare

FIG. 577.—**Quarter-crack.**

it thin every time the horse was shod, and that the broad, level buttress was not suited for that ; hence the preference for the little scooping, crooked searcher. As these incidents have had a disastrous effect on shoeing, which we have scarcely in any degree begun to relieve, I will quote from Mr. Coleman's work of 1798 :—

" 'Those who supposed that the weight of the animal was chiefly supported by the horny sole, have attributed a function to that organ which it does not possess ; but, although the laminæ are capable of sustaining the animal, yet, as they are elastic, and at every step elongate, the horny sole is necessarily pressed down in the same degree, and by first descending and then ascending, as the laminæ dilate and contract, the horny sole contributes very materially to prevent concussion. This union of the crust with the coffin-bone sustains the weight of the animal ; the crust supports the weight even when the horny sole and frog are removed ; if the sole and frog in reality supported the weight, then the foot would slip through the crust when the frog and sole were taken away.

" 'The sole, frog, and bars were taken away from both the fore feet of a horse ; the feet were then alternately lifted by placing the hands on the loins of the horse ; he kicked, all his weight was then sustained by the laminæ of the fore feet, and yet this made not the smallest degree of change in the situations of the bones.

" 'From this experiment, therefore, it is, that the union of the sensitive laminæ with the horny laminæ is sufficiently strong to support the whole weight of the animal on two feet.

" ' The first thing to be attended to is to take away the portion of the sole with the drawing-knife ; and to avoid pressure, the sole should be made concave or hollow. If there be any one part of the practice of shoeing more important than the rest, it is this removal of the sole between the bars and the crust. In common practice these parts are removed by an instrument called the buttress.

" ' The removal of a proper quantity of horny sole has been represented to be a

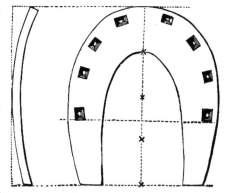

FIG. 578.—**French Shoe.**

delicate operation, and in the hands of common smiths liable to do mischief. But any smith capable of paring a hoof cannot fail to be equal to removing part of the sole with the drawing-knife. That the practice may be faithfully executed in the army, a farrier from each regiment of cavalry has been permitted to attend the college to learn the practical part of shoeing.'

"The foregoing passages, abounding as they do in errors, give evidence of the manner in which some of the greatest changes in the practice of horse-shoeing have occurred since its history has been written, and changes which have led to the worst possible results. Once, however, the notion got possession of the minds of the men at the wheel, that the bottom of the foot, its arched sole, was not designed to support the weight, but to yield to pressure downward; everything had to give way to that idea. The sole and frog were torn away, and because,

Fig. 579.—**An Old Quarter-crack Grown Down.**

Fig. 580.—**Quarter-crack.**

during the barbarous experiment, the connection did not yield, and the bone protrude like a finger through a torn glove, negative evidence was taken in confirmation of the theory framed; the paring away of the horses' soles with the drawing-knife was thus established, and the army, by sending farriers to learn the new system, became the means of enforcing the absurd and cruel practice of thinning the sole throughout this kingdom and the colonies.

"It is interesting to see the differently constituted mind of Mr. Moorcroft on the natural bearing of the question in 1800. He says :—

"'The sole ties the lower edge of the crust together, and by its upper part forming a strong arch, it affords a firm basis to the bone of the foot, and by its strength it defends the sensitive parts within the hoof.'

"This is true. We fail to discover a single passage in any work or any traditional account to show that any objection was raised to the continuance of the use of the buttress in England, any more than over the rest of the world, where it had been adopted from time immemorial, until, along with his other new theories about shoe-

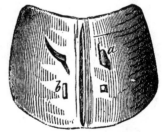

Fig. 581.—**Toe-crack.**

Fig. 582.—**Toe-crack.**

ing, Mr. Coleman believed it to be the wrong thing to employ, and then a crooked knife and a coarse rasp were adopted as weapons that might do more destructive execution than the one dismissed."

George Fleming, in his work on "Shoes and Horse-shoeing," says :—

"This evil of paring or rasping must be looked upon as the greatest and most destructive of all that pertains to shoeing, or even to our management of the horse.

Nine tenths of the workmen who resort to this practice cannot explain its object, and those who have written in defense of it say it is to allow the descent of the sole and facilitate the lateral expansion of the hoof.

"Fancy our gardeners cutting and rasping the bark off our fruit-trees, to assist them in their natural functions, and improve their appearance ; and yet the bark is of no more vital importance to the tree than the horn of the sole wall and frog are to the horse's foot.

Fig. 583.—**Quarter-crack.**

Fig. 584.—**Effect of Founder.**

"*The sole, frog, and bars must on no account, nor under any conditions, unless those of a pathological nature, be interfered with in any way by knife or rasp.* As certainly as they are interfered with, and their substance reduced, so surely will the hoof be injured. Nature has made every provision for the defense. They will support the contact of hard, soft, rugged, or even sharp bodies, if allowed to escape the drawing-knife ; while hot, cold, wet, or even dry weather has little or no influence on the interior of the foot, or on the tender horn, if man does not step in to beautify the feet by robbing them of their protection, perhaps merely to please the fancy of an ignorant groom or coachman.

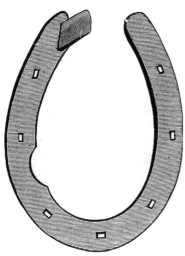

Fig. 585.—**Shoe for Quarter-crack.**

"If we closely examine the upper surface of the sole of a hoof that has been separated from its contents by maceration, we will find it perforated everywhere by myriads of minute apertures, which look as if they had been formed by the point of a fine needle. If we look also at the vascular parts of the foot that have been in contact with this horny surface, it will be observed that they have been closely studded with exceedingly fine, yet somewhat long, filaments, as thickly set as a pile of the richest Genoa velvet. These are the villi, or papillæ, which enter the horny cavity, and fitting into them like so many fingers into a glove, constitute the secretory apparatus of the frog as well as the sole. Each of the filaments forms a horn tube or fibre, and passes to a certain depth in a protecting canal whose corneous wall it builds. When injected with some colored preparation, one of them makes a beautiful microscopical object, appearing as a long, tapering net-work of blood-vessels, surrounding one or two parent trunks, and communicating with each other in a most wonderful manner. These filaments are also organs of tact, each containing a sensitive nerve, destined to endow the foot with the attributes of a tactile organ.

"This distribution will enable us to realize, to some extent, the amount of injury done by paring. The horn thrown out for their defense and support being removed by the farrier's knife, and perhaps the ends of these villi cut through, the meager pellicle remaining rapidly shrivels up, the containing cavity of each vascular tuft as quickly contracts on the vessels and nerves, which, in their turn, diminish in volume, disappear, or become morbidly sensitive, through this squeezing influence. The feet of a horse so treated are always hot, the soles are dry and stony, and become unnaturally concave. The animal goes tender after each shoeing, and it is not until the horn has been regenerated to a certain extent, that he steps with anything like ease. Until the new material has been formed, each papilli experiences the same amount of inconvenience and suffering that a human foot does in a new, tight boot.

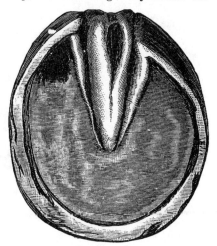

FIG. 586.—**Gifford's Foot as it Appeared Before Treatment.**

"This tenderness is usually ascribed to the nails and other causes ; and the horse, in the stable, rests on one foot, then on the other, as if he suffered uneasiness or pain. * * *

"All the preparation any kind of foot usually requires for the shoe may be summed up in a few words; leveling the crust in conformity with the limb and foot, and removing as much of its margin as will restore it to its natural length, rounding its outer edge at the same time, and leaving the sole, bars, frog, and heels in all their natural integrity."

Osmer, an old writer of good standing, in 1751 said : —

FIG. 587.—**Shoe Fitted for Curing Corns. From Coleman.**

"I believe there are many horses that might travel their whole lifetime unshod on any road, if they were rasped round and short on the toe ; because all feet exposed to hard objects become thereby more obdurate, if the sole be never pared ; and some, by their particular form, depth, and strength, are able to resist them quite, and to support the weight without breaking ; and here a very little reflection will teach us whence the custom arose of shoeing horses in one part of the world and not in another. In Asia there is no such custom of shoeing the horse at all, because the feet acquire a very obdurate and firm texture from the dryness of the climate and the soil, and do really want no defense. But every rider has a rasp to shorten his horse's feet, which would otherwise grow long and rude, and the crust of the hoof would most certainly split."

He continues by saying,—

"From the good that was found to arise from putting shoes on horses which have naturally weak feet from being brought up on wet land, the custom of putting shoes on all kinds of feet became general in some countries. Our ancestors, the original shoers, proposed nothing more, I dare say, in their first efforts, than to preserve the crust from breaking way, and thought themselves happy that they had skill enough so to do. The moderns also are wisely content with this in the racing way.

FIG. 588.—**Position of the Spreaders for Opening the Quarter.**

"In process of time the fertility of invention and the vanity of mankind have produced a variety of methods; almost all of which are productive of lameness; and I am thoroughly convinced from observation and experience, that nineteen lame horses out of every twenty are lame of the artist, which is owing to the form of the shoe, his ignorance of the design of nature, and maltreatment of the foot, every part of which is made for some purpose or other, though he does not know it.

"I suppose it will be universally assented to, that whatever method of shoeing approaches nearest to the law of nature, such is likely to be the most perfect method.* * *

"The superfices of the foot around the outside, now made plane and smooth, the shoe is to be made quite flat, of an equal thickness all around the outside, and open and most narrow backward at the extremities of the heels; for the generality of horses, those whose frogs are diseased, either from natural or incidental causes, require the shoe to be wider backwards; and to prevent this flat shoe from pressing on the sole of the horse, the outer part thereof is to be made thickest, and the inside gradually thinner. In such a shoe the frog is permitted to touch the ground, the necessity of which has already been seen. Added to this, the horse stands more firmly upon the ground, having the same points of support as in a natural state.

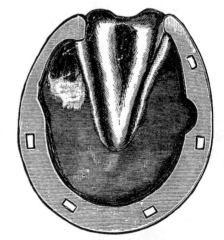

FIG. 589.—**The Shoe as it Appeared when on, with the Quarters Opened Out.**

"Make the shoes as light as you can according to the size of your horse, because heavy shoes spoil the back sinews and weary the horse; and if he happen to overreach, the shoes, being heavy, are all the more rapidly pulled off.

"Those who think it frugality to shoe with thick and heavy shoes, and seldom, are deceived, for they lose more by it than they gain ; for thereby they not only spoil the back sinews, but lose more by it than if they had been light."

It is conceded by all the best modern authorities that the French author above referred to, whose work was published in 1750, was the great father of a correct system of reform in shoeing. It was supposed in his day, as it is in a great measure now, that a

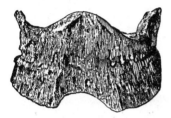

Fig. 590, 591.—**Sand-crack, or Fissure in Front of Hoof.**

A deep substance of horn is found beneath the fissure at the lower part of the hoof, where a corresponding cavity is formed by absorption in the coffin-bone.

horse could not travel without having heavy, unwieldy shoes on, and that the greatest skill was exhibited in the amount of cutting and rasping done on the feet.

He boldly proclaimed that all this was injurious, and tried to prove it by the most convincing arguments. The principles of treatment,

Fig. 592.—**Flat, Convex Sole.**

though given a hundred and thirty years ago, are just as important now as they were then. He says :—

"In the state of nature, all the inferior parts of the foot concur to sustain the weight of the body ; then we observe that the heels and frog, the parts said to be most exposed, are never damaged by wear, that the wall or crust is alone worn on going on hard ground, and that it is only this part which must be protected, leaving the other parts free and unfettered in their natural movements."

Fig. 593.—**Flat, Weak Sole.**

In advising tips or thin-heeled shoes, he says :—

"Thin tips extending back to the middle of the quarters, allow the heels to bear upon the ground, and the weight to be sustained behind and before, but particularly in the latter, because the weight of the body falls heaviest there.

Fig. 594.—**Foot Referred to in Text as it Appeared.**

"The shorter the shoe is, the less the horse slips, and the frog has the same influence in preventing this that an old hat placed under our own shoes would have in protecting us from slipping on the ice. * * *

"It is necessary, nevertheless, that hoofs which have weak walls should be a little longer shod, so that the gradually thinning b r a n c h e s reach to the heels, though not resting upon them. For horses which have convex soles, these l o n g shoes should also be used, and the toes should be more covered to prevent the sole touching the ground. This is the only true method of preserving the foot and restoring it. A horse which has its feet weak and sensitive, ought to be shod as short as possible, and with thin branches, so that the frog comes in contact with the ground ; because the heels, having nothing between them, are benefited and relieved. (See Fig. 479.)

"Crescent shoes are all the more needful for a horse which has weak, incurvated quarters, as they not only relieve them, but also restore them to their natural condition. Horses which have contusion at the heels (blains, corns), should also be shod in this way ; and for cracks (seime, sand-cracks) at the quarter, it is also advantageous.

"The sole or frog should never be pared ; the wall alone should be cut down, if it is too long. When a horse cuts himself with the opposite foot, the inner branch of the shoe ought to be shorter and thinner than the outer.

"Rasping the foot destroys the

Fig. 595.—**The Shoe as it may be Fitted to Support Weak Heels.**

strength of the hoof, and consequently causes its horn to become dry, and the horny laminæ beneath to grow weak ; from this often arises an internal inflammation, which renders the foot painful, and makes the horse go lame. * * *

" When a horse loses a shoe, a circumstance often occurring, if the hoof is pared, the animal cannot walk a hundred steps without going lame ; because in this state the lower surface of the foot being hollowed, the horse's weight falls upon the crust, and this, having no support from the horny sole, is quickly broken and worn away ; and if he meets hard substances on the road, he all the more speedily becomes lame. It is not so when the sole is allowed to retain its whole strength. The shoe comes off, but the sole and frog resting on the ground, assist the crust in bearing the whole weight of the body, and the animal, though unshod, is able to pursue his journey safe and sound. . . . . It is necessary to be convinced of another fact ; that is, it is rare that a horse goes at his ease and is not promptly fatigued, if the frog does not touch the ground. As it is the only point of support, if you raise it from the ground by paring it, there arises an inordinate extension of the tendon, caused by the pushing of the coronary against the navicular bone, as has been mentioned above, and which, being repeated at every step the animal takes, fatigues it and induces inflammation. From thence often arises distentions of the sheaths of tendons (moletts-vulgo, ' windgalls ') engorgements,

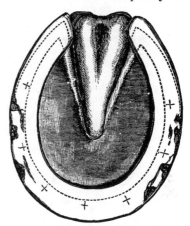

Fig. 596.—**Points Showing where the Horn is Strongest to Drive the Nails In.**

and swelling of tendons, etc., that are observed after long or rapid journeys. These accidents arise less from the length of the journey, as has been currently believed, than from the false practice of paring the sole. . . . We always find ourselves more active and nimble when we wear easy shoes ; but a wide, long, and thick shoe will do for horses what clogs do for us,—render them heavy, clumsy, and unsteady. * * *

" The feet become convex by hollowing the shoes to relieve the heel and frog, because the more the shoes are arched from the sole, the more the wall of the hoof is squeezed and rolled inward, particularly toward the inner quarter, which is the weakest ; the sole of the foot becomes convex, and the horse is nearly always unfit for service. * * *

Fig. 597.—**The Same as would Appear with the Shoe On.**

" The reason why it is dangerous to pare the feet of horses is, that when the sole is pared, and the horse tands in a dry place, the horn becomes desiccated by the air which enters it, and removes its moisture and its suppleness, and often causes the animal to be lame. * * *

"It is the pared foot that is more affected with what is termed contracted or weak inside quarter, and which also lames the horse.

"It also happens that one or both quarters contract, and sometimes even the whole hoof, when, in consequence of its smallness, all the internal parts are confined in their movements ; this is due to paring, and lames the horse.

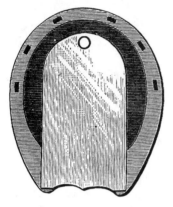

Fig. 598.—**Original Shoe Fitted with Plate On.**

Fig. 599.—**Form of Bar Shoe which would be a Good Support for Weak Heels.**

"There also occurs another accident : when the quarter becomes contracted, the hoof splits in its lateral aspects, and the horse is lame. This accident is termed a sand-crack (seime)."—*Lafosse.*

Though not generally known, this system of shoeing has long been in use in India. Freeman, in his work published in 1796, who

Fig. 600.—**Same as 598 with Plate Removed.**

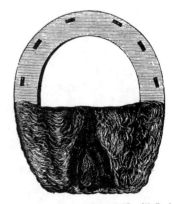

Fig. 601.—**Heel of Shoe 598 with Pad of Oakum Attached.**

is yet considered good authority, strongly advocated this system of shoeing. He gives the following statement, which explains itself :—

"The instance in which I was disappointed was that of a horse kept entirely for a riding-horse, and which was consequently almost daily under my own inspection.

This horse had very strong feet, one of which was smaller than the other, with the toe turning out and the frog almost wasted. The bars of the foot, before he was turned out, were scarcely visible, but upon examining them after he had been out

Fig. 602.—Bearing-surface of Shoe to Prevent Striking.

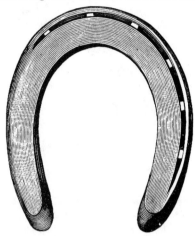

Fig. 603.—Forward Shoe to Prevent Striking.

about three months, they were found to have increased surprisingly. Notwithstanding this, they were not strong enough to counteract the pressure of the quarters ; and the foot itself seemed to be rather decreased, which is contrary to what is usual ; for after having been turned out for a certain time, they generally become larger. So particular a case led me to turn my mind to a particular method of cure. This I should hardly have found out, if chance had not at that time put into my hands Lieutenant Moor's "Narrative of Captain Little's Detachment." On page 93 of this book is the following passage :—

"'The bigotry with which all sects of the Hindoos adhere to their own customs is very well known ; still when these customs are strikingly injudicious, and totally abstracted from all religious prejudices, perseverance degenerates into obstinacy, and simplicity into ignorance. So it is with the Mahrattas in abiding by their present practice of cutting the hoof and shoeing horses ; they cut away the hinder part of the hoof in such a manner that the pastern almost touches the ground, and the frog is suffered to grow so that the hoof is nearly a circle, in which form the shoes are made, the hinder parts almost touching, and so thin that a person of ordinary strength can easily twist them. Instead of making the back part of the shoe thick-est, they hammer it quite thin, making the fore part thickest, and the shoe, gradually becoming thinner, ends in an edge.'

Fig. 604.—Shoe to Prevent Interfering or Clicking.

"This mode of shoeing in a country where, from the nature of the climate, the horse's feet probably are very strong, did not strike me to be quite so injudicious as the author above mentioned represents it. I determined, therefore, to try on this particular horse a shoe in some respects similar to those described, that I might see whether it would alter the shape of his foot ; since it is said to make 'the frog grow so

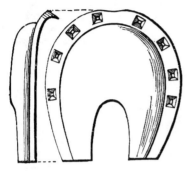

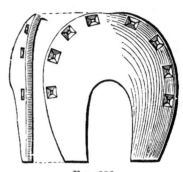

Fig. 605.—Form of Shoe Adapted for Protection of the Foot and Aiding Mobility—From the French.

Fig. 606.
Ground View of Same.

that the hoof is nearly a circle,' which was the very effect that in this case I wished to produce. I therefore ordered my smith to make a shoe at my own forge in the form I generally use (which will be hereafter described), with the following exceptions : The web of it was to almost cover the sole, room being given to admit a picker ; and as it proceeded to the heels, the web on each side was to be continued as far as the cleft which separates the bars from the frog. He was to make the fore part the 'thickest,' and to hammer it so thin at the heels that it would 'end in an edge,' by which a person of ordinary strength could easily twist it.

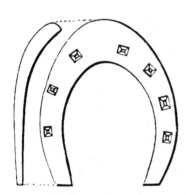

"I own I apprehended that this shoe, from being so thin at the heels, would bend in different places, and thereby injure the foot. But as it was constantly under my own eye, I knew that if that circumstance should happen, the injury could not be material in the short time it

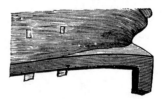

Fig. 607.—Form of Shoe Adapted to Hind Foot to Aid Mobility. Used by the French.

Fig. 608.
Shoe Raised from the Heel.

would be permitted to go unnoticed. But this did not prove to be the case. After the horse had worn this shoe a day or two only, I found the action of the leg was more free than it had ever been before ; for the bars with their covering touched the ground ; the extremities of the web on each side, by being so very thin, having bent a little over them, but they were prevented from injuring them by being extended to the cleft which separated the bars from the frog. This pressure of the web on the bars was an assistance to them in the expansion of the quarters ; and the shoe was kept so wide at the heels that the exterior parts of it could not hurt him. This shoe, therefore, acted exactly contrary to other shoes, which, as I before mentioned, are generally an impediment to the expansion of the heels, whereas this became an assistance to it.

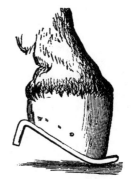

" In three weeks I took off this shoe to examine the state of the foot. His frog was found to be increased, and in a better condition than I had before seen it. The same shoe

FIGS. 609, 610.—Shoes Adapted for Stiff Joints.

was therefore replaced for three weeks more, at the end of which time his foot had become considerably larger and straighter. In a week or ten days more the horse was to go thirty-six miles on a turnpike road.

"Although this kind of shoe had succeeded so well in a riding-horse, I had some

FIG. 611.—French Shoe for Aiding Mobility.

doubts about venturing it on the road. However, I at last determined to risk it, and had another shoe put on of exactly the same pattern, in which he performed his journey without any injury, so that I have ever since continued to adopt it, having found it to answer beyond any expectation I had formed of it; for that foot which was before smaller than the other, with the toe turning out, has, by the use of this shoe, become of the same size, and so straight that there is now scarcely any difference between the two feet."

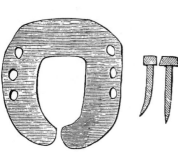

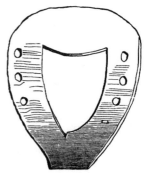

FIG. 612.   African Shoes.   FIG. 613.

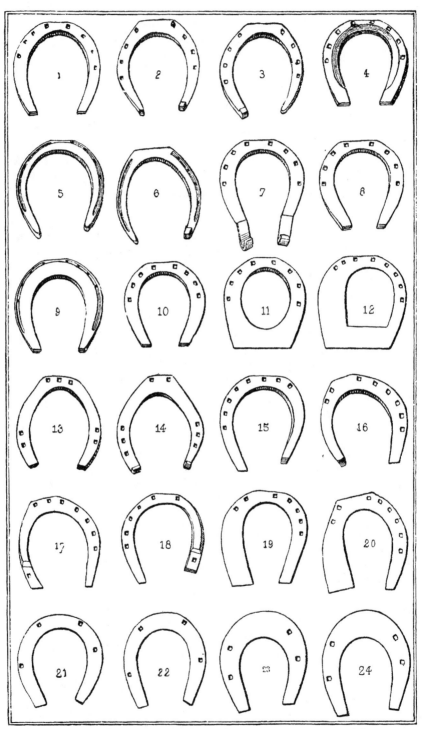

Representative Model Shoes of Different Kinds.   From the French.

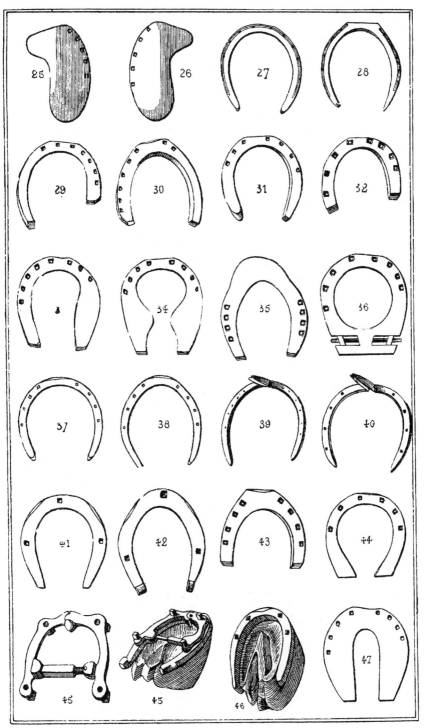

Representative Model Shoes of Different Kinds. From the French. [397]

We give here a few specimens of shoes from Cæsar Fiaschi's work, published in England in the 16th century. The figures of shoes he gives are twenty in number. No. 1. Fore-shoe without calkin ; 2. Shoe with the calkin ; *à 'l Aragonaise* on one side, and the other side thickened ; 3. *Lunette* shoe, or "tip" ; 4. Three-quarter shoe ; 5. Beveled shoe, with the *Aragonaise* calkin on one

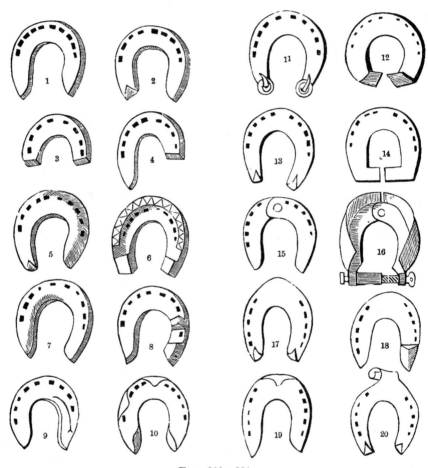

FIGS. 662—681.

branch, and the other thick at the heel ; 6. Shoe with *sciettes*, or projecting toothed border, thickened toward each heel to prevent slipping ; 7. Thick-sided shoe, thin toward the inner border, and seated like the English shoe ; 8. Shoe with buttons, or raised catches on the inner branch, and thickened on the heel of the same side ; 9. A shoe which has the inside heel and quarter much thicker and narrower than usual; 10. A shoe with crests or points toward the ground surface on the toe and quarter, and *barbettes* at the heels; 11. A shoe with the calkins doubled over, and provided with rings; 12. The foot surface of a shoe with the heels turning up toward the foot; 13. Shoe with two calkins; 14. A *bar* shoe; 15. A jointed shoe to suit any size of foot; 16. A jointed shoe without nails, and secured by the lateral border and the heel-screw; 17. A hind shoe with calkins; 18. A shoe with one of the branches greatly thickened at the heel; 19. A hind shoe with a crest or toe-piece; 20. A hind shoe with the toe elongated and curled upward, probably for a foot the back tendons of which were contracted, causing the horse to walk on the point of the toe.

Below, in Figs. 682–685, are given a variety of old Roman shoes found in England, France, and Switzerland, and supposed to be from nineteen hundred to over two thousand years old.

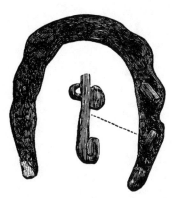

Fig. 682.

Fig. 683.

Fig. 684.

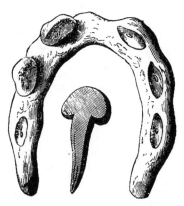

Fig. 685.

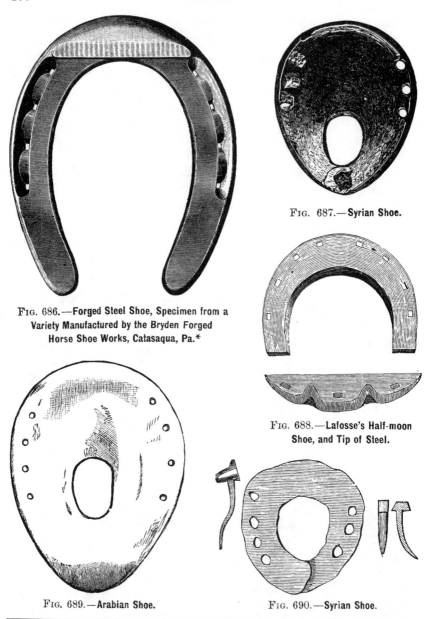

Fig. 686.—Forged Steel Shoe, Specimen from a Variety Manufactured by the Bryden Forged Horse Shoe Works, Catasaqua, Pa.*

Fig. 687.—Syrian Shoe.

Fig. 688.—Lafosse's Half-moon Shoe, and Tip of Steel.

Fig. 689.—Arabian Shoe.

Fig. 690.—Syrian Shoe.

* This, with other cuts of model shoes manufactured by this company, were by special request forwarded to me for insertion among models of good working shoes, but were received too late to be put in proper place. The patentee, Mr. Bryden, is known to me personally as a man of rare skill as a student of the foot. I am indebted to him for many valuable points on the treatment of the foot, and the shoes manufactured under his supervision are so good in all respects that I would strongly urge upon shoers and others interested to give them a trial.

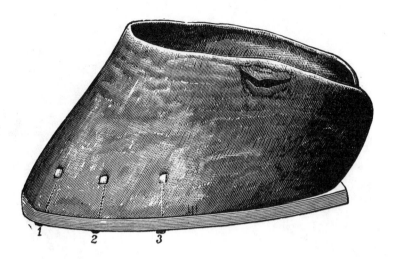

Fig. I.

  The shoe properly formed, adjusted, and nailed on the hoof of a five-year-old horse that had never been shod but once.

Fig. II.

  The foot as it is ruined by bad treatment. The shoe and nails are too large; the nails too many in number and driven too deep. The shoe is set back too far. The hoof is rasped away so much as to weaken it and destroy its symmetry.

PLATE I.

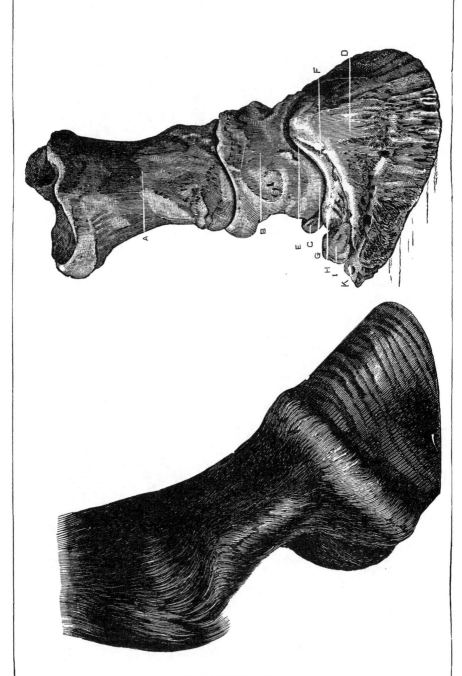

PLATE II.

PLATE II.*

A front view of the bones of the fore feet of a horse in their relative position.

A. The pastern bone.

B. The coronary bone.

C. The navicular bone.

D. The foot bone.

E. The point of insertion of the tendon of the extensor muscle.

F. A concavity to give attachment to the ligament which unites the foot bone to the coronary bone at G.

G. Coronary bone.

H. A continuation of the same concavity, to which the cartilage of the foot bone is attached.

I, I. The upper and lower processes of the foot bone.

K, K. A groove in the foot bone, which receives a division of the main artery, coming round from behind.

K, L. A groove receiving another division of that artery, which proceeds round the extreme edges of the foot bone.

---

*The plates here given are selected from the author's special book on the horse, "Facts for Horse Owners," in which are forty plates. In the extra edition these plates are printed in colors.

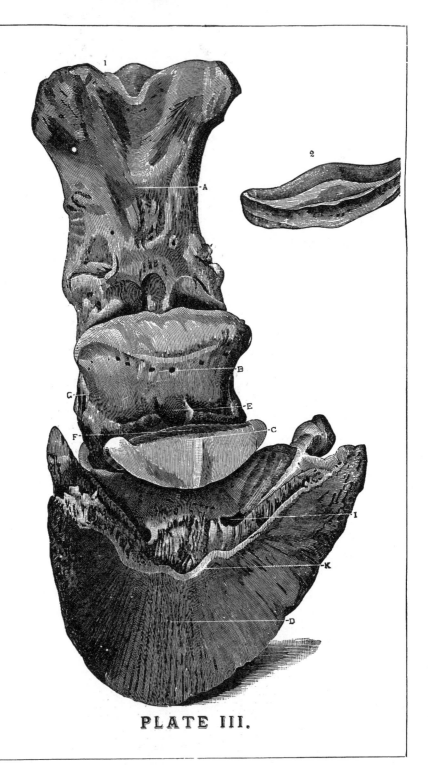

PLATE III.

PLATE III.

Fig. I.

A back view of the bones of the fore foot in their relative
situation.

A. Pastern bone.

B. Coronary bone.

C. Navicular bone.

D. Foot bone.

E. A cavity which in the natural state is filled with fat.

F. The upper surface of the navicular bone, from which two ligaments
arise, and pass round the lateral depression in the coronary bone,
marked G.

G. Points of attachment on each side of the ligament which unites the
navicular bone to the foot bone.

I. Two grooves in which two main trunks of the arteries are continued
into the foot bone.

K. The line of insertion of the tendon of the flexor muscle.

Fig. II.

A view of the anterior and inferior surfaces of the navicular bone detached from the other bones.

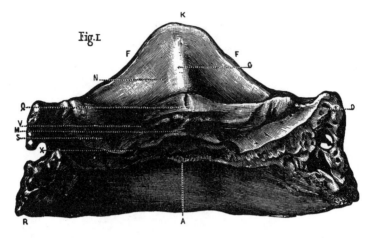

Fig.I.

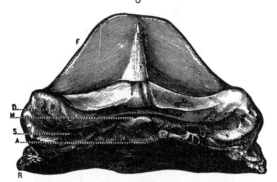

Fig.II.

Fig.III.

Fig.IV.

Fig.V.

PLATE IV.

PLATE IV.

This cut represents the third phalanx seen from its posterior part ; and the navicular bone,—inferior, superior, and anterior views.

Fig. I.

Posterior Part of the Third Phalanx (ADULT).

A. Semi-lunar crest.
D. Basilar process.
F. Superior border.
G. Spreading out of the articular face.
K. Anterior view of the pyramidal eminence.
M. Posterior view of the inferior face.
N. Glenoid cavity of the superior face.
Q. Portion of the articular surface corresponding to the anterior border of the navicular bone.
R. Retrossal process.
S. Edge of the plantar fissure.
V. Posterior border of the third phalanx.
X. Plantar orifice for passage of blood vessels.

Fig. II.

Posterior Part of the Third Phalanx (COLT).

A. Semi-lunar crest.
D. Basilar process.
F. Superior border.
M. Posterior view of the bone.
R. Retrossal process.
S. Plantar fissure.

Fig. III.

Inferior Face of Navicular.

C. Transverse ridge.
E. Anterior border.
H. Extremity of the bone.

Fig. IV.

A. Median ridge or bulge of the superior face.
D. Anterior superior border.
E. Anterior inferior border.
G. Posterior border (is very thick, and cribbled or pierced with vascular orifices).

Fig. V.

Anterior Face of Navicular.

E. Soft part hollowed under the anterior articular facet.
H. Articular facet corresponding to the posterior facet of the third phalanx.

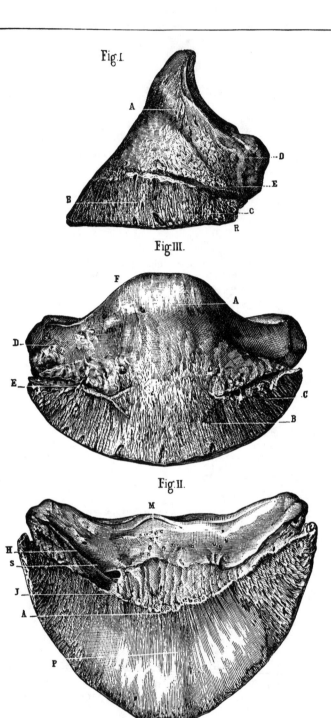

Fig. I.

Fig. III.

Fig. II.

PLATE V.

PLATE V.

This plate represents the third phalanx of the colt, seen from its lateral, anterior, and inferior faces.

Fig. I.

Lateral Face.

A. Base of the pyramidal eminence.
B. Vascular porosities.
C. Patilobe eminence.
E. Pre-plantar fissure.

D. Basilar process.
K. Pyramidal eminence.
R. Retrossal process.

Fig. II.

Anterior Face.

A. Pyramidal eminence.
B. Porosities and vascular imprints
C. Patilobe eminence.
D. Basilar process.
E. Pre-plantar fissure.
F. Superior border.

Fig. III.

Inferior Face.

A. Semi-lunar crest.
H. Plantar fissure.
J. Imprint of the insertion of the perforans.
P. Inferior face.
S. Edge of the plantar fissure.

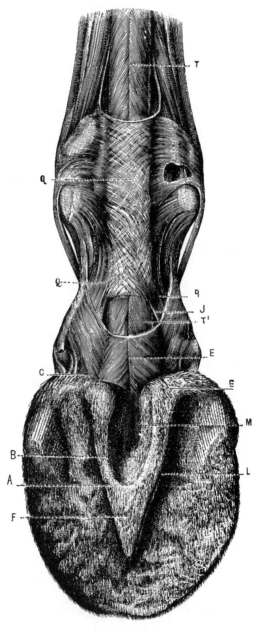

PLATE VI.

PLATE VI.

This figure represents the posterior face of the digital region, flexed backward in a manner to show in its full extent the inferior or plantar face of the foot.

The skin has been lifted from above the third phalanx, and the enveloping sheaths of the tendons are dissected. The velvety tissue is preserved.

A. Median part of the pyramidal body (fleshy frog) of plantar cushion, or sensitive tissue of the sole.

B. Branches of the pyramidal body.

C. Cartilaginous bulb.

E. Angle of inflection of the branches of the pyramidal body.

F. Point or apex of the fleshy frog.

J. Interval of separation of the two branches of the perforatus.

L. Lateral lacunæ of the pyramidal body.

M. Median lacunæ of the pyramidal body.

Q, Q. Fibrous sheath of union of the two branches of the perforatus.

R. Branches of theperforatus directing th emselves towardtheir point of insertion at the second phalanx.

T. Tendon of the perforatus.

T'. Tendon of the perforans at its passage between the branches of the perforatus.

V. Strengthening sheath of the plantar aponeurosis.

X. Lateral bands of the strengthening sheath of the plantar aponeurosis, which cross the direction of the branches of the perforatus to go and attach themselves on the lateral parts of the first phalanx.

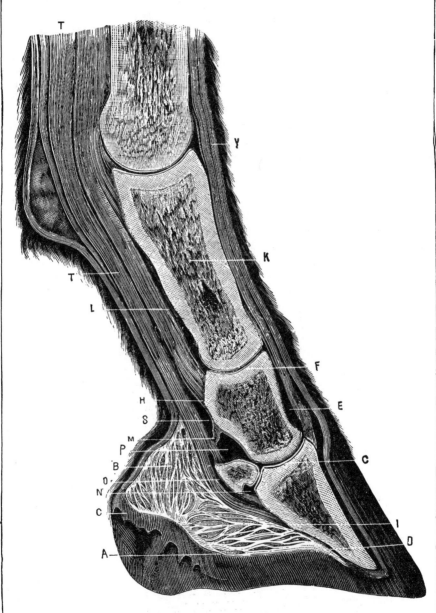

PLATE VII.

PLATE VII.

This plate shows a longitudinal section of the digital region in its median plane.

Its object is to show the spongeous substance in the interior of the bone, the fibrous intersections in the plantar cushion of the articular and tendinous synovial sheaths, and of the plantar cushion (or pad) in the interior of the hoof under the third phalanx and the navicular bone.

A. Inferior part of the pad (cushion).
B. Ligamentous bands (filaments) representing the structure of the fibrous body forming the plantar pad.
C. Enveloping fibrous membrane of the plantar pad.
D. Point of insertion of the plantar pad to the inferior face of the bone of the foot.
E. Spongeous substance of the interior of the second phalanx.
F. Articulation of the first phalanx with the second.
H. Branches of the perforatus at its insertion to the lateral parts of the second phalanx, or small pastern bone.
I. Insertion of the plantar aponeurosis to the semi-lunar crest.
K. Interior of the first phalanx.
L. Section of the perforatus tendon.
M. Transverse ligament of the yellow fibrous tissue uniting the anterior face of the perforans to the posterior face of the os coronae, etc. (2d phalanx).
N. Diverticulum of the sheath of the articulation of the foot between the little sesamoid and the third phalanx.
O. Little sesamoidal sheath.
P. Capsule of the articulation of the foot set superiorly against the *cul du sac* of the great sesamoidal sheath.
T. Perforans tendon.
Y. Metacarpo-phalangial articulation, or fetlock joint.

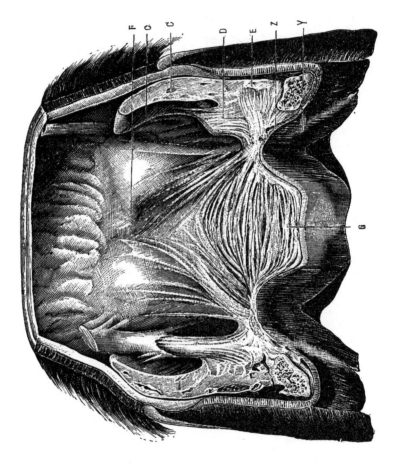

PLATE VIII.

PLATE VIII.

This plate represents a transverse section of the posterior part of the foot behind the phlanges, between the two fibro-cartilages.

It shows the disposition of the bulbs of the plantar pad, or cushion, the stratified layers of the pyramidal body, the hight of the cartilages of the hoof, and the direction of the bars.

B. Bulb of the plantar pad (or cushion).

C. Internal face of the fibro-cartilages, or lateral cartilages.

C'. Hight of the hoof.

D. Part of the lateral band of the reinforcing sheath of the perforans.

E. Point of junction of the inferior border of the cartilages with the substance of the plantar pad, or cushion.

F. Longitudinal depression of the anterior face of the plantar pad.

G. Stratified layers of the plantar pad in the pyramidal body.

Z. Superior surface of the bars.

Y. Thickness and direction of the bars.

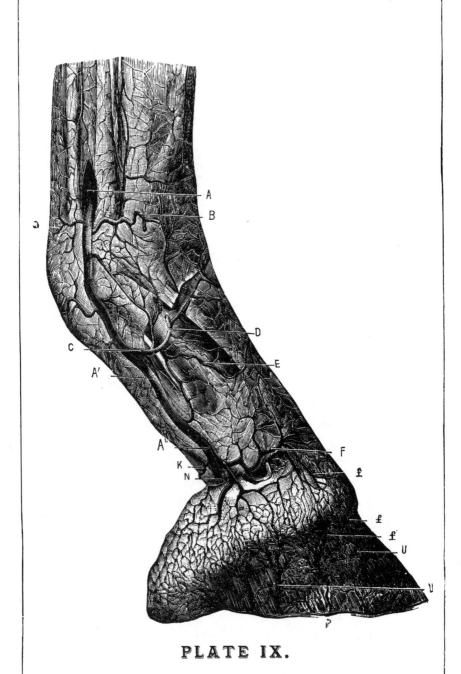

PLATE IX.

PLATE IX.

The figure shows the superficial disposition of the digital artery on the lateral face of the phalanges.

A, A′, A″. Digital artery from its emerging point above the great sesamoids to the point where it disappears under the plate of cartilages in N.

B. Anterior transverse branch at the metacarpo-phalangial articulation.

C. Perpendicular artery.

D. Ascending branch of the perpendicular artery.

E. Descending branch of the perpendicular artery.

F. Transverse branch forming with the corresponding one the superficial coronary circle.

f. Descending ramuscules in the pad of the superficial coronary circle.

f′. Ascending ramuscules of the podophyllous tissue, or sensitive laminæ.

G. Posterior transverse branches of the metacarpo-phalangial articulation.

K. Artery of the plantar pad, or cushion.

P. Circumflex artery.

U, U. Ascending terminal divisions of the digital artery; they emerge from the porosities of the third phalanx, and send ramifications to the podophyllous tissue.

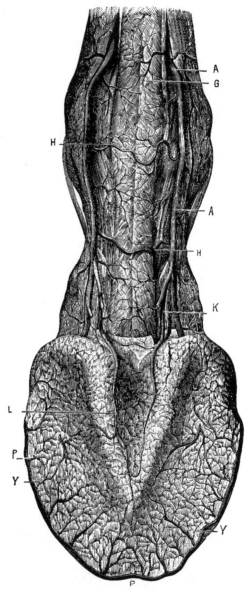

PLATE X.

PLATE X.

Arterial Vessels.

The figure represents the superficial disposition of the digital artery at the superior face of the first two phalanges and at the inferior face of the third.

A, A'. Digital artery in its passage along the phalanges.

G. Posterior transverse branches of the metacarpo-phalangial articulation.

H. Branches above one another at intervals.

K. Artery of the plantar pad, or cushion.

L. Internal branch of the artery of the plantar pad.

P, P, P. Circumflex artery.

Y, Y. Solar arteries, or arteries of plantar surface.

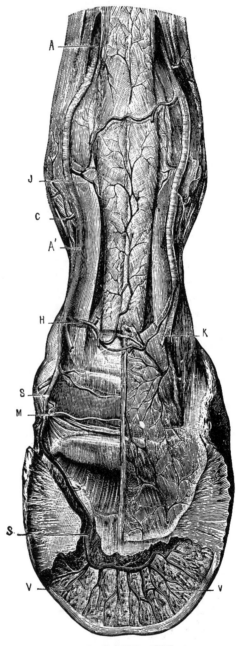

PLATE XI.

PLATE XI.

Arterial Vessels.

The figure shows the deep disposition of the digital artery at the posterior face of the first two phalanges, and in the interior of the third seen from its inferior face.

A, A'. Digital artery.

C. Perpendicular artery at its point of origin.

H. One of the branches running posteriorly, destined to the perforans tendon, in which it ramifies itself.

J. Deep-seated branch.

K. Point of origin of the artery of the plantar pad.

M. Deep transverse branch, completing behind the front superficial coronary circle.

S. *Plantar* artery or posterior terminal branch, in the plantar fissure, and in the semi-lunar sinus, where it forms with its analogue the *semi-lunar* anastomosis.

V, V. *Radiated* divisions of the digital artery emanating from the convexity of the semi-lunar anastomosis, and following the direction of the descending canals of the third phalanx to go and contribute to the formation of the circumflex artery at the exterior circumference of the notched border of the bone.

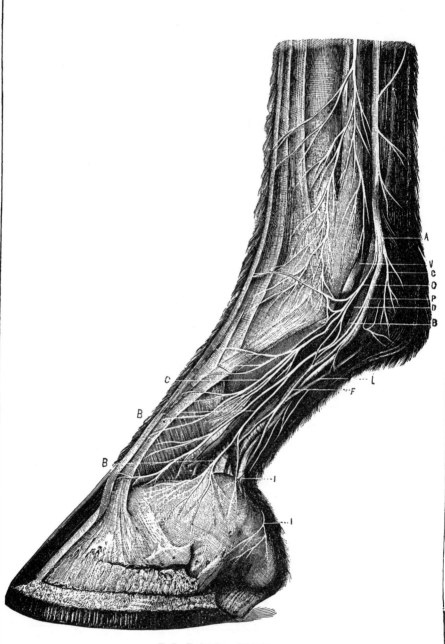

PLATE XII.

PLATE XII.

This figure represents the principle nerves of the digital region.

The plantar nerve occupies the same situation, but the divisions which emanate from it are more numerous and more anastomotic.

P. Plantar nerve.

A. Point of emergence of the plantar nerve above the sesamoids.

B, B. Cartilaginous branch.

C, C. Cutaneous branch.

D. Digital artery.

F'. Bulbous branch.

G. Transverse branch behind the metacarpo-phalangial articulation.

I. Nerve of the plantar pad.

L. Lateral band, or filamentous stay, of the proper tunic of the plantar pad. It crosses obliquely from backward forward, and from upward downward, the direction of the plantar nerve.

V. Digital vein.

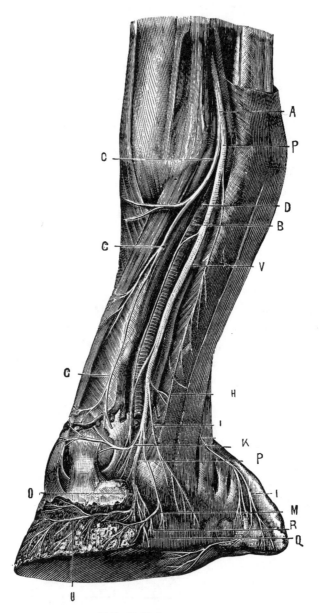

PLATE XIII.

PLATE XIII.

This figure represents on the digital region, seen from three-fourths behind, the disposition of the plantar nerve on the posterior face of the phalanges of the terminal divisions in the interior of the bone of the foot.

P. Plantar nerve.

A. Point of emergence of the plantar nerve above the sesamoids.

B. Cartilaginous branch.

C. Cutaneous branch.

D. Digital artery.

H. Occasional divison destined to the cartilaginous bulbs.

I, I. Branch of the plantar pad.

K. Transverse coronary branch.

M. Podophyllous division.

O. Pre-plantar nerve.

Q. Descending branch in the patilobe fissure.

R. Arterial ramuscules accompanying the digital artery in the plantar fissure.

V. Vein following sometimes behind the plantar nerve in all its phalangial course. This vessel does not always exist.

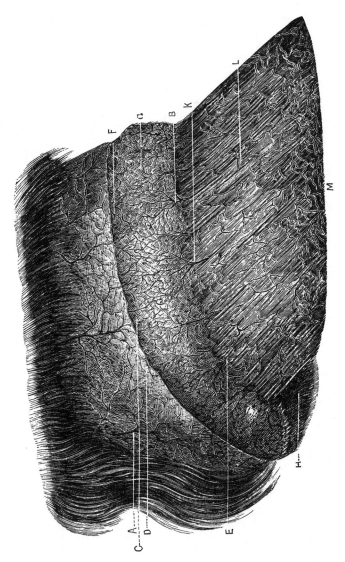

PLATE XIV.

PLATE XIV.

The object of this figure is to show the disposition of the capillary vessels in the tegument of the digital region seen sidewise.

A, A. Arterial vessels of the skin.

B, B'. Arterial vessels of the coronary band, or cushion.

R. Villosities of the coronary cushion. This vessel does not always exist.

This figure represents the principal perioplic bourrelet, the coronary groove and the podophyllous tissue or sensitive laminæ.

A, B. Principal coronæ (or cutidura) with the villosities covering it.

C. Superior border of the coronary cushion.

D. Perioplic coronary groove.

B. Perioplic (pad) covered with little horny substance.

F. Inferior border of the cushion.

G. Podophyllous tissue, or sensitive laminæ.

H. Villosities of the inferior extremity of the podophyllous laminæ.

E. Arterial vessels.

K. Small arterial branches.

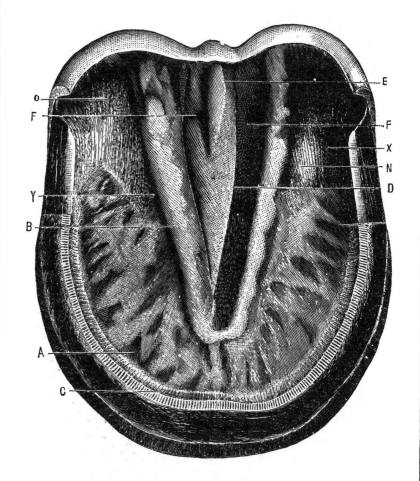

PLATE XV.

PLATE XV.

This figure represents the superior face of the floor of the hoof, formed by the sole and the frog. The wall has been cut at the level of the sole, in order to show the termination of the horny leaves in the edge, or border of the sole

A. Circular digital cavity at the point of reunion of the sole and the wall.

B. Superior border of the frog.

C. Termination of the horny leaves in the edge of the sole.

D. Cavity formed by the superior face of the frog.

E. Ridge of the frog, or frog stay.

F. Groove of the superior face of the frog.

G. External face of the glomes of the frog.

N. Keraphyllous tissue at the internal face of the bars.

O. Cutigeral cavity at the level of the angles of inflection.

X. Bottom of the angle of inflection.

Y. Point of termination of the bars at the lateral parts of the frog.

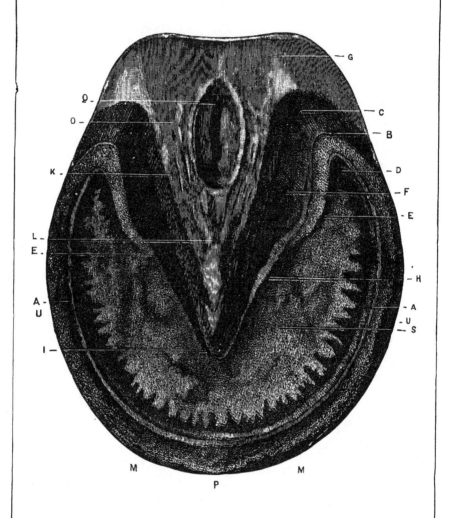

PLATE XVI.

PLATE XVI.

View of the hoof from its inferior face.

P. The wall.

S. The sole.

L. The frog.

A. Line indicating the commissure of the sole and the wall, known as the linea alba, or white line.

B. Angle of inflection of wall of the heels (buttress).

C. Superior border of buttress.

D. Region of the heels of the foot within the angle known as seat of corn.

E. Inferior border of the bars.

F. External face of the bars lining the lateral lacunæ of the frog.

G. Glomes of the frog, or bulbs of the heels.

H. Terminal extremity of the bars at the sides of the frog

I. Point of the frog.

K. Branches of the frog.

M. Regions of the *mamellas* of the hoof.

P. Region of the toe of the hoof.

Q. Median lacuna of the frog.

U. Region of the quarters.

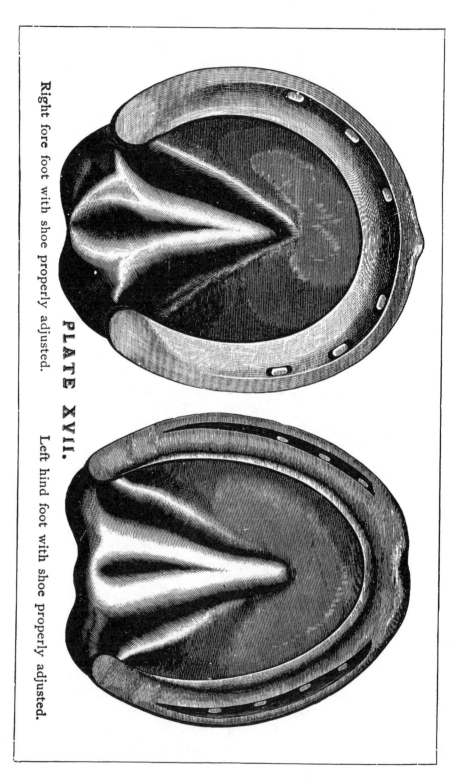

PLATE XVII.

Right fore foot with shoe properly adjusted.

Left hind foot with shoe properly adjusted.

DISEASES

AND THEIR TREATMENT.

CHAPTER XXI.

THE CIRCULATION.

THE phenomenon of the circulation is of so interesting and remarkable a character, and its condition has such an influence
upon the health, that I think it advisable, as an introduction to
the Medical Department, to make some reference to it. There are
so many diseases and difficulties of a serious character which are the
result of derangements of circulation, that it certainly seems necessary to give some explanation of it, that the reader may be impressed the better with the necessity for such prudence and care as
would prevent its disturbance. The writer thinks it also advisable,
instead of giving a labored description, which may be easily obtained from any physiology, and which but few would take the
trouble to read, to do this mainly by the aid of illustrations, a variety of which have been included at considerable expense.

GENERAL PLAN OF THE CIRCULATION.

The blood is circulated through the body for the purpose of nutrition and secretion, by means of one forcing-pump ; and through
the lungs, for its proper aeration, by another ; the two being united
to form the heart. This organ is therefore a compound machine,
though the two pumps are joined together, so as to appear to the
casual observer to be one single organ. In common language, the
heart of the mammalia is said to have two sides, each of which is a
forcing-pump ; but the blood, before it passes from one side to the
other, has to circulate through one or the other set of vessels found
in the general organs of the body or in the lungs, as the case may
be. This is shown at Fig. 692, where the blood, commencing
with the capillaries on the general surface, passes through the

veins which finally end in the vena cava *b*, and enters the right auricle *c*. From this it is pumped into the right ventricle *d*, which, contracting in its turn, forces it on into the pulmonary artery *e*, spreading out upon the lining membrane of the

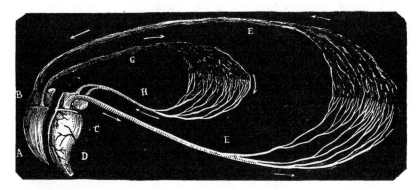

FIG. 691.—Theoretical Plan of the Circulatory System.

H, D, C, E, the canal for red blood; E, B, A, G, canal for blue blood. The arrows indicate the course of the blood. The two canals are represented in their middle portion, A, B, C, D, as isolated; but in nature they are enveloped at this point in a common sac that concurs to form the heart.

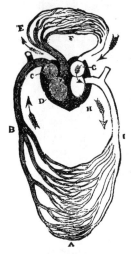

FIG. 692.—Plan of the Circulation.

lungs, to form the capillaries of that organ at *f*, from which it is returned to the left auricle *g* through the pulmonary veins. From the left auricle it is driven on through the left ventricle ; and this, by its powerful contraction, forces the blood through the aorta *i*, and the arteries of the whole body to the capillaries *a*, from which the description commenced.

While the venous blood is on its way to the heart, when near it, it is met by the thoracic duct (see *k, y*, Fig. 694), which conveys into this returning blood the nutritive property of the food extracted from it by the digestive organs. With this new supply of nutritious matter, the blood goes to the heart and lungs to be oxygenized by contact with the air, and thus be continued through the heart and arteries as before explained. The system takes up its material for its wear and tear through the capillaries or hair-like tubes, which are interposed between the two great divisions of the vascular system, arteries and veins. These little tubes are so small that they are from $\frac{1}{1000}$ to $\frac{1}{4000}$ of an inch in diameter. The smaller are found in the retina of the eye and brain, the larger in the liver and lungs. The worn-out tissue of the body is also taken up by the blood, and carried off through the bowels, lungs, kidneys, and skin, which are the natural sewers or depurative channels of the body. *The quantity of blood* that a horse contains is about $\frac{1}{10}$ of his weight.

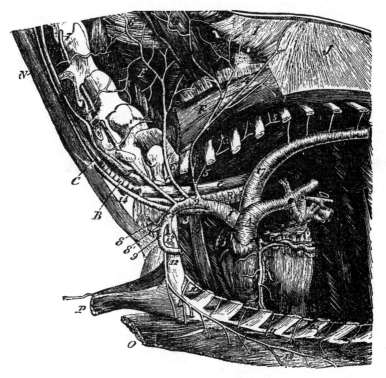

Fig. 693.—**Distribution of the Anterior Aorta.**

1. Anterior aorta; 2. Left axillary artery; 3. Right axillary artery; 4. Dorsal artery; 5. Subcostal artery; 12. External thoracic artery; 14. Carotid artery; 17. Posterior aorta. A, pulmonary aorta; B, trachea; E, superior branch of the iliospinal muscle; F, inferior branch of the same; G, great complexus muscle; I, I, originating aponeurosis of the splenius and the small anterior serratus muscles; N, sterno-maxillaris muscle; O, P, great pectoral and sterno-prescapularis muscles turned downward.

A horse weighing 1,000 pounds would therefore have about 100 pounds of blood, or nearly 50 quarts. Fat horses have proportionately less blood than those that are lean ; and it is claimed that wild animals generally have more blood in proportion than the domestic ones. Forty pounds of blood have been taken from medium-sized horses without serious injury ; and it requires the extraction of about $\frac{1}{5}$ of the total weight before life is destroyed. It is a remarkable fact that this large amount of blood in the body makes its entire round of circulation in the short period of from two to three minutes. This has been proved by the following experi‑ ment, which has been made and repeated many times at the Columbia Veterinary College, New York : The jugular vein was opened on one side of the neck, into which saline matter or poison was injected ; on the opposite side the carotid artery was tapped. In fif‑ teen seconds the first traces of the substance injected could be detect‑

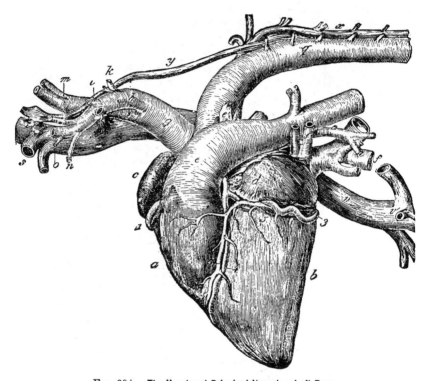

FIG. 694.—The Heart and Principal Vessels ; Left Face.

a, Right ventricle; b, Left ventricle; c, Right auricle; d, Left auricle; e, Pulmonary artery; f, Pulmonary veins; g, Anterior aorta; h, Left axillary artery; i, Right axillary artery, or brachio-cephalic trunk; p, Carotid arteries; q, Posterior aorta; x, Vena azygos; y, Thoracic ducts; z, Embouchure of that vessel, placed near the origin of the anterior vena cava.

ed in the blood ; in twenty seconds it was found very plainly. But while it is known that the main body of blood makes the shorter pulmonary circuit, that part going to the extremities most distant from the heart requires much longer time ; but it is assumed that all the blood in the body makes its entire circuit in the short period of from two to three minutes.

I refer to this fact, which is not familiar to the average reader, to show the great importance of not subjecting the horse to such in‑

fluences as will derange the circulatory system. The remarkable energy of the circulation through the blood-vessels is very finely illustrated by spreading and tying apart the toes of a frog's foot, and examining the web through a good microscope. The field of observation will appear like an immense plain cut up with large rivers intersected by numerous small streams, all running with the rapidity of a torrent, the larger currents running much the faster. The blood-corpuscles are also clearly distinguishable. Something of an idea of this can be seen by referring to Figs. 696 and 697, which

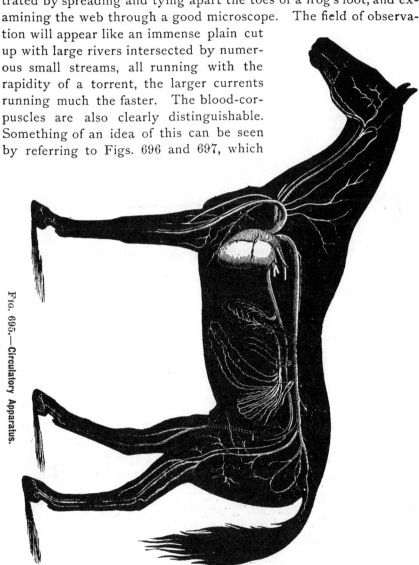

Fig. 695.—Circulatory Apparatus.

represent such a view of the circulation through the web.

When the circulation is in its natural state, that is, distributed properly to all parts of the body, it implies a state of perfect health, but if, from any cause, it is withheld or forced from any part of the body, there is not enough blood in that part, while there will be an excess in other parts. Thus, if the horse is exposed to a cold wind or is chilled by a current of air striking the body, the blood will be forced from its surface to the internal organs, accumulating where there is most freedom for it, or where it is weakest; usually in the lungs and surrounding parts, kidneys, bowels, and sometimes in the feet, the first indication of which would be a shivering fit, followed by fever. Now, it is evident that the object should be, when there is such disturbance, to equalize the circulation again, or force it back to its natural channels as quickly as possible, and that treatment by which this can be done most easily and quickly will be the best. The circulation is really controlled by the nervous system. If the nervous system is from any cause weakened, so that it is unable to act with the usual vigor, there is less ability to resist the influence of disturbing changes, and the horse is, as it is termed, more liable to take cold, which means a disturbance of the circulation.

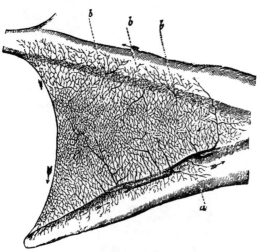

Fig. 696.—Web of Frog's Foot Stretching between Two Toes, Showing the Blood-vessels and their Anastomoses.

a, a, Veins; b, b, b, Arteries, the capillaries being between.

Hence a horse, when warm and exhausted after a drive, if given a little too much cold water, would be liable to have colic, founder, etc.; or if allowed to stand in a cold current of air, to have an attack of pneumonia, or some other indication of vascular disturbance before referred to, which would be scarcely felt if cool, and the nervous system in a vigorous condition.

It is evident also that the quality of blood being dependent upon the food taken, and the condition of the air breathed, it is necessary that the food should be clean and of good quality. No moldy grain, hay, or other food unfitted for proper nutrition, should be given, and the stable should be well ventilated with pure air at all times, and all poisonous gases, particularly the ammonia which is formed from the urine, should be allowed free egress from the stable, as the animal cannot be expected to keep in good health while compelled to inhale such malaria.

It is needless to explain the bad effects upon the depurative organs of the derangement of the circulation by which these channels are to a greater or less degree " clogged," or unable to do their proper work.

Now, it is within the province of every owner to prevent these troubles by employing care in feeding, exercise, etc., which is much better and easier than to try to cure them when sick. It is far easier to prevent a house from getting burned up by not letting the fire get started, than to depend upon the power of putting it out, for with the best of energy it may cause a destruction of the building. So in the cure of diseases ; it is a great deal better and safer to

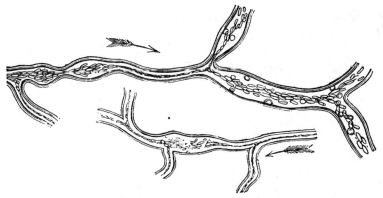

FIG. 697.—Irregular Contraction of Small Vessels in the Web of a Frog's Foot after the Application of Stimuli.

take such measures as will prevent them, for derangements once started will often, in spite of the best of treatment, greatly injure, if not destroy, the animal. It is certainly the owner's duty to guard his horse against unnecessary exposure, or merciless driving until in a profuse perspiration, and then leaving the animal in some cold, bleak place without even a blanket, or but a very poor apology for one, and that thrown on carelessly, while the owner is perhaps enjoying himself with his friends in some drinking saloon, toasting his shins, and the poor horse stands shivering at the door. The effect of such bad treatment will not then have time to develop itself, but will be seen in a few hours, or at farthest on the following day, by a *cold or cough*, running at the nose, or an attack of pneumonia, laminitis, or other cause of trouble.

The three principal points in preserving the health of a horse are feeding, air, and exercise. In the first place, irregularity of feeding, even of the best of food, will produce disease; but when with this is combined the giving of tainted or musty hay or grain, the difficulty is greatly aggravated.

Fig. 698.—Sweat Gland, Magnified 40 Diameters.

b, b, Canal; c, Gland; d, Opening on surface; e, Perforated epidermis.

Ventilation.—The stable should be neither too hot nor too cold. The horse will show the effect in a few days by coughing or having slight irritation of the mucous membrane of the throat.

A horse can take cold as easily by going out of the cold air into a hot stable, as he can by going from a hot stable into cold air, and *vice versa.* It is the sudden change of temperature which produces the change on the mucous coat of the larynx and of the throat.

The clothing of the horse in the stable should be neither too heavy nor too light. If kept too warm, he will be more likely to take cold when he goes out to exercise on a cold or chilly day.

To keep a horse doing well, constant attention is necessary to little things —watchfulness in driving; if the road is heavy, and the horse shows fatigue or is warming up excessively, hold him up and let out on smooth, descending pieces of road — a very little driving without regard to this prudence will often get a horse " off his feed," if not cause sickness; properly clothing and protecting a horse when warm after a drive; care not to give so much cold water as to chill; if there is chill or inclination to fever, or the horse is " off his feed " after a drive, giving a little fever medicine, with any other prompt measures to relieve the derangement at its commencement, may prevent a very severe attack of congestion or inflammation, if not save the life of the horse. It is in attention to these little things that the real key of the owner's success lies in the care of his horses.

The simplest and best methods of treatment for all the ordinary causes of sickness and lameness will be found on the following pages.

I would add in this connection that there are really but few diseases which are very dangerous or common to horses, and if the owner can be so aided as to successfully manage these difficulties, such knowledge must be invaluable to him. These difficulties comprise colic, inflammation of the lungs, founder, navicular-joint lameness, and shoeing. A horse may die in a few hours from a severe attack of colic, if not promptly treated; yet it is a difficulty easily managed, if one knows what to do, and it is done promptly. An attack of pneumonia is a very serious thing; but during its first stages it is easily controlled if taken in hand at once. A horse that is *foundered*, if not treated promptly, is practically ruined, as a change of structure quickly results; yet every case of acute founder

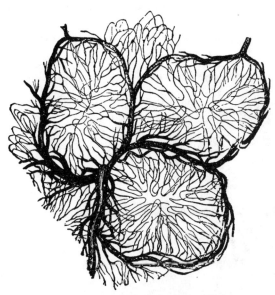

FIG. 699.—Horizontal Section Through the Middle Plane of Three Peyerian Glands, Showing the Distribution of the Blood-vessels in their Interior.

or laminitis is curable, and not only this, but the treatment is so simple that it is not at all difficult to comprehend or apply. In shoeing, a horse badly or improperly shod, no matter how good the feet, if the hoofs are thin, is liable to be soon practically ruined.

The treatment for these difficulties will be found to be particularly careful and thorough. There are, of course, many other difficulties

FIG. 700.—Section of the Liver of a Rabbit, with the Hepatic or Introlobular Veins Injected.

which it is important to know how to manage, for which the best practical treatment is given.   In fact, the medical department of this work will be found entitled to the fullest confidence, and must

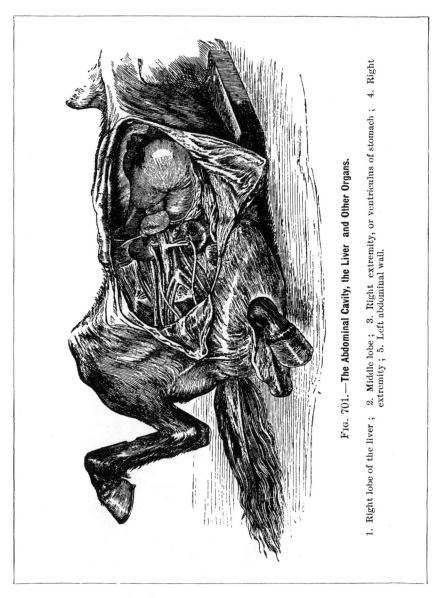

FIG. 701.—**The Abdominal Cavity, the Liver and Other Organs.**

1. Right lobe of the liver ;   2. Middle lobe ;   3. Right extremity, or ventriculus of stomach ;   4. Right extremity ; 5. Left abdominal wall.

be accepted as invaluable to horse owners.   The writer would, however, recommend that in all critical cases the safest course is to employ a competent veterinary surgeon, if available.

CHAPTER XXII.

DISEASES OF THE BONES.

THE skeleton of a horse is made up of 242 bones; and as these bones are the hard frame-work of the animal body, serving for the support and attachment of the softer textures and the protection of delicate organs, they are consequently liable to the same accidents and diseases as the other parts of the body. They are composed of animal and earthy matters, in the proportion of one third of the former to two thirds of the latter. They are covered externally by a sensitive and vascular membrane called the periosteum, and lined internally by a similar membrane called the endosteum. They enter into the formation of the joints, their ends being held together by the ligaments, and their adjoining surfaces being covered by cartilage or gristle, with a lubricating fluid between, called synovia, or joint-oil, to prevent friction and facilitate the motion of the joint.

Diseases of the bones are not very numerous in the lower animals; the most common are *Exostosis*, in which we have an enlargement or bony tumor thrown out on the surface of the bone; when between two bones, and uniting them together, it is called *Anchylosis Caries*, generally defined to be an ulceration or disintegration of the bony texture; *Necrosis*, which is the entire death of the whole or part of a bone; *Osteosarcoma*, which is a disease more particularly of the ox tribe, in which we have a tumor on the bone, partly bony and partly fleshy, occurring commonly on jaws or ribs; and *Enchondroma*, consisting of a cartilaginous or gristly tumor on a bone; it is more common in man, but is also seen in cattle, and occasionally in the horse.

ANCHYLOSIS OF BONE.

Anchylosis is simply extensive exostosis, in which we have the ends of two or more bones united by bony matter, as shown in ring-bone, spavin, splint, etc.

Symptoms are enlargements round the joint, which is stiff and inflexible, and in some cases the animal is lame.

Treatment.—If there is lameness, blister or fire, as may be thought necessary, so as to complete the union of parts. The motion of the joint cannot be restored by any treatment.

CARIES OF BONE.

Caries is generally defined to be ulceration or disintegration of

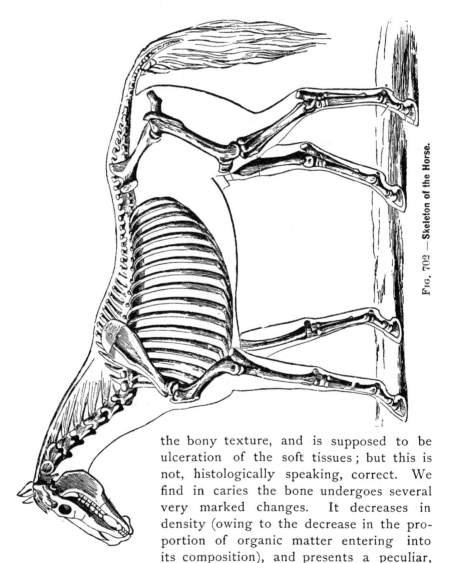

FIG. 702 — **Skeleton of the Horse.**

the bony texture, and is supposed to be ulceration of the soft tissues; but this is not, histologically speaking, correct. We find in caries the bone undergoes several very marked changes. It decreases in density (owing to the decrease in the proportion of organic matter entering into its composition), and presents a peculiar, worm-eaten appearance, which enables us always to recognize a carious bone in the dried state. (See specimens in chapters on "Navicular-Joint Lameness" and "Laminitis.")

Causes.—It may arise from whatever produces inflammation of the bone, or arrests or suspends its nourishment. It is a frequent sequel of fracture in the ribs, sometimes from neglect or mismanagement of poll-evil, or fistula of the withers ; in cattle, sometimes from "foul of the foot." Whatever destroys the periosteum may produce caries.

Fig. 703.—**Exostosis.**

1. Splint; 2. 3. Enlargements caused by injury.

Symptoms.—The surrounding tissues are swollen ; there is an opening into the diseased bone, from which acrid, bad-smelling matter discharges, in which float speculæ of disintegrated bone. On examining the bone, it presents a fungus, which readily bleeds when touched ; on pressing the finger into it, sharp processes of bone are felt, which are the bone breaking up. The bone is easily punctured with a probe or knife.

Treatment.—This, in most cases, is a very tedious affair. In the first place, the wound must be freely opened, and the parts touched with dilute hydrochloric acid several times a day. Mineral and vegetable tonics must be given. When practicable, as on the withers, the diseased portion should be cut off with a fine saw. Occurring in a joint, we must endeavor to produce anchylosis of the joint, the treatment of which has been explained as for spavins, etc.

Fig. 704.—**Splint, and Small Wind-gall.**

Fig. 705.—**A Splint after Cure.**

NECROSIS OF BONE.

Necrosis is generally defined to be the entire death or mortification of a bone. It differs from caries, in which the bone is discharged in particles, whereas in necrosis not unfrequently the whole bone dies, and becomes encased in a new bone of exactly the same shape, which is perforated by numerous holes, through which the old bone exfoliates.

Causes.—In man it not unfrequently arises from constitutional causes,—scrofula, etc. ; but in the lower animals it generally arises from local causes, mechanical injuries, extensive destruction of the surrounding soft parts, especially if it involves the artery supplying nourishment to the bone. In young thoroughbred horses, we are familiar with it from sore shins, which arises from the animal being put in training too young. The concussion sets up inflammation of the periosteum, which may be followed by caries, but more commonly necrosis of the cannon bone.

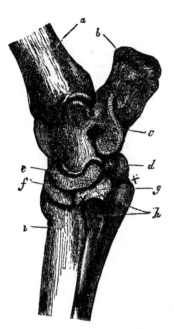

FIG. 706.—**Back Inside View of the Bones of the Hock.**

a, Tibia; b, Os calcis ; c, Astragalus; d, Cuboides; e, Navicular; f, Outer cuneiform; g, Middle cuneiform; h, Splint; i, Cannon, or shank.

Symptoms.—The external appearances do not differ very materially from caries. We have sinuses penetrating bone, from which there is a copious discharge of most offensive-smelling matter, in which are occasionally discharged pieces of dead bone which have escaped through the holes in the new bone. This is called the process of exfoliation. It is easily distinguished from caries by the surface of the bone not being worm-eaten, but smooth, and penetrated by numerous holes. Again, it is not soft, as in caries ; it cannot be punctured with the probe, and it is as heavy as in health, if not heavier.

Treatment.—It must be treated on the same principle as caries. The sinuses must be kept open, frequently washed out, and some stimulant injected, as hydrochloric acid (diluted), and tonics, and good food must be given from the first.

EXOSTOSIS, OR BONY ENLARGEMENT.

Exostosis is, in general, the consequence of periostitis, or inflammation of the vascular membrane covering the bone, though it doubtless also arises from other causes. It sometimes comes on without having attracted the least attention, or produced the least apparent disturbance to the animal, and may appear on any bone in the body, or on any part of a bone, sometimes so small as to escape observation altogether, and sometimes very large. It may be caused by external injury, or it may be the result of constitutional disturbance, more commonly the former. Its nature, causes, symptoms, and treatment will be better understood by taking the most common example of splint, spavin, and ring-bone.

SPLINT, OR SPLENT.

Splint is a hard, bony tumor occurring on the inside of the shank or cannon-bone of the fore leg, usually well up near the knee, which is well represented by Fig. 704. It is situated partly on the splint-bone (from which it takes its name), and partly on the cannon. Young horses are most subject to splints. The periosteum in them being more vascular than in old animals, it is more liable to inflammation, which is very readily induced in the unsolidified bones of the young horse when exposed to concussion or external violence. It occurs on the inside, because the center of gravity falls through that part ; when there is splint or enlargement on the outside, it is usually caused by an injury. Sometimes the opposite foot striking the part will cause so much inflammation as to produce considerable soreness and lameness, followed by thickening and enlargement of the part.

Symptoms.—At the start there may be no enlargement, nor anything to indicate the seat of trouble. The horse appears all right on a walk or on soft ground ; but if moving rapidly on a hard road, and especially down hill, considerable lameness will be shown. Running the fingers along the edge of the bone from the knee down, and pressing with the ends of the fingers, inflammation or enlargement will soon be discovered, both by heat and tenderness, and in time by enlargement.

FIG. 707.—**Bones of Leg and Foot.**

Treatment.—If the inflammation is up near the joint, it will usually be more serious, and cause more lameness ; but as a general thing, splints require but very little treatment, and in time will **get** well of themselves if let alone. During the acute stage, treat simply with cooling applications. Cold water turned for some time from a pump or by other means of letting a steady stream strike the part, which should be continued for at least fifteen minutes, and repeated two or three times a day, would be best. If this is not done, then tie several thicknesses of cloth around the part, and keep wet; but this will not be so good as the first method. The following is a favorite remedy for any local inflammation :—

F<small>IG</small>. 708.—**Union of All the Bones of the Hock without Enlargement.**

F<small>IG</small>. 709.—**The Same, with Excessive Bony Enlargement.**

Muriate of ammonia...... 2 dr.
Vinegar ....2 oz.
Water... ....2 oz.
Spirits of wine...........4 oz.
Mix.

The simplest and quickest way of relieving the lameness, and that which is now practiced very generally by veterinary surgeons, is to cut through the periosteum over the part. This is done by catching up the skin between the thumb and finger at the lower edge of the splint, and with a knife or other instrument making an incision in it; then pass up under it a probe-pointed bistoury, or a

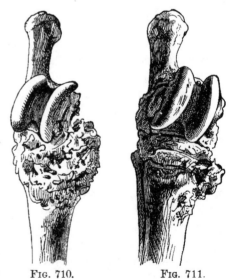

F<small>IG</small>. 710.

F<small>IG</small>. 711.

Showing a Bad Condition of Spavin.

common nicking-knife, to the top, and cut down to the bone. The part may now be treated as for simple inflammation; afterward, simply by cooling applications. The usual treatment is, after the acute stage has passed off, to clip the hair and blister once or twice.

Or, a more effectual way would be by firing, the best way of doing which is by the pyro-puncture process; but this is seldom necessary.

I give several excellent remedies for splints and ordinary enlargements, either of which may be used ; also a number under the head of Special Remedies, given near the close of this book, all of which are very good. The following is also used with much success :—

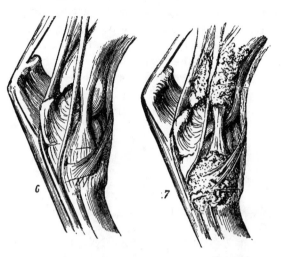

F<small>IG</small>. 712.—**Healthy Hock Dissected.**   F<small>IG</small>. 713.—**Diseased Hock Dissected.**

Oil of origanum........	1 oz.
Oil of turpentine.........	1 oz.
Alcohol............................	½ oz.

To be applied night and morning, for a few days at a time.

SPAVIN.

The causes of spavin are numerous — altered bearing, predisposition from conformation or malconformation of the limb, but proceeding mainly from hard work, sprains, or any cause which excites inflammation of this part. But the most common cause lies in the breeding of horses, as very often a colt is bred from a spavined sire or dam, or both, when the colt is sure to inherit the same defect.

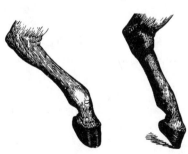

F<small>IG</small>. 714.—**Action when Natural.**   F<small>IG</small>. 715.—**Action of Badly Sprained Leg.**

Symptoms.—The first symptom usually shown in spavin is a stiff moving on the toe, which causes a peculiar quick catching up of the leg, especially in trotting. This varies according to the amount of inflammation and its location, from being scarcely noticeable at first, and passing off entirely after going a little ways, to severe lameness or stiffness of the hock, which greatly improves or disappears when warmed up during a sharp drive of a few miles, but appearing much worse after such a drive when the blood is again cooled. The hock is observed to be less freely used than the other. He is worse on the hard road. He limps considerably when he strikes his toe on a stone or the ground. If the leg be taken up and the joint forcibly extended or flexed, he will limp quite badly. Spavined horses generally lose condition, and from the pain caused by rising they frequently stand for a long time.

FIG. 716.—A Healthy Hock.   FIG. 717.—A Jack Spavin.

If it is the result of a strain, causing acute inflammation, the lameness will not pass off by exercise so readily as it will after it becomes chronic.

An enlargement usually makes its appearance from the fifth to the sixth week. Any prominence can be seen by standing in front of the horse about three or four feet from the shoulder, and looking back across the hock, or by standing behind the horse and looking forward across the hock.

The effort the horse makes to relieve the heels by walking upon the toe, indicates the necessity of removing the shoe, raising the heel-calks, hammering down or cutting off the toe-calks, and rounding the toe.

Care must be taken not to mistake a natural fullness, known as "rough hocks;" and it is always advisable to compare the one hock with the other. We frequently have inflammation or spavin uniting the small bones without the least outward enlargement. Fig. 708.

Quite often, before any enlargement appears, the trouble may be mistaken for hip lameness. But in this difficulty there is a peculiar dragging motion, and for want of muscular action the hip is sametimes fallen in or wasted, while in spavin the leg is lifted and brought forward easily, traveling mostly on the toe, and shows marked improvement by exercise.

Treatment.—If there is heat during the first few days, use cooling applications, such as an ounce of sugar of lead to half a pail of ice-water, about two weeks, when the inflammation may pass off. A dose of physic may also be given. Or a very simple way, and according to my judgment the best, is to throw a strong stream of cold water against the part for twelve or fifteen minutes, repeating two or three times a day as before explained. If past the first stage, and the case has become chronic, the only reasonable treatment is counter-irritation and rest, or keeping up sufficient local inflammation, without dissolving or blistering the skin, to arouse nature sufficiently to produce anchylosis, or a union of the bones involved.

There are two methods of treatment for this: First, if not very serious, by blistering; second, by what is termed "firing." This is done in two ways: First, by burning lines over the skin with a feather-edged iron

FIG. 718.—**Small Spavin.**

sufficiently close and deep to produce an extensive external inflammation, but without breaking or destroying the skin; second, by burning small holes into and around the diseased parts. On the following page are given a few of the best practical remedies.

FIG. 719.—**Very Large Spavin.**

Blistering is adapted for only simple cases, so that when serious, firing is the most reliable and effectual treatment. In case of either blistering or firing, the hair should first be clipped from two to three inches above and below the enlargement, and out to the middle of the hind and fore part of the leg. A favorite remedy used by one of the best practitioners in the country is prepared and applied as follows :—

Biniodide of mercury.................3 dr.
Iodide of potass ....1 dr.
Iodine in crystals, pulverized........1½ dr.
Blue ointment (mercurial) ....1 oz.
Lard................................1 oz.

Mix, and apply to the seat of the spavin three days. When the parts become sore, omit the treatment for the same length of time; then apply once in three days for two weeks, after which stop all treatment.

Or either of the following blisters may be used, which are among the very best : —

Finely powdered cantharides..................................1 oz.
Powdered euphorbium.....................................2 dr.
Lard... 1 oz.
Tar...2 oz.

Mix.   This is a very strong blister, and is regarded as very good.

Another favorite perscription is :—

Corrosive sublimate ....2 dr.
Lard..1 oz.
Tar...½ oz.
Cantharides.. ....2 dr.

The following will also be found efficient :—

Equal parts of biniodide of mercury and cantharides, and three parts each of tar and lard.

The blister should be thoroughly rubbed on with the hand about ten minutes.   Twenty-four hours afterward apply a little vaseline or oil, and repeat night and morning until the action subsides.   This will prevent the skin from cracking, as well as lessen the pain.   After which, wash with castile soap and warm water.   In no case should more than one leg be blistered at a time, especially if the horse is thin-skinned and sensitive, as it produces serious disturbance and fever.   A variety of prescriptions for blisters will be found under the head of the best remedies used, if it is desired to use blisters ; also the most famous secret quack cures will be found under that head ; but it is not advisable to use them.

FIRING.

For firing, put the horse in stocks.   If this is not convenient, the next best way is to bring a rope around the neck and fasten to the well leg ; or still better, buckle a soft strap around the fetlock, and from a ring attached to the strap, pass a rope around the neck of the horse and draw short enough to raise the foot from the ground. Next put on a twitch, with the stick part at least twenty inches long ; it should be so arranged as not to hurt the horse until the instant of touching with the iron, when the head should be thrown up a little with a slight jerking motion, to divert his attention from the pain of the firing.

I give two illustrations of the firing part of the iron, reduced in size about one third.   The larger the iron, the longer it will retain the heat.   The blade should be of steel (of the form given in the illustration), a little more than a quarter of an inch thick at the back, and gradually thinned down to the edge, which should be about one sixteenth of an inch in thickness, and nicely rounded.

The handle may be nothing more than a straight round bar of iron from sixteen to seventeen inches long and turned back at the end. It is necessary to have at least two irons, so that while one is being used, the other can be heating.

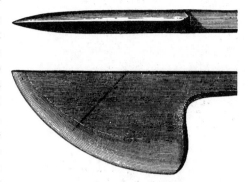

FIG. 720.—Feather-edged Firing-iron. Three-fourths Size.

FIG. 721.

It should be heated to a dull red color, and when taken from the fire the edge quickly run over a board or plank to make it smooth. When the edge is turned dark, draw perpendicular lines on the leg, as shown in Fig. 722, from top to bottom. They should be about two inches apart at the top, and not drawn deeply. Lay the edge where desired to start from, and draw steadily and gently to the bottom. Then commence at the top and make cross lines, obliquely, about half an inch apart. Start the point of the iron from the line at the right or left, and draw toward the center, as shown in Fig. 722.

The skin should not be penetrated or cut through, as it would leave a blemish. The cuticle is simply to be destroyed, and a dark-brown impression left upon the skin, from which there will exude a glutinous substance soon after the operation. If the iron is red or too hot, there will be great danger of burning through; though if the operator is dextrous he can use it quite safely by drawing it proportionately light and quick, but the work cannot be so well done as with an iron that is of a dull-red color, or quite dark at the edge. With such an iron, if the first line is not drawn quite deep enough it can be repeated until the right depth upon the cuticle is obtained, which will be indicated by its color. If the lines are drawn much nearer than half an inch, there will be danger of sloughing, while if too far apart there will be proportionately less inflammation produced. They should be of a certain depth and distance apart, and crossed as little as possible, to avoid breaking the skin. If this is done neatly, when the healing process takes place, the creases formed by the iron will be drawn together, the hair grown over, leaving no visible trace of the firing. After the operation, the horse should be put in a box-stall. On the following day a little grease, vaseline, or oil should be rubbed over the part, which will keep it soft and prevent cracking. This may be repeated at any time afterward, should it appear too dry. Should any of the cracks break and threaten to make a sore, dust on a little of the magic healing powder, which will stop it immediately, unless very severe. No bandaging or any such means should be re-

FIG. 722.—View of Lines as they Should be Made with Feather-edged Firing-iron.

FIG. 723.—Bad Method of Firing. The Lines Cover too Small a Surface.

sorted to. Simply see that the horse does not bite or rub the parts.

This method of firing is the one that has been most generally used. It is very painful to the horse, and requires considerable practice to do it well, although there is no particular sleight or secret in doing it beyond making the lines cover rather a large surface, and as near each other as can safely be done without causing so much inflammation as to extend across the division, and blemish by breaking or destroying the skin between. The next point is depth of the firing. This can be learned reliably only by practice. The deeper the firing, the more extensive the inflammation produced, though in no case should it be carried deep enough to break the skin, as this will surely cause a blemish, while in very slight firing there will be proportionately less inflammation, and to that degree less effective.

THE PYRO-PUNCTURING PROCESS.

The method of firing now found to be most effective for this difficulty, and that used most generally by the best practitioners, is the pyro-puncturing process. It is much easier done, more simple, not so liable to blemish, and far more effective. I give two forms of iron ; one representing about three sixteenths of an inch, the other about an eighth of an inch or less, in diameter. The rule is, the larger the iron the farther apart must the holes be made, and the smaller the iron the closer together. The principle is to make the punctures as near as can be done safely without producing so much inflammation as to cause the skin to break or slough between them. The average distance apart is from three fourths to one inch for the larger iron, and half an inch for the smaller iron, observing not to go near the vein.

Fig 724.—**Dots Showing Usual Number and Location of Punctures in Firing.**

If the horse is valuable, it is best to use the smaller iron, as there is less danger of blemishing. The part of the iron used should be suficiently long to enable puncturing as deep as desirable. I give illustrations of two such irons ; one representing the round part drawn out with considerable bulb behind to give sufficient body to retain heat ; the other a bulb of iron with a hole punched, into which is fitted a piece of steel or iron wire of suitable size. These fine-pointed irons for pyro-puncturing should be used only when at a white heat, and never when cooled to a red heat. The reason for this is that there is much less pain felt when the iron is at a white heat, as the sensibility is almost immediately destroyed. It is desirable to have three or four irons heating at once, so as to be sure of having one continually at white heat.

The method of using it is to barely touch the skin at first, to mark the points to be punctured, which should be extended out some little distance beyond the line of enlargement or immediate seat of trouble (as shown in Fig. 724). Then repeat, burning much deeper each time, until the holes are made to a depth of about three eighths of an inch, more or less, according to the severity of the case. Where there is much enlargement, penetrate to the bone proper over that part. When the firing is complete, rub on thoroughly a strong blister. The following simple Spanish-fly blister is good :—

Spanish flies...1 oz.
Liquid tar............... ....½ oz.
Lard...2 oz.

Mix, and rub on thoroughly from five to ten minutes, putting on a pretty thick application, and leaving on about forty-eight hours, when wash off with warm water and soap. When dry, rub on some grease or lard ; and let the animal rest three weeks.

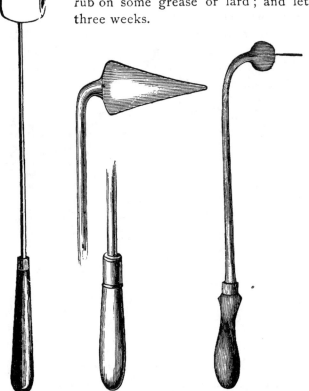

The principle is to keep the horse quiet long enough to give time for exudate to be thrown out and unite the parts involved, and this requires from three to five or eight weeks, and in some obstinate cases possibly even longer, depending upon age; the younger the horse, the more easily and quickly this will be done, while the older the horse, and the less constitution, the

FIG. 725.—Small Pyro-puncturing Iron. FIG. 726.—Large Pyro-puncturing Iron. FIG. 727.—Small Pyro-puncturing Iron. The Wire too Small.

slower and more difficult it will be to do. In any event, it must be continued or repeated, until the lameness disappears, after which work moderately for awhile.

If, after a couple of months or so, there is any perceptible lameness or soreness, an ordinary biniodide of mercury blister may be applied once or twice, as the case requires, or the firing may be repeated, as before stated. The point is to keep up sufficient counter-irritation to make the cure complete. It will also aid in removing any enlargement that may remain.

RING-BONE.

The treatment for ring-bone, splints, curbs, and spavins is practically the same. If there is inflammation, the result of recent strain, use cooling applications, and give the horse rest until it passes off, when counter-irritation by blistering or firing must be resorted to.

FIG. 728. — **Joint Anchylosed in Ring-bone, without Enlargement. The Roughened Appearance of the Bone the Result of Inflammation of the Periosteum.**

A ring-bone is a bony excrescence, or enlargement, about the pastern, most frequently occurring in the hind leg. Sometimes it does not cause much lameness, while again the lameness may be very severe, and perhaps incurable.

FIG. 729.—**Ring-bone. The Joint Anchylosed and Enlarged.**

This will depend much upon the location of the enlargement upon the joint. Should it be upon the center of the bone, it may not occasion any trouble; but if upon the margin of the joint, it is liable to cause much lameness. Fig. 729, taken from a photograph, is a front view of an enlarged anchylosed joint, or ring-bone; Fig. 730 is a view of another specimen cut through the center, showing the joint grown solid. I include an illustration of quite a bad ring-bone, and the same clipped, lined, and also dotted to show how the firing should be done by the pyro-puncturing process.

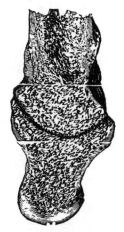

FIG. 730.—**Longitudinal Section of Joint after Anchylosis.**

At first there may be a somewhat tender and yielding enlargement, which, in the course of time, becomes a hard, bony formation. Second, the horse may make an effort to relieve the pressure from the heels or toe, according to the location of the inflammation. Should he raise the heels, then raise the heel-calks and round the toe. If on the other hand he seems to throw pressure upon the heels, then lower the heel and round the toe.   In the fore feet, at any rate, it will be necessary to round

Fig. 731.—Ring-bone as it Usually Appears.

Fig. 732.—As a Ring-bone Should be Fired by the First Method.

the toe sharply, which will greatly relieve the strain upon the joint by enabling the foot to roll easily, or turn upon the toe.   The best method of doing this is by the Roberge shoe, illustrations of which are given in "Shoeing," pages 282, 283.   Clip the parts, as shown in Fig. 722, then blister or fire, as explained for spavin.

Fig. 733.—Method of Firing by the Pyro-puncturing Process.

There should be no blistering or firing around the heel under the fetlock, as this would cause breaking or an irritation of the skin, which would be very annoying and difficult to heal.

SIDE-BONE, OR FALSE RING-BONE.

Side-bone, properly speaking, is not exostosis, but ossification of an already existing structure, it being ossification of the lateral cartilages of the os pedis, or bone of the foot.   It is most common in the fore feet, especially where the pasterns are short and straight.

Symptoms.—The lateral cartilages, which in health are soft and flexible, become enlarged, project above the hoof, and are hard and bony.   While the inflammatory process is going on, there is heat and pain in the part, and consequently lameness, which in most cases ceases when the ossification is completed ; but there is always a degree of stiffness observable, and the lameness is apt to return if the horse is much used on the road.

Causes.—Short, upright pasterns predispose to them ; they are most common in heavy draught horses, used for teaming on the road. Sometimes it arises from a tread from another horse, which causes inflammation of those structures, which is followed by ossification of the cartilage.

Treatment.—The same principles must be observed in all these cases. Rest is most essential ; continued cold applications, by making him stand up to the fetlocks in soft clay, with cold water frequently applied, would be the proper treatment until the acute stage has passed, after which repeated blistering, or, if thought necessary, firing would be advisable.

CURB.

This is a swelling upon the back part of the hock about five or six inches from the point (an illustration of which is given in Figs. 734, 736). If there is heat and tenderness, with more or less lameness, use cooling applications. The quickest way to reduce inflammation of this kind is to direct a stream of cold water against the part for ten or fifteen minutes, and repeat at intervals. It would relieve considerably to raise the heels of the shoe, and when the inflammation subsides, blister repeatedly. If this does not succeed, fire the part.

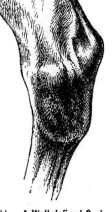

734.—**A Well-defined Curb.**

Curbs are not usually difficult to manage. I include a remedy which is very effective in removing chronic enlargements of this kind. It was first brought to my notice by being used upon one of my baggage-horses during one of my campaigns in Ohio. I purchased this horse cheap on account of his having a large curb, which, though it did not cause lameness, blemished the leg badly. I noticed my manager, Dr. Williams, occasionally rubbing on some medicine. It seemed to me like a waste of time to attempt doing anything for it, and so expressed myself. He said, "Wait, and I will show you the effect." He simply applied the remedy two or three times a week, and in two or three months, to my surprise, the enlargement had almost entirely disappeared. Since then several cases of morbid joint enlargement have been cured by applying this remedy occasionally for two or three months, one especially bad, caused by an injury down near the hoof. The following is the remedy :—

```
Oil origanum...........................................1 oz.
Oil of spike...........................................1 oz.
Oil of amber...........................................1 oz.
Spirits of turpentine..................................1 oz.
Camphor................................................1 oz.
```

Mix thoroughly, and rub on the enlargement two or three times a week.

The following is the treatment used by one of the most successful veterinary surgeons in this country :—

First, put on a high-heeled shoe, then take boiling water, and with a sponge have the curb well bathed for about ten minutes. Then apply the following liniment :—

```
Aqua ammonia..........................................1 oz.
Tinct. of iodine......................................2 oz.
Glycerine.............................................3 oz.
```

Apply to the part two or three times a day, until quite sore.

Then stop for a few days, when repeat the medicine as before, and so continue until again sore.

BOG SPAVINS AND THOR- OUGH-PINS.

This disease may be called wind-galls of the hock, caused, usually, by strain and overwork,

Fig. 735.—**An Ordinary Curb.**

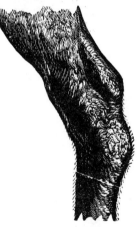

Fig. 736.—**A Very Bad Curb.**

but principally by lunging back upon the hind legs. When the swelling is inside and front of the hock, it is called a bog or blood spavin. This is caused by a distension or rupturing of the membranes which cover the synovial cavity of the joint. The swelling is soft, and yields to the pressure of the finger.

Thorough-pin is of the same character—an enlargement on the back, inside of the upper part of the joint, where in its natural condition is a hollow. This swelling extends across under the tendon, forming a tumor between the calcis and thigh bone. It is simply a rupture of the synovial membrane, allowing the synovia to escape. By pressing upon one side, the swelling is pushed through to the other side ; and sometimes there is connection with the swelling in front. These enlargements rarely cause lameness, though sometimes they may cause inflammation of the parts involved.

There is no satisfactory treatment for these difficulties. One of

FIG. 737.—**Bog or Blood Spavin.**

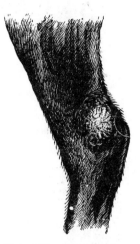

FIG. 738.—**Thorough-pin.**

the best remedies during the acute stage is to rub on soft soap and salt. Rub on the part thoroughly at night and wash off in the morning, for two or three times. This will sometimes work wonderfully well. Have used it repeatedly with the best success. This remedy will work well on acute cases, but its effect is not satisfactory upon old, confirmed cases ; for if the enlargement is brought down, sharp driving or straining of the parts will usually bring back the trouble. Blistering sharply is the treatment usually pursued. If this fails, firing is the last resort. There is no difficulty in bringing down an enlargement of an ordinary bog spavin by blistering, but as soon as the horse is put to work or strained in the least, it is liable to come back again.

I consider trusses and all that sort of thing of no special account in this difficulty. I have been told repeatedly of parties who punctured these enlargements to allow the secretions to run out, that in each case so much inflammation was excited in the joint as to cause the loss of the horse.

FIG. 739.—**Capped Hock.**

Blood spavin is supposed to be caused by a distension of the large vein which passes through the integuments involved in bog spavin. I do not know any distinction between them worthy of mention, especially as there is no treatment given other than that named.

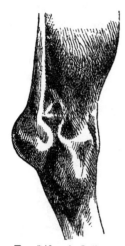

FIG. 740.—**An Ordinary Capped Hock.**

CAPPED HOCK.

This is an injury or bruise at the point of the hock, and is usually caused by striking the parts against some hard object. If the inflammation is acute, use cooling applications. When the inflammation has subsided, use any ordinary stimulant or blister recommended for the purpose.

WIND-GALLS.

Wind-gall was the name given to those soft, puffy swellings found at the back part of the fetlock joint, from a supposition that they contained air. They consist of enlargement of the little sacs, or bags, which are always found to contain a mucous fluid wherever tendons pass over joints, as at the back of the fetlock. This form may be termed *simple wind-gall*. In other cases, the distension is caused by an increased secretion, and bulging of the capsular ligament of the joint itself. This form may be distinguished as *complicated wind-gall*.

Few horses that have done any work are free from them, and unless dependent on some more serious lesion than simple distension of these *bursæ mucosæ*, they are of no consequence.

Causes.—Hard work is the well-known cause of wind-gall. In rapid motion or heavy draught

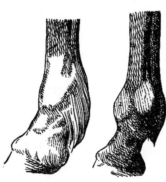

FIG. 741.—**Natural, Healthy Joint.**   FIG. 742.—**Showing Two Enlargements.**   FIG. 743.—**Clearly Marked Condition of Wind-gall.**

the friction of the tendons is greatly increased; consequently an increased secretion of synovia is required, and takes place in all synovial sacs during exercise; but if the action be not so violent as to strain the parts, it is speedily reabsorbed. On the other hand, if the exertion be inordinate, these little *bursæ mucosæ* become injured, inflammation is set up, and they become permanently enlarged.

Again, the exertion may be so violent as to cause sprain of the tendon, which extends to the capsule, or the joint itself may suffer, and cause distension of the capsular ligament, constituting complicated wind-gall, which is more serious.

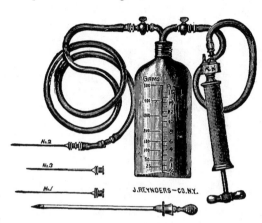

FIG. 744.—The Aspirator.*

Symptoms. — Simple wind-galls are little puffy swellings, seen at the sides of the tendons as they pass over the fetlock joint, most common on the hind leg. They are soft even when the weight is thrown on them. It is very important to be able to distinguish between simple and complicated, or between the harmless and what is not harmless. If situated between the tendon and the suspensory ligament, it depends on distension of the *bursæ* through which the tendon passes; if it feels hard when the other leg is held up, and is accompanied with a

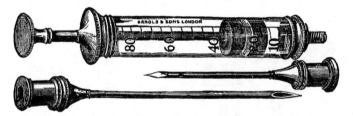

FIG. 745.—Hypodermic Syringe that Would Answer.

slight lameness, the tendon is implicated. When placed in front of the suspensory ligament, between it and the bone, it is accompanied with increase of synovia in the joint itself.

Wind-galls generally appear suddenly.

Treatment.—There are three methods of treatment: First, during the acute stage they can be easily removed by any firm but even pressure by pads and bandages, with cold water frequently applied.

---

* This cut was furnished by John Reynders & Co., Manufacturers of Surgical and Veterinary Instruments, etc., 303 Fourth Avenue, New York City, N. Y., of whom any veterinary instruments needed can be obtained.

Second, when it has been long neglected, or the case is complicated, counter-irritation or any good stimulating liniment or light blister may be used. The biniodide of mercury ointment may be well rubbed in several times, or a cantharides blister may be used.

Third, letting the synovial fluid out. This is done with an instrument called "the aspirator," which is a bottle attached to a small suction-pump, or more properly, a syringe attached to a bottle, and worked so as to draw out the fluid. The method of operating is as follows: Force the needle of the aspirator into the wind-gall, and draw off the fluid. When it is all drawn, inject a little of the following solution into the part:—

Tinct. iodine	½ oz.
Iodide of potassium	20 gr.
Water	3 oz.

Bandage well and keep the parts wet with cold water, the bandages to remain on from three to five days. This produces an adhesive inflammation of the part. This treatment can be used with safety in all cases where there is enlargement of the sheaths of the tendons. It cannot be safely used in what is called a blood spavin, because there is danger of puncturing the vein, and second, may extend into the true hock joint, which would induce so much inflammation as to produce a stiff joint or even suppuration of the coverings of the bone, which would finally destroy life. The hypodermic syringe, shown in Fig. 745, may be used.

FIG. 746.—**As the Horse Usually Rests his Toe upon the Ground.**

NAVICULAR-JOINT LAMENESS.

It is estimated that this is the cause of fully nine tenths of all serious and obscure cases of lameness in the fore feet. If neglected or not treated properly, in from three to six months such changes of structure, or degeneration, take place in the parts as to make cure impossible, when it is termed "groggy, or chronic lameness." In reference to the cause of this lameness, a very able author says:—

This is a strain that does more mischief than any other, and entirely from the circumstance of its producing scarcely any lameness in the walk. A horse, therefore, when strained in the coffin joint, and having no lameness, or scarcely any, in the walk, is usually put to work, or what is nearly as bad, is turned to grass without any regard to the situation, where he is often liable to be driven about. If, instead of this, it were treated like other strains, whose symptoms are more apparent, and which produce a greater degree of lameness, it would soon get well, and with greater certainty than a strain in the back sinews. But as it is a strain in the coffin joint, it is the most intractable kind of lameness we meet with, because it is nearly always neglected at its first occasion.

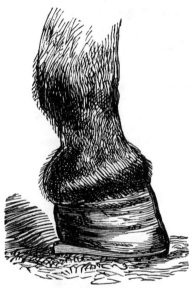

Symptoms.—It sometimes occurs in an instant, as by a horse stepping on a round stone, running in the field, etc., when he may at once be quite lame; at other times its progress is slow. Some peculiar formations of the foot are more subject to it than others. When the result of sudden strain, there will be considerable heat in the back part of the foot, with well-marked lameness. When it comes on gradually, a slight tenderness is observed, particularly at starting, which goes off with exercise. This gradually increases; the foot is found hot, and as a result of increased heat, contraction may set in, the hoof becoming dry and brittle. He steps on his toe, and when standing, points his foot, that is, places his foot in front, resting on the toe; and if both feet are involved, which is not uncommon, alternating the feet. Contraction is not an invariable symptom, as feet are subject to it that are entirely free from contraction.

Fig. 747.—Usual Appearance of Foot with Chronic Coffin-joint Lameness.

Often the foot is found to be round and apparently healthy, the most careful examination by the owner or smith not enabling them to locate any cause for the trouble. In ordinary cases the horse will show no apparent lameness while on a walk; but on a trot may flinch considerably, showing a great tendency to stumble.* Driving

* In some cases, usually fast trotters, the horse may at first only point, and gradually show a little soreness or stiffness at starting, or what is termed bobbing — dropping the head. Irritation in these cases is induced very slowly, as hereafter explained. The principle of treatment is the same,—prompt removal of the cause of irritation, developing healthy circulation in the parts, and aiding mobility.

28   a

down hill, or on a rough, cobbly road, will greatly aggravate the

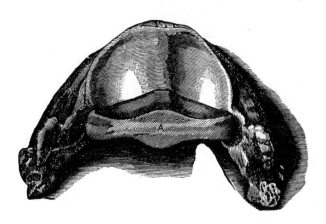

lameness, because going down hill increases the force of concussion; and a stony or uneven road so wrenches and strains the joint, or exposes the frog to such incidental pressure, as to greatly increase the pain and soreness. In some cases of

FIG. 748.—**Back View of Coffin-bone and Navicular-bone Attached in Place.**

acute strain, the lameness may be quite marked, the horse being scarcely able to walk, and when he does, keeping the foot flexed by walking upon the toe, and when standing, resting the toe upon the ground.   As this acute stage passes off, which will usually be in one or two weeks, the animal will seem to have grown much better, at times perhaps appear quite well, then grow suddenly worse again, depending upon the part of the joint involved and the road he is traveling on. He will go better on hard, smooth, sandy roads, but on soft, yielding ground, is liable to grow lamer, if the sole is thin and the frog prominent, because of the increased pressure upon the frog, and thence upon the parts involved, by the foot setting into the ground.   As the lameness continues, more or less change of structure takes place in the foot, a gradual drawing in of the quarters, the foot becoming perceptibly smaller than the opposite one, the heels higher, the frog smaller, and the sole more concave, the hoof showing a more glossy, hard appearance.   The shoe will invariably be worn round at the toe. A result that often follows is a shrinking

FIG. 749.—**Back View of the Bones of the Foot.**

or wasting of the muscles of the shoulder, called "sweeny," which is caused by a want of properly exercising them. The symptoms are about the same, so far as the lameness goes, whether the mischief has extended to ulceration or not, the history of the case only guiding in enabling to determine how far this has gone. Of course these conditions will vary in degree, as there may be only a slight extent of ulceration, or a high degree of simple inflammation. Yet, in the former case, the lameness will not be so marked as in the latter, notwithstanding the prospect for recovery will be much less.

We will now presume a horse, without any apparent cause, to show a little lameness, and we desire to make a careful examination. First, is there any possible cause from recent shoeing, such as a

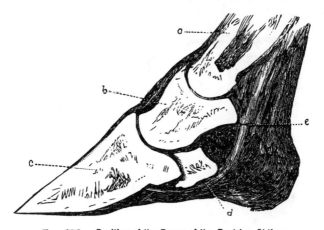

Fig. 750.—**Position of the Bones of the Foot too Oblique.**

a, Pastern bone; b, Coronary bone; c, Os pedis, or coffin-bone; d, Usual seat of the lameness; e, Perforans tendon.

badly fitted shoe, driving the nails too close, or pricking? Let the shoe be taken off carefully, by raising each clinch in succession, and pulling the nails out. Now tap and examine all parts of the foot carefully, and especially if there is any bruise or corn at the inner heel, or at any part of the sole, which will be noticeable by being red, and sensitive to light tappings of the hammer or to squeezing of the pinchers. It is always best to make the most thorough and careful examination, so as to give assurance of being able to point with more certainty to the difficulty under consideration. Pressure with the thumb over the middle of the flexor tendon, on its inner side or its outer, as deeply as can be reached in the hollow of the heel, the foot being bent back, causes pain; or catching the foot in one hand and the ankle in the other, and while twisting a little, pressing against the tendon, will cause considerable flinching. Tapping lightly upon the bar or sole, on each side of the frog, will cause flinching. Next, if the horse is taken by the head and turned short round, he will show increased lameness.

Upon an examination of these cases by the owner or horse-doctor, if no cause of trouble is discovered in the foot, the lameness

is supposed to be in the shoulder. Now, there is no lameness that reveals itself more plainly than shoulder lameness ; because when the muscles of the shoulder or arm are strained or injured, the mobility is so seriously impaired that the limb is lifted and brought forward with a sort of dragging motion. It is easy to see if a man were to injure his shoulder or arm, that with the greatest effort he would scarcely be able to lift it to put on his coat. But were the trouble in his hand, or below the elbow, he could do it without the least difficulty. The effect is the same upon the horse. By moving him back and forward, if the trouble is in the foot, or below the knee,

Fig. 751.—**Tendons and Ligaments of the Foot.**

the foot will be raised and carried forward naturally, but put down tenderly, as if trying to protect it from the force of concussion ; whereas, if in the shoulder, as explained, the mobility of the limb is greatly impaired, which is shown by the difficulty with which it is raised and brought forward.

I would call particular attention to these symptoms, from the fact that after an examination by persons who do not understand the nature of the difficulty, and finding no apparent trouble in the foot, the conclusion is arrived at that it must be in the shoulder, which is treated with liniments, blistering, etc., as explained, without doing any good, not only punishing the horse unnecessarily, but occasioning a loss of valuable time.

I would also remind, in this connection, that when the lameness continues in one foot for some time, on account of throwing the weight so much upon the opposite foot to relieve the lame one in standing or walking, there is liability to bring on the same trouble in the well one,—a not uncommon occurrence,—when the lameness will be equally marked in both fore feet. The horse will grow worse when the heel is lowered by putting on a thin shoe, or by losing the shoe, and will go better when the heel is raised, and especially so if the toe is rounded so as to aid mobility.

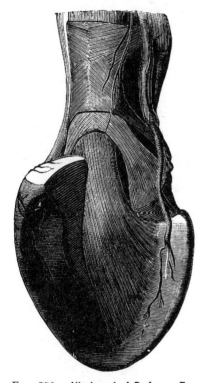

Causes.—The coffin joint is composed of three bones ; viz., the lower or pedal bone, and the navicular and pastern bones. (See Fig. 772.)

It will be seen that the navicular bone extends across the back edge of the coffin joint ; that the flexor tendon passes down under it, and inserts itself into the lower surface of the pedal bone. This supports the navicular bone when weight is thrown upon the limb, as the back part of the small pastern rests upon the navicular bone. Now, if from any cause irritation is set up in the synovial membrane of this small bone, or of the sheath of the tendon which supports it, or of the surrounding parts, whether by sprain, concussion, injury, contraction, improper shoeing, changing the obliquity of the foot, that is, raising or lowering the heel too much, allowing the toe to grow too long, or any cause of changing the proper adjustment of the foot, etc., the effect is practically the same in causing inflammation and lameness.

FIG. 752.—**Attachment of Perforans Tendon to Bottom of Pedal Bone. From Manikin of the Foot.**

The best authorities agree that the most common indirect causes of this lameness are raising the frog from the ground and contraction. An old author of high standing says :—

When the foot is in its natural condition, the frog is its strong point of support; and if this support is removed by paring, or by the use of thick-heeled shoes, which raise the frog from all possible contact with the ground, the support is weakened, and there is necessarily great strain thrown upon the tendon. This is caused by pushing the coronary against the navicular bone, which, being repeated at every step or jump the horse takes, strains the tendons, or causes inflammation. By contraction, because in proportion to the drawing together of the heels, there will be a compressing or forcing upward of the arches of the commissures and horny frog against the tendon and navicular joint, impeding the action of the joint generally, and liable to cause inflammation of the synovial membrane, ulceration, and change of structure ; it also destroys the natural position of the limb, by making the pastern joint more perpendicular, which, as has been mentioned, increases the jar of the coronary on the pedal bone. So that we have involved the lower surface of the navicular bone, its synovial membrane, the flexor tendon which plays over it, and sometimes the upper surface, when it is called coffin or navicular joint lameness.

Fig. 753.—Inferior Articulating Surface of the Navicular
Bone in a Healthy Condition.

Fig. 754.—Indications of Disease.

Fig. 755.—Inflammation Progressed so Far as to Cause
Caries of the Bone.

All leading authorities concur in the correctness of this statement.

Treatment.—The first and most important condition of cure is *rest;* the horse should be at once taken from all work ; he must not be, as is commonly the case, allowed to run even in pasture, or anywhere where there would be any freedom to run or walk around much ; give him simply the limits of a large, level stall. Remove the shoe by raising the clinches, and pull out the nails one by one ; then cut off or hammer down the toe-calk, and partly turn up the toe like the ground

surface of an old worn-out shoe. Next, raise the heel-calks from five eighths to three quarters of an inch, fit the shoe nicely to the foot, and nail on, being careful not to wrench or hammer it unnecessarily in doing so. Two important points are gained by this : First, raising the heels from the ground throws the articulation of the pastern bone well forward upon the pedal bone, relieving pressure of the navicular bone from the tendon supporting it ; second, the removal of all pressure of the frog from the ground, which aggravates the inflammation, and rounding the toe aids mobility, and thereby lessens the strain upon the joint.

If there is much
lameness and heat in
the foot, provide a tub
or box, in which put
water as hot as can be
borne with the hand,
and sufficient to come
up even with the
ankle, and let the
horse stand with the
foot in it for about an
hour, keeping the
temperature up to the
point stated. Now
take a bag or cloth,
into which put a suffi-
cient quantity of bran
to envelop the foot
thoroughly, and tie
loosely around the

Fig. 756.—Showing the **Effect of Long-continued Inflammation in the Foot. This is Caries of the Navicular Bone
and Pedal Bone Greatly Reduced in Size.**

foot or ankle ; pour on hot water moderately, and then let the horse
stand, allowing the poultice in the meantime to become cool. If

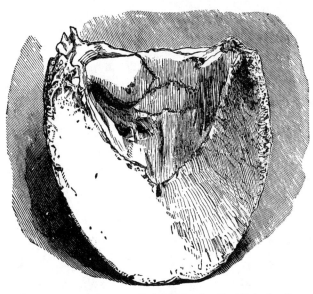

Fig. 757.—The **Navicular Bone Fractured. Foot Bone Greatly
Reduced in Size, Weakening the Fiber.**

there is much in-
flammation and
lameness, this
method of hot
fomentation may
be repeated two
or three times
during the day,
until all the in-
flammation sub-
sides. The usual
method of apply-
ing hot fomenta-
tions is to take
several thick-
nesses of blanket
or rugs, and after
wringing them
out of water as
hot as can be

borne, bring them around the foot loosely, and repeat at short intervals as they become cool ; or a lot of bran or mud can be put into a box, and hot water poured on until at the temperature desired, when the foot can be placed in it up to the ankle, as before explained. The general practice is to tie a poultice of bran around the foot, and keep wet with cold water until the inflammation subsides, which would be good treatment ; but if there is much inflammation and lameness, I would certainly advise, as far as practicable, hot fomentations continued for about an hour, then alternating with cold, and repeated two or three times each day ; but letting the poultice or cloths remain on until cool will be sufficient for reaction from the previous application of heat.

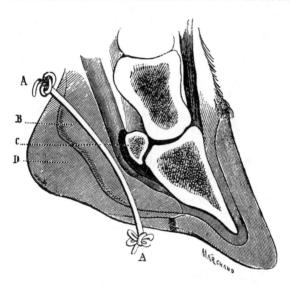

FIG. 758.—**As the Seton Should be Inserted into the Foot.**

A, A, the seton; B, the sensitive frog; C, navicular bone; D, insensitive frog.

If cold applications are used, it is important that there be sufficient bran or wet cloths tied around the foot and ankle to keep the parts thoroughly wet and cool, until inflammation subsides, in addition to which the bottom of the foot should be kept stuffed with flaxseed meal, or anything that will aid in keeping the foot moist and cool. If this is done, after about a week the attack will usually pass off. After the acute stage has passed off—and the wet cloths should be kept on until that time, even if there is no lameness—it is good practice to apply a sharp blister around the heel and coronet. It is in any event necessary, and may be even repeated once or twice, should there still remain any lameness. In the meantime, as before stated, the horse should be kept quiet, and if there is much lameness, there should be given in the first place a small dose of physic, with laxative, cooling food. This is all that is necessary to do in any ordinary case, and especially at an early stage.

It is next important not to expose the horse to conditions that would strain or injure the foot until fully over the effects of the injury. Consequently, the horse should at first be driven very moderately for two or three months, or more. If the road is rough, frozen, or stony, there is such danger of straining, wrenching, or bruising the foot, and thereby causing a relapse, that the horse should not be driven, if it can possibly be avoided.

If there is any contraction of either cr both quarters, there should be a special effort to overcome this also during the treatment. (See "Shoeing.") In opening the foot with the spreaders, great care should be taken not to produce any irritation. The

FIG. 759.—**The Navicular Bone Fractured.**

quarters should be opened gradually. When the lameness has entirely disappeared, bring the frog again slowly to the ground to the extent it will safely bear. If any soreness is indicated, raise the heel a little, keeping the foot moist to prevent contraction; and when the soreness passes off, again gradually lower it. It is always advisable to call in a veterinary surgeon if one is available. In extreme cases a frog seton is advised. This, of course, can be attempted only by the surgeon.

LAMINITIS, OR FOUNDER.

Laminitis, or Founder, may be described as simply congestion or inflammation in the feet. It may be severe or moderate, according to the degree of disturbance. If inflammation runs high and is allowed to continue, it is liable to produce so much disorganization as to induce loss of the hoof, which is, however, rare; or so much change of structure in the feet as to make the horse ultimately so stiff and sore or so much of a cripple as to become practically worthless excepting for slow, easy work. This loss of substance and change of structure is shown by a variety of illustrations.

There are two stages of this disease, acute and chronic. The first produces a high state of excitement and inflammation of the sensitive lamina, and more or less of the internal structure of the

FIG. 760.—Position of Horse when Suffering from a Severe Attack of Laminitis.

foot generally; the second, a morbid or insensitive feeling of the parts generally. The first or acute stage can be invariably cured, if treated properly, which is not at all difficult to do; the second, or

FIG. 761.—As the Horse Usually Lies Down when Suffering from Laminitis.

chronic, stage is not curable, but may be palliated to a limited extent.

Symptoms.—At first, if the result of exhaustion and chill, there will be the marked effects of great disturbance of the circulation, so that there may be a general stiffness and soreness, with high, quick pulse, etc., which will be soon followed by tenderness, congestion, and inflammation of the feet. To relieve the pain in the feet he endeavors to throw his weight upon the hind ones. He advances them in front, resting principally on the heels, when the hind ones are drawn well under him, something like the position shown in Fig. 760. On backing him, he backs with evident reluctance; when forced back, he drags one foot after the other, evincing considerable pain in doing so. When moved forward, he walks on the heels, his movements being slow and difficult. He will often be found lying down, as removing weight from the feet gives relief; and while down he will usually point with his nose toward the feet. Sometimes the inflammation may be in but one of the fore feet, or sometimes in the hind feet, which is not common; and in some isolated cases inflammation may be in all four feet; but is usually limited to the two fore feet.

Fig. 762.—Showing the Foot Broken and the Outer Margin Turned up. The Effect of Founder.

Causes.—Laminitis is very apt to occur from overtasking the feet by pounding them over a hard or rough, frozen road, or leaving the horse standing while heated and exhausted, and especially where a current of cold air strikes him; indirectly by prick or binding with nails, or continued injury from a badly applied shoe, or any cause of continued strain or injury to the feet; driving through a river while warm; washing the feet while warm and neglecting to dry them; frequently also from overloading the stomach by eating too freely of oats or other grains, as we

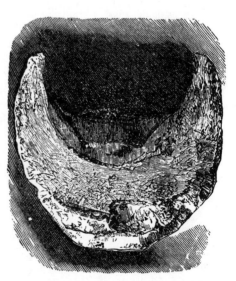

Fig. 763.—Showing the Bone Greatly Reduced in Size and Broken. The Effects of Severe Laminitis, or Founder.

often see when a horse gets loose during the night and gets to the oat-bin; or drinking too freely of cold water when heated and ex-

Fig. 764.—**Arteries of the Foot Injected.**

hausted. It may also be caused by inflammation passing from other parts of the body to the feet, but not often ; but by whatever cause, it is the same, namely, excess of blood in the feet.

Treatment.—It is evident that when such a large volume of blood as passes through the foot is obstructed, and active inflammation is set up, that there must not only be great local but general disturbance, and that it is not only necessary but of importance to relieve this as quickly as possible, if results would be prevented which would destroy the health and mobility of the foot. The inflammation is primarily limited to the sensitive lamina and sole, which, if allowed to go on, seriously involves the periosteum and bone, when it is called peditis, which is of a more serious character, and specially referred to farther on. I will first give the treatment pursued by Dr. Summerville,* a practitioner of great experience and success, with whom I studied. I include it mainly because I know of its effectiveness

from personal experience. If the case can be treated as soon as the disease begins to develop, bleed from the neck vein from four to eight quarts, according

1. Transverse section of the hoof.

2. Horny laminæ.

3. Vascular laminæ.

4. 5. Small cells between the podophyllous and the keraphyllous tissues.

6. Section of the tubes of the hoof.

As will be seen, this beautiful structure is entirely destroyed in the front part of the foot, as shown in Fig. 775.

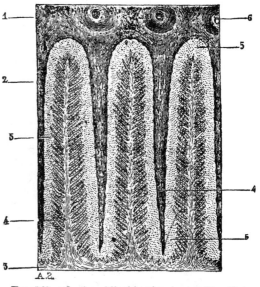

Fig. 765.—**Section of Hoof Laminæ Largely Magnified.**

* Dr. William Summerville, No. 127 Erie St., Buffalo, N. Y.

to the size and condition of the horse ; that is, if the horse is large and fat, and consequently full of blood, and the attack severe, then the larger quan-

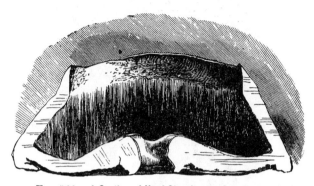

Fig. 766.—A Section of Hoof Showing the Sole Bent and Bulged Downward. The Effect of Founder.

tity mentioned may be taken. Afterward give a purgative ball, not enough to physic severely, but to open the bowels freely, which, as explained definitely under the head of "Physicing," for an average-sized horse should be from 4 to 7 drachms aloes, 1 drachm ginger, bar soap enough to make a mass, and made into a ball. After the fore shoes have been removed, poultice the feet thoroughly with bran and cold water, as follows : Fill two small bags, sufficiently large to hold three or four quarts, with bran, put a foot into each, and tie loosely around the top with a string. Keep wet either by pouring on water, or by putting each poulticed foot into a bucket of water. This manner of poulticing should be kept up for four or five days, when the shoes may be tacked on and the horse exercised a little. Cloths wet with cold water should be tied around the coronet, and the soles stuffed with flaxseed meal, or any other means of keeping the feet wet for a week or two can be used.

Fig. 767.—Front View of the Pedal Bone in a Healthy Condition.

The horse should have tepid water to drink, and warm bran mashes during the operation of the medicine. If the disease is stubborn, which is rarely the case, a second ball may be given after an

interval of four or five days. All the cases coming under my observation in the Infirmary during the year in which I was connected

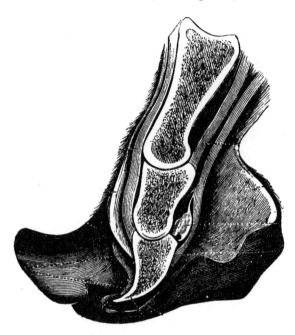

with it, and all
that have been
treated under my
supervision since
then, invariably
yielded to this
treatment. If the
case has run two or
three days with-
out treatment
or has not been
treated properly,
I would advise
opening both toes
by thinning out
their soles, and
the feet put into
moderately h o t
water so as to ex-
tract a quart or
more of b l o o d
from each. If this
cannot be done,
then open the

Fig. 768.—**Showing the Extreme Change of Structure and Injury
to the Foot.   The Effect of Laminitis.   The Pedal Bone
Displaced in an Extreme Degree. From the French.**

veins freely at the coronet.   If treated as directed, it is rarely that
the attack will not pass off in four or five days.

Dr. Charles Meyer advises the following mode of treatment,
which he has used with great success :—

If the animal is taken within the past twenty-four hours, have the shoes removed, and put the feet into a tub of hot water.   Wind flannel wrappings or bandages around both legs up to the elbows, and keep them constantly wet with hot
water for from two to three hours.   In the meantime have the horse well covered
with blankets, and give the following remedy:—

Fluid extract aconite....	30 drops.
Oil of sassafras.	1 oz.
Saltpeter....	2 oz.
Linseed-oil.	1 pt.

This is to be given at once.   There will be a profuse perspiration in from fifteen
to twenty minutes.   Keep the blankets on about six hours, then remove and put on
dry ones.   Keep wet swabs on the horse's feet, and stand him on wet clay.   All
stiffness and soreness in the feet will be removed in from thirty-six to seventy-two
hours.   In the meantime give one of the following powders :—

Bicarbonate of potash.............. ....3 oz.
Nitrate of potash....... ... .6 oz.

Make into six powders, and give two every eight hours until well.

Fɪɢ. 769.—Showing the Great Change of Structure Produced by Severe Inflammation.

Dr. William Shepherd, of Ottawa, Ill., in an address before the State Veterinary Association, advised treatment as follows :—

In the treatment of acute laminitis, as soon as possible after having discovered

Fɪɢ. 770.—Internal View of Fig. 769, Showing the Great Displacement of Pedal Bone. The Dotted Lines Show the Point to which the Foot Should be Trimmed.

that the animal has been foundered in the feet, or has acute laminitis, which is the same thing, have the shoes taken off, place the feet in a deep tub of warm water in which some hay has been put to form a soft foundation for the tender feet to rest on. Keep them there for about an hour, then take them out and put them in warm poultices, composed of equal parts of slippery-elm bark and linseed meal. Be sure the poultices envelop the whole hoof. Have a deep, soft bed placed under the animal

Fig. 771.—Showing the Direction of the Bone-cells as Thrown out from the Podophyllous Tissue.

Give a purgative, which should be one half of the ordinary dose, as superpurgation is apt to follow otherwise. If Barbadoes aloes be the agent employed, four drachms will be found sufficient. Give a dose of aconite, say ten drops, every twenty minutes, until the animal has been thrown into a profuse perspiration. Cover him with warm blankets. The poultices should be changed twice a day, and after taking them off put the feet in water, as above recommended. Continue this treatment for three days at least. Feed no grain, simply bran mashes, vegetables, and hay. When shoeing the animal, see that the shoes are wide-webbed, the hoof-surface being convex, still leaving sufficient flat surface for the wall of the hoof to rest comfortably on. If it is a valuable beast, have him turned out on lowland pasture in about two weeks after the commencement of the attack. Should he be stabled, keep damp swabs on while he is housed. This treatment is applicable to either acute or sub-acute, which I have here treated as one disease, and which, in fact, it is.

Fig. 772.—Position of the Bones of the Foot in a Healthy Condition.

Dr. Hamill Advises

if there is simply a congestion of the extremities and fever, to treat as a fever locally and generally. Give as sedatives aconite and niter internally, with cooling applications locally to the feet. If the inflammation is so extreme as to cause a destruction of the suspensory power of the laminæ, then it is advisable to bleed quickly. If purgatives are advisable, give calomel and aloes in the proportion of 1 to 2 drachms of calomel to 4 to 7 of aloes.

CHRONIC FOUNDER.

When the inflammation is very intense, and is allowed to continue very long, there is an exudation or lymph thrown out that separates the wall from the sensitive laminæ at the toe. In time there are immorphus horn cells grown from the sensitive laminæ, or phodofilous tissues of the coffin-bone, making a soft, spongy horn, which, pressing againt the wall in front, forces the anterior part of the bone downward against the sole, making it bulge downward, and in some cases perforating it, with a corresponding falling in of the wall above, producing what is termed a drop sole, which will be more or less marked according to the amount of disorganization. I give two very interesting specimens of extreme cases in Figs. 769 and 770. The first was obtained by me of Prof. Cressy, connected with the Massachusetts Agricultural College, now of

FIG. 773.—The Sole at the Toe Broken Through. The Effect of Severe Inflammation in the Foot, or Acute Laminitis.

FIG. 774.—The Substance of the Bone Greatly Reduced in Size. The Effect of Acute Laminitis.

Hartford, Conn.; the second from a specimen furnished by the Columbia Veterinary College, of New York City. They are drawn half size, and are exact reproductions of the originals. When there is inflammation in the feet, involving the bones, it is surprising to what degree the pedal bone is liable to become absorbed or changed in

29   a

form, and have its texture weakened.   Figs. 776 and 777, which were also obtained from Prof. Cressy, show the great amount of

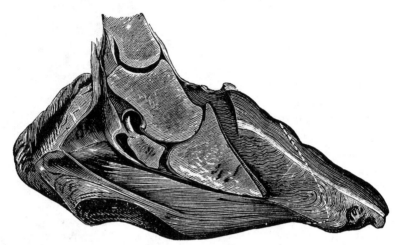

FIG. 775.—A Sectional View of Fig. 771.   An Exact Drawing of Specimen Showing Grain of New Growth of Soft, Spongy Horn.

change and absorption that may be produced from this cause. They represent the superior and inferior views of a bone that had been very much absorbed and turned up at the outer edge, cut in two, and united to sections of an ordinary healthy bone, to show the extreme change produced in its form. The part outside the dotted lines was so porous that it could be looked through as plainly as through the texture of coarse cloth, and its fiber was so weak that it would crumble between the fingers. Fig. 778, also obtained from Prof. Cressy, is another interesting specimen showing the upper view of another bone of the same character. Fig. 779 is a side view of this bone, taken on an exact scale, showing the remarkable bending up of the edges, and its thinness, it being not over

FIG. 776.—Posterior Sectional View of Pedal Bone, Showing Changed and Weakened Condition from the Effect of Inflammation.

three quarters of an inch at the pyramidal process, or front of the joint. Fig. 780 is a bottom view of the same kind of bone, and was obtained of the Columbia Veterinary College. Being engraved from a photograph, it did not work up so well. Instead of being flat, as it appears, the outer edges were bent upward over a quarter of an inch, with the edges ragged and broken.

I include also a specimen showing effect of inflammation by the pressure of the toe-calk and excessive rasping of the wall. These re-

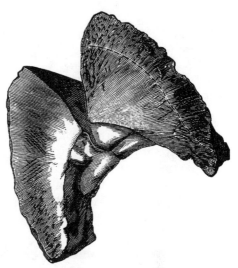

FIG. 777. —Inferior View of Bones Shown in Fig. 776.   Part to the Right Diseased.

markable changes of structure in the foot generally, especially in the pedal bone, when compared with that in a state of health, we see to be very great, and explain the destructive effect of inflam-

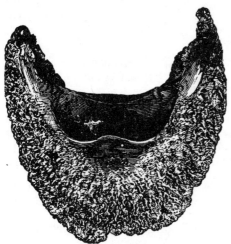

FIG. 778.—Showing Absorption and Change of Form in Pedal Bone,—the Effect of Inflammation.

mation when allowed to continue for any length of time. Reference can also be made to the many interesting specimens following the section on "Navicular-Joint Lameness" showing this. Many of these specimens will show not only the navicular, but the outer edge of the pedal, bone to be fractured.

In some extreme cases where inflammation runs high, and is allowed to continue very long, this separation of the wall from the internal structure may be continued so far as to cause ulceration of the coronet and loss of the entire hoof; but this is rare.

There is no cure for chronic founder. All that can be done is

Fig. 779.—**Side View of the Above, Showing Bending up of the Edges, etc.**

to palliate it to the best advantage. Some good practitioners, when they suspect any exudation at the toe, and a separation of the laminæ, open the toe, so as to give free vent to it. This I would regard good practice.

When there is some dropping of the sole, the best way to produce a healthy condition of circulation and cell-growth is to put on tips or very thin shoes that will allow pressure upon the sole. (See "Tips" in "Shoeing," pages 334 and 389.) Better still, in addition, would be allowing the horse to run on soft or gravelly ground. (See Treatment for Peditis.)

PEDITIS, OR INFLAMMATION OF THE OS PEDIS.

When there is severe inflammation of the feet (laminitis) the periosteum (membrane covering the bone) and the pedal bone sometimes become involved, when it is termed Peditis.

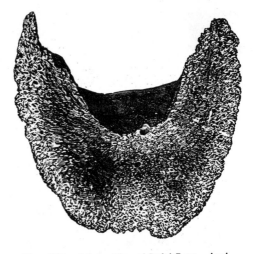

Fig. 780,—**Inferior View of Pedal Bone.   Last Referred to in Text.**

This is indicated by the horse showing intense pain, getting up and lying down often. No local treatment seems to check the structural changes that go on ; it will run from one to two months ; the horse has a ravenous appetite all the time, and as a rule does not lose flesh. If temperature rises, give sedative treatment,—opium, aconite with nitrate of potassa in small doses (not over 1 ounce a day, divided into two parts and given in water). When the temperature gets down to 102°, stop internal treatment, and treat locally about as follows : It is necessary to have a stall with a soft bottom, as saw-dust, ashes, etc. Occasionally it is best to dampen the ashes a little during the day, and rake them up so as to form a yielding body to the feet. Throw a little bedding over it at night, and also during the day, to give the horse a chance to lie down.

Treatment.—Apply cooling applications, such as cold swabs ; that is, cover the feet with two or three thicknesses of blanket, and keep wet with cold water. After the acute symptoms subside, blister. The point is to lower the fever, and check the flow of blood to the feet.

CHAPTER XXIII.

CATARRH.

REFERENCE is made under the heads of "Circulation" and "Diseases of the Air-Passages," especially on pages 406 and 483, to the importance of guarding the horse from such variation of temperature or serious disturbance of the circulation as would produce conjestion of those parts; and what is said on such pages should be studied in connection with this subject.

Catarrh, or "cold in the head," is an affection of the lining membrane of the nasal chambers and cavities of the head. It consists of a conjested or inflamed state of that membrane, giving rise to a glairy discharge from one or both nostrils, and when the head of the windpipe (larynx) is implicated, accompanied by a cough.

Causes may be classed under predisposing and exciting, as the majority of young horses under five years of age may be said to be predisposed to this affection. The exciting causes are sudden variations in the state of the temperature; undue exposure to cold when an animal is in a heated state, especially after a hard day's work or drive; standing in stables badly ventilated, or any place exposed to cold draughts. Perhaps the most common cause in young horses is placing them in warm stables in the fall of the year immediately on taking them off the pastures. A sudden change from a cold to a hot temperature is more likely to cause catarrh than a change from a hot to a cold one.

Symptoms.—If the horse is standing in the stable, he will appear dull, and incline to hang his head in the manger; the mouth is hot, and the pulse quickened and weak; the coat is staring, and the lining membrane of the nose is reddened and injected. If the larynx is involved, steady pressure on that region will cause coughing.

This is the congestive stage, which speedily passes off, and exudation takes place from the vessels, causing a discharge from the nostrils, at first watery, gradually becoming thicker, and of a yellowish color. In some instances this matter becomes pent up within

the sinuses of the head, and comes away in large quantities every three or four hours. A watery discharge from the eye is also very often an accompaniment of catarrh. If these symptoms become aggravated, the appetite is impaired, the bowels are costive, and the feces passed are of a clayey nature, the legs and ears are cold, and the breathing accelerated. Catarrh, if improperly treated, or the animal kept at work and exposed to sudden changes of temperature, is very apt to descend to the chest, and is a prolific source of other and more se-

Fig. 782.—**Suffering From Cold.**

rious diseases, as inflammation of the lungs (*pneumonia*), or of the covering of the lungs (*pleurisy*), or of the bronchial tubes (*bronchitis*).

In the majority of cases catarrh is but a simple affection indicated by a little increase of pulse, a slight discharge from the nose and eyes, the hair roughened, not much appetite, and some cough, which is sometimes severe, and if the patient gets anything like proper usage or treatment no very serious results generally follow.

Treatment.—At once place the animal in a comfortable, well-ventilated, loose box, as should be done in all affections of the chest ; blanket warmly, give aconite or some of the fever medicine ; if the case is serious, as stated, it may run into general inflammation of the air-passages, as bronchitis or laryngitis ; also hand-rub and bandage the legs ; the clothing and bandages must be removed twice a day, and the body well rubbed over. Give one or two drachms of aloes in solution, combined with one half drachm of powdered ginger. Steam the head by means of a nose-bag partly filled with scalded bran, into which put an ounce or two of turpentine. Hang the bag on the head same as in cut, being careful not to have it so tight around the nose

Fig. 783.—**Nose-bag.**

as to heat or scald it, and be oppressive. Many horses have been suffocated by having the bag brought too tightly over the nose. A few repetitions of this will cause the nose to run freely. Nurse by giving bran mashes, boiled oats, etc. Rest and care will usually do the rest. In mild cases it is not necessary to use the nose-bag. A few doses of tartar emetic and nitrate of potash may be given daily in a bran mash, and the throat rubbed with a stimulating liniment. If there is much inflammation of the throat and air-passages, any good liniment may be applied on the throat and around the chest, and bandaged as shown in the figure.

LARYNGITIS, OR "SORE THROAT,"

consists of inflammation of the mucous membrane of the head of the windpipe (larynx). It is generally called "sore throat," and is a very common affection among horses, occurring in a variety of forms, being sometimes of a very acute nature, and running its course with great rapidity; in other cases of a milder type, and assuming what may be called a sub-acute form.

Causes are similar to catarrh, as undue exposure to cold and variations in the temperature; but in some seasons it ap-

FIG. 784.—Simple Method of Covering the Throat.

pears as an epizootic disease, large numbers of horses becoming affected with it about the same time. These cases are always of a typhoid nature, more especially when occurring in stables insufficiently ventilated.

FIG. 785.—Method of Covering the Throat and Chest for Laryngitis. From Mayhew.

Symptoms of "sore throat" are well marked. The horse holds his head stiff, with his nose poked out, showing the muscles of the neck prominently; he has considerable difficulty in swallowing; if he attempts to drink, part of the water is returned through his nostrils; the throat is painful to the touch, and the least pressure excites a violent fit of coughing. At the commencement of the disease it is difficult to distinguish it from "distemper" (strangles). By the third or fourth day the difference can be easily seen ; the usual tumor of distemper does not appear. The pulse varies ; in some cases but little altered, in others very quick and weak. The coat is also staring, and the functions of the kidneys partly arrested. In severe cases the breathing becomes heavy and laborious. By the third or fourth day from the beginning of the attack, a greenish yellow matter is discharged from the nostrils.

Treatment.—The general and local treatment should be very much the same as for cold or catarrh, with the addition of a free use of counter-irritants to the throat, as mustard well rubbed in, or any good stimulating liniment, or even a light liquid blister. Aim to keep up the strength by feeding soft, easily digested food ; a bran

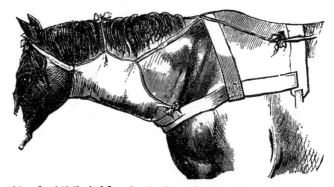

FIG. 786.—Good Method of Covering the Throat for Fomenting or Applying Stimulants for Laryngitis.

mash with a little boiled oats in it, carrots, etc. ; any food that he can eat easily.

When the bowels are constipated, as is often the case, clysters of soap and water must be freely used. When the cough is severe and hacking, the following ball may be given once or twice a day :—

Camphor...1 dr.
Powdered opium...1 dr.
Ext. belladonna...2 scr.

If the horse is threatened with suffocation, the windpipe should be opened, and a tube inserted. (See description of operation under head of " Tracheotomy.")

One of the leading practitioners of the country dictated to the writer the following as his best treatment :—

Counter-irritation of the larynx. The best internal remedy would be :—

Ext. belladonna...2 dr.
Chlorate of patash ....1 oz.

with a sufficient quantity of honey to be made into the form of an electuary, and appiled with a spoon to the back of the tongue. Also use one-half ounce doses of chlorate of potash put into a pail of water, and allowed to remain in front of the animal.

STRANGLES, OR HORSE DISTEMPER.

This is another form of sore throat occurring mostly in young horses from two to five years old, and which is familiar to every one. Its design seems to be to throw some poisonous matter from the system, and the object should be to keep the strength of the animal up, and hasten suppuration.

Fɪɢ. 787.—**Horse with Strangles.**

The exciting causes are similar to catarrh, transition from cold to heat, as from the pasture to the stable, change of stable from the country to the city. It occurs most commonly in spring, and is usually seen in cold, damp weather.

The general symptoms are very much the same as explained in the previous difficulties. The distinguishing points are, the horse is out of sorts ; the neck becomes sore and stiff ; an enlargement appears between the branches of the jaw, which is hot and tender ; there is some discharge from the nose. In ordinary cases the tumor goes on to suppuration ; a copious discharge of thick yellow matter takes place from the nostrils ; in about a week the tumor has matured, become soft, and points, and either bursts or should be opened ; continues to discharge for some time, and gradual recovery takes place. But if the case is very severe it will grow worse, often threatening to cause suffocation. The horse is able to eat or drink but little, and strength is lost rapidly.

Fɪɢ. 788.—**Simple Method of Covering the Tumor when Stimulated.**

Treatment.—Provide a comfortable, well-ventilated stall ; clothe warmly ; rub and bandage the legs ; nurse by giving bran mashes, boiled oats, carrots, etc. Bowels should be opened by injections.

Use freely a poultice made of wheat bran and warm vinegar, changing as often as the poultice becomes dry, using the eight-tailed

FIG. 789.—The Eight-tailed Bandage.

bandage until the enlargement becomes soft and can be opened, when relief will be prompt. Or the following treatment may be adopted, which is very good, and in some cases may be preferable : Take spirits of turpentine, two parts ; spirits of camphor, one part ;

FIG. 790.—The Eight-tailed Bandage as Adjusted.

laudanum, one part. Put this on the neck with a brush, if convenient, or in any way to apply it without exciting pain, three or four times a day until soreness is caused. After each application, have ready three or four pieces of flannel,

which should be a good thick article ; put these over the parts, and bind on with the eight-tailed bandage. Or hot fomentations and

poultices can be freely applied to the tumor, so as to encourage the formation of matter. When the tumor points, open it by cutting through the skin, and if necessary enlarge the orifice by pushing in the finger, also small doses of saltpeter should be given in the feed, or the following powders night and morning :—

FIG. 791.—Opening the Abscess in Strangles.

Niter..	1½ oz.
Tartar emetic.....................................	6 dr.

Mix and make into six powders.

Sometimes the inflammation is so deep as to cause serious soreness and swelling of the throat. In this case the horse must be nursed carefully by feeding warm gruel; the drink should be warm; grass or anything that will tempt the appetite should be given.

GLANDERS AND FARCY.

I consider these difficulties mainly to enable the detection of them to prevent their spreading, as they are extremely contagious to both men and horses. They are incurable, and to guard against the possibility of danger when a case is suspected, the only safe way is at once either to isolate or to destroy the animal.

I depend mainly for my explanation of these diseases upon several old authors.* They fully agree with the statements of modern authors that it is practically useless to tamper with glanders. Farcy in its early stage can be controlled without difficulty, but the medicine injures the constitution seriously, and in addition, it is rarely that the disease will not soon break out again or develop glanders.

FIG. 792.—**An Ordinary Case of Farcy.**

Symptoms.—The distinctive appearances which glanders present may be slow in their development, and may continue for years, during which he may feed and work well, constituting *chronic glanders;* or they may run on rapidly, and in two or three weeks are well marked and soon come to a fatal termination, when it is called *acute glanders.*

The coat is rough and staring; he is usually hide-bound; the belly drawn up, and constitutional disturbance exists, the pulse being easily excited; the membrane lining the nostrils is of a leaden hue; the glands inside the lower jaw where the pulse is felt become enlarged, hard, and nodular like a mass of peas or beans, especially on the side from which the discharge takes place—usually the left, sometimes the right, or even from both; the discharge is clear and watery at first, becoming thicker and sticky, accumulating around the nostril; cough may be present, but it is not an invariable symptom. As it advances, the discharge increases, becomes purulent, of a greenish color,

FIG. 793.—**A Farcy Bud.**

sometimes mixed with streaks of blood; it is of a heavy specific gravity, and if dropped into water, sinks to the bottom; it has a very offensive smell; the gland on the affected side becomes hard and adherent to the side of the jaw; ulcerating tubercles form on the nostrils, which have a mouse-eaten appearance, being raised and irregular at the edges, and depressed in the center; they run into patches, and spread

---

* Turner, Youatt, M. Volpi, White, and others.

over the whole nasal septum ; weakness and emaciation set in. The ulceration in some cases extends to the cartilages, and even the bones are sometimes implicated, when occasional bleedings ensue. Cough is troublesome ; farcy buds appear in some cases over the body, and he dies a disgusting and loathsome spectacle.

Farcy.—Farcy and glanders are essentially the same disease, and depending on the same specific poison in the blood, but manifesting itself in a different locality. It often occurs in connection with glanders, but is also seen independent of it, running into glanders as it progresses.

Symptoms.—It usually affects the superficial absorbents of the hind limbs in the

groin, extending downward on the inside of the thigh, following the line of the lymphatics, also along the absorbents of the neck and shoulders ; little tubercles, or farcy buds, form, which in some cases become indurated and lie dormant for a time, but in most cases they go on to ulceration, producing angry, irregular ulcers similar to the ulceration in glanders ; the virus being conveyed along the absorbents, the buds extend in knots ; lines of corded and inflamed absorbents are felt extending from below upward, the hair being rough and bristling along their course ; by and by swelling of the legs sets in ; as it goes on he becomes emaciated ; the ulceration attacks the nostrils, and glanders and farcy are combined, and

Fig. 794.—**A Piece of Farcied Skin. From Mayhew.**

death relieves him at last.*   A disease called watery farcy must not be mistaken for genuine farcy.

As there is liable to be considerable difficulty experienced in diagnosing glanders from common running of the nose from cold, strangles, or nasal gleet, I include the best description I can find of the symptoms as they progress :—

The earliest symptom is an increased discharge from the nostril, small in quantity, constantly flowing, of a watery character and a little mucus mingling with it. Connected with this is an error, too general, and highly mischievous, with regard to the character of this discharge in its earliest stage of this disease, *when the mischief from contagion is most frequently produced.* The discharge of glanders is not sticky when it may be first recognized. It is an aqueous or mucous, but small and constant, discharge, and is thus distinguished from catarrh or nasal gleet or any other defluxion from the nostril. It should be impressed on the mind of every horseman that this small and constant defluxion, overlooked by the groom and by the owner, and too often by the veterinary surgeon, is a most suspicious circumstance.

Dr. James Turner, an old English veterinary surgeon before referred to, deserves much credit for having first or chiefly directed the attention of horsemen to this important but disregarded symptom. If a horse is in the highest condition, yet has this small aqueous constant discharge, and especially from one nostril, no time should be lost in separating him from his companions.†

---

* Fig. 794 is a very good illustration of a bad case of farcy photographed from life.

† Mr. Turner, during his experiments, referred to a fine mare that had simply a slight running of mucus from one of the nostrils, which he pronounced glanders, and highly contageous.

This discharge, in cases of infection, may continue, and in so slight a degree as to be scarcely perceptible, for many months, or even two or three years, unattended by any other disease, even ulceration of the nostril, and yet the horse being decidedly glandered from the beginning, and capable of propagating the malady. In process of time, however, pus mingles with the discharge, and then another and a characteristic symptom appears. Some of this is absorbed, and the neighboring glands become affected. If there is discharge from both nostrils, the glands within the under jaw will be on both sides enlarged. If the discharge is from one nostril only, the swelled gland will be on that side alone. Glanders, however, will frequently exist at an early stage without these swelled glands, and some other diseases,

Fig. 795.—A Bad Case of Farcy. Photographed From Life by Prof. Cressy.

as catarrh, will produce them. Then we must look out for some peculiarity about these glands, and we shall readily find it. The swelling may be at first somewhat large and diffused, but the surrounding enlargement soon goes off, and one or two small distinct glands remain ; and they are not in the center of the channel, *but adhere closely to the jaw on the affected side.*

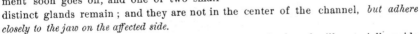

The membrane of the nose should now be examined, and will materially guide our opinion. It will either be of a dark purplish hue, or almost of a leaden color, or of any shade between the two ; or if there is some of the redness of inflammation, it will have a purple tinge ; but there will never be the faint pink blush of health, or the intense and vivid red of usual inflammation. Spots of ulceration will

Regardless of his advice, the mare was sold. Months afterward he found a number of horses in a stable suffering from glanders, all having undoubtedly taken the disease from this mare, she having been worked and stabled with them. A large number of cases are referred to by others, caused by being put into the stalls that had been occupied by horses showing the above symptoms ; in one case one horse was the means of inoculating a whole troop of army horses, making it necessary to destroy them all. So it is best to be on the safe side, by taking the greatest possible precaution when a case is suspected.

probably appear on the membrane covering the cartilage of the nose,—not merely sore places, or streaks of abrasion, and quite superficial, but small ulcers, usually approaching to a circular form, deep, and with the edges abrupt and prominent. When these appearances are observed, there can be no doubt about the matter.

When ulcers begin to appear on the membrane of the nose, the constitution of the horse is soon evidently affected. The patient loses flesh ; his belly is tucked up ; his coat unthrifty, and readily comes off ; the appetite is impaired ; the strength fails ; cough, more or less urgent, may be heard ; the discharge from the nose will increase in quantity, it will be discolored, bloody, offensive to the smell ; the ulcers in the nose will become larger and more numerous, and the air-passages being obstructed, a grating, choking noise will be heard at every act of breathing. There is now a peculiar tenderness about the forehead. The membrane lining the frontal sinuses is inflamed and ulcerated, and the integument of the forehead becomes thickened and somewhat swelled. Farcy is now superadded to glanders, or glanders has degenerated into farcy, and more of the absorbents are involved.

At or before this time little tumors appear about the muscles and face and neck, following the course of the veins and the absorbents, for they run side by side ; and these the tumors soon ulcerate. Tumors or buds, still pursuing the path of the absorbents, soon appear on the inside of the thighs. They are connected together by a corded substance. This is the inflamed and enlarged lymphatic ; and ulceration quickly follows the appearance of these buds. The deeper-seated absorbents are next affected ; and one or both of the hind legs swell to a great size, and become stiff, and hot, and tender. The loss of flesh and strength is more marked every day. The membrane of the nose becomes of a dirty, livid color ; the membrane of the mouth is strangely pallid. The eye is infiltrated with a yellow fluid ; and the discharge from the nose becomes more profuse, and insufferably offensive. The animal presents one mass of putrefaction, and at last dies exhausted.

As stated before, chronic catarrh is a discharge from the nose, affecting only the lining membrane of the nose ; and there may be also enlargement of the glands, staring coat, and debility, so that it is sometimes difficult to distinguish one from the other during the early stage of glanders. Then, again ulcerated teeth may produce the same symptoms of discharge from the nose of a very offensive character, which may be taken for glanders. So that, when there are the characteristic symptoms of glanders, it is very important to look closely to the condition of the teeth — is there any enlargement or ulcerous secretion in their neighborhood, which may extend into the nasal cavity ? When the horse is valuable, and there is any doubt about the case, the best way is to inoculate some worthless horse with some of the virus ; if glanders, it will show itself very quickly.

The usual method of doing this is to first cut off the hair from the side of the neck or other part of the body about the size of a half dollar ; then take a lancet and pass it under the cuticle, or scarf-skin, only deep enough to bring a few drops of blood. The matter is to be introduced into this opening with a thin slip of wood of the form of the lancet. If the matter is glanderous, the part will become sore in two or three days, and a scab will form on it, which, in a few days will be thrown off, leaving a peculiar kind of ulcer, which will often spread rapidly, causing a painful swelling of the adjacent parts, with corded lymphatics and farcy buds. In about a fortnight the glanders will appear.

Prof. Robert Jennings, of Detroit, an old veterinarian of much experience, speaks in the *Veterinary Journal of Comparative Medicine* of a number of cases supposed to be glanders, which proved to be caused by ulceration of the teeth, which he cured without difficulty. Could refer to a number of cases of this character if necessary. The test of inoculation would of course be conclusive.

Treatment.—The following are favorite prescriptions for farcy :—

Arsenic..5 gr.
Ext. nux vom...1 dr.

For a drench in a pint of water twice a day.—*Prof. Williams.*

Sulphate of copper......................................1 dr.
Iodine...1 dr.

This amount in a pint of water twice daily.—*Prof. Williams.*

Sulphate of copper......................................½ dr.
Sulphate of zinc..½ dr.
Anise-seed..3 dr.

Make into a ball with common mass, and give once a day.—*Prof. Gamgee.*

Sulphate of copper......................................1 dr.
Calomel...1 scr.
Common turpentine.............................3 dr. to ½ oz.

Licorice powder, enough to form the ball.—*Prof. Coleman.*

Three drachms of sulphate of copper given every night in the food until the animal refuses to eat. After a few days repeat ; but if the case is bad, give the medicine in water as a drench, if he will not take it in his food.—*An Old Practitioner.*

The following, which was obtained by the writer years ago in Ohio, was regarded as very valuable for the cure of farcy. It was claimed to be a great secret, and was repeatedly sold for fifty dollars as a specific for farcy :—

Sulphur...¼ lb.
Saltpeter...½ lb.
Black antimony..1 oz.

If acute, give one tablespoonful twice a day. If sub-acute, once or twice a week.

Two parties who have used the above assured the writer that they had cured farcy with it, and regarded it as a very valuable prescription.

The ulcers are to be opened and dressed with disinfectants, and treated as for an ordinary ulcer, great care being taken not to get any on the person, as, should there be the least abrasion of the skin, it would inoculate the system.

It is proper in this connection to state that glanders may be developed in consequence of being kept in low, damp, badly ventilated stables, when debilitated by hard work and insufficient nourishment ; also as a sequel of weakening complaints, such as neglected or improperly treated strangles, influenza, etc.

When glanders is known to have existed in a stable, or is seriously suspected, it is advisable to thoroughly cleanse the manger, etc., so as to prevent the possibility of contagion. The most careful experiments have proved that glanders can only be communicated by the virus ; and though it may be dried and lay for even a year, it has still sufficient vitality to impregnate with the disease. It has been supposed that the only way to get rid of it would be to tear down the stable and build it anew — an old veterinarian of much experience so stated to the author as his opinion.

But the following precautions are now regarded to be entirely sufficient : The manger, rack, or whatever there has been within the reach of the horse, upon which matter could be thrown or could touch,— and this will include partitions and every part or object in the vicinity,—should be scraped, and scoured with soap and water, and then thoroughly washed with a solution of chloride of lime, about a pint of the chloride to a pailful of water ; the walls should be whitewashed ; the pails newly painted, and the iron work exposed to a red heat ; the halters, clothing, etc., used upon the case should be burned. The only means of preventing the disease is to keep the stable cool and well ventilated. Hot, close, and badly ventilated stables, it is claimed by all authors, are strong causes of the disease.

There are many jockeys who make it a business to trade for horses of this character, fix them up by cleansing the nostrils, etc., and trade them off. As before stated, during the early stage it can only be detected by slight running from the nose. Such villainous practice cannot be too severely condemned as a crime, which should be promptly punished to the extent of the law.

Chronic Cough

is often a sequel of sore throat (laryngitis), as also of distemper (strangles), and is a disease from which, when once fairly established, complete recovery seldom occurs. It consists of a chronic inflammation of the many glands imbedded within the lining membrane of the larynx, causing an irritation of that highly sensitive organ. The cough is easily excited by pressure externally, and is of a deep, hollow nature, differing materially from the loud sonorous sound of a healthy cough.

It is often associated with other diseases of the chest, as broken wind, thick wind, etc. The cough is generally most severe in the morning or after meals, and is always aggravated by gross feeding. In many cases chronic cough interferes but little with a horse's usefulness, especially if he is used for ordinary farm work ; but it must be considered an unsoundness.

Treatment.—If the horse has been affected for some time, treatment is generally very unsatisfactory, and must be more of a palliative than a remedial nature. If only recently, treatment may be undertaken with better chances of success. Give the cough ball as recommended for laryngitis, and apply the following liquid blister, or any good counter-irritant, externally, and in some cases great benefit will attend the use of setons.

> Olive-oil, oil of turpentine, aqua ammonia, equal parts.

To be shaken well, and rubbed on with the hand.

If occurring from intestinal disorder, the treatment of course must be directed to the proper seat. The medicinal treatment is greatly assisted by feeding the animal properly and regularly, giving small quantities of food at a time ; carrots in winter, and green food in summer should be given. Feeding nice clean corn-stalks is much better than hay ; if hay is fed, it should be bright and clean, or the dust shaken out of it, and dampened a little, and of this only a limited quantity should be given. If a greedy eater, either remove from his reach the bedding, which he will be likely to eat, or put on a muzzle. The following are also excellent cough remedies:—

> Camphor..1 dr.
> Powdered opium..1 dr.
> Powdered digitalis..1 dr.
> Calomel..1 dr.

Make into a ball and give every second morning until six doses are given.

> Tar-water..½ pt.
> Lime-water...½ pt.
> Powdered squills...1 dr.

This drink every morning in obstinate coughs. As a sedative to allay the violence of the cough,—

> Niter..4 dr.
> Powdered opium...2 dr.
> Prussic acid (dilute)......................................1 dr.

Mix in a pint of mucilage or linseed tea, and give half a tumblerful three times a day.

An old writer says : " I have known an obstinate cough cured by drenches composed of a syrup made of molasses and vinegar ; also by a decoction of garlic with linseed-oil. Barbadoes tar and oil with balsam of sulphur, have also been employed as remedies for a cough."

The following is also an excellent remedy :—

Gum ammoniac...2 to 3 dr.
Powdered squills.........   ....1 dr.
Camphor...1 dr.
Ginger..1 dr.
Castile soap..2 dr.
Oil of anise-seed...20 drops.

Syrup and flour enough to form a ball.

A favorite prescription for curing cough : Put into alcohol all the

Fig. 796.—**The Act of Coughing.**

tar it will cut ; add one third in quantity of tincture of belladonna. Dose, from one to two teaspoonfuls once or twice a day.

A simple remedy which will sometimes work very nicely is :—

Fluid extract belladonna 10 to 15 drops in a tablespoonful of water on the tongue three or four times a day. If there is swelling of the glands of the neck, rub on a sharp stimulant or mild blister.

The writer has used this very successfully, and, in fact, mainly depended upon it when on the road, for allaying attacks of coughing.

HEAVES, OR BROKEN WIND.

Heaves are indicated by an increased action of the flanks. The inspiration is natural, but the expiration requires two efforts to expel the air. There is at times a short cough or grunt while the air is being expelled from the lungs. Heaves are never found in the racing stable where the horses are properly fed. They are always found among cart or team horses which are fed upon large quantities of coarse food or hay. The seat of the disease is found in the air-cells of the lungs, in the form of enlargements and sometimes ruptures of the cells. The cause of the disease is the immense quantity of hay forced into the stomach, the greedy animal perhaps, not being satisfied with his allowance, eating the bedding. The bowels and stomach press hard against the diaphragm, and the lungs not having room to expand, the air-cells are enlarged or ruptured, and the horse is said to have the heaves. Much has been said by different authors in relation to the curability of the heaves. Some advocate one means, some another, among which is feeding on the Western plains, or upon prairie hay, which is said to contain a "resin weed;" but like many other remedies, it is only palliative.

In 1842 Capt. Squiers, of Buffalo, N. Y., who commanded on the steamboat *Dewitt Clinton*, owned a valuable trotting mare called Caroline. She had the heaves badly. He took her, in the spring of that year, to Chicago, and turned her out to pasture on the prairie, for the purpose of curing the disease. In the fall he brought her back on his boat, with a quantity of prairie hay to keep her during the winter. But upon returning again to timothy hay, the heaves returned as bad as before sent west. (The writer was personally acquainted with Capt. Squiers, he being proprietor of the Courter House at that time, where the writer boarded with him.)

Prairie hay and grass is more laxative than timothy hay, and the animal cannot eat half as much in a given time of the former as of the latter. Consequently it promotes a condition favorable to respiration, by stimulating the bowels, and also prevents pressure upon the lungs. I think there are several other means of treatment equally as good as prairie grass or hay ; one is corn-stalk fodder. My reason is founded on this basis, that it is by saccharine matter that most animals subsist, and the less compass occupied in the bowels the better. One quart of oats is equal to an armful of hay, and three pounds of corn leaves contain more sugar than six times the bulk of timothy hay. It will be seen, then, that the cause, treatment, and cure are marked in these few words ; that is, that heaves are produced by pressure upon the diaphragm by too much food in the stomach and bowels, and is cured by lessening the quantity of food to occupy the same space. After the horse is turned out to grass a few days, the heaves will usually disappear, from the fact that the bowels are generally relaxed by exercise and pure air. The only treatment which will prove to any degree effective, is to give one of the following remedies :—

Powdered ginger.............. ....½ oz.
Capsicum................. ....¼ oz.

Form into a ball, and give three nights in succession ; then omit two or three nights, and give again two or three nights in succession. Or—

Tincture of phosphorus ....8 or 10 drops.

Give in the drink several times a day for eight or ten days.

The horse should have regular exercise, and be watered often with a small quantity at a time, and have straw instead of hay to eat. Under this treatment heaves will disappear. *

---

* The foregoing is a synopsis of Dr. Summerville's lecture to the writer on " Heaves."

Prof. Law, in his *Veterinary Adviser*, says :—

Overfeeding on clover hay, sainfoin, lucern, and allied plants ; on chaff, cut straw, and other bulky and innutritious food, is the main cause of heaves. In Arabia, in Spain, and in California, where there is no long winter feeding on hay, and in our Territories where clover is not used, heaves is a disease that is virtually unknown ; it has advanced westward just in proportion as clover hay has been introduced as a general fodder for horses, and it has disappeared in England and New England in proportion as the soil has become clover sick, and as other aliment had to be supplied. The worst conditions exist when a horse is left in the stable for days and weeks, eating clover hay, or even imperfectly cured, dusty hay of other kinds, to the extent of thirty pounds and upwards daily, and then is suddenly taken out and driven at a rapid rate. Violent exertions of any kind, and diseases of the lungs, are also potent causes. It is mainly a disease of old horses, but may attack a colt two years old. Finally, horses with small chests are most liable, and thus the disease proves hereditary.

Treatment.—Turning out on natural pastures, feeding corn-stalks and other laxative food, will relieve, and even cure, mild and recent cases. Feeding on dry grain, with carrots, turnips, beets, or potatoes, and a very limited supply of water, will enable many broken-winded horses to do a fair amount of work in comfort. Hay should never be allowed except at night, and then only a handful clean and sweet.

The bowels must be kept easy by laxatives, the stables well aired, and sedatives (digitalis, opium, belladonna, hyoscyamus, stramonium, lobelia) used to relieve the oppression. If a white discharge from the nose co-exists, tonics should be given as for chronic bronchitis, to which wild cherry bark may be added. Tar-water as an exclusive drink may be given, and a course of carminatives (ginger, caraway, cardamoms, fennel) may be added with advantage. But nerve tonics, and above all arsenic in five-grain doses daily, and continued daily for a month or two, are especially valuable.

No broken-winded horse should have food or water for from one to two hours before going to work.

The usual method of treatment adopted by "jockeys," is to feed the horse on cut rye straw, to feed very little hay, and to feed all aliments dampened. Rye straw is cut as you would cut hay, then mixed with bran or middlings, into which a handful of salt is added, and dampened with water. This is fed every night. Oats and other grain is always dampened. Draught horses fed in this way seldom show any sign of heaves.

Prof. Law regards the following as the best preparation for heaves :—

Arsenic (Fowler's solution.)....................................1 oz.
Belladonna ext... ..1 dr.
Tinct. of ginger.......................... ....½ dr.

Mix with a pint of water for a drench and give every morning for a month or two.

A favorite remedy for heaves, used by Prof. Dick, principal of Edinburgh College, and undoubtedly of great value, is :—

Camphor, digitalis, opium, calomel, of each, 30 grs.

Make into one powder or ball, and give once a day for a week. If no improvement is noticeable, omit the calomel, and give for a week or two longer.

Spanish brown	2 oz.
Tartar emetic	2 oz.
Resin	4 oz.
Ginger	2 oz.

Mix and give two teaspoonfuls twice a day in the feed.

Vegetable tar, in mass	½ oz.
Gum camphor	½ oz.
Tartar emetic	1 dr.

Form into balls, one of which is to be given once a day.

Indigo	1 oz.
Saltpeter	1 oz.
Rain-water	1 gal.

Mix and give a pint twice a day in the feed.

ROARING.

This is a very annoying difficulty, for which there is no satisfactory treatment. Like chronic cough, it often follows an attack of laryngitis or of distemper (strangles), and in these cases we believe it is owing to a wasting (atrophy) of the muscles of the head of the windpipe (larynx), whereby its caliber is diminished, and when the air rushes in during violent exertion, a roaring sound is produced. The senseless and cruel practice of tight-checking, in addition to the throat-latch being often buckled so tightly as to obstruct the breathing, is also a very common exciting cause.

Symptoms.—When the horse is not excited, and so long as the air passes in a uniform rate through the larynx and windpipe, the animal does not feel any inconvenience ; whenever he is excited or galloped, causing a rush of air, the roaring noise is produced. The sound in ordinary circumstances is only produced on inspiration, but in very severe cases the sound is audible both on inspiration and expiration.

In some horses, roaring is difficult of detection. There are several tests which can be resorted to with the view of detecting it. It may often be readily detected by taking the horse firmly by the head and striking him suddenly on the side, causing him to start forward ; if a grunting noise is emitted, it is always a suspicious circumstance. But the better test would be to gallop the horse sharply for some distance, then pull him up quickly, and by applying the ear to the nostrils or to the windpipe, any abnormal sound will at once be noticed. A good test in the case of draught horses is to compel them to draw a heavy load.

Treatment must be principally palliative ; much can be done by generous and regular feeding, and never allowing the animal to overload his stomach and bowels. Occasional doses of laxative and sedative medicines tend to relieve the more distressing symptoms.

In the early stages, continued applications of tincture of iodine is beneficial when applied to the throat. With this the following mixture must be used internally :—

```
Powdered prickly-ash bark.................................4 oz.
Powdered belladonna leaves.......................... ......3 oz.
Powdered licorice root....................................6 oz.
```

Mix the above with molasses into a soft mass, and give a piece as large as a black walnut on the back of the tongue, with a flat stick, twice a day. This must be continued for at least one week, after which give the remedy once a day for two weeks.

Have the hay well dusted, and moisten all feed given the patient. The above treatment will always cure, or give relief, providing the disease is not too far advanced.

Great relief is sometimes experienced by putting a seton on each side of the neck for some time. Sharp blistering may also be tried, but is not nearly so effective as setoning.

The following treatment for the cure of roaring, or whistling, as it is termed, has been used by Mr. E. D. Conklin and others in Cleveland, O., and they claim the most satisfactory results. Mr. Conklin, who is a large owner of horses, and perfectly reliable, states that he cured one very bad case ; could not pull a load two rods up hill without blowing and choking down ; was completely cured in six weeks. Has tried it in a number of cases, and always with satisfactory results. The treatment was introduced by Dr. Johnson, of Cleveland, who claims he can cure any case. As there is no really satisfactory treatment for this difficulty in regular practice that I know of, I give this remedy and state my authority. It can be tried with safety.

```
Fowler's solution........ ................................1 oz.
Sulphuric acid.............................................20 drops.
```

Give the horse in the evening 30 drops of the mixture in about a wine-glass of water, on the tongue. Spongia Tosta, first dilution (a homeopathic remedy), 10 drops in the morning, to be repeated alternately for from four to six weeks, giving more or less, and for a longer or shorter time, according to the severity of the case, until a cure is effected.

Dr. Johnson also found that when the horse is choking with severe inflammation of the throat, called distemper, diphtheria, etc., that giving successively spongia, aconite, and belladonna, after intervals of fifteen minutes, and repeating, is very effective. This prescription was given the writer by Dr. Johnson. Since then Mr. Conklin, in conversation with the writer, stated that in relieving heaves he found it of decided value. Filling a sponge with the spongia preparation, and squeezing it into the nostrils and mouth a few times will give relief. He regarded it very effective and valuable for this purpose.

BRONCHOCELE.

Bronchocele, or morbid "enlargement of the thyroid gland or body." These are two small glands situated one on each side of the windpipe (trachea), about three inches from the head of the windpipe (larynx); they are ductless glands, having no excretory duct, and are largely supplied with blood-vessels and nerves.

Stallions seem to be the most affected by this. It is a tumor usually on one side of the windpipe, and the character of the swelling varies according to its duration. It may be soft or firm, and it may affect the whole gland, or only one side of it; the tumor seldom causes pain, and the animal appears not inconvenienced by it, although very large. The tumor varies in size from that of a hickory nut to as large as a man's hand. It has been regarded by some as a cause of roaring, but it is evident that it has nothing to do with that difficulty.

Treatment.—Iodine and its compounds seem to have the best effect in removing this enlargement. One part of iodine to six or seven of lard, to be applied daily; and at the same time administer twice a day in solution 1 drachm of iodide of potassium.

NASAL GLEET

is the name applied to a chronic, glairy discharge from one or both nostrils, of a whitish muco-purulent matter, the result usually of neglected catarrh. The general health of the animal does not seem to suffer; he looks well, feeds well, and works well.

Nasal gleet is not an uncommon disease, and many horses have been destroyed, supposed to be affected with glanders, when in reality they were only suffering from nasal gleet. It is on this account that I have been so explicit in describing glanders.

Causes.—It is very often the result of catarrh in a chronic form, as stated, induced by further exposure to cold, and want of a proper supply of nutritive food. It may also occur in cases where it cannot be traced to a catarrhal attack of the air-passages; and it occurs oftener in aged than in young animals.

Symptoms.—The first noticeable symptom is a yellowish discharge from one or both nostrils. The lining membrane of the nose (schneiderian) is altered in color ; it becomes of a pale leaden hue, but does not exhibit ulcerative patches, as in glanders. The discharge may vary both in quantity and quality. It is often retained for some time within the sinuses, and comes away in considerable quantities. In other cases the discharge is continuous, and collects about the nostrils ; the sub-maxillary gland, in cases of long standing, becomes tumefied, but not adhering to the bone as in glanders ; the frontal and nasal bones are affected, and present an enlargement

FIG. 797.—Nasal Gleet.

or bulging out over the seat of the disease. If tapped with the point of the finger, a dull, heavy sound is produced, showing that matter has collected within the sinus. In ordinary cases it is a long time before it materially affects the horse in his working capacity. When the bones are greatly diseased, and the matter collects within the nasal sinuses, it interferes with respiration, causing laborious breathing.

Treatment.—Although a formidable disease, even the worst of cases may recover if properly treated. The successful treatment in all cases where this disorder has existed, has been on the tonic principle. Bleeding and purging are positively injurious. Give good food and moderate exercise, sponge the nostrils with tepid water, or steam the head, as described for catarrh, once or twice a day, and administer mineral or vegetable tonics, as—

Sulphate of copper............................... ....3 oz.
Powdered gentian..1 oz.

Make into twelve powders, and give one in the food morning and night ; or, the sulphate of iron in two-drachm doses twice a day.

The nasal cavities may be injected with a weak solution of sulphate of zinc or of alum ; or of sulphate of copper, about five grains to an ounce of water. When the bone is diseased, and matter collected within the sinuses, it is necessary to trepan the bone. After operating, inject the sinus with tepid water twice or thrice a day, followed by injecting any of the astringents already recommended. The opened sinus sometimes fills up with a fungus growth, which must either be removed by the knife or by means of caustics.

I include here treatment reported in the *Journal of Comparative Medicine and Surgery* for January, 1883, by John Lindsay, D. V. S., of Huntington, Long Island, which has been so effective that I think it worth while to copy his report in full ·—

July 5, 1881, I was called to examine a horse at Clay Pits, Long Island. This animal was supposed to be suffering from glanders. As he was a valuable work-horse, the owner did not wish to destroy him without my advice.

The horse was a bad case to look at. He was discharging very offensive matter from both nostrils, which had the odor of pus coming from a necrosed bone. The horse was much reduced in flesh and very weak. On examination I found him to be suffering from nasal catarrh, and on my stating this to the owner, he wished me to try to cure him. The disease was of three years' standing. At first I thought of trepanning, but having no instrument, I concluded to try injecting the nostrils, knowing from experience that if I could reach the necrosed bones with my solution I could make a cure.

Mixing up one ounce of Calvert's crystallized carbolic acid No. 2, to one pint of water, I injected two ounces into each nostril twice daily. After three days of this treatment, there was a marked improvement, which after this was less pronounced; but there was a gradual and steady change for the better. At the end of two weeks the animal had improved much in general health, and at the end of four months was entirely cured, and there has been no return of the trouble up to date.

July 24, 1882, I was called to see a horse suffering from a very offensive discharge from his nostrils of one year's duration. At times there was a marked subsidence of the discharge, followed by acute exacerbations. When I saw the case, it was in one of the acute attacks. Upon examination, I diagnosticated nasal catarrh.

I ordered the same treatment as used in the above case, and in two months a cure was effected, with no recurrence.

August 10, 1882, I was called to see a horse which could not breathe easily, and the owner feared the animal was developing heaves. The breathing was labored, and there was marked evidence of obstruction of the nasal passages. There was not, however, the double action of the flanks commonly observed in horses. Upon inquiring, I found that two months previous to my visit the horse had suffered with a severe discharge from the nostrils, which had since ceased. But two weeks after the nasal discharge stopped, he had trouble in breathing.

I came to the conclusion that the horse had been afflicted with chronic nasal catarrh, and that the turbinated bones were plugged with thick pus. He was placed under the same treatment as the other two cases, and in three days began sneezing, and blew from his nose two large masses of thick and cheesy pus, followed by a return of the discharge.

The continued use of the injections, however, terminated in a complete cure of the case in one month.

INFLUENZA — EPIZOOTIC — CATARRHAL FEVER.

This disease has been so common since 1871, and it has caused such serious losses, that it may well be regarded with great apprehension by owners. On this account I have been induced to make a special effort to obtain the most reliable and practical treatment for its successful management. So much depends, in the treatment of this disease, upon good conditions of care and nursing, that is, careful housing, keeping up the strength, etc., which in the country must be mainly dependent upon the owner, and it is so easy to cause the loss of a case by a little carelessness or bad treatment, that it is especially important to give such details as will enable a successful treatment of this disease. To accomplish this, I not only give the very best explanation of the difficulty and treatment directed by one of the most prominent veterinary surgeons of the country, but the treatment practiced by Dr. Meyer, who informed the writer that he had treated thousands of cases without losing a single one, complications excepted ; that of true pink-eye he never lost a case, and consequently must be accepted as entirely reliable and of great value.

Influenza, etc., belongs to the class of diseases called epizootic, which are distinguished by extending over a large tract of country, and attacking a number of horses at the same time. In its nature it resembles an epidemic form of catarrh, but it is essentially different, and is easily distinguished from that complaint by its epizootic character, and the marked prostration, and low typhoid form of fever which always accompanies it. It does not affect horses alike in all seasons ; some years it is apt to involve the lungs principally, with a marked tendency to dropsical effusion, whereas in others the liver and digestive organs are chiefly implicated.

Causes.—It is usually supposed to arise from "atmospheric causes,"—some changes which are said to exist in the atmosphere which are not easily explained. It occurs mostly in spring or autumn, and is most commonly seen in overcrowded, badly ventilated stables, situated in malarial districts. City horses are more liable to it than those in the country, and coarser breeds are more subject to it than finer breeds. Poor and overworked horses are especially subject to the fever.

The disease at times comes on as an epizootic. While it is considered decidedly contagious, many veterinarians claim no infection. Dr. Meyer informed the writer that while the fever was at its hight, in one stable where the sanitary conditions were excellent, and containing one hundred and seventy horses, not an animal was taken with the fever ; while in badly ventilated stables, and under poor conditions, the disease was rampant.

Symptoms.—It is early characterized by weakness, a quick, weak pulse, hot mouth, shivering, dullness, watery eyes. The lining membrane of the nose is reddened, accompanied by a watery discharge, which soon becomes thick and purulent, accompanied by sore throat and difficulty of swallowing ; the appetite is impaired, and the bowels costive. These symptoms, instead of abating, as in catarrh, increase, the breathing becomes hurried, and there is lifting of the flanks. The low form of fever is characteristic, as also its occurring in spring or fall, and attacking a number of animals in the same way, distinguishing it from common catarrh.

In some seasons the lungs are primarily affected, and there is great weakness, with a tendency to dropsical effusion ; water accumulates in the chest ; the heart and its coverings are seriously involved ; often the eyelids, lips, and whole head are greatly distended with fluid. In other cases the liver and bowels seem to suffer most, causing great thirst, general uneasiness, costive bowels, and light-colored feces, sometimes covered with slimy mucus, and rapid prostration. "When unfavorable termination occurs, the dullness increases to stupor, the extremities get colder, the breathing more difficult and abdominal, the pulse quicker, weaker, and more irregular, until death supervenes."

PINK-EYE.

Symptoms as Given by Dr. Meyer.—The symptoms are shown in a staggering gait, hanging head, trembling, shivering as from cold, loss of appetite, watery discharge from the eyes, one eye closed, especially the left one. The pulse is quickened and weak, from 50 to 60 in the minute, and the breathing is hurried, temperature 104° to 106°. The bowels are bound and the urine scanty. The disease is often complicated with bronchitis, pneumonia, pleurisy, etc. A pinkish color of the mucous membrane of the eyelids is always present in this disease. There is a discharge from the nostrils, swelling of the limbs, which are tender to the touch. The animal is weak, lying down most of the time. The body seems to be hot all over. The head hangs low, and the horse seems to be suffering from pneumonia. The only difference between pink-eye and pneumonia is, that in the former the pink-eye is noticeable, and the horse lies down, while in the latter he does not."

Treatment.—The general principles laid down for the treatment of common catarrh, are applicable to the treatment of influenza ; bleeding, purging, or any method of treatment that would tend to diminish the strength, must be avoided, as the debilitating tendency is great from the first. He should be placed in a loose box, the body clothed, and the legs bandaged. If noticed while the shivering fit lasts, one or two ounces of acetate of ammonia may be given with advantage. The bowels should be gently opened by a pint of castor-oil and one or two drachms of calomel, supplemented by injections of soap and water. When the rigor has passed off, and the fever runs high, the fever medicine should be given in doses of fifteen to thirty drops, every hour and a half, or tincture of aconite in doses of about ten or twelve drops may be given. He should be encouraged to drink water holding small doses of niter in solution ; should he not drink it, he may have a few mouthfuls of water every hour or two, which of itself is excellent for reducing fever. He should have green food when procurable, or a little boiled oats, and bran mash, or anything else he will eat. When the throat is very sore, and the cough troublesome, rub on the throat a counter-irritant, as directed for sore throat, and give the following ball night and morning :—

Camphor...1 dr.
Opium...1 dr.
Nitrate of potash...2 dr.

Make into a ball with linseed meal and molasses.

Should the lungs or bronchial tubes become involved, indicated by the heaving flanks and careful breathing, use counter-irritants of mustard or good strong liniment, or hot fomentations to the sides until there is relief, as directed for pneumonia. From the first, tonic treatment will be found beneficial in counteracting the debilitating tendency of the disease.

When all inflammatory symptoms have disappeared, tonics will greatly aid the recovery.

Dr. Meyer's Treatment.—Good nursing and good air are indispensable ; the patient should be well blanketed, and fed on anything he chooses to eat ; the stable should be purified by throwing air-slaked lime in the stalls, etc. ; and from the first, begin by giving the following remedies every eight hours :—

Carbonate of ammonia..1 oz.
Cinchona bark, powdered.....................................2 oz.
Nux vomica,   "   ....½ oz.
Digitalis leaves, "   ....2 dr.
Gentian root,   "   ....3 oz.

Mix and make into eight balls.

Give as much water as the patient chooses to drink, to which add some saltpeter. About two ounces a day should be used. The above balls should be used after the second day by giving one morning and night ; when feeding is resumed, discontinue the remedies, and continue with good nursing. Will cure in six to eight days. Bathe with hot water and salt.

It is also necessary to exercise quite slowly at first, as a very little overdoing or exposure is liable to bring on a relapse, which is almost sure to be fatal.

Congestion of the Lungs, Pleurisy, Inflammation of the Lungs.

It is explained in the article on "Circulation" (page 406), that when a horse is exposed to cold, or to conditions which derange the circulation, such as changes of temperature, especially after severe exertion or exhaustion, standing in a current of cold air, etc., thus forcing the blood from the surface of the body to the internal organs, it will in most cases go to the lungs and surrounding parts, when it would be termed pleurisy, pneumonia, or congestion of the lungs, with possible complications with other parts.

This is so common, and fatal in its effect, if neglected or not treated properly, that it is very important to have the nature and treatment made so simple and plain to owners and stable-keepers that, in the absence of competent professional aid, they may easily understand and combat it successfully during its insipiency, when it can as a general thing be easily managed.

We will first briefly consider the structures involved in pulmonary affections. The windpipe (trachea), after entering the chest, divides into the bronchia, or bronchial tubes. These divide

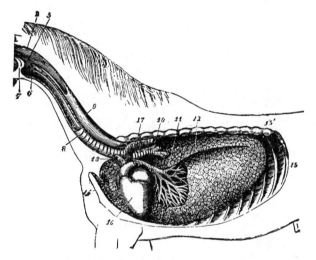

Fig. 798.—**Showing the Respiratory Organs.**

8. Trachea; 9. Esophagus; 10. Section of left bronchus; 11. Ramifications of right bronchus ; 12. Right lung; 13. Left lung seen from above; 14. Sternum; 16. Heart ; 17. Posterior aorta ; 18. Anterior aorta.

and subdivide into smaller tubes, finally terminating in the air-cells. The lungs are made up of clusters of these cells ; of a large mass of pulmonary texture called the parenchymatous structure or substance of the lungs ; of blood-vessels, both functional and for the nutrition of the organ ; of nerves and lymphatics ; and the whole inclosed in a serous membrane called the pleura, which is made up of two portions, one portion being reflected over the lungs (pleura pulmonalis), while the other lines the inside of the ribs and diaphragm (pleura costalis). The lungs are exceedingly light in proportion to their size, and are very vascular organs ; consequently they are very liable to diseases of an inflammatory character ; and the precursor of inflammation is congestion. A good idea of the circulation in these parts can be obtained by a study of Fig. 804.

Bronchitis is inflammation of the lining membrane of the tubes of the lungs and lung cells, which is considered in another part of this work ; but as it is frequently connected with lung difficulties, I refer to it again in this connection.

Pleurisy is inflammation of the pleura (or serous membrane which covers the lungs and thoracic cavity), before referred to.

Pneumonia is an inflammation of the lung tissues, or parenchyma of the lungs. If we had bronchial pneumonia, we would have an inflammation of the lining membrane of the tubes and the parenchyma of the lungs ; if we had pleuro-pneumonia, we would have an inflammation of the pleura, or membrane, and the parenchyma, or tissues of the lungs.

Congestion of the lungs consists in an increased determination of blood to the capillaries of the air-cells. When one or the other (right or left) lobe of the lungs is so engorged with blood forced into them that they are unable either to receive or discharge blood in proper quantities, thereby interfering materially with the process of respiration, it will, consequently if allowed to go too far, cause direct suffocation and death. It may exist as an independent disease, or accompany other affections of the chest. The distinguishing symptoms of each, with treatment, will be given farther on. In order to simplify the treatment, I refer next to the nature and effect of inflammation.

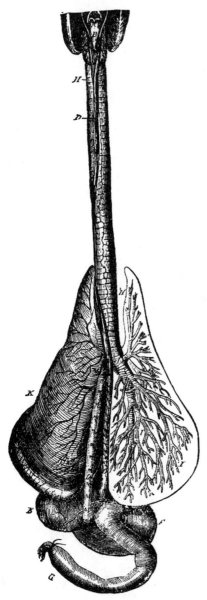

Fig. 799.—Trachia and Bronchial Tubes.

H, trachia ; I, ramifications of bronchial tubes ; L, chobaic artery.

It is first an increased action of the blood-vessels. The consequence is an increased amount of blood to the part. The next change to take place is a collapsed condition of the walls of the vessels. Now there follows an enlargement of the blood-vessels; then the blood passes the walls of the vessels through the tissues outside of the vessels. The next change is the breaking down of the cellular tissues—normal cells; next a rapid growth or proliferation of abnormal cells. To go through symptoms: If an external injury, for example, there would be, first, pain caused by the pressure upon the nerves. The heat following would be caused by the

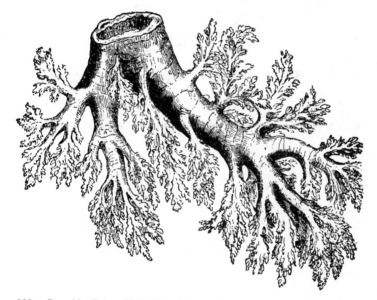

Fig. 800.—**Bronchial Tube, with its Bronchules and Ultimate Ramifications. Natural Size.**

chemical changes that are going on within the part. The redness is due to the passing of the blood from the vessels into the tissues; the swelling is due to the breaking down of normal cells and the rapid formation of abnormal cells. The object in all cases, whether internal or external, is to equalize the circulation as quickly as possible.

There are two methods of treatment: If we know the cause, as, for example, the animal having stood in a draught of air or been exposed to cold, chilling weather, alcoholic stimulants would be the best treatment, not only giving alcohol internally, but rubbing it on the legs, and covering the body with warm blankets. Rub the elbows and hocks to the feet, with the hand or a brush, quickly, and cover with warm flannels. If not successful, or if inflammation, before explained, sets in, there will now be a rapid rise in temperature, when there may be a strong stanic pulse ; in that case sedatives would be required. Tincture of aconite has stood the test for years. About ten drops Fleming's tincture four or five times a day, with from an ounce to an ounce and a half of nitrate of potass divided into two powders and given, one in the morning and one at night, or the fever medicine, hereafter given, can be used.

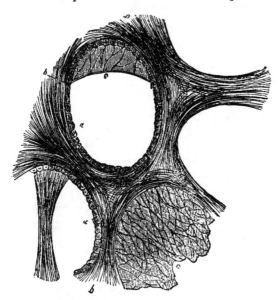

FIG. 801.—**Air-cells of Lung, with Intervening Tissue.**

a, Epithelium ; b, Elastic trabeculæ ; c, Membranous wall, with fine elastic fibers.

In the early stage, external means of irritation can be freely used with good results, but are not admissible when the disease has thoroughly set in, as they only aggravate the trouble. If the pulse is weak, stimulants are required, such as carbonate of ammonia, 2 drachms ; camphor, pulverized, 1 drachm ; and nitrate of potass (as before). Give in one dose three times a day —the potass to be given in water separately. (See also article on "Pulse.")

The termination of inflammation will be either in resolution— that is, a clearing of the lungs, what is known as a gray hepatized state—or in a breaking down of lung tissue, which may develop into an abscess, or tubercles, or gangrene, or death of the lung tissues.

If the horse is young, and strong, and vigorous, not as much stimulant should be used as for an old horse.

If ammonia arises from bedding in stable, it should be neutralized by sprinkling on a little chloride of lime ; too much of it would have an aggravating effect upon the mucous membrane.

CONGESTION OF THE LUNGS.

Symptoms.—It is first noticeable by the horse having a severe chill or shivering fit. He refuses his food, hangs his head between his fore legs or upon the manger, will not move or lie down, breathing quick, panting-like. The nostrils are expanded, the head thrown forward; the countenance expresses pain and great prostration. (See Fig. 802.) The pulse is sometimes full and quick, but generally quick and weak, scarcely perceptible; the membrane of the nose and eyes bright red, tending to purple; ears and legs are very cold, with a cold, clammy sweat at the extremities.

When occurring after a hard ride or drive, the horse will become tired and sluggish in his action; he will perspire profusely,

Fig. 802.—Horse with Congestion of the Lungs.

and almost refuse to proceed, except with the greatest difficulty; he will stand with his elbows turned outward, heaving violently at the flanks; as before explained, the nostrils are dilated, and the ears and extremities cold; the pulse is oppressed, or almost imperceptible at the jaw; the mucous membranes of the nose and eyes are reddened. When of a milder nature, as often occurs in horses suffering from catarrh, which have been subjected to a fast drive and exposed to cold draughts, he is seized with a trembling fit; the ears are cold, and the respiration hurried, when the ear applied to the chest can plainly detect the imperfect breathing.

The inability of the horse to take sufficient air into the lungs, causes great and rapid prostration, and the horse will often, from extreme pain, lie down and get up, resembling colic *(Summerville);* but the coldness of extremities, prostration, and condition of pulse, will, if carefully examined, enable an understanding of the real

31   a

cause. A choking noise is sometimes heard coming from the throat. In some cases a little blood may be thrown from one or both nostrils. Extreme prostration and laborious breathing, and bleeding from the nostrils, show a condition of severe congestion.

Causes.—The most common cause is violent exertion when the horse is in an unfit state for severe work ; as, for instance, a horse in high condition is taken out of his stable and driven rapidly for five

Fig. 803.—View of the Horse's Chest Indicating the Position of the Ribs and Extent of the Thorax over which Auscultation is Performed.

or six miles ; this induces an increased quantity of blood to the lungs, more than they can dispose of in their weakened condition from want of regular exercise. It is also caused by impure air, in horses standing in crowded, badly ventilated stables, and is often a sequel of catarrh.

Treatment.—In acute cases it must be energetic. Clothe the body well, and administer stimulants, as—

Sulphuric ether...... .... .2 oz.
Laudanum ....1 oz.

To be given in half a pint of cold water ; or nitrous ether may be given in place of the sulphuric.

If no medicinal agents can be conveniently procured, give a quart of warm ale, or a tumblerful of gin, whisky, or brandy, mixed up with hot water or sugar. Have him put into a warm place, with plenty of ventilation, as pure air is an indispensable adjunct in the treatment of all pulmonary diseases. If no relief follows, and there is danger of suffocation, take from four to six quarts of blood from the neck vein, rub alcohol or other stimulant on the legs, rubbing well with the hand, and apply hot cloths to the sides and loins, and cover up with dry blankets, so as to induce a free perspiration, and thereby assist in relieving the lungs.

There is some difference of opinion among practitioners in relation to bleeding for congestion. Dr. Summerville, who is a very able and successful practitioner, instructed the writer as follows : "If there is much congestion, it is necessary to give prompt relief, which can be done best by taking four to six quarts of blood quickly from the neck vein ; stimulate the sides and legs, and give fever medicine as for pleurisy." While he condemns bleeding for pleurisy or inflammation of the lungs, he says, " In a severe attack of congestion,

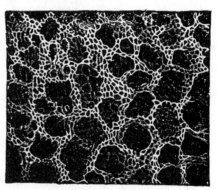

Fig. 804.—**Arrangement of the Capillaries around the Air-cells.**

bleeding cannot only be resorted to with safety, but, as above stated, is indispensable ; but must not be carried too far, merely to assist the lungs to throw off the load of blood forced upon them, and to give the medicine prescribed a chance to operate." Prof. Williams also advises the same treatment. While he condemns bleeding as a general rule, he advises, where congestion is so great as to endanger asphyxia, bleeding a little (from four to six quarts) promptly.

Pneumonia—Inflammation of the Lungs,

as before explained, is inflammation of the substance of the lungs.

Causes.—It is often a sequel of neglected or improperly treated catarrh. It may also, as stated, be accompanied by pleurisy. A frequent, and we may say the most common, cause is exposing the horse while warm to a sudden change of temperature, by allowing him to stand in a cold draught of air, etc. ; getting chilled or wet ;

washing the belly and legs immediately after exercise and allowing the horse to get chilled ; removing from a warm to a cold or
from a cold to a warm stable ; or cold applied to the surface of a
heated animal, by which the blood is driven from the skin and extremities to the internal organs. Any slight cold or sore throat
may run into pneumonia. Driving rapidly against a cold wind, especially after being confined to the stable for some time, is a com-

Fig. 805.—Usual Position of the Horse when Suffering from Shivering.

mon cause, and a horse should be watched carefully after such an
exposure ; also breathing impure air in overcrowded, badly ventilated
stables, or standing in an open, draughty stable.

Any exposure to cold and wet, sudden chills, housing in very cold, draughty
stables. Horses kept in ill-ventilated stables are undoubtedly rendered susceptible
to many diseases, and to pneumonia among the rest ; but they will bear impure air
even better than cold draughts blowing directly upon them. I have repeatedly observed that the slightest cold contracted by a horse kept in a draughty stable has
almost invariably been succeeded by pneumonia, and that if the animal was not removed to a more comfortable situation, the disease tended to a fatal termination.
— *Williams.*

Symptoms. — Pneumonia is almost invariably ushered in by
shivering, and coldness of the surface of the body. The breathing
becomes hard and full, panting-like. The pulse is full and oppressed,
running up to from sixty to eighty beats per minute, differing in its
character from the pulse of pleurisy, which is hard and wiry. The
ears and legs are cold ; the membranes of the eyes and nose are

reddened ; the animal stands persistently with his elbows turned out, to give more freedom to the lungs. He stands with his nose toward the window or door, where he can get fresh air.

A healthy horse breathes at an average of ten times in a minute, viz., ten inspirations and ten expirations ; and the time occupied by the inspiratory movement is longer than the expiratory. In pneumonia the expiration is as long, if not longer, than the inspiration, and these movements are very much quickened, being an effort of nature to compensate for the impaired action of the lungs. When a cough is present, it is freer and less painful than the cough of pleurisy. By ap-

Fig. 806.—As the Horse Usually Stands when Suffering from Inflammation of the Lungs. From Mayhew.

plying the ear to the sides of the chest, in the early stage a crepitating sound is heard, which becomes altered as the disease progresses ; but in a general sense it is easily distinguished by the horse standing with the legs spread, the head thrown forward, breathing quick and hard, and ears and legs cold.

Treatment. — Blanket warmly and put in a comfortable stall where there will be pure air, and give the following fever medicine :—

Fig. 807.—Horse in the Last Stages of Inflammation of the Lungs. Mayhew.

Tincture of aconite........1 oz.
Tincture of belladonna... 2 drs.
Water....................3 oz.

Of this give from 15 to 30 drops on the tongue every 20 or 30 minutes, or about 10 drops tincture of aconite every two hours, more or less, according to the severity of the case. If the case is severe, apply strong stimulants to the legs, breast, and sides of the chest, as before explained, such as mustard made into a paste and rubbed in thoroughly, or a liniment composed of aqua ammonia reduced one half with water, and rubbed in well so as to invite circulation to surface and extremities.

Blankets wrung out of hot water applied to the sides in the early stage (for details see " Fomentations "), is preferred by many. If this is done at the time the fever sets in, either in pneumonia or pleurisy (the treatment for which is practically the same), with a few doses of the fever medicine, it is rarely the horse will not be relieved next day ; but if not, recovery will not commonly take place before the fifth or sixth day. Give from 2 to 3 drachms nitrate of potass two or three times a day. When there is improvement, which will be denoted by the pulse becoming full and regular and the expression and actions being lively, give less fever medicine and at longer intervals. Should too much be given, it will be noticed by falling of the pulse, sweating, trembling, and anxious eye, when it should be discontinued, and stimulants would be indicated.

Nurse by giving simple food, such as a little bran with boiled oats, linseed meal, cooked carrots, with a little good hay. If there is much weakness, give moderate doses of whisky or brandy, from 4 to 6 ounces two or three times a day, being governed by its effects. If the bowels are bound, move them by enemas. Recovery will be greatly aided by the use of stimulants and tonics ; liquor acetate of ammonia in 2 ounce doses three or four times a day, may be used.

The best veterinary surgeons now all agree that bleeding is not only unnecessary but injurious in treating pneumonia and pleurisy.

PLEURISY.

As before stated, pleurisy is inflammation of the pleura.

Symptoms.—It may be sudden or gradual in its attack, the

horse showing indisposition, sometimes for days previous. He will be dull and heavy in action for a day or two, unwilling to lie down, pulse not much disturbed, or there is a chill, or shivering fit, which lasts from one to three hours, when fever sets in ; breathing at flanks a little accelerated, countenance is anxious, the head is sometimes

Fig. 808.—Usual Appearance of a Horse Suffering from Pleurisy. From Mayhew.

turned toward the side ; does not lie down. As the disease advances, the symptoms become more marked. The ears and legs become cold ; the pulse, from being a little accelerated, grows quicker, hard, and full ; the head is hung forward ; stands up persistently ; breathing hurried; the membrane of the nose and eyes red.

Turning the horse round, or hitting against the chest, back of the shoulder, will cause a kind of grunt.

The ear applied to the chest will detect a rough, rasping noise, and there is generally present a short, painful, suppressed cough, easily excited by pressure on the larynx.

Causes are similar to those of pneumonia, such as variations in temperature, exposure to cold while warm, standing in a draught of cold air, impure air, etc. Pleurisy occurs as an independent disease, or, as before stated, may be accompanied by inflammation of the lungs. If neglected or not treated properly, is a very dangerous disease.

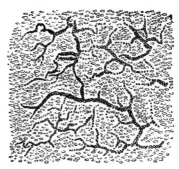

Fig. 809.—The Pleura as it Appears when Inflamed, Magnified.

Treatment is practically the same as for pneumonia. Put in a cool, well-ventilated stall ; give fever medicine ; blanket the body, neck, and legs warmly ; if at all serious, using stimulants on the extremities, and hand-rubbing thoroughly, with hot fomentations to the sides ; the general treatment, in a word, is the same as for pneumonia. Should there be cough, or soreness of the throat, it is to be treated in connection, as directed for laryngitis.

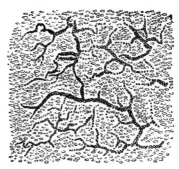

Fig. 810.—Section of Pleura Showing Blood-vessels Greatly Injected with Blood.

I wish now to call attention to what must not be done. First, give no physic nor oil for any form of inflammation of the lungs. Cathartic medicine is poisonous, such as aloes, oils, or tartar emetic. There is so much nausea during the operation of these medicines, and debility from their effect, that they do harm. There is such great sympathy between the bowels and the lungs, that they hasten the cause of inflammation of the lungs, often causing death within a few hours after administering them. Next, do not bleed

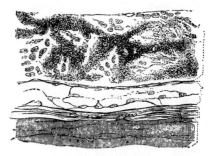

Fig. 811.—Showing Adhesive Inflammation of the Pleura.

for pleurisy, as so doing will cause debility of the capillaries of the part, which would induce hydrothorax, or dropsy of the chest.

This will be somewhat puzzling to owners and stable-keepers, and especially to those who may be guided by Youatt and other good old authorities who invariably advised this treatment.

The better to aid my readers, I include also the directions given by Prof. W. W. Williams, president of the new Veterinary College of Edinburgh, Scotland :—

1. Place the animal in a well-ventilated loose box, but where the air is not too cold.

2. Clothe and wrap the body, extremities, and head in suitable but not too heavy cloths.

3. Give it as much water as it will drink, adding to the water, if there is much fever, about an ounce of niter, or 20 to 30 drops of tincture of aconite, to the bucketful.

4. If the bowels are bound, loosen them by injections of oil or warm water.

5. If there is much weakness, give two drachms each of carbonate of ammonia and camphor, in the form of a ball, twice daily.

6. Let the food be simple, laxative, cooling, and nutritious, as bran, boiled linseed meal, good hay, or cooked carrots or turnips.

7. If moderate diarrhea or profuse staleing come on, they are on no account to be checked, as this is an effort of nature to throw off the disease.

8. If there is great exhaustion, moderate doses of whisky may be given, but there is no use of pushing them, unless their good effects are soon seen.

The attention of the writer has been particularly directed to the value of the fever medicine before recommended in the treatment of pleurisy and pneumonia. During the year of his stay in Buffalo with Dr. Summerville, it was invariably used for all cases of chills and fever with remarkable success. Indeed, the writer does not remember a single fatal case, even of those that had been caused by exposure, or from badly ventilated stables, or of an epizootic character, when treated within a reasonable length of time. The usual course was blanketing the horse comfortably warm and giving this medicine, in about the proportion and at the intervals stated, the size and the condition of the case determining how much to give. A great many times while on the road the writer has had occasion to use this medicine for chills and fever, and always with success. Indeed, if this is given promptly, with anything like ordinary care, aided by other means as directed, there need be but little danger of failure. The point is, as repeatedly stated, to take the case in hand promptly at the start ; watch closely the condition of the animal that has been exhausted, or hard-driven, and exposed to cold, especially during chilly, rainy weather, and if any indication of chill is noticeable, give a little of the fever medicine once or twice, and blanket warmly, and it is rarely any serious trouble will follow.

The medicine is put up by Dr. Summerville & Sons, and stable-keepers will do well to order it of them. Address, Dr. Wm. Summerville & Sons, 127 Erie St., Buffalo, N. Y.

DR. MEYER'S TREATMENT FOR PNEUMONIA.

In conversation with Dr. Meyer on the treatment of pneumonia and pleurisy, he stated that he treated them with decided success without using aconite, which is recognized as the best sedative for fever. I requested the details of his method of treatment, which I here include as an important addition to what I have already given on the subject :—

Have the animal well blanketed and cared for in a roomy stall, where there is plenty of circulating air, and give one of the following balls every eight hours:—

    Carbonate of ammonia...1 oz.
    Pulverized chincona bark....................................2½ oz.
    Pulverized nux vomica ....½ oz.
    Pulverized digitalis leaves ....3 dr.
    Pulverized gentian ....2 oz.

Make into eight balls.

Also give the following in water twice a day :—

    Nitrate of potash .... 6 oz.
    Bicarbonate of soda ....1 oz.

Make into six powders.

Have the animal's chest rubbed with alcohol two or three times a day for the first two days. Feed nutritious food, or anything that may tempt the animal to eat. The medicine must be continued until the animal commences to lie down, which will be from the sixth to the eighth day.

DR. MEYER'S TREATMENT FOR PLEURISY.

Symptoms rather obscure. Animal dull, dejected, off his food, sweats easily, pulsation from 60 to 80, small and weak, temperature 102½° to 104°; above this is sure death. Sometimes there is a cough from commencement, but often or in about half the cases there is no cough. During the first three or four days the extremities and ears are alternately hot and cold, appetite almost wholly lost. The fecal and urinary secretions are considerably lessened. The membrane of nose and eyes are injected. Tongue is generally foul, belly tucked up, does not lie down. The thoracic walls are fixed, breathing almost wholly abdominal, the elbows turned. If made to move suddenly, especially turning short around, there is a groan or growl. Breathing quick or catching-like and short. Often the right side only is affected.

Treatment.—Hot applications to the chest. This can be done best by wringing blankets out of hot water and applying them to the chest,—two or three blankets, one over another, and all covered with oil-cloth or other blankets so as to keep in the heat. Rub limbs with alcohol ; they may also be loosely bandaged. One of the following balls should be given every eight hours :—

Powdered opium..½ oz.
Muriate ammonia..1½ oz.
Powdered chincona bark...3 oz.

Mix and make into six balls.

Give the animal anything he will eat or drink. If the horse is taken during the early stages, this will cut it short in from 48 to 60 hours.

If in an after stage swelling begins to show itself below the chest walls, that is, between the fore legs, and extending backward, shows the least symptom of the trouble known as hydrothorax, give the following remedy: Fluid extract digitalis, from twenty to twenty-five drops, more or less according to the size of the horse, every four hours, and continue until the swelling begins to lessen, then the intervals of giving the drops should be lengthened to eight hours. If the swelling is very large, the skin should be punctured in from twenty to thirty places, and the parts bathed with hot water three or four times a day.

Hydrothorax, or Water in the Chest.

This is a sequel of pleurisy when neglected or not treated properly, and which can scarcely be said to be curable. When pleurisy is running into this difficulty, there may be some appearance of recovery; the breathing and fever are not so intense; the horse will perhaps eat a little; the skin looks sleek and glossy; these signs of improvement may continue for several days, but if the pulse is gradually increasing in frequency, and its strength diminishing, there is undoubtedly water forming in the chest.

When this has taken place to any great extent, there is difficulty in breathing, and a flapping of the nostrils; the eyes are clear and unnaturally prominent; the intercostal spaces bulge out, and the ear applied to the chest can only detect the respiratory murmur above the surface of the fluid; the legs and breast will swell; the circulation becomes more and more impaired, the pulse getting weak and indistinct.

Prof. Williams states, in relation to the cause of hydrothorax: "Of the termination of pleuro-pneumonia in hydrothorax, I have only to say that since I have abandoned the heroic or counter-irritating treatment [he advises hot fomentations to the chest; discards all blisters and irritants], hydrothorax has been almost unknown to me. For this the principle of treatment is stimulants, tonics, and diuretics." I give the treatment of a leading authority, who advises as follows :—

Give a pint of warm ale combined with one ounce of nitrous ether three times a day; blisters applied to the sides, and iodide of potassium in 1 drachm doses twice a day; feed the animal on nutritious and easily digested food.

When a large accumulation of fluid takes place, it must be removed by tapping. The puncture is usually made in the intercostal space between the seventh and eleventh ribs, near the junction with the cartilages. The space between the eighth and ninth is usually recommended.   An incision is first made with a lance through the skin, the trochar and canula is carefully pushed through the muscles and pleura, directed slightly upward and backward, keeping it close to the anterior border of the ninth rib, so as to avoid wounding the intercostal artery; when the trochar is withdrawn, the fluid flows freely through the tube ; sometimes it gets obstructed by coagula of lymph, which should be cleared by inserting a small whalebone staff. Care must be taken not to allow air to enter the cavity, as death has often occurred from this cause during the operation.   It is advised before making the incision to draw the skin aside so as to form a valvular wound, at the same time taking care to prevent the entrance of any air.   The operation may be repeated in a day or two on the other side ; but in most cases the relief is but temporary.   In any event tonic treatment, such as sulphate of iron, tincture of gentian, stimulants and diuretics, iodide of potassium, are to be depended upon if successful.

Hydrothorax was a very common result of pleurisy, when treated by bleeding, blistering, etc.   The congestion or inflammation in the first place is due to debility, and bleeding only increases it ; and especially when the bleeding is repeated, though for a time there was apparent relief, fever and increased debility followed, resulting usually unfavorably.

The treatment advised for pleurisy, if the case is attended to promptly, even though very severe, will be found so effective as to leave but little probability of any serious effusion taking place.

TYPHOID PNEUMONIA.

Cause is mainly attributed to those influences which interfere with the general health and vigor of the animal, among which stand pre-eminently overcrowding, improper ventilation, confinement in damp, filthy stables, drinking bad water, holding in solution decomposing, organic matters, insufficient nourishment, and undue exposure, together with what may be termed, generally, atmospheric causes.

Symptoms.—The horse is off his feed, disinclined to move, appetite gone, pulse weak and low ; will sometimes eat a little, will not lie down, stands hanging his head, is listless and stupid, not much cough, rarely any discoloration of the membrane of the nose or eyes ; urine scanty and high colored ; feces hard and coated. After two or three days the membrane of the nose and eyes is a little discolored or red, pulse quicker, 65 or 70, breathes quicker. About the fourth or fifth day there is usually a discharge from the nostrils, of a blackish brandy-colored serum.

Treatment.—As the word typhoid means low, it is necessary to watch it carefully in that stage, which will last, as described in the symptoms, the first four or five days, when in many cases the pulse may run down to thirty.   Stimulants should be used at this stage, such as a little brandy and water or whisky and water. A gill or two of liquor to be given as a drench ; or what is much better, take carbonate of ammonia, from one to two drachms, powdered ginger root, one to two drachms, made into a ball with honey or molasses, and given twice a day. It should be remembered that this treatment alone is intended only for the low stage of the disease. When the pulse seems to rise to fifty or sixty about the fifth or sixth day, the patient should then be treated as for pleurisy, with fever medicine. Under the influence of the latter treatment the pulse will recede and resume its natural number of beats (forty). In this form of disease the horse is extremely pros-trated at first, the whole system being inactive. The pulse may run up in time to seventy, or even eighty.

The horse should be kept moderately warm, clothing thoroughly the head, neck, and extremities ; he should have a comfortable, well-ventilated stall ; open the bowels by enemas ; give tepid water to drink, in which is a little nitrate of potash, as advised for pneumonia. Nurse the horse with anything he will eat,—a handful of wet hay, a carrot or two, an apple or a potato, or anything of an alterative nature.

Be careful not to exercise too soon.

BRONCHITIS.

Bronchitis, or inflammation of the mucous membrane of the bronchial tubes, is often associated with inflammation of the lungs, but also occurs as a separate affection.

Causes are similar to other pulmonary diseases. It is a result of laryngitis or catarrh ; or it may depend on atmospheric influ-ences, and in these cases it is always accompanied with great weak-ness and prostration.

Symptoms.—There is a short, dry, and husky cough, speedily becoming more prolonged. When a horse gives a natural cough, he opens his mouth a little ; but when laboring under this disease, he keeps his mouth closed, trying to suppress the cough. As the disease advances, the mouth becomes hot and dry, the ears and ex-tremities alternately hot and cold, the pulse not hard and wiry as in pleurisy, but soft and compressible, and the respirations are quick and hollow. If the ear be applied to the breast, a rattling sound can easily be detected ; the bowels are inactive, and the appetite is gone. Death may occur in from three to five days.

Treatment the same as for laryngitis, explained on page 455; counter-irritation to the throat, and if there is fever, give fever medicine or aconite, as for pneumonia. If the cough is very distressing, give the following every night and morning :—

Extract of belladonna ....1 dr.
Powdered digitalis ....2 scr.
Camphor ....1 dr.
Powdered opium. .... 1 scr.

COLIC.

There is no disease about which there seems to be so much difference of opinion among horsemen as that of colic. When the horse is taken sick suddenly, showing the symptoms of colic, the owner, or some neighbor called in who is presumed to know, is most

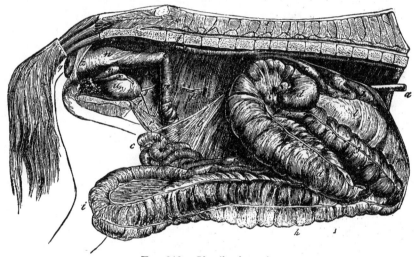

FIG. 812.—Digestive Apparatus.

likely to assume the trouble is caused by bots ; another perhaps believes it is belly-ache ; while others who may be present are likely to be equally positive in supposing the trouble to be caused by something else. The treatment, too, is usually on the same principle, equally doubtful, if not ridiculous. The first and most common remedy is plunging a knife into the roof of the horse's mouth to bleed, "*so as to give blood to the bots, or relieve the colic, or whatever it is*"; this hap-hazard cutting is liable to sever the palate artery, and endanger the horse's bleeding to death. The next resource is likely to be that of running the horse up and down the street, or kicking him in the belly, giving sweet milk and molasses, etc. No one would pretend to be able to explain definitely the nature of the trouble ; but they *believed* it was this, that, or something else, and the consequence was that the poor horse was liable to be tortured for hours, often killed, by cruelty or repeated dosing with remedies that were not applicable to the case. While it is true a horse may show the symptoms of colic, from a variety of causes, which would mislead the judgment of even good practitioners, it is so exceptional as to be scarcely worth referring to here.

It was stated in another part, by the writer, that he employed a veterinary surgeon of unusual skill and experience to instruct him in his method of treatment for the cure of such diseases as are most common and dangerous to horses in this country, including the prescriptions used by him for the same.

The first morning, while waiting in the office for the commence-

ment of this instruction, the doctor came in hurriedly, saying, "There is a horse here that has the colic; I wish you to observe his condition carefully; notice what will be done for him; in the meantime read every authority in the library on the causes and symptoms of colic, but do not read the treatment, as the treatment given in books is not reliable, and would only mislead you."

Fig. 813.—First Stages of Spasmodic Colic Somewhat Exaggerated.   Mayhew.

As directed, I noticed carefully the condition of the case and the effect of the treatment, which was favorable. In the meantime I read up on the subject, and that evening I was given a lecture on colic, when the doctor informed the writer that he had killed hundreds of horses before he knew how to treat it successfully; and that the treatment given in books, and generally advised, could not be depended upon to cure colic with anything like certainty; that even veterinary surgeons of very high standing could not feel any certainty of being able to cure colic; that it was found especially difficult to cure flatulent colic, or tympanites. "Now," said he, "we can cure every case that comes into this stable, if we can have an opportunity of treating them within a reasonable length of time, or before there is a collapsed condition of the circulation.

The opportunities for treating colic in the Infirmary were very many. The Erie Canal heads at that place, which necessarily concentrated a large number of canal horses in the vicinity, which, with those of the city, brought to the Infirmary almost every day a number of horses suffering with colic; and during my experience there of a year, there was not a single death from this cause; and since then, extending over a period of twenty years, I have used the same treatment in the cure of a great many cases, and had it used under my supervision, without the loss of a single case ; this treatment I give first, having the utmost confidence in its great value.

There are two forms of this disease, namely, spasmodic and flatulent colic. The first is wholly of a spasmodic nature, and if not promptly relieved, will, in severe cases, run into inflammation of the bowels, causing speedy death. The second, while exhibiting the same general symptoms, shows marked enlargement of the belly, from generation of gas, which, if not checked and neutralized, results

Fig. 814.—**First Stage of Spasmodic Colic.**

fatally, by rupturing the diaphragm, causing suffocation and death. The advantage of this treatment for colic was, first, in making a fair trial of the best antispasmodic, laudanum ; then, if it failed to give relief, or if there was relapse, bleeding promptly, which not only gave relief with more certainty, but prevented a tendency to inflammation, thereby making a cure when medicine proved unavailing. Second, in giving peppermint for flatulent colic. He found by experiment that peppermint was the only remedy he could depend upon for neutralizing the distending gas ; and its combination with ether, as the best for giving relief.

Causes.—The common causes of colic are a sudden change in the feed ; very often during the summer, when running at pasture, if taken up for a day, and a feed of oats or dry food given, it is apt to cause gripes; feeding new oats or new corn is a common cause; applications of cold water to the body; drinking freely of cold

FIG. 815.—**Second Stage of Spasmodic Colic.**

water when heated, especially if hard well-water, often gives rise to a severe attack; worms and other intestinal irritants may induce it; costiveness and unwholesome food often cause it; overloading

FIG. 816.—**Third Stage of Spasmodic Colic.**

the stomach, or being put to work on a full stomach, will give rise to it.

Symptoms.—The animal is suddenly seized with pain in the bowels, becoming restless and uneasy, crouching, sometimes striking up toward the belly with the hind foot, looking round to his flanks, evincing great distress ; he gets down after several apparent efforts, rolls about, sometimes on his back, sometimes quite over.* (These symptoms are in part illustrated by Figs. 814 – 816, which are ideal, but will serve to give an idea of the symptoms. Fig. 813, which I copy from Mayhew, is considerably exaggerated, the head being held too high, showing too excited and nervous an expression, and the hind leg brought too near the body. Fig. 814 shows a common symptom during the early stage.) Profuse perspiration breaks out over him. The paroxysm soon passes off, and he gets up, shakes himself, and begins feeding ; during the interval the pulse is unal-

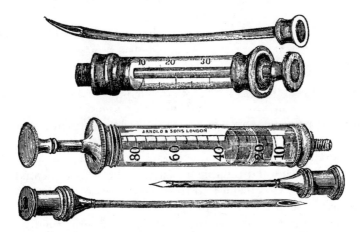

Figs. 817, 818.—Forms of Graduated Hypodermic Syringe Frequently used in Treating Colic.

tered ; the legs and ears are natural in temperature. After an interval of longer or shorter duration, the attack returns, perhaps with increased violence, when he gathers himself, falls down and rolls about as before. As the disease advances, the symptoms become more severe.

Youatt, in his description of colic, contrasts its symptoms with those of inflammation of the bowels, and though not exactly according to modern authorities, it will materially aid the reader in determining the difference ; so I include it. I would also refer the

---

* He may also act as if he wanted to make water, which he cannot do, there being a spasmodic contraction of the urethra. Hence the desire to give diuretic medicine. Straining in this way is usually prompted by a desire to relieve the muscles of the belly. No diuretic medicine should be given, as the horse cannot pass urine until the attack of colic ceases, or it is taken from him with a catheter. It is very seldom necessary to use the catheter. In fact, it is not necessary to pay any attention to this symptom. As soon as relieved of the colic, the horse will pass water freely.

reader to the description of each by Dr. Meyer, which follows on page 500.

COLIC.	INFLAMMATION.
Sudden in its attack.	Gradual in its approach, with previous indications of fever.
Pulse rarely much quickened in the early stage of the disease and during the intervals of ease, but evidently fuller.	Pulse very much quickened, but small, and often scarcely to be felt.
Legs and ears of natural temperature.	Legs and ears cold.
Relief obtained from rubbing the belly.	Belly exceedingly tender to the touch.
Relief obtained from motion.	Motion evidently increasing the pain.
Intervals of rest.	Constant pain.
Strength scarcely affected.	Rapid and great weakness.

If not checked, or there is not relief, it runs into inflammation of the bowels, which is very fatal, and the point is to combat and overcome it before running so far as to resist treatment.

This disease being wholly of a spasmodic character, it must be counteracted by antispasmodic treatment; and laudanum being the most powerful and reliable antispasmodic, it is indicated.

Treatment.—Give from two to three ounces of laudanum and a pint of raw linseed oil.* If not better in an hour, give two ounces of laudanum and the same quantity of oil. If there is not relief in a reasonable time after the second dose is given, take from six to twelve quarts of blood from the neck vein, according to the size of the horse and the severity of the attack.† Always in bleeding make the orifice large, and extract the blood as quickly as possible.

In the Infirmary the practice was, as stated, to try the medicine, and as soon as convinced it was not sufficient to relieve the case, no time was lost in bleeding. Or, if a case was brought in that had been suffering some time, not only medicine was given, but bleeding was resorted to at once.

TYMPANITES, OR FLATULENT COLIC.

Symptoms the same as in spasmodic colic, with the difference of

---

*This is the dose advised for a large horse. For a medium or small-sized, nervous-tempered animal, two thirds the quantity would be equally large.

† It will rarely be found necessary to resort to bleeding if the case is attended to promptly, and in only very serious cases, where the horse is fat and large, is so large a quantity of blood to be taken. In ordinary cases, six to eight quarts would be sufficient.

there being so great an accumulation of gas in the stomach and intestines that the belly is swelled. This disease will often prove fatal in from one to three hours. It is generally very sudden in its attacks, often occurring while the animal is at work, particularly during warm or changeable weather; but it is generally caused by indigestion, producing gases in the bowels and stomach.*

Fig. 819.—**Early Stage of Flatulent Colic.**

Treatment.—Blanket comfortably, so as to keep up evaporation, and immediately give the following as a drench:—

Peppermint	2 oz.
Sulphuric ether	2 oz.
Water	1 pt.

Shake up thoroughly, and keep covered with the hand or cork before administering. If not relieved, it should be repeated in one

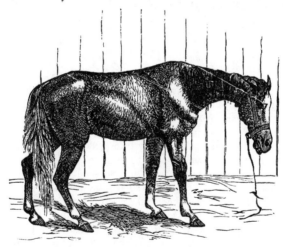

Fig. 820.—**Advanced Stage of Flatulent Colic, or Tympanites.**

---

* There are two locations for this disease, the stomach and the colon and cœcum ; but in either it requires the same treatment, as it is generally produced by the same causes. When in the stomach, it will be distinguished by eructations, or belchings of gas through the œsophagus, or gullet. If in the colon or cœcum, the horse is violently swollen along the belly, flanks, and sides. The pulse is rarely disturbed until the disease advances, when it will become quickened, running to its hight quickly, and receding as rapidly, if fatal. If to terminate fatally, it will become weaker and slower until it is almost imperceptible. If the animal is allowed to fall down suddenly, while the pressure of gas upon the walls of the stomach is very great, there is a liability of rupturing the diaphragm, which would cause almost instant death from suffocation.

half to three quarters of an hour. If the horse is small, and the attack not severe, less may be given ; while if very large, and the attack severe, even more may be given.*

During my practice of late years, when I had a case of colic, I usually gave the following preparation :—

Peppermint ....1½ to 2 oz.
Sulphuric ether...1½ to 2 oz.
Laudanum ....1 oz.
Soft water ....1 pt.

After shaking thoroughly, I gave this immediately. I have found it in all cases to give relief. It is particularly valuable to non-professional men who cannot, during the early stage, tell the difference between spasmodic and flatulent colic, and on this account it is the preparation the writer would advise. Stable-keepers should always keep it on hand, in readiness for an emergency, as it is very important to be able to treat this disease promptly.

If the horse is subject to attacks of colic, which are usually produced by irritating matter in the bowels, it can usually be relieved by giving one or two sharp doses of physic.

Dr. Meyer's method of treatment is so good, explaining as it does some symptoms, with other points of treatment not given, that I include it in full :—

First, there is a switching of the tail, followed by a pawing with the fore feet, and acting as if there were an inclination to lie down. Usually gets down and rolls, looks at the belly, rolls, then up again, and seems at rest for a few minutes, when he goes through the same actions again. The pulsation is full and strong, about natural. By looking at the inner surface of the eyelid there will be some sign of inflammation. When the attack is running into inflammation of the bowels, or becomes seated, there will be an inclination to sweat, an anxious expression in the eye, increased respiration, the pulsations from 70 to 80, small and weak. The inner lining of the eyelid will be plainly injected or reddened, the animal at times looking toward the flanks; walks almost in a circle ; makes attempts to lie down, coming down about half way, gets up and walks around again, which may be repeated a number of times ; finally succeeds in getting down, which he does very carefully, then will lie outstretched for a few moments ; will make an attempt to rise, and will sit up like a pig, as shown on page 504.

In colic, the horse throws himself down carelessly, rolls around in a careless manner, and then jumps up,—an important sign of death. After the case has been treated for some time, he may seem easier ; but if allowed to have his own way, and he wanders off to some unusual place, it is positive proof that he is beyond medical aid.

Treatment for Colic.—2 ounces laudanum, ½ ounce spirits of camphor or 1 drachm gum camphor, 2 ounces sweet spirits of niter, 2 drachms fluid ex. belladonna. Mix

---

*The ether disturbs the breathing, making the horse apparently distressed, breathing laboriously, which will pass off in a few hours.

with one half pint of water, and give as a drench. If the patient is no better in one hour, repeat, and, if constipated, use warm water injections.

"Flatulent colic, treatment the same as above. In the early stage, if after about half an hour the patient seems no better, give two ounces of essential harts-horn in water, with warm water enema. If by this time there is no flatus, or break-ing of wind, and the animal's abdomen or belly is very much distended, and is belch-ing up air out of the nostrils, and commences to tremble in his legs, an operation will have to be performed. Take a lance or knife and make a slight incision through the skin on the right flank, (the ox is always punctured on the left flank, and the horse on the right,) at a point where the tympanitic sound is most marked. As a rule, this point is midway between the edge of the last rib and the hip bone, and about six inches from the lateral processes of the spine—about where the cross mark is on Fig. 822. Take trocar and canula, put the point into the incision previously made with the knife. Direct the instrument inward, slightly downward and for-ward, and hit it a sharp blow with the flat of the hand to send the instrument through to the hilt. Now draw out the trocar, when the gas will escape. When the escape of gas has ceased, put a finger over the opening of the canula to prevent the air from filling in, and withdraw. When withdrawn, rub slightly with the finger over the wound, and leave it alone. Before performing the operation, give four ounces of vegetable charcoal which has been kept dry, mixed with one quart of

FIG. 821.—**Trocar and Canula.**

milk. The horse will have instant relief after the operation. If he remains quiet, feed nothing for about twelve hours. Give flaxseed tea to drink. After the expira-tion of this time, feed bran mashes, with oatmeal or ground oats, and continue from four to six days, when the animal will be well. When there is no hope by medicine, this operation is the only treatment that promises success. Should the horse be un-easy after the operation, give one of the balls used for inflammation of the bowels, which should be repeated once in from four to six hours until quiet.

During the warm months Dr. Meyer usually performs this oper-ation from twenty-five to thirty times, to save life. His loss is about one in ten.

I would add that during my experience in Buffalo, I had no oc-casion to perform this operation, the treatment given proving in every instance effective. This operation, according to standard authorities, has been regarded as seldom successful. I think the reason is that the case has been allowed to go too long before re-sorting to it. In a conversation with Dr. Meyer in relation to it, he stated that he regarded it as very valuable treatment, enabling him to cure a large proportion of cases which otherwise would be beyond help. As it may in some cases be found necessary to perform this operation, I give a diagram of the body, showing the location of the point to be punctured, and also add an excellent illustration of the method of performing it upon cows or oxen that may become bloated,—a very common occurrence in cattle that are turned into a clover-field, and eat too much. (See Stock Department, page 132.)

When a horse is taken suddenly sick, especially after a drive, or after having been given cold water or a change of food, looking at his side, and acting as if he wanted to lie down, etc., simply catch him by the ear, and if it is warm, and the pulse is natural, it is always accepted as a proof of colic. Now, what can be done provided you have none of the medicine recommended? Give about a tablespoonful of ginger in a pint of hot water, well stirred; or giving as a drench from four to six ounces of good whisky or brandy, is sometimes very effective.

Hot fomentations to the sides and belly are also very effective, using woolen blankets wrung out of water as hot as can be borne, and covered with two or three other cloths to retain the heat, and to be repeated as they cool. A hot bran poultice would be somewhat better, as it would retain the heat longer. (Full directions for giving fomentations will be found under that head.) The fever medicine, given in doses of from a drachm to half an ounce, has also been found very efficient.

Fig. 822.—The Cross Showing the Location to be Punctured.

INFLAMMATION OF THE BOWELS.

Enteritis, also sometimes called red colic, may occur as a primary disease, but more often it is seen as a consequence of colic or constipation of the bowels. It generally proves fatal. As an idiopathic affection, that is, occurring independent of any other disease, it may occur from any of the causes of colic, particularly overloading the stomach.

Symptoms.—The animal is noticed to be unwell; he is dull and stupid; refuses food; has shivering fits, the mouth becoming hot, and extremities alternately hot and cold, the pulse being quick, small, and wiry. He looks toward his flanks; the bowels are costive; after a time pain sets in, and is continuous and violent; he rolls about, the sweat pouring from him in streams; the eyes are blood-shot; the belly hot and tender. He does not throw himself violently down, as in colic, but lies down cautiously, and tries to steady himself on his back. As it goes on, the symptoms are augmented, the legs and ears get deadly cold, the pulse becomes weaker, and soon is imperceptible ; the mouth gets cold and clammy ; extravasation of blood is going on in the bowels ; mortification sets in, the pain ceases, and he may stand up. He is dull and stupid, surface of the body cold, mouth cold, twitching of the muscles, and retraction of the upper lip. He soon falls violently to the ground, endangering the lives and limbs of the attendants who happen to be near him, and after a few struggles expires. After death, the bowels are very much inflamed, and the inner surface black and clotted

Fig. 823.—First Stage of Inflammation of the Bowels.

with extravasated blood. Death sometimes occurs in from six to eight hours, and even in shorter time. When occurring in consequence of colic or constipation, it is very difficult to determine the exact transition from spasm to inflammation.

Treatment.—In the outset, especially when occurring as a primary affection, and not as a consequence of another disease, copious blood-letting will be advisable—from four to six quarts, or sufficient to make an impression on the pulse. He should be turned into a well-littered loose box, and allowed to roll as he pleases. The bowels are obstinately constipated, but drastic pugatives are apt to increase the inflammation ; our utmost efforts must therefore be directed to open them by copious injections (of linseed tea, soap and water, tobacco-smoke, or infusion of tobacco), back-racking, etc. A quart of linseed-oil, with two ounces of laudanum, should be given, and repeated, in half the dose, every one or two hours, if required. Fomentations of hot water must be constantly applied to the belly, or bags wrung out of boiling water. Where, from the violent tossing of the animal, this is impracticable, blister the belly with tincture of cantharides or mustard and turpentine.

If the symptoms do not moderate in a few hours, the pulse continues full, and the legs and ears not very cold, a second bleeding may be advisable ; but this is seldom the case, as the prostration is

rapid, the pulse becoming small, wiry, and almost imperceptible, and the legs and ears deadly cold. In this case bleeding but hastens the fatal termination.

When it has continued eight or ten hours, if it takes a favorable turn, the pulse becomes fuller, the surface warmer, and he will lie for some time stretched out, apparently asleep, being weakened from the

FIG. 824.—A Sure Indication of Inflammation of tne Bowels.

disease and bleeding, and probably partially narcotized from the laudanum. In this stage he must be made comfortable, and covered up in straw or sheets. We usually "bury" him in straw. This restores the balance of the circulation, often causing him to sweat ; and after lying thus for one or two hours he will get up relieved, and begin to feed.

• No hay must be given him. After a little he should be encouraged to drink well-boiled gruel, or eat a thin bran mash. Injections must be continued until the bowels are freely opened. For a few days he must be kept warm ; a few mouthfuls of cold water may be given every hour ; gentle walking exercise and sloppy diet must be continued for some time. About the fourth day, even though the bowels have become regular, he should have a purgative (from six to eight drachms of aloes, made into a ball), to remove ingesta, and restore the secretions to their natural condition.

7

The following is the treatment advised by Dr. Summerville :—

This disease is generally caused by constipation of the bowels, hard driving, overpurging or looseness of the bowels, or drinking cold water when warm. Constipation is, however, the principal cause of the disease, and when this is the case, the first and most important condition of relief is to get an action of the bowels.

Symptoms.—For the first few hours the horse is uneasy, paws, looks around at the side, the pulse is slightly accelerated and wiry. As the disease advances, the intermissions between the attacks become less, pulse quicker, running from seventy to eighty beats in a minute, in some instances even faster; lies down and gets up, shows much pain, no swelling of sides; now begins to exhibit fever, bowels constipated, urine highly colored and scanty.

Remedy.—Give a quart of raw linseed-oil. If constipation is very great, add from four to six drops of croton-oil.

If scours, or overpurging, sets in, give an ounce and a half of tincture of opium with six ounces of water. But in order to suppress the inflammation, it is necessary to bleed immediately from the neck vein from six to ten quarts of blood, according to the strength and size of the animal. In extreme cases bleeding may be repeated to the extent of four to six quarts in three or four hours. If much pain exists in constipation, give from one to three ounces of tincture asafetida. Feed lightly for a week at least, giving gruel, roots,

Fig. 825.—A Symptom of Inflammation of the Bowels, or Great Internal Pain.

grass, and bran mashes, and keep quiet. Do not exercise for several days if there is danger of a relapse. This is a dangerous disease, and requires prompt treatment.

Treatment advised by Charles A. Meyer :—

The first stage of inflammation of the bowels is when the animal sits on his haunches like a pig, gradually gets up, and walks around as if in great agony; makes attempts to lie down, and when he does, goes down very carefully; may make a few rolls; will gradually straighten out again, attempt to rise, and sits on his haunches again like a pig. This position is a sign of bowel inflammation, and to save the patient the treatment must begin in earnest. Should the patient be fat and plethoric, bleed from the neck from two to eight quarts, according to the size of the horse. Apply a strong rubefacient to the abdomen, of 1 lb. of strong mustard, 2 oz. aqua ammonia, and water sufficient to make into a plaster; rub in well, and cover with paper, to keep in the heat. Then give the following medicine :—

Opium, pulverized	4 dr.
Subnitrate of bismuth	2 oz.
Chloroform	4 dr.
Nux vomica, pulverized	2½ dr.
Licorice root	Q. S.

Make into four balls, give one every 4 to 6 hours, according to the uneasiness of the patient, which must be kept quiet, and these balls will do it. Feed soft, nutritious food, warm water, and no hay, for about one week.

SUPERPURGATION, DIARRHEA, ETC.

An over-relaxed state of the bowels may arise from various causes. In some animals it is favored by peculiarities of conformation, as is seen in *washy* horses, animals with long legs, open ribs, and flat sides, with tucked-up bellies, such being liable to purge from the simplest cause.

Change of feed, especially from dry to green, or unhealthful food, and sometimes through nervous excitement, is apt to produce scouring. It is usually the evidence of something wrong, and the effort of nature to remove it. Some irritant or undigested food being lodged in the bowels, the intestinal fluids are poured out in superabundance to remove it. The incautious use of purgative medicines is a common cause of superpurgation. It often occurs in the latter stages of debilitating diseases, when it is always an untoward symptom, betokening a breaking-up of the vital powers. The presence of little white worms *(ascarides)* is occasionally the cause. It sometimes follows the drinking of cold water when an animal is in a heated state.

Symptoms.—The symptoms vary according to the nature of the case, and the causes that give rise to it. It may be simply an increased fluidity of the contents of the bowels, as is seen in washy or nervous animals, unaccompanied by pain or constitutional disturbance ; or, on the other hand, it may be (as in superpurgation) attended by pain, expressed by uneasiness, pawing, looking to the flanks, etc. He strains frequently, and the feces are very watery ; the pulse is small and hard. Rapid and increasing weakness and emaciation, loss of appetite, and unless means are speedily adopted to check it, inflammation of the bowels is apt to set in.

Treatment.—Great care must be exercised in feeding and watering washy horses, dry feed being best suited to them. They should not be allowed to drink too freely of water, especially before work. In many cases it may be necessary to give them some starch or chalk mixed up in the feed. In all cases, the main point is to discover the cause. If arising from improper food, it must be changed at once.

If some irritant be suspected, nature must be assisted in her efforts, by giving a quart of linseed or castor oil, followed up by starch or well-boiled flour gruel, keeping the animal warm. If worms are suspected, or seen in the dung, one or two ounces of spirits of tur-

Fɪɢ. 826.—General View of the Horse's
Intestines, Showing the Distribution of
Blood to them by the Great Mesen-
teric Artery.   The Animal is Placed
on its Back, and the Intestinal Mass
Spread Out.

A. The duodenum as it passes behind the great mesenteric artery; B.
free portion of the small intestine ; C.
ileocæcal portion; D. cæcum; E. F. G.
loop formed by the large colon; F. F.
point where the colic loop is doubled
to constitute the suprasternal and dia-
phragmatic flexures; pelvic flexure.

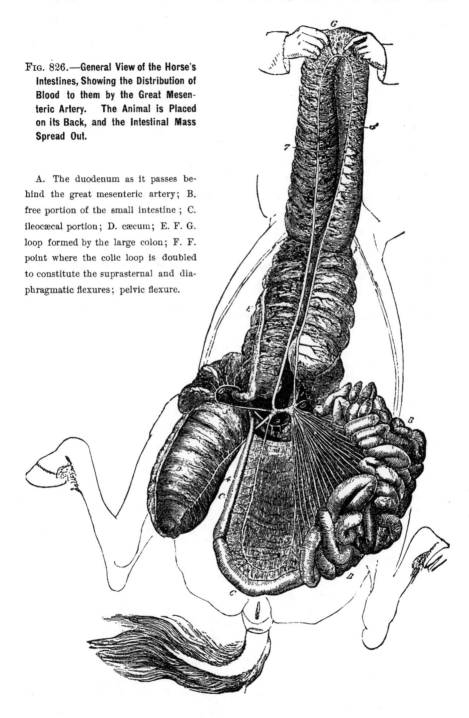

pentine, or any of the vermifuges recommended, should be added to the oil. Should it not yield to this, neutralize the acids in the bowels by giving an ounce and a half of prepared chalk and a dram and a half of powdered catechu, mixed in a pint of water. Give once or twice a day until purging ceases. Keep the animal without exercise, and do not give much water to drink.

If this disease should arise from nervous excitement, give a drachm of powdered opium in the food once a day for three or four days. Or give the following astringent drench :—

Powdered opium..1 dr.
Prepared chalk ....4 oz.
Gum acacia........................ ....1 oz.

Dissolve in warm water, and give in well-boiled flour or starch gruel. It may be given two or three times a day, the gruel being given frequently. If very severe, injections of solution of catechu and starch, with a little tincture of opium, should be given.

The belly may be stimulated with liquid blister. He must be kept perfectly warm, and the legs bandaged. Care must be taken not to induce an opposite state of the bowels by the injudicious use of astringents. An ounce each of carbonate of soda and ginger should be given daily for some time after recovery. Rest and good dry food are necessary for some time.

CONSTIPATION.

Constipation is a condition the very opposite of the above, in which we have a diminished action of the bowels, the dung being dry and voided with difficulty, leading to dangerous "stoppage of the bowels." It arises from various causes, especially from being fed on dry, fibrous food. If in pasture in the fall, when the grass is tough and fibrous, with perhaps a scarce supply of water, the fibrous ingesta are liable to become felted together, and impacted in the bowels. Want of exercise, and feeding too much grain, are also prominent causes.

It is sometimes accompanied by inflammation of the bowels. Horses that are kept up, or not worked regularly, and especially if fed on dry food, should have an occasional bran mash with plenty of water to drink, or small doses of laxatives ; aloes is the simplest and best, from two to four drachm doses, with green food. If accompanied by colic, or inflammation of the bowels, back-raking, etc., must be resorted to until relieved. Green grass is about the best laxative.

All horses, especially those advanced in years, should be watched carefully, and when there is any tendency to constipation, it should be prevented, as before stated, by giving bran mashes, carrots, and raw potatoes ; or, if thought advisable, a little oil or physic, with regular exercise and sufficient water, and there will usually be no difficulty. It is very important to look to this condition ; neglecting it, colic, inflammation of the bowels, etc., may result.

WORMS.

Worms are most commonly found in the stomach and bowels ; they are also sometimes met with in almost every part of the body. Investigation shows there are over thirty kinds of worms that infest the horse. Dr. Robert Jennings, about thirty years ago, at that time a resident of Borden Town, New Jersey, now of Detroit, Michigan, informed the writer that he had traced out thirty different kinds in

FIG. 827.—**Symptom of Worms.**

the horse, and among others exhibited a piece of muscle that was perforated by a large number of little white worms from one to two inches long.

Mr. White, an old author, says :—

I have found worms in the wind-pipe, in the mesenteric artery, in an abscess in the substance of the abdominal muscles, and according to Lafosse, they have been found also in the pancreatic and salivary ducts.

FIG. 828.—**The Appearance of a Horse that is Troubled with Worms.**

There are but three or four that are very common. First, the *teres lumbrici*, a large worm from four to ten inches long, that lives in the intestines. It looks like the common earth-worm, yellowish white, and tapered at both ends. Second, the *ascaris*, commonly called needle or thread worm, of a dirty white color, usually from one to two inches long. They are sometimes found in thousands. They have been observed chiefly inhabiting the mucous coat of the cæcum, on the surface of which, it is supposed, they are developed in little cells, which, when matured, burst, producing considerable irritation, and often serious inflammation of the parts. They are also sometimes found to infest the rectum in large numbers, and to relieve the irritation they produce, the horse rubs his tail.

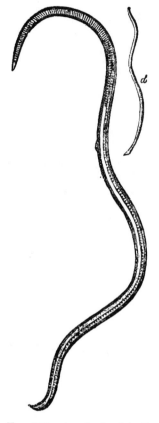

FIG. 829.—**Ascaris Lumbricoides.**

A. female ; D. male (natural size).

Varieties of *strongyli* and *oxyures* also occur, and are sometimes mistaken for *ascarides*. They are, however, distinct species ; the former is tapered, and terminates in a spine ; whereas the latter is blunted, with a head like a leather sucker. The *strongyli* inhabit the cæcum, colon, and duodenum ; the *oxyures*, the mesentery, spermatic cord, and in fact almost every organ in the body. The common whip-worm, or long thread-worm, technically called the *trichocephalus dispar*, are found in the cæcum. They resemble a whip, the shank being about a third, and the thong two thirds of the length, usually about two inches. *Bots*, which inhabit the stomach, will be referred to especially following this article.

There is also a small thread-like worm, called *filaria*, from a half inch to an inch and a half long, which travels all through the system. This is the worm that sometimes gets into the eye and grows there. The *tape-worm* is sometimes found in the horse, for which I give a specific remedy used by Dr. Meyer with great success. (I give illustrations of a few worms, though not of all that I desired, on account of the difficulty of obtaining them. They will not, however, be of any special interest or importance to the general reader.

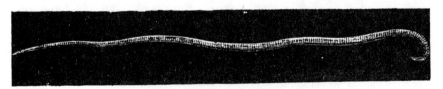

FIG. 830.—**Ascaris Marginata, Enlarged.**

Hence those obtained are put in without regard to much technical explanation.)

Symptoms of worms are debility, feebleness, sluggish movements, emaciation, staring coat, hide bound, skin covered with blotches, irregular and capricious appetite, tucked up belly, pallid appearance of the lining membrane of the lip, badly digested feces ; rubs the tail, and when fundament worms exist, a whitish substance will be found about the fundament. Many horses have worms, and their presence is never suspected till they appear in the dung. Troublesome diarrhea is sometimes produced by the presence of ascarides in the cæcum, which are sometimes found in vast numbers in the rectum.

Treatment.—The horse should be put on bran mashes for a few days, then give him nothing but water for eight or ten hours, then give the following drench :—

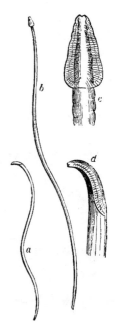

Fig. 831,—**Ascaris Mystax.**

a. Male; b. Female ; c. d. The expansion of its anterior part seen from the front and side.

Linseed-oil	1 qt.
Spirits of turpentine	2 oz.

In an hour after give a warm bran mash, and the next morning give a dose of physic. If thought necessary, in about a week this may be repeated.

Dr. Summerville claimed there was no better medicine for the destruction of worms than calomel, and advised it to be given in the following combinations : —

Calomel	3 dr.
Tartar emetic	1 dr.

Mix, and divide into three powders, one to be given at night for three successive nights, to be followed in twenty-four hours with a good purging ball. Or,—

Aloes	4 dr.
Tartar emetic	1 dr.
Ginger	2 dr.

Calomel about the size of a bean, and molasses enough to make into a ball. To be given every morning for three days.

Dr. Hamill found, in treating inflammation of the extremities caused by injuries, such as getting a nail in the foot, where excessive, that occasionally after giving a dose of aloes and calomel large numbers of worms were expelled. Would advise from two to four drachms calomel, with aloes according to size and temperament of the horse.

This is also corroborated by Dr. White, who advises to give one or two drachms of calomel with a dose of physic ; or the calomel at night, and a dose of physic in the morning. Or give a drachm of calomel for three successive nights previous to the physic.

The following for worms was given the writer by a veterinary surgeon of very high standing : —

Take hickory-wood, sumac-wood, and ordinary white ash, and burn to ashes. Feed a large spoonful twice a day for three days. Then follow up with a cathartic.

FIG. 832.—**Young Fila-**
ria Thread-worm.

A. young worm as rolled up in the body of the mother ; A. the same unrolled in a drop of water; a. Head, with the protuberances and mouth; b. Origin of the tail, with the anus (backside).

Prof. Gamgee's favorite remedy : —

Asafetida... ....2 dr.
Calomel and savin....................1½ dr. each.
Oil of male fern........... ....30 drops.

Mass sufficient to form a ball to be given at night, and a purge in the morning.

Dr. Sheldon, formerly of New York City, depended mainly upon santonine, by the use of which he claimed great success, and which he also claims never fails to clean the worms out of a horse. He treated as follows : —

First, give bran mash. In 24 hours give one drachm of santonine, which should be dissolved in water ; then mix in a quart of starch, and give as a drench ; in 30 minutes give aloes in solution sufficient to move the bowels promptly.

I also include a favorite horse-jockey remedy, which is regarded very good : —

Aloes......... ....1 oz.
Spirits of turpentine......................3 oz.
Eggs.......................................6.

Make into an emulsion, beaten together ; give to the horse after being fed with two or three bran mashes.

Dr. White says : —

A run at grass in the spring is perhaps the best ready of all, for it is the most effectual means of invigorating the digestive organs and purifying the blood. When it is not convenient to turn the horse out, he should be fed green grass in the stable.

The following was given the writer by a special friend (a veterinary surgeon of high standing), as the treatment he would advise for the cure of worms ; and though in part a repetition of what is given, it is so good that I include it : —

First, *lumbricoides* can be removed by drastic purges of aloes, or aloes and calomel. If calomel be given in from two to four drachm doses, on a fasting stomach of twelve hours, then fast from ten to twelve hours afterward, after which give small doses of aloes

or saline purges, it will destroy nearly all traces of worms or parasites in the stomach and intestines, even clearing out bots. The
best general treatment advised is santonine, areca nut, and male
fern. Of santonine, better known as worm-seed, the dose is from
one to four drachms, according to the size and temperament of the
horse. For the small, nervous, well-bred horse, the smallest dose
would be sufficient; while for a large, coarse-grained cart-horse the
larger dose of four drachms will be necessary. Of the same quantities of powdered areca nut and male fern, about one ounce is the
average dose. All vermifuge medicine should be taken while fasting, as better results will thereby be obtained; let the horse fast

FIG. 833.—Strongylus, Enlarged.

ten or twelve hours before giving the medicine, and nearly as long
afterward. It is not necessary to give physic after either of these
medicines. Nearly all the parasites in horses can be expelled by
the judicious use of calomel.

BOTS.

As among most owners and horse-doctors, every obscure lameness in the foot is supposed to be in the shoulder; so, when a horse
is taken sick, nine times out of ten it is supposed to be caused by
bots. If the horse turns up his upper lip, looks at his side, shows
uneasiness, paws, and rolls, it is taken as a sure sign of bots.

It is claimed that as a rule bots are harmless parasites, seldom
producing much mischief, and to be found in almost every horse that
dies, sometimes in great numbers, adhering to the coats of the
stomach; but about this there is much difference of opinion.

Prof. Law on the subject : —

Bots are the larvæ of the *gadfly*, which are noticed to be so common, pestering
the horse during the summer and autumn, darting at him around his legs and sides,
and depositing their eggs on the hair of the parts. These eggs are caught by the
horse when he licks the parts in defending himself, and swallowed. In the stomach
they develop rapidly. By the aid of the hooks around their heads they attach
themselves to the mucous membrane, mainly of the left half of the stomach (see Fig.

33   a

834), but often also to other parts, such as the right side of the stomach, the duodenum, or small gut leading from the stomach, and the throat. There they steadily grow in the winter, and in spring pass out in the dung, burrow in the soil, and are transformed into the gadfly. The disturbance they cause depends on their numbers and the portions of the canal on which they attach themselves. In the throat they produce a chronic sore throat and discharge from the nose, which continues until the following spring, unless they are previously extracted with the hand. In the left half of the stomach, which is covered with a thick, insensible cuticle, they do little harm when in small numbers; hence Bracy Clark supposed them to be beneficial in stimulating the secretion of gastric juice.

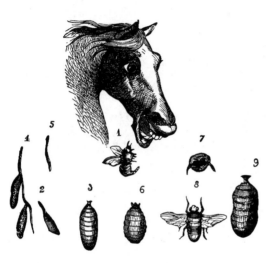

FIG. 834.—**The Gadfly Depositing Eggs, and Full-grown Bots.**

1. The female fly about to deposit an egg ; 2. the egg magnified ; 3. the bot ; 4. the eggs magnified, attached to a hair ; 5. the newly hatched bot ; 6. the bot full grown ; 7. the head of a bot magnified ; 8. the male fly; 9. the chrysalis.

When very numerous, and above all when attached to the highly sensitive right half of the stomach or the duodenum, they seriously interfere with digestion, causing the animal to thrive badly, to be weak, and easily sweated or fatigued, and even determining sudden and fatal indigestion. This last result is especially liable to occur in spring or early summer, when the bots are passing out in great numbers, and hooking themselves at intervals to the coats of the sensitive bowels in their course. They will sometimes accumulate in such numbers as actually to block the passage.

In discussing the subject, White says : —

They are generally attached to the cuticular or insensible coat of the stomach ; but sometimes clusters of them are found at the pylorus, and even in the beginning of the first intestine, named the duodenum. In one case they were so numerous in this last situation as to obstruct the passage completely, and cause the animal's death.

Feron, an old writer, says he has paid particular attention to this subject, and has found that when in large quantities, they are very destructive to horses ; that he has seen several horses whose stomachs had been pierced quite through by them, the bots making their way into the abdomen.

James Clark, of Edinburgh, an author of high standing, quoted in " Shoeing," relates a case of a horse's stomach being perforated by bots.

In " White's Farriery," vol. 2, page 73, Dr. White says : —

I have seen several horses destroyed by these worms. In some of them they caused inflammation of the lungs ; in one frenzy, or mad staggers; and in one horse, the pylorus was completely plugged up with them. There is a remarkable sympathy or consent between the stomach and lungs, and it is owing to this that they sometimes cause inflammation of the lungs. In the cases which have occurred in my practice, the most remarkable circumstance was the great depression they occasioned.

Symptoms.—There is no way, so far as I know, and I have consulted a great many veterinary surgeons on the subject, of determining the symptoms of bots. A horse is taken sick, showing all the symptoms of colic ; he is treated for that difficulty, is cured, and the trouble is presumed to have been colic. According to the best authorities I can find, the conclusion is that the symptoms of bots cannot be distinguished from other diseases of the stomach and bowels ; that sometimes, when occurring in dense clusters around the pylorus or in the first bowel, they interfere mechanically with digestion, and keep the animal weak and emaciated, and subject to slight attacks of colic, capricious appetite, and irregular bowels. Beyond these indications, which may be identified with other difficulties, there is no way of determining whether they are the cause of annoyance.

Treatment.—This is doubtful. I give that which has been advised as the most effectual. White says : —

Fig. 835.—**Eggs Greatly Magnified.** The most likely means of expelling bots is to keep the horse without food during the night, and give him in the morning a quart of new milk sweetened with honey ; and about ten minutes after, give four, five, or six ounces of salt in a quart of water.

Dr. Feron remarks that—

Common oil given in large quantities has sometimes succeeded in detaching bots from the stomach. It is the only medicine that seems to have any effect in making them loosen their hold on that organ.

Blaine says that the continued use of salt mixed with the food appears to be obnoxious to them ; for sometimes under its use their hold gives way, and they are ejected.

The popular remedy for bots is sweet milk and molasses, which is more safe than reliable. The following is recommended : —

3 drachms each of aloes and asafetida, rubbed down in hot water, and when

cool add an ounce each of turpentine and ether. To be given every second day for a week, leaving out aloes if bowels become too open.

To relieve pain and uneasiness, any of the colic mixtures are to be given.

Prof. Law advises giving potato juice to feed and quiet the bots, adding some colic medicine if thought necessary.

In a report by Dr. Adams in relation to the subject, published about fifteen years ago in the " Medical and Agricultural Register," he stated, having made the following experiments at different times on bots *three-fourths grown*, that—

When immersed in rum, they live 25 hours ; decoction of tobacco, 11 hours ; strong oil of vitriol, 2 hours, 18 minutes ; essential oil of mint, 2 hours, 5 minutes. Were immersed without apparent injury in spirits of camphor, 10 hours ; fish oil, 49 hours ; tinct. aloes, 10 hours ; brine, 10 hours ; solution indigo, 10 hours. A number of small bots, with one that was full grown, were immersed in a strong solution of corrosive sublimate ; the small ones died in one hour, but the full-grown one was taken out of the solution, six hours after its immersion, apparently unhurt.

INFLAMMATION OF THE KIDNEYS.

Inflammation of the kidneys is generally caused by hard work, by slipping, throwing the hind parts so suddenly under the belly as to produce undue tension of the lumbar vertebræ, or from sudden colds by being exposed to rain and cold, the eating of musty hay or oats, or unhealthful food of any kind. Too powerful or too often repeated diuretics produce inflammation of the kidneys, or a degree of irritation and weakness of them that disposes to inflammation, from causes that would otherwise have no injurious effect.

Symptoms.—Less or more fever of the system generally, and unwillingness to move, particularly the hind legs, dung hard and coated, very sensitive to pressure on the spine. The horse looks anxiously around at his flanks, stands with his hind legs wide apart, and straddles as he walks, shows pain in turning ; the urine is voided in small quantities, and is usually high colored, and sometimes bloody ; the attempt to urinate becomes more frequent, and the quantity voided smaller, until the animal strains violently, without being able to pass any or but very little urine. The pulse is quick and hard, full in the early stage of the disease, but rapidly becoming small, though not losing its character of hardness. Introduce the hand into the rectum. If the bladder is found full and hard under the rectum, there is inflammation of the neck of the bladder. If the bladder is empty, yet on the portion of the intestines immediately over it there is more than natural heat and tenderness, there is inflammation of the body of the bladder. If the bladder is empty and there is no increased tenderness and heat, there is inflammation of the kidneys.

Treatment.—If the pulse is high, about sixty, take five or six quarts of blood, and give a fever ball; to be repeated in three hours if not better. Fever ball: 4 drachms Barbadoes aloes, 1 drachm tarter emetic, 2 drachms ginger, calomel about the size of a bean, molasses sufficient to make into a ball. Counter-irritation must

next be excited over the seat of the disease. The loins should be fomented with hot water or covered with mustard poultice, or, better, heat a peck of salt in an oven, place it in a bag, and put it over the part affected. If the case is severe and protracted, a sharp blister may be used. *No diuretics are to be given, as they would simply aggravate*, and make the disease worse. After the bowels are open, give aconite, and treat as for fever. After recovery, the horse should be kept very quiet for a month, and if in season,

Fig. 836.—A Prominent Symptom when the Urinary Organs are Involved.

turned out to grass. If in winter, feed with light, mushy diet; exercise lightly by leading, if the animal be valuable and it is desired to aid recovery by extra care.

PROFUSE STALING (DIURESIS).

Profuse staling, sometimes called diabetes, consists principally of simple, increased secretion of urine, without any apparent structural disease of the kidney, or much alteration of the composition of the urine, so characteristic of this affection in man.

Causes.—It arises in a great measure from feeding musty or heated hay, exposure to cold, etc. Frequently it occurs as an accompaniment of acidity of the stomach, or from the improper use of diuretics, as niter, saltpeter, resin, etc., which are frequently given in large quantities for some time by grooms and ignorant persons, not knowing the harm they are doing thereby. It is of these ingredients also that most of the "condition powders" kept for sale, which are often liberally fed, are composed. It is not prudent, or at all necessary, to give such medicine, excepting for specific purposes, and then very cautiously.　Intelligent owners give but very little medicine.　Instead, they give bran mashes, etc., with good air, regular exercise, and grooming.

Symptoms.—The intense thirst first attracts attention ; he is constantly craving for water, and rapidly loses condition ; the coat becomes rough and staring ; he passes large quantities of clear urine, his litter being constantly wet.　He will be seen poking among his litter, which he often eats with avidity in preference to good hay. If it goes on unchecked, great prostration sets in, the heart beats tumultuously, the throbbing being often visible at the side, the pulse being irregular and intermittent.

Treatment.—It is generally very easily checked if taken in time ; a complete change of diet is indispensable ; give good sweet hay ; carrots are recommended.　The bowels must be freely opened. Iodine in doses of two drachms, once or twice a day, is claimed to be a never-failing remedy, very useful in correcting the thirst and checking the flow of urine.

The following ball may be given night and morning :—

Iodine ....1 dr.
Iodide of potassium ....1 dr.
Barbadoes aloes...1 dr.

Licorice and syrup sufficient to make a ball.
Or, give one of the following balls every night :—

Powdered opium.......................................½ oz.
Powdered kino ....1 oz.
Prepared chalk ....1 oz.

Mix with molasses, and make six balls.

Tonics should be commenced early.　In some cases it can be arrested by making him drink water with pipe-clay or pease-meal shaken up in it.　A run at pasture will often cure it.

INFLAMMATION OF THE BLADDER (CYSTITIS).

Causes.—It may arise from the too free use of diuretic medicines, or from the injudicious use of fly blisters of turpentine ; sometimes from the presence of concretions or gravelly deposits in the bladder, or an extension of spasm, or inflammation of other organs.

Symptoms.—Almost the same as those of inflammation of the kidneys.　Frequent voiding of urine in small quantities, quick pulse ; looks frequently at flanks, paws violently, tender when pressed upon under the flanks.

When the body of the viscus is the seat of the disease, it becomes very irritable, the urine being passed almost as soon as it reaches the bladder, the act of staling being almost constantly going on.

The other symptoms are nearly analogous to nephritis; when examined by the hand in the rectum, it is found empty, hot, and tender. When the neck of the bladder is the seat of the disease, it will be found distended with urine, and, instead of frequent staling, we have almost complete suppression of urine.

Treatment.—The treatment resembles that recommended for nephritis, which see. Should the contraction of the neck continue, a gum elastic catheter should be introduced, or a little warm oil may (in the mare) be injected into the bladder. Small doses of bicarbonate of soda or potash should be given to neutralize the urine, which is usually acid.

Here the principal object is to lower inflammation and relax the muscular contraction of the neck of the bladder. Bleed largely, almost to fainting; give physic as for inflammation of the kidneys, or a quart of linseed-oil. A drachm of powdered opium, made into a ball, or given in drink every two or three hours, and blister over the loins. Give aconite, as for inflammation of the kidneys.*

RETENTION OF URINE.

The most common cause is keeping the animal active, not giving time to urinate, and a spasm of the neck of the bladder or gravelly concretions; any cause of irritation may cause spasm. Symptoms are the same as in inflammation of the kidneys, except standing very wide behind, and when walking, a straddling gait resembling a cow with a very full bag.

The most prompt treatment is to use the catheter, and scarcely anything more is necessary. But if one is not obtainable, bleed freely, and give a strong opiate: 3 oz. tinct. opium, in half a pint of water.

BLOODY URINE

is generally the result of injuries of the loins, unwholesome food, violent exercise, etc.

Treatment.—Give plenty of linseed tea to drink; if the animal refuses it, drench him. Give internally, once a day, one of the following pills: sugar of lead, 1 oz.; linseed tea, 2 oz. Mix with molasses and divide into eight parts.

---

* If possible, call a veterinary surgeon, who will introduce a catheter, which will relieve the animal immediately.

DISEASES OF THE NERVOUS SYSTEM.

The nervous system consists of the brain, which is lodged in the cavity of the skull (cranium) ; the spinal cord, lodged in the cavity of the vertebral chain ; and numerous little white cords, called nerves, which are given out from the brain and spinal cord, and distributed to the different parts of the body, especially those parts endowed with sensibility, and under the control of the will. Besides this system of nerves, there is another set, independent of the cerebro-spinal axis, called the sympathetic or ganglionic system, which supplies the organs of nutrition and other viscera, blood-vessels, etc. It consists of numerous small centers, called ganglia, extending in two great chains from the head to the tail, on each side of the bodies of the vertebræ, closely associated with the other system by intricate communication.

Inflammation of the Brain (Phrenitis).

Phrenitis is not a very common disease, though the substance of the brain itself, or, as is more commonly the case, its membranes, or coverings, become inflamed. It has received various appellations, such as *mad staggers*, *sleepy staggers*, etc.

Fig. 837.—**Symptom of Inflammation of the Brain.**

Causes.—The causes are not thoroughly understood. Injuries to the skull, *metastasis*, or the transference of inflammation from some of the other organs, high condition and overwork, undue exposure to a hot sun, all seem to be favorable to its production. Horses that are too highly fed are subject to this, while moderately fed horses are scarcely ever inclined to it.

Symptoms.—It is usually ushered in by dullness and persistent drowsiness ; he stands with his head between his legs, or sometimes resting against the manger or leaning against the wall ; the eyes shut, and the pupils dilated ; the pulse is full, soft, and slow ; the breathing is heavy and loud ; he is very difficult to arouse, and when startled, he looks dreamily about ; may take a few bites of hay, but soon drops asleep again ; the bowels are costive, and the urine scanty and high colored.

In a day or two the symptoms are mitigated, or it goes on to the second stage, when the pulse becomes quick, general excitement takes the place of lethargic stupor ; the countenance is wild and excited looking ; the eyes are blood-shot and staring ; delirium sets in ; he dashes himself furiously about, reels and staggers, often throws himself violently down ; lies trembling, blowing, and convulsed ; his blood-shot eyes like to start out of their sockets ; he will soon get up, rear and plunge forward, breaking everything around him, evidently unconscious of the injuries he is sustaining ; and, what is characteristic of the complaint, his destruction is carried on evidently without purpose, as is evinced in rabies, or madness. The convulsions become more frequent and continuous, and death ends his misery in from twenty to twenty-four hours.

Treatment.—Copious blood-letting must be at once resorted to ; no time should be lost in giving a strong dose of purgative medicine. One or both jugulars may be opened, or where, from the restlessness of the patient or danger in working about him, this is impracticable, the lancet should be plunged into the temporal artery, which will be found about three inches below the ear, between it and the nostril.

The following drench should be given :—

Barbadoes aloes ....6 dr.
Carbonate of soda........................ ....½ oz.
Croton beans, powdered 15

Three drachms of aloes may be given every three hours, with copious injections every hour, till the bowels are freely opened. Sedatives should also be used, such as extract of hyoscyamus and calomel, a drachm of each shaken up in a little thin gruel, given every two hours. Seldom is repetition of blood-letting advisable ; cold water should be constantly applied to the head ; a small hose made to play upon it in a constant stream, where it is convenient, will be found very useful.

The favorite prescription of a very successful practitioner is: " Give on the tongue every six hours about one drachm of the extract of conium." He gave this after the horse had fallen.

Dr. Summerville's explanation and treatment of this difficulty are so plain and good, that I include them : —

Is first noticeable by dullness or sleepiness of the eyes, an unwillingness to move, general heaviness of the system. This disease is frequently called *megrims, fits,* and *mad staggers ;* but in part only one disease, according to the extent of such disease as the animal may be affected with.

The cause of staggers is an undue flow of blood to the brain, which rarely or never occurs in any animals except those in a plethoric (fat) condition.

Some writers and practitioners assert that there is a disease known as stomach staggers. I have never seen a case where it was necessary to treat the stomach, but always direct attention to the brain, as being the seat of the disease, which may be properly called *head staggers.*

In case of megrims, or fits, it is merely a lesser attack, or pressure of the blood-vessels on the brain, and *mad staggers* is a greater pressure of the same vessels on the same part. The brain is divided into two parts, namely, cerebrum and cerebellum, which occupy a horny box in the head. The blood-vessels passing over the brain and coming in contact with the skull, become distended by an increased quantity of blood, and produce the feeling which is thus exhibited.

There is but one cure for this disease, and that is, remove the cause. Bleed largely from the neck—ten, twelve, or fourteen quarts, or until the symptoms of fainting. After the horse is convalescent, a sharp dose of physic should be given to regulate the bowels. I would advise owners of such horses to dispose of them. Once taken with the disease, they are subject to a repetition of the attack when the blood-vessels become filled again.

Note.—Small doses of aconite (of the quantity for fever) may be given three or four times a day as a good preventive. Turning to pasture horses that may be liable to this disease will prove both injurious and dangerous.

When driven in the hot sun, the head should be protected with some sort of covering, which is now used very generally in many large cities, or a large sponge, kept wet with water, may be tied on the back of the head.

MEGRIMS, OR VERTIGO.

The form of nervous complication known as megrims is not uncommon. Its nature is but imperfectly determined.

Causes.—It is often connected with worms or other derangements of the stomach or bowels, said also to depend on over-accumulation of blood in the head. The late Professor John Barlow found tumors in the choroid plexus of the brain. In these cases, it is often connected with over-feeding, and its consequence is derangement of the digestive organs.

It is most commonly seen in harness horses, usually during hot weather, occurs generally on a heavy pull going up hill, probably from pressure of the collar interrupting the return of blood from the head ; or "the long-continued constraint the bearing-reins put the head to," may prove the exciting causes in animals predisposed to it.

Symptoms.—All at once, when going along the road, he is observed to jerk up his head in a convulsive manner ; he seems giddy, reels, staggers, may fall down and lie for a few moments insensible ; he gets up, looks stupidly about, shakes himself, and proceeds as if nothing had happened.

At other times he merely stops, experiences a few convulsive movements of the head, with slight giddiness, which by letting him stand for a few minutes soon passes off. He is ever after subject to these fits, especially during the hot summer months.

Treatment.—When depending on organic changes in the brain, it is incurable, and is subject to these attacks from time to time. When a fit comes on on the road, stop him at once, throw the collar forward off his shoulders and let him stand ; if convenient, pour a stream of cold water over his head. Bleeding in the mouth has been recommended, but is quite empirical ; it soon passes off. When occurring in a young horse for the first time, he should be well physicked out, and if worms are suspected, treat as recommended for worms. Tonics are often beneficial, especially arsenic given in doses of from three to five grains daily. Megrim subjects are dangerous hacks, and should only be used where they can do no harm to life or property.

Sun Stroke.

This is liable to occur during the hot summer months, particularly in large cities. It is usually caused by overwork or hard driving in the sun. Horses that are fat and young, and old, feeble horses are most subject to it. Wearing a sun-shade or a large sponge saturated with water on the top of the head, giving cool water occasionally, and sponging out the nostrils, and wetting the head, with of course moderate work or driving, are the best preventives. A very good plan, when driving through the country, where accessible, is to tie a few branches well covered with leaves so as to come over the head. They also serve to keep the flies away.

For light driving, a breast-strap is better than a collar, because it permits more freedom of the circulation.

Symptoms.—In severe cases the horse will suddenly stop, pant violently, possibly drop to the ground and die in a short time.

When the attack is mild, he will flag in his gait, be unsteady in his limbs, spread his legs in standing, and totter. The head is held low, the eyes protrude, the nostrils are dilated, the pupils of the eyes smaller than natural, and the breathing rapid. Pulse is quick and weak, the heart beating violently and irregularly. Relief must be prompt.

Treatment.—Unharness, and throw pails of cold water over the whole body, especially on the back of the head, neck, and spine. Next, rub the skin energetically with rough cloths or bagging, or anything convenient. Then repeat the douching. The best of all medicine, it is claimed, is quinine. The quickest way to get its effect would be to inject from 25 to 50 or 60 grains under the skin with a hypodermic syringe. This is the remedy used in the East Indies, and is claimed to be the very best in giving relief.

As a prompt diffusable stimulant during the severe depression, the following may be given : —

Sulphuric ether.. ....2 oz.
Water...1 pint.

Given as a drench.   Or, 15 to 25 drops tincture of aconite, in a pint of ale.

After the attack has passed off, the horse should be turned out where he will be well protected from the glare of the sun by trees, etc., and allowed to rest for a few weeks ; and if it can be avoided, he should not be driven afterward in the hot sun.

Azoturia, Partial Paralysis, Spinal Meningitis, etc.

Under these and other names we will notice a disease which is at times very common in this country, and very alarming in its aspect, from the suddenness of its attack and severity of its symptoms, producing almost complete loss of power of the hind quarters.

Causes.—It usually occurs in horses which are being "fed up," or which have been accustomed to hard work, and are allowed to remain in the stable for a few days, having a liberal allowance of good feed ; the system becomes plethoric, more blood being formed than the system can dispose of, whereby the vascular organs are overloaded, and consequently, under increased action caused by exertion, they are apt to become congested.

Symptoms.—The animal is apparently in excellent health and spirits.   He starts off lively ; but before he has gone far, he suddenly stops, crouches, seems very much distressed.   The sweat rolls off him in streams ; he blows and heaves at the flanks ; he cannot move for a few minutes.   He drops on his hind quarters ; can hardly drag them after him.   When made to move, he drops as if his leg was dislocated or broken.   The pulse is very high, from sixty to eighty, and the muscles of the quarter are swollen and hard.   In some cases he gets down, and cannot get up again ; but seldom is loss of power at first complete, or sensibility entirely lost.   The urine is generally very high colored ; we have seen it black or coffee colored, which is a sure proof of the trouble, and always voided with difficulty.

Treatment.—When seen in the early stages, abstract six quarts of blood,* remove the urine with a catheter, and give from 7 to 8 drachms of aloes.   Persistently apply hot-water cloths to the loins,

---

* There is some difference of opinion as to the propriety of bleeding. Some of the best practitioners do not now bleed for this difficulty, and while I should regard it good treatment, it may be omitted, as physicking, with other treatment, will usually give sufficient relief; but if the case is very hearty, short-necked, and full blooded, bleeding would seem to be advisable.

and cover them up well with dry blankets, changed every half hour. Give 20 drops of tincture of aconite in a little cold water every two hours, till the fever subsides. If the pain is very severe and twitching, give the following drench :—

Sweet spirits of niter...2 oz.
Tincture of opium .... 2 oz.
Cold water ....1 qt.

Mix.

Injections of soap and water should be given, and the legs well rubbed and bandaged. It is important also that he be turned gently, about every three hours, and that his bedding be made as comfortable as possible. According to modern practitioners, who have had decided success in the treatment of this disease, it is not at all necessary to put in slings. In fact, the better recoveries are made without putting in slings ; neither should he be urged to get up too soon ; will usually do so of his own accord when able, but may be helped a little.

In most cases it will yield to this treatment, and in three or four days he will be convalescent. However, in many the loss of power increases ;. he makes frequent efforts to get up, but cannot support himself behind. In these cases the spine should be freely blistered with mustard and turpentine, or with the strong ammoniacal liniment. Good nursing and care are everything ; in fact, indispensable. Give restricted diet, carrots, bran mashes, etc. When all fever and acute symptoms have subsided, and recovery of power is tardy, give the following ball night and morning :—

1 drachm nux vomica in powder, made into a ball, with linseed-meal and extract of gentian. Or, 2 grains strychnine, made into a ball in the same way.

The nux vomica or strychnine, whichever is used, should be gradually increased, until to the maximum of what the system will bear without serious disturbance, when it should be stopped, or the dose diminished. He should be well bedded up with straw, and as before stated, turned as often as once in every three to four hours. It often runs its course in from thirty-six to forty-eight hours, usually, however, in from three to six days. It is more fatal in stallions and geldings than in mares. If a veterinary surgeon is available, he should be called in promptly when this disease appears.

In a conversation with Dr. McBeth of this city (Battle Creek), on the foregoing disease, he informed the writer that he had treated a great many cases during his practice, with success ; that a short time before, directly after a severe storm, which was the cause of keeping the animals idle while kept on their usual amount of food, he had six cases, as a consequence, in one week, all of which made good recovery. One case had been down forty-eight hours, another some eighteen hours, and a third about twelve hours before he was called. This success induced me to make the request that he would give me, in the fewest words, the outline of his understanding of the disease, with his treatment, which I give here as dictated by him :—

This disease is generally common to horses that are worked hard, then stand still with regular feed. When put to work, or when driven, perhaps not going more than a quarter to half a mile, begin to sweat profusely, and in a few minutes afterward show great weakness in the back, acting as if having lost power to move the hind legs; in fact, appearing stiff all over. If not helped quickly, the horse is liable to fall down.

The cause of the disease is the horse making more blood, while idle, than the system can appropriate. When put to work, the muscles in the lumbar region become congested, and the consequence is the horse loses power to raise or control his hind parts. If treated properly, will usually regain his strength in from twenty-four to thirty-six hours.

Treatment.—First give a sharp cathartic, also apply counter-irritants over the region of the kidneys, using sheep-skin or counter-irritants; also use the catheter. Give small doses of spirits of niter, with 10 to 15 drops aconite added, from four to six hours apart. When fever subsides, give nervine tonics with strychnine in one half grain doses, or powdered nux vomica in one half drachm doses, in from two to four hours apart. If not very serious, about four hours apart.

If the horse is not able to rise, must not let him lie on one side longer than three hours at a time. These cases are nervous and must not be excited. They must be handled very gently and walked around very carefully.

After this article was written I received a *U. S. Veterinary Journal* for December, 1883, published in Chicago, Ill., in which I find an excellent essay on this subject read by W. L. Williams, V. S., before the Illinois State Veterinary Association, and as an additional aid to successful treatment, I copy that advised by him :—

The great essential in treatment is careful nursing, without which success is rarely possible in severe cases. As soon as the first symptoms appear, keep the animal as quiet as possible. If able to stand comfortably, have him stand as still as possible ; if recumbent, procure him a good bed of straw at once, and by as quiet means as possible try to prevent any effort at getting up. This can usually be done readily by having a steady man hold the head, or he can be assisted by another man keeping the lower fore leg flexed against the chest by means of a strap upon the foot. Should the animal be standing, but growing more and more liable to fall, lose no time in getting him into the most comfortable place at hand. When already down, unless the weather be inclement or the location unfavorable, do not attempt to move him for two or three hours, when he should be removed to a well-bedded, comfortable loose box or shed. He can with little difficulty be rolled on a low sled or a farm gate, when a good span of horses will readily drag him to the stall door, and five or six men will soon place him where desired. Pass the catheter early, and keep it up twice or thrice daily so long as the animal remains recumbent. Remove the shoes from the fore feet to prevent bruising of the chest and elbows while lying ; apply hot cloths or slightly stimulating liniment to the loins and quarters. Keep the bowels open by moderate cathartics and enemas, and thus assist the kidneys in execrating the effete materials from the blood. The kidneys usually act freely enough, but should they not do so, diuretics should not be given during the early stages, as they would most likely increase the already excessive congestion. Allow plenty of fresh water and good, nutritious, easily digested food, if the animal will eat.

After the second or third day, should there be great debility, vegetable tonics with alcoholic stimulants should be given in moderation. The animal should be turned from side to side three or four times daily, but on no account urged to get up, nor should slings ever be used, as they only aggravate the case and retard the recovery. When the animal is fit to be up, he will get up alone without urging.

Should some degree of paralysis remain after two or three weeks, nux vomica conjoined with diuretics are to be used. In mild cases, a gentle cathartic, with a day or two of rest, is sufficient. The progress is favorable, most cases making a rapid and complete recovery. In the more severe cases, if the animal becomes quiet after 12 to 30 hours, with regular, not much quickened pulse, the appetite returns, and the animal lies a large part of the time upon his chest ; recovery may be looked for, although the animal may be unable to rise for five or six days.

When the animal continues restless and weak, will not lie upon his chest except when held, refuses food almost entirely, the pulse becomes weaker and quicker, with considerable elevation of temperature, the case is to be considered a very grave one.

PARALYSIS.

The horse is taken suddenly, falls down, and is unable to rise. Sensation almost completely lost in posterior extremities. No increase in the pulsation ; temperature will be found at 102° to 103°. The usual remedy is to give a sharp cathartic (see "Physicking"), and have the animal placed in slings. Next apply stimulating embrocations to the spine, and give one of the following balls every eight hours :—

Alcoholic extract belladonna.....1 oz.
Bromide potass................4 oz.

Liquorice root sufficient to make into six balls for the first stage.

This treatment should be persisted in for the first four days, thoroughly bathing the animal's hind quarters with mustard water, and keeping up the stimulants to the spine until sore. The application of a fresh sheep-skin or a hot salt bath to the loins would be still better.

Fig. 838.—**Short-necked Horses Most Subject to this Trouble.**

There is another difficulty which resembles spinal paralysis, namely Azotaria (treatment for which is given under that head). As in the first case, the animal drops, and loses all power to get up. In spinal paralysis there is a loss of sensation, and a constant dribbling of urine, and involuntary fecal passage.   Temperature 102° to 103°.   No perceptible change of color in urine.   In Azotaria the animal has suddenly partial loss of sensation, the urine and feces not voided.   No perceptible rise in temperature.   The urine, if withdrawn from the patient, will be of a coffee-brown color.   The animal is uneasy, struggling and sweating over the flanks, and in great pain.

This difficulty is usually found in short-necked horses that are fed too much grain.   Scarcely ever find horses in moderate condition subject to it.—*Dr. Meyer.*

TETANUS, OR LOCK-JAW.

This disease is wholly of a nervous character, being a peculiar irritability of the nervous system, inducing constant spasmodic contraction of the voluntary, and after a time the involuntary, muscles, and is very fatal unless treated skillfully and carefully. It is more common in the extreme South than in the North; and is more liable to occur during the warm months.

FIG. 839.—**Symptoms of Lock-jaw.**

Symptoms.—In the first stage there is a disinclination to move; then the tail becomes erect and quivers, the ears set back, and the conjunctiva is thrown over the pupil of the eye, and the head is elevated, with the muzzle and facial muscles contracted, the nostrils open, and the whole expression of the countenance haggard and excited, evincing great suffering. (A good idea is given by Fig. 839.)

As the disease advances, the muscles all over the neck and body become stiff and rigid, and the legs have the appearance of a four-footed stool. The animal has little or no power to move.

For the first few days the teeth remain apart, but as the disease advances, the muscles of the jaw become so contracted as to bring them close together. Hence the name "locked-jaw."

The bowels are constipated, the urine scanty, and passed with difficulty. The pulse is usually not very high, but is easily raised by excitement; he is very nervous, starts and quivers when any one approaches him. His appetite remains good, and from inability to feed, his hunger amounts to starvation ; he will make every effort to suck up gruel or fluids, when, from the fixity of the jaws, he is unable to masticate. The breathing, at first not much altered, becomes difficult and loud. The symptoms generally reach their climax about the third or fourth day.

The causes of this disease are numerous. It commonly occurs in consequence of wounds, when it is called *traumatic* tetanus ; in which case it is not developed until about the period the wound is considered healed ; it may occur from causes not apparent, when it is distinguished as *idiopathic* tetanus ; but it is generally produced from a wounded nerve or bunch of nerves, pricking the tail, and

very often from docking, punctured wounds in the feet from glass or nails, and sometimes from exposure to cold. Summerville says, "I have known one case to occur from fright." Worms and other intestinal irritation sometimes give rise to it. The pulse is almost normal for the first few days. As the disease advances, the pulse quickens, and the animal is compelled to stand on his legs un-

FIG. 840.—A Test for Lock-jaw.

til death, if it terminates fatally. If favorably, a relaxation of the muscles begins from the fifth to the seventh day.

Treatment.—First, as the disease is of a nervous character, quietness is of the greatest importance. The animal should be removed to an isolated place, or cool, dark, roomy loose box, by himself, and the cause of the disease found. If from docking, the next joint should be taken off the tail. If from a wound in the foot, the wound should be opened up and made new, and an application of digestive ointment inserted, so as to produce a healthy flow of matter. Or, as soon as opened up, diligently foment with warm water, after which cover with belladonna, and apply poultices of linseed meal and opium or hyoscyamus to soothe and allay the irritation, and give promptly at the same time a strong purgative, such as—

Aloes (Barbadoes) . . . . .7 dr.
Calomel . . . . .2 dr.
Given in solution or ball, as most convenient.

Injections of alkaline solution of aloes should also be given, as it is of the greatest importance to get the bowels open early. Bella-

34   a

donna in half-drachm doses should be given four or five times a day. If it cannot be given otherwise, place it up in the cheek, when he will suck it up.

He must be kept perfectly quiet, and the box cool and dark, no one being allowed to go near him but the attendants, and they must go about him noiselessly. A newly flayed sheep-skin should be laid over the loins, and well covered up to excite perspiration. Very high authorities claim that blisters and other irritating treatment must be avoided. He must be treated as in a nervous fever, while average good authorities advise having the spine rubbed well with a strong liniment, such as one part aqua ammonia, two parts sweet-oil ; to be repeated daily until the back becomes sore. He should be allowed all the nutriment he will take ; and when he cannot eat, sloppy drinks of linseed tea, barley water, well-boiled oatmeal gruel, etc., should be frequently placed within his reach.

It may run its course in four or five days, or it may continue for one or two weeks. It very often proves fatal.

Dr. Mc Beth, of this city, who has had excellent success in the management of this disease, informs the writer that he has recently had two very severe cases, both *idiopathic.* The worst, owned by W. M. Merritt, of this city, had run four days, with jaws entirely fixed, before being called. His treatment is, first sharp cathartic, aloes, with enemas to encourage action of the bowels, with half-drachm doses of belladonna, in some cases even more ; in this case, being a very desperate one, he gave drachm doses of solid extract, every three to four hours, with counter irritation over the spine, and generous nourishment as described.

He of course found great difficulty in giving the medicine, being compelled to push the aloes up into the mouth with a piece of stick, until a sufficient amount was taken up to produce a free action of the bowels.

STRINGHALT.

This is a peculiar jerking or pulling up of the hind legs when walking or trotting, familiar to every one. It is most severe during cold weather when the horse is led out of the stable, also after a hard drive, and is much better when driven and warmed up. Many horses that have but a slight touch of it may move off showing so little evidence of it as to escape notice. If suspected, back the horse up hill, especially after standing awhile, or when cool, and he will show it most clearly.

It is claimed that colts suffering from worms, and horses suffering from derangement of the digestive organs, will show some temporary jerking of one or both hind legs, from which they recover under good keeping and mineral tonics. The writer has never known a case of stringhalt to be cured. There are a great many theories and pretended cures, but I know of none worthy of mention.

THUMPS, OR SPASMODIC ACTION OF THE DIAPHRAGM, commonly called thumps, is caused by severe and long-contin-

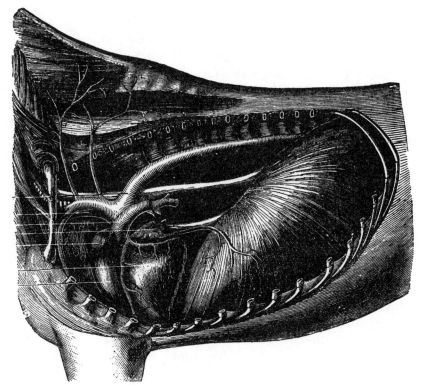

FIG. 841.—The Circulatory Apparatus Indicating the Position of Heart, Arteries, and Diaphragm.

ued driving and hard work. Horses of a nervous temperament having too much cold water given to drink on a cold morning, nervous irritation, severe work or excitement from any cause, may excite this trouble.

Symptoms.—A sudden jerking or twitching of the muscles of the sides and flanks; pulse wiry, quick, and low; more or less fever; extremities natural.

Treatment.—This disease being of a purely spasmodic character, but in this case wholly of a nervous nature, bleeding must be omitted, and must be treated wholly by giving spasmodic remedies. Give asafetida, in a dose of from 1 to 3 ounces of the tincture, mixed in a half pint of water. Given as a drench, it will stop it almost instantly.

If necessary, the medicine may be repeated in two hours. Keep the horse well clothed, and all exciting causes away from him. The bowels should be kept loose and regular, by giving bran mashes and moderate exercise.

LYMPHANGITIS—WEED—MONDAY MORNING LEG.

This disease is attributed to high feeding and insufficient exercise, generally in working-horses. Those having worked steadily are kept standing in the stable for a few days, given all they can eat, when on a morning the animal will be found lame. This usually occurs in dray horses. The owner comes in late Saturday night, and feeds ; on Sunday he gives an extra allowance, enough to last all day ; the horse eats all. Perhaps the owner does not come again until the following day, when he finds his horse is unable to back out of the stall. For this reason the disease is called by some Monday morning leg. It usually affects one of the hind legs, and is an inflammation of the lymphatics. The left leg is usually affected.

The leg is swollen, is favored and held from the ground ; the swelling extends on the inner side from the foot up to the body. There is heat, and great tenderness to the touch. Horses that have once been attacked by lymphangitis are liable to a recurrence time after time, until the limb assumes permanently an enlarged condition.

Treatment.—Clothe the animal warmly and give a moderate purge, and bathe the affected limb with very hot salt water 3 or 4 times a day. After each bathing, apply the following lotion :—

    Tincture of arnica...2 oz.
    Water ....1 pt.

Feed no oats or stimulating food, simply bran mashes, to which add plenty of salt ; after the third or fourth day feed one of the following powders morning and night :—

    Iodine of potass ....2 oz.
    Bicarbonate of potass ....1½ oz.
    Powdered gentian root ....3 oz.

Mix and make into 10 powders.

In 8 to 10 days, when the symptoms have disappeared, if any

swelling remains, there being no pain, apply for a few times an ointment.

Mercurial ointment ....2 oz.
Iodine ointment ....1½ oz.
Vaseline ....4 oz.

Make into a salve.

THE PERITONEUM.

The peritoneum is the thin serous membrane which lines the cavity of the belly, and is reflected over the organs contained within it, forming a complete covering to them. It also suspends and retains them in their proper relative positions by its folds and reflections, vulgarly known as the caul (omenta). This membrane also secretes a delicate serous fluid for the purpose of lubricating the surface, so as to prevent friction during the ceaseless motions of the viscera. It is also the matrix over which the blood-vessels are distributed to the organs contained in the belly ; hence the inflammation of these organs is apt to extend along this vascular-investing membrane, constituting peritonitis.

PERITONITIS.

Peritonitis occurs in two forms, acute and chronic. Acute peritonitis, as a primary disease, is not very common in the horse.

Causes.—It is usually caused by external violence, as from being hooked by a cow's horn, or staked in jumping a fence ; it also sometimes follows castration, operations for hernia, and other operations involving a division of it, and occasionally from exposure to damp and cold, especially when heated.

Symptoms.—It usually sets in with shivering fits, general uneasiness in the region of the abdomen ; quick, short breathing ; pulse quick, small, and wiry ; tenderness on pressure on belly ; lying down and rising frequently ; he moves about uneasily in his box, and is very feverish ; the bowels are costive, and he strains occasionally. The pain is not so violent as in colic or inflammation of the bowels, for which it is apt to be mistaken.

Treatment.—Relieve the bowels by injections, give a brisk purgative, as six drachms of aloes, with a drachm of calomel. Drachm doses of extract of belladonna or hyoscyamus should be given every hour, for three or four doses ; or tincture of aconite, from fifteen to twenty drops every two hours, in a little cold water, till the fever is subdued. Apply smart counter-irritation to the whole surface of the belly by rubbing in a strong liquid blister. The treatment of peritonitis does not differ very materially from that of enteritis, or inflammation of the bowels, which see.

THE STOMACH.

The stomach is that pouch or bag into which the food passes from the gullet, and in which it undergoes the primary and essential changes in the process of digestion.   The stomach of the horse is a comparatively small organ ; its shape is generally compared to the air-bag on a pair of bag-pipes.   It has two openings, the *cardiac*, into which the food enters from the gullet, and the *pyloric*, through which it passes into the bowels, or gut.   Its inner surface is lined by two distinct membranes, a *cuticular* and a *villous*.   The former lines the cardiac portion, and is white and wrinkled ; the latter covers the pyloric, and is yellowish red, soft and velvety to the touch.   The latter is the true digestive stomach.   In it the gastric juice is secreted, and the essential process of chymification, or the formation of the food into chyme, goes on, the former being merely for macerating and further triturating the masticated food.

INDIGESTION.

Indigestion in one form or another is very common in the horse.   It occurs in two forms, which may be distinguished as acidity of the stomach, or heart-burn, and acute indigestion, or total arrestment of digestion.

ACIDITY OF THE STOMACH.

Acidity of the stomach arises from bad food and irregular feeding.

Symptoms.—The animal is observed to lose condition ; the skin is dusty and unthrifty ; he is continually poking and picking among the litter, licking out the corners of the manger, occasionally stretching out the nose, and pouting the upper lip.   If turned out, he licks earth or sand, and evinces a depraved appetite ; at work he is easily sweated ; his bowels are irregular, the dung being light-colored and glazed.

Treatment.—Change the feed, give sweet, well-cured hay, a few bran-mashes, and gentle walking exercise.   Give him the following laxative ball : —

Barbadoes aloes...6 dr.
Ground ginger...2 dr.
Carbonate of soda...2 dr.

Make into a ball with molasses or lard.

Place a lump of rock salt in his manger, and give a little carbonate of soda or magnesia twice a day in the feed.   When recovery begins, give him tonics for some time, with gentle exercise.   If he persists in devouring the litter, muzzle him up for a few days. This, if neglected, is apt to run on to diabetes or jaupis.

ACUTE INDIGESTION.

Acute indigestion is very common in this country, especially in the spring, from the continuous hard work, and necessarily liberal feeding. It is usually induced by overfeeding, that is, eating too much at a time, more especially when the animal has been fatigued and hungry. It sometimes occurs from his breaking loose in the night, and gorging himself at the corn-bin. Another frequent cause is overloading the stomach with clover or green feed when wet; this often induces violent and fatal indigestion.

Symptoms.—Digestion may be arrested, either by "the food undergoing no change, forming a dangerous load, or running rapidly to frightful fermentation." In the former case the animal is dull and stupid, the pulse is slow, and the breathing oppressed; he is stiff, and inflammation of the feet, or *acute founder*, is apt to set in. If he have access to water, it speedily sets up fermentation, gas being rapidly evolved; the stomach is greatly distended, the belly swollen, colicky pains set in, he rolls about in great agony, looking wistfully at his flank, kicking his belly with his feet; he tosses about in despair, the bowels being unmoved. He gets up and down frequently, the sweat rolls off him in streams, and in many cases death puts an end to his sufferings in from four to six or eight hours, caused by rupture of the stomach or bowels, or violent inflammation of the intestines.

Treatment.—It is more easily prevented than cured, by simply attending to the following rules: Never let a horse get too hungry; never give him too much at a time; never put him to work on a full stomach; and never let him drink too freely after eating, and we will seldom see this fatal disease.

Treatment must be prompt to be effectual. The following drench will be found useful: —

Barbadoes aloes......... ....8 dr.
Liquor ammonia...1 fl. oz.
Or, spirits of turpentine ....2 fl. oz.

Dissolve the aloes with a little carbonate of soda, in nearly a quart of warm water, and add the other.

Rub the belly well, and apply cloths wrung out of boiling water diligently to it. Give copious injections of soap and water, or a mild infusion of tobacco or tobacco-smoke. If no relief is obtained in one or two hours, give at intervals of an hour, two drachms carbonate of ammonia, ½ ounce ginger (powdered), in gruel.

CHAPTER XXIV,

THE FOOT.

PRICKING IN SHOEING, STEPPING ON NAILS, GLASS, ETC.

THE foot is made up of the coffin-bone (os pedis), the lower end of the small pastern bone (os corona), and the navicular bone (os navicularis), with the tendon of the flexor pedis, which passes over the navicular bone, and is inserted in the sole of the coffin-bone, a variety of illustrations of which I give. The surface of the coffin-bone is covered by laminæ or thin plates, running from above downward, fitting into corresponding plates on the inner surface of the hoof. The sole is also covered by a sensitive structure which is villous, that is, presenting elevations and depressions, which fit into reciprocal horny villi on the sole of the foot. At the back part of the sole we have the sensitive or fatty frog, covered in a similar manner by the horny frog. These, with the coronary ligament (which occupies the groove in the upper margin of the wall of the hoof, and from which the hoof grows), and the coronary frog-band, blood-vessels, nerves, and lymphatics, constitute the foot of the horse. (To make this more plain, I include drawings of different views of the hoof; reference can also be made to illustrations in " Shoeing.")

Accidents and injuries of the foot constitute the principal bruises,—stepping on stones, sharp bodies, treads, etc., and are also causes of lameness. It is liable to injury from various causes, as occasionally participating in constitutional derangement; but by far the greatest amount of injury arises, directly or indirectly, from shoeing.

Sometimes, from carelessness, a nail penetrates the sensitive part of the foot (usually called the quick). Sometimes the nail itself does not penetrate, but is driven so close as to cause the wall, in its course, to press on and bruise the quick, (something like Fig. 843,) giving rise to inflammation, and usually terminating in suppuration.

Serious trouble is also liable to be caused by driving the nails deep and clinching them tightly, as this will bend the nails more or less inward upon the soft parts, causing a binding, uncomfortable

(536)

pressure that produces a soreness, and sometimes very serious in-flammation.

Symptoms.—Lameness may appear in a day or two, sometimes not for a week. The foot is found to be hot and tender, and the least tap with the hammer causes pain ; in moving, the animal sets the foot down so as to throw the pressure off the tender part, and when standing he will rest the foot. Sometimes the leg swells con-siderably ; the swelling is sometimes painful, and is very apt to mis-lead the inexperienced.

Treatment. — Remove the shoe, and having with the hammer or pincers discovered the faulty nail, thin the sole around it, and with a fine drawing-knife follow the course of the nail till the matter is evacuated ; make a free vent for it, and immerse the foot in a warm poultice for a day or two. When the symptoms subside, the

FIG. 842.—The Horse as he Usually Rests the Foot when Lame.

shoe may be applied, and the sole filled with tow and tar, or Friar's bal-sam, tincture of myrrh, etc., retained by cross slips or a leather sole, care being taken not to bruise the sole. The crust at the injured part should not rest on the shoe. (For further details, see page 349 in "Shoeing.")

If the nails are driven so deep as to bind, which, as before stated, is a very common occurrence, particularly in feet with thin hoofs, the first thing to do is to remove the nails ; if much inflam-mation, poultice until relieved ; then let the shoe extend farther out under the crust, and drive smaller nails, using care not to drive deep.

If a nail has been driven into the foot, get the horse to the sta-ble as quick as you can, and take off the shoe. If not done before, remove the nail, glass, or whatever it is, from the foot carefully. See that no part remains, and remove a little of the hoof from around the opening. Drop a few drops of Friar's balsam or com-pound tincture of benzoin into the orifice, both of which can be ob-tained in almost any drug store. If this is not obtainable, use the simple digestive ointment (given under head of "Cuts"), and cover the foot with a large flaxseed poultice. If the injury is at all severe, give a sharp dose of physic, and let the animal stand quiet. The object is to keep down the inflammation. *No hot oils or anything stimulating is to be applied.* If there is much inflammation, omit digestive dressing until after it is reduced by poulticing, when dress with digestives.

There is liable to be tenderness if the sole should strike the ground afterward, as there may be inflammation of the periosteum, to relieve which, put on a high-heeled shoe, and blister around the coronet. The sole is sometimes bruised by the shoe pressing upon it, causing much inflammation and lameness. Take off the shoe, poultice for twenty-four hours or more ; fit the shoe so as to remove all pressure from the sole ; if sore yet, continue the poultice ; if matter is formed, treat as you would any simple ulcer, with a healing astringent. Several good preparations are given in another part of this work.

Foot Lameness.*

Symptoms.—Horse goes gradually sore, walking tender either behind or before.

FIG. 843.—**Rucking.**

As a rule comes in one foot; if in the hind foot, tries to put the heel down first. Not much fever in the feet. No apparent cause ; hard to locate the trouble. The only diagnosis is by tapping the wall of the foot, which will give a hollow sound. It is all due to want of cell-growth or nutrition of horn cells, which will cause the wall or hoof to separate from the true foot. At the start the horse may travel sore or tender, growing worse gradually for two or three months ; finally the horse becomes very lame. There is no fever ; no pain by pressure or hammering. The only point noticeable is by the hollow sound of the wall when hammered upon.

By examining the sole of the foot at the point where the sole and wall are united, by pricking there with a probe, a granulating substance will be found—little dry fibers of horn, which are the dead horn-cells. These can be found and pricked clear up to the coronary band, without causing any feeling to the horse.

Treatment.—Clean out the foot properly, and pour nitric acid into the crevice made until all the dead part is cleaned out. Then put on a plain shoe so as to protect the sole and wall ; fill out the bottom with oakum and hot tar ; next fire all around the coronary band, the same as for ring-bone, and apply a sharp blister, and allow the horse to stand five or six weeks. If by the third week there is no sign of healthy horn, the blister may again be applied. But there is usually after three or four weeks a good noticeable growth of healthy horn.

After this, but little more can be done than to exercise the horse moderately, until the new growth of horn-structure has grown down.

---

* Dictated by Dr. Charles A. Meyer.

SEEDY TOE.

This is the name given to a dry, mealy secretion of horn, which is sometimes seen to take place between the horny and sensitive sole at the toe. It is seldom seen in this country, owing to clips being not much used.

Causes.—It is generally caused by large clips being hammered firmly on the toe, bending in the hoof, and bruising the part.

Symptoms.—Pain and lameness, with heat and tenderness, on pressure at the toe. The horn is dry and mealy, and matter is generally found at the bottom of it.

In bad cases, horny processes are found pressing inward, producing absorption of the coffin-bone, with a tendency for fungus growths to shoot up, producing a very troublesome disease.

Treatment.—In a simple case, open it up, cut down to the bottom, add poultice for a few days, when the shoe may be applied ; remove the pressure by cutting down the crust, and fill it up with tow and hot tar, when it will soon get well.

In bad cases, with fungus and bony absorption going on, free incisions must be made; sometimes it will be necessary to cut through the wall. Caustics must be freely used, such as muriate of antimony, dilute hydrochloric acid, etc., with pressure judiciously applied ; the process may be arrested, and the part healed.

When there is want of cell-growth, with a separation of the wall from the inner structure, which is very common in horses that have been driven hard, or been partially foundered, another high authority advises the following, which is practically the same as that given for foot-lameness :—

Treatment.—Thorough and repeated blistering around the coronet. Next pour boiling hot tar or even corrosive substance, such as muriatic acid, butter of antimony, spirits of salts, etc., into the cavity formed.

Whenever there is a separation of the wall from the sole, with weak or slow growth of horn, this is effectual if there is any life in the parts.

In severe cases, as first explained, the firing-iron is necessary, first cleaning out the dead part and filling in with hot tar, etc.

This is added in order to give a little more extended idea of the method of treatment.

GRAVELING.

A small stone, gravel, or dirt becoming imbedded under the shoe at the point of the heel between the bar and frog, usually the inner heel, and working through the sole into the quick, is called graveling. If not removed, it will in time work up through the coronet, or cause matter to form which will burrow between the wall and the sensitive sole.

The horse shows more or less lameness on the trot; is aggravated when driven over hard ground or trotted fast. If not interfered with, the lameness continues for about three months, when the gravel usually works through the coronet, making a small break in the skin, after which the lameness disappears; but should the matter be confined to the sole and surrounding parts, it is liable to cause considerable disturbance and injury to the foot.

When a horse shows lameness without any apparent cause, this part should be carefully examined, 1. To discover if the sole is broken at the point of the heel; 2. By slight tapping against the wall of the part with a small stone or hammer, to find if there is any unusual sensibility; 3. By resting the hand gently upon the part, to see if there is any increased heat, which would of course point to the seat of trouble. Sometimes gravel works into the sensitive part in consequence of the sole being denuded to relieve a bruise or corn. The point is to remove the cause of irritation. If much inflammation and pain, poultice; this will lower inflammation, and aid in soaking out and removing any foreign matter accumulated. When this has been done, saturate a pledget of tow with tincture of myrrh, or tar ointment, or Friar's balsam, and insert into the part, covering it completely. Next, fit a shoe so there will be no pressure upon this part, and nail on. It will usually be found necessary to put on a bar shoe until the heel is grown down again and will bear pressure.

BRUISE OF THE SOLE.

The sole is liable to bruise from the shoe being improperly seated, sometimes from sand or gravel being impacted in the web of the shoe, or by "picking up" a stone, which, getting wedged in the foot, bruises the sole.

Symptoms.—Lameness first attracts attention to it; in removing the shoe, the sole is found tender, and the foot hot; on paring the sole, it is found discolored at the bruised part.

Treatment.—A few days' rest may be necessary, with the foot immersed in a poultice, or stopped with some emollient dressing; and by using a leather sole or felt pads for a short time, it disappears.

TREADS, OR CALKS.

Injuries to the coronet are very common, especially in the Northern States during the winter months, when horses with sharp calks are driven or worked on rough, icy roads or deep snow, particularly in the woods. Treads, or calks, usually happen on the hind foot, by the horse accidentally setting one foot on the other, or another horse stepping on it. In ordinary cases, if not cut very deep, all that is necessary to do is to cut the hair from the edges, sponge or clean out any hair or dirt that may be driven in, and pour on a little kerosene oil, followed by a little hot tar, or the parts covered with hot tar will be sufficient.

But if the cut is deep, it will sometimes prove to be a very serious difficulty, and require prompt attention to prevent serious inflammation of the parts. The first thing to be done in such a case is to carefully remove any dirt or other foreign matter. When thoroughly clean, it may be bound up with a pledget of tow dipped

Fig. 844.—The Coronet as it
Usually Appears when
Badly Calked.

Fig. 845.—As the Hair Should
be Clipped from the Edges
of the Injury.

in tincture of myrrh, or compound tincture of benzoin, or Friar's balsam, which, if available, will be found an excellent remedy. The point is now to prevent any excessive inflammation. Keep the horse quiet, feed bran mashes, etc., no grain ; and if there is enough inflammation to cause much soreness, cover the foot with a large hot poultice. If the soreness becomes at all excessive, at once use hot fomentations, following up for at least one or two hours three or four times a day ; after which keep the leg tied up with wet cloths, or poultice. If there is extreme pain, give an anodyne, or inject a little morphine under the skin, as a horse cannot endure pain very long, and continue fomentations industriously ; this, at all events, must not be neglected.

In very severe cases it may be necessary to put the horse in slings, if he will not lie down. When the inflammation subsides, but little more is necessary to be done than to let the parts alone, dressed with any of the preparations before given.

To illustrate the seriousness of these cases sometimes, I will refer to an accident of the kind to one of my own horses. One of my men, who had special charge of and drove a favorite pony, took it into his head during the winter to have the calks pointed with steel and made very sharp. While the pony was standing in his stall, with one foot resting against the opposite, he was suddenly startled by some one approaching, when, throwing his weight upon the elevated foot, the inside calk was driven well into the coronet of the opposite foot. I was kept ignorant of the accident for several days, when it was made known to me by discovering the horse to be lame. The

FIG. 846.—As the Foot was Held During the Period of Greatest Inflammation.

injury at the surface did not seem to be serious, but it was deep. In consequence of being driven on the road, the inflammation soon became so serious that it was necessary, at great inconvenience, to leave the horse behind a couple of weeks, the part in the meantime being thoroughly poulticed and fomented. The inflammation passing off, and being entirely free from lameness, he was again put to his work on the road, when the roads were breaking up. Driving him through the deep mud for a few miles again brought on such serious inflammation of the parts as to necessitate a constant application of fomentations for hours at a time, night and day, for several days, to overcome it.

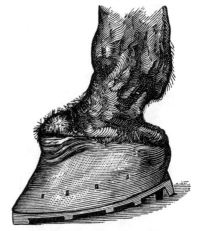

FIG. 847.—The Usual Appearance of a Foot Badly Calked, and Neglected or Improperly Treated.

Fig. 846 is an illustration

of how he stood when he suffered most severely. I also give specimens of the usual method of sharpening the calks in winter, and as they should be rounded or filed to prevent serious injury. Owners should not neglect to look to this matter very carefully. The toe and inside calk especially should be rounded sufficiently to prevent any serious cutting. Concave shoes should be used in winter ; with such, calks

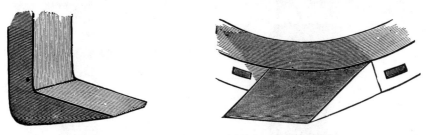

Fig. 848.—Calks as They are Usually Sharpened in Winter.

need not be long or sharp to give sufficient hold. Particular care should be taken not to have any calks or sharp shoes on when there is an

Fig. 849.—As the Calks Should be Blunted or Rounded to Prevent Cutting.

effort to subdue a horse. This caution must not be disregarded, as a horse under such circumstances is liable to cut himself dangerously.

OVERREACH.

When a horse, in a fast pace, overreaches the fore with the hind foot, the inner rim of the shoe cutting a semi-circular flap on the heel or quarter, it is called an "overreach." It should be treated as a tread ; but when practicable, the edges should be brought together by a wire suture, and bound up with Friar's balsam or compound tincture of benzoin.

QUITTOR.

In all cases in which matter forms in the foot, whether from pricks, corns, bruises, or treads, unless it has free openings to escape by, it acts as an irritant, extending in every direction, through the tissues, and at last working its way to the coronet, where it bursts, producing a very troublesome disease, and requiring both patience and perseverance to effect a cure.

Symptoms.—It is recognized by the small aperture at the coronet, which seems almost overgrown with " proud flesh." The dis-

FIG. 850.—A Good Rep-
resentation of an In-
jury by Over-
reach.

FIG. 851.—As the Edges of
the Wound Should be
Trimmed before
Dressing.

charge is glairy and constant. On examining it with a probe, sinuses are found running in all directions. The quarter is enlarged and bulging, and the lameness severe and protracted.

As I cannot do better than give the treatment used by Mr. Gamgee,* which is recognized as the very best, I will give it in full :—

After taking off the shoe, and doing all that is necessary to the hoof, I prepare to inject a mixture, for the pharmaceutical combination of which I say nothing, though I can say a great deal for its practical efficiency. To prepare the mixture, take bichloride of mercury, one drachm ; rectified spirit, one ounce; after rubbing and dissolving the sublimate in the spirit, add half a drachm of liquor plumbi acetatis. By means of a small syringe, elastic gum, or pewter, with small tube two inches in length, and bulbous end, I inject the mixture down the sinus. This requires to be carefully but very effectually done. The direction of the syringe must

---

*Joseph Gamgee, formerly professor in the new Veterinary College, Edinburgh, Scotland.

therefore be changed from the vertical to the oblique, in both a forward and a backward direction, the object being to infiltrate the mass as far as it can be penetrated by the innumerable small sinuses converging to the outer channel. To do this part well, one strong man is better than several hands, if the horse's head be held steady, and an assistant hand the instruments, etc. I take the horse's foot forward upon my knee, and, as a rule, succeed in performing the operation without giving much pain to cause the horse to resist ; though difficulty, requiring a little exceptional care, may occasionally occur when previous treatment and torture have been resorted to. Now for the effect that follows : The foot is released and placed on the ground, and once or twice the animal stamps, indicating that a smarting is produced by the caustic agent; but in a brief space of time that passes, and signs of ease are manifest. On examining the foot in as short a time as four hours after the operation, I have found the tumor sensibly subsided, and all the symptoms favorable. We have been in the habit (members of my family used this excellent remedy before me) of repeating the injection of the preparation the second time after the lapse of twelve to twenty-four hours, and again, after a similar interval, a third time. And this general rule seems to me to recommend itself, and admit of explanation in this way : At first all the structures are so engorged that the agent cannot be forced through the morbid deposit ; but in proportion as the diseased structures are reached, they are destroyed, and shrink, and in each succeeding application the fluid caustic is pressed round the withered, wasted substance, until the whole comes away in the space of a week or little more, when the cure is advanced far, and thereafter rapidly effected. This represents the progress of a good cure. Sometimes the application has to be repeated several times, at intervals of two or three days ; but where delay is essential, I diminish the activity of the preparation by adding a double portion of spirit.

FIG. 852.—**An Ideal Representation of a Foot Showing Bad Condition of Quittor.**

The following treatment for quittor was given the writer by one of the most successful practitioners in the country, who claims it will cure any case, in fact, leaving nothing to be desired when used properly :—

In the first stage of quittor inject into every part carefully two or three times a day the following lotion :—

Corrosive sublimate ....½ oz.
Goulard's extract ....2 dr.
Alcohol ....4 oz.

After the fourth day inject twice a day equal parts of the following mixture :—

Potassa chloras ....2 oz.
Potassa permanganas...1 oz.
Hydrochloric acid...½ oz.
Water ....8 oz.

This is a splendid thing for quittor, and also fistulous withers. Of late, I have great success with it.

A bar or three-quarter bar shoe, should be used for some time, and the diseased quarter cut down to keep it from pressure ; and in course of time the foot will become useful, if not sound.

THRUSH.

Copying the language of a standard authority, "Thrush is inflammation of the lower structure of the sensitive frog, during which pus is secreted with or instead of horn." It is most common in the hind feet, and also occurs in the fore. It occurs at all ages, and is frequently seen in the colt running in the straw-yard, arising from the acrid moisture of urine, dung, etc., softening and corroding the frog, and extending to the sensitive structures above. It is also seen in roadsters whose feet are not exposed to acrid moisture. In them it is caused by contraction, or the insinuation of sand and dirt into the cleft of the frog, producing irritation, followed by suppuration of the sensitive frog, causing it to secrete unhealthy horn, and discharge offensive matters.

It may sometimes be constitutional, as we often observe it appear just as the coat is being changed, and other constitutional changes are taking place in the system.

Symptoms.—There is seldom much lameness, unless the animal steps on a stone, or sand or gravel gets into the cleft ; but it is always attended by a tender, gingerly action. The cleft of the frog is deeper than in health, and a thin, acrid discharge oozes from its sides and bottom, emitting a characteristic and fetid odor. If not checked, it extends, and the frog becomes loose and ragged ; scales fall off in layers, exposing the sensitive parts, which are tender and contracted. If neglected, the entire foot may be involved, and it may degenerate into canker.

Treatment.—No time should be lost, and no case, however slight, should be neglected. The foot must be thoroughly cleaned, and all loose, detached parts freely removed. The secreting surface should be exposed, and calomel dusted on, and pressed with a spatula or thin slip of wood into every crevice. Keep the foot thoroughly dry, and more than one or two dressings will seldom be required. Sometimes it readily yields to cleanliness and simple dressings, with hot tar placed in the cleft with tow, and retained with cross slips, or applications of sugar of lead or sulphate of zinc. Or, after the parts have been washed, and the diseased part removed as directed, apply powdered sulphate of copper to the parts, and fill up all parts with cotton packed in so as to keep out all dirt. If necessary, this should be repeated in a few days.

It is generally advisable to give some opening medicine, and attend to the general health and exercise.

CANKER.

Canker of the foot is apt to supervene in cases of neglected or badly treated thrush, quittor, or puncture, and often follows bad cases of grease. It is most common in heavy draft-horses, that are kept in damp, filthy stables, and is most prevalent about large cities.

Symptoms.—In this disease we find a morbid state of the sensitive sole and frog, and instead of sound, healthy horn, fungus excrescences are thrown out, with an offensive acrid discharge. When aggravated, the whole becomes covered with a growth of fungi, which are like shreds of leather in appearance, with a great tendency to spread over or underrun the sole, separating the horny from the sensitive parts. It is very difficult to get the horn to grow again.

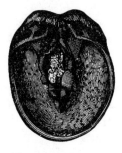

FIG. 853.—The Foot, Showing Canker.

Treatment.—In no case is so much patience required as in canker,—in fact, it is generally considered as incurable, from the difficulty experienced in suppressing the fungus, and getting the horn to grow again. All loose and detached horn must be carefully removed, so as to give free vent to the irritating matter. As much of the fungus as may seem practicable, without much bleeding, should be removed by the knife or cautery, and followed up by some escharotic, such as acetate or sulphate of copper, nitrate of silver, butter of antimony, or sulphuric acid. Whatever caustic is used, it must be applied every day; for if neglected one day, it is apt to underrun the sole, and may lose more than it will regain in a week. Firm pressure is very beneficial, and should be constantly applied by means of tow, firmly impacted, and retained by means of slips of wood or hoop-iron slid under the shoe; and the foot must be kept perfectly dry.

The caustic may be occasionally changed. To destroy the fetor, chloride of zinc or chloride of lime may be dusted on, or even occasional dressings of dry lime will be useful. With a dressing of tar, in which verdigris and nitric acid, two drachms of each to one pound of tar, are well mixed, and applied with a degree of firm pressure, at least every second day, the worst cases can be cured..

Moderate work, if it can be done without the foot getting wet, will expedite a cure. The following is highly recommended as a dressing : Take equal parts of pine tar and lard, melt over a slow fire, and add sulphuric acid very slowly until ebullition (boiling) ceases. Apply this to the parts.

SPRAINS, BRUISES, ETC.

Sprains are so common, and so liable to spoil a horse when neglected or not treated properly, and in addition the treatment is so simple and easily applied, that the subject is worthy of more than ordinary attention. On this account I have introduced several illustrations, showing the parts in the fore legs that are most liable to such injury.

Sprain may be said to consist in an overstretching of the part (be it muscle, tendon, or ligament) to such a degree as to cause rupture of some of the fibers of which it is composed, in consequence of which inflammation is set up, and effusion takes place, producing enlargement around the part.

The reason why sprains take so long to recover is, the lacerated fibers have to be absorbed, and new ones formed in their place, or, as is often the case in repeated sprain of the same part, their place is filled up by organized lymph, leaving a permanent thickening.

Causes.—Natural weakness of the part sometimes predisposes to it. It may arise from whatever exposes the part to inordinate exertion, as, for instance, slipping on ice or on a rolling stone, awkward stepping, galloping on rough or uneven ground, and a common cause is allowing the feet to grow too long,

Symptoms—In severe cases the part is swollen, hot, and tender ; the limb is thrown into a position that relaxes the sprained part. If extensive, we have symptomatic fever, and he refuses his food, the mouth is hot, pulse accelerated, etc., which passes off when the more acute symptoms subside. Lameness, of course, is continuous, thus differing from disease of the joint, in which he is always lamest at starting, getting less lame as he gets warmed up.

Treatment.—No matter where the location of the sprain is, or what part is injured, the principle of treatment is the same, when we have three indications presented : First, to allay the inflammatory process ; second, to promote absorption of the decayed fibers ; and third, to hasten the production of new ones. Most authors recommend either local or general depletion by bleeding from one of the large veins near the seat of injury, or from the jugular vein of the neck. This, however, I think is now-a-days very wisely dispensed with, and in my opinion is altogether unnecessary.

The bowels must be freely opened, and kept open by laxative and easily digested food, such as bran mash, linseed tea, roots, etc. The continued application of heat or cold to the parts aids greatly in checking the inflammatory action. If pain and swelling are excessive, hot fomentations continued for an hour or two, alternated with cold water, will be found to give most relief. (For particulars in fomenting, see "Fomentation.") Gentle and equable pressure, by means of a judiciously applied bandage, is very beneficial in sprains of the leg.

Rest must be given from the first, and the patient must be turned into a loose box. Having by these means succeeded in subduing the inflammation, one or two applications of an absorbing blister will generally remove any enlargement that may remain. Should the thickening and lameness prove obstinate, the firing-iron may be resorted to. (For an explanation of the method of using this, see "Firing in Spavins.")

SPRAIN OF THE BACK TENDONS.

Should a horse, when traveling or running with much force, step on a hub or stone in a way to bring an uneven strain upon one or more of the ligaments or tendons of a limb, there is liable to be caused such a severe strain as to result in serious lameness and injury, which, if neglected or not treated properly, often leads to permanent lameness and injury of the horse. This is especially common in sprain of the back tendons.

The principal seat of strain in the fore limb is in the tendons at the back part of the leg, usually called sprain of the back tendons, or back sinews. As these tendons (flexor perforans and perforatus) are the chief agents in producing the motions of the limbs, acting like levers over the pulley-like surfaces on the ends of the bones in

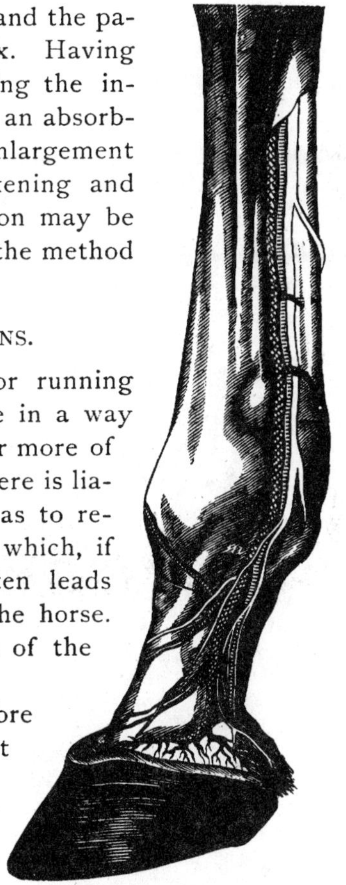

FIG. 854.—The Leg with Skin Removed, Showing Arteries. See Plates in Part on Shoeing.

their passage down to the foot, they are consequently very liable to be overstretched and strained, sometimes in a very slight degree, and sometimes to a considerable extent. It may be necessary here to notice the arrangement of these two tendons. The muscles (perforans and perforatus) arise from below the elbow-joint, pass down through a theca at the back of the knee; below the knee they become tendinous; the first is one of great strength, nearly round, and is inclosed in the other, which forms what is termed a sheath for it; half-way down the cannon, the perforans is joined by a strong ligament (the metacarpal); the two tendons pass down together through a sheath formed for them at the back of the fetlock; the latter splits into two divisions, having the perforans passing between them; they are inserted one into each side of the lower pastern bone (or corona), the perforans, passing down, is inserted into the sole of the coffin-bone, just in front of the navicular joint, over which it passes. A good illustration of these different parts is given in Fig. 855.

Fig. 856 will be found an especially fine illustration of the perforans and perforatus tendons above the fetlock, an explanation of which is also included. A point here is very nicely explained by White, who says:—

Between these two tendons there are in two parts thin vascular membranes by which they are joined together; these membranes appear to serve as bridles, allowing the perforans tendon to move a little way within the perforatus, and then preventing any further motion. The situation of those membranes is about midway in the

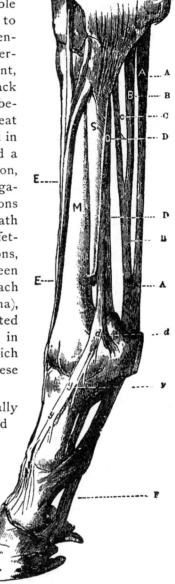

FIG. 855.—**Tendons and Ligaments of the Fore Legs.**

A. flexor perforatus; B. flexor perforans; C. metacarpal ligament; D. superior sesamoidal ligament; d. Bifurcation of the sesamoidal ligament; y. Continuation forward of branch of the sesamoidal ligament; F. continuation of the flexor perforans tendon, afterward inserted into the lower side of the os pedis; E. extensor tendon; M. great metacarpal, or cannon shank bone; S. splint bone.

pastern. If the coffin joint happens to be extended in a way the animal was not prepared for, both these membranes are ruptured. The consequence is an effusion of blood between the two tendons, whereby all motion between them would be effectually prevented, were the animal left to obey his own instinctive feelings.

In most of the so-called cases of clap, or sprain of the back tendons, the ligament, and not the tendons, is the seat of the injury.

Causes. — Whatever tends to throw unusual stress upon these parts may produce it, such as galloping on uneven ground, allowing the hoofs to grow too long, thereby increasing the leverage on the tendon ; sometimes it occurs in leaping, often while jumping around in play.

Symptoms.—The animal is very lame, the part is hot, swollen, and tender ; the limb is held forward, so as to relax the part ; in some cases he can hardly touch the ground. On taking up the foot and pinching with the fingers, he evinces the pain he feels. If the outer tendon (perforatus) is injured, we have a bulging out behind, interrupting the evenness of the line which characterizes the tendons. If the perforans, it is felt

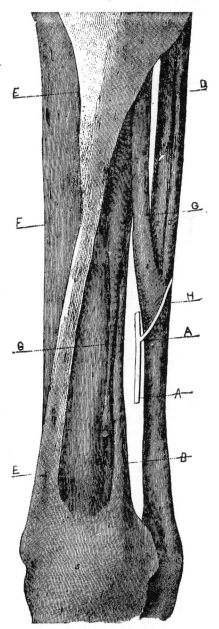

Fic. 856.—**Flexor Tendon, etc.**

A. the outside nerve, or that part of it where the branch H communicates; B. the suspensory ligament; C. the great ligament of the back sinew; D. the two back sinews, or flexor tendons; E. E. the exterior tendon; F. the cannon, or shank bone; G. the splint bone; H. the back sinews and their great suspensory ligament, apparently joined together; this, however, is not the case; it incorporates only with the perforans tendon, marked figure 2, and so intimately that they form one and the same substance at the part marked by the letter *i;* the perforatus, marked figure 3, forms a sheath for the perforans as already described in the article on "Strains; " 5, the fetlock-joint.

between the ligament and the perforatus ; and if the metacarpal ligament, as is most generally the case, it can be felt between the bone and the tendon.

Treatment.—As before stated, the first condition of cure is rest. The animal must be turned into a loose box, and if the injury is severe, the swollen limb must be well fomented with hot water ; cold may be preferable, if slight. This must kept up for more than an hour, when the following cooling lotion may be well rubbed in, and a thick woolen bandage applied, well saturated with it, and kept wet with cold water :—

| Fig. 857.—Showing the Back Tendons Considerably Thickened in Consequence of Repeated Injury or Strain. | Fig. 858.—Showing the Effect of Hard Driving. | Fig. 859.—Enlargement of the Tendons from Interfering or Banging. |

Niter (saltpeter)...2 oz.
Sal-ammoniac ....2 oz.
Common salt..4 oz.
Spring water..... ....1 pt.

Or, the following :—

Saltpeter .... 4 oz.
Sugar of lead..... ....1 oz.
Muriate of ammonia.....................................1 oz.
Common salt..1 pt.
Cold water..2 gal.

Perhaps the simplest and best home treatment would be about as follows :—

Make a bag as long as the limb—an old trouser's leg of good size, sufficiently long to extend from the hoof to above the knee, would be the thing. Tie a string rather loosely around the foot below the fetlock. To keep it in place, secure a wide tape or strip of cloth to the upper edge of the bag, pass it over the shoulder, and fasten to the opposite edge ; next take bran, to which add a little salt, and pour on it as much boiling water as will bring it to a thin consistence. While hot as the horse can bear, fill the bag with it. This will form a poultice around the part, and keep it moist and sweating. It can be kept hot by pouring on hot water occasionally, and should be renewed, if necessary, in twenty-four hours, and so continued until the inflammation subsides. In all cases of severe sprain, a purgative should be given ; it reduces the fever, and acts as a counter-irritant. In any event give opening, easily digested food.

Having in this way reduced the inflammation, if the swelling still remains, apply a good strong liniment or blister. The biniodide of mercury ointment is best in these cases, and should be repeated :—

Biniodide of mercury...1½ dr.
Lard..1 oz.

A run at pasture will generally complete the cure. Sometimes, by repeated sprains, the tendons become considerably thickened (as shown in Fig. 857), in which case firing is preferable. Sometimes, from repeated sprains, the tendons become contracted, causing the animal to go on his toe ; in these cases, the operation of tenotomy, or cutting the tendons, is advisable.

The following treatment for sprains, which is given for insertion by a leading practitioner, will be found good :—

First wash with very hot water five or ten minutes at a time, then apply the following mixture :—

Tincture opium ....2 oz.
Chloroform ....1 oz.
Fluid extract aconite.....................................1 oz.
Soap liniment ....7½ oz.

To be applied two or three times a day after bathing the parts with hot water.

If constipated and feverish, a slight purging ball should be given. If the case has run two or three days, and is assuming a sub-acute stage, then stimulating liniment must be used. The following may be used :—

Aqua ammonia ....2 oz.
Spirits of camphor......................................2½ oz.
Alcohol..7½ oz.

To be rubbed on two or three times a day until the skin becomes sore.

Breaking Down.

The suspensory ligament is one of the strongest in the body; it is placed immediately behind the cannon-bone, from the head of which it rises; passing down, it divides, one division going to each of the small bones at the back of the fetlock (ossa sesamoides). (See Fig. 855.) This ligament is the great main-stay of the fetlock joint, and sustains the most of the weight at this part, consequently we frequently find it snaps asunder under the great weight thrown upon it in leaping, galloping, etc. It is sometimes broken above the division; but more commonly, one or both bifurcations are torn.

Causes.—Violent exertion, or sudden jerks, as is the case in leaping, galloping, or jumping from a hight.

Symptoms.—It is sometimes mistaken for rupture of the flexor

Fig. 860.—**Method of Applying the Bandage.**

Fig. 861.—**Showing the Leg Bandaged.**

tendons; but this is so improbable an occurrence, that we are almost skeptical of its occurrence at all. If it does occur, it is extremely rare. In rupture of the ligaments, the fetlock descends to the ground; but when raised, the animal can flex the foot, which he could not do were the tendons ruptured. It usually occurs near the sesamoides, when we have swelling, heat, and pain.

Treatment.—Slinging is almost indispensable to keep the limb steady. Splints and bandages should be judiciously applied, and a high-heeled shoe put on so as to keep the parts *in situ;* and the inflammation must be regulated by the constant application of cold, laxative medicine, and cooling, easily digested food, sparingly supplied, when reunion will take place, but a permanent thickening is generally left. When the animal is able to use the limb, the slings and splints may be dispensed with, and it may be fired or blistered to consolidate the new fibers, and form a permanent bandage to the part. The horse can never afterward be passed as sound, nor will he stand much hard work.

SPRAIN OF THE FETLOCK.

FIG. 862.—**Turco's Leg as it Knuckled Forward.**

The ligaments of the fetlock j o i n t are s o m e t i m e s sprained, g i v i n g rise to swelling of the joint, pain, and lameness. Its nature, causes, symptoms, a n d treatment differ so little from those of other parts that it is only necessary to state that the treatment is the same.

But suppose we have a strain of the extensor tendon or of the ligaments of the fetlock joint, and the horse must be moved. In that case it would be necessary to apply a woolen bandage over the part carefully, drawing it tightly, and holding it in place by sewing it on. But as soon as the stable is reached, this bandage must be taken off, and a loose one put on. If there is not very much inflammation, simply lameness and weakness, good treatment would be keeping the bandage thoroughly wet with hot vinegar and salt, by pouring it on. In one instance, one of my horses, Turco, was so seriously sprained that he could scarcely step, the

FIG. 863.—**Showing Tendons and Ligaments of the Hind Leg.**

joint knuckling forward as shown in Fig. 862. It was absolutely necessary to drive him eight or ten miles. By bandaging the leg tightly as described, he went along quite well; but as soon as the stable was reached, this bandage was taken off, and a loose one put on, which was kept wet as explained; and being compelled to drive him every day, this treatment was repeated; and though he was driven over one hundred miles in two weeks, he was at the end of that time entirely over the effects of the sprain.

At another time, when in Maine, Tommy sprained the tendons of one of his forward legs so seriously that he could scarcely step. We simply raised the heel-calks of his shoe, rounded the toe, and bandaged the parts loosely, and kept wet as explained. Next morning the ankle was tightly bandaged, when he was able to do considerable work in the ring, and walk through to the next town, ten miles. This course was repeated, and at the expiration of about two weeks, he was all right, though in the time driven about one hundred miles.

Sprain of the Perforans Tendon, or Navicular-Joint Lameness.

The symptoms are very fully explained under that head, page 432, but I would here state again, that in an acute stage, the principle is rest, with hot fomentations or cooling applications; next aiding mobility of the parts involved to prevent irritation, by the construction of the shoe, etc., as explained in "Shoeing," Figs. 562–576.

Shoulder Lameness.

This is not very common, but is liable to happen from the limb slipping sideways while running in a pasture, or slipping accidentally on a wet plank, or ice, etc.

To guard against error in diagnosing affections of the shoulder, it must borne in mind that all muscular tissue is apt to waste if it is deprived of its usual amount of exercise, as we frequently see in the shoulder, the shoulder shrinking on one or both sides, while the real seat of the disease is in the feet; therefore it is very necessary to be able to distinguish shoulder lameness from many other affection with which it is apt to be confounded. Many horse doctors and those about horses are apt to attribute every lameness they do not understand, and whose seat is not self-evident, to an affection of the shoulder.

We have seldom any recognizable tumefaction, nor much heat, unless it be recent and violent. When the horse has strained the shoulder, the limb is brought forward with a peculiar dragging motion, as shown in Fig. 864 ; whereas if the trouble is in the foot, the limb will be raised and brought forward without much difficulty, but put down tenderly to lighten the concussion. While standing,

FIG. 864.—**As a Horse will Travel with Lame Shoulder.**

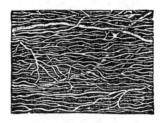

FIG. 865.—**Distribution of Capillaries in Muscle.**

the joints will be somewhat relaxed, the heel raised, with the toe resting upon the ground. In shoulder lameness, the head will be carried low, the limb brought forward with a good deal of difficulty and pain, and without ability to bring it in front of the other.

Treatment.—Give a dose of physic, foment the shoulder and inside of the arm close to the chest with hot water, which is to be continued for at least one hour, and to be repeated as long as there is inflammation ; give fever medicine three times a day ; give food of a light, opening nature, such as grass, bran mashes, etc., and keep him quiet in a box stall until the lameness disappears. One of the liniments for sprains, etc., may be used after the acute stage passes off. This is about all that can be done, though some bleed from the inner plate vein during the acute stage. This method is

FIG. 866.—**Method of Putting on Bandage.**

not now often practiced, however. When the case becomes chronic, blisters and setons may be employed with good success.

LINIMENT FOR SHOULDER LAMENESS.

```
Aqua ammonia...................................................2 oz.
Spirits of camphor.............................................2½ oz.
Rectified spirits of vini......................................7½ oz.
```

First, foment the part with hot water; then rub as near dry as possible, and apply the liniment twice a day until the skin is quite sore, and then stop for a few days; if the lameness is not gone by this time, renew the treatment as before.

SWEENEY.

This is a sprain of the muscle which fills up the posterior cavity on the outer side of the shoulder joint (outer tubercle of the head of the humerous). It occurs mainly in young horses when first put to plow, or in others going on uneven ground, and stepping unexpectedly into holes. In the endeavor to recover the equilibrium on stepping into a furrow or hole, this muscle which forms the outer support of the joint is injured, and there results heat, swelling, and tenderness on the outside of the joint, and a most characteristic gait. The horse may walk, or even trot, without much apparent lameness; but standing directly in front of him the affected shoulder is seen to roll outward from the body to a far greater extent than the sound one. Soon the muscle begins to waste rapidly, and in bad cases the shoulder-blade may be denuded until it appears to be covered by nothing but skin.—*Law.*

FIG. 867.—**Internal Aspect of the Left Fore Leg.**

A badly fitting collar often gives rise to it. A prominent cause also is some injury to the foot, which would prevent a proper use of the muscles of the shoulder, and thereby cause an atrophied, or wasted, condition of them. So that when there is wasting of the part, the foot should be carefully examined to see if there is any cause for it, and if so, removing the cause will of itself be sufficient to make a cure.

Symptoms.—At first, though it is seldom noticed, the muscles swell up, are hot and tender; in the course of a few days, the swelling has disappeared, and the muscles are becoming fast absorbed. In many cases this goes on till the bone can be felt. There is little or no pain on pressure in this stage, and no positive lameness ; but there is a peculiar rotary motion of the limb, from the other muscles having no counter-balancing power. This is sometimes mistaken by non-professional men for dislocation of the shoulder joint. This, however, cannot occur, unless it is accompanied by severe laceration, or even fracture.

Treatment.—In the first instance, rest and hot fomentations are indicated, which, as the process of reproduction begins, should be followed by stimulant embrocations or mild blisters, frequently repeated, with moderate walking exercise. In this case, we must trust more to nature than medicine ; and in time the muscles will be reproduced, and by gentle work and well-fitting harness he will become as sound as ever. Many do nothing for them, but turn them to pasture, and in most cases they come up all right.

The simplest and most effective treatment for filling up the shoulder is the rubbing on thoroughly with the hand of soft soap, to which a little salt has been added. This do four or five times in the course of a week. This simple remedy, which is very effectual for this purpose, has been kept as a great secret by a leading horseman in Toledo, Ohio, who has repeatedly sold it for five dollars, first showing its effect in filling up the shoulder, when he could easily sell the prescription.

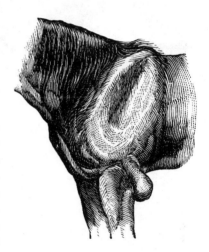

Fig. 868.—**An Ideal Representation of the Shoulder with Sweeney.**

HIP LAMENESS.

Sprain of the whirl, or round bone, as it is commonly called, consists of a sprain of the round ligament of the femur, which holds the ball in the socket. Sometimes it is almost torn asunder ; but so strong is this articulation, that dislocation cannot occur, except as an accompaniment of fracture.

Symptoms.—Very seldom any external swelling unless it is very severe, and the muscles surrounding the joint are involved ; when by making him stand square on his hind legs, and standing directly behind him, and comparing one hip with the other, any enlargement can be easily detected. Sometimes we have heat and tenderness ;

but in most cases these are absent.   One characteristic symptom is stepping short, the lame leg is not brought so far forward as the other one, and he drops on that quarter.   The tendon of the glutæus maximus, as it passes over the trochanter, is frequently the seat of

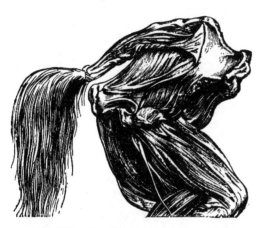

the lameness.   In this case we have swelling, heat, and pain on pressure, with short stepping.   When the horse stands in stable, he will stand square on both hind feet ; and when moved, the lame side is elevated and dragged along for want of muscular action.

FIG. 869.—**Deep Muscles of the Hip and Thigh.**

Treatment.—The first condition, as in all cases of lameness, is rest, with fomentations, alternated with cooling lotions, etc., until the inflammation is subdued, followed by repeated blisters, which must be freely used, as the disease is deep-seated.

Apply hot fomentations to the part two or three times a day, which should be continued an hour or more each time, alternated with the pouring on of cold water.   When the acute stage passes off, clip the hair closely from a large surface ten or twelve inches in diameter over the part, and apply a sharp blister ; a better condition of counter-irritation will be produced by applying at the same time two setons, which are to be extended under the skin about six inches each, something of the form as shown in Fig. 870.   (For special instruction, see "Setons.")   If need be, repeat the blisters.   Recovery usually takes place in from one to two weeks ;

FIG. 870.—**Setons.**

but is sometimes a very serious lameness, and must be attended to thoroughly and promptly.

The following is the treatment advised by very able practitioners :—

Give a laxative, and apply hot fomentations to the part two or three times a day. After each fomentation apply a strong stimulating liniment. Continue this treatment until the skin is sore, then cease the treatment, and apply the following for a few days :—

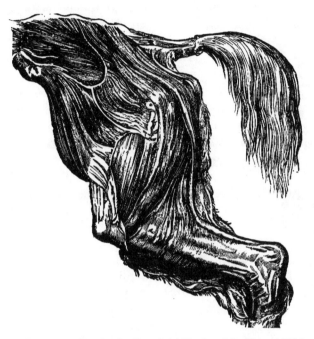

FIG. 871.—Showing the Superficial Muscles of the Hip and Thigh.

Soft soap...6 oz.
Alcohol.. ....12 oz.

Apply twice a day until well.

KNUCKLING OVER.

Knuckling, or standing over, is very common in cab and stage horses. It gives the animal an ungainly, worn-out appearance. It may occur on one or both knees, which are bent forward, and are very shaky, or the fetlocks may be knuckled forward. Veterinarians differ as to the real nature of this condition, or as to the part really at fault. Some suppose that it is from "a relaxed and lengthened state of the extensor muscles ;" others "of the ligamentous tissue at the anterior part of the joint ;" others "an inordinate contraction of the flexors, to such a degree that the equilibrium of the flexors and extensors is destroyed." Dissection, however, fails to confirm these

36   a

views. It appears to us to depend on contraction of the ligaments at the back of the joint.

Causes.—It is generally caused by too hard work when young, particularly continued road-work, which causes the joints to start forward, as shown in Figs. 872, 873.

Symptoms.—It requires but to be seen to be recognized. Instead of the beautiful, symmetrical form of the limb, the joint is thrown forward, throwing the shank-bone more oblique and the pastern-bone more straight, giving the animal a jaded, tottering appearance.

Treatment.—Some blister, or fire and blister; but we think this does no good whatever. All we can do is to give rest; leave the rest to nature. Turn him into a large loose box or small paddock, and feed him well, and it is astonishing how the patient will sometimes improve.

Drs. Hamill and Meyer treat ordinary cases of sprung knees with very marked success, by lowering the heels and lengthening out the toes somewhat; this can be done both by paring the heels down some, and using thin-heeled shoes;

Fig. 872.—**An Ordinary Case of Sprung Knees.**

then rubbing on the legs once or twice a day alcohol, or any good stimulant. The case seems to improve even under moderate work. Very bad cases are incurable.

BROKEN KNEES, OR OPEN JOINT.

It is a very common occurrence in the horse, generally arising from accidents, kicks, blows, stabs, etc. It is most common in the knee and hock; but all the joints of the limbs are liable to be punctured or laid open by some accident or injury.

Open joints are generally divided into lacerated and punctured. In the former we have the skin, ligaments, etc., cut

Fig. 873.

through, and the joint laid open, as is often seen in the knee. In the latter we have merely a small opening (it may be only sufficient to admit the probe) into the joint, from which trickles the synovia, or joint-oil.

All cases are alike dangerous, and are characterized by the same general symptoms, and are liable to be attended by the same consequences. They differ only in degree, according to the importance and extent of the cavity exposed.

Causes.—The causes of open joint are almost invariably external injury—in the knee from falling. The horse stumbles; falls upon his knees; and should the ground happen to be gravelly, hard, or stony, the knees are liable to be lacerated or cut through.

In other joints the injury is usually caused by being accidentally stabbed or cut.

Symptoms.—In giving an opinion in these cases, we must bear in mind that the joint is not always open, although we have a discharge of synovia from the wound; we may have it from the theca, or sheath, of some tendon, and it requires close examination in some cases to say which it comes from. What we imply by the term *open joint*, is where the skin, ligaments, tendons, etc., have been cut through, and the articulation laid open.

FIG. 874.—Broken Knees.

FIG. 875.—The Same with Hair Clipped from Edges of Wound.

In the first place, the animal is very lame. On examining the wound with the probe or finger, it is found to penetrate the joint; we have a clear, oily fluid, which is very smooth and slippery to the touch. The discharge may be very trifling, still it is not the less dangerous. In most cases we have symptomatic fever, which often runs so high as to cut the animal off. It is recognized by the quick pulse, hot mouth, irregular heat of the surface, costive bowels, and the excruciating pain the animal evinces.

Treatment.—This is the most important part of the subject. In the first place, the animal must be removed to a comfortable stall or loose box with a high roof, and well ventilated; he must at once be placed in slings, which should be gradually tightened until his toes barely touch the ground.

The wound must be washed out with tepid water, all gravel or dirt removed, and the real extent of the injury ascertained. The limb must then be placed in splints, well padded, and held together by leather straps. A very convenient plan for the knee is to take three slips of wood, about three inches wide, and half an inch thick, reaching from the elbow to the foot, with the edges beveled and well padded, and nailed together with three straps, which buckle in front. This, placed one at each side, and one behind, prevents flexion or extension of the joint entirely, and leaves it open to be dressed at pleasure, without undoing the splints. A large poultice of linseed or oatmeal should be applied cold, and continued until the granulations spring up from the bottom to close the wound. This simple plan of treatment is infinitely more soothing, and at the same time more successful, than the former methods of plastering it up with lime, flour, powdered blue-stone, oxide of zinc, white vitriol, etc. To some, these may seem very convenient and effectual methods of stopping the discharge, and, doubtless, in some cases they may succeed if circumstances are favorable ; but in many cases when an artificial plug is thus formed, it merely plugs it up for a little time. By and by, ulceration of the skin occurs, the plug falls out before the internal parts have healed, and the consequence is, that we have a far larger and more dangerous wound than before. In changing the poultice, be sure not to remove any of the coagula of synovia that may have formed around the opening. The poultice must be simply removed and changed, without washing the wound.

When the granulations become extuberant, they can be regulated by squeezing a sponge of cold water over it, or dust on a little oxide of zinc. Nothing, however, must be injected into the wound, as is sometimes done. Punctured wounds of joints must be treated on the same principle ; the joint must be kept perfectly still, and the granulations encouraged by poultices, etc.

Very often there are wounds in front of the knees, usually caused by falling or striking against some hard object, which may be more or less severe, according to circumstances. In a simple case of abrasion, but little if any treatment will be necessary ; if much bruised, with skin broken, tie short to a high rack to prevent lying down. Bandage the part tightly, and keep wet with a mild astringent, such as—

Sugar of lead..½ oz.
Carbolic acid.. 50 or 60 drops.
Water..1½ to 2 qts.

Keep the horse quiet until the inflammation is subdued.

The best lotion in my judgment for these bruises and superficial cuts of the skin, is calendula. It has the best effect in reducing inflammation of a bruise and cut of this kind of anything I know of. (See Calendula in list of medicines used.)

FRACTURES.

Owing to the difficulty experienced in keeping the bones of the leg of the horse in place to enable their reunion, with the expense and trouble involved, in addition to the fact that if even treated successfully the horse is supposed to be of but little value afterward, there is but little encouragement given by veterinary authorities for the successful treatment of such cases. But the success of Dr. Mc Beth, of Battle Creek, Mich., in treating ordinary fractures, has been so marked, and by such simple treatment, too, which is, I believe, peculiar to himself, not being, so far as I know, laid down in veterinary works, that I am induced to give his method of treatment, which he kindly explained to me with permission to publish, as it may serve to occasionally save a valuable horse.

He tells me that within the past two years he has treated three cases with perfect success. The first, a yearling, with a split of the ossafraginis, or short coronary bone of the fore leg. The second, a four-year-old, a fracture three inches above the fetlock joint of the off hind leg. Third, an oblique fracture, involving the fetlock joint one inch above the joint of the fore leg of a seven-year-old. His method of treatment is as follows :—

After providing himself with the best quality of plaster-of-Paris, he prepares from three to four splints made from strips of hickory wood, about an inch and a half in width and a fourth of an inch thick, of suitable length, or pieces of band iron about one eighth of an inch in thickness, with the ends thinned down somewhat, and if necessary, the edges and the bar bent to fit the form of the part ; he next provides bandages of suitable strips of cotton cloth, about three inches and a half in width. While the horse is standing naturally, the limb is brought forward a little, resting easily and naturally upon the ground, when the bones are held gently in a proper position. The part is first covered with a bandage of one thickness of the cloth ; next a little of the plaster, after being prepared, is put on the cloth under the splints, so as to level off the inequalities of the surface, and give an even bearing to the splints. The bandage is now started from the bottom, with the aid of an assistant ; a little of the plaster is laid on quickly with the knife, in a layer of from one fourth to three eighths of an inch thick, when the bandage is brought quickly over it, and drawn tight enough to cause the water to ooze through the cloth ; this is continued, the bandage being lapped about one half of an inch, until carried beyond the edges of the splints, when the process is reversed to the bottom, and then again to the top, making in all three layers, which forms a strong, unyielding cast about an inch or a little more thick around the part, when the horse is given freedom to take care of himself in a large, comfortable stall.

An important condition of success is in the preparation of the plaster. First, it should be of the very best quality ; next, as the plaster will set very quickly, not more than enough for one layer should be prepared or attempted to be put on at a time. Put in a tin dish about as much plaster as will be necessary for one coat or layer over the part. Pour on sufficient water to wet it well, and stir thoroughly for one minute. Being all ready, instantly commence putting on, laying on as stated, until the plaster becomes too hard, when make another batch, and continue the process, and when that is used, making more, and continuing until finished.

If the skin is broken, or there is a serious cut, as the splints are being put on, avoid covering the spot with wood or iron, and in the course of from six to ten hours, a hole should be made through the plaster to it, when it is to be treated as an ordinary wound. The point is to make the casing so long and tight as to thoroughly support the limb, without being too heavy or clumsy, yet not to obstruct the circulation.

In each of the cases referred to, there was no swelling or other trouble, and consequently no after treatment. The horse was let alone, and in about eight weeks the cast was taken off, when there was found to be a complete union of the parts without any noticeable deformity.

Dr. Mc Beth tells me this method of management is original with himself so far as he knows, and certainly its simplicity in connection with his success, entitles him to considerable credit. Plaster has been employed, I understand, for this purpose, but was put on in such a way as to form a mass excessively heavy and clumsy, and consequently not favorable to success.

Of course, when such an accident occurs, if a practitioner is available, he should be at once called in. The treatment is included mainly for the benefit of practitioners.

DISLOCATION OF THE PATELLA, OR " STIFLE."

This is most common in colts, from the outer condyle not being fully developed, allowing the patella to glide off and on at every step.

Causes.—It occurs generally in young animals, and is most common on hilly pasture where the soil is gravelly ; the feet becoming worn and tender, causes him to relax the stifle in walking, when the patella is apt to slide off. It sometimes occurs from external violence, or from interstitial absorption of the condyle.

Symptoms.—The limb is extended backward, the foot is bent up, and the animal drags the limb as if it were cramped and he was unable to draw it forward. Cramp of the muscles of the legs is not unfrequently mistaken for dislocation of the patella. But cramp is easily known from the suddenness of the attack, from there being no enlargement of the stifle, and from the bending up of the foot.

FIG. 876.—**The Horse as he Usually Appears when Stifled.**

Treatment.—It must be returned to its place as soon as possible, which can be easily done in the following way : Make one or two assistants pull the foot forward, while you push the stifle back, and at the same time push the patella forward, when it will slip into its place, and the animal will walk off almost as sound as if nothing had happened. If it is followed by lameness or swelling about the joint, rest must be given, and to prevent its recurrence, the stifle may be blistered.

A very good plan with colts, in which it frequently occurs, is to remove the patient to a loose box, with a level, even floor ; and to put a shoe on, with a tip projecting in front about two or three inches, slightly turned up, which will keep the muscles attached to it on the stretch, and so prevent its slipping out again. This may be worn for one or two months, as required.

A good deal of a secret in relieving a horse when stifled, is to take short hold of the bridle or halter, so as to throw the head up with a jerking motion, and quickly force the horse back upon his heels. It is rarely the peculiar exertion will not bring the patella back into place ; when, by walking the horse back and forth a little, he will be found all right.

STIFLE-JOINT LAMENESS.

Besides dislocation of the patella, or knee-cap, from laceration or extension of the lateral ligaments, we frequently find the stifle joint itself diseased. The condyles may be diseased, or the semilunar cartilages may be displaced. Sometimes the tendinous origin of the flexor metatarsimagnus (the principal muscle in bending the hock joint) is torn or strained. This is always a serious lameness, owing to the flexibility of the part involved.

Causes.—The causes are the same as in other joint-slips, blows, wrenches, etc.

Symptoms.—In moving, the limb is held as straight as possible ; it is moved of a piece, as it were, the stifle is turned outward at every step, and the leg is swung around, and placed farther forward than in hip lameness. In most cases we have heat and swelling. If made to stand on the limb, the capsular swelling can be felt, and pain is evinced on pressure.

Treatment.—Rest must be given. If the cartilages are displaced, they must be replaced by careful manipulation ; hot fomentations, or continued cold applications, must be applied ; and in the latter stages, repeated blisters or setons should be resorted to.

CUTS OR WOUNDS.

In ordinary cases they are easily managed. All that is neces-

Fig. 877.—Syringe for Washing out Wounds.

sary to do is to clip the hair from the edges of the wound, remove any hair or dirt from it by sponging the part with warm water, and dress it with any of the healing preparations or digestives hereafter given, which will cause a secretion of yellow matter, and a healthy granulating process. Each day following, to be cleansed by sponging out with a lather made of castile soap and warm water, and the application of the medicine repeated.

In a very serious, deep, or contused wound, if any large blood vessels are severed, they should be tied up. Arteries will throw the blood out in jets, and veins in a steady stream. If an artery is cut, it must be stopped promptly ; if it cannot be tied up, it can usually be stopped by touching it with a hot iron, or applying any good styptic. (See "Styptics.") Simply covering over with cobwebs will usually answer a good purpose. Clip the hair from the edges, also any bits of loose skin which would be liable to slough off ; but it is always advisable to save every bit of skin that can be kept alive ;

the part to be sponged out daily, and the dressing repeated. The injury will heal from the bottom, gradually filling up, by what is termed a granulating process. If there is serious inflammation, swelling, and pain, poultice ; but if poultices cannot be used to advantage, or if pain and swelling are very severe, hot fomentations must be applied and continued without intermission until it subsides ; then dress daily as directed. Care must also be taken to keep the horse quiet in a comfortable stall, free from the annoyance of flies, and fed with easily digested, laxative food ; if there is much tendency to fever, give a small dose of physic.

If the cut or wound is deep, dress with a tent, which is simply a wad of tow dipped in digestive ointment, which will be referred to farther on ; the cavity is not to be filled with the tent, but only the bottom, and then the wound will heal up as it ought ; if the wound is merely syringed out, or dressed superficially, it is liable to close over at the surface, and appear healed, while at the bottom the matter is spreading and burrowing, forming a sinus; in case there is too rapid granulation, or proud flesh, check it by touching with a little caustic.

Fig. 878.—Severe Lacerated Wound.

Fig. 879.—Incised Wound.

When the wound fills up, and there is not skin enough to cover it, dusting over it a little of the magic healing powder, or any of the astringents given, will cicatrize it quickly. If a wound is indolent, or does not seem to granulate, simply use a stronger stimulant ; if serious, use a caustic, which will remove the unhealthy parts, and set up a healthy condition of granulation. A very good simple stimulant to rouse an indolent ulcer to action, is an ounce of blue vitriol, pulverized, to a pint of water ; and for a simple healing or granulating effect, a lighter preparation, or about 2 drachms to a pint of water ; to be used as a dressing once a day. If the wound is deep so as to make a pouch of accumulated matter, it must be syringed out from the bottom every day, or better, a dependent opening made from the bottom, and kept open by a piece of tape or string passed through it, to let the matter pass off.

For deep, incised wounds, from pitch-fork, etc., the following is claimed to be excellent :—

Saltpeter.... .... .1 lb.
Water..1 gal.
Best whisky...1 qt.

Inject into the wound with a syringe three times a day until a cure is effected. It prevents inflammation or a tendency to sloughing or mortification. A gun-shot wound, a foot deep, in the thigh of a horse (the ball could not be found, remaining in the leg) was cured in two weeks by this treatment.

In any case of sinuses being formed, they must be opened up to the bottom, and made a simple wound, when it is to be treated as for a wound. Or, the pipes destroyed by a caustic introduced and repeated until the unhealthy part is sloughed out to the bottom. A very simple and effective caustic is that made of blue vitriol, either in strong solution, when it could be injected, or a little powdered fine in the form of a tent, which is simply a little rolled up in a strip of thin paper, twisted at the ends, and pushed to the bottom with a

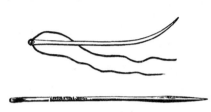

Fig. 880.—**Small Suture Needles.**

Fig. 881.—**Large Suture Needles.**

probe. Several parcels of this kind, one after another, can be pushed in until the sinuses are filled. In four or five days a core will be formed, which will usually destroy the sinuses to the bottom ; if any remain, it can be ascertained, and the dressing repeated upon that part, until it is all made a clean wound, when it can be treated as before described with a simple digestive preparation.

If there is an injury to the bone, ligament, or tendon, and not treated properly, a small sinus is formed, from which matter will ooze. In such a case, a probe must be introduced, and its extent ascertained ; if the sinus extends to the bone, which can be known by the probe striking it, a free opening should be made to the bottom, if the situation will admit, the diseased surface scraped off, when it can be treated as before explained, by the use of Friar's balsam, etc. (See " Friar's Balsam.") If all dead matter is not removed, sinuses are almost sure to again form after the wound is healed, when the whole treatment must be repeated.

Punctured wounds of the tendons, and the capsular ligaments of the joints, which often happen in the hind or fore legs, should be first touched with lunar caustic by making the stick pointed, and in-

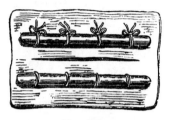

FIG. 882.

sert into the wound an eighth of an inch or more ; then if necessary, poultice. This class of wounds, it is found, do not do well by the treatment pursued in other wounds. So long as there is freedom of the synovial fluid in pasing off or any irritants are permitted to enter such a cavity, they seem only to aggravate it. The point is first to stop this, which can be done best as directed, or by touching lightly with a hot iron ; keep the animal quiet, and use an astringent dressing ; if inflammation is excessive, poultice, and there will usually be no trouble.

If clean cut, or the wound is of a character that will permit the edges being brought together, as in cases where the skin is widely separated, the point is, after sponging out the part so as to remove any foreign matter, to bring the edges together, and hold them in apposition, if it can be done without the skin sloughing, until healing by first intention takes place ; but this can seldom be accom-

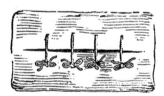

FIG. 883.

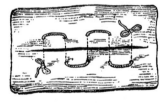

FIG. 884.

plished, excepting to a partial degree, in the horse, on account of the amount of muscular action of the skin ; but in many cases it must be resorted to, and will enable holding the edges together sufficiently long to allow the wound to heal without leaving much of a scar.

The stitches, which should be from three quarters to an inch apart, can be made by means of a curved, flat needle, with silk or linen well waxed. I give illustrations of different methods of doing this, which should make it sufficiently plain to be understood. First by stitches ; or by approximating the edges by stitches passed around a quill or small piece of round twig placed on each lip of the wound, termed *quilled suture.* Or, pins may be passed through the lips at suitable distances, and a little tow or thread twisted around each, like the figure 8, as shown ; or the edges may be held together by strips of sticking-plaster. A good adhesive plaster can be made by melting about two parts of Burgundy pitch to one of tallow, and spreading while hot upon cloth ; cut in strips of proper length and breadth, draw the edges of the skin together, and lay on while hot ; the parts to be dressed with a weak solution of carbolic acid, about in the proportion of one part to twenty or thirty parts water. The writer has had excellent success by the use of calendula, tincture of the garden flower called marigold. This should be

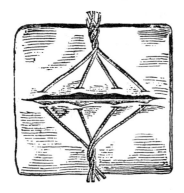

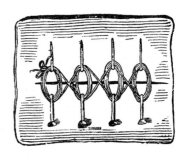

Fig. 885.   Fig. 886.

diluted with about one fourth to one third of water ; or any good antiseptic may be used.

The following for this purpose, obtained from one of the best practitioners in the country, is included :—

In wounds where the muscles are badly contused and lacerated, the following wash has taken the precedence above all other remedies, and by far supercedes carbolic acid. It acts as an antiseptic, and prevents excessive granulation. Take 1 oz. white vitriol or sulphate of lime, to 16 oz. water. Syringe the parts out well with the lotion, after being well cleansed, twice a day. By taking 1 oz. of white vitriol to 4 oz. of water, and penciled on the parts with a camel's-hair brush two or three times a day, it will cut down the excessive granulations commonly called "proud flesh."

For a healing or digestive ointment, the following is unrivaled :— ·

Palm-oil....	2½ lbs.
Lard	2 lbs.
Gum turpentine	½ lb.
Bees-wax	¼ lb.
Calamine	1 lb.

Simmer all together over a slow fire, and it will be fit for use. Put a little in the wound once a day. Wash the wound with warm water and castile soap before applying the ointment.

This is the favorite prescription of one of the best practitioners in the country, and is among the very best for the cure of cuts, pricks, and incised wounds in the feet, etc., that has ever been used. It sets the wound to running yellow matter quickly, and produces a healthy granulating process.

Turpentine and hog's lard, equal parts, simmered together, with a small quantity of powdered verdigris stirred in, is also a fine healing preparation for cuts and wounds.

The following is also a fine healing preparation, good for old sores or injuries in the feet, etc. :—

```
Tincture of myrrh.....................................1 oz.
Tincture of aloes.....................................2 oz.
Water.................................................1 pt.
```

To be applied once a day.

Healing ointment for cuts, galls, etc. :—

```
Oxide of zinc, pulverized fine........................4 dr.
Carbolic acid......................................... 6 gr.
Lard..................................................1 oz.
```

Melt the lard and stir in the zinc. Add the carbolic acid and mix thoroughly. Apply once a day. Will cause a healthy discharge from a foul ulcer.

Magic healing powder :—

```
Burnt alum............................................½ oz.
Prepared chalk........................................1 oz.
Pulverized gum camphor................................1 dr.
Calamine, pulverized..................................2 dr.
```

Mix, sprinkle on the sore.

When a wound will not heal, or there is not skin enough to cover it, dust on a little of this powder, and it will cicatrize it quickly. It is good for galls, saddle wounds, or other parts where the skin is thin or broken, providing there is no inflammation and condition requiring healing astringents. This is the original recipe for the famous magic healing powder, and has often been sold as a great secret, for from ten to twenty-five dollars.

A good healing preparation, especially for cuts or incised wounds in the feet: Tar and hog's lard, equal parts, melted together, removed from fire and stirred till cold.

The following hoof ointment has been in use in the British army, and used by British farriers with decided success. It is also

highly recommended by our most eminent veterinarians in this
country :—

Mutton tallow	2 parts.
White resin	2 parts.
Barbadoes tar	2 parts.
Yellow beeswax	1 part.
Castor-oil	1 part.

Melt the resin and the beeswax together, then add the tallow.
When melted, add the tar and castor-oil, then remove from the fire
and stir until cold.

This ointment is mostly used for diseased conditions of the
feet.   It is also effectual for the cure of many of the most troublesome skin diseases.   Blotches and cracks of the heels, to which so
many horses are liable in winter, are cured by nothing so readily as
by this ointment, well rubbed in, after the parts have been thoroughly washed with warm water and soap.   This ointment is also
good for cattle, sheep, and sporting dogs.   It is also one of the very
best hoof ointments.   See " Hoof Ointments."

INJURIES TO THE TONGUE.

The tongue is often injured by violence, pulling it out in giving medicines, either by the restlessness of the animal or clumsiness
of the operator, often by being tied up with a " hitch " of the halter
in his mouth ; by running back, he sometimes cuts it nearly
through.   A very common cause also is the use of a severe bit.

Treatment.—If not too much lacerated, the divided edges
should be brought together by the metallic suture, and dressed frequently with the following lotion :—

Alum	1 oz.
Borax	1½ oz.
Honey	1 oz.
Water	1 qt.

If it is nearly cut across, it may be necessary to remove it, and
tie the blood-vessels, and dress frequently with the above lotion.

Tincture of marigold, called calendula, is so good for bruises
and cuts of this character, that I think it worth mentioning.

When in Painsville, Ohio, in 1869, a horse was brought in by a
leading gentleman.   He stated that the horse had the habit of pulling recklessly ahead against the bit, so much so that he could not
be stopped, offering to wager that he would pull six men with the
bit.   Upon trial, with a breaking bit on, he pulled eight men around
the ring.   His tongue, becoming caught under the bit, was cut fully
half off, and the mouth so badly bruised that it became terribly

swollen in a short time. I had a few ounces of calendula with me, which I had obtained to try its effect if opportunity presented. I reduced some of it one third to one half with water, and bathed the mouth and tongue with it thoroughly, repeating two or three times in a couple of hours.

Being compelled to leave for Madison the same evening, I directed the owner to bathe the part with the preparation four or five times a day at least until my return. I remained at Madison one day, went to Geneva the next, when I again returned to Painsville to fill my engagement there, being absent three days. Upon examining the case I was surprised to find all swelling and inflammation gone, and the tongue entirely healed.

A horse having lost a part of the tongue, cannot drink without plunging the head deep in the water.

CUTS OR BRUISES OF THE CHEEKS.

To cure cuts or bruises of the cheeks, use inside—

Tannin ....1 dr.
Borax ....1½ oz.
Water...3 or 4 parts.

Swab the inside of the wound once a day.

For the outside dressing, use—

Tincture myrrh....... ....1 oz.
Tincture aloes ....2 oz.
Water...½ pt.

Mix, and swab the parts once a day.

Wash or sponge the parts with warm water and castile soap before each dressing.

The writer once had a case of very serious bruising and ulceration of both cheeks of a horse. This treatment was prescribed by Dr. Braily, formerly chief veterinary surgeon in U. S. cavalry service, and is particularly effective for such injuries.

During first or acute stage the persistent use of hot fomentations, alternated with cold, will usually prevent serious trouble. This should not be neglected in any serious case of such injuries.

SORE MOUTH.

The lips frequently become sore at the angles of the mouth from cutting or bruising of the bit. Tincture of myrrh and aloes, equal parts, applied to the sore, will soon cause it to heal.

FISTULA OF THE WITHERS.

The principle of treating fistula of the withers and poll-evil is the same as for treating other deep-seated ulcers explained; the only difference is that they are more complicated on account of their location, and require, if anything, more careful treatment.

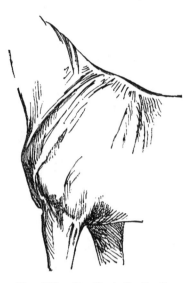

Fistula of the withers is caused by an injury to, or bruising the top of, the first vertebra of the neck, or the ligament covering it. At first there is simply inflammation, with some swelling, making the part very tender and sore; if this is not arrested or dispersed, matter will form and penetrate in different directions around and between the dorsal vertebræ, and under the shoulder blade, before it comes to the surface. Consequently the fistula may extend to both sides, and if neglected, may seriously involve the bones, in which case the cure will be proportionately more difficult.

Fig. 887.—Shoulder in Healthy Condition.

At its early stage, when there is simply inflammation and soreness, cooling applications, such as pouring cold water upon it, or directing a small stream from a hose against it, and repeating, is good. The part can be kept wet by the following lotion, and then if the inflammation does not abate, give a dose of physic and apply an iodine or sweating blister:—

Saltpeter....................4 oz.
Sugar of lead................1 oz.
Muriate of ammonia..........1 oz.
Common salt............... ..1 pt.
Cold water..................2 gal.

Lay on a few thicknesses of cloth, and keep wet with it.

Or the following may be used:—

Tincture of arnica...........8 oz.
Water ....1 qt.

Fig. 888.—Showing a Bad Case of Fistula.

If, however, matter forms, the sooner the abscess is opened the better. When this is done, the extent of the injury, or of the sinus, if any has formed, must be carefully ascertained with a probe, or by introducing the finger. If this cannot be done to advantage, then the pipes must be destroyed by the introduction of the caustic tents, as explained for treating deep-seated ulcers, under the head of "Cuts or Wounds," so that it will make a clean sore ; then a depending opening for the matter to run off must be made by passing a seton from the bottom outward, and sponge or syringe it out once a day with a strong suds of warm water and castile soap. It must be borne in mind that if allowed to heal over with pus, or any unhealthy matter remaining at the bottom, matter will continue to form, and finally break out anew, making, if anything, a more complicated condition of ulcer. The point is to see that all foreign matter, sinuses, or unhealthy bone, are thoroughly removed. Sinuses can be removed either by cutting away or sloughing off with caustics as explained, and the diseased bone by scraping. Syringe out the

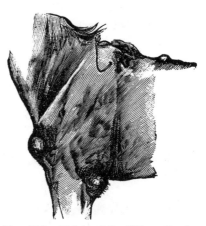

FIG. 889.—**Fistula of the Withers Showing Seton.**

parts well, first with castile soap and water, then with a mild solution of blue vitriol, or carbolic acid and water ; after which treat as before with digestive ointment, tincture of myrrh, etc., as advised under head of "Cuts or Wounds."

FIG. 890.—**Good Method of Covering the Parts.**

Soon after leaving the road, my old trained horse Gifford was threatened with fistula of the withers. When able to examine the case, I found there was severe inflammation and swelling of the parts, which were so painful the horse would not allow them to be touched. The veterinary surgeon in charge had applied a sharp stimulant, the effect of which was intensified by covering the parts

with a couple of thick blankets. The horse was very fat, and there were indications of matter forming, which as the horse was extremely sensitive, would cause great trouble in dressing the parts, which would be necessary for some time. I expressed my fear of this result, but the doctor thought differently, assuring me that he had every reason to believe the inflammation would disperse in time. I left, giving him full liberty to manage the case in his own way, and was gratified on being informed shortly afterward that the inflammation was dispersed, and in this way a cure was effected. The serious condition of the case, and the success with which it was treated, induced me, for the benefit of my readers, to write to the doctor for the details of the treatment used, which I here include :—

The treatment pursued in the management of Gifford was as follows: Take two pounds salts, four ounces cream of tartar, mix well, divide into nine doses, and give one dose once a day in his feed. For the local treatment, I took of the tincture of iodine and cantharides, equal parts, and applied to the shoulders every day for ten or twelve days ; after which, I used a stronger solution two or three times a day for three or four weeks. The case was a very bad one.

POLL-EVIL.

Poll-evil is caused by being clubbed back of the ear, striking back of the head against an obstruction, pulling hard upon the halter, or checking the head high, so as to bring undue pressure upon the ligaments of the parts, which will be shown by the inflammation and swelling over the first vertebra of the neck. If this inflammation is allowed to continue, the posterior part of the occipital bone, and sometimes the atlas bone, also the strong tendon over them, will be involved, causing serious ulceration of the parts, unless taken in hand promptly. The principle of treatment is precisely that of fistula of the withers. First, cooling applications, a dose of physic, and a cooling, opening diet.

A favorite prescription for dispersing inflammation of this kind, used by an old author, is,—

```
Tartarized antimony, crystallized and finely powdered............2 dr.
Olive-oil.................................................2 dr.
Hog's lard...............................................1 oz.
```

Vaseline can be substituted for the oil and lard. When properly rubbed on the part, this will act as a powerful blister, but does not blemish. Should matter form, it must be opened to the bottom ; and, after being cleansed out, ascertain how far the matter has burrowed, or the degree to which sinuses have formed. It is not prudent to do any more cutting at this part than simply to make a sufficiently deep incision to give an opening for the matter to pass off. If sinuses have formed, caustic tents are to be introduced, as before explained, until a clean sore is made. If the bones are involved, they must be scraped ; next, a **depending** opening made by running a seton from the bottom outward. Sometimes the matter extends across the neck to the opposite side. In such a case, the best way is to run a needle across between the muscles, and out on the opposite side, making an outlet on both sides.

The after treatment is the same as for fistula of the withers, being careful to remove all foreign growth, or diseased bone. Dress first with slightly caustic solution, then with digestive ointment, as explained.

I will include here a remedy which is claimed to be very effectual in the cure of poll-evil, fistula of the withers, etc. Burn corncobs, and fill the cavity to the bottom with the ashes. It may be necessary to repeat two or three times before a cure is effected. The ease with which this can be applied makes it worthy of trial.

Fig. 891.—**Showing Seton.**

The following remedy is used by veterinary surgeons of my acquaintance as a remedy of great value, and is kept a secret. The point in using it is, to saturate a little tow with it, and push it to the bottom of the ulcer, so that it will touch every part of it. In about twenty-four hours the diseased part can be separated from the healthy flesh with the finger, from the top to the bottom, and taken out, when it is to be dressed as a simple wound :—

Acetate of copper (verdigris)	4 oz.
Sulphate of copper (blue vitriol)	4 oz.
Alum	4 oz.
White precipitate (white mercury)	1 oz.
Nitric acid	2 oz.
Honey	1 lb.

DISEASES OF THE EYE.

The eye, or organ of vision, is composed of three tunics, or coats, and of the same number of humors. To the external coat (sclerotic and cornea) it owes its form. The middle tunic is made up of the choroid, or vascular, coat of the iris, or the thin curtain suspended in the aqueous humor, and perforated in the center by an opening called the pupil, or pupillary opening, which in the horse is of an elliptical form ; in man it is round. The inner coat is called the retina, or nervous covering, and is the terminal expansion of the optic nerve.

The humors are three in number, and they serve as reflectors of the light. They are: the aqueous humor, crystalline lens, and vitreous humor. The last is the largest, and occupies about four fifths of the whole interior of the globe, or eyeball. The appendages

FIGS. 892, 893, 894, 895.—Different Types of the Eye in Health.

of the eye are the eyelids, eyelashes, and the membrana nictitans, generally called the haw, which is situated in the inner or lower angle of the eye. It is connected with the different muscles of the eyeball. By the contraction of the straight muscle of the eye, the haw is forced outward, and is one of the beautiful arrangements that nature has provided for the protection of so delicate and sensitive

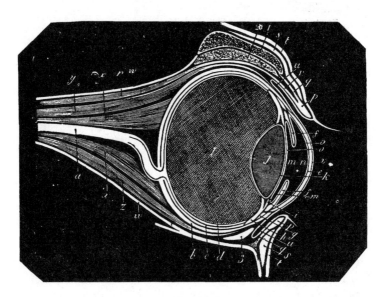

FIG. 896.

a, Optic nerve; b, Sclerotic; c, Choroid; d, Retina; e, Cornea; f, Iris; g, h, Ciliary circle; i, Insertion on crystalline lens; j, Crystalline lens; k, Crystalline capsule; l, Vitreous body; m, n, Anterior and posterior chambers; o, Membrane of aqueous humor; p, p, Tarsi; q, q, Fibrous membrane of eyelids; r, Elevator muscle of upper eyelid; s, s, Orbicularis muscle of eyelids; t, t, Skin of Eyelids; u, Conjunctiva; v, Membrane covering cornea; x, Posterior rectus muscle; y, Superior rectus muscle; z, Inferior rectus muscle; w, Orbital membrane.

an organ. The eye is wholly covered by a thin membrane called the conjunctiva.

SIMPLE OPHTHALMIA, OR INFLAMMATION OF THE EYES,

is a common disease among horses, and consists of inflammation of the conjunctival membrane covering the eye.

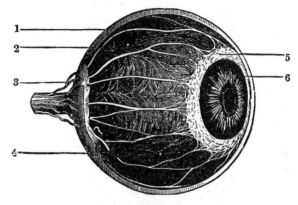

FIG. 897.

1. Sclerotic coat; 2. 4. Veins of the choroid; 3. Ciliary nerves; 5. Ciliary ligament; 6. Iris.

Causes.— It may be produced by many different causes, and perhaps the most common is from the introduction of a foreign substance into the eye, as a hay seed or chaff pickle becoming lodged in the external covering (cornea), or by direct injury to the eyes, as from the blow of a whip, or something of the kind. When from a blow or direct cause of injury, but one eye will be affected, while if from cold, etc., both eyes will be involved. It is also caused by allowing horses to stand in foul stables, especially in the

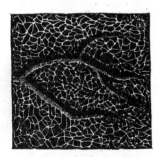

FIG. 898.—**Capillaries of the Vascular Layer of the Retina.**

summer months, whereby ammoniacal gases are generated, proving very injurious to the eyesight. It proceeds from exposure to cold, and is often an accompaniment of catarrh.

Symptoms.—The eyes are weak ; the conjunctiva, or inner lining of the lids, inflamed ; water running from the eyes ; the lids partly, if not wholly closed, according to the severity of the case. Bluish or white film, the result of inflammation, comes over the cornea, extending no deeper than the surface, and may vary from slight cloudiness to entire opacity.

Treatment.—This must, in a great measure, depend upon the cause ; therefore it is of the greatest importance to make a careful examination, especially if but one eye is affected.

If there is any foreign matter in the eye, remove it promptly, which can be done either by means of a feather or a pair of forceps. The eye should be fomented with tepid or warm water, and the horse kept in a darkened stable or loose box ; next, the eye may be kept constantly moist by means of a sponge or cloth wet with tepid

or cold water, and applied over the eye ; or better, Goulard's extract, used in the proportion of 1 drachm to a pint of water. If accompanied by great pain, the following lotion should be applied around the eye several times a day :—

Watery infusion of opium	1 oz.
Goulard's extract	4 oz.
Water	12 oz.

When the cloudiness or opacity of the cornea is tardy in being removed, the eye should be stimulated daily with the following collyrium :—

Nitrate of silver	5 gr.
Distilled water	1 oz.

Fig. 899.—**Good Method of Covering the Eye.**

Apply by means of a feather or camel's-hair brush.

If he must be used or kept in the sunlight, the eye should be kept covered with a blue cloth tied loosely over it. It is very important to attend to any such form of local inflammation promptly ; not only treating properly, but, if possible, taking him from all work, since, if neglected, or the inflammation aggravated by heating the blood, the sight is liable to be destroyed, or run into periodic ophthalmia. It is somewhat wonderful how much injury the eye will recover from, when treated with any kind of care.

Twenty years ago, when driving horses without reins was regarded as a great feat, in training them to drive in this way, it was sometimes necessary to use the whip very severely over the head,

Fig. 900.—**Reversed View of the Above.**

when the eye was liable to be struck, and so seriously injured as to close it and make it entirely white from inflammation in a short time. Yet, in every case, by bathing with cold water, keeping in a dark place, and if moved, keeping the eye covered with a cloth, in a few days the eye entirely recovered.

Once, while training Gifford, one of my old pair of trained horses, he ran accidentally against the corner of a stair, striking the eye so severely as to instantly destroy his power of sight ; the eye was entirely closed, and red with inflammation. In this case I simply kept the eye covered with a cloth kept constantly wet with water in which was tincture of aconite in the proportion of about 40 drops to half a pint of water. There was entire recovery within a week. This mild preparation has proved for me very efficient in reducing local inflammation.

SPECIFIC, OR PERIODIC, OPHTHALMIA,

is the most severe affection to which the horse's eye is liable, and is very common in this country. The parts principally and primarily involved are the internal structures of the eye, and the changes which occur vary in degree according to the severity of the attack.

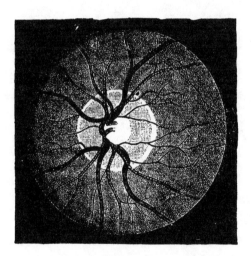

Fig. 901.—**Physiological Papillæ, as Seen with the Ophthalmoscope.**

Causes.—The great cause of this affection can be traced to an hereditary predisposition, always ready to burst forth when exposed to certain exciting causes, such as injuries of any kind, as before explained, being kept in very dark and ill-ventilated stables, and then suddenly exposed to the glare of a hot sun ; and, like simple ophthalmia, it may follow continued exposure to cold.

Symptoms.—Among the first symptoms is a watery discharge from one or both eyes, and on being exposed to the sunlight he exhibits a peculiar uneasiness, with a partial closure of the affected eye. As the disease advances, the eyelids become swollen, and if turned upward, the conjunctiva appears reddened and injected ; the eye looks smaller, and retracted into its socket ; the interior of the eye reveals a peculiar muddy or turbid appearance, showing floating flakes, and a yellowish or whitish deposit at the bottom of the chamber. Fig. 902 is designed to show, on an enlarged scale, something of this change. The symptoms are very like those of simple oph-

8

thalmia, and often lead to the supposition that the eye has received a blow or other injury.

The above symptoms become more and more aggravated, and the patient becomes affected constitutionally ; the circulation is increased, the mouth hot, and the appetite impaired. These symptoms may continue for several days, and then gradually disappear, or they may be prolonged for weeks, and end only with the destruction of the eye. A prominent and well-marked symptom of this disease is its shifting from one eye to the other ; in many cases, one eye has no sooner recovered than the other becomes affected. At other times, recovery is rapid, and to all appearances the eye looks perfectly healthy ; in a short time, however, the disease returns, and often with increased severity. These occurrences or shiftings take place in from three weeks to a month or more. As the disease advances still further, the eye begins to clear, the cornea becoming transparent, leaving a slight muddiness in the anterior part (cham-

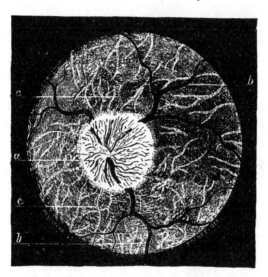

Fig. 902.—**Inflammation of the Optic Nerve.**

a, Papillæ of the optic nerve congested; b, Enlarged veins, connected by exudation round the papillæ; c, rather diminished arteries.

ber) of the eye ; the pupil diminishes in size, and the disease gradually terminates in more or less opacity of the chrystalline lens or its capsule, constituting cataract.

Treatment.—As a general rule, the treatment of specific ophthalmia is very unsatisfactory, but still medicinal remedies are found beneficial in palliating the disease. The horse should be placed in a comfortable and darkened loose box, with a plentiful supply of pure air. A brisk dose of purgative medicine should be administered, and if much constitutional fever is present, ten drops of the tincture of aconite should be given every three hours, until six or eight doses are given. Bleed from the facial vein, and follow by fomentations of hot water to the eye. After the third or fourth day, cold applications are preferable to hot. The extract of belladonna may be applied around the orbits, and also administered internally, in doses of two scruples three times a day. When the acute inflammatory symptoms are somewhat abated, the absorption of the effused products should be aided by a stimulating collyrium, as,—

Sulphate of zinc.................................... ....10 grs.
Distilled water................. ....1 oz.

or any of the eye-waters advised under that head.

Fig. 903.—**Generalized Atrophical Choroidites.**

a, Papillæ of the optic nerve, preserving its rosy color; b, c, Atrophied choroid, showing the white tint of the uncovered sclerotic; d, e, Blood-vessels of the retina: f, Pigmentary deposits of the choroid.

The following simple treatment, used by a very successful practitioner, has by special request been written out for me :—

When the lids are swollen, and not due to any disease, such as pink-eye, etc., but to a cold, and injuries of numerous descriptions, the eye should first be bathed with hot salt water for a few minutes, then turn the lower lid down and drop on the lid and eye-ball, with an eye-dropper, the following collyrium:—

Sulphate of atropa...................... ....10 gr.
Sulphate of zinc .... 1 dr.
Aqua rosæ ....6 oz

Drop on the diseased eye 15 to 10 drops two to three times a day. This remedy is a certain cure in most all eye troubles.

In diseases of the eye due to liver complaint, first give a strong cathartic combined with 1 to 2 drachms of calomel, and treat the eye as above.

AMAUROSIS, OR GLASS EYE,

consists in either partial or complete paralysis of the optic nerve, or its terminal expansion, the retina.

Causes.—Injuries to the brain, causing an extravasation of blood upon the deep origin of the special nerve of sight (optic), from disease of the internal coat of the eye (retina). It occasionally occurs as a sequel of stomach staggers or indigestion. We have also known it to occur in pregnant mares. Percival mentions several cases of amaurosis occurring in mares with foal, where vision was perfectly restored after parturition.

Symptoms.—The eye has a peculiar glassy appearance ; the horse carries his head very high, and is continually moving his ears, and his action is high, lifting his feet as if he were stepping over some obstacle. He is easily alarmed by any noise. The pupil is dilated, and loses its natural elliptical form. If the glare of a lighted candle is brought to bear upon the eye, the pupil refuses to contract, thus showing that nervous influence is lost.

Treatment.—The horse should have rest, and a strong dose of purgative medicine given. If supposed to arise from effusion or pressure on the nerve (optic), blisters and setons to the poll are recommended, and diuretics should be used. In some instances the powdered nux vomica, in doses of one scruple twice a day, has been used with advantage. If amaurosis has continued for a lengthened period, it is incurable, and treatment in such cases would be entirely useless.

CATARACT

is the name applied to a deposition of a pearly white substance within the eye, and is a very common affection in this country. It consists of an effusion of lymph, either on the middle humor (crystalline lens), or on its capsule, and is variable in size, sometimes not larger than the head of a pin, while in other cases it covers the whole lens.

Causes.—It is generally a result of repeated attacks of specific ophthalmia, or it may even supervene upon a first attack ; it may follow a severe injury to the eye.

Symptoms.—The eyesight is either partially or completely gone, and when covering the greater part of the lens, it is easily known by its pearly white appearance. When small, it is somewhat difficult of detection ; the eye is smaller than in health, and the pupil becomes greatly contracted when exposed to light. It may be detected by placing the animal in a bright light, and carefully examining the eye ; if the eye appears smaller than the other, it indicates something amiss with it. He should then be placed in a darkened stable, and allowed to stand quietly for ten or fifteen minutes before being subjected to an examination. Stand in front of him, and bring a lighted candle close up to the front of his eye, when any alteration in the structure of the lens can be readily detected.

Fig. 904.—**Partial Cataracts, or Small White Specks within the Pupil of the Eye.**

Treatment of the horse is useless, as when permanently established, it cannot be removed. When the cataract is confined to one eye only, it interferes but little with the horse's usefulness for ordinary work.

The cornea is frequently injured from the puncture of a nail, allowing the aqueous humor to escape, and perhaps injuring the crystalline lens, completely destroying the vision. When the injury is confined to the cornea, the humor may be reproduced. The part should be diligently bathed, either with hot or cold water, and the fomentations must be applied several times a day ; and the eye supported by means of a wet sponge or cloth, which tends to subdue the acute inflammation and allay the pain, and by keeping the eyelids closed, it supports the lacerated parts.

After a few days it may be necessary to stimulate the part, when any of the stimulating applications recommended for simple ophthalmia may be used.

The membrana nictitans, or haw, sometimes becomes enlarged, the result of an injury, or from being implicated in other diseased conditions of the eye. Even in its healthy state, we have known it to be mistaken (by ignorant persons) for an abnormal structure, and barbarously removed. It is not an unusual circumstance to hear persons boast of the rapidity with which they can remove this beautiful and most essential appendage to the eye.

DROPSY OF THE BELLY (ASCITES).

Ascites consists of a collection of serous fluid in the cavity of the belly. It is not very often seen, unless in connection with some other disease.

Causes.—It is usually the result of chronic peritoneal inflammation, or a sympathetic extension, or accompaniment of "water in the chest" (hydrothorax), chronic disease of some important organ contained in the belly, which it invests. Occasionally it occurs in conjunction with enlarged liver or spleen. Sometimes also from impeded circulation, consequent on abnormal tumors pressing on some important vessels ; and unquestionably, as in the human subject, some animals have a dropsical tendency (diathesis).

Symptoms.—The animal is observed to be dull and inactive, the bowels are costive, and the urine scanty ; he is always thirsty, watery swelling appears between the fore legs, which soon extends backward along to the sheath or udder ; the belly is large, and when struck, emits a dull, heavy sound. As it goes on, the breathing becomes rapid, and the pulse quick and small, the thirst intense. the appetite fails, the enlargement of the belly becomes more perceptible, the external swelling greater, and the breathing much increased ; as death approaches, the pulse becomes imperceptible, and as Blaine remarks, "the peritoneal inflammation produces colicky symptoms frequently, and in this way being occasionally but little disturbed, and at other times very ill, a few active symptoms carry off the poor beast."

Treatment.—When the watery effusion is extensive, few cases recover ; however, much can be done to arrest it in the early stages ; the prospects of recovery, of course, depend a good deal on the cause of complaint ; when accompanied by hydrothorax, it almost invariably proves fatal. The strength from the first must be harbored, stimulants must be given from the beginning ; open the bowels by an active purgative, smart friction being frequently applied to the belly, or if the swelling is considerable, it should be supported by bandages ; should the state of the patient permit, walking exercise should be persevered in. The following ball should be given daily :—

> Iodine...1 dr.
> Iodide of potassium ....1 dr.

Linseed meal and soft soap sufficient to form a ball.

Occasional doses of sweet niter and warm beer should be given. Free scarifications with a lancet or sharp knife should be made in the swelling.

Tonics should be more early used than they generally are ; a very good tonic ball in these cases consists of—

Sulphate of iron ... .2 dr.
Iodine .... 1 dr.

Made into a ball with linseed meal and soft soap. Or,—

Ginger...2 dr.
Gentian..2 dr,
Sulphate of iron ....2 dr.

Molasses sufficient to make a ball.

When medical treatment fails, temporary relief may be obtained by *tapping*, which consists in puncturing the belly, in the line between the navel and the sheath or udder, taking care not to injure the bowels or any important vessels, in doing which the belly must be tightly bandaged, and kept compressed.

ANASARCA, OR SWELLED LEGS.

If plethoric, fat legs and sheath swelled. When standing in the

FIG. 905.—Thickening of the Tendons, Caused by Banging or Striking the Part.	FIG. 906.—The Leg in its Natural Condition.	FIG. 907.—The Leg as it Appears when "Filled" or Swelled.

stable without any of the usual symptoms, should first be given a strong cathartic, and twenty-four to thirty-six hours after give the following powders in the feed morning and night :—

Sulphate of iron................................. ....1½ oz.
Powdered digitalis leaves.. ....2 oz.
Nitrate of potassa.. ..6 oz.
Powdered nux vomica...½ oz.

Make into twelve powders, and give in feed morning and night as above directed, until the animal's feces become of a blackish color, then stop.

By this time the horse should be well. If the case is weak and debilitated, omit the physic and powders, and give good, nutritious food. In the meantime the horse in either case should have gentle exercise.

It is bad practice to bandage. The application of bandages with stimulating liniment prevents the free circulation of the blood, thereby causing not only debility of the capillaries, or small blood-vessels, but also irritating the skin. It in all cases gives temporary relief, but does not cure. The treatment before given is the only one to be depended upon.

Inflammation of the Veins (Phlebitis).

Owing to the practice of bleeding horses for all ailments, which is still very common among people through the country, phlebitis is not uncommon. It consists of inflammation of the coats of the vein, involving the surrounding cellular tissues also.

Causes.—When it occurs, it almost invariably follows the operation of bleeding, arising from some mismanagement in performing it, or securing the integuments after. Rusty fleams, carelessness in pinning it up,—as in pulling the skin out, allowing blood to filtrate the cellular tissues,—bringing the edges unevenly together, or, as in cases we have known, pinning the vein itself to the skin. Certain states of constitutional predisposition of the veins to take on inflammatory action are said to exist.

Symptoms.—It is easily distinguished by the inverted edges of the wound, which are red and swollen, and discharge thin serum, which soon gives place to pus. The vein above the incision is hard, hot, and tender, and considerably enlarged. The swelling extends upward to the head ; the inflammation extends to the surrounding tissues ; the side of the neck is swollen ; the neck is stiff, and the head extended. The symptomatic fever runs high.

Treatment.—The head should be tied up, and almost constant fomentations of hot water applied for several days. The lips of the wound should be touched with the cautery or lunar caustic. A full dose of purgative medicine should be given. When the acute fever has subsided, the wound should be blistered throughout its entire extent, and repeated if required, the head being kept elevated, and the horse's feed placed within his reach.

These cases often terminate in complete obliteration of the

vein ; but in course of time the smaller vessels of the neck enlarge, and take the place of the lost jugular. He is not suited to be turned to pasture, as the head is apt to swell. He can never after be passed as a sound horse.

THROMBUS.

Thrombus is the name given to a round tumor which sometimes occurs around the puncture made in bleeding.

Causes.—It is usually the result of pinning up the wound by drawing the skin out, allowing the blood to be extravasated into the cellular tissues ; also from the opening in the skin not being opposite the opening in the vein, or too small to allow the blood to escape freely ; often from the tissues being irritated by repeated striking of the fleam, or " perhaps from spontaneous inflammation and serous effusion in the divided integuments and membranes themselves."

Symptoms.—It is easily recognized by the appearance of a round, full swelling surrounding the opening a short time after bleeding.

FIG. 908.—**The Barbarous Method often Resorted to, of Burning out the Lampas.**

Treatment.—It should be opened again, the coagula squeezed out, and the edges of the wound again brought together, and a pad or sponge saturated with a strong solution of Goulard's lotion, or cold water constantly applied for an hour at a time, the pad being supported by a broad bandage round the neck. The head must be tied up for at least twenty-four hours. It usually subsides in a day or two. Should swelling remain, it should be blistered and treated as in phlebitis.

LAMPAS.

Lampas is the name given to a slight enlargement of the bars or ridges on the palate behind the incisor teeth. It is mostly confined to young horses, and is a natural conjestion of these parts, consequent on the shedding of the teeth. It is not so much a disease as a natural and salutary process, which in general is best let alone, and in which cruel remedies, such as firing, should never for a moment be thought of. If much inflamed, a slight scarification, with sloppy feed for a few weeks, will suffice to remove it. In older animals, similar swellings are sometimes seen arising from indigestion ; a slight physicking will generally remove them, without resorting to such *outré* practices as " cutting out the lampas."

DISEASES OF THE SKIN.

The skin is a membrane of variable thickness, which covers the whole body, and is reflected inward by all the natural openings, so as to line, by its internal reflections, the eye, the nasal cavities, the mouth, etc., etc. Skin diseases in the lower animals generally do not prove so inveterate as in human beings.

SURFEIT

is an affection of common occurrence among horses in the spring and summer months, and is an eruptive disease, showing itself in the form of small tumors, or pimples, and extending along the neck, or over the whole body.

Causes.—It very often proves a sequel to some derangement of the digestive organs ; as from feeding for a lengthened period on one kind of food, and more particularly if it is of a stimulating or heating nature. It is also apt to occur in horses that are in high condition, when subjected to violent exercise, causing them to sweat freely, and then being exposed to sudden chill ; in this form it is often met with in colts when being first put to work.

Symptoms.—It appears suddenly ; small pimples or tumors arise on different parts of the body and neck, and particularly underneath the mane ; in some instances they disappear rapidly by absorption, while in others they burst and discharge a thin fluid : the hair comes out, and small scales form, which are easily pulled off. At times this affection proves very irksome and troublesome to the horse, causing him to rub violently against his stall, or bite at the parts affected. In its simple form it appears to inconvenience the animal but little, and is generally easily removed.

Treatment.—In the first place the food should be changed, and a mild purgative given, as Barbadoes aloes, four to six drachms ; the kidneys should be made to act freely, and for that purpose the following ball may be given daily for four or five days :—

Nitrate of potassa..3 dr.
Camphor.. 1 scr.
Oil of juniper...1 dr.

With soft soap and linseed meal sufficient to form an ordinary-sized ball.

In inveterate cases, small doses of calomel and opium may be used with success. The eruptions should be thoroughly cleansed with soap and water, and afterward dressed with a mild solution of the chloride of zinc, about twenty grains to a pint of water. He should have regular exercise and good grooming, using the wisp instead of the curry-comb. Surfeit differs from mange in not being contagious.

URTICARIA, NETTLE RASH, HIVES, ETC.,

shown by pimples, or elevations, on the skin, may go and come within twenty-four hours, generally due to a disturbance of the stomach, such as gastric derangement. In any case not serious, the symptoms are as follows: The horse probably not having taken well to his feed (apparently all right), a few hours later the whole body will be covered with little eruptions or elevations all over the skin.

The treatment for it should be as follows: Give a cathartic, and have his body well bathed with strong salt and water. This bathing may be repeated two or three times within twenty-four hours; feed lightly, and reduce the amount of grain feed.

This disease is caused by overfeeding and want of exercise; is always common to fat horses, and makes its appearance during the spring and summer months.

MANGE

is another eruptive disease, and is very contagious, and is caused by the repeated attacks of minute insects which burrow into the skin; these insects are called *acari*, and can be easily seen by means of a magnifying glass. (I include illustrations of two varieties of mange parasites.)

Causes.—In the majority of cases it is the result of contagion, either from coming in direct contact with a mangy horse, or it may be carried by means of his harness or blankets. It is also generated by uncleanliness and insufficient nourishment; the skin, from being allowed to become covered with dirt, loses, in a great measure, its highly important function in maintaining an animal in health.

Symptoms.—Generally, the first symptom observed is the animal's rubbing his head and neck against the stall or manger; small pimples appear, and the hair falls off; the skin is dry and hard, and upon the hardened patches may be seen small red spots. A horse affected with mange is kept in a constant state of irritation, which soon reduces him in flesh.

Treatment.—He should be separated from other animals, and thoroughly washed with soap and water every second or third day, afterward dressed with the following application :—

38   a

FIG. 909.—**Symptoms of Mange.**

Linseed-oil. . . . . .4 oz.
Oil of tar. . . . . .4 oz.
Sulphur. . . . . .3 oz.

Mix, and rub well into the affected parts. Or—

Oil of turpentine. . . .4 oz.
Oil of tar. . . . . .4 oz.
Linseed-oil . . . . .6 oz.

Mix.

Alternately with the above application mercurial ointment may be used. The horse should be given a generous diet, and moderate and regular exercise. In inveterate cases arsenical solutions are beneficial, but must be used with caution. All clothing, harness, etc., which have been used on a horse affected with mange, should be thoroughly cleansed before they are used again. The only means of preventing this disease is to keep both animal and stable in a cleanly condition.

The following is recommended by a very successful veterinary surgeon :—

Take the horse in the sun, and scrub him thoroughly all over with castile soap and water, then wash him well from head to tail with gas water, in which put 2

FIG. 910.

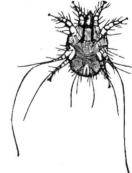

FIG. 911.

Mange Parasites.

drachms white hellebore to the gallon. He must now be put in another stall, distant from the one in which he has been standing. Thus treated, it rarely requires more than one washing to effect a permanent cure. The harness should be thoroughly scrubbed, and put away for six or eight weeks. These precautions are necessary to success in this otherwise troublesome disease.

HEN LICE.

It is not known to many that hen lice and common human body lice grow on horses with great rapidity. Hen lice especially are sometimes very troublesome. Prof. Bouley, in 1851, first called attention to them.

FIG. 912.—**One of the Tests for Mange.**

Symptoms.—When a horse is taken suddenly with irresistible itching, sometimes acting half frantic in his efforts to relieve himself by scratching, biting, striking up with his hind feet, and stamping, examine him carefully for hen lice. This trouble is to be particularly looked for where hens have access to, or roost in, the stable. There is liable to be an eruption of very small vesicles under the skin, the hair falling off in small, circular spots. In a few days these spots are liable to extend.

When neglected, or not attended to, the horse is liable to lose his appetite, grow thin and weak, on account of the constant annoyance and irritation to which he is made subject.

Treatment.—Remove the cause. Hens should never be kept near a horse stable, nor allowed to roost in it. Wash the animal with a decoction of tobacco or staphysgia ; whitewash the stable, and observe cleanliness. If subject to human lice, and the animal is poor, with long hair, clip it off, and wash the animal with a decoction of stavesacre,

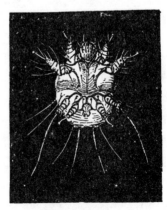

FIG. 913.—**Mange Parasite.**

one ounce of the powdered seeds to a pint of water, taking care that the animal does not lick himself for some time after the remedy has been applied.—*Williams.*

An ounce of arsenic to a pail of soft water, with which to wash the horse thoroughly in a warm place, is claimed to be a sure remedy for destroying either kind of lice.—*Summerville.*

RING-WORM.

This is not a common disease among horses. It consists in a parasitic growth of organic cells in the surface of the skin. Ring-

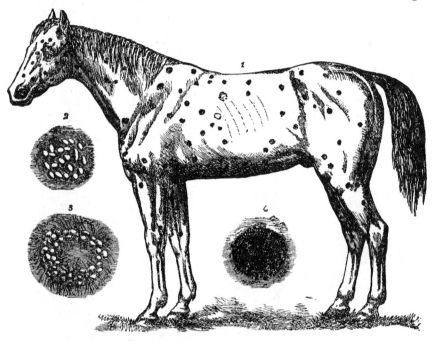

FIG. 914.—Herpes—Vesicular Ring-worm.

worm is a common affection in man, and is said to be communicable from him to the lower animals. Like other diseases of the skin, it is also generated by uncleanliness.

Symptoms.—The hair falls off on various parts of the body, especially about the face, eyelids, cheeks, neck, and thighs, leaving small and apparently ulcerated patches, which appear white and scaly, and have a peculiar tendency to spread; the animal loses flesh, and his coat becomes dry and dirty-looking.

Treatment.—Ring-worm, if attended to in the early stage, is easily cured. The affected parts should be well cleansed, and touched with a mild caustic, and dressed daily with the following ointment :—

Iodine.... ....1 dr.
Lard...1 oz.

Or, in place of the ointment, a liniment composed of—

Sulphur	1 oz.
Iodide of potassium	6 dr.
Iodine	3 dr.
Oil of tar	10 oz.

May be used daily.

HERPES—VESICULAR RING-WORM.

The treatment for this disease consists in purgative, low diet, and local applications of sedative lotions.

SCRATCHES, MUD FEVER, AND CRACKED HEELS

are very common occurrences among horses, especially in the spring and autumn months, and the hind legs are oftener affected than the fore ones.

FIG. 615.—A Very Bad Case of Scratches.   FIG. 916. An Ordinary Case of Scratches.

Causes.—They are very often the result of keeping horses standing in damp or filthy stables. Clipping the hair from off the legs is regarded as a very serious cause of scratches, as it leaves the skin so bare that it cannot as readily resist the effects of irritants of any kind as when protected by its natural covering ; but the most common cause is the habit of washing the legs with cold water, and not drying them thoroughly afterward. The sebaceous glands in the hollow of the pasterns become inflamed, their secretion is increased, the skin cracks, and discharges an ichorous matter.

Symptoms.—They usually cause lameness, more or less severe, according to the severity of the attack, always most painful for the first few steps. The hollows of the pasterns are swollen, red, hot, and tender, with transverse cracks which open at every step, and often bleed, especially in cold weather.   A good illustration of this is shown by Figs. 915 and 916.)

Treatment must be regulated according to the extent and duration of the disease.   In all cases the horse should be kept in a dry place, with an abundance of clean litter; the heels should be thoroughly cleansed, and if painful, poultices of linseed meal applied for several days.   If the horse is in high condition, and the legs much swollen, a full dose of purgative medicine must be given, followed by two or three doses of diuretic medicine, as,—

Nitrate of potash..3 dr.
Resin..3 dr.

With soft soap sufficient to make an ordinary-sized ball.

After poulticing, the parts should be dressed once or twice a day with the following lotion :—

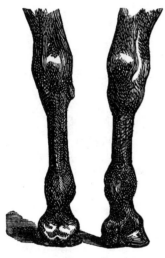

Sulphate of zinc ....6 dr.
Acetate of lead..................1 oz.
Water..........................1 pt.

Occasionally scratches prove very troublesome and difficult to cure ; if the ulcerations extend, it will be necessary to change the dressing, and dry powders, such as oxide of zinc, calomel, etc., should be tried.

The following is included from a very successful practitioner, as his favorite treatment :—

First, wash the parts off well with warm water and soap, dry thoroughly, and apply the following ointment twice a day:—

Oxide of zinc....................3 oz.
Carbolic acid....................2 dr.
Lard..........................10 oz.

Fig. 917.—**Showing the Legs in Healthy Condition.**

Mix.

If the case is serious, internal remedies must be resorted to.   First give a laxative, then feed twice a day one of the following powders:—

Sulphate of iron...1½ oz.
Pulverized gentian root....................................3 oz.

Make into eight powders.

The following is one of the very best remedies ever used.   It was given the writer by a drunken horse doctor for the cure of a very serious case of cracked heels, old Turco, my favorite trained horse, being the case, and it cured him quickly after all other treatment had failed. See particulars in "Facts for Horse Owners," page 1010.

Resin	2 oz.
Copperas	2 oz.
Alum	2 oz.
Beeswax	1 oz.
Tar	1 pt.
Tallow	size of hen's egg.

Boil over a slow fire, skim, and add a handful of the scrapings of sweet elder. When cool, it is fit for use.

Another remedy, for which much is claimed, is the following :—

Sweet-oil	6 oz.
Borax	2 oz.
Sugar of lead	2 oz.

Mix.

First wash clean with soft water and castile soap. When dry, apply once a day.

Sometimes a horse will irritate or break the skin by getting a rope or strap around the leg, which, if neglected, will cause a great deal of trouble by inducing scratches or cracking of the skin. The leg should be immediately poulticed with flaxseed meal, until all inflammation subsides. The horse in the meantime should have bran mashes, with a small dose of physic.

If, however, it has been neglected, and scratches or ulceration of the skin follow, it must be treated the same as for an ordinary case of scratches. I have found that tying a thickness or two of flannel loosely around the part for a few days after treatment, is very beneficial.

For Scratches and Cracked Heels.

The following remedy of great value is given by one of the leading veterinary surgeons in the United States :—

Take of oxide of zinc, one drachm ; veterinary cosmoline, one ounce ; powdered gum benzoin, ten grains ; camphorated spirits, one drachm ; mix thoroughly. The mode of application is a matter for attention. It should be gently rubbed upon the cracks with the finger, so as to distribute it in a moderately thick layer over the whole of the affected part, and to insinuate it as much as possible under any crusts that may be formed in the disease. Once properly applied, it will prevent further crust from collecting, while it serves the several purposes of a new cuticle to the abraded skin, a water-dressing, and a barrier to the oxidizing action always present in inflammation. The heels must not be washed after the application of the ointment ; they may be wiped with a soft napkin as much as may seem necessary, but when the ointment is once applied, it should not be removed by washing without good reason. Or the following liniment may be successfully applied : Take of Goulard's extract, English glycerine, and skunk oil, two parts each ; liquor ammonia, half a part ; mix. Agitate before using, and apply with a soft brush twice a day.

Hoof Ointment.

Used by Joseph Gamgee, V. S., formerly professor in the new Veterinary College, Edinburgh, Scotland, over forty years. It is also used as a remedy of great value for skin diseases, referred to particularly in "Scratches and Cracked Heels."

As a preventive of the injurious effects resulting from changes from humidity to dryness, and *vice versa*, I have used a hoof ointment, which I have found an admirable adjunct to all other good management.

When I began to see that humidity impaired the texture of the hoof, I had recourse to oil, lard, or tallow, with the view to exclude moisture ; but my experiments were attended with questionable effect, except in the case of mutton tallow, which, during wet weather, I found beneficial.

The following is the formula, as improved : —

Resin........ ....2 parts.
Mutton tallow...2 parts.
Barbadoes tar..2 parts.
Yellow wax..1 part.
Castor-oil............... ....1 part.

Given on page 983 of " Facts for Horse Owners."

To be combined according to pharmaceutical rules.

This ointment is a perfect antiseptic, and as soon as it is applied to horses' feet with bad thrushes, the offensive odor ceases.

Directions for Use.—The ointment should be applied after the feet are washed clean and become dry, and is most effectually applied by rubbing in with the hand.

Take a piece the size of a walnut, press it on the sole at the point of the frog, then into the commissures ; and lastly, rub it well into the sole and frog, and then extend it over the wall and round the coronet, using as much as may be sufficient to cover these parts effectively. It may be repeated about every fourth day ; and the evening, after work, is the best time ; or once a week will suffice to keep the feet in good condition under ordinary work.

Good for Skin Diseases.

Though I have called the preparation a hoof ointment, it is as effectual for the cure of many of the most troublesome skin diseases as it is good for the preservation of the feet. The breaking out of blotches and cracks of the heels, to which horses are so liable in winter, after the very objectionable practice of clipping and trimming, is cured by nothing so readily as by this ointment, well rubbed in, after the parts have been thoroughly washed with warm water and soap. In the same way as directed for horses' hoofs, the ointment is good for the feet of cattle, sheep, and sporting dogs.

Grease.

This may be considered as an aggravated condition of scratches, and is induced by the same general causes. In the early stage, it consists in inflammation of the sweat glands, followed by an offensive, white, oily discharge from the heels. The acrid character of the discharge often causes large portions of the skin to slough away, leaving ugly sores behind.

Symptoms.—There is generally more or less swelling of the legs, which, if not speedily relieved, is followed by a discharge ; the hair falls off, and the skin is reddened and inflamed. The parts are very painful and hot, and in many cases the least pressure of the hand will make the horse twitch up his leg, and continue to hold it up for some time. In other cases, when made to move about in his stall, or when taken out of his stable in the morning, he will keep twitching up his legs as if he were affected with stringhalt. Exercise appears to relieve the pain, as after being walked for ten or fifteen minutes, he goes quite free. As the disease advances, the skin cracks, and the discharge increases, becoming more and more purulent and offensive. (A good illustration of its appearance at this stage is given in Fig. 919.) The swelling increases, not being confined to the heels, but involving the front of the fetlock joint, and in some cases extending upward to the hock. The cracked condition of the legs and heels undergoes a change of structure, and fungoid granulations spring up similar in form to a bunch of keys ; this is called the "grapy stage," which may vary considerably in structure, at one time being very vascular, bleeding readily when touched ; in other instances it loses its vascularity, and becomes hard and horny ; from between the crevices of the grapes an ichorous, glairy discharge continues.

Fig. 918.—A Bad Condition of Grease.

There is a small parasite, called *sarcoptes hippopodus*, which is sometimes found in chronic cases of grease (Fig. 919). Williams says this class of insect may be also common to mange. The disease induced by it is called foot mange. Attention is drawn to a horse with this disease by his rubbing his fore legs, or striking constantly with the hind ones during the night. The seat of the disease, and the ready detection of numerous parasites in clusters where crusts or scabs form about the horse's heels, suffice to enable us to diagnose the malady.

Treatment.—Without cleanliness, all medicinal remedies are useless. The heels should be washed with soap and water every day, and the general comfort of the animal attended to. If the patient is in high condition, a dose of purgative medicine must be given, and the animal restricted to a cooling diet, as carrots, bran, etc. ; or, if in summer, green food is preferable. The following lotion may be applied daily, which, in mild cases, will generally suffice :—

Chloride of zinc ....30 gr.
Water..1 pt.

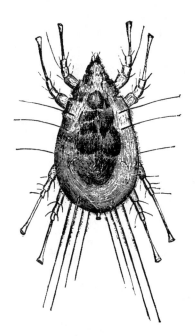

FIG. 919.—**Sarcoptes Hippopodus.**

In cases of long standing, the hair must be cut off, and the parts softened with linseed-meal poultices ; to which may be added charcoal, yeast, or bleaching powder. After removing the poultices, dust the parts over with oxide-of-zinc powder, or apply the following ointment every morning, to be washed off at night :—

Acetate of lead.............1 scr.
Soft soap...................4 dr.
Lard ....4 dr.

As in other skin diseases, small doses of Fowler's solution of arsenic are generally attended with beneficial results.

TUMOR ON THE SHOULDER.

Very often, in consequence of continued chafing of the collar, which may be neglected, serious inflammation is caused, sometimes followed by a deep cyst of matter beneath the large flat muscle which covers the front of the shoulder. The tissues around the part become thickened and indurated so that it is frequently difficult to detect any fluctuation of matter, yet it may be assumed, when there is considerable swelling, that has continued for some time, and matter exists, there will not be recovery until it has been removed. In slight cases only, a little nut-like induration usually forms without matter.

Treatment.—In cases where injury is recent, if the horse must be used, change the collar, so that, if possible, no chafing or pressure will be brought upon the part. Bathe the shoulder with hot and cold water according to the severity of the case, or two or three thicknesses of wet blanket may be slung over the shoulder. Bathing the part thoroughly with arnica which has been reduced about one third with water, is a favorite remedy for chafes and bruises. The following liniments for external inflammation are very good :—

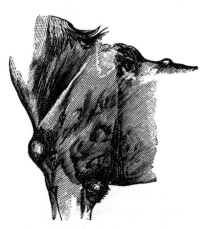

> Wormwood ....2 oz.
> New England rum.........1 qt.

Steep the wormwood in the liquor, and apply the preparation thoroughly to the shoulder. Or,—

> Goulard's extract ....1 oz.
> Vinegar.....................2 oz.
> Spirits of wine............3 oz.
> Water......................1½ pt.

FIG. 920.—**Showing Tumor on Elbow.**

Cover the part with two or three thicknesses of cloth kept wet with this.

An excellent remedy for bruises and soreness, caused by kicks, etc., is made by putting into whisky all the camphor which it will cut or dissolve. Bathe the part thoroughly with this.

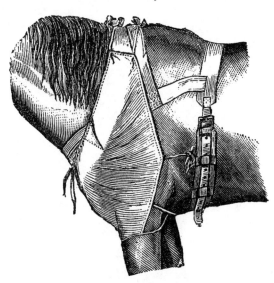

FIG. 921.—**A Good Method of Covering Shoulder with Wet Cloths or Poultices, when Seriously Chafed or Inflamed.**

If a tumor forms, open it with a knife, and treat like an ordinary wound ; or the matter can be drawn off with a trochar and canula, until the sac is reduced, when it can be opened. If a solid tumor forms, a straight verticle incision is to be made through the skin over the mass, and dissected out, when the skin is to be brought together with stitches, and treated as a simple wound.

Tumor on Point of the Elbow.

These are, in most cases, caused by the heels of the shoe when the horse lies with his fore limbs bent under him.

Treatment.—If in its acute stage, hot or cold applications may be used; if very much swollen, bathing with hot water will be best. When the acute stage passes off, apply an iodine or biniodide of mercury blister; if serum is secreted, it is recommended as the simplest treatment, to draw it off with a canula and trochar, and inject the sac with compound tincture of iodine, diluted with twice the quantity of water. Or, open the sac freely at the lower part, and heal like a common wound. If a hard mass is left beneath the skin, it is to be dissected out, and the skin brought together with a couple of stitches, and treat as a simple wound.

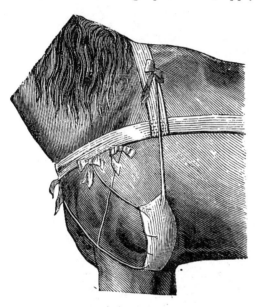

Fig. 922.—A Good Method of Covering or Poulticing the Elbow when Injured.

Sallenders

is a name given to an eruption on the front of the hock joint, consisting in a scurfiness of the skin, accompanied by an ichorous discharge, and falling out of the hair.

Causes.—High feeding without exercise, disorder of the digestive system, uncleanliness, and bad grooming. In stallions of the heavy draught breed it is a very common affection, and proves difficult to remove.

Treatment.—Dress the parts with mercurial or iodine ointments, keep the legs dry and clean, and give regular but not severe exercise, and occasionally a dose of laxative medicine. When only slight, the following lotion may remove them :—

Corrosive sublimate .... 20 grs.
Water..1 pt.

Apply twice a day.

MALLENDERS

is the name given to a similar affection located at the back of the knee. The treatment must be the same as for sallenders.

SADDLE AND COLLAR GALLS,

a very common occurrence among horses, are caused by uneven pressure of the saddle or collar ; the skin becomes excoriated, and the hair falls off. Large inflammatory swellings appear, which may form into abscesses, or the skin may become indurated and thickened.

Treatment.—The parts should be fomented with warm water, and some simple or cooling lotion applied, as,—

```
Acetate of lead ...........................................1 oz.
Water........................................  ...................1 pt.
```

If abscesses form, they must be freely opened, and well fomented

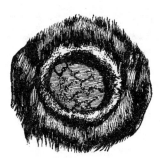

or poulticed. When the skin becomes indurated, forming what are called sitfasts, they must be dissected out.

The following is said to be an excellent healing lotion for saddle or collar galls :—

FIGS. 923, 924.—**Sitfasts. The Result of Saddle and Collar Galls.**

```
Sulphate copper. .1½ oz.
Sulphate zinc.....1 oz.
Sugar of lead ...1½ oz.
```

Put in three pints of water. Swab on the parts two or three times a day. Reduces inflammation, and sets up healing granulation of parts.

TENOTOMY.

As the name indicates, it consists in division of the tendons in cases of morbid contraction, giving rise to knuckling over the fetlock, causing the whole weight to be thrown on the toe. It is only applicable to cases in which we have no anchylosis of the joints.

The horse being cast and properly secured, the leg is taken out of the hobbles, and a rope attached to the foot, which is held by assistants. A longitudinal incision is made about an inch in length, a little in front of the tendons, and below any point of thickening that may exist. A common small-bladed scalpel, or the curved tenotomy knife, is passed in, care being taken to avoid the artery vein and nerve, and the tendons are divided ; the skin behind must not be cut, as the ends of the tendon may protrude, giving rise to fungus growths. The foot should now be easily brought into its natural position ; if not, some force should be used to bring it back "by placing the knee against the front or projecting part of it, at the same time laying hold of the foot with one hand, and the upper part of the leg with the other, and using considerable force." This is sometimes necessary to break up adhesions which may have formed. A stitch or two should be put in the wound, and a thick woolen bandage kept constantly wet with cold water should be applied for some days. If much inflammation ensues, a poultice should be applied, and some purgative medicine given.

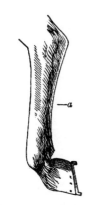

FIG. 925.—Showing the Position of the Foot Before being Operated Upon.

a, Point to enter the knife for cutting the tendons.

If the fetlock descends too much, the heels should be raised. If adhesions take place during recovery, a tipped shoe should be put on the foot. In from two to three months he will be fit for work.

In a conversation with Dr. Hamill about this operation, in explaining the simplicity and success of the operation, he referred to a case in point. To make the matter more clear to the general reader, I made the request that he would write out a statement of the method of treatment used by him, with a drawing showing the position of the foot before being operated upon ; also drawings of his method of adjustment for holding the foot in position after the operation, which are here given :—

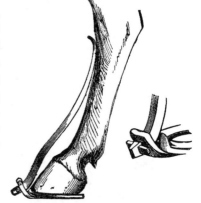

FIG. 926.—Drawing of the Shoe and Bar Used for the Treatment of the Case Referred To.

TENOTOMY, OR DIVISION OF THE TENDONS.

This is one of the simplest, as well as one of the most useful operations in equine surgery, as it will restore to normal position and strength a limb which has been so much deformed by contraction of the great flexor tendon of the foot, as to leave an otherwise good horse utterly useless. This contraction causes what is known as knuckling, or descending forward and downward of the fetlock joint toward the ground.

The operation is as follows : The horse is secured (in some cases throwing down is unnecessary), the leg is flexed or bent at the knee, a very small incision is made through the skin on the inside of the leg, at the inner border of the tendon, where it stands out freest from the "cannon bone," at *a*, Fig. 925. Then insert a probe-pointed tenotomy knife, keeping it pressed as close to the tendon as possible to avoid cutting the artery, which may be better protected by pressing with the fingers of the left hand toward the bone, all the soft tissues lying in front of the tendon. Press the knife in until the skin is reached, but not cut, on the opposite side ; turn the edge toward the tendon, cut carefully backward, while an attendant straightens the limb, until both tendons are severed, if necessary, to let the limb out straight. But a small wound is best for the healing process. And where adhesions have taken place, force is

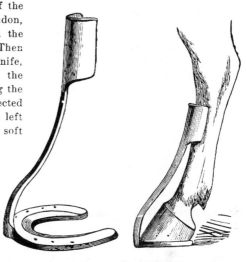

FIG. 927.—**Drawing of Model Shoe and Bar Designed for this Purpose, and its Adjustment.**

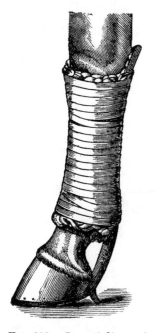

FIG. 928.—**Form of Shoe and Bar Used by French Veterinarians.**

required to straighten out the foot, with the *brace* or *stay shoe.* (See Fig. 927.) With a little antiseptic dressing occasionally to the wound, recovery will take place early. As a much better " set " limb can be had with use of the *stay shoe,* it may be added that one can be easily made by welding a bar of the desired length on the old shoe, setting it to the position of the sound limb, then packing and bandaging all together just above the point of operation. (See illustrations 927, 928.)

The *adjustable brace shoe,* shown in Fig. 926, is also simple, which is taken from the very shoe actually in use on one of the worst cases of contraction of the flexor tendon ever in New York City. A horse belonging to Messrs. Smith & McWilliam, Manhattan Gas Works, N. Y., was a large, powerful draught horse, between fourteen and fifteen hundred weight, used at very heavy work. Through some sprain to the off hind limb, he kept walking on the toe for about five or six months. Every known remedy was tried to prevent knuckling, both as regards medical treatment and shoeing, Heavy plates of steel were welded in front of the toe of the shoe. During another six months, he kept going over, until finally he walked on the anterior face of the hoof, with the fetlock joint resting on the ground. Fig. 925 shows the position in which the foot was carried. The limb appeared to be paralyzed above the joint. When he was down, he was quite helpless, had to be helped up, and in the end could hardly be made to stand alone. The owners decided to have him destroyed, although only eight years old, but first acquainted their veterinary surgeon. He advised tenotomy, which was performed in the month of March, 1878. In a few weeks the horse worked on Mr. Smith's farm at heavy plowing, and other farm work. Shortly after, he was taken back to the city, put to the same heavy work again, when he worked for two years, and never afterward showed the slightest lameness, or even weakness, in that leg.

CASTRATION.

The following article was, by special request, written by Dr. Chas. A. Meyer, who is an expert of the very highest order in the performance of this operation:—

CASTRATION BY THE LATEST METHOD.

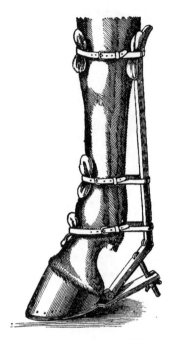

Fig. 929.—**Form of Bar and Shoe Used by French Veterinarians.**

Advances and progress have been made in all branches of the sciences and arts, and the art and science of surgery has been one of them. The nature, temperament, and disposition of the horse is better understood, and the educated veterinarian often risks his life for the benefit of stock raisers. We will, therefore, speak of the most improved method of castrating the stallion, as it is now, and will in the future, be performed with more ease and success. The old method of castrating the stallion, which so often injured the animal by breaking his back, injuring his limbs, spraining his muscles, and frequently disabling him for life, is now prevented. The method as now performed is to castrate the animal standing, using no ropes to tie

Fig. 930.—**Miles's Ecraseur.**

his legs, no hard usage, no clamps, and is less liable to cause tetanus, erysipelas, sclerous cord, etc. The operation is as follows:—

Put a halter on the animal, speak to him kindly, lead him to a corner, and quietly back him into it. Have the groom hold the halter-rope with the right hand, rather short, and place his left hand or arm over the face of the horse, and turn the animal's head to the left, or nigh side. The operator should have a sharp castrating knife, a pair of scissors, and, the most important instrument of all, the ecraseur (as shown in Fig. 930), called Miles's Ecraseur. The operator should stand on the nigh side, midway between the fore and hind legs (say nothing to the horse), grasp the scrotum gently in the left hand above the testicles, now with the knife held about 8 to 10 inches from the scrotum, make a slash into and through the coverings of the testicles, cutting into them proper. While the cut is made with the fore fingers at the back of the scrotum, raise the several coverings, and the testicles pop out. This must be done quickly. Then step back, apply the chain of the ecraseure about an inch above the testicle, and quickly tighten the chain. When a firm tortion is on the chain, gradually tighten the same, when a peculiar grating sensation will be felt. Do not cut clear through the cord with the chain. Then take your scissors and cut below the chain, when the testicle will fall to the ground. Gradually loosen the chain, which should require about half a minute, and repeat the same operation on the second testicle. You will not have any bleeding, and the animal will stand perfectly quiet.

This was at one time performed by a few men, who traveled through the country castrating, and who captivated the stock raisers by their clever way of operating, and who look upon it as a secret, of which there is no such thing. The whole secret lies in this: The testicles are endowed with a profuse plexus of nerves, and are a highly sensitive organ. By making a sharp, quick incision in the testicle, the pain is so intense that the animal becomes unnerved, and is under complete control of the operator. In this lies the whole secret. In some cases, the stallion makes a few sharp, quick kicks with one leg, but they are so as not to get in close proximity with the operator, being straight out behind. There is no danger to either the operator or the horse. Nothing is applied to the wounded part, which is to be left alone ; a slight swelling will be visible for a few days, which is natural, and must be to produce a healing of the parts. The percentage of loss is very slight, and only then due to complications, such as colds, etc. I have never yet seen an animal die from being operated upon by this method.

THE OLD METHOD,

as practiced by an old man named Gould, who resides near Bath, Steuben Co., N. Y. He is known in that and surrounding counties for his success in castrating horses, claiming to have never lost a case, and that there was but little swelling after the operation. The writer took particular pains to see the old man operate, and learn his secret.

The horse was laid down, and tied in the usual manner. He washed the parts thoroughly with warm water, and then greased them with lard. The clamps were of the usual kind. It was the preparation he put on the clamps that made his success, he said.

He put on the clamp, first, rye flour paste ; on this he sifted equal portions of red precipitate and corrosive sublimate, mixed together in powder. In twenty-four hours the clamps were taken off. This method of treatment has been pursued for many years by a friend of the author, and he claims, with unfailing success, never having lost a case, and it is followed by no appreciable swelling.

INJURIES AND DISEASES OF THE PENIS.

Causes.—The penis or yard of the stallion more particularly is liable to injury, from being kicked in covering, or sometimes it gets injured by awkwardness of the groom in serving mares ; also from being cruelly struck with a whip or stick while in a state of erection. Warts and excrescences frequently cover the surface of the organ.

Symptoms.—We may have injuries of more or less severity, from a slight scratch to deep and severe laceration of its substance ; or, on the other hand, the blow may have merely bruised, without breaking, the skin, producing want of power to retract it, and often accompanied by enormous swelling of the organ. When long out, the glans assumes a reddish-brown color, and the surface is cold, with very little sensibility. This is known a *paraphymosis.* Sometimes these swellings subside, but thickening and enlargement of the lower part remains, preventing retraction within the sheath, proving very troublesome and unsightly. Warty excrescences are easily recognized, and may occur on any part of the organ.

Treatment.—Injuries from kicks and blows must be treated on the general principles of subduing inflammation. If it hangs pendulous, it must be supported by a broad bandage round the body, and copious effusion with cold water, or iced water in summer, constantly applied ; if very hot and tender, accompanied by fever and constitutional disturbance, hot fomentations may be more applicable ; whichever is employed must be persevered in for some length of time. Purgatives should be given, and low diet, for some time.

Unless there is extensive laceration of the substance of the organ, nothing more than cold applications are required ; should it prove tardy in healing, Goulard's lotion, or a mild solution of sulphate of zinc, will prove beneficial. When it continues, and the tumefaction increases, free and deep longitudinal scarification must be made on its surface, and repeated in a few days, if necessary. Sometimes charcoal poultices are required to cleanse the wounds and soothe the part.

FOULNESS OF THE SHEATH AND YARD.

In geldings the penis becomes diminished considerably in size, and, from want of the sexual desire, seldom protrude it without its covering, the sheath ; consequently the sebaceous secretion of the glands in the prepuce accumulate, forming a black, soft, fetid substance, with a strong persistent uric odor. This sometimes becomes irritating, and gives rise to uneasiness, and should be occasionally washed out with warm water and a soft sponge, taking care not to scratch or bruise the inner surface, as troublesome swellings sometimes ensue.

More trouble, however, arises from the accumulation of little round " beans " (as horsemen call them), of a soft clayish appearance, in the cavity in the head of the penis, surrounding the end of the urethra, sometimes obstructing the passage of the urine by pressing on the urethra, or even stopping up the orifice itself, giving rise to difficulty in staling, and uneasiness.

The sheath should be washed out with soap and water, and the hand, well oiled, should be passed up, and the penis drawn out, when the accumulation should be removed, taking care not to scratch or bruise the parts.

PARTURITION, OR FOALING.

The period of gestation in the mare varies from eleven to thirteen months. Usually about ten days before foaling she begins to "make bag," the udder enlarges, and a thin, milky fluid can be drawn from the teats, and a glairy discharge escapes from the vagina, giving warning that the foal is about to be dropped. When the time approaches, she becomes uneasy, getting up and down frequently. Presently the true labor pains begin, the womb contracts on its contents, assisted by the diaphragm and abdominal muscles ; the whole body is convulsed with the effort ; the mouth of the womb becomes dilated ; the water-bag appears and bursts ; and when the presentation is natural, a few efforts force it out— sometimes inclosed in the membranes, which must be immediately removed ; and if the cord does not give way itself, it being sometimes thick and strong, a ligature should be put on it about four inches from the belly, and the remainder cut away. In general, mares are best left to themselves at this important period ; but care should be taken that they do not get into awkward positions, as against a wall, or the sides of the box.

ABNORMAL PRESENTATIONS.

The natural position of the foal at birth is with the head resting on the two fore legs. When in this position, and the parts natural, it soon comes away without very much exertion. In many cases, however, the foal is found in such positions as to prevent its escape without assistance. In all cases of protracted labor, where the pains continue without effect, assistance may be required. The hand being raised in temperature by washing in warm water, should be introduced to ascertain the cause. In some cases the neck of the womb will be found not sufficiently dilated, but the foal is found in its natural position. In such cases it may be gently dilated with the hand, or left alone, when nature will often overcome it herself. In cases of natural presentation, we must not be in too much of a hurry to deliver; harm is often done by injudicious interference. One or both fore legs may be doubled back, with the head presenting. In this case, push it back, and pass the hand down the leg if possible; get them up into the passage, either by the hand or looped cords passed round the fetlock, when, by slight traction, it will generally be brought away. The legs may be presented in the passage, and the head either doubled down under the brim of the pelvis, or turned over the shoulder down on the flank. In this case, it should be pushed back bodily, and the head sought for, when a loop must be placed, if possible, on the lower jaw; it must now be pushed back, while the head is to be pulled forward, and brought into the passage. This case is often very troublesome, from the difficulty sometimes experienced in reaching the head. It is sometimes necessary to remove one of the legs by cutting the skin round the fetlock, and with the embryotomy knife dividing the skin of the leg as far as the shoulder, and separating it with the fingers, when it can be removed. A cord should be attached to the loose skin to aid in traction, when the head can in most cases be reached. We have had occasion to remove both legs in the same manner before delivery could be effected.

Sometimes the buttocks and tail only are to be felt; this is often a troublesome case, especially when the legs dip under the pelvis. It must be pushed well in, and the hind feet, if possible, secured and brought into the passage. Often, however, it is very difficult to do, when, as recommended by Prof. Dick, " the contents of the abdomen must be removed at the rectum; the pelvis divided at the symphysis, when a cord being attached, and force used, the hind legs will get into the place of the viscera, and the quarters collapse so as to allow of extraction." The whole four feet may be presented in the passage; the simplest way of delivering in this case is to feel for the hocks, and slip loops on the hind feet; and by pushing back the fore ones, it may be removed by the hind legs.

It is impossible to describe minutely the details of procedure in these cases, as, from difference in collateral circumstances, such as size, age, length of time she has been in labor, swelling of the parts, etc., etc., different plans of treatment must suggest themselves to the operator. The principles to be observed are these: endeavor to get it into its natural position, in which position it is easiest delivered ; failing in that, get it into the next easiest, viz., the hind legs first ; that impracticable, remove those parts of the foal which offer most resistance, care being taken in so doing not to bruise or lacerate the mare. In no circumstances are tact, coolness, and steady perseverance more required than in a protracted case of labor ; however, the dictates of humanity no less than professional duty demand that we shrink not from the most difficult. For difficulties incident to parturition, such as inflammation, flooding, etc., see Chapter XX, page 183, Second Part.

BLISTERS.

Before a blister is applied, the hair must be cut off from the part as closely as possible. The blistering ointment is then to be well rubbed into the part with the hand ; and after this has been continued about ten minutes, some of the ointment may be smeared on the part. In blistering the legs, the tender part of the heel, under the fetlock joint, is to be avoided ; it may be better to rub a little hog's lard or vaseline on it, in order to defend it from any of the blisters that may accidentally run down from the leg. When the legs are blistered, all the litter should be removed from the stall, and the horse's head should be carefully secured, to prevent his rubbing the blistered parts with his nose. On the third day he may have a cradle put around his neck, and be turned loose into a large box, or a paddock, or an orchard. In a field he would be apt to take too much exercise. About a week or ten days after the blister has been applied, the parts should be oiled with some olive-oil or vaseline. If flies are troublesome, and make the horse restless, they may be kept off by the tar ointment, or tar and train oil mixed.

COUNTER-IRRITANTS.

THEIR USES, HOW TO EMPLOY THEM, ETC.,—WILLIAMS.

In all painful affections, warm fomentations or poultices must as a rule be prescribed. In the course of some days, however, if the pain is subsiding, and the parts seemingly relaxed, much benefit will be obtained by making a change to cold, mild astringents and bandages, to promote absorption of the exude.

The congested capillaries may be relieved by local bleeding, but the parts upon which such an operation is performed are very few, except about the coronet of the foot. An incision into the coronary plexus will reach the vessels at once ; the utility of this is, however, very doubtful, except in rare cases. Bleeding at the toe, although much practiced by many, is not to be commended.

Purgatives are very useful during the first stages of lameness, reducing the inflammation. A full dose of aloes may be given with advantage, the diet being properly regulated and restricted to bran mashes, a little hay, and the water to be chilled.

After the acute signs of inflammation have subsided, if the lameness still remains, the application of the so-called counter-irritants will be rendered necessary. These consist of rubefacients, blisters, setons, and the actual cautery. The actions of these remedies differ only in degree, in rapidity, and in performance, not in the nature of the exudation which they produce. Without entering into any speculative discussion upon the question, superficial irritants are beneficial in all cases of chronic lameness, whether it be caused by disease in bone, cartilage, ligament, tendon, or any other structure ; and they are often more decidedly beneficial when applied to the diseased structure itself than to the skin covering it. For example, a lameness arises from bone spavin ; its eradication is much more certain and rapid when a pointed cautery is applied to the diseased bones than when the hock is fired in the ordinary way. Again, a spavin has been fired and blistered repeatedly without benefit ; the bones are "punched" (a barbarous operation, and only to be performed in extreme cases), violent inflammation is excited in the diseased bones, which for a time increases the lameness; but this gradually subsides, and the original lameness is found to be removed.

I am of the opinion that the curative action of external irritants is not due to their producing metastasis or counter-irritation ; but that they excite within the originally diseased structure a reparative inflammation, partaking in its nature of what is described by Virchow as the "secretory inflammation," which, superseding the original diseased process (whether that be inflammation pure and simple or its effects, ulceration, caries, or a formation of a low form of fibrous tissues), excites the formation of reparative material by which the breaches are united, ulcers healed, and diseased action removed.

To illustrate this view, I will bring forward two familiar examples: 1. The healing of a sinus or fistula, after the application of a blister, or of the actual cautery to the skin contingent to it ; and 2. The removal of phlebitis (inflammation of the vein in the neck after bleeding) by a blister.

In the first instance, we find that a sinus heals after a blister or cautery, by the formation of an organizable exude, which completely fills up the cavity of the sinus ; and, in the second, we find that a blister assists in the obliteration of the inflamed vein, not by removing the inflammation from it, but by promoting the formation of a large quantity of reparative lymph, and hastening its further development into fibrous tissues, by which the vessel is transformed at the inflamed part into a fibrous cord. Now if the curative action were due to the removal of inflammation, we should find that in the first case the relief would be only of a temporary nature, the sinus would still remain, being generally the cause and not the effect of the morbid action; and in the second, that the inflammation being removed from the coats of the veins, the vessel would, upon removal of the clot, become pervious. But such is not the case. Let the clot be removed ever so often, it is sure to form again, and nothing has the power of overcoming the inflammation of the vessel until it has been transformed into an organized cord, a process most materially hastened by the application of a blister.

I think it may therefore be accepted that external irritants—whether they be simply rubefacients, producing a mere redness of the skin, vesicants or blisters, which cause elevations of the cuticle by fluid underneath it, or cauterization and setons, which promote the suppurative action—remove lameness by assisting nature in a process of repair.

Rubefacients may be employed in the less severe forms of lameness, in sprains of tendons, or in slight affections of joints, along with rest and fomentations, after the more acute symptoms have passed away.

It is usual to apply blisters in all cases of some standing, when organic changes in the parts involved are suspected. Before a blister is applied, the hair should be clipped from the part, which, if dirty, ought to be washed, and when dry, the blister applied with smart friction for about ten minutes. To obtain the full effect of a blister, a quantity of ointment is to be thickly laid on after the rubbing in is completed.

The best agent is cantharides, in the form of acetate, tincture, or ointment, to the limbs, the ointment in preference ; one part of cantharides to twelve parts of lard or palm-oil. If prepared with a temperature equal to the boiling point of water (212°), it will be sufficiently *strong* and will *never blemish.* It is a mistake to think that the powdered flies should be mixed with the vehicle when it is nearly cold. An ointment so prepared will require three times the quantity of cantharides. The heat melts the cantharidine.

Hints upon Blistering Generally.—No more than two legs are to be blistered at one time, and three weeks at least must be allowed to elapse before the others are blistered, and between each re-application. It is a bad practice to blister extensively in very hot weather ; and it is a mistake to suppose that blisters to the loins and back are more apt to irritate the urinary organs than when applied to any other part of the body, provided that it be carefully and properly done.

The evil results of blistering are: 1st. The production of strangury, by the absorbed cantharidine irritating the urinary passages. This is a very rare occurrence, provided the blister has been applied to a moderate extent of surface ; but if four legs, or even two, be extensively blistered at one time, the occurrence of such may be laid down to the indiscretion of the practitioner. In some cases, however, very moderate blistering may be followed by strangury, and when it does occur, it is best treated thus : First wash the blistered surface with warm water, in which a little alkali has been dissolved ; dress it with oil, give the animal demulcents to drink, such as cold linseed tea, and administer a few doses of opium and bicarbonate of soda.

2d. The production of a considerable amount of nervous irritability, fidgetiness, quickened pulse, and injected mucous membranes, with loss of appetite. These symptoms are due to a nervous temperament ; and if not very severe, had better not be interfered with. Should they become alarming, the animal must be treated as in the first instance ; the fomentations being continued for a longer period to the legs. It may be here mentioned that fomentations should not be hot, but soothingly warm.

Sometimes blisters, no matter how carefully applied, produce excessive swellings of the limb or limbs, with a tendency to suppuration and sloughing of the skin. These results are generally due to the animal's being in bad health, and in a condition tending to anasarca or to erysipelatous disease. The treatment must consist of purgatives or diuretics, as the case may be ; fomentations, astringent lotions, and gentle exercise, as soon as the pain is sufficiently subsided to admit of the animal's being moved about. In many cases the swellings involve the sheath of the penis, and the under surface of the abdomen. Punctures are very useful in such parts, by allowing the escape of the contained fluid. I have seen tetanus arise from a very limited blister to one fore leg.

If the effects are not sufficiently apparent in about thirty hours after the blister has been applied, a very little more, or what is remaining on the skin, which may be sufficient, should be gently rubbed in ; and in about forty-eight hours after the application the part is to be washed, and every trace of the blister removed ;

a little oil being now applied, or, what suits better, perhaps, an emulsion of sweet-oil, carbonate of potash, and water. It is a mistake to keep the parts soft too long ; the eschars should be allowed to accumulate, and to desquamate gradually.

Firing, or the application of the actual cautery, is a much more severe irritant than a blister, and often removes pain very rapidly when repeated blisters have failed to do so. In bone diseases, and in all cases of chronic lameness, it is of great benefit, and seems to act by powerfully exciting the healing process in the part diseased. The firing may be in lines, and superficial, the transverse method being the least calculated to blemish ; or it may be in points, and deep, by pyro-puncture (see treatment for spavins, ring-bones, etc.) into the diseased structure. This latter method is the more easily performed, and the more effective.

Nothing is more calculated to dispel the idea of the correctness of the counter-irritation theory than the dissection of a part which has been recently fired (say three days after the operation), when it will be found that the skin, subcutaneous tissue, and the bones,—when they are superficially situated, such as those of the hock, pastern, etc.,—are involved in the inflammatory action so produced. Thus a bone spavin lameness is removed by the inflammation excited by the cautery in the diseased bones, providing a supply of material for the purpose of uniting them together into one immovable mass ; or as in caries of a ginglymoid joint, for the repair of destroyed structure, as already explained.

Setons act very satisfactorily in some cases of bone diseases, especially those accompanied by external heat of the part ; they produce a discharge of pus, and their action can be continued for a much longer time than that of blistering or firing. In tendinous or ligamentous lameness, with much thickening of the integuments and subcutaneous structures, setons should not be employed, as they leave much additional thickening, and are not so effectual as the actual cautery.

HOT FOMENTATIONS.

This is so often advised for acute inflammation, sprains, etc., notwithstanding the simplicity of its application, I think it advisable to give such details as will serve to aid the owner in its use. The use of hot and cold water alone, intelligently applied, will be found a very safe, simple, and effective remedy for allaying inflammation, pain, and congestion.

The principle is to apply all the heat the animal will bear, but not enough to scald or burn. It is best accomplished by wringing through a common clothes wringer a woolen blanket (a common horse-blanket will do) out of boiling hot water, fold it quickly into four or more thicknesses, and place it over the affected part. Cover the hot cloth well with dry blanket. If continued or repeated long enough to relax the skin, cold is to be applied to tone it up, when, if necessary, the heat is to be again continued.

For Acute Pleurisy.—To relieve the pain, apply hot fomentations over the seat of the pain, from one to three hours, or till the pain subsides. The fomentations should be renewed every five or ten minutes, and at the conclusion should be followed with a heavy, cold compress for about ten minutes. Ice compresses instead of the fomentations will sometimes afford relief when all other means fail. After ice-compresses have been applied for an hour, they should be followed by a hot fomentation, and then apply the cold compress again until the pain subsides.

For Colic.—Apply hot fomentations sufficiently large to cover the abdomen or belly of the horse, in quick succession, for an hour or so, till relief is obtained. And at the same time give a copious injection of hot water into the rectum, of from 110° to 118° F. A gallon or two of water should be used for this purpose. Any kind of a syringe will do, but the Fountain Syringe is much to be preferred above all others. Sometimes the fomentation is all that is necessary to give relief, and sometimes injections alone will give great relief.

For Strains and Sprains.—Apply hot fomentations vigorously, changing them every five or ten minutes till the pain and swelling subside. Apply a cold compress for the last application, and the compress can be left on continuously, but it should be covered with the woolen cloth.

For a Cold.—If the cold is located in the head, a fomentation can be applied to the head, and should be extensive enough to cover most of the neck. This can be done by folding a blanket lengthwise about four thicknesses, and just winding it spirally around the horse's head so as not to cover the eyes; and if one blanket is not sufficient, another blanket can be wound around the head and down the neck in the same manner. The fomentation should be well covered with a dry blanket, and if it is so hot that the horse cannot bear it, the hot folded blanket, after being wrung out of hot water, should be folded in a dry one, so as not to burn him. In this case, it is not necessary to add another dry blanket over the fomentation.

If the cold seems to be settled all over the horse, several blankets may be joined at the edges, and thrown over the horse so that the edges hang down to the ground, forming a kind of tent for the horse to be under. The edges of the blanket behind and before the body can be pinned together. Then place a vessel with hot water under the horse, and a hot brick or hot flat-irons can be thrown into the water to produce a vapor, which should be continued until the horse is in a profuse sweat. Then he can be sponged off, beginning with cool water, and ending with cold water, or sprayed with cool water, then with cold; or the water can be poured over the body, if it is not convenient to spray. The animal should then be warmly blanketed, and in the course of 20 minutes if he does not sweat, or has ceased to sweat, he should be dried thoroughly by wiping with cloths and rubbing with the hand, until perfectly dry. Care should be taken that the temperature of the room in which this treatment is given does not fall much below 50°, and would be better to be about 65° or 70°, and there should be no draught. The treatment can be made much more effective by placing the horse's feet in as hot water as he will bear, while the vapor bath is being given.

Another method is a hot-blanket pack, which is sometimes more convenient, and is just as effectual. The hot-blanket pack can be given by wringing a heavy blanket out of hot water, and folding it; then folding it in a dry blanket and putting it around the body of the horse. It will require at least two such blankets to to reach over the body of the horse. He should then be very heavily blanketed, so as to keep the heat of the hot cloths in, and produce perspiration. The hot-blanket pack should be followed by cool sponging, spraying, or pouring, the same as after the vapor bath. The after-treatment should be the same as after a vapor bath.

POULTICES.

The simplest and cheapest poultice can be made by pouring boiling water on about a peck of bran, so as to make a very thin mash; or linseed meal could be added to it. Boiled turnips make a good poultice, which would also be improved by the addition of a little linseed meal.

Poultices are generally too small, confined, and dry. A poultice should be made large, so as to cover the parts thoroughly, and keep them moist. When a horse gets a nail in the foot, or it is calked, or when there is any local inflammation from an injury, covering the parts with a warm poultice will be found a very simple and good way of keeping down inflammation. If it is desired to poultice the leg for a sprain of the tendons, a flannel bag can be made for the purpose, or an old pant's leg, if convenient, can be pulled up over the leg; tie a string loosely around the foot below the fetlock, and fill the bag with the poultice above the knee, which can be kept up by tying a piece of listing, or a strip of flannel over the shoulder. Poultices are also useful applications for promoting suppuration in inflamed tumors, and when there is irritation or inflammation in the heels, such as scratches, cracks, or grease. The poultices commonly employed for these purposes are of an emollient character. The following is a standard formula :—

Linseed meal .... 1 lb.
Bran..2 qts.
Hog's lard..2 to 4 oz.

Boiling water enough to make a soft poultice.

Or, turnips thoroughly boiled and mashed, any quantity, linseed meal enough to form the poultice. A good poultice can be made of carrots, grated fine. Either of these simple poultices may be converted into an anodyne poultice by the addition of opium ; into a fermenting poultice by the addition of yeast, and by substituting oatmeal for linseed meal ; into an astringent poultice by the addition of Goulard's extract, sugar of lead, or powdered alum ; and into a detergent poultice by the addition of white or blue vitriol.

In obstinate cases of virulent grease, where there is much pain, and a stinking, dark-colored discharge, and especially when emollients are found ineffectual, the detergent poultice has quickly cured the disease, and in such cases even a solution of corrosive sublimate has been used with the best effect. But emollients should always be fairly tried, and some diuretic medicine given.

THE PULSE.

The arteries are the vessels which convey the blood from the heart to the system. "The blood nowhere passes through an artery so rapidly as it is forced into it by the ventricles of the heart, on account of the resistance offered by all the tubes against which it is forced. The consequence is, that when it receives the wave of blood, both the diameter and the length of the vessel is increased, and this is followed by a recoil and recovery of its previous position, owing to the elasticity of the tube ; these operations constitute the pulse, which is felt when the finger slightly compresses an artery."—*Bennett.* Hence the pulsations of the artery correspond with the beatings of the heart, and consequently indicate the irritability of that organ, or the system generally. The average pulse of the horse is from thirty-two to forty beats per minute. The smaller and more nervous the horse, the quicker the pulse ; while the larger and coarser bred, the slower. The most convenient places to feel the pulse are at the arm, on the inside where the artery (*radial*) passes over the head of the bone, or on the under part of the lower jaw. It can be felt easiest and best at the lower jaw, a little behind, where the submaxillary artery comes up and winds round to gain the cheek. (See Fig. 931.) Pass the finger down the jaw up near the neck on the inner edge, and a cord-like ridge will be felt, which, upon gently and firmly pressing it with the end of the finger, will plainly be felt to throb and beat. (See Fig. 932.)

"Frequent reference is made to the state of the pulse in different diseases, such as colic, pneumonia, laminitis, etc., etc. Hence it should be studied carefully. For example, during the early stage of colic, the pulse will be hardly affected, and the ears and legs will be natural in temperature ; while in inflammation of the bowels the pulse will be quick and wiry, ears and legs cold, etc. In fever it is quick, wiry, and light, indicating the extreme or not of disturbance in the circulation."—*Youatt.*

There are four general principles, or points, which must influ-

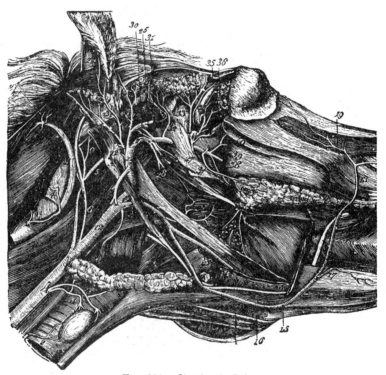

Fig. 931.—Showing the Pulse.

1 and 12, Carotid artery and its branches; 13, Submaxillary artery.

ence the course of treatment in all diseases. If there is high temperature, 102° to 107° (107° to 108° is fatal), the first point is to reduce the fever. In first stage, aconite internally is best ; externally, wrapping the body and extremities to equalize the temperature.

The heart's action is the next great point. Thirty-four to forty beats to a minute is normal ; below that indicates debility. If it is a quick, wiry, or thready pulse, it indicates inflammation of the intestines or abdominal organs, which calls immediately for sedatives. Take, for example, general colic treatment. Usual colic dose :—

Laudanum ....1 to 2 oz.
Sweet spirits of niter......................................1 to 2 oz.
Tincture belladonna.......................................1 to 2 dr.
Linseed-oil ....¾ to 1 pt.

If tympanites (flatulent colic), would add to the above one half to one ounce tincture jamaica ginger, and one half to one ounce aromatic spirits of ammonia, with a few drops tincture nux vomica, every half hour, until relieved.

Quick and feeble pulse indicates the lungs being involved. Moderately rapid, and throbbing or bounding pulse would indicate inflammation of the extremities, such as laminitis, and is to be treated as such. While an irregular pulse-beat, whether fast or slow, would indicate the heart itself being involved, which is to be treated by giving medicines that act upon the heart, such as alcoholic stimulants, belladonna, and digitalis. The first two stimulate the heart, the last is a heart sedative. Of alcohol, brandy, etc., give 2 to 4 ounces, with same

Fig. 932.—**Feeling the Pulse.**

quantity of water for a dose ; tincture of belladonna, 10 to 12 drops, which may be given in small doses every hour for an unlimited time, or in 1 to 2 drachm doses twice a day, not to be longer than a few days. Digitalis, being a heart sedative, must be used with greater caution ; from 15 to 60 drops of the tincture may be given twice a day for two to four days, or until the heart's action becomes slower. This drug has accumulative properties—that is, it may not seem to act for some time ; and then act with such great force as to be fatal.—*Hamill.*

GIVING BALLS.

Medicine is most commonly given to horses in the form of a ball or bolas, the size of which should not exceed that of a hen's egg. Though named a *ball*, it is generally rolled up in a cylindrical form, about one inch in diameter, and two and a half in length. In giving a ball, the horse's tongue is drawn out on the off or right side, and held firmly with the left hand, while with the right the ball is quickly passed over the tongue into the pharynx, or top of the gul-

FIG. 933.—Bad Method of Giving Ball.

let.   The hand should be kept as near to the roof of the mouth as possible in giving the ball; there will then be much less danger of being wounded by the teeth.   The moment the right hand is withdrawn from the mouth, the tongue is let loose, and the ball generally swallowed.

Balls cannot be conveniently given unless wrapped up in paper;

FIG. 934.—Approved Method.

but for this purpose the softest and thinnest should be chosen.   In holding the tongue with the left hand, while the ball is introduced, great care is required, as the rough and violent manner in which this is sometimes done often injures the tongue, or lacerates the under part of it.   The muscles by which swallowing is effected may also be seriously injured in this way.   In violent colds, strangles, etc.,

there is often so much
soreness of the throat as
to render swallowing very
painful and difficult; in
such cases, neither *balls*
nor *drenches* should be
given, as they are sure
to do mischief by irritating the throat, and may
even suffocate the animal
by getting into the wind-
pipe.

FIG. 935.—**After Giving Ball.**

PHYSICKING.

It is always best, if possible, to prepare the horse for physic by
giving a bran mash twenty-four hours previously, as the medicine

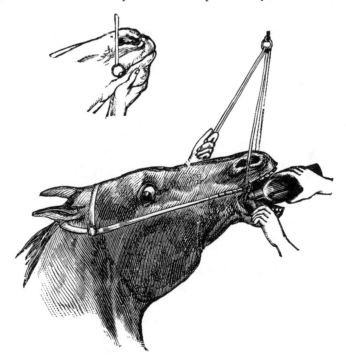

FIG. 936.—**Giving a Drench.**

will act more favorably, and there is less danger of superpurgation.
Five drachms of aloes (Barbadoes aloes are always used for horses)
will act as forcibly after a mash as seven without. Again, the quan-

tity of physic should be adapted to age and size. The rule is to give one drachm for each year up to seven. Eight drachms is the largest given at one dose. The following is a good physic ball :—

Barbadoes aloes, pulverized................ .... 7 dr.
Bar soap... 4 dr.
Ginger ....1 dr.

The usual way is to mix the ingredients in this proportion, then reduce to the weight intended, and give.

For alterative balls simply give from one to two or three drachms of mass, as above prepared, two or three times a week, for a week or two. The following are the details advised :—

The horse should be fed with bran mashes for two or three days, and have moderate but regular exercise, or be worked with moderation. He should be allowed only a moderate quantity of hay, especially if he has a voracious appetite ; and if inclined to eat his litter, he should be prevented by a muzzle, or by being tied up to the rack in the day-time, or what is still better, by having his litter removed during the day, and by applying the muzzle at night after he has eaten his allowance of hay. If in low condition, some oats may be mixed with the bran mashes ; but eight to ten pounds of good hay are a sufficient allowance for a day and night. On the morning when the physic is given, neither hay nor mashes should be allowed, until two or three hours after it has been taken. Some practitioners, however, direct a small, thin mash of bran only, to be given about an hour after, for the purpose of dissolving or mixing with the physic. This, however, is unnecessary, though supposed to render the effect milder and more expeditious. But this is not the case ; physic should be given fasting. During the day, the horse may have walking exercise for about half an hour, once only, and be fed with bran mashes, and have the chill taken off his water. Grooms generally consider exercise unnecessary or improper on the day the physic is given ; and on the following day, when the medicine generally operates, they are apt to give too much exercise. But as soon as the purging has taken place in a sufficient degree, which is generally the case about the afternoon of the day after it is taken, exercise is unnecessary and improper. And should the purging continue, or be found to be going on the following morning (that is, on the morning of the third day, including that on which the medicine was given), it should be restrained by gruel made of arrow-root or fine wheat flour, with which the horse should be drenched if he refuses to drink it. Should the purging continue after this, about half an ounce of tincture of opium may be given with a little gruel.

Horses sometimes appear sick, and refuse their food, after taking physic, either during the afternoon or evening of the same day, or the following morning. This is generally caused by a neglect of the preparation above directed, by the stomach being loaded at the time the physic is given, or by the horse feeding improperly too soon afterward; and not unfrequently by the physic being too strong. When this sickness is observed, the horse should have walking exercise; and if it be on the same day the physic is taken, and the uneasiness be considerable, let a clyster be administered; nothing more is necessary. Should it continue, however, the following morning let him be again exercised, and have some water with the chill off; and if the purging does not come on, and he appears to make fruitless efforts to dung, let the clyster be repeated, which, with repetition of the exercise, will generally produce the desired effect. A horse should be clothed, and not exposed to rain or cold wind during the operation of physic; and when its operation has ceased, he should be gradually brought back to his usual diet and work.

Cathartics improve digestion and chylification by cleansing the intestines and unloading the liver, and if the animal is afterward properly fed, will improve his strength and condition in a remarkable degree. Diuretics carry off the excrementitious matter of the blood by the kidneys, and thereby produce a similar effect, but not in so essential or permanent a manner; for if the system of feeding, which renders the blood impure, be continued, it will soon return to its original state. Cathartics are always useful when the appetite and digestion are bad, and this is known by a voracious or depraved appetite, both for food and for water, rumbling of the bowels, and a frequent discharge of wind from the anus. This is the case in a remarkable degree with broken-winded horses, and generally in such as have chronic cough, or are crib-biters. Cathartics should not be given too strong or too frequently, as they may thereby weaken instead of strengthen the digestive organs, and produce the effect they were intended to remove. Cathartics should always be made with soap, in the following manner, and then, if given upon an empty stomach, they will be carried off, and will not be dissolved until they get into the large bowels, where their effect is intended to be produced; that is, carrying off all the excrementitious matter that may be lodged in them. When given in this way, they never produce sickness or pain in the stomach, but always operate without pain or danger.   The following is a good cathartic ball :—

Barbadoes aloes, powdered............................ 4 dr. to 1 oz.
Hard soap...3 to 4 dr.
Ginger..1 dr.
Water... 1 dr.
Oil of cloves...10 drops.

Beat the soap, oil of cloves, and water together in a mortar, so as to form a paste, and if necessary use more water.   This being done, add the powdered aloes and ginger, and beat the whole into a ball.

BLEEDING, OR PHLEBOTOMY.

The operation of blood-letting is now almost discarded in modern practice.   It is simple, and can be performed by almost any

Fig. 937.—Raising the Vein.

one with a steady hand.   For its performance a fleam and blood-stick are required ; the star of the fleam should be large at the shoulder, to make a sufficient opening to allow a free flow of blood, and the blade should be broad, to prevent its sinking in when the vein is deep.   The jugular vein of the neck is usually selected to bleed from.   The head should be moderately raised and slightly turned off, the eye next the operator being covered by the hand of the assistant holding the head.   The left side is easiest operated on ; the vein is raised by the pressure of the third and little fingers of the left hand, which holds the fleam.   It is most superficial about two inches from the angle of the jaw, consequently this point is usually selected for the operation. The vein being raised, and the hair smoothed down by the moistened finger, the star of the fleam is placed in line with the course of the vein, with one smart tap of the blood-stick the skin and coats of the vein are punctured, and the blood will flow. When sufficient has been abstracted, the edges of the wound should be carefully taken together, and hairs and clot carefully

Fɪɢ. 938.—Method of Placing the Fleam.

wiped away; a small pin is passed through them, and a little tow wound round it, and the point of the pin cut off. The head should be tied up for a few hours to prevent his rubbing the pin off.

SETONS.

Setons are similar in their action to rowels, and are used for much the same purposes. They are usually made of broad white

Fɪɢ. 939.—The Orifice Closed after Bleeding.

tape. In inserting a seton, the skin is cut with the roweling scissors as above. A seton needle, which should be large and well polished, is passed in and pushed under the skin as far as is necessary; another cut is then made in the skin, through which it is passed out; the needle in its course should separate the skin on each side from its cellular attachments. The lower opening should always be so placed that the matter will have a dependent outlet. The ends of the seton should be tied to circular pieces of leather, so as to prevent its being pulled through. It is necessary to wash it frequently with warm water, and pull it up and down often, to keep it open, dressing it occasionally with digestive ointment to keep up the discharge.

THE ROWEL.

Rowels are used as counter-irritants in treating deep-seated inflammations; and whenever any morbid disease is to be stopped, as in grease and in thrushes, they have long been favorite remedies among horsemen.

In applying a rowel, the skin is to be taken up between the finger and thumb, and a cut is made in the skin with the roweling scissors, and with the hook on the handle of the scissors, it is separated from its cellular connections for about two inches, and a dossil of tow, or a circular piece of leather, with a hole in it, previously dipped in digestive ointment, is inserted, which must be cleaned and moved every day. A discharge is soon set up, which has a tendency to remove any deep-seated, morbid action.

TRACHEOTOMY.

It sometimes happens that from the tumefaction of strangles, the impaction of foreign bodies, and other sudden causes of obstruction, the life of the patient is threatened from suffocation. It is found necessary to open the windpipe to avert the untoward result, until the cause of the obstruction be removed.

It consists in making an incision through the skin and muscles in the mesian line down on the trachea, or windpipe, cutting through two rings of this tube, and inserting a bent tube, which is usually made of block-tin, with a broad flange, to which tapes or straps are attached to tie it round the neck. It is usually employed to give temporary relief; but I have known horses to work with a tube in the windpipe for years. It must be frequently taken out and cleaned. When the cause of the obstruction is removed, the tube is withdrawn, and the edges of the skin being scarified, they are carefully brought together, and treated as a simple wound.

EMBROCATIONS

are external applications in a liquid form, that are rubbed on a diseased part, as in strains and indolent swellings, and as an auxiliary in the treatment of internal inflammation. They are of a stimulating nature, and greatly assisted by friction. Of this kind are opodeldoc, soap liniment, etc.

EMBROCATION FOR HARD, INDOLENT TUMORS.

(No 1.) Olive-oil.... ....4 oz.
       Camphor..4 dr.

Mix.

(No 2.) Mercurial ointment .... 2 oz.
            Olive-oil .... 2 dr.
            Camphor .... 2 dr.

Embrocations of a more stimulating kind are sometimes employed in swellings of the joints, old strains, or other local affections, such as soap liniment with liquid ammonia, olive-oil, and oil of turpentine ; but blisters in such cases are generally more effectual.

Embrocations are often improperly employed, as in recent strains, or inflamed tumors, and other cases where emollient or cooling applications are required. Both strains and bruises are at first attended with a degree of inflammation proportionate to the violence of the injury, and the susceptibility of the injured part ; therefore they require, at first, such treatment as is calculated to subdue inflammation, as explained under head of " Sprains," etc.

ANODYNE LINIMENT.

Castile soap.................................. 4 troy oz.
Spirits of camphor........................... 2 troy oz.
Oil of rosemary............................... ½ oz.
Alcohol....................................... 2 pt.
Water... 4 oz.

Good for sprains, bruises, rheumatic pains, etc.

LINIMENT OF AMMONIA, OR VOLATILE LINIMENT.

Strong solution of ammonia .... 1 oz.
Olive-oil .... 2 oz.

Mix.

To this, camphor or oil of turpentine is sometimes added ; and the solution of ammonia is, for some purposes, joined to the soap liniment.

MUSTARD EMBROCATION.

Flour of mustard .... 4 oz.
Liquid ammonia .... 1½ oz.
Oil of turpentine................................ 1 oz.

Water, a sufficient quantity to bring it to the consistency of cream. Flour of mustard mixed into a thin paste, with water only, is a powerful stimulant, and may be employed with good effect in cases of internal inflammation, either of the bowels or lungs.

SOAP LINIMENT.

Hard soap....................................... 1 oz.
Camphor .... 1 oz.
Oil of rosemary................................. 1 oz.
Rectified spirits .... 1 pt.

Cut up the soap, and let it stand with the spirits until dissolved, then add the rest. Good for sprains, bruises, etc.

CAUSTICS

are substances which burn away the tissues of the body by decomposition of their elements, and are valuable to destroy fungous growth and set up healthy action. They are, consequently, often required to destroy proud flesh, kill the virus in poisoned wounds, stimulate old ulcers, excite healthy action in fistula, and remove warts, tumors, etc.

Corrosive sublimate, in powder, acts energetically; nitrate of silver is excellent to lower granulation; sulphate of copper is not so strong as the above, but good; chloride of zinc is a powerful caustic, and may be used in sinuses, in solution, seven drachms in a pint of water; verdigris, either in powder or mixed with lard, is good as an ointment, in proportion of one to three parts. Carrying this treatment to extreme implies using a hot iron, the actual cautery.

Vegetable Caustic.—Make a strong lye of hickory or oak ashes, put into an iron kettle, and evaporate to the consistency of thin molasses; then remove into a sand bath, and continue the evaporation to the consistency of honey. Keep it in a stoppered, ground glass jar.

This caustic is very valuable in fistulas, cancers, scrofulas, and indolent ulcers, particularly where there are sinuses, necrosis (or decay) of bone, and in all cases where there is proud flesh; and also to excite a healthy action of the parts. It removes fungous flesh without exciting inflammation, and acts but little except on spongy or soft flesh.

RHEUMATISM.

When a horse is taken suddenly lame, or appears stiffened, without any apparent cause for it, and especially if the lameness seems to shift from one part to another, it may be suspected that it is rheumatism. Horses of a nervous temperament, that are housed closely and pampered, are most liable to this trouble.

It is very important that there should be no exposure to rain or cold, especially after being warmed up; and, in fact, when there is a tendency to rheumatism, the same care, precautions, and principles of treatment are to be observed that are generally used in human practice.

I may refer here to a point in the treatment of rheumatism, of great value, not only to horse owners, but to the profession generally. In conversation with an old veterinary surgeon, of great experience and skill, in speaking of the virtues of aconite in certain derangements of the circulation, he stated that years ago his wife had been subject to attacks of rheumatism of the most severe character.

There was one physician whose treatment seemed to be wonderfully successful in giving relief. Whenever she was taken suddenly, he was accustomed to immediately call in this physician. The lady being taken with a violent attack, and he going hurriedly for the physician, he found him just leaving to call on a patient that needed his immediate attention. Upon his making known his business, the physician said, " I cannot possibly go now ; but if you will go and get a preparation of aconite [which he described], I guess she will come out all right." Said he, " I went and got the aconite, and gave as directed. She got well, and," he added in a laughing way, " I never went back for him afterward ; and if taken in time, I'll warrant it will cure any case of rheumatism."

A year or two afterward, being suddenly exposed to a cold, chilling rain, in the fall, without being provided with suitable underclothing, I was taken with a severe attack of rheumatism in the right side and arm. I was in the country, where I could not obtain any medicine, and was compelled to wait for thirty-six hours, until I reached a point where there was a drug store, and obtained a little of the ordinary tincture of aconite. Of this I took six or eight drops three or four times a day. Within twelve hours I was sensibly relieved, and within two or three days I was well. During the succeeding twelve or fourteen years I had several severe attacks, and each time was entirely relieved in from a few hours to a few days, by the use of the same remedy. But I was careful to take it promptly on the first appearance of the trouble.

During my professional experience I was constantly subject to rheumatic attacks, there being a constant predisposition to them, compelling me to exercise the greatest precaution. To illustrate some of these attacks and the effects of the remedy, I would mention that there was such a constant inclination to it in the right arm and shoulder that every change of weather would be felt by me. For example, in Natick, Mass., when getting out of bed in the morning, the arm being strained a little, a violent attack set in, and in an hour or two I could not raise my arm to a horizontal position, the pain being so intense as to be almost unbearable. I immediately obtained a little aconite, took it as before stated, and by four o'clock that day I could easily raise the arm to the head, and in two or three days the trouble was all gone.

The last attack was in the hip, occurring about three years before this writing (1887). It also set in upon getting out of bed in the morning. The pain soon became intense, and I could scarcely walk. This attack seemed so severe that I felt doubtful of being relieved by my old remedy. I concluded, however, to try it, and, to my surprise and gratification, in twenty-four hours I was relieved, and in a few days the trouble had disappeared.

I give these details, the better to illustrate to my readers the peculiar value of this simple remedy, with the desire to aid them. When, in consequence of a strain, there may be inflammation in the sheath of a tendon, or any muscular injury, this remedy would be certainly indicated. In one instance where I was strained myself in riding a mustang pony, one of the tendons of the right leg was so strained that I was made seriously lame. I supposed of course it would pass off in time, but after a period of three months it became if anything increased, and was a very serious matter. A physician of large experience, whom I consulted, directed me to take small doses of aconite (about six to eight drops of the tincture three times a day). In three days the lameness entirely disappeared, and the pain causing it never returned.

Whenever afterward any of my horses were so injured or strained as to cause lameness, no matter whatever else I did, I gave this remedy in about the same proportion relatively, and there was in all cases a very satisfactory recovery. The remedy prescribed for pneumonia (p. 485) is about the best preparation, I think, to be used. I used, when obtainable, the "fever medicine" recommended in the same chapter, and given also on page 877 in my large book on the horse, with very full facts of its use and manufacture. When rheumatism is suspected, whatever else is done, I would advise giving from twenty-five to thirty drops of this preparation on the tongue, the same as recommended for colds, pleurisy, pneumonia, etc. In one case only that I knew to be a sharp attack of rheumatism, did I prescribe this when on the road, when there was entire relief.

The ordinary nature and symptoms of and treatment for rheumatism, as given by our best authorities, are as follows :—

Rheumatism is an inflammation of the joints, tendons, ligaments, or muscles, caused by an unhealthy condition of the blood, accompanied by stiffness and lameness. The inflammation frequently changes its seat, and is rarely followed by suppuration. It is often a result of influenza, colds, and catarrhs, and sometimes is occasioned by exposure to cold and damp.

Acute Rheumatism,

or rheumatic fever, starting with a lameness, with or without swelling of a joint, accompanied by dullness, quickened pulse, and heated skin, soon causes a poor appetite, a constipation of the bowels, and high coloring of the urine. An almost constant symptom is an affection of the synovial membrane. In severe cases the affected animal stands with difficulty, the limbs are much swollen, and the regions of the joints are bulged out, soft, and puffy.

The remedies for acute rheumatism should be speedy and effective. The use of salicylic acid, with proper nursing, is recognized as about the best remedy. The following formulas, in the order given, are highly recommended by leading practitioners :—

Salicylic acid .... .1 oz.
Bicarbonate of soda..1 oz.

Mix in a pint of water or gruel, and give as a drench three or four times a day.

Nitrate of potash ....½ oz.
Powdered colchicum ....1 dr.
Oil of turpentine . ...1 oz.

To be mixed with linseed-oil and given at one dose, night and morning.

Also,—

Calomel.. ...20 gr.
Quinine .... 20 gr.

The following is highly recommended as a liniment :—

Compound soap liniment....................................16 oz.
Liquor of ammonia..2 oz.
Tincture of cantharides........... ....2 oz.
Tincture of opium..2 oz.

To be well rubbed in, and the affected limbs incased in warm flannel.

CHRONIC RHEUMATISM

does not change its locality as often as the acute form. This form usually attacks a joint, and results in ulceration of the cartilage and the increase of bony deposit surrounding it. The lameness caused by chronic rheumatism is exceedingly obstinate, and yields only to long-continued treatment. It returns on the least exposure. There is little fever attending this form of the disease, and the general condition of the patient during the continuance of the disease may be good. Hot fomentations, fully explained on page 616, would be the simplest, speediest, and most effective method of relieving severe pain and inflammation.

The following remedy may be safely employed :—

Carbonate of potash...1 oz.
Nitrate of potash...1 oz.
Iodide of potash...2 dr.

Give in a pint or two of water ; to be repeated once a day for two or three days, and then omit a day or two, or lessen the amount.

WARTS.

These are very common to horses, and quite annoying to most owners to manage, and it is very important to know how to treat them. Warts are of three kinds. The first is of a cartilaginous nature, and is contained in a sac, or shell, grown from the skin, and when this sac is divided, its contents drop out, leaving a clean cavity, which pretty soon vanishes. The operation is a comparatively painless one. The second kind is also cartilaginous, but is not in a sac, adhering to the skin, and growing large, with a rough crown and a vascular body. When severely injured, it rarely heals, but ulcerates in a tedious manner. This is the same species of wart usually found on the human hand. The third species is hardly of the same nature as the others, consisting of a cuticular case, inclosing a soft granular substance.

When the warts are found to be inclosed in a well-defined cuticular shell, the quickest and most humane practice is to take a sharp-pointed knife, and run the blade through each in succession. The edge should be cut away from the skin, and the knife being withdrawn with an upward, cutting motion, the sac and substance are both cut open. The inside may then be easily removed, and the part touched with this solution :—

Chloride of zinc.. 1 gr.
Water................... .... 1 oz.

When the growth proves to be of the fixed cartilaginous kind, it should be at once removed, and this is best done with a knife, and the excrescence should be thoroughly cut away. The bleeding that will follow may be controlled by means of a hot iron.

Should excision be objected to, caustics may be applied, such as strong acetic acid, butter of antimony, nitrate of silver, or lunar caustic. (See caustics on page 630.) Afterwards treat as an ordinary sore.

ADDITIONAL PRESCRIPTIONS.

ALTERATIVES.

POWDERS.

No. 1.—Tartar emetic...2 oz.
       Niter (saltpeter) ....4 oz.

Mix.

Divide into twelve powders, one to be given twice a day in the food. Useful in catarrh, influenza, and skin diseases.

No. 2.—Sulphur.. 3 oz.
       Niter... ....2 oz.
       Antimony...1½ oz.

Mix.

To be divided into six powders, one daily in the food. Useful in skin diseases.

BALLS.

No. 1.—Barbadoes aloes....................................10 dr.
       Castile soap..12 dr.
       Powdered caraway seed............................12 dr.
       Powdered ginger...... ....4 dr.

Molasses or palm-oil sufficient to form a mass. Divide into six balls, one to be given every morning till the bowels are freely opened. Useful in hide-bound, costive bowels, and skin diseases.

DIURETIC ALTERATIVES.

BALLS.

No. 1.—Powdered resin.......................................4 oz.
       Castile soap..3 oz.
       Venetian turpentine...................................2 oz.

Powdered caraway sufficient to form the mass. Divide into balls of a convenient size ; one daily, till diuresis is produced. Useful in swelled legs, dropsical effusion, weed, etc.

ANTI-SPASMODICS.

No. 1.—Sulphuric ether ....1 oz.
       Infusion of opium......................................2 oz.
       Peppermint water.....................................1 oz.

Mix.

To be given in a quart of cold water. Useful in flatulence, spasm, etc.

No. 2.—Ether and chloroform, of each........................½ oz.
       Tincture of opium........ ....2 oz.
       Tincture of cardamom ....1 oz.

To be given in a quart of water. Useful in colic.

No. 3.—Spirits of ammonia (aromatic) ....2 oz.
   Dilute hydrocyanic acid..... ....20 drops.
   Tincture of ginger.......................................2 oz.

To be given in a quart of beer, well shaken. Useful in spasmodic colic., etc.

ANODYNE DRAUGHT, OR DRENCH.

No. 4.—Tincture of opium.............. .... ½ to 1 oz.
   Spirits of nitrous ether............................1 to 2 oz.
   Essence of peppermint *.........................1 to 2 dr.
   Water..1 pt.

ANODYNE CARMINATIVE TINCTURE.

No. 5.—Best Turkey opium......................................1 oz.
   Cloves, bruised.......................................2 oz.
   Jamaica ginger, bruised ....3 oz.
   Old Cognac brandy..............................1 qt.—*White.*

DRENCH FOR STOMACH STAGGERS.

No. 1.—Barbadoes aloes...............................5 dr. to 1 oz.
   Calomel ... .2 dr.
   Oil of peppermint............................ .....20 drops.
   Warm water.. ....1 pt.
   Tincture of cardamom ....2 oz.

Mix, and give at one dose.

ASTRINGENTS.

No. 1.—Powdered opium..1 dr.
   Powdered catechu....................................2 dr.
   Powdered chalk.......... ....1 oz.

To be given in arrowroot, starch, or thick flour gruel. Useful in diarrhea or superpurgation.

No. 2.—Powdered catechu and alum, of each...................2 dr.
   Powdered opium....................................1 dr.
   Powdered ginger............................. .....2 dr.
   Oil of cloves........ ....10 drops.

Molasses to form a ball. Useful in superpurgation, diarrhea, etc.

DRYING POWDERS.

No. 1.—Prepared chalk..4 oz.
   Sulphate of zinc......... ....1 oz.
   Charcoal ....1 oz.
   Armenian bole......................................2 oz.
Mix.

To be finely powdered, and dusted over raw surfaces. Useful for healing wounds.

ASTRINGENT LOTION

No. 1.—Sulphate of zinc......... ....6 dr.
   Sugar of lead.... ....1 oz.
Mix.

---

* Essence of peppermint consists of the essential oil of peppermint dissolved in spirit of wine, one part of the former to three of the latter.

To be dissolved in a quart of water. Wet the wound twice a day with the lotion, well shaken. Useful for wounds, bruises, etc.

ASTRINGENT OINTMENT.

No. 1.—Resin ointment........................ . ...4 oz.
      Oil of turpentine...1 oz.
      Powdered sulphate of copper........... ....½ oz.

Mix, and make an ointment. Useful for tardy sores and fungus growths.

BLISTERS.

OINTMENTS.

No. 1.—Lard... .... 1 lb.
      Turpentine... 4 oz.
      Powdered flies.. 3 oz.
      Biniodide of mercury........... ....6 dr.

To be thoroughly incorporated. Useful for splints, spavins, ring-bones, and enlargement of glands.

No. 2.—Lard .... 1 lb.
      Beeswax .... 4 oz.
      Biniodide of mercury................................2½ oz

Melt the lard and wax, and add the biniodide, and stir till cold. Useful for enlargement of bone or glandular tissues.

COLLYRIA (EYE-WATERS).

No. 1.—Nitrate of silver............................2 to 10 grains.
      Rain, or distilled water.............................1 oz.
      Infusion of opium................................5 drops.

Mix.

To be applied to the eye with a feather or camel's-hair pencil. Useful in opacity of the cornea, specific ophthalmia, etc.

No. 2.—Sulphate of zinc.................................½ dr.
      Acetate of lead.......................................1 dr.
      Distilled water........ ....16 oz.

Mix.

To be used as above.

COMPOUND CAMPHOR LINIMENT.

Camphor ....2 oz.
Spirits of lavender............................... ....1 pt.
Liquor ammonia....................................6 oz.

Mix.

Useful in sprains, or as a mild blister.

COMPOUND IODINE LINIMENT.

Iodine ....1 part.
Soap liniment ....8 parts.

Mix, and shake well. Useful in sprains, thickened tendons, enlarged glands, etc.

CONDITION BALL.

No. 1.—Powdered ginger...................................... 1 dr.
Powdered gentian...................................... 3 dr.
Sulphate of iron ....2 dr.

Molasses sufficient to form a mass. To be made into one ball. Improves the appetite and stimulates digestion.

CORDIAL DRENCH.

No. 1.—Good old beer (warm)...................................1 qt.
Powdered ginger.................................$\frac{1}{2}$ oz.

Shake well. To be given in exhaustion, and recovery from debilitating diseases.

VETERINARY AROMATIC POWDER.

Powdered caraway seeds.......... ....6 oz.
Powdered allspice...................................... 4 oz.
Jamaica ginger, powdered...........................2 oz.
Licorice powder............................. ....2 oz.

Mix.

This is a good cordial powder, and may be given in a dose of two or three drachms in warm ale, in such cases as require the use of cordials. If the form of a ball is preferred, it may be obtained by beating up a dose of the powders with a little molasses.

COUGH BALLS.

No. 1.—Calomel ....1 dr.
Opium ....1 dr.
Camphor ....1 dr.
Digitalis..1 dr.

Made into a ball, with molasses. One daily, till six are given, when a gentle laxative should be administered.—*Dick.*

No. 2.—Digitalis..$\frac{1}{2}$ dr.
Camphor ....1 dr.
Tartar emetic ....1 dr.
Linseed meal..1 dr.
Nitrate of potass...................................... 3 dr.

Made into a mass, with Barbadoes tar. Useful in chronic cough. Used as above.—*Spooner.*

DRENCH FOR A COUGH.

Bruise 3 ounces of fresh squills in a mortar, or 4 to 5 ounces of garlic, and macerate them in 12 ounces of vinegar in a slow oven or on a hot plate for one hour ; strain off the liquid part, and add to it one pound of treacle or honey. The dose in bad coughs is 3 to 4 ounces. If there exists much irritation, a tablespoonful of tincture of opium may be added to every 6 ounces.